Why We Make Movies

BLACK FILMMAKERS TALK ABOUT
THE MAGIC OF CINEMA

George Alexander

Harlem Moon
Broadway Books
New York

Photo Credits

Grateful acknowledgment is made to the following for permission to use their photos in this book: Bill Duke—photo by Dexter Browne; Camille Billops—photo by Camille Billops; Carl Franklin; Charles Burnett—photo by John Oh; Debra Martin Chase; Doug McHenry—photo by D. Stevens; Ernest Dickerson—photo by Shane Harvey; Euzhan Palcy—photo by Guy Viau; Forest Whitaker; Fred Williamson; George Tilman, Jr.—photo by Philip V. Caruso; Gina Prince-Bythewood—photo by Sydney Baldwin; Gordon Parks—photo by Toni Parks; Haile Gerima—photo by Jezebel Filmworks; John Singleton—photo by Eli Reed; Julie Dash—photo by Keith Ward; Kasi Lemmons; Kathe Sandler—photo by Dwight Carter; Keenen Ivory Wayans; Lee Daniels—photo by Andrew Song; Malcolm D. Lee—photo by David Lee; Manthia Diawara; Melvin Van Peebles—photo by Chico De Luigi; Orlando Bagwell—photo by Mel Wright; Ossie Davis—photo by Anthony Barboza; Reginald Hudlin; Spike Lee—photo by David Lee; St. Claire Bourne—photo by Robert Benson; Stanley Nelson—photo by Diallo McLinn; Warrington Hudlin; William Greaves—photo by Deane Folsom.

Published by Harlem Moon, an imprint of Broadway Books,
a division of Random House, Inc.

PRINTED IN THE UNITED STATES OF AMERICA

HARLEM MOON, BROADWAY BOOKS, and the HARLEM MOON logo,
depicting a moon and a woman, are trademarks of Random House, Inc. The figure in
the Harlem Moon logo is inspired by a graphic design by Aaron Douglas (1899–1979).

Visit our website at www.harlemmoon.com

First edition published 2003.

Book design by Tina Thompson and Erin L. Matherne

Library of Congress Cataloging-in-Publication Data

Alexander, George, 1963–
    Why we make movies : Black filmmakers talk about the magic of cinema / George Alexander.
        p. cm.
    ISBN 0-7679-1181-4
    1. African Americans in motion pictures. 2. Motion pictures—Production and direction. 3. African American motion picture producers and directors—Interviews. I. Title.

PN1995.9.N4 A43 2003
791.43'023'092273—dc21   2002038869

10 9 8 7 6 5 4 3 2 1

To my loving sister Adrienne Michelle Alexander Scott, I miss you more than words in a book or pictures on a movie screen could ever say.

ACKNOWLEDGMENTS

Writing a book is no easy feat. I am forever grateful to God for blessing me with a career that I truly love. I wish to thank my parents, Lionel and Velma Alexander, for supporting me in all of my endeavors even when I seemed foolish to the rest of the world; my late big sister, Adrienne, to whom this book is dedicated, for loving me unconditionally; my brother and sister-in-law, Lionel III and Cynethea Alexander, for their moral support; my brother, Alton, for being a good brother; my nephew, Alexander Adrian Scott, for always cheering me on and assuring me that all would work out fine; my aunt, uncle, and cousin in Los Angeles, Georgie and Lynwood and Lyn Davis, for their ongoing support, great meals (especially Lyn's spareribs), airport pickups, pep talks and holidays.

I wish to thank Doubleday/Harlem Moon vice president and executive editor Janet Hill for believing in me all along and being a great friend. I'd also like to thank Lourdes Liz for giving me my first professional writing job and for being a round-the-clock cheerleader, personal advisor, marketing guru, shoulder to lean on and confidante. I must express my utmost gratitude to my dear Spelman sister in Los Angeles, Sherri McGee, for getting me writing gig after writing gig when I was just getting started. I shall never forget it. You are the best! I have to thank my wonderful friend and producing partner, Monique L. Jones, for buying into my creativity from the beginning. We will make our movie, Mo!

My heartfelt thanks goes to 2002 MacArthur Fellow Stanley Nelson and to George Tillman, Jr., for agreeing to be sample chapters in my book proposal. You made it all happen. I have to thank Warrington Hudlin for not only agreeing to be in this book but also for being a tremendous help in my securing people like his brother Reginald, Melvin Van Peebles, and for his generous advice. Camille Billops for her ongoing mentoring, never-ending giving spirit and the usage of tape after tape from the Hatch-Billops Collection. Dahlia Welsh for her excellent research assistance.

Growing up in Mobile, Alabama, was sometimes as magical as the movies, and I am blessed to have some of the kindest, most supportive family and extended family from Mobile, who though scattered near and far, are still always there when the storms of life start raging, at any hour, no matter how dark: Robert Alexander, Sr., Angela Alexander and Roy Cuthkelvin, Robert Alexander, Jr., Allison Alexander, Michael Alexander, Veronica Gayles, Patricia Davis Garrett, Joyce Dixon Minnard, Jennifer Childs, Damian Bracey, Victor Crawford, James Frederick and Tracy Watson, Angela Turner, Phillip Cusic and Lolita Rhodes Cusic, Charlotte Greene (your spiritual guidance is heavenly), David Thomas, Gregory Parker, Ashley Shipman, Tony Hailes, Burton LeFlore, Alvin Hope.

I am also thankful for my longtime great friends Al and Carole Bush of Charlotte, North Carolina and their sweet children, Elyse and Kailin. I promise to be a better godparent. I promise!

The Morehouse, Clark College (now Clark Atlanta) and Spelman clan always comes through: my girls Jaquelyn and Kathryn Flowers, Larry and Rachel Strawn, Carolyn Taylor McQueen and Gary McQueen, Harris Bostic, Tony and Melanie Pinado, Stanley and Karen Washington, Kelvin and Celia Walker, Karl and Sheila Humphrey, Dwayne and Anita Reade, Katrina and Alan Smith, Kim Bronson, Avery and Trina Byrd, Kevin Ross, David T. LaVelle, Justin Sanders, Charles Reese, Avery O. Williams, Scott and Chantal Ellis, Gregg Baty, Jay and Meryl Jackson, Sean Moss.

The New Yorkers: Jeff, Rachel, Noah and Ruby Hastie for everything, Lisa E. Davis for her excellent legal advice and friendship, Sheila Bridges, Warner Johnson, Judge and Mrs. Milton Richardson, Kay Shaw, Richard Clark, David Ushery, Terry C. Lane, Mark Thiesfeld, Manfred St. Julien, Da Kim, Doug and Deidre Traynor, Robin Whitley, Lana Garland, Bobby Garland, Todd Wilson, Marcella Lowery, Manuel Hughes, Shannon Ayers, Jim Holden, Elin Morgan, Cliff Virgin, III and Benilde Little, Harriette Cole, Michael Roberson, Keith Brown and Maria Perez Brown, Lorrie King, Bernard Bell, Nicole Moore, John Yull, Musa Jackson, Geraldine Moriba-Meadows, Darlene Currie, Jon Shoates and Laura Washington, Liz Hamburg, Michele Blackwell, Tracyann Williams, Mark Adams, Leander Sales, Tad Smith and Caroline Fitzgerald, Valerie Jo Bradley, Michelle Materre, Marie Brown, Bernard Gugar, Dawn Wilson, Glenn Schembri, Pamela Johnson, Michael Paul, Arnold Lewis, Dr. Ian Smith, Preston Kevin Lewis, Bret Mollison, Anasuya Isaacs, Richard Shropshire, Patrick Bass, Tatia Williams, Mondella S. Jones, Jerolyn Minter, Denise Gillman, Sheryl Huggins, Albert S., Jyll Taylor, John McGregor, Lynn Richardson, Gesla Kruse, Deidre Marcelle, Michelle Reid, Aaron Feodor, Daryl Ince, Valisha Graves, Aaron Talbert, Erik Talbert, Kim Singleton and Thomas Mitchell. Gennell Jefferson for all of your great meals whenever you visit L.A. from Chicago. All of the beautiful people of my Harlem block whose names I don't know but whose bright faces and daily greetings tell me that life is wonderful. My agent, Victoria Sanders, of Victoria Sanders & Associates and the rest of the crew there: Diane Dickensheid, Imani Wilson and Meilan Carter. I must thank Chris Burge, Lynette Jefferson, Hermann and Peggy Mazard and the rest of the faithful of the Wednesday-night Bible study in Manhattan. Prayer is powerful! I wish to thank Frederick Douglass Creative Arts Center (FDCAC) president and cofounder Fred Hudson, who is the most giving and compassionate writing instructor on the planet. I also want to thank Trudy Stallings, Jo Matos and the entire community at FDCAC. Olivia Smashum, Maria Weaver,

John Murchison, Ariel Paredes, Elaine Brown, Eric Othello Butler, Jason Mulderig, Julie Anderson and Alyce Emory at HBO; Jeff Friday at Film Life; Stacy Spikes, Joy Huang and Andre at Urbanworld Films; Mable Haddock and Terry Scott at the National Black Programming Consortium; Thelma Golden and Sandra Jackson at the Studio Museum in Harlem; Selena Wong at Showtime; Illinois State Senator and my Morehouse brother Ken Dunkin, Randy Crumpton, Deborah Kerr and Agape Papas of the Chicago International Film Festival. The Graveses, Caroline Clarke and Tariq Muhummad at Black Enterprise (BE) for my first print job. Sonya Donaldson, Sakina Spruell, Alfred Edmonds, Derek Dingle and the rest of the people at BE for the many assignments. Keith Clinkscales, Leonard Burnett, Roy Johnson and Debra Jackson at Vanguarde Media.

The Angelenos: Adisa, Tina Andrews & Stephen Gaines, Martin Jacobs, Emma McFarlin, Pearlena Igbokwe and Timothy Robinson, Cassius Titus, David Wyatt, Kriss Turner, Lisa Gay Hamilton, Vince Pepe, Charlton Blackburne, Michael Mayson, Nichelle Protho, Angela Northington, Peter Graham, Terilyn Shropshire, Kenneth R. Reynolds, Mark Cheatham, Deborah Berger, Eric Payne, Rodney Charles, Lance Gatewood, Vanessa Morrison, Karen Peterkin, Brett Andrews, Lori Lakin, Tracy Burnett, my late neighbor Rose Cornsweet, Kendall Stevens, Wendell Pierce, Wendy Worthington, Carol Mayes, Niva Dorell, Don D. Scott, Rene Simon Cruz, Sharon Cobb, Ena Frias and Ntare Mwine, Tracy Lawrence and Roland Poindexter, Karen Hunte, Chris Smith and Salaam Coleman, Roz Stevenson, Ava DuVernay, Sharon Johnson, Tamika Lamison, Erik Washington, Tonya Lee Williams, Charlie Morton, Treva Etienne, Charles King and Jenean Glover, Stacy Evans, Rhonda Penrice.

My publicists and staff at Rohr Talent and Management in Los Angeles are incomparable: Steve Sato Rohr, Sandra Messick, Ryan Smith. THANKS!! I owe you! The awesome Doubleday Broadway Publishing and Harlem Moon people: Catherine Pollock, Laura Pillar, Brian Jones, Meredith McGinnis, Emma Bolton, Tracy Jacobs, Katia Nelson, Toisan Craigg. Hollywood Black Film Festival: Tanya Kersey-Henley, Sylvia Moore, David Daniels. For the staff members, assistants, publicists, agents and others who helped along the way: John Singleton's awesome assistant, Jamaica Carter, who always gives 200 percent; you get first prize. Tracey Lyles, Julia O'Farrow, Rodney W. Gray, Ali Hileman, Lisa Cortes, Jackie Bazan, Don Juan, Suzanne O'Donnell, Lia Martin, Ramona Knepp, Deborah McGee, Maia Medre, Lana Campbell, Johanna Fiore, Tracey Lyles, Rod Gailes, Jason Lam, Heidi Lopato-Slan, Lisa Schoenberger, Michael Connor, Robert Weaver, Felecia McEachin, Ada Babino, Letifah Martin. The staff of the Donnell Media Center of the New York Public Library for their excellent service. Support your local library, folks! The staff of the Schomburg Center for Research in Black Culture. Candace Howell and the Metro New York Chapter of the National Black MBA Association.

CONTENTS

INTRODUCTION

Movies. I've always loved the movies. Since my earliest memories of watching *The Wizard of Oz* every year on TV and the weekday-afternoon TV "Big Show" in my hometown of Mobile, Alabama, featuring old classics like *The Creature from the Black Lagoon*, *King Kong* and *The Fly*, to family gatherings to watch our Super 8 home movies of road trips, First Communions and Christmases—movies have always played a major role in my life.

I shall always remember those Saturday matinees with my mother at the old Downtown Theater in Mobile where I saw those mesmerizing Disney animation masterpieces like *Lady and the Tramp*, *Sleeping Beauty* and *Snow White and the Seven Dwarfs*.

Graduating from animation to more live-action fare, I somehow persuaded my father to let me tag along with him and my teenaged brother and sister to see Gordon Parks's *Shaft* at Mobile's fabled Roxy theater. Admittedly, I hadn't a clue as to what was really going on, but that MUSIC, that MUSIC by Isaac Hayes along with Richard Roundtree's strut, his afro and leather jacket have remained treasures in my mind as the ultimate in Black male coolness.

I also had a stint in front of the camera when my first-grade teacher at Most Pure Heart of Mary School, Sister Mary Margaret, picked me to be one of three actors in a film produced by local high school students. It was a hip, silent piece set to Beatles music. What an exciting moment for me. There was a screening, I was introduced to the audience; I had my star moment.

I later became a huge fan of '70s B horror movies like *Frogs*, about killer amphibians, and *Stanley*, about rattlesnakes. And don't forget *Godzilla*. Those movies were fantastically horrifying, and I'll never forget *Godzilla vs. the Smog Monster*, which I saw with my good friends Alton and Craig Stevens and their mom, Lois Jean.

Like most kids, I'm sure, I knew early on that movies had the power to excite, instill fear, make one laugh or cry. But spoil my beach visits? I didn't realize that was possible until I saw Steven Spielberg's *Jaws* in 1975. I had been a water lover since I was a toddler, but *Jaws* terrified me so much that I refused to water-ski on Fowl River in Alabama the entire rest of that blood-curdling summer no matter what assurances the grown-ups gave me that there were no sharks in the freshwater river. But I just couldn't get that poor little boy on that yellow raft from *Jaws* out of my mind. I wasn't going to end up like him—lunch.

Despite my love of movies, I never saw myself having anything serious to do with them. Yes, I was in a children's theater growing up and had a few bit parts, but that and the student film were it as far as the role entertainment played in my life. Off to college, I studied business like a good Morehouse College Man, and later even earned a Columbia MBA. But the world of high finance just wasn't for me. I was severely disenchanted and spent many painstaking hours contemplating my future. Living in Brooklyn in the late '80s and early '90s, I couldn't help but be influenced by all of the energy that Spike Lee was generating. He was transforming the world and I had lived in Clinton Hill, a neighborhood bordering the legend-in-the-making and oh-so-funky Fort Greene. And Spike was the mayor of the land. Perhaps movies would be my thing.

At the suggestion of my good college buddy Harris Bostic II, I enrolled in a Saturday-morning screenwriting class at the New School for Social Research in Manhattan, and my life has never quite been the same since. There I found the magic, vibrancy, and humor that were missing from my world. I was forever on a new course. From the first day of class I knew my banking days were numbered. I would later take film classes at the School of Visual Arts and direct a couple of short films, screen one at Lincoln Center with the Black Filmmaker Foundation, and embark on a journey to the silver screen.

A few years after my first screenwriting class, I made the most important and best decision of my life—I quit banking—and I've never looked back. But my father has always told me that nothing worthwhile in life is ever easy, and so it has been with film. Pursuing my film industry fantasies has been the most exciting and most difficult challenge of my professional life, and one I wouldn't trade for anything.

But last I heard, fun, dreaming and wishing don't pay bills. Peddling my scripts, taking meetings and trying to make it all happen in Hollywood, I quickly realized that getting a break in Tinseltown is more than just not easy—it's EXTREMELY HARD. Yes, I'd saved and planned, but I needed to make some extra cash.

Enter journalism. With a few good friends at HBO, I queried my wonderful friend Lourdes Liz about writing for a segment of the company's Web site dedicated to urban content. She and Sybil Berry agreed to let me, and with that "yes" I got the opportunity to interview great directors such as Forest Whitaker, Kasi Lemmons, Stanley Nelson and Ernest Dickerson. I've always loved hearing people tell their stories. During my interviews with the above-mentioned directors, I got a chance to hear about their childhoods, their craft, family life and a host of other things. The sad thing about it was that for my given writing assignments, I wasn't able to use most of the material. I thought to myself, "This would be a great book. These guys have the most incredible stories, and I'm sure there are other people who'd want to hear them." But a book? Me? I wanted to write screenplays and make my own movies. Why would I write a book about Black directors?

Fast-forward several months later to a reception at Harlem's illustrious Aaron Davis Hall. I was talking with editor Janet Hill and I said, "Janet, I have a book idea." She said, "What is it?" "A book on Black filmmakers," I said. Her response: "I've been wanting to do that book for years. Now I have a writer!"

Jump-cut to book proposal, agent, submission, committee, approval, book deal, to the piece of work I'm honored to have you holding in your hands.

Writing *Why We Make Movies* has been the most fascinating experience of my entire life. Never before have I had the opportunity to engage, to be inspired by, to listen to, to eat with, to laugh with, to visit, to be captivated by, and to be encouraged by some of the most brilliant minds in the universe. My meetings with each filmmaker were like a master class, with the erudite teacher instructing the humble and eager student. I entered this theater with respectable knowledge of cinema, and as I continue to journey with this project I realize that my trip has only just begun; there's much more exhilarating learning and living to do.

On the pages that follow, you will have a chance to slow-dissolve into the thoughts, meanderings, visualizations, the still photographs, the slow-pan shots, the slow disclosures, the dramatic builds, the payoffs, the closeups and the dress rehearsals of living cinematic geniuses—the best of the best.

It should be understood, however, that this book is not meant to be a "best of" listing, nor is it exhaustive. In fact, the most painstaking part of this experience was having to select only 33 names. There are unquestionably many other directors and producers whose talents, contributions and creative visions make them eligible for inclusion: Sidney Poitier, Oprah Winfrey, Antoine Fuqua, F. Gary Gray, Isaac Julien, Irene xenabu Davis, Madison Davis Lacy, Sam Pollard, Charles Stone III, Damon Dash, Tim Story, Carol Mayes, Clark Johnson, Raoul Peck, Theodore Witcher, Cauleen Smith, Adisa, Tim Reid, Paul Hall, Mario Van Peebles, Monty Ross, Kevin Hooks, Rusty Cundieff, Tracey Edmonds, Suzanne de Passe, Christopher Scott Cherot, Reggie Rock Bythewood, Debbie Allen, Neema Barnette, Gene Davis, Michael Jenkinson, Thomas Carter, Carl Seaton, Diana Williams, Rick Fujuyiwa, Preston Holmes, Mark Brown, James Lassiter, Gary Hardwick, Partrik-Ian Polk, Eric LaSalle, Kevin Sullivan, Ice Cube, Jeff Clanagan, Master P, Hype Williams, Denzel Washington, the Hughes brothers, Larry Clark, Kathleen Collins, Billy

Woodberry, Jacqui Jones, Louis Massiah, Nelson George, Damon Lee, Will Packer, Rob Hardy, Bridgette Davis, Pearl Bowser, Joe Brewster, Kwyn Bader, Christine and Michael Swanson, Clyde Taylor, Alison Swan, Craig Ross, Marc Cayce, Jeff Byrd, _____ (insert your name if I forgot you). These are only some of the names that come to mind.

I have attempted to present the reader with a broad range of cinematic voices whose works are not only important for today or just yesterday, but will continue to speak to and inform us and the world for years, decades and perhaps generations to come. From pop culture legends like Gordon Parks and Ossie Davis, to Spike Lee and his *She's Gotta Have It*, to Orlando Bagwell of the historic and mesmerizing *Eyes on the Prize* series, to Julie Dash, to Keenen Ivory Wayans and his hilarious *Scary Movie*, I have sought to take you on an odyssey across the plains of Black America's contributions to the magic of cinema in the voices of its creators. Not the historian, not the movie buff, not the opinion maker, not the civil rights leader, not the politician, not the critic— the filmmakers themselves do the talking. There is one exception: Prof. Manthia Diawara of New York University is the only critic included, but he also *makes* movies.

So grab your popcorn, your soda and your Goobers and take a seat. The show is about to begin.

Enjoy!

GEORGE ALEXANDER

The Pioneers

Gordon Parks

Perhaps no other living person personifies what it means to be a renaissance man more than the legendary Gordon Parks. Born November 30, 1912, in Fort Scott, Kansas, the youngest of fifteen children, Parks is an internationally acclaimed photojournalist, filmmaker, art photographer, novelist, poet and composer who has been making his mark on world culture for more than half a century.

Parks made his first film, *Flavio*, in 1964, a documentary film short based on a photographic essay he did for *Life* magazine. Parks went on to make his feature film debut for Warner Brothers with his autobiographical *The Learning Tree*, making him the first African American to direct a major studio film. The film is based on Parks's novel of the same name; Parks adapted the novel, directed, wrote, produced and scored the film.

The Learning Tree was followed by *Shaft* in 1971. Based on the book, *Shaft* became an international hit, igniting what was to be called the blaxploitation movement. The character John Shaft became a pop culture icon, influencing everything from hairstyles to dress to street attitudes. And Isaac Hayes won the Academy Award for Best Original Song.

Parks went on to direct *Shaft's Big Score!*, *The Super Cops*, *Leadbelly*, *Solomon Northup's Odyssey*, *Moments Without Names* and *Martin*. In the year 2000, HBO presented a documentary on Parks's extraordinary life titled *Half Past Autumn: The Life and Works of Gordon Parks*, produced by St. Clair Bourne and Denzel Washington.

— — —

GA: *Your film career was actually preceded by your work as a photographer. What sparked your interest in photography in the first place?*

GP: I was working on the railway, the route from Chicago to Seattle, Washington and on to St. Paul, Minnesota. While in Chicago, and I would spend some time during my layovers going to a movie, a museum, or doing whatever to kill time. This time I went to the theater in Chicago, and as I was leaving the theater the newsreel came on and it was the bombing of the American gunship the *Panay* by the Japanese. So I decided to stay and watch it, and it was a real shock. The photographer who did it stayed right by his gun and the ship sank, and just as the film ended over the loudspeaker someone announced: "Norman Alley, the photographer who shot this wonderful footage, is backstage." Norman Alley then came out on stage in a white suit, took his bows, and there was applause. [Laughs]

GA: [Laughs]

GP: And I thought that was a very impressive thing. I never forgot that, and when I got to Seattle I looked through the window at the pawnshop and there was a camera in the window. So I went in and asked about it and the guy sold it to me for, I don't know, it was $12.50 or $7.50. I shot some film on the West Coast over the next few days, fooling with my camera, and I took it to Eastman Kodak in Minneapolis, where I was living, to get it developed. I didn't even know how to load the camera. A guy loaded it for me. The guy at Kodak asked me, "How long have you been shooting?" I said, "Well, I just started, that's my first roll." They said, "First roll?! This is excellent. You sure it's your first roll?" I said, "Yeah, it was my first roll of film." He said, "Well, you keep this up, we'll give you a show in our window." Well, I kept it up and they gave me a show in their window.

GA: *You later broke into fashion photography, having met Frank and Madeline Murphy, who owned a womenswear store in Minneapolis. Tell me about that. The shot [for the Murphys] of the woman seated in the evening gown is exquisite.*

GP: Well, I doubled-exposed everything except that shot. I went by the store to look for fashion work, and Frank Murphy was kicking me out of the store, and Mrs. Murphy came to my aid. She asked him, "What does the young man want?" Frank said, "He wants to shoot fashion. I'm telling him to get out. They do fashion photography in London or Paris." I felt smaller and smaller. Mrs. Murphy said, "Well, how do you know he can't shoot fashion, Frank?" Just like that. I was surprised, and he was surprised. She asked me if I shot fashion, and I lied and said, "Yes, ma'am." She asked me if I had my work with me. I said, "No, ma'am. My work is at home." She said, "Well, I'm going to give you a chance. You come by here tomorrow after six o' clock and I'll have models and clothes. How many models do you want?" I said, "Ahh, three" [holding up three fingers]. [Laughs] "How many gowns?" I said, "Twelve." All guesswork. There was this friend of mine, Harvey Goldstein, who owned a camera shop on the university campus. He said, "Man, you're crazy. You can't shoot—you don't have film, the right camera, you don't have lights. And you can't shoot fashion." I said, "Well, Harvey, you can fix all that up in one day. You're going to let me have all the equipment, and I'll take care of the fashion." That's where it started. I had double-exposed everything but one picture, it turns out. That one picture that you saw of the woman on the couch, it was good. My wife said, "Well, why don't you take that one and show it to her." I called Harvey and asked him if he would blow it up for me to 16 x 20. The next day I had the picture sitting on an easel outside the door when the Murphys came in. They saw it and Madeline said, "It's beautiful. Where are the rest of them?" [Laughs] I told the truth. She said, "Would they all have been that good?" I said, "That's the worst one of all." [Laughs]

GA: [Laughs]
GP: She bought it and said, "Well, let's do it over, but no more double exposure." I said, "All right." So years later I did my first big story for Vogue, I think it was ten pages of color, and I got a cable from Madeline saying, "I just saw the Vogue magazine and I see you're not double exposing anymore. I'm coming to New York this weekend, and I'd like to take you to the Plaza for dinner." I said, "Fine." During dinner I said, "Madeline, you know, all these years I've wondered why on that particular day you came to my rescue. You'd never seen me before and I was telling you I had talent" and she said, "Oh, you did have talent, otherwise we wouldn't have seen all of those beautiful pictures in Vogue." I said, "Why did you come to my aid when Frank had me out the door?" She said, "Oh, well, I think maybe, Gordon, I was just mad as hell at Frank that day." [Laughs]

GA: [Laughs]
GP: I said, "I'm glad you were."

GA: Great. How did you develop your eye for fashion? Were you always curious? They say that the artist can see things that the rest of the world can't see.
GP: I wonder myself, at times, how I developed an eye for fashion. I looked at fashion books: Vogue, Harper's Bazaar and different books that I saw. I always appreciated well-dressed women, and

somehow or another it stuck. I was obsessed with it. They even recognized that when I went to work for *Vogue*—that I had an eye for fashion beyond what some of the other photographers had.

GA: *There's a sense of elegance in your photography that is extraordinary.*
GP: Yeah, especially when you come off of a farm in Kansas. [Laughs]

GA: *Tell me how* The Learning Tree *came about, making you the first Black studio director.*
GP: I didn't start out to become a filmmaker. It was by accident. Most still photographers have sort of an urging to go into motion pictures because they get a little frustrated with seeing the still image sitting there and the camera moving and the image not moving. So you want to turn it around a bit. I was fortunate inasmuch as my first film *The Learning Tree* was about my childhood, it was autobiographical and it was difficult to do.

I would never have expected to direct a film. But John Cassavetes called me because he had read the novel *The Learning Tree*, which was my first novel, and said that he thought it should be made into a motion picture. I said, "Well, that would be fine, John, I'd like to see it made into a motion picture." He said, "I think you should direct it." I said, "There are no Black directors in Hollywood, and there are not going to be any." He said, "Well, why don't we try?" I said, "Go ahead and be my guest." He responded, "Would you come out here day after tomorrow?" I said, "Yeah." He said, "Meet me at Warner Brothers Studio at 12:00 P.M. It's in Burbank."

And I met him. He had read both *The Choice of Weapons* and *The Learning Tree*, and had given them to Kenny Hyman, who was running the studio at the time. But he and Kenny were at odds. Cassavetes had done a film for him and they weren't speaking, but Cassavetes said, "I'll introduce you to him, then I'll leave." That's the way it happened. I think the first thing Hyman asked me was if I wanted to write the screenplay. I said, "You mean, you want me to direct this film?" He said, "Yeah, I want you to direct this film." Just like that. He said, "Which book would you like to direct first?" I said, "Well, what do you mean?" He said, "Well, I've read *A Choice of Weapons*, and I read *The Learning Tree*. I said, "*The Learning Tree's* first. I'd rather do that first." I thought he was putting me on—you know—a Hollywood put-on. [Laughs] So I said, "Well, I'd be happy, but I don't know any screenwriters. I don't know anyone out here." He said, "Why don't you write the screenplay yourself? You wrote the novel." I said, "Okay"—I thought he was still putting me on. He said, "Cassavetes tells me that you're a composer. Maybe you could compose the music for it?" I said, "Okay. Why not?" You know now it's going this far. "That'll be fine with me," I said. Then he said, "Since you're going to be the first Black director in Hollywood, you should have a lot of control, and maybe you should produce it for Warner Brothers as well." I said, "Why not?"

I still didn't believe him until it flashed across the news and the newspapers from the release that Warner Brothers's public relations put out that they were going to do my film and I was going to direct it. I signed contracts and began to believe it. But I had never done any of these things. It was my first novel, and I'd never directed or produced any film, so I had to go get the best people I could find.

GA: *There's also a story behind the novel, The Learning Tree. How did it come about?*

GP: I'd never written a novel. But I knew Carl Mydans, one of the *Life* magazine photographers I talked with, was a good writer. He was a reporter for *Life* and a photographer as well. He said, "You talk so much about your childhood in Kansas. You should write a novel about it." I said, "I've never written a novel, Carl." He said, "You ever try?" I said, "No." He said, "Well, go home this weekend and try." I went home that weekend and tried, and it turned out to be a best-seller in five languages, and I tell a lot of students, Black students especially, "Luck's going to come your way, you just have to be ready for it when it comes. If it comes and you're not ready for it, it'll say, 'Well, see you later. Next year. I was here, but you weren't ready for me.'"

GA: *There's so much truth in the novel and in the film. Do you think that's what people respond to in the work—the humanity?*

GP: Well, all I could go on was honesty and humanity and what had happened. I didn't have vast creative experience. I didn't feel creative, especially at that time. I had to go on what had actually happened and some people who have lived it—they revisit it through me. I think that's why the book took off, not only in America but in several countries, including Germany and France.

GA: *What was your actual process for making the transition from a phenomenal life as a still photographer—Life, fashion, poverty work—to motion pictures. How did you prepare?*

GP: Well, I didn't have much time to prepare myself. I had been assigned to the film overnight. All I could do was rely on what experience I had with photography. Working for *Life* magazine, I had been assigned to different stories that required the use of certain lenses for the effects I wanted to get. It meant getting a cinematographer, hiring one who understood me, understood my story, liked my story and could understand certain technical things that I would try to achieve. I liked the work of Burnett Guffey, because he had done *Bonnie and Clyde* and a couple of other films. But he was retired and wasn't going to come out of retirement. But when he read the book he said, "I want to do this." He liked the book. We had our little differences on the studio set one day before we went out to shoot the film in Kansas. I showed him a couple of setups and I wanted to see how he'd react to them. He said, "You can't do them that way." I said, "Well, why don't we try, just try?" He said, "Okay." So we did it his way and we did it my way. We looked at the rushes that evening and he said, "You win hands down. You can do it." Well, I had used similar lenses for still photography. I knew how I wanted my subjects to move—I had made those moves before, I had been through all of those experiences.

GA: *So you took your still photography experiences and applied them to motion pictures?*
GP: Yeah, and finding the right characters, the right actors, to perform, like Kyle Johnson [who played Newt, the Gordon Parks character], who was like me more or less, and Marcus, who was the antagonist. I knew all of those boys; they had different names—the dirty cop Kirky [Laughs], he lived not too far from where I lived. He had his old motorcycle, we found his old clothes, but he had actually died by then. But it was all so real. It was like revisiting the whole thing all over.

GA: *I've read in the transcript from a PBS interview with Phil Ponce where you said that as a still photographer your subject is so much more important than the photographer. Does the same apply in motion pictures?*
GP: Well, your subject matter is the main thrust. If your views are entangled with the subject matter's views, then fine, but if not, you'd better stay away from your own views and go with your subject matter. Because that's what your story is all about, that's what your screenplay's all about, and the director has to always be in control. He has to be able to change things in a minute, in a second, even though it's written out in another way. Luckily for me, I wrote my first screenplay myself. The other screenplays, well, I had to make changes. When I did *Shaft*, sometimes I had to make changes right on the spot. I'd say, "No, we won't do it that way, we'll do it this way." But Roundtree [Richard Roundtree, who played John Shaft] would say, "Well, it says here . . ." I'd say, "I know. It says that, but don't say it that way. Change it." Because when Roundtree's asleep or having a sandwich at night or out with his girlfriend, I'm sitting up figuring out the next day's shoot and how I'm going to do it.

So I have it thoroughly in my mind and the changes I have to make for the next day—if I will make any changes or not, if I'm getting what I want and if the actors are giving me the kind of performances that I want. All of that has to be taken into consideration, and then the personalities of the actors themselves have to be taken into consideration for the next day's shoot. Some consider themselves overnight stars and give you all kinds of trouble. You have to look at them and evaluate and say, "Are they worth it?" If not, send them home and find someone else.

GA: Have you ever had to send anyone home?

GP: Yeah. One extra I sent home. He got a little bit too important.

GA: What film was that?

GP: The Learning Tree. Then I had to send a man who was the set designer home, back to California. There were problems with my being a Black director. I think the man whom I chose to be my assistant, Bill Conrad [off-site producer from studio] was somewhat put out. He disliked the fact that I was doing exactly what he wanted to do all his life. He had an image of himself as being another Orson Welles. He wanted to direct, he wanted to compose. The studio gave me a choice of five men who would be of assistance to me. I met with them for lunch, and he was the most obstinate during lunch—he hardly spoke, hardly shook my hand—but the rest of the guys were all fine. Kenny Hyman asked me, "Well, you met them all, now which one would you like to have?" I said, "Well, Conrad." He said, "That ornery son of a bitch? Why do you want him?" [Laughs] I said, "Does he know his business?" He said, "Yeah, he knows his business." I said, "I want him." He said, "Why?" I said, "Because I want to be his boss." [Laughs]

GA: [Laughs] You like a challenge.

GP: I think he [Conrad] thought eventually I would flake out and he'd take the film over. His assistant was named Jimmy Lydon, and they were sending back reports to the studio that the film was underexposed and that I was doing this and I was double exposing or underexposing. Well, what they didn't realize was that the film was going back to Hollywood, they were looking at it and they were telling me, "Beautiful, beautiful." So I told him, I said, "Look, Lydon, no more reports out of here unless I see them. And you should know that those people are looking at the film back at the laboratories and they're telling me that it's beautiful and you're telling them that I'm underexposing or double exposing. That's for me to decide." He said, "I didn't intend to do you any harm." I said, "Well, you did do me some harm." I said, "I just don't want anymore, otherwise we'll part." After that, Bill Conrad said, "Hey, you're doing great. I'm going back to Hollywood. See you later. Good luck. If you need me, holler." Later on, we became sort of friendly. He became an actor—he did Jake and the Fat Man and Cannon on TV—and later on he invited me out on his yacht.

GA: What was it like adapting the novel The Learning Tree into a screenplay?

GP: I was in a position where I could do it. Had I been a director working with another screenwriter's work, that would have been more difficult. But having lived this story (it's autobiographical), and being the director and the screenwriter, I had complete control. So if something didn't work, I was able to get rid of it without feeling badly about it. If it worked for me, it worked. There were times when I was confused, and I admitted to myself that I was confused [Laughs] and did something about it.

GA: *Given that you're a photographer, how did you work with your cinematographers?*
GP: Burnett Guffey was a very good cinematographer—he had a lot of experience, his rolls were good, he knew what I was after. He was my cinematographer on *Shaft*, *Leadbelly* and so forth. All of the cinematographers I worked with would ask me to take a look through the camera before we'd start shooting. The Japanese cinematographer with whom I did one film knew me and knew what I was after. All of his setups were complementary to what I thought, what I felt. The direction can go all the way down to the music. For instance, when Isaac Hayes did the music for *Shaft*, and I had to work with him—having been a musician myself, I was able to help.

GA: *What's the process for composing the music for a film?*
GP: You get your footage first, then you sit down and look at it and decide where you need music. You don't want too much music, you don't want music in moments unless it's completely necessary—especially if someone is killed, a funeral, or if someone is happy, a cabaret scene. It all depends upon what your screenplay says.

GA: *When you did Shaft, did you have any idea that it would become such a pop culture icon? It's one of the most popular films in history.*
GP: I'm not sure if you know it or not, but in 2000 the Library of Congress selected *Shaft* as one of the most important films of all time. *The Learning Tree* had made it quite some time ago, but I didn't know that *Shaft* would make it, so I have two films now. I'm happy about that. I had no idea when we were making *Shaft* that it would become the great landmark that it would. I thought we had a good film and the studio thought we had a good film. Jim Marbury who ran MGM at the time said you'd better take this film to England and show it to the English press. I said, "Jim, they're not going to understand this film in England." He said, "Why not?" I said, "Well, I just don't think they will." He said, "Take it. Set it up." I set up the press in London, that's where they did it. I went there. And one Brit reporter said [in British accent], "What does Shaft mean, really?" [Laughs] I stuck my finger up in the air and I said, "It means 'up yours'!"

GA: [Laughs]
GP: One reporter said [British accent], "The blokes are going around calling each other mother, mother, mother. [Laughs] What does that mean?" [Laughs]

GA: [Laughs]

GP: A female reporter said, "It means motherfucker!" Just like that.

GA: [Laughs]

GP: I said, "Thank you! I couldn't say it!"

GA: [Laughs]

GP: So when Shaft opened, it opened all over the world, and it's still playing in different parts of the world. But actually, one of the best films I ever did was Leadbelly, I think.

GA: And the studio didn't push that film the way you thought they should have.

GP: Well, Frank Yelburn at Paramount was responsible for the film, but Frank lost his job just as we finished shooting. Frank loved the film. The guy who followed Frank had never heard of Leadbelly, so he didn't want to put his new money into Frank Yelburn's film because Frank had made seven films. And this guy killed about six or seven of Frank's films. He would have killed Leadbelly, but Charlie Champlin, a critic with the Los Angeles Times, had seen it and said that he thought it was the best film of the year. Otherwise this guy would have killed it. But I think Leadbelly was probably one of my best films.

GA: It's a fantastic film. You later did some PBS films, like Solomon Northrop's Odyssey, about a young Black man born a slave in the 1840s. What motivated you to do that work?

GP: I left Hollywood after Leadbelly. I got disgusted because I had put an awful lot of effort in it, it was a good film. The studio head told me that it was a beautiful film and that the studio was going to get behind it. He then went upstairs and told his assistants to kill it. It was invited to two or three festivals and won first place. I took it to Europe, and audiences stood up and cheered.

GA: Tell me about the short documentary film you did set in Brazil, called Flavio.

GP: After I returned to America after finishing shooting a story on Flavio in Life magazine in Rio de Janeiro, my friend said, "You know, no one is going to believe this. You should go back and do a film on this." And that's what I did. I came back and did a short film, but I used three 35mm cameras because we needed to shoot as quickly as possible. The government did not want that story to get out.

GA: The Brazilian government didn't?

GP: The Brazilian government didn't. It was a disgrace to them. Luckily, I got my motion picture film out. But when the story was published in Life, the government had that particular flavela [very poor neighborhood] destroyed, although they just moved the people to a different flavela. But there was no running water, no toilets—the whole mountainside was a disaster, with people dying and little kids dying before they got to be twenty years old. Flavio had about six months to live when they found him. When I went back to Brazil when they did the HBO film on me [Half Past Autumn], he was in his forties.

GA: Were you happy with Half Past Autumn?
GP: Yes. And it's been very successful for HBO.

GA: Would you like to direct again?
GP: I've been offered to direct this novel I've written, The Sun Stalker. I wrote the novel, but I'm not that anxious to direct it. Well, not something that big. It would need to be shot in Ireland, England, Scotland, Venice, Paris, and Germany, which means carrying a crew from America and picking up people everywhere you go. It's just too much. I'm not as young as I used to be.

GA: [Laughs] You're a photographer, a poet, composer, a filmmaker. But what is an artist?
GP: Well, you're asking a big question. Being an artist is being able to interpret the most vivid, the most outstanding things in your imagination or vision. If you're a writer, you try to write in a way that's not normally done. For instance, you could write a sentence the way everybody else could write it, but write it differently. The same goes for taking a picture. When you're pointing a camera at someone—not the ordinary shot, but something that goes for the person's personality. With music it's whom you love, whether or not it's Rachmaninoff, Satie, or whether it's Prokofiev, Duke Ellington, whoever it is, you have your own interpretation of that. If you're a pianist, you sit down at the piano and do your own thing, express your own feelings. I feel that it has to come from the heart. It's not so much the eye as it is the heart. The heart works as a conduit to express what you're feeling. In other words, just have a piece of glass next to your heart. You project what the heart is feeling. And that's the way it is with any artistic approach.

GA: How does an artist get to the place of being able to create from the heart? How do you source that honesty within yourself?
GP: It takes time. First you have to master your concept. In photography, first you have to master the camera so you will know what to tell it and the lens to do and when you want it to do it, then get lost in it. It's the same with writing. Last night, for instance, I spent three hours working on

one paragraph. There were different ways I could twist it and make it turn. But I wanted to do it in a way that wasn't ordinary. So when I finally finished, I said, "Mmm, I like it." That was at 4:30 in the morning. I had to give it a lot of thought. Anyway, I would have written it, people would have understood it, but I wanted to do it in such a way that they not only understood it, but they appreciated it as art and not just as a sentence out there. With this book [a memoir] I'm writing, my writing is better than it's ever been in my entire life. I started writing on my eighty-ninth birthday November 30, 2001.

GA: *What's your secret to longevity and creativity? You move around faster than some of my friends who are in their thirties.* [Laughs]
GP: Well, you have to work a lot if you have three-ex wives. [Laughs] They're all my good friends. Hell, if you don't work at something, you fall apart. I don't believe in these guys who retire at fifty-five or sixty years old. If you can, fine, but you need something to keep yourself going. Right now, if books are not enough to hold me together, I'm working on a piano concerto and a piece for the Chinese cellist Yo-Yo Ma. I'm also working on three new movements now [November 2002]. I just like to do these things—they keep me going, otherwise I'd fall apart. I'm approaching ninety, and I had two Achilles tendons removed a couple of years ago. If I hadn't had those removed, I'd still be skiing. This spring I may go back on the tennis court. Without the Achilles tendon, you lose that cushion. So I mean the thing about it is to just keep going. There's a lot to distract you. There are a lot of reasons to say that you can't do this or you can't do that, but you know yourself and your body better than anybody else—even better than the doctors. You can diagnose your problem better than the doctor can. *The Sun Stalker*, a novel I wrote about J. M. W. Turner, is being published on my ninetieth birthday.

GA: *Your family was very important to you in your development. Tell me about that.*
GP: My father was a great man, my mother was a great woman, my brothers and sisters were great people. There were fifteen children altogether, and I was the youngest of the whole lot. I learned a lot from them, I got a lot of love from all of them. That's the thing that saved me. When I got through writing my memoir and I wondered how in world was I alive, I know it's the love that they gave to me when I was a youngster. It kept me going. I try to give that love to the rest of the world. I'm a little surprised sometimes by all of the responses I get from around the world, all of the letters from people, foreign people I've never heard of. They've read my books, seen my pictures, and say that I've changed their lives and so forth, and it makes me feel very good. Some people can't understand why I don't understand it. All I was doing was doing what I was

supposed to do—give what was given to me. I was given love, understanding. Why do I want to possess it without passing it on to somebody else and giving someone else a helping hand when I can? I don't have time to do it all the time, but I try. People say, "Why you do this, why you do that?" I say, "Somebody helped me. So I like to give someone else a helping hand." A lot of people did help me, and they weren't all from the Black race. Count Mrs. Murphy, Harvey Goldstein, Alexander Lieberman at *Vogue*, Wilson Hicks at *Life*. All those people, I don't know. When people ask how I did it being a Black man, well, I just did not allow color to enter the picture when I went to *Vogue* or when I went to *Life* or anyplace else. Here's my work. Here I am. If you can use me, fine—if you can't, goodbye. It never hurt me. Even if you refused me, it wouldn't send me away with a ton of regrets because my color happened to be different from yours.

GA: Where did you get that strong sense of self?
GP: It came from my mother and my father.

GA: What are your thoughts on Black cinema today?
GP: I don't look at many films. I get all of the Academy films. But films are difficult, and a lot of them don't hit the mark. They get too involved in politics and this or that and the gimmicks. They lack the honesty that some of the films used to have, and when they lack the honesty they lack the power. I haven't looked at many films lately. I'm too busy writing, too busy with poetry, too busy with music. I've been asked to do films recently by different people, but if I don't like the screenplay, I don't bother. I don't do it for money right now. I have to love it. That goes for everything I do. With *The Sun Stalker*, which I just finished, people ask me, "Why an English painter from the nineteenth century?" I say, "Because I loved his work." [Laughs]

GA: Who were your creative influences when you started your career?
GP: Well, there are certain photographers I admired when I started off, certain filmmakers, composers, writers like Richard Wright. In music, Rachmaninoff is my favorite. Erik Satie is one of my favorites. Prokofiev. I'm all over the place. It's difficult to say which directors I like.

GA: What advice do you have for aspiring directors?
GP: To do anything well, you have to have a purpose other than just money. You have to have good feelings about the universe, about people, about helping it become a better universe. Become what God wanted us to become when he put us in this universe—to make a contribution. You should not just take up space here without showing your thanks to the power for having put us

here, and that's what I try to do. I try to make my day worthwhile, my life worthwhile. If you don't have good thoughts about good things, you'll never make good photographs. You're not going to make good pictures and you're not going to write good books or anything else. You're not going to write good music. You might think that you're being successful, but in the end you're not unless you're making some sincere contribution—especially to our youth, because our youth are tomorrow. Without our youth, there is no tomorrow.

Melvin Van Peebles

Anyone who has ever seen Melvin Van Peebles's independently produced *Sweet Sweetback's Baadasssss Song* (1971) knows that they've never witnessed a film quite like it. An urban film before the term became commonplace in film parlance, *Sweetback* presented an edgy and controversial image of Black America and, along with Gordon Parks's *Shaft* and Ossie Davis's *Cotton Comes to Harlem*, helped catapult in the blaxploitation era.

Though called by many "the father of Black modern cinema," Van Peebles will not hesitate to tell anyone that the success of *Sweetback* made him a pioneer not only in Black independent cinema but in all of independent cinema.

The Chicago-born Van Peebles made his feature film debut in Paris with *The Story of a Three Day Pass* (1967) and later the independently produced *Sweetback*. His other directing credits include *Don't Play Us Cheap* (1972), *Identity Crisis* (1989), *Vroom, Vroom, Vroom* (1995) and *Le Conte du Ventre Plein*. Also an accomplished novelist and composer, he performs his music across the United States and Europe.

- - - -

GA: What role did movies play in your life growing up? Were you a movie buff?
MV: There was nothing called "movie buff." You'd just go to the movies.

GA: What were some of your favorites?

MV: There were no fucking favorites, man. You were in a movie. You saw everything. You'd go see your triple features—they had triple features. I remember when I made my first film in San Francisco. A guy came to my door—I'll never forget this. I was living in a little apartment, and the guy knocked on the door and he said, "My name is Roger Ferragalo and I hear you're doing movies." I said, "Yes, sir." He said, "Well, welcome to the Bay Area Cineastes Club." I said, "Yeah. What's a cineaste?" The guy said to me, "You're a disciple of whom? You like Eisenstein or Kurosawa or Orson Welles?" "Who's that?" I said. I'd never heard of any these people. I didn't know anything about *Citizen Kane*. I didn't know shit about *Potemkin*.

GA: So what made you decide that you wanted to make movies?

MV: What happened was when I left college, I was going to go to Europe. I had gotten myself a ticket and I was going because I hadn't been yet. But thirteen days out of college, I was in the Air Force and I was an officer. I had graduated from college when I was still twenty, so I was an officer while I was still a minor—I couldn't buy a drink. And I stayed in the Air Force for what seemed a long time, in that I was the first Black officer that had graduated—ROTC had just been initiated at Ohio Wesleyan, and everywhere I went they couldn't believe I was an officer. I looked like I was about fifteen, plus I was Black. [Laughs] This was the tail end of the Korean War. So then I ended up as a navigator and years later ended up as a navigator on a jet bomber—the first jet bomber that ever came out, the B-47.

GA: So what did you do after leaving the Air Force?

MV: I moved to Mexico and lived there for about six months, and then I came back. I really hadn't come to the analyzation of the question when I was young, "What did I want to be?" Well, I didn't think I wanted to be a presser or own a tailor shop like my father, but I had this enormous specialty military training course. So I applied to fly at TWA, on one of the other airlines, make good bread and have a nice life. However, they didn't say it, but they weren't taking minorities into the cockpit. So as far as teaching or any of that other shit, with my big mouth, I would have lasted about five minutes. I ended up driving cable cars. If I had to come back to the States, I said, "What's the best city in the States?" The best city was San Francisco. So I drove cable cars there, and while I was driving cable cars I also started to write, because as much as I liked painting, none of the people I knew or enjoyed talking to knew anything about art or cared anything about art.

GA: These were the people in your circle in San Francisco?

MV: Well, I didn't have a circle. But just the people, Jimmy Boy and Catfish and so-and-so. They didn't know anything about Modigliani or Monet, and I didn't feel that had any resonance in the everyday life of our people. Where are the Negroes? The people that I like, that I have something I want to say to. And I thought I'd write. I'd write novels. I thought I'd teach myself to write. So watching the people who kept getting on and off the cable car, I thought, "Huh. I bet I could write an article about this." Then I analyzed things in a not-so-artistic way. What would be the gimmick, I guess is the best word. Well, I'd write from the point of view of a cable car guy—a day in the life of a cable car. So I started it, and the article grew and grew and grew into a book—a photo essay book—The Big Heart. It was published and it got rave reviews. The photographer was a little old German lady named Ruth Bernhard.

GA: What was your process? Did you have an agent?

MV: I didn't know what an agent was. I was talking with somebody on the street as I was walking to work one day. We just happened to begin to talk, and I was telling her what I was doing and she said, "I know somebody who's a photographer." That's how I met Ruth Bernhard. Then the guy who ran the cable car fired me because he didn't think niggers should read, let alone write. I said, "How come you're firing me?" "Because your profile shows that you're going to have a big accident," he said. "Have I had a big accident?" "No, but your profile . . ." I had been working there almost a year. Not that I'd had one, but my profile. . . . So I went to work in the Black university, which is the post office. I call it the Black university. But before I left the cable car, someone who had gotten on the car said, "You know your book's a movie? Who laid it out?" I said, "Me." "Who was the photo editor?" I said, "Me." He said, "Your book is just like a movie." I said, "I'll go into movies." That was 1957. How do you go into movies? Now, I suppose it would be a daunting idea if I had known about all of the other things I did before I did them. So I called the guy who I heard had a camera. He was a still photographer, and I said, "I want to make a movie." He said, "That's great." He was very encouraging, and he asked, "What's the subject of the documentary?" I said, "It ain't gonna be no documentary. I want to tell a story. Just like the things you see in the movies." He said, "Yeah?" "Yeah," I said. I asked him how much it would cost, and he asked, "Are you going to shoot in sixteen or thirty-five?" I said, "What's that?" He said, "Sixteen- or thirty-five-millimeter." I said, "Oh, okay. What's that?" He explained what they were, and after the explanation I did a calculation, and at that time, if I used 16mm film I realized I could make a feature film, according to my calculations, for $500. I said, "All right, we're going to do it." Of course, what that $500 turned out to be was ninety minutes of 16mm film. He said that he had a camera and that I could use it.

GA: *Did you have a script?*

MV: I don't know if you'd call it a script, I had what I wanted done. When you put it down in different ways, you'd call it a script. The film was called A King. Anyway, so we started shooting, and then we had to send the film to the lab. I had forgotten about the developing. Developing hadn't been calculated in my price. After I got it developed, I said, "Now we're going to look at it." He said, "No, no, no, no. You never look at the negative. You've got to make a print from your negative." I said, "What? Huh?" My first feature turned out to be eleven minutes long. Plus, I lost the sound. That's how I went into music, because I couldn't afford any musicians and I needed a soundtrack.

GA: *Had you played an instrument before?*

MV: No. And I couldn't remember what I wanted, so I went to the piano. Since I couldn't read the music, I just numbered all the keys on the piano, and I've been doing that up to now. Somebody else puts it down for me. But I'm teaching myself to read a little bit. I did three short films: A King, Three Pickup Men for Herrick and Sunlight. So I went down to Hollywood with my films and I was offered a job as an elevator operator and I said, "I want to write and direct." Because I could get blindsided sometimes, forget I ain't a white boy. I'd keep getting blindsided. Finally, you're very aware of it, but then there are still times where you're just not thinking about it—the implications of that. But the guy said, "You don't have knack for this [directing]" . . . I said, "Fuck this. I'll go back to my second love—celestial mechanics." So I wrote to the University of Amsterdam, and applied to study astronomy. I told them that I would come early to brush up on the language, and they accepted me. On the way over there, I took my films and gave them to a guy named Amos Vogel in New York who ran something called Cinema 16 there. I leased my films to him and went on to study astronomy.

Anyway, while I was studying astronomy, one day I came back home and there was a letter for me. It said, "What are you doing? You are a genius, dada, dada, dada, dada, da. Don't waste your time. You should be in film." I'm in Amsterdam studying astronomy. He may not come when you call him, but he's always right on time—this Vogel guy got invited to France to bring some of his films. He sent my films along with some of the others, and the people saw this film and they went fucking wild. Now, the white people here had been telling me the usual kind of stuff. So I hitchhiked to France from Amsterdam, and they loved me and they took me to this little private theater above one of the big theaters on the Champs Élysées; it was in the evening, and they showed my films. Everyone said, "Oh, wonderful." Then we come down, their limos pull up, everybody kisses me, but then they drive off. I'm standing there on the Champs Élysées. I can't speak a word of French, ain't got a jingle in my pocket. And Amos Vogel is in New York. They just happened to see the films through him. I'm in the middle of the street with no bread, two wet cheeks, three cans of film and not a penny. So I begged. I was a beggar in the streets of Paris. I had been married through the service until halfway through Holland. And [my wife] just said that I worked too hard and that she wanted to see the world. So she took off to see the world.

GA: *How long did you beg in the streets?*
MV: Actually, I haven't stopped.

GA: [Laughs] *That's a good one.*
MV: [Laughs]

GA: *I'm going to do your kind of begging, how's that? You can teach me some tips. "Begging According to Melvin Van Peebles." That could be a book. Where did you live?*
MV: Under the bridge. I had no money. Then little by little I learned the language and I met some people, nice enough people, and little by little I began to make it there. After I learned enough French, I became a journalist.

GA: *So your wife and your children had left by the time you went to Paris?*
MV: Yes, they had already left.

GA: *Did you really think that it was possible for you to make it in film?*
MV: You don't know if it's possible. You just know that it ain't impossible. I get so tired of motherfuckers coming and telling me, "I'm broke, but I'm going to try hard, and I'm going to make it because I try hard. I'm not going to starve." You don't know if you're going to make it or not. If you like it, just try it. There's no guarantee. We're made to believe that if you work hard and do everything that somehow you'll win, but there's no guarantee.

GA: *You have to enjoy pursuing it—is that what you're saying?*
MV: Sometimes you don't even enjoy pursuing it, but I'd rather do that. I'd rather drink muddy

water and sleep in a hollow log than let the motherfucker win the other way. No, I'm going to keep on at it. Fuck it. I've been known to fight on occasion. Someone will say, "How did you know you could beat that motherfucker?" I didn't know I could beat him. That had never entered my mind. I just wasn't going to take it. There's a difference. That's a major difference. It's a different mind-set. Because if you know you're going to win, then you've got this other thing on your shoulder, such and such. No, I just wasn't going to take it. I didn't know this was going to be a success. People talk about *Sweetback*. Man, I was just hoping I would get the money back so that the people I had borrowed from, buddies of mine, wouldn't kill me. No biggie. People say, "You're such a financial wizard. With *Sweetback* you own the film negative." I said, "I ain't got partners. Not because I was brilliant, but because nobody would do it with me." I played the role of Sweetback not for any reason except that I could find no one who would play it for me who knew anything about cinema. An actor would say, "Put in a few more lines for Sweetback." I'd say, "Well, he doesn't talk a lot."

GA: *Tell me about working as a journalist in Paris.*

MV: I was walking down the street one day and I said, "I don't believe that." You don't believe what, Melvin? Because I was alone and I realized I could read French. Suddenly I was reading the headlines and I didn't even realize I could even read them. And there was a murder, and I guess we Americans see more "Perry Mason" or more this, that or whatever it is. It sounds cornier than a motherfucker to me. I went to the newspaper and said, "Listen, I don't think this is the way it happened." The story was about a murder on an American air force or army base. It was a stroke of luck. It was August, and if you don't know France, in August everyone goes away, so I was hired to write the story.

GA: *You did your first feature film,* The Story of a Three Day Pass *in France. Tell me how that came about.*

MV: I discovered a French law that said that French writers could have a temporary director's card. So I went to the Centre de Cinema and I walked in and they're not used to hearing nigger shit. I went there and said in French, "I came to pick up my director's card. Yeah, you know the French law says that a writer can have a director's card. That's what the law says. Well, I write in French. I'm a French writer, right?" The guy looked at me: "Yes."

GA: *What was your process for actually making the film?*

MV: I had a director's card and I waited a couple of weeks, then I went back to the Centre de

Cinema and said, "I want to apply for a grant. You know, French directors can apply for a grant. I have my French director's card." The guy said, "Yes." So I applied for this grant and I wrote a movie that was flattering to the French. But I didn't know it was flattering to the French. I was just telling the truth. Anyway, I was hoping I'd get $30,000 and they gave me $300,000, about a third of the film's budget. Afterwards, I'd be walking down the street and people would be crossing the street going, "Hey, Mel. How you doin'?" Everybody in the world said he was my pal because I was directing and producing and so forth. I shot some in Paris and some of it in Normandy—Un Fleur, Deauville. And the film won the San Francisco Film Festival in 1967. What happened there was that everybody freaked. When I came to San Francisco as a French delegate, nobody knew I was American, let alone Black. I show up and the best little old lady with blue hair was announcing my film. I said, "Lady." She said, "Don't bother me." I said, "Lady." She said, "I'm busy, son. Excuse me." I said, "Yo, lady. I am Melvin Van Peebles." That's when America changed—right then and there—because my presence at the festival freaked everybody. Everybody said to me, "Melvin, why are you over there with those frogs? Why aren't you here making movies? You're a talent at making movies." I said, "Motherfucker, the last time I asked you for a job, you told me to go be an elevator operator." He responded, "Well, well, well, ahhh . . . that was it . . . ahh, thank you."

GA: *And you eventually did work in Hollywood. You went on to make* Watermelon Man *(1970) for Columbia Pictures. What was that like, and did you see yourself pursuing a Hollywood career at this point?*
MV: It was a very different, very different experience. But I never saw myself pursuing any career. I just saw myself doing what I wanted to do. If that coincided, good. If it didn't, oh, tough. I felt that there was a whole audience that felt the same way I felt years earlier when I started in film. You asked me earlier why I started in film. I just got tired of seeing shit. That's not the world I know, so I thought that even with my little films, I'd show the world what I knew.

GA: *So you said your experience on* Watermelon Man *was very different from your experience in France. How so?*
MV: It didn't turn out to be any different than other Hollywood experiences for people. The Hollywood directing experience is a lot less independent; there's a different ethic versus the French. Plus you have to add the next veneer of the racial aspects of it. Very little of it was blatant racism, but a lot of it was benign, unconscious racism. I remember when I originally got the script, I thought it was a mistake because guys were telling me that they were looking for a director but they couldn't get the right cast. They named some names like Jack Lemmon, Alan Arkin. Then

they sent me the script and I read it over the weekend and I said, "Yeah, you dummy, you sent me the wrong script." He said, "No, that's the right script." I said, "Right script? This guy is Black." He said, "Yeah, but he starts off white." I said, "But he's only white for the credits—maybe five minutes. Why don't you get a Black guy and paint him in white face—instead of having a white guy being in the rest of the movie in Black face? Is that possible?" In essence, the king can play the valet but the valet could never play the king." I just said it like that. He said, "Fine. Okay." But anyway, that's not what I wanted to say. That's why I did *Sweetback*. I did *Sweetback* because I wanted to do a movie that told it like it is. How I saw things. What happened was, I was sitting down trying to come up with the money. Then I said, "Well, if I had the money, I would go to this lab. I would get this and this. Since I had a three-picture deal at Columbia after *Watermelon Man*, one of the things that happens in Hollywood is that the director gets to choose the film lab he wants, the equipment he wants to rent, et cetera. So all of these people try to be in good graces with the director, so I went to these different places and said that I wanted to make a little film and asked, "How much do I owe you?" They said, "Oh, that's okay, Mel. Don't worry about it. We'll work that out." Because I implied that I was shooting this little porno film. So that's how I got the money. I had some cash in the film and I got a lot of credit around town. By the time they got wise and wanted to cut off my credit—the film was getting a little longer than people thought. I said, "Well, you could, but if you did that . . ." He asked, "So when will you be paying?" I said, "I don't know, because if I don't finish the film I don't know when I'll be able to pay you. I'd have to go back to the post office at $59.00 a week. It's gonna be a long time." He said, "Well, just hurry up and try to keep it slim, okay?"

GA: Did you present the script for Sweetback to Columbia?

MV: Yes. But my agent wouldn't even present it. So that saved me that 10 percent and Columbia dropped me from my deal there.

GA: Sweetback is a controversial film. It's heralded by some as having started the blaxploitation movement. Did you feel you were creating a movement at the time—did you think you were a pioneer—or were you just making the movie you wanted to make?

MV: I was just doing what I wanted to do. As I said, I thought that I could make this movie, it could make money, et cetera. But don't forget, when *Sweetback* was finished I had to hire a white man to pretend he was the boss to release the film. And even after that, only two theaters in the entire United States would show the movie. All of the fanfare about the film happened long afterward.

GA: You also composed the music for Sweetback and you sold the soundtrack.

MV: I invented the whole thing because I had no money. I said that I'd write a tune and I'd have the Black deejays play the tune. I found this group that nobody had ever heard of and it was Earth, Wind & Fire. Before *Sweetback*, no one used a movie soundtrack as the selling feature, a publicity point for a film. If a studio was releasing a musical, the album would come out two or three months later, maybe. It wasn't used as a selling tool.

GA: That's pretty incredible.

MV: My album was on a record label. I was on A&M Records and they dropped me. Everybody's thrown me down the fucking steps. I don't give a shit. I've been thrown down the steps, I was born and bred in a briar patch.

GA: Now you own the masters to most of your films, correct?

MV: Yes.

GA: Is that important for Black filmmakers, owning their masters?

MV: Son, that ain't what I do. I knock the door down and let the people get in any way they can get in. I would not intimate that everybody else follow my way of doing things. There are other ways of doing things—you get it to work, how you want it to be, and that's fine.

GA: You've successfully done acting, music, film, plays, books. How do you mix them all and do them well?

MV: I have no idea. I just do what I like. I would say that's basically the case, except in acting, in which you're doing what somebody else asks you to do. Otherwise, if I have an idea I put it down. Then I give myself the luxury of finding out the format in which it would best work.

GA: What's your creative process? When you're writing, what's your structure?

MV: Until recently, there was no trustworthy infrastructure. That is, I couldn't go to anyone who would look out for me. So I had to do it myself, I had to do the business myself, which was very time intensive. Now there are African American lawyers—and in many of the more esoteric aspects of the entertainment business they were not available before. I can now avail myself of them, but before I had to do it all myself. I had to teach myself, which was very labor-intensive. I had to teach myself how to write, how to read contracts, how to distribute my work, et cetera. You couldn't trust everybody, and that was very time consuming.

GA: But once you actually start working on a project—a screenplay, a play, et cetera—what's that process like?

MV: It depends. As a loner . . .

GA: Would you define yourself as a loner?

MV: I wouldn't define myself as a loner. I'm just alone. [Laughs]

GA: Who or what are your creative influences when it comes to your work?

MV: Why go to a secondary source? What happens is, if I'm going to, for example, do a piece of music—I was walking down the street about six months ago and, oh, BAM! This idea hit me. It was a beautiful idea. What I did was, I prepared the work. Then at that juncture I listened to all the work of the moment and of the niche that I was thinking of it for.

GA: What do you think about Black films today?

MV: In general, it's very simple. I'm pleased that we are beginning to be able to make movies. I'm not sure that we have enough sophistication. Movies in America are pretty much still controlled by the producing structure.

GA: Do you mean the Hollywood studio system?

MV: Movies are controlled by the system period.

GA: Do you think Black filmmakers have a moral responsibility to bring certain positive images to the screen?

MV: Listen, I have trouble coming back from the toilet without my pants leg wet without figuring out things for anybody else. One thing that I am pleased with is that I've gotten to see a lot of the starts of various revolutions. I was very, very fortunate in that I wanted to make it possible for Black people to be able to make movies. As part of that, being in a capitalistic society, was to make it economically feasible. Part of the economic feasibility was to produce movies that made money. Up until *Sweetback*, no Black movie had ever hit it big. But don't forget, Sundance dedicated a retrospective to me, because I'm not the father of Black modern cinema, I'm the father of American independent film—independent films were not taken seriously—any independent film. America is so Black/white oriented, though, we all say, "Gee, he's the father of Black independent film," but smart people know that I'm the father of the whole independent movement, period. They weren't taken seriously before. And I wanted Black filmmakers to do it, but not because of me. Do whatever they think. When I started what has now evolved into what is known as rap, I just wanted us to have a format that would allow dissertation in song. Everybody thought I was crazy when I did my first music. You ever heard of the album *Brer Soul*? Then Gil Scott Heron picked it up. Ask him and he'll say, "Well, Melvin started it." See, I did a lot things and a lot of other people say, "Oh, you started Blacks on Broadway" [with *Ain't Supposed to Die a Natural Death*]. Yeah, I did. We didn't have Blacks on Broadway, not behind the scenes running the shit. And we didn't have music in the format that became rap, like *Brer Soul*. Because I felt that the musical forms were too restrictive at the time. You only had ballads, et cetera, which didn't allow you to run the story down.

GA: *What inspired your documentary film* Classified X *(1997), which examines the historical treatment of Blacks in American cinema?*
MV: A French television company financed it. They wanted to do an anthology about Blacks [in film].

I said, "I ain't interested. I will tell you my point of view. Period. You want that, fine. And I will do it my way, I'm the fucking boss or forget it."

So I made sure that I was the boss, I own 50 percent of the print, plus I'm the writer, the producer and the narrator. I got to do it exactly the way I wanted to and had it written in my contract. A French television company financed it with slightly deficit financing. We got other financing from around the world. But I was the boss, and people said, "Why don't we try to get American money?" I said, "You gotta be kidding. I don't want American money, because they're going to want to tell me what to do."

So when we made the movie, I sold it to four or five countries—Germany, France, England, Australia. The overall part of this is that I sold it to other countries, so that when I came to the States, people in the first few companies said, "Yeah, it's nice, but I don't know . . ." Then I said, "You know, that's interesting, because I've already sold it in England and other places."

Then they had to shut up, because they will find some so-called technical reason to make what is in actuality a political decision.

GA: *Is there something in film, TV or music you'd like to do before you leave the planet?*
MV: I guess . . . remember in *Key Largo* when Edward G. Robinson had slapped Claire Trevor and Humphrey Bogart had gotten on his case and he said, "What do you want, Johnny Rocko?

I'll tell you what you want. You're just a greedy, me, me, me. . . . All you want is more, more, more." And Edward G. Robinson looked at him and said, "Yeah, that's right. That's what I want—more. That's what I want—more." That's all I want is more. More, more. I've got this great foolproof system in the morning. I look at the paper, I read the obituaries. If I'm not there, I get out of bed.

William Greaves

Born in Harlem, William Greaves began his career as a professional actor, playing the lead in the Shubert Production *A Young American*. He went on to work on the Broadway stage, on television and in films and was featured in the 1949 film *Lost Boundaries*. He also played the romantic lead in 1947's *Miracle in Harlem* and is a member of the prestigious Actors Studio.

In 1951, Greaves left his acting career to pursue work as a filmmaker and left the United States for Canada, where he joined the production staff of the National Film Board of Canada. Greaves's documentary films include, most recently, *Ralph Bunche: An American Odyssey* (2001), narrated by Sidney Poitier. Other films include *Ida B. Wells : A Passion for Justice* for PBS (1989), *Black Power in America: Myth or Reality?* (1987), *Booker T. Washington: The Life and Legacy* (1983), *From These Roots* (1974), and *The First World Festival of Negro Arts* (1966).

From 1968 to 1970, Greaves was the executive producer and cohost of the groundbreaking public affairs network televison series *Black Journal*. Greaves's films have earned more than seven international film awards, an Emmy and four Emmy nominations. In 1980 he was inducted into the Black Filmmakers Hall of Fame and that same year was honored at the first Black American Independent Film Festival in Paris. He is also a recipient of an "Indy," the Special Life Achievement Award of the Association of Independent Video and Filmmakers.

In addition to his documentary work, Greaves executive-produced the hit motion picture *Bustin' Loose* (1981), with Richard Pryor and Cicely Tyson. He also produced three other feature films: *Ali, the Fighter* (1971), starring Muhammad Ali and Joe Frazier, *The Marijuana Affair*, starring Calvin Lockhart and Ingrid Wang, and the recently rediscovered avant-garde *Symbiopsychotaxiplasm: Take One* (1968).

— — —

GA: *Tell me about growing up in Harlem. How did you become a great filmmaker?*

WG: I would tell you my age if I told you I was a Harlem Renaissance baby. But around that time—1936—I mean, I grew up in the center of Harlem, 135th Street and Lenox Avenue to be specific. It's now called Malcolm X Boulevard, which is where the Schomburg Center for Research in Black Culture is. I grew up there, and later on I knew some of these legendary people. Countee Cullen was a teacher of mine in Frederick Douglass Junior High School at one point, and various other people in the Harlem Renaissance. I was a kid, but I would see, for example, filmmaker Oscar Micheaux carrying these bags and going into a bar and grill called The Big Apple on 135th Street and Seventh Avenue, which was across the street from his office. He'd set up his projector and show his films, because he had to do a lot of his own distribution. I didn't know who he was or what he was or anything. The point I'm making is that my Harlem growing-up experience was a marvelous experience. I got to know all these different people who were very conscious. Harlem was a very politically, socially, culturally conscious place—much more, I think, than today.

GA: *How did you evolve? You started off in engineering at City College of New York and later got into dance, correct?*

WG: Yes, I started in engineering at City College in 1943. I went to Stuyvesant High School in New York City. That was my major launch pad other than the Frederick Douglass Junior High School I went to in Harlem. My father liked the idea of my being an artist until I wanted to go to high school. I wanted to go to Music and Art High School, but he said, "No, no. Go study a trade." So I chose Stuyvesant High School in New York City, which is a science school. This pleased my father, but Stuyvesant was and still is a very competitive high school. In fact, it's the most competitive high school in New York. You have to take a test to be accepted, and I got in. As a matter of fact, I just found out recently that I graduated in the top 10 percent of my class. Many years later, Stuyvesant did a whole tribute thing on me and gave me an award as one of its most distinguished graduates. Stuyvesant was a great experience, because Stuyvesant moved me towards technology and science and things of that kind, all of which has proved helpful to me as an artist. I took a very competitive examination and got into City College here in New York, but I ultimately dropped out because I got involved in African dance with Asadata Dafora's dance company and then was invited to join the original Pearl Primus Dance Company. In 1945 I then went on to audition for a theater group, the American Negro Theater.

GA: *What led you to dance?*
WG: A Haitian friend of mine, Mark Desgraves's life involved dance. Mark's father was a professor, he taught Afro American, African and Haitian history, about Toussaint L'Overture, Henry Christophe, and Jean-Jacques Dessalines, and all those people who were leaders in Haiti at the time of the revolution against Napoleon. So he used to teach us every Saturday morning, and it was wonderful. Mark danced in a Haitian dance group, and both of us were good social dancers. We used to go to the Renaissance Ballroom in Harlem and dance with the girls.

GA: *Then from dance to acting. Tell me about that.*
WG: From dance to acting and songwriting, and a whole lot of things that were creative.

GA: *Yes, and even Broadway.*
WG: Broadway, yes, as an actor. I performed in the original companies of *Finian's Rainbow* (1947) and *Lost in the Stars* (1949). Both were hit plays. I had featured roles in *Lost in the Stars* and the hit movie *Lost Boundaries*.

GA: *I know that you were somewhat disenchanted with the roles for African American actors when you were acting, leading to your making your own films. Tell me about that.*
WG: Well, after you've studied African history, and the highly advanced civilizations that flourished in Africa in antiquity, you're not ready to play "Stepin Fetchit" roles in movies on Broadway, not in a racist society.

GA: *[Laughs] Can you talk about your African studies and how that influenced you creatively?*
WG: While I was an actor, I used to go up to the Ethiopian library in Harlem and take classes with William Leo Hansberry, who was the uncle of Lorraine Hansberry. He was also a history professor at Howard University. In that class were some people whose names you may know. I hate to say classmates of mine—I was the mascot of the group, I was the young kid, young Turk. But people like John Henrik Clarke; Jean Hudson, who was the head of the Schomburg; J. A. Rogers, who was a historian; and George Haynes, Richard B. Moore . . . a number of very interesting people who were very much involved with the retrieval of our lost history.

GA: Where exactly was this Ethiopian library in Harlem?

WG: It was in Harlem on 138th Street, not far from the Stanford White houses. So while I was in the theater I could go there on the weekends for these classes. I always had a sense of my own sort of dignity, and I never liked the stereotypical depictions of us on the movie screens of America that were going on with people like Stepin Fetchit, Rochester and Hattie McDaniel, and so on. With all due respect to them, they had to make a living, so God bless them. But I just didn't want to subject myself to any of that, and I never did. I did a film called *Lost Boundaries*. In that film, you'll see that the types of roles I played were a precursor to those played by Sidney Poitier and Harry Belafonte, who were all friends of mine at that time growing up. But at that time, I was at the head of the pack until getting into this African history thing. I became so progressively excited about African history and I began to learn that I could make these documentary films about the truth—about who we are as a people—and I became so excited that I stopped acting. [Laughs] And I left the country for Canada in 1952 when I couldn't break into the racist film industry here.

GA: So you actually attempted to make films in the United States before going to Canada?

WG: Oh, yeah. I tried to get into the American film industry, but by 1952 the era of the "race films" had come to a close. By "race films" I mean those films that were made by and about Black people, that were not derogatory like the products of Hollywood. All of those nonstereotypical Black films were put out of business because of the changes in the politics of segregation and discrimination in America. After World War II, Black people could go to the theaters downtown, where whites went, and all that stuff. So a lot of the race films lost their market. But when I tried to get into the mainstream industry I wasn't allowed to, because the apartheid nature of America was still very strong at that time and it was vicious. So what I did was, I said, "To hell with this, I'm not going to hang around here and let this crazy, psychotic place make a fool out of me." [Laughs] I left the country and I got on the production staff of the National Film Board in Canada, which was a great experience. I started off as an apprentice, assistant editor, assistant director, and then I became a sound editor and then an editor and then chief editor of a very important, award-winning unit there. I then went on to become a writer and director. I went through the whole pathway of filmmaking.

GA: How long were you in Canada?

WG: Eleven years.

GA: You did a memorable documentary in Canada called Emergency Ward? Tell me about that.

WG: Right, it was shot in the cinema verité technique, which at that time was very revolutionary.

As a matter of fact, the National Film Board brought cinema verité to America in 1957. We were involved with cinema verité before a lot of the people in the U.S.—like Maysles, Wiseman and Pennybaker—were involved in it. They got into it about two or three years after the Canadians.

GA: *You also did some work for the United Nations.*
WG: Yes, I worked for the United Nations from 1961 to '63 and then I left the U.N. once I got the opportunity to set up my own company in 1964. I then did work on contract for the United States Information Agency (USIA) under George Stevens, Jr., who was the head of the Agency's film unit.

GA: *What type of films did you do for the U.N.?*
WG: I did a film on the flight of an airliner called *Cleared for Takeoff*. As a matter of fact, when I left the National Film Board I became a public information officer for films and radio for the International Civil Aviation Organization, a U.N. agency up there in Canada, and eventually ended up in the U.N in New York.

GA: *What was it like working with the U.N.? Was it exciting?*
WG: Yes, it was a very fascinating experience, because I flew around the world twice making a film about the flight of an airliner around the world, and the international cooperation was critical to ensure safe air travel. So that was very interesting. Alistair Cooke was the on-camera talent, and I directed the film and wrote the basic script.

GA: *Tell me about the film you did for the USIA called* The Wealth of a Nation.
WG: They wanted to do a film showing in Cold War terms that America was friendly to dissent and very much a free society where people could speak their minds freely. So they asked me to do this film called A Nation of Dissenters about people who challenge the authorities. I started working on it, and it came to pass that when they realized that I was focusing on various popular dissenters, they decided that they didn't really want that much dissent. [Laughs] It took a long time to do the film; we had to redefine the parameters of the original theme. The new theme was what it meant to be in a nation in which there is freedom of individual expression. We did this film and it was interesting, and I moved around the country filming, and it was very mind-expanding. From there on, I just kept working on social-welfare films for the government. The United States government was my biggest client, because without the government I wouldn't have been a film-maker. Racism was still so rampant in the movie industry, as far as people of color behind the

camera were concerned, that even though I had all these credentials—I could write, produce, direct and all of that—I couldn't get any work from the mainstream film industry here. As a matter of fact, I think during the 1960s I was probably the most experienced Black filmmaker in the country. I don't think any of them, even Gordon Parks and various other people, had my depth of filmmaking experience. I had eighty films under my belt. But never mind that, it still didn't cut any ice with the industry, and I'm very glad in a way, because it forced me to be an independent, as I might have ended up in some Hollywood studio and been coerced into selling my soul. [Laughs]

GA: Your film First World Festival of African Arts is incredible. How did that come about?
WG: I did that for USIA, the United States Information Agency. If you see that film you'd never know that it was a U.S. government propaganda film, because it wasn't. From my point of view, it talked about our heritage as a people and it traded on the concept of Negritude. Well, Leopold Senghor was the president of Senegal and had become a very important person in the French parliament, but he was also a poet. Amiee Cesaire at the time was a very major intellectual from Martinique and Alioune Diop was an important political philosophical figure, and the three got together and put on this First World Festival of African Arts, which the USIA got wind of and decided to send a crew to Africa to film a piece of the festival for a news clip for the Agency's *Screen* magazine. When I got there I said, "Wow, this thing is fantastic." And I realized that the significance of the whole event was major. So I was able to do this film, which actually was only supposed to be this *Screen* magazine film but ended up being determined by Senghor and Diop and other organizers of the festival, to be the official record of the festival. The Russians were there with a large film crew of more than fifteen to twenty in terms of people. So were the French, Belgians, Italians and other countries there with large film crews. I only had three on my crew. There was me and my cameraman—both of us did the camera work. Believe it or not, I trained my chauffeur to record sound, and so we made this film with only a three-man crew.

GA: That's amazing.
WG: Yeah, and then I brought the footage back to America and cut it. As a matter of fact, I shot a sequence with Langston Hughes, and he is in the opening of the film mingling with fishermen bringing in their nets of fish from the ocean. I invited him to see a rough cut and he really loved it. I took the style of his poem "The Negro Speaks of Rivers" and used variations on it throughout the film. And it was the most popular United States Information Agency film in Africa for about ten years.

GA: That's great. Given your extensive coverage of Black people in your films, some call you the Chronicler of the Black Experience. How do you feel about that?

WG: Well, chronicler, I've been called a griot, the dean and—I don't know, all those marvelous accolades, which are very nice. It's encouraging to have that kind of attention, respect and so on, but fortunately, I think I'm a little too old for it to go to my head at this point. I just sort of listen to it for whatever it's worth.

GA: You've covered so many wonderful aspects of African American history, but we seem to live in a society that doesn't value history at all. Does it concern you sometimes that audiences, especially young audiences who could benefit the most from your stories, may not appreciate them?

WG: One of the most depressing experiences occurred this past year when we showed the Ralph Bunche film to an audience of high school seniors in Westchester [County, New York]. The town in which we showed the film is largely white, and so they decided to draw the audience from the schools in the greater area. Knowing that, here I am, a Black filmmaker showing this film about a Black man. And they got the idea that they ought to bring in some Black students from the other communities, like Mt. Vernon, New York. They wanted them to learn about their history. It was interesting to me that some of these Black kids took to it, but some of them were asleep by the end of the film. None of the white kids were asleep, which was interesting to me. It tells you the degree to which we have been and are being mentally enslaved by not getting our kids to focus on the whole range of things that have occurred in the past that really have to do with their present and future, that has to do with their minds and ultimately their families and communities.

But fade out, fade in, I was down at Spelman College in front of an audience of young Black female students, and after it was over students came up to me and complimented me on the film. One girl, I saw her sort of push her way through the crowd that was around me and she said, "Mr. Greaves, I enjoyed your film very much. It really meant a lot to me, and I think I learned a great deal that I didn't know. Dr. Bunche was a very important man, and I want you to remember me, because I'm going to be president of the United States someday." I looked at this girl and I said [Laughs], "This is fantastic." I said, "Right on, sister!" Also, at Morehouse I had an audience of about six hundred Black male students.

GA: I went to Morehouse.

WG: Oh, did you? The Morehouse students were quiet as mice, just vacuuming it up, the information in the film. It was marvelous. I said, "Jesus Christ. This is why I want to make movies—to get this kind of reaction."

GA: They gave you hope that it's not in vain.
WG: Oh, yeah. But to answer your question, when they go to sleep, that really kills me.

GA: When we first started talking, you mentioned that a lot of those in media don't understand the power of the media. The interesting thing about your film Black Power in America: Myth or Reality?, was that power was discussed consistently—the movers and shakers of power.
WG: Sure.

GA: I like the way you talk about power in the film. Do Blacks have power in the media today, and how can that power be used more responsibly and to empower?
WG: Well, you know, with all due respect, BET has a lot of power but they're not using it properly at all. Some of the things they do, yes, I'm sure they're community-based, but there's a lot of silliness that goes on, and I guess part of it is marketing. There is a market for that, but I don't feel that there's a kind of will there to educate. Ebony magazine and Jet magazine, the Johnson publications, you feel that even though they are commercial that they've got Lerone Bennett there [the Black historian], they're trying to do something positive along with being commercial.

GA: Absolutely.
WG: But with BET you don't get that impulse, that feeling.

GA: Well, in speaking of Jet, you can frequently read something very informative about Black people in that magazine that hasn't been chronicled elsewhere.
WG: Exactly.

GA: For example, they'll cover someone being awarded an honorary degree someplace, someone who was hired at a university, or if an important Black figure has passed away.
WG: [John] Johnson in a way is unheralded, because on the one hand the nationalists, militants and progressives want to get this show on the road and feel he's going too slow. But he has done more to help an overall consciousness raising than any other publisher that we have that I know of. He's done those series on Black history and all kinds of things, long before they were doing it

in the white media, so he really is to be, in a sense, applauded, and I'm sorry that he doesn't run BET instead of the other Johnson. [Laughs]

GA: *And now BET's owned by Viacom. One thing that I notice in your films is that a great deal of your subjects seem to have nobility. They have honor and courage and you're able to bring this out in the films, whether it be Ralph Bunche or Booker T. Washington. How are you able to illuminate such a quality in these African Americans?*
WG: I think it's in the choices that we make.

GA: *Yes.*
WG: I choose people who are interesting and who are into mental liberation, psychological emancipation. Those are the people who I feel should be role models and an inspiration for people who will someday become leaders in human affairs. We have a political problem in America of gaining full first-class citizenship status, and it's an ongoing problem, so it makes sense to choose those kinds of people. Because, as Paul Robeson said, "The Negro artist has to choose freedom or slavery." For him, he had made his choice.

I was having dinner with his son [Paul Robeson, Jr.] last night. We talked about the future film that he and I wanted to make about his father's life. I'm certainly encouraging it as much as possible. But the quality that you're picking up is the quality of the people who mentored me, like William Leo Hansberry, and people whose names you wouldn't know, like Taiyi Seifert, Austin Briggs Hall, Prince Akiki Nyabongo. There are numbers of people who were close friends and colleagues and mentors, people like Sam Countee, an artist, a very talented man.

There are these various people who I was fortunate to be tutored by and work with, like Lee Strasberg at the Actors Studio, and Elia Kazan, the director who was one of my teachers there. At the film board in Canada I had some great mentors up there, like Tom Daly. I was also very heavily involved in spiritual development and being mentored by Sri Aurobindo, an Indian philosopher and mystic who I never met in person. He died in 1950, but his writings were very influential in my thinking. As a matter of fact, in *The First World Festival of Negro Arts*, you'll see a lot of his influences. Langston Hughes and Sri Aurobindo were the two spiritual forces behind my creation of that film.

GA: *Tell me about your film Ralph Bunche: An American Odyssey.*
WG: I'm very pleased with the Bunche film now, because we worked very hard on it. It was going to be a six-part series, and then we couldn't get it into the PBS system at that length, so we had to

cut it down to four parts and then to three parts and then finally to a two-hour special. We got help from the Ford Foundation, the MacArthur Foundation, the Cosbys and various other foundations like the National Black Programming Consortium, National Endowment for the Humanities and the Corporation for Public Broadcasting.

GA: You worked on this film for a long time?

WG: Well, yes, see because we actually rough-cut eighteen hours of film on Bunche's life. First we did six hours of this long version in fine cut, then fine-cut another four hours, and each time we had to take the thing apart and put it back together again. There were enormous problems in getting the financing for these different stages, and then finally we couldn't get the completion funds for a PBS airing unless we cut the Bunche story down to two hours, so we had to squeeze all of this into a two-hour film. Now, what we're doing are these fourteen teaching modules, which are thirty minutes each and they are film productions in and of themselves.

So all in all we've done a total of fifteen completed films on Bunche's life, because Bunche was a tremendous figure in the pantheon of international and national leaders. He was really a superb human being, brilliant and at the same time very much dedicated to humanity—Black, white, green. He was a real role model for all human beings. So we're now doing production on various facets of his life—fourteen different facets of his life, most of which didn't appear in the two-hour PBS TV special. The miniproductions will be useful for teachers in universities, colleges and high schools.

So working on this project has been an awesomely arduous, difficult, painful, frustrating experience, and unless you have the commitment—the psychological, psycho-spiritual commitment—to the subject matter you're working on, it can be very painful and destructive to your health and everything else. As you say, I've been around in this thing for quite a long time. But because my psycho-spiritual center is not in making some executive in Hollywood happy by bringing in a lot of profits from a silly film—and I'm not disparaging people who do that—but I'm just simply saying that's not where I come from. Where I'm coming from is the psycho-spiritual liberation of people of color and the psycho-spiritual liberation of the white community as well. That's what I'm all about. [Laughs]

So I have more energy to deploy in that area, because I don't feel I'm prostituting myself by doing something because it pays a lot of money. Mind you, I love money and all of that too. [Laughs] Don't misunderstand me, but I like to make money doing what I want to do rather than what someone else wants me to do. Maybe that's an aberration, but I don't think so.

GA: *Was it challenging doing the Bunche documentary from a book, making an adaptation?*

WG: No, the book was very, very helpful. Without Sir Brian Urquhart's book [of the same title] I would not have been able to have done this film as well as it is done. I could have done the film, but it would not have had the kind of scholarship that is invested in it, and then, of course, I had twelve scholars working with us too. But Brian Urquhart was Bunche's closest friend and colleague, and his replacement as Under Secretary General of the United Nations. When I showed the film to Kofi Annan and his executive suite saw the film, they freaked out. Annan said, "This is a film on one of our heroes. It's got to be seen by everyone in the U.N. system and beyond." So he said, "I want this film to be shown at the major U.N. facilities and agencies throughout the world." We gave the U.N. 117 prints of the film, and it's now traveling around the country under the umbrella of the Human Rights Watch Festival in roughly twenty-five cities. My company is distributing it to schools, colleges, universities, libraries and special-interest groups, because another interesting part of my life as a filmmaker, an independent filmmaker, is that because of the racism and apartheid nature of this country when I started out I couldn't get my films shown. I said, "Well, screw these folks, I'm going to distribute it myself," which is what I began doing, and I'm glad that I did. I have only racism to thank for that, because it's made me much more self-reliant in the sense of the Booker T. Washington tradition, I guess. I have been able, with the help of my wife Louise, who is in charge of our distribution area, to get our films out there to all these different film libraries, universities, et cetera.

GA: *You've also distributed films by other producers and directors. Tell me about that.*

WG: Well, Gil Noble, who I think very highly of, is a wonderful film producer. He actually has a television show (Like It Is), and he gave me one or two of his films—*Fannie Lou Hamer* is one—to distribute. He was going to give me more but then decided to change direction. He wanted to put his films out in another context, but he hasn't gotten that going yet. I may end up distributing more of his stuff, because we're still very good friends and respect each other's work. But we haven't distributed that much work of other filmmakers. We did distribute one called *Witness to Apartheid* by Sharon Sopher, but unfortunately we're not a big enough distributor to take on other people's films. At some point we probably will.

GA: *Tell me about your film Symbiopsychotaxiplasm: Take One and what inspired you to do it?*

WG: It came about as a result of my interest in mysticism, science, philosophy and creativity. It's a mix of all those different disciplines. It's very confounding and very difficult to decode. When people see it, they just can't understand it. As a matter of fact, it was shot in 1968 and I finished it in about 1970, 1971, and we couldn't get it distributed anywhere. The distributors couldn't understand it at all. They didn't know what it was all about, and one astute critic seemed to understand it. He said, "This is so advanced in it's thinking that it won't be marketable until thirty or forty years from now," and sure enough, the goddamn film now is moving inexorably into a marketable position.

It's been at about fifteen international film festivals, and the Sundance Channel acquired it and is showing it. Also, Steve Buscemi, Steven Soderbergh and I are planning to do a sequel of it if we can get the financing. Steve Buscemi was at Sundance when it was shown there, and it was a big success at Sundance.

GA: *He fell in love with it.*
WG: He did, he really did.

GA: *You've been very successful outside of the Hollywood system, but you did executive-produce a very funny and successful Hollywood film, Bustin' Loose, starring Richard Pryor. How did you get involved with that project?*
WG: Well, I was one of several Black producers approached by MCA New Ventures, which was a subsidiary of MCA, a sister company to Universal Pictures. They were supposed to be helping Black productions, so they asked my company to take on a project called *Heaven Is a Playground*. We developed it and everything, but the bottom line is that we never got the financing for the film, but the management team at Universal, especially Ned Tanen, who was the president, were impressed with the way in which I conducted the whole project and offered me *Bustin' Loose* to executive-produce.

They also wanted me to come on staff there, which I turned down because by then I had my own company and I had my own freedom of action to do the films that you've seen. That to me seemed more of where I was coming from than to go to Los Angeles and become a Hollywood producer. The stuff that one does out there has a short shelf life; it's a big deal for a few months, then it's gone and it usually has no lasting nourishing, psychological or social impact over a protracted period of time. But our films [William Greaves Productions] are practically indestructible. From These Roots was done in 1974, First World Festival in 1968. They are constantly being used by the academic and special-interest communities. They certainly have a long shelf life.

And the Bunche film is going to be around for fifty years. My feeling is that an advocacy film or a film that's an educational tool or a social-force film can do the work of a major advocacy organization like the NAACP or any of these organizations if the film is strong enough. You see this very starkly in *Birth of a Nation*, which was able to mobilize public thinking with respect to the African American in a very significant way. All of these various right-wing and racist organizations like the Ku Klux Klan couldn't have achieved that level of impact without the help of that evil film.

GA: *Given the power of film and the fact that more African Americans are using it as technology advances, why don't we see more people using it that way to empower and as a means to effect social change?*

WG: Well, I think it has to do with society as a whole. It's not only Black people, it's white people, it's all people in modern society and particularly as modern society is being promoted in America. There is a tendency in America to denigrate intellectual development and education and to gravitate towards instant gratification of sensationalist media. Violence, sex, comedy, all that silliness. It's Roman circus time. It's very much Roman circus time. So when you're involved in the circus you don't have time for intellectual and political, sociological and cultural development. So that's the problem, and the Black community is the victim of this dynamic, as is the white community and the Latino community, and all communities in America are in the grip of this media—not disease but epidemic [Laughs]—the epidemic of the media. The media is in epidemic mode, creating diseases of the mind of all kinds. It's polluting the mind in a variety of ways, and most people are not aware of it. And unhappily, most Black media people are not aware of it. I don't know what to say about it other than the fact that not only are most Black media people not aware of it, but most white media people and most Latino media people, and most Asian, are not aware of it.

GA: [Laughs] *It's a societal problem, you're saying?*

WG: It's a society-wide problem and people who are conscious in this society—Black or white and all other in between—are very disturbed by what I'm talking about because they can see that it's true, and this media pathology can be very dangerous to the society. It becomes almost a national security problem to have a society that is silly, immature and dysfunctional. [Laughs] Such a society can be very vulnerable to all kinds of destruction both from within and without.

GA: *We have events like September 11 and everyone's caught off guard and surprised, but the day before some of the hottest stuff on the news was about which celebrity is getting married or something trivial like that. We feed our brains with all this stuff as if it's really important, so when the terrorism that's been cooking all along occurs, we're blown away by it.*

WG: You've got that right. You stated it very, very acutely, very clearly. It was the long arm of a very hostile reality knocking over those trade towers, and we Americans, especially white Americans, were totally unprepared for that.

GA: *Yes, because we've been so caught up with what movie's going to open number one at the box office.*
WG: Yeah, yeah.

GA: *Having been an actor and a member of the highly selective and prestigious Actors Studio, how has your acting training prepared you as a director?*
WG: Oh, it's been marvelous—the core of acting, the capacity to empathize with characters and the human condition and the human animal and so on. My work with actors is very strong, largely as a result of my work at the Actors Studio and being trained by Lee Strasberg. Also, I'm constantly being prepared as a director, because I teach acting and I've done it for quite a number of decades. I have moderated some of the sessions when Strasberg was out making a movie or something like that. I also taught acting for the screen at the Lee Strasberg Institute up until his death. I was one of the five or six people who would substitute for Strasberg in running the sessions at the Actors Studio, and I still teach there from time to time. So managing actors and directing actors is a skill that I long ago developed, and if you saw some of my directing you would see the effects of that training.

GA: *Would you like to do more feature film work?*
WG: I'd love to do more feature films—I've only done four, but I'd love to do more. But it's very difficult to raise money for these things, and getting people to finance films that are on the wavelength of the things that I've been talking to you about. Paul Robeson, Jr., and I tried for about seven years to get the money to make a film about his father's life. I tried very hard to get money to do Langston Hughes's *Sweet Flypaper of Life,* which is a very wonderful story written by Langston Hughes and Roy De Carava.

GA: *The great photographer.*
WG: Right. So Roy and Langston got together and did this book and I got hold of the book through Liska March at the Actors Studio and turned it into a screenplay. Langston read the screenplay and was very excited about it, and Roy was too. I took it up to the Sundance Lab and worked on it with Robert Redford, Paul Newman, Karl Malden, James Brooks, and they were all very excited to do the film, but I couldn't raise the money. The Hollywood studios wouldn't back it.

GA: It all comes down to the money.

WG: Yes, because *Sweet Flypaper of Life* dealt with the rehabilitation of a young Black man in Harlem by his grandmother, and it was a very compassionate piece. And that didn't seem important to the moguls of the media in Hollywood. I really would like to do that film.

GA: What's the general challenge in doing documentary films and getting people to really appreciate them?

WG: Consciousness raising. The American audience is very down on education and media, and particularly documentaries. Let me put it this way: Documentaries are becoming more popular in a way, but the more popular they become the more trivial, even silly they also get. [Laughs] So we're caught between a rock and a hard place.

GA: What are some of the types of documentaries that you find silly?

WG: What you see on the History Channel or Biography. It's better than nothing. I'd rather see them on the screen than some of the other stuff. But when you turn off the set you almost say, "Well, what was that all about?" I don't think you have that reaction when you see Ida B. Wells or the Bunche film. You say, "Gee, I'm going to read the newspapers more carefully. I'm going to get involved with social reform movements," et cetera.

GA: You talked about directing in an article by Maria San Filippo in Senses of Cinema on Symbiopsychotaxiplasm, and you said, "My problem is to get out of nature's way and let nature tell her story. That's what a good director does." Can you elaborate?

WG: The whole business of the creative spirit—I don't want to get into the mystical aspect—the creative process is a very tricky phenomenon. Much of it turns on intuition, impulse, inspiration, spontaneous response in the formulation of a work of art. The good director respects and encourages these dynamics in the actors and other artistic workers that he assembles to execute his vision of a scene. The good director is ever on the lookout for these qualities and gives actors and other film artists the freedom to spontaneously tap these hidden reservoirs of inspiration when they appear from the hidden depths of the subconscious, which is the genius part of the actor's craft. So this business of "getting out of one's way" really is spontaneously allowing yourself to respond to these various gifts of nature from the subconscious that leads to a kind of freshness, a creative freshness, which is what you want as both a director and an actor, and it's hard to get an actor to be like that, because most actors and directors are into too much control. They control their behavior and they don't give their own spirit and/or those of their coworkers the freedom to be creative, truly creative!

GA: There's a lot of censorship.

WG: Exactly, precisely, and that tendency to control makes the performance stiff, not fresh and predictable, to an audience watching.

GA: Out of all your films, of which one are you most proud—which is your greatest achievement?

WG: Right now it's *Ralph Bunche*. But the films I've done have stood the test of time very well—*From These Roots, Ida B. Wells, Black Power*. I have quite a few films, but I'm really more excited about *Ralph Bunche* right through here than I am about any of the others, although I recognize that they were very good. I'm fascinated with *Symbiopsychotaxiplasm*, because it's a very daring leap into the unknown, in terms of what we're talking about—this whole thing about creativity and spontaneity, letting things happen by themselves. It's such a creative film because the creator of the film has decided not to be a meddler in human nature and behavior, has decided to let the event unfold in and of itself out of the basic circumstances that he has devised. So it's a tour de force, and if you see the film, you will see how the crew gets furious with me because I won't control them. Because I've given them so much freedom—too much, they complain. It's beyond the traditional, conventional notion of improvisation for an actor. And, well, you read the Maria San Filippo article. She does a very good job in sort of capturing that aspect.

GA: What advice would you give to someone looking to break into film right now, especially into documentaries?

WG: The only thing I can think of that really makes sense is that making movies is so hard, so tough that you damn well better make sure that you're making a film about something that you really and truly care about. Unless you have that passion at the core center of your interest in a particular project, if it's something that you really have a burning need to put out there in the form of a film, you're in danger of making a lousy film. If you make a lousy film, they're not going to throw money at you to make another lousy film. The whole business of making a film requires long hours each day, energy deployed working out creative, artistic, philosophical solutions, narrative solutions, a myriad of solutions that have to do with audience response, the politics of the community and all of that. You have to go through all of that plus the business of managing and looking at this stuff and retaining it in your head, and unless you really care, you're not tapping into your genius, because your genius comes from your subconscious, your emotional life, all of those things over which you're not much in control, but nonetheless energize and cause you to think and clarify and reason, with inductive reasoning and deductive reasoning and all kinds of thought processes. And unless you're powered by that burning core need to reveal the truth of what it is you're feeling, my advice is to forget it because you'll just do crappy films and they won't achieve much, maybe an ulcer, or some other psychosomatic complaint.

Occasionally, a person who is poorly motivated may end up doing something very exciting, but it's largely a fluke. It'll happen once, but it won't happen over and over again. The higher batting average comes from your level of commitment. The Tiger Woods effect, the early Marlon Brando effect, the Jessye Norman effect, the Michael Jordan effect, Ali, all those people are very, very energized and committed to what they're doing. What I'm talking about, I guess, is what Stanislavski and Strasberg would call the use of genius, the liberation of genius in a particular mode of activity, human activity, whether it's filmmaking or sports or whatever. If you can connect with the thing that really matters to you in that particular area, then you've got a chance to succeed.

GA: We started our talk discussing history, and that being a critical factor in your life in terms of the stories you tell. Do you think that history could be critical to other Black filmmakers in terms of broadening their understanding of who they are as a people and the types of stories they tell?

WG: I think it would help tremendously if they studied their history, because they would find out that two, three, five, ten, fifteen, twenty thousand years ago the Africans, especially the Ethiopians and the ancient Egyptians, were very much involved in the business of human evolution and the civilizing activities of the human animal and they would become progressively, I would say, inspired and proud of their heritage and would understand the obscenity of the kind of position in which we not only find ourselves but are constantly being attempted by others to keep us in this secondary subservient position in the world. A lot of progress has been made in this country. There's no question about it, and as a matter of fact, I would have never come back to America if it had not been developing along democratic lines as a society, and it certainly has been more than most societies on the face of the Earth, but having said that, it still has a way to go. Especially today, when winds that are hostile to the human spirit are gaining ferocity. Learning not only African but history in general would be very, very useful for any of these young people. Charles C. Seifert, the man who started the Charles C. Seifert Ethiopian History Library in Harlem, said, "A race without a knowledge of its history is like a tree without roots." It's true.

So I would say to other Black filmmakers and those of other oppressed people, what you want to do is get to the roots of your culture so that your creations can flower and make life beautiful in a sense not only for yourself but for the people in general. That's my thought in a nutshell. Know who you are. As Shakespeare says, "To thine own self be true." Somehow or another I feel that we need to have people in the media who understand what the media is all about. I regret to say that most of the media people we have in film and in other media are not aware of how central and pivotal they can be either to the psychological and spiritual liberation of people of African descent or all people of color, for that matter. And realistically speaking, most white people themselves are enslaved by the media and aren't aware of it and need to be liberated from the adverse negative impact of what purports to be positive educational and mass media.

GA: *Explain what you mean by your statement that people of color and white people are enslaved.*
WG: A lot of white people labor under the delusion that they are superior to Black people, and that's a slave mentality because they've been trained to think that way, and as a result it interferes with their efficient relationships—more productive and creative relationships—with people of color here in America and worldwide. America suffers in terms of a genius pool of intellects like Ralph Bunche, who can help this country become that center of a golden age for the world. People like Ralph Bunche can help turn this country into something extremely positive. It's positive enough in many respects, but it constantly needs reminding of its creed, the Bill of Rights, the Declaration of Independence. It needs to be constantly returned to that source. This is something that we as a people have been constantly moving the country towards, its creed, and the fact that it should live out as fully as possible the tenets, the dictates of the American creed and the Declaration of Independence.

If there was less prejudice, less racism and all of that in this society you would get a bigger contribution by African Americans, Latinos and so on, and you'd get a much bigger contribution to the country by women, for that matter. Women still have problems in second-class citizenship in a way. You get a much richer society in terms of the genius of all these different groups being much more liberated than they are at present. So when I say that whites as well as Blacks are enslaved, they are buying into, very often, this notion of superiority and it's very counterproductive.

Ossie Davis

Erudite, wise, warm, and committed to African American progress are just a few words to describe writer, actor, director, producer and social activist Ossie Davis. Born in 1917 in Cogdell, Georgia, Davis is arguably one of the deans of African American cinema, a living legend. As an actor, Davis has performed in more than ninety films, including *No Way Out* (1950), *Let's Do It Again* (1975), *Jungle Fever* (1991) and *Miss Evers' Boys* (1997). Davis got his start on the stage in the title role in Robert Audrey's 1946 play, *Jeb*. He is also known for his role in Lorraine Hansberry's award-winning Broadway play *A Raisin in the Sun* (1959), as well as the 1961 film version of the play.

In 1970, Davis made his feature film directorial debut with the hit movie *Cotton Comes to Harlem*, based on the famed writer Chester Himes's novel. The film, which stars Godfrey Cambridge and Raymond St. Jacques, is considered, along with Gordon Parks's *Shaft* and Melvin Van Peebles's *Sweet Sweetback's Baadasssss Song*, to be one of the most important films of the blaxploitation era. Davis went on to direct *Kongi's Harvest* (1970), *Black Girl* (1972), *Gordon's War* (1973) and *Countdown at Kusini* (1976).

Davis wrote the 1963 play *Purlie Victorious*, which starred his wife Ruby Dee. His most recent play *Last Dance for Sybil*, which starred Ms. Dee, Arthur French and Earle Hyman, premiered in New York in November 2002.

Davis and his wife, Ruby Dee, have shown their unending commitment to the social elevation of African Americans by giving of their time, energy and resources to causes in support of the race. Davis eulogized both Malcolm X and Martin Luther King, Jr.

■ ■ ■ ■

GA: *Tell me about growing up in Georgia and the role that creativity played in your life. How did you become the person you are today?*

OD: Well, now, if you can imagine a little boy in Georgia thinking about creativity, then you can imagine what I can't. I grew up as a little boy in Georgia, and I lived a full life as a little boy going to school, church, hanging out with Mama and Daddy and my friends, going down to the watering hole, swimming, hunting rabbits with slingshots and living the full life of a country boy. Movies were silent in those days and we only got a chance to see them maybe on the weekend, and then Black people had to sit in a special section. So movies were certainly not a pleasant experience for me. I remember, of course, what I saw. I was impressed by the cowboys, and I remember always seeing somebody Black making a fool of themselves, and I laughed just like the white folks laughed. I didn't identify with him [the Black person]. Man, that essentially is what movies were to me. I left the South in 1935, and when I came north, movies were a little bit more a part of what was available. I went to the moving pictures, and I think I liked westerns and I liked, I suppose, what most everybody else liked up to and including World War II. Then we came out of World War II, and in about 1949 came the television, and I watched that. I don't remember it having a profound effect on my life, certainly not like the theater. I'm a theater person. I like live theater, getting up on the boards and walking where there's a live audience out there ready to hug you or throw things at you, depending on how they felt about your performance. Until this day, I prefer the live theater to motion pictures, although motion pictures by now are the most powerful statements being made today.

GA: *Given that film is such a powerful medium, what do you think is the role of film? One could argue that it's just entertainment, but one could also argue that it goes beyond that. What are your thoughts on the role of film?*

OD: Well, essentially, film is a part of the entertainment industry, and by that I mean those things in society which are meant to distract you, that which is meant to lead you away from reality, that which is meant to take your mind off of things, off your troubles and all of that. It's the great American drive toward trivializing every damn thing. I suppose if movies didn't start the drive toward the trivial, movies certainly made it a national phenomenon. I never thought of movies as making major statements, although I was impressed with *Grapes of Wrath, They Shall Not Die, For*

Whom *the Bell Tolls*, and wonderful little motion pictures I saw did make important statements. The first motion picture I was in, *No Way Out*, had to do with Black folks struggling to be treated fairly in the country and it was not a bad statement, so I liked that. But I've never sat down and said, "Oh, movies! You great cultural phenomenon. Let me look at you, let me examine you, let me describe you in all those wonderful ways." I knew even as a child that there was a bullshit connection. I felt like P. T. Barnum did: "Suck up on every minute. Throw something out there and let him stumble over it." I knew about minstrel shows, carnivals, circuses and movies, and when I came north I knew about vaudeville. However, movies were just one part of the entertainment industry at that time.

GA: *When and why did you begin to write scripts?*

OD: I started writing because I felt like writing when I was a kid in high school, and my father and mother were both good storytellers, they were master storytellers. A lot of the stories they told were traditional stories coming from the common culture, like Br'er Rabbit, Br'er Fox, Br'er Bear, ghost stories, humor stories. But some of the stories they told were things from their lives, and they were quite wonderful to me as a boy and I remembered them all. Somehow I wanted to put them in book form. So from the first day I went to school, that was basically what I was going to school for—to learn how to write so that I could write those stories down. Now, ultimately I did write, I somehow drifted into writing drama rather than stories and tales, but the impulse was the same. It was really the joy of telling a good story well, and I felt I had the talent to do that. Even in high school I wrote a little play which we put on, and that pleased me very much. So I said that when I got to college that's what I was going to do. When I did get to college, that's what I firmly had in mind.

GA: *You went to Howard University, studied theater and were mentored by Alain Locke. What was it like going to Howard and studying theater?*

OD: Well, that's a difficult question to deal with, because it's like asking, "What's it like to be alive?" I mean, I was there, I was a student, Locke was an exciting instructor, he seemed to think that I was a talented man. As a matter of fact, in my later semesters he lent me money to pay tuition, which I paid him back, and it was he who suggested that if I was serious about becoming a playwright that I should go to New York, go to Harlem, where there was a little theater group being formed, and that I should join that group and study everything I could about writing plays, particularly since I had come from the South and had never been in a theater when I first met him. So he said, "Go study, learn, find out what theater is all about, then you will know whether you can write for it or not." And I was so impressed with his suggestion that I didn't stay to finish college. I saved up a little money, hopped the train, got off at Penn Station, got up to Harlem, found the Rose McClendon Players, asked them to let me join, they did, and I've been in the theater ever since.

GA: *You've done quite a bit in your career on stage and on screen, having been in many movies. But what was it like making that transition to actually directing a movie like* Cotton Comes to Harlem?

OD: It seemed to me to be a matter of natural progression. I would say out of experience that directing a film is an extended form of writing. A good director is also a good writer, though he may not use words. In the motion picture he would tend to use images, but he's telling a story, and a good director tells stories with images and a good writer tells it with words. So when I got my chance to direct, I knew instinctively what I wanted, how I wanted it, and most of the pictures in the film are framed by the cinematographer and not the director. The director deals with the characters and the actors who play the characters. When I got to be a director, it was merely an extension of what it meant to be a writer. It's like instead of talking to yourself when you write, you would be talking to the same character, but it was a live person across from you. Then the cinematographer would decide where to put the guy or how to move him so that the camera would be satisfied. And that was all.

When I got into film directing I was lucky, because Sam Goldwyn, Jr., was the producer on *Cotton Comes to Harlem* and he hired the best crew available—the top cinematographer, top sound people, costumers, all the attendant crafts were headed by experts and they could tell me how to do things and where to do it better than I could because they were speaking from experience. Life has always been for me a case of one thing leading to another, and I've never really been totally surprised going from one thing to another. The wonderful thing is that when you're going from one thing to another, you soon find out that one thing is very closely akin to another. Oftentimes you don't know if you've shifted gears or turned the corner. It's still life and you're still truckin', moving along as best you can.

GA: *Did you study any specific films or directors when you decided to get behind the camera?*

OD: No. I hadn't the slightest desire to get behind the camera. I hadn't the slightest idea. I didn't get involved in *Cotton Comes to Harlem* as a director. I was hired as an actor, and Sam Goldwyn, who produced the film, knew that although the novel was by Chester Himes, the screenplay had been done by a white writer, Arnold Perl, who incidentally was a friend of mine. Goldwyn was concerned about whether or not a white writer could really get to the juice of the Black experience. So when I first read the screenplay he kept asking me, "Is that authentic, is that how Black folks would do things?" And I said, "Yeah, yeah, yeah." Finally, I said to him, "Look, Sam, you hired two actors—Godfrey Cambridge and me—and we know what it is to be Black, so if we're shooting a scene and we get someplace and we don't think it's Black enough, we'll Blacken it up." So he said, "Could you Blacken it up now?" I said, "What do you mean?" He said, "Could you read the script and the little places where you think you might want to make changes, could you make the changes now?" I said, "Well, I guess, yeah, I could do that if I had to." He said, "Well, I'll pay you. Here's the script." So I took the script as a favor to him, and because he was paying me a few bucks and started working on a few scenes where the white writer hadn't quite gotten it right and sometimes had it completely wrong.

Finally, I began to make changes, and the one thing about a script, when you change one thing, particularly if you change it substantially, you're bound to have to change another to accommodate the first change. So when I changed one thing, Sam said, "Well, look, I like that, I like it very much, but if you're going to do that on page fourteen, how can you do this on page sixteen?" I said, "Yeah, well, I guess I'll have to change page sixteen too." He said, "Yeah, yeah, go ahead. Change it, I'll pay you." So I started working on the script on a piecemeal basis, and wound up finally rewriting the whole script top to bottom. Meanwhile Sam kept asking me, "Who do you think would be a good director?" And I didn't know and I didn't really care; it was just a job. Getting a director was his responsibility, not mine. So he kept coming up with directors, all of whom were white. Everyone he brought up I said, "Oh, man, he's great, he's a top man."

So Sam knew that I really wasn't paying any attention trying to help him solve the problem, and I think he wanted a Black director, and the only one out there in the seventies that anyone knew anything about was Gordon Parks, and I don't know what Gordon was doing at that time. But we kept naming directors, then finally Sam came to me and he said, "I've found the director I want." I said, "Who is it?" He said, "Well, come out to the house for dinner and I'll tell you." I was working in Los Angeles at the time on Night Gallery, I think it was, and one day after shooting I drove out to his house, he sat me down, gave me a couple of stiff martinis and I said, "Sam, who's the director?" He said, "Okay, have a drink." I said, "Okay. Sam, who's the director?" He said, "I'm going to tell you. Let me fill up your glass." So I got semi-stoned and then I said, "Sam, damn, man. Who've you got to direct the damn thing?" He said, "You." I said, "What?" He said, "You. I've gone to United Artists, I've checked, all the money people find you acceptable and so do I, so you're going to direct the film." I said, "The hell you speak. This ain't for directing." He said, "But I want you to direct." I said, "Well, give me two days to think it over."

I took the script, brought it home and showed it to Ruby and she found the script likable; she wasn't knocked out by it. But she agreed that maybe if I wanted to direct it, why not? So eventually I let myself be persuaded to direct Cotton Comes to Harlem. Of course, at Sam's suggestion, and he was wise, I didn't try to direct and act in it too. So we went out and got Raymond St. Jacques to come in and play opposite Godfrey, and I got to direct. But my being a director was Sam's idea, not mine.

GA: Cotton Comes to Harlem is a classic. Did you have any idea that the film would become a classic while you were making it?

OD: No, I didn't, and I wasn't impressed then and I'm not impressed now. I did the best I could, I looked at it, I liked what I saw, I laughed. There are only one or two places where I might have done things differently. I accept the movie for what it is. And it's a damn good film. According to Sam, it was one of the first films that began to draw Hollywood's attention to the fact that you could make a film for Black folks, and even if white folks didn't come, that film could make money. That hadn't been so before. Hollywood had made A Raisin in the Sun (1961) and lost money, they'd made Gordon Parks's The Learning Tree (1969) and had not made money, so when my film came along and it made money and made good money, even when United Artists and the others were sort of in trouble anyway, my film, I think, led the way to blaxploitation films, which Hollywood in the next ten years milked and received the benefit of.

GA: What do you think were the elements in Cotton Comes to Harlem that made it such a hit within the Black community?

OD: The humor and the authenticity. I had lived the life that was in the script and that Chester Himes had written about, or I knew someone who had lived the life. So most of the stuff that was in the film was sort of common knowledge on the streets. I had loved these characters anyway, because I had read the book. I think I wasn't trying to prove anything, I wasn't trying to go anywhere, I was just trying to have a good time in the sense that I used to have a good time standing on the street corner lying with the other guys, just that sense of creative fun and bullshit and this is how life is in Harlem. So I think the audience caught on to that and enjoyed it.

GA: Cotton Comes to Harlem will always be heralded as a seminal work. How did you get involved with the subsequent films that you directed?

OD: In this business one thing follows another. If you get out there and draw attention to yourself as an actor, or writer or a director, before one door closes another will open. Everyone will be coming to your door with the next project. For the next two or three years I had things to do that came my way. I certainly didn't go out looking for them. And I did them. I liked Black

Girl. I also liked a film I shot in Africa called *Kongi's Harvest* (1970). I think I was the first African American film director to go to Africa to make a feature, and then I went back three or four years later to make another feature—*Countdown at Kusini* (1976). So I had about five films in the can.

GA: *Now, you did the film* Countdown at Kusini *in 1976 with Delta Sigma Theta sorority as the producers. Great organization. How did that come about?*

OD: Well, the Deltas felt that instead of just bitching to Hollywood about the Black film fare coming from Hollywood, maybe they could come up with films of their own. Blaxploitation films were popular and making money, and the Deltas said, "If we make a film and we have eighty thousand members in our organization, out of our membership alone we could almost make a film a success [by buying tickets for the film]. So why don't we make a film?" At that time, I had a son-in-law who was Nigerian, and he had a script by a white writer and the Deltas took a look at it, Ruby and I took a look at it and I felt we could do it, so we arranged through my son-in-law to get the rights to do the film. And also at that time, I was chairman of the North American Section of the Black and African Festival of Arts and Culture, which was going to be held in Nigeria, so I had been going to Nigeria and coming back.

So we went to Nigeria and worked out the details and ultimately made the film. When we came back we tried to work out a way where the Deltas could certainly get access to their own membership as the audience. This is what happened. At that time, there was a producer at Columbia Pictures who had been our agent, and I don't want to give his name because of some of what I'm about to say. But the Deltas showed him our film, and he said that he liked it very much and that he wanted to distribute it. And he set aside $300,000 from Columbia for the film prints and advertising, which we got. Then we opened the film and we went into distribution, but we found that in many places our film would open and then, a couple of nights later, our film would close. Now, the reason for that was that you deal with two entities after you make the film. First in this process, you have to deal with a distributor, and the distributor has to deal with an exhibitor. The Columbia representative who was distributing the film dealt with the exhibitor and said, "We're going to give you picture A [a good film], which you want very badly, right? But in order for us to give you picture A we're going to put these dogs [poor films] in the agreement, too—pictures, B, C and D. So the exhibitor, in order to get picture A, gladly accepts films B, C and D. In the case of *Countdown at Kusini*, which the exhibitor was essentially forced to take, the exhibitor would honor the commitment to show the film for a couple of days and then pull it. That was so he could tell the Columbia people, "Well, I tried to show your film, but the people didn't come." Now, the Deltas would open the film in each market with a big gala, but they needed a little more time for the film to stay around to make their membership aware of the film. By the time the Deltas got their membership lined up, the film had already been pulled and there was nothing we could do about it. So the film by and large was a failure. If the exhibitor had been able to keep the film for four or five days so that the weekend could come and the message could have gone out to the Black church, we could have kept the damn thing there for a week or ten days once we got our own community organized.

The Deltas are not in the business of distributing films, and we found out later that the Columbia man never gave us the rest of the monies that he'd set aside for prints and advertising. The presumption, of course, is that he took it for himself, and that was one of the ways that people in Hollywood could make a fast buck. So I think because we weren't slick enough and smart enough to know how to deal with that, particularly since it was being handled by people who had no knowledge of the business at all—the Deltas—we were almost a perfect setup to fail.

But the Deltas' plan—if they themselves had known how to execute it—still made sense. If you have eighty thousand people to whom you can sell tickets, all you have to do is make a film that is budgeted under what eighty thousand tickets will recoup, and the difference between what you have to pay out to make the film and the money that comes in is profit. So all you have to do is start out with budgeting it carefully, then promoting it and raking in the profits. We knew the theory, but the legwork and footwork the sisters didn't know, there was no way they could. And I didn't know—I'm not a producer either. So in the end, it was not a project that did what it was supposed to do.

GA: *That's unfortunate. Do you think such a strategy with some of the national Black organizations partnered with the right producers and studios could work today?*
OD: Oh, yeah. You can do that, but the first thing you would have to do would be to secure a promoter and distributor, somebody who would know the theory, know which papers to put it in, know the audience, et cetera. You can't just go out and do it with the program committee of the organization. You have to know people who are pros and work with them.

GA: *What are your thoughts on the 2002 Oscar wins for Denzel Washington and Halle Berry?*
OD: One of things I hate most about Hollywood is the whole Oscar idea, but having said that, I'm very glad, even at this late date, that Halle and Denzel did win, although I was sorry that the films themselves were so negative and to sometime degree perverse. But it's still better late than never, and better something than nothing. We've [Black people] always had to come into the American

kingdom from the whorehouse or the shithouse; they wouldn't let us in the front door. I've seen Denzel do better work than the crooked cop in *Training Day*, and I've certainly seen Halle do better work than what she did in *Monsters Ball*, but goddamn it, they got it and I'm pleased, and I'm glad they gave old Sidney that lifetime award. So to me the Oscar situation was a positive one. I still think the whole Oscar setup is bullshit, but I think that if you're going to have bullshit, at least have equal-rights bullshit—let Black folks be involved too. So, yes, my response to the Oscar situation is positive.

GA: *You and your wife, Ms. Ruby Dee, seem to be the consummate professional artists. You've both enjoyed lengthy, full careers. What exactly is the job of an artist?*

OD: The job of the artist is to communicate. All art is entertainment, but all entertainment is not art. You have to learn how to be an artist and also an entertainer. They differ in quality and in scope sometimes, and you have to accomplish them both, but whether you are an artist or an entertainer you have to be professional, have standards, be craftworthy, know what is good from what is merely sufficient. An artist has to know what is excellent from what is meretricious, and must insist from himself that quality be maintained no matter who the hell is looking. You have to satisfy yourself, and sometimes the first thing that comes out is not satisfactory. We can entertain, but we are also artists, and for the artist, things must be kept in perspective: the social perspective, the economic perspective, the political perspective—all of these have to be considered when you're dealing with art. Art is a form of truth; entertainment need not be.

GA: *You and Ms. Dee have also used your art and celebrity to positively influence the civil rights movement in this country. Is that also the artist's responsibility?*

OD: It's a responsibility for the two of us, because that's how we define ourselves. But it would be hard to come into the business professionally like we did in 1945 and '46 without being in the middle of a battle that was being fought—the battle to include Black folks in the American experience, particularly as it related to art and entertainment—since the battle was in full swing. Paul Robeson and Lena Horne were already on the scene, and everything we did had to be judged as to whether it was good for Black folks or bad for Black folks, or it grew out of a situation affecting Black folks like a lynching, or you were in a campaign to bring out the vote and someone called on you to recite a poem or something like that. We didn't have the luxury of just thinking of ourselves as artists or celebrities. We knew that all Black folks were looking at us, all white folks were looking at us, and if we did the wrong thing there would be hell to pay. But at the same time, every time we did the right thing, that moved us up higher on the ladder toward acceptance in

America. Therefore, there was no way for us not to be involved. We were involved whether we were personally involved or not. People were looking at us, judgments were being made on the basis of how we behaved or took care of business.

So we were in the thick of struggle when we stepped on stage for the very first time. And one struggle led to another, so Ruby and I started out in struggle and we're still in struggle, because there's still a lot to be struggling about. Now, there may be people who came along then, and certainly people coming along now, whose jobs do not have to meet those stringent conditions. They may be actors, young people who do not feel they have to prove themselves. They have the right to vote—that's already guaranteed—the right to open access, the fight for inclusion has been won and they don't have to go and picket to get the job they want, so the struggle may not touch them and they may not be sensitive enough or lucky enough to understand that there are other areas of struggle that must be addressed now. So the struggle might leave them untouched altogether, and we certainly understand that. We don't say that everybody has to go through the same bullshit that we had to go through, no. Each generation has to find its task and assignment and do it. We certainly got involved in ours, and we still are, but that doesn't make us any better or any worse than anybody else.

GA: *There's a profound statement you made, and I read it in an essay on "Howard Legends" by Naijean Bernard at Howard University. You say, "The profoundest commitment possible to a Black creator in this country today, beyond all creeds, crafts, classes and ideologies whatsoever, is to bring before his people the scent of freedom." Could you please comment on that?*

OD: Certainly. Freedom is a dangerous concept unless you know what it is with which you're dealing. Freedom is like a sharp knife, a loaded pistol, gunpowder and a match. If you don't know what you're doing, you're going to blow yourself to hell. Freedom in the artistic sense means, from our point of view, that state of excellence that you arrive at only after lots of discipline and blood and sweat and tears and grunting and groaning and being constrained. Ultimately, you become worthy of your craft, you become free, you become an artist. Young people today think freedom is merely the right to stand up and be themselves—they don't have to worry about training, they don't have to worry about voice, they don't have to worry about how they walk, how they sound, how they talk or whether what they do has any impact on the struggle. That to them is a sense of freedom, but to me freedom is the last gift that you have and it's only given to you because you have finally, through struggle, become a master of your craft. So it has to embody tradition, exercise, rehearsal, practice, practice, practice. It has to embody refinement of craft, discipline, organization, thinking long and hard about the affect of what it is that you do and what it is you say, then finally you graduate into freedom. It's not a gift given to you; it's a state to be won. That's what I mean by freedom.

GA: *Incredible. You've been in a number of films with Spike Lee. Tell me what it's like to work with him.*

OD: Well, that's one of the most joyous experiences we can have, because Spike pays you on time, and I've worked with Spike more than I have with any other director. Spike has given me about five jobs and paid off every time—how are you going to beat that? [Laughs] Spike is a creative, bold, self-contained independent filmmaker. Spike is to film what Malcolm X was to struggle. Wherever he goes, something exciting is liable to happen. So you don't get too close, because you might get the shit knocked out of you. But you stand and you salute because you know a unique talent has come into your presence. He's a damn good creator, a good Black man, and I suspect him to be a good husband and father too. He's started a family and I have the old keen eye on him, and so far he's up to muster. Within the confines of industry, Spike is one of those creative, artistic pioneers. Spike is one of the few men I know, Black or white, who could have sat down at that table with Sam Goldwyn, Louis B. Mayer, H. B. Warner and David O. Selznick—authors of Hollywood. Spike could have sat with those men and been their creative and intellectual equal, and I can say that about few people, Black or white.

GA: *What advice do you have for people who want to work in the entertainment field as directors, actors and writers but who also want to be artists, to reach that high ideal?*

OD: I would say that you must deepen yourself, study yourself, study your history, study your craft, study your art, try to find something that you respect in everything you do, and if you can't respect it, walk away.

GA: *What legacy would you like to leave on the planet for the rest of us and for generations to come?*

OD: I would like to leave a legacy of struggle. I would like my life to say, to all who paid attention, that this was a man who had the great benefit of knowing what struggle was and how necessary struggle is to the formation of character. There will always be good and evil in the world no matter how perfect we may think we are, and the struggle is between the two. I've tried my best always in the struggle to choose the best side and to give it all I had, even if at times I might have been called on to give my life. I struggled, I looked for the best in every situation and I've been blessed.

Fred Williamson

When meeting Fred Williamson for the first time, one is greeted with the familiarity and warmth of an old high school friend, the good-looking guy who got all of the girls then and who still has the looks and aplomb to get the prettiest girls now. Decidedly charismatic and witty with tough-guy charm, Williamson first gained notoriety as a superstar professional football player, nicknamed "The Hammer" for his defensive talents on the gridiron, with the Oakland Raiders and the Kansas City Chiefs. For the Chiefs he played in Super Bowl I in 1967.

A 1960 architectural engineering graduate from Northwestern University, Williamson worked briefly as an architect after his football career ended before setting out for Hollywood, where he quickly assumed the role of Diahann Carroll's love interest on her late-sixties, early-seventies hit television series *Julia*. He later gained roles in Robert Altman's M*A*S*H* (1970) and with Otto Preminger in *Tell Me That You Love Me, Junie Moon* (1970), starring Liza Minnelli. Williamson received an Emmy nomination for his work on the seventies hit series *Police Story*.

It was while working with Altman and Preminger that Williamson decided to pursue directing and producing, and he launched his Po' Boy Productions in 1974. Since then he has directed or starred in close to forty films produced under the Po' Boy banner (making him one of the most prolific Black director/producers) including *No Way Back* (1976), *Adios Amigos* (1975), *South Beach* (1992), with Peter Fonda and most recently, *Down 'N Dirty* (2000) and *On the Edge* (2002) for Blockbuster.

GA: Tell me about growing up.

FW: I was a thug.

GA: Were you?

FW: Yeah, I was a thug because I was pretty. I was good-looking at a very young age. I was so good-looking I was pretty, so people used to pick on me because they thought "pretty boy" was not a tough guy, so I had to fight all the time to survive, to show that you could also be a good-looking kid and fight. What happened was that I immediately became a leader. It was a quality that was God-given to me, and people started following me around. I was never a guy who would sit in the background and watch the world go by. I always wanted to be a part of the world and participate in everything. I grew up in Gary, Indiana, and Chicago, and I was class president until senior year, when a lot of jealous students cast some votes not to have me elected and we had a second election. I wound up winning it anyway. So I guess my leadership qualities followed through into my being an astute student in high school—not because I wanted to be bright or be brilliant, I just wanted to be the best in the class. I wanted to live up to the expectations that my friends and so-called followers had elevated me to. So I graduated number seven in a class of three hundred and twenty, which allowed me to get in the universities that I wanted to go to. I had sports scholarships—basketball, track and football—from all the major colleges around the country. Ultimately, I picked Northwestern, because it didn't have any Black students.

Acting was never in my background. I'm an architect. I studied architecture, and when I came out of school I worked for Bechtel Steel in San Francisco several years at the same time I was playing football for the Oakland Raiders. I used Bechtel as my off-season job. Still then, acting was not a part of my future, and being a ghetto kid, I just could never foresee getting on that little tube where I saw all these people acting doing their thing. That was something for the ultra society of white folks.

GA: Being a pro athlete and an architect would be your career, you thought?

FW: That would be the whole thing, yes, yes. But when I stopped playing football and started sitting at a desk, that lasted for about nine months. The desk and the walls started to close in on me. I couldn't make the transition comfortably. I started looking around for something else to do. You've got to remember, this was the sixties, and high school was in the fifties, when Black was not cool. Anything that you did and accomplished as a Black man meant that you definitely were going against the society and going against wherever they wanted you to be. The problems at that time were big. These kids who are making a lot of money and doing big-time things in Hollywood now just don't understand what was happening back in the fifties and sixties. They don't totally realize that they were still sicking dogs on people back in the sixties. They were still hosing them down on the corner, beating them up with sticks and billy clubs back in the sixties. In Chicago, they tried to keep you confined in a certain area—the so-called ghetto.

GA: What was it like attending Northwestern with there being so few Black students?
FW: Being a rebel and the kind of guy that I was, everywhere that I went I felt like I belonged there and they didn't belong there, and that I owned the joint and they were on my property. So I had a rash of white girlfriends that upset the college tremendously, but there was nothing they could do about it because I was their star. All they could do was talk nice to me and say—their favorite expression to me was, "Please, Mr. Williamson, be a little more discreet, will you?" [Laughs] I learned that the toughest guy in high school was the guy who did nothing. There were two or three guys I looked up to. And they were touted as the baddest motherfuckers in school and I ain't never seen 'em fight nobody. I learned that image is everything. Image is everything. So I became one of them. I didn't talk, I didn't say anything, so people were always trying to figure me out. And I was big enough and strong enough to carry that image, that persona, and that's all you have to have.

GA: You're too much. [Laughs]
FW: That's because I'm good at what I do, which is selling me. It depends what day of the week you talk to me, but I understand image and I know how to cultivate it and deal. That's like my movies—my movies all have this persona and the same image. If you see a Fred Williamson movie, there ain't gonna be no singing, no dancing, and I'm gonna kick some ass, I'm going to have some pretty ladies, and I'm gonna do my thing and I'm going to ride off in the sunset.

GA: How did you break into the film business from football and architecture?
FW: Back in the day, there was no money in pro football. We weren't making any money. My signing bonus as the number-two draft choice was $1,600 in one-dollar bills; my starting salary was $9,500. I had to work in the off-season in order to sustain. So I knew that the only thing available to me was selling cars or selling machines—if I wanted to get away from architecture I had to go be a salesman or something. One night I was watching television—for several weeks I'd been watching Diahann Carroll on Julia—and I noticed that every week the guest star role on the show was a new boyfriend. Right away that gave me an idea to go to Hollywood and tell the producer, Hal Kanter—I went and told him, to make a long story short, I told him that Diahann Carroll was a prostitute. She was a whore.

GA: Huh? You told him just like that, in those words?

FW: Yes. He said, "What do you mean?" I said, "She's dating a new guy every week. That makes her a whore. That means she's screwing somebody each week." He said, "Well, you know, we're getting a little problem from the NAACP about the show about the same thing." I said, "I'm your man. Give her a regular boyfriend—I'm the man. You ain't got nobody in the show better-looking than me, right? I know I can handle her." He said, "You ever acted before?" I said, "I did A Raisin in the Sun and Carmen Jones up in college for five years." I hadn't done anything, man. If he had asked me which character I played, I would have been dead.

GA: [Laughs]

FW: [Laughs] So he said, "Okay, I'll write a show for you. I like your style. I'll write a show for you called "Dancing in the Dark." The show was about a pro football player who retired from football, met Diahann Carroll and we fell in love. So I was on the show. It worked out pretty well and they signed me to a contract.

GA: What was it like working on the show with Diahann Carroll—a star?

FW: Hey, man, everything is a new experience. As long as she stayed pretty and brushed her teeth every day, everything worked out well. There's nothing worse than a pretty girl with funky breath. But Diahann kept her teeth clean and she had a nice smile. I mean, you can get along with anybody, man, if you're from the ghetto and you understand that all you have to do is be nice and get a check. You understand that real good. But if you're from another part of the world, where you can have your silver spoon and you don't have to be nice and you don't have to worry about the check, then that's different.

GA: You later did some work with director Robert Altman on the movie M*A*S*H. Tell me about that.

FW: We were shooting Julia at Twentieth Century Fox and I was in the commissary, and Bob Altman came down and he said, "Hey, you're the Hammer, right?" I said, "Yeah." He said, "I'm making a movie and it's about football players and I don't know shit about football—would you put this football shit together?" So I brought him all of the football players. My buddies were Buc Buchannan, Super Nat. Also, at that time there was a semipro team in Santa Barbara, so I brought them all in because I wanted to do contact football, and he [Altman] let me direct those football sequences. That was really my first movie experience. I made more money in that movie than I made in my whole goddamn football career.

GA: *Wow. And you got the directing bug after that?*

FW: I didn't get the directing bug, no. What I wanted was to—again, we're talking '70, man. There were no Blacks in Hollywood. There was Jim Brown, Poitier, no one was really breaking into the business in '70. So I still was not satisfied, because I saw myself as a hero. I saw myself as Clark Gable, John Wayne, all these people, but Hollywood didn't see me that way. I figured the only way I could do that was to start making my own movies. When I did *Julia*, I never left the set. I got into the business with the idea of learning this business of the business. So I watched how they moved the camera, I asked questions, I talked about the lights. I learned everything, so by the time *Julia* finished, I knew how to take a camera apart, put it together in the dark, I knew about lighting, I knew how to do everything. I went to Paramount and said, "Listen, let's make a western." This was about 1971 or 1972, right after *Julia*. They said, "Well, what kind of western do you want to make?" I said, "I want to make one with a Black cowboy. I want to call it 'Nigger Charley'." The man almost jumped out of the window. I said, "Listen, you don't understand. Really, that word doesn't have a big impact, because too many people have misused it and said it too many times so it doesn't mean anything." We were still kind of in a negative experience, we were on the edge of it, 1972. He said, "Well, how much does it cost?" I said, "I can make this movie for $600,000." We went to Arizona and we made a film called *The Legend of Nigger Charley* [directed by Martin Goldman], and that film made about $30 million. Larry Spangler produced it.

GA: *And they were banking on you as the star.*

FW: Exactly. Then we had a whole line of them, from *Black Caesar* to *Hell Up in Harlem*, to *Bucktown*. The timing was right, because we needed heroes. We needed Black heroes. We didn't need any more comics. We didn't need any more funny people. Richard Pryor took care of that. Richard Pryor was the funniest man in the world. But we still didn't have any heroes, man. We didn't have anybody standing up kicking people's ass, and I made it real clear that I kicked everybody's asses. I was equal opportunity prone. I kicked white people's, Black people's, yellow people's and pink people's asses. See, you couldn't say that Fred Williamson was after whitey, because I was after everybody who was wrong and bad in my pictures. When the smoke cleared, I was the only one left standing. So my movies were not "get whitey."

GA: *You also always wanted to get the girl, you told me when we spoke for Black Enterprise (Dec. 2001).*

FW: I had three rules in Hollywood: (1) You can't kill me; (2) I win all the fights and (3) I get the girl at the end of the movie, if I want her.

GA: If you want her.

FW: If I want her. [Laughs] Those are my three rules.

GA: [Laughs] How did Hollywood producers and studios receive your rules when you presented them?

FW: That was never my goal. My goal was never to be part of Hollywood, because I knew that Hollywood was not going to let me attain what I called success—let me attain the hype—because I was too far ahead of my time. Now it's a whole other game. They give us five Black stars every ten years and push them up and make them stars, and then every five or six years they give us a new crop of people. In '70 they weren't interested, man. They weren't interested in putting us up nowhere. Every time we made a movie that was a success, they'd say, "It's lucky and we can't afford to invest in a Black film." Because you go to a celebrity party in Beverly Hills and the president of Paramount is talking to somebody and the person asks, "Well, what's your big picture this year?" and the president responds, "*The Legend of Nigger Charley.*" That don't work.

GA: [Laughs]

FW: [Laughs] That don't work at a Beverly Hills party. That don't sound good. Even if it made cash, that doesn't sound good. They jumped on the bandwagon for about two years. A couple of major studios made a couple of films, but the films topped out at about twenty to twenty-five million bucks, which is not going to pay their light bill.

GA: So at the end of the day, you didn't want to pursue Hollywood?

FW: No, my whole concept in life was to be doing what made me happy, being what I wanted to be so I wouldn't have to hurt nobody, be pissed off and go around the world kicking people's ass and hurting somebody to be happy. It was about attaining what I felt made me feel good and I was free to do what I wanted to do and be gainfully and consistently employed. Most of the brothers who came through the seventies with me in the movies ain't working now. And if they are working, they're not doing the same work that they were doing in the seventies, with this positive-image thing. They're just actors looking for work who go and sit in a room with fifty other guys and try to read for one little part with some little white producer sitting there looking at you like you're a piece of meat, because when they send out the sheets every week about what parts are available, there's always some little line in there that says, "Forty-five-year-old Black guy to act something like . . ." They give you some example of how they want you to be, and it's always somebody else. It's not anything that carries the show. What carries the show, you don't have to specify. You say, "Good actor who has ba, ba, ba." But when they say, "Black," they audition fifty of ninety unemployed Black actors, about fifteen minutes apart, which means you have the whole goddamn little room and hallways filled up with every fucking Black actor who's unemployed, sitting there waiting to go in—short ones, fat ones, dark ones, baldheaded ones, full of hair, dreadlocks—all reading for one fucking part.

That shit hasn't changed. That's the way it was in the sixties and seventies, and that's how it is today. And I believe in seniority. What's the point of working so much and becoming a viable and marketable commodity when you have to go through the same rigmarole? I don't mind going reading for the part if I know that I have a possibility of getting it, but let me read for the producer and the director, and give me a time that's independent of all the others who are sitting out here in this goddamn room who don't have the background that I have. I mean, give me some respect. If you don't give me no respect, then I ain't interested. I'll go find a job somewhere else.

GA: *And you went and did your own thing with* No Way Back. *Tell me about that.*
FW: Right, I decided to do my own thing with No Way Back. We had made all of these films and I was talking to the president of AIP [American International Pictures], Sam Arkoff. I said, "How do these films do in Europe?" He said, "Well, films with Black stars don't do well in Europe." I couldn't understand that, because of all the girlfriends that I had who were Spanish and German and Italian. I said, "Well, how can that be?" He said, "Well every film that has a Black star in it is sold across the board at $3,000 per film." I said, "No, no, no. That's not right." So I made No Way Back for $75,000. I took my first film under my arm to the Cannes Film Festival in 1975, and I've been going to Cannes ever since. In Cannes, I gave the maître d' of the Carlton Terrace one hundred bucks—because I'd be there two weeks—to save a table for me. I spread out my fliers, hired me some models out on the beach and gave them $25 apiece to put these T-shirts on with the name of the picture on it and I set up my little office on the terrace. My first customer was Greece. A guy came by and said, "Oh, Williamson. We like your movies. We make a lot of money with your movies. I want to buy your movie. Three thousand." I said, "Naw, no way. Forget about it. There's no way that you're going to buy my movie for $3,000. Because anytime you want a Fred Williamson movie now, you've got to come directly to me."

GA: *Before they were going to AIP?*
FW: Yes. AIP had most of the Black films at that time. Sam Arkoff made Foxy Brown, Slaughter, Coffy—all those films. And what was happening was that AIP had been sold a bill of goods by the white distributors in Europe because they were playing on America's prejudices. They understood that if they said that Black ain't nothing over there, they could get away with it, because people

over here readily believe it and readily accept it because that's the lifestyle they live. But what they were doing was buying it [a film] for $3,000 and laughing like a dog all the way to the bank because the films do good business over there. It doesn't have to be a good picture. Their attitude toward Black is totally opposite of what the attitude toward Black is in America. In Europe and in all of the other countries, it's a whole other ball game. Every country came to me at the festival and I turned them all down, and by the end of the festival, the last two days, they came by again, one at a time, and said, "Okay, we'll pay your price, but you have to go back and not tell them what we bought." So l left there with my sale with No Way Back, which I made for $75,000 and I made $270,000 at Cannes.

GA: Great. How did you raise the $75,000 to make the film in the beginning?

FW: I went to Lewis Horowitz at Imperial Bank [The Lewis Horowitz Organization in L.A., now a division of Southern Pacific Bank], and he believed in the value of my making the movie. First of all, I had to convince him that I could make the film for $75,000, and I did so by telling him that I'd wear all hats. I'm the producer, I'm the writer and I'm the star, so I don't have to pay anyone. All I have to do is buy the film and the camera and pay the other people. Since there were no stars in it, I was the only one in it who had any value, so that's why I could make it for $75,000. He loaned the money, and when I came back I gave him his check—$75,000 plus interest—so the money was out for about three months.

That is the ignorance, even today. They're quick to tell you that if you have a Black lead in a film, it doesn't have a European value. They'll tell you that today. They think that today.

GA: That seems to be a constant argument. Halle Berry recently said the same thing in The New York Times before the 2002 Oscars.

FW: But see, that's a whole other story. What pisses me off about Halle Berry—it's not about Halle Berry so much as it is about how Hollywood perceives interracial affairs. They'd put a white guy with a Black chick making out like a dog, but I haven't seen a brother making out with Roberts [Julia Roberts].

GA: I liked Monsters Ball a lot, but you have a point. That's true.

FW: I haven't seen that happen, and to me that's disturbing. It's just that nobody's talked about it. Halle Berry was doing it, Angela Bassett had a love scene. Three or four of our top so-called Black females have had fantastic, great love affairs with white stars.

GA: Whitney Houston in The Bodyguard.

FW: Yes, Whitney Houston also. Now, you turn it around the other way. See, I ain't seen Wesley Snipes kiss nobody. I ain't seen Samuel Jackson swap spit with nobody. They're put in these situations, and you wonder why they don't. Denzel could have slobbered all over Roberts in *The Pelican Brief*. They were running and holding hands, escaping from everybody. The situation was definitely there, and the way it ended with them standing out on an airfield, looking at each other, gazing into each other's eyes like there's going to be a romance, then she gets on the plane and leaves and he goes off. They don't hug, they don't kiss, they don't swap no spit. What's the deal with that, man? You're going to tell me Hollywood has changed, Hollywood is growing? Hollywood has gotten smart.

They know how to do the same shit to pacify Black people and the NAACP to keep them off their backs by giving them jobs and making them feel like celebrities and stars. The way to be is for them to decide. Hollywood has to decide to give you the part, to go with you. If they feel they can control you, then they give you the part, then they give you another part and another part. That's what makes you a star. You just don't decide to be a star in this business. Hollywood decides if they're going to go with you and put you in a big-budget film—then gives you another one, then gives you another one to keep it going. How many Black stars in this goddamn business can do movies without a white counterpart? None. Who has starred in a movie without a white counterpart and had some success? Denzel hasn't done one. Snipes hasn't done one when he didn't have a white counterpart.

GA: Will Smith in Ali was a box-office disappointment.

FW: The movie has to have a main white counterpart.

GA: Why is that the case, do you think?

FW: I think it's the subject matter that they pick, and we all know Ali, so there's no way you can give me Ali. Put it on television and we'll watch it, but we ain't gonna file out, because we lived with that. We know the real Ali. We all know him. You can't give me a movie and tell me this is about Ali. You can make it a documentary and show me some footage with Ali. That's what Ali did with *The Greatest* with the real Ali, and that wasn't no big success, but they didn't spend a lot of money on it. This second Ali, they spent a ton of money [$107 million]. It was no way they could've gotten it back [according to *Variety*, the film grossed $80.8 million worldwide]. Give us the right subject matter and we'll go do it.

GA: In terms of Black films performing in foreign territories, some Black filmmakers tend to accept this argument, but you've spent time abroad and understand those territories, which positions you to market your films overseas. Is that what makes the difference?

FW: Again, even if you don't accept it, it doesn't really matter. If you don't have any control over your project, you have to believe. I just made a deal with Blockbuster called Down 'N Dirty. They said, "We'll keep domestic." I said, "Fine, give me the foreign, you can have all of the domestic," and I'll make more money than they will. But they don't understand. And I try to tell them, "Look, why don't we split it—you take fifty percent of the world, then we'll both make a lot of money?" They said," No, you take Europe and we'll take all domestic." I said, "Fine, okay. Good." That's, again, their misunderstanding that a film with a Black lead won't make money. Now, there are some films with Black leads that won't make money like films with too much ethnic comedy. The Europeans don't relate to the ethnic comedies.

GA: Could you expound on what you mean by that?

FW: Well, there are no ghettos over there. When they play my film, they play in the same theater where they play Stallone or where they play any action star, because there are no ghettos. But here in America, they know that if they have a Black film they can play it in Harlem, South Central, South Side of Chicago. Well, they don't have that Black audience to cater to in Europe. They don't understand ghetto slang and inside jokes that deal with the ghetto. All that internal stuff they don't relate to, because they don't understand it. It's like comedy. What's funny here ain't funny over there, and what's funny over there ain't funny here. The only person who has been able to transcend that as a standup comic has been Jerry Lewis. Jerry Lewis was stepping in buckets and falling down stairs, which was funny back in the day, but he can do the same thing in Europe, step down, step in a bucket and fall downstairs, and they'd laugh like crazy.

GA: Physical comedy works, is what you're saying. The visual.

FW: Snatching the tablecloths off and the shit's still there, and trying to do that magic shit and everything comes off the table.

GA: Right, right.

FW: They relate to all of that. That's why I can do an action film—a kick in the mouth needs no translation. Ouch in America is ouch in Rome. So there are certain things that don't need translation. As long as you keep a film in the genre where it doesn't need a translation to get the punch line, then it's easier and they don't really care if it's a Black lead or a white lead, as long they understand it and like it. Then they'll deal with it.

GA: *What tend to be your strongest markets overseas?*
FW: I think where a Black does business is where there's less prejudice, which is Europe. The strongest markets there are France, Italy, Germany and Spain.

GA: *Do they dub?*
FW: They do subtitles. Sometimes they dub them, but they want to hear the actor's voice. Most of the people who dub them are the Japanese and Chinese people, because they are so particular about what they do. But they usually give me a nice voice. When I say, "Sit down and shut up, man," they say it in Japanese. So they give me somebody who's cool. But they dub over there because most of the Japanese people don't understand English anyway. They have people over there who do dubs who are just as big a star as the people who do acting, because they have distinctive voices, and so when they hear that voice, those people are big celebrities too.

GA: *You've also done a number of films using foreign presales, correct?*
FW: After I did No Way Back, I decided that if I wanted to up my budget and not increase my risk—I didn't want to be in a position where I didn't pay the bank back and create that kind of reputation. My first movie cost $75,000, and if I wanted to go up to $150,000–$200,000, my risk would become greater. So what I would do was go to all the markets. I went to Cannes, MIFED, and I would pre-sell the film, get the contracts, then bring the contracts back to Lew Horowitz at Imperial Bank, and he would lend me money against the contracts because that's as good as gold. It means that once you deliver the film they give you the money. That's how I did all of my other films.

GA: *You've been quite successful using keen entrepreneurial skills to build your film career.*
FW: Everyone who's in my position and even bigger has the power to do that.

GA: *Why don't we see more Black actors, directors and producers raising money in foreign markets?*
FW: Because it's about business, man. Everybody wants to stay at home, have the phone ring and have someone stroke him and tell them how great they are. If Denzel wanted to do it or Snipes wanted to do it and not be part of the Hollywood system and really make some films that they

wanted to do—or maybe they are. We don't know. Maybe what they're doing they really want to do. But it would be easy for them, man, to set up for themselves a little company and physically go and say to a buyer in Italy, "Here, I want $250,000 for my next picture. Give me a contract and you'd have it for $250,000. They'd snatch it up in two seconds. Then he'd bring the contracts, take the money and make whatever dream film he wanted to make. Why don't they do it? Only they can tell you, but I know that they have the power to do that. Not only Black stars but whites. Any white actor who's reached a certain status can just start his own company, do his own presales, then make his own movie. But if you're making $20 million or $10 million a picture, why do you need the aggravation—if that's not your motivation? That just so happens to be my motivation.

I'm very happy I'm not making $5 to $10 million a picture. I would be very hard to live with, because I would have lost this energy that's necessary for me to survive in this bullshit world. Once you lose the energy, then you become defensive. You become like these idiots here (in L.A.). They go out and don't know how to act. They become defensive people. You can't walk up to them, you can't talk to them. They think that they're a whole other species of the human race because they're making $10 million, so they become defensive people, they become unapproachable and they become different people. I'm glad I'm not like that. I have to have this energy of being on all the time, and all the time being aware of the marketplace and all the time making deals and spending fifty percent of the day on the phone calling Europe, calling producers, calling distributors. That's my life, that's my style, and I enjoy doing it. See how good I look at the age I am now?

GA: Well, it's pretty amazing. How do you do it?
FW: I'm wheeling and dealing, man. I'm stress-free. I ain't sitting at home waiting for the phone to ring, wrinkling my brow, saying, "Ain't nobody called me in two weeks. Goddamn, what I'm a do?"

GA: You're in control of the process?
FW: Yeah, when you're in control of that, then you become in control of yourself. You control yourself, what else is there?

GA: You have a certain level of freedom, because if you're not careful the business will beat you down if you allow it to do so.
FW: Listen, the more money they make, the more depressed they become. All the people who get in trouble . . . and you're always reading about the ones you shouldn't be reading about. But they

become defensive, man. They don't have that inner drive to do things themselves. Most of these actors can't go to the grocery store by themselves, man. Somebody's got to take them there or they've got to send somebody just to buy some bread, peas, beans and shit.

GA: [Laughs]

FW: It's amazing how helpless a lot of these so-called big stars are. They can't do anything for themselves because they're surrounded by yes people.

GA: *What are your thoughts on Black cinema and Black popular culture today?*

FW: Well, there's the rap music and pop music. There's some positive value in the movie business from the standpoint that it has brought back a lot of the old films that were made in the seventies that the younger generation never got to see. But rap music is reaching back for it, because when they hear James Brown on the *Black Caesar* soundtrack doing "Poppa's Got a Brand New Bag," they say, "Wow, that's great music." So some of hip-hop music deals with old music. And the do-wop is slowly starting to come back—the do-wop era with the Flamingos and the Drifters and those groups—so it has had a positive impact on that. And it has grown.

See, that's what happened in the seventies when we were making our films. They weren't around long enough to grow and become a different kind of film. We were in a hurry to get them out. We were too busy selling hard action, hero stuff, trying to be the hero and make the right film, that we never really got to enjoy what we accomplished, because we were always put on a different level, being a role model or being the hero. We were too busy fighting. Now they just accept it. You want to be a movie star? Go to Hollywood. A kid in the ghetto looking at that says, "I'm going to do that. I'm going to Hollywood." Hey, man, that never happened in the sixties. You could never sit and watch the others and say, "I'm going to Hollywood to be a movie star." Now people like Townsend can come in and say that they made a film for $100,000 in credit cards, which is all bullshit—the film cost more than that—but it made good press and it got people to pay attention to it who maybe never would have paid attention to the film. But back in the fifties and sixties, you never could have even thought of doing that. But because so many of us have gone before them, they have this freedom to do that.

So it's still a growing process, because we don't have control. We don't have control of the product and the subject matter, so it's still a growing process. Until we do that, we're not really going to get the kind of film we really want to see. What kind of film is that? But again, when the smoke clears we should be standing. Because when they talk to me about a film, they want to kill me and have Schwarzenegger avenge my death. No, kill Schwarzenegger and let me avenge his death. That kind of stuff comes at you. Like Roundtree [Richard Roundtree of Shaft] did the film City Lights with Burt Reynolds and Clint Eastwood, and he was killed in the first five minutes. That's not the way I want to go. Let one of them die and let me stay throughout the whole film talking about them.

GA: [Laughs] Still standing, huh?
FW: [Laughs] Exactly.

GA: What are your hopes for Black cinema going forward?
FW: I don't have any hopes. I'm a realist. I understand where it is, and I understand that it ain't gonna change until we change. There ain't no hopes. Hopes don't change a damn thing.

GA: Okay. [Laughs] You are the hope, huh?
FW: I guarantee that I'm part of the hope.

GA: What advice do you have for aspiring directors?
FW: Stay the fuck home. The only way to be a part of this business is that you have to learn the business of the business. If you learn the business of the business, then you have a possibility of being successful on both sides of the camera. If you come to be an actor, keep your ass home. But actors and directors suffer the same consequences of people having to critique you and give you a job. If you come with your hand out, you have fewer chances of gaining success in anything. You have to bring something to the table in order to get something. You have to remember that there are a whole lot of people ahead of you, wanting to do the same thing that you want to do, who have more seniority, who've kissed more ass than you have, so you have a lot of ass-kissing to catch up on when you come out here. Keep that in mind. So if you're not bringing anything to the table but a desire, you have no shot. You'd better bring something more to the table than a desire.

GA: What legacy does Fred Williamson want to leave on the planet?
FW: That I did whatever I wanted to do, whenever I wanted to do it, as many times as I wanted to do it. That's my legacy.

Michael Schultz

Milwaukee, Wisconsin, native Michael Schultz has been making his imprint with the moving image for more than thirty years. Schultz began his career directing for the stage and was a founding member of the internationally famous Negro Ensemble Company. In 1969 he directed Hal Halbrook and Al Pacino on Broadway in Does A Tiger Wear a Necktie, which garnered Schultz a Tony Award nomination.

Moving to film, Schultz made his directorial debut with To Be Young Gifted and Black, a television film based on the writings of the late Lorraine Hansberry. But it is the urban classic film Cooley High (1975) for which Schultz is perhaps most widely known. Set in a high school on the south side of Chicago in the 1960s, the film is a coming-of-age tale of friendship, love, boyhood and striving to beat the odds of a precarious urban life—all set to a fabulous Motown soundtrack. Cooley High is a pure celebration of some of the best of African Americana. After the success of Cooley High, Schultz directed another classic, Car Wash (1976), with Richard Pryor, Bill Duke, the Pointer Sisters, George Carlin and Ivan Dixon. Car Wash received awards for best music and the jury prize for superior technique and Schultz was nominated for the Golden Palm at the 1977 Cannes Film Festival. In the 1980s, Schultz directed a young Denzel Washington in Carbon Copy.

During the 1990s, Schultz focused his career on the small screen and directed a number of telefilms and several two-hour movies for the George Lucas–created Young Indiana Jones

Chronicles. His episodic television credits include some of the most popular shows on television: *The Practice, Boston Public, Touched by an Angel* and *JAG*.

Schultz has also entered the world of animation, working closely with David E. Kelly and Lucas. He is the artistic driving force behind ImajiMation Studios, Inc., a company specializing in a unique art form called urban anime, a blend of the Japanamation style with that of hip-hop's urban sensibilities. ImajiMation has created work for Adidas, Ford Motor Co., R. Kelly, Toni Braxton and UPN, and is now developing a hip-hop driven animated feature film called *Blok Hedz*.

— — — —

GA: *Tell me about growing up in Milwaukee. Were you creative?*

MS: No, actually I was more of a sports person and I loved school, so I was more into science and the Boy Scouts. But I come from a family of two children—a younger brother and myself. When I was four years old my parents split, so my mother was a single mother. She and my grandmother raised us, and my mother took us to plays and ballets, but I don't ever recall being interested in it. I wanted to be Colin Powell. My main goal coming out of high school was to go to the Air Force Academy and to be a general in the Air Force. I was second highest in the state of Wisconsin [on the entrance exam], and they were only taking one person from each state. I got an appointment to West Point as a consolation prize, but I turned it down because I didn't want to be in the Army, I wanted to fly jets.

When I didn't get accepted to the Air Force Academy, I decided I'd go to the University of Wisconsin to study aeronautical engineering. I was going to be an astronaut. I thought that if I can't fly in the military, I'll just fly rockets. But I discovered in my freshman year that I was not cut out to be an engineer. So my first two years of college were kind of exploratory, finding out what I really didn't want to do. I then decided to drop out, because I really didn't know what I wanted to do, but because I had all of these high scores in the military [tests] when I dropped out of school—it was during the Vietnam conflict—I was immediately draft material. I had to go back to school in order to prevent being fodder in the war. I said, "If I'm going back to school, it will have to be for something I love."

I transferred from Wisconsin to Marquette University in Milwaukee, where they had a great theater department, which was really just tolerated by the university and not sanctioned by it, because theater was a tool of the devil—Marquette is a Jesuit school. And what was great about it was that if we didn't sell tickets, we didn't have money to buy costumes or for sets or lights, et cetera. It was like being in a real commercial environment within a university setting, and it was like being in an Off-Broadway theater. You had to exist by the quality of the work. To be a part of the group, you had to do everything: dance class, acting class, design lights, design costumes and build sets. Everyone who went to the theater school came out with an ability to do many things, not just act. But I didn't want to do any of that. I discovered that I wanted to direct.

GA: At that time, did you see yourself as just directing theater?
MS: No. Well, during my sophomore year at the University of Wisconsin I spent most of the time in the campus movie houses watching Fellini, Zefferelli, Antonioni and Bergman—all of these great foreign films. I just loved the power of the medium when it was used in a non-Hollywood way. I said, "I'd love to be able to do that," but I had no idea how to get started because there were no role models. Gordon [Parks] hadn't started yet. Melvin [Van Peebles] hadn't started. The only role model I had was Sidney Poitier, and I didn't want to be an actor. [Laughs]

GA: Was there a memorable film by Fellini or Bergman that influenced you?
MS: I can't recall the titles, but they were just brilliant discourses on humanity and human interaction and man's relationship to society and to God. The one thing that disturbed me during this period was that there were no Black images to be seen because it was after the 1940s and before the blaxploitation period. There was a period when we were just absent from the screen and also absent from the theater. My desire was to change that—to have our stories somehow represented in the media and to be able to tell the fascinating stories most of which are still untold.

GA: And so after college you went to New York?
MS: Yes, after college I went to New York and started directing in a theater that was run by John Lithgow's father [Arthur] at Princeton University at the McCarter Theater. And that's where I got my first professional directing job, directing Waiting for Godot, and that was followed by The Emperor Jones. They wanted me to be in the acting company, which I agreed to do if I could direct one of the plays for the season. They hired me to direct The Emperor Jones because it dealt with a Black character and they couldn't find a director for Waiting for Godot. I'd seen Zero Mostel and Burgess Meredith do it on Broadway, and I didn't think they had done it right. Although they got tremendous accolades, to me they missed the point of the play. So I went to Arthur Lithgow and said, "Look, I know this play. I can direct this play. If you don't like the job I'm doing, you can fire me. I don't need to do Emperor Jones. I directed Waiting for Godot, got great reviews, directed Emperor Jones, completely different, and got great reviews for that.

I came back to New York in 1968 and put my résumé on Douglas Turner Ward's desk, because my wife told me they were just starting the Negro Ensemble Company. And Ward didn't know that there were any Black directors besides Lloyd Richards, so he hired me to direct the first play that season, called *The Song of the Lusitanian Bogey*. It was a fascinating, highly dramatic sing-spiel, which was a cross between a dramatic play and a musical. It was about the Portuguese oppression of Mozambique and Angola. It was a highly, highly political and very powerful drama. It won the Obie for best directing for Off-Broadway that year [1968]. Out of that I got my first Broadway job, directing a play called *Does a Tiger Wear a Necktie* in 1969, and I cast Al Pacino and Hal Holbrook. I was always blessed with not only being in the right place at the right time, but having the ability to do the job and being prepared for the opportunities that opened up.

GA: *And you received a Tony nomination for that play. What was that like?*
MS: It was great, because just to be a serious play and to be on Broadway is an amazing thing in and of itself. I thought we should have won, but *The Great White Hope* won that year.

GA: *What was it like working with Al Pacino and Hal Holbrook?*
MS: It was great. Even in Al's early days he was a consummate professional, very meticulous about everything, very consistent, always thinking and very creative and very powerful on stage. Holbrook was an old pro and he had a great young cast, which included my wife Gloria (credited as Lauren Jones), who was also nominated for a Tony for acting.

GA: *How did you make the transition from directing for stage to directing for film and TV?*
MS: In college I had the chance to switch over from theater to TV because halfway through my career they added a television department—which meant cameras and all of the technology I was interested in. But I was learning so much about working with material and working with actors and all of these classic plays, great writing, I felt that if I made a reputation in the theater as a director someone would ask me to direct a movie. And after I did *Does a Tiger Wear a Necktie*, which opened to good reviews, a producer came backstage one night and offered me the film *To Be Young Gifted and Black*, which was based on a play about Lorraine Hansberry. Her ex-husband Robert Nemiroff put it together from a combination of segments of her work: her plays, essays, speeches, poems, doodlings as a writer. It was a very brilliant look at Black America through a very talented young writer's eyes who died at the young age of thirty-four.

So for me it was the perfect segue from theater to film, because it was about a theater person. I had read all of the theory books about film and all of the Russian filmmakers—Eisenstein and

Potemkin (1925) and how to edit and how to direct—but I had never had my hands on the technology. So what the producer, Bob Fresco, did was he put me with a very good director of photography and a really good editor. I knew what I wanted to see in terms of storytelling. They kept me in check in terms of making it look right for film, but I hadn't the foggiest clue about the technical aspects of making a film. When the producer offered me the project I said, "Yeah, I'll do it in a second. Give me the script." So he hands me the play, and I said, "Where's the script?" And he said, "You have to write it, and we have three weeks before we have to be in rehearsal." He had raised the money to shoot the film on videotape, but he saw the value of the piece and was hustling to get enough money to do it on film and wound up shooting it on 16mm using fifty-five locations in thirteen days. [Laughs]

GA: That sounds like madness. [Laughs]
MS: If I had known any better I probably would have said no, but I said yes. And I had great actors in it: Ruby Dee, Roy Scheider, Barbara Barrie, Blythe Danner, Claudia McNeil and my wife was in that.

GA: What was it like working with Ruby Dee?
MS: Ruby was fabulous. She's wonderful, another consummate pro.

GA: Speaking of a pro, what makes a pro?
MS: Someone who does the work no matter what, no matter how they're feeling, no matter what's going on in their lives in the outside world. They are there when they need to be and they deliver the goods. To me, that makes a pro. That was a great experience, because creatively I could do anything I wanted to do. It was very intense, creatively stimulating, and I could do anything imagistically.

GA: Given how influential cinema can be, has it influenced the choices you've made as a director in terms of the movies you've chosen to do during your career?
MS: Absolutely. I've turned down many, many films that I felt portrayed elements that I did not want to put out there in the public mind. I've never done any really violent pictures. The violence that's in my films is there to illustrate a lesson. The reason being is that I've always thought that what we put up on screen has an impact on not only our children, but on the society as a whole. A lot of people in Hollywood will say, "Well, that's just entertainment." But you're putting those images in the psyche of every individual who looks at them, and it changes their thought process.

GA: Do Black filmmakers have a responsibility in terms of the choices they make regarding the images of Black people they bring to the screen? Many argue that it's so hard to break into the film business that once you get a break you have to take it because you may not get another one.

MS: Unfortunately, a lot of people give in to that temptation—get the break and do whatever it is—because the business isn't controlled by people who have our interest in mind but only the need to make a dollar. So the content really doesn't matter to the people who say yes or no to what the content is, it matters to us as a people what the content is. I never thought I'd see in my life-time the blaxploitation period come back. I never thought I'd see Stepin Fetchit come back.

GA: Is that your commentary on today's Black films?

MS: To a great degree, unfortunately. Not to say that there hasn't been some really good films. But the mass of material has kind of taken the image of Black America back many, many steps.

GA: What types of films specifically bother you? Some of the romantic comedies?

MS: Like Booty Call? [Laughs] Actually, I used to have to see every Black film that was made just to chart the curve as to where we were going, but I think maybe three or four years ago I couldn't take it anymore. It was just an unending stream of bad Black movies that had characters in them that were just unconscionable, I thought. [Laughs]

GA: Do you think the material you see as unconscionable has something to do with the way we view ourselves in society?

MS: I don't know if it is so much the way we see ourselves, but it's definitely the way the larger society sees us and that they're willing to pay for certain images and certain stories and not willing to pay for other stories. As a matter of fact, other stories frighten them; stories that deal with strong, tough Black male characters and even female characters, frighten the established moviemaking order. Films that deal with any revolutionary themes scare them to death. Unfor-tunately, the stories that we've done about certain periods of slavery have been so poorly done that they've also scared off whatever Black audience there was because "nobody wants to see that slave stuff." [Laughs] So we as a people have not done a good job of managing our own images. Jews, on the other hand, as a people, have done an incredible job of managing their images.

GA: That said, what can Black filmmakers do to improve this situation? We know it costs a lot of money to make films and Blacks don't control the distribution channels. But what can Black filmmakers do to ulti-mately make things better?

MS: I see little sprouts of hope every now and then. For example, the Black film festivals around the country have gotten more and more popular, and audiences are going to see films there that they can't see in the Hollywood vein of storytelling. The Pan African Film Festival in L.A. and the film festival in Chicago are constantly flooded with people, and to me that's a very hopeful sign that there's an audience out there ready and willing to try new stuff and hungry for other images. We as entrepreneurs haven't really tapped that audience, haven't really taken the bull by the horns and built our own studios and done our own thing. Even the guys who have done it, like Bob Johnson at BET, have really just done it for their own benefit, to amass a certain amount of wealth and not really care about what material they put out. It just takes some pioneering in order to improve things. There's the African Heritage Network and that may do something, but in terms of filmmakers we haven't gotten together, pooled the talent, found the businesspersons and pooled the resources to really create our own Black Hollywood. I think the only way that you control your image is that you control the financing of it. I would just take a page from the Jews who built Hollywood, and they built it for a reason. Not only could they make money, but they could also put out alarms whenever the specter of anti-Semitism rears its head.

GA: We as Blacks must learn to do that ourselves.

MS: Exactly. If we had some courageous businessmen who could make the necessary alliances—and now that technology is getting to a point where it doesn't have to be done in a huge studio, it doesn't have to run through the normal pipeline. Independent film has gotten more and more play as people are finally getting tired of the standard Hollywood tripe, even though the big blockbusters still exist. Eight out of ten films are still disappointments, and now I sense that younger audiences are going for newer stuff and we just have to do our own banking.

GA: Cooley High is of course a classic. Actually, that film, in my opinion, has influenced a number of other Black films, like House Party and School Daze. How did you get involved in Cooley High?

MS: It came from one of my early pictures that shall remain nameless—that never got released—but I was working with an editor who then in turn was working with a producer named Steve Krantz. He told me he was developing a movie that I'd be really perfect for directing, and it was called Cooley High. So he made the contact, I got the script and I read it. I was in New York and they were out in Los Angeles, and I told him, "Well, it has some good stories in it, but it's not a movie. It's just a random collection of stories, and this script really needs some serious work."

GA: *And the writer was Eric Monte.*

MS: Yes, but what I discovered when I got out here and met with the producer was that the producer was rewriting Eric Monte's work, trying to bring some coherence to it. I was directing television at the time—*Rockford Files, Baretta, Starsky and Hutch.* I came out to L.A. to do television, but at the same time I was talking about working on the script for *Cooley High.* And when I found out the producer was rewriting the script, I said, "Look, just give me two or three weeks with Eric alone and I'll see what we can come up with." So I realized that Eric was not a writer, but he was a very good storyteller with these great stories about growing up in Chicago. So I hired a stenographer and made a deal with Eric that I would come over to his house every day and we'd work for eight hours a day from ten to six and just talk, and she'd write down the story. He'd tell stories about growing up and I'd tell stories about my growing up, and we eventually got it all down on paper, and then I started culling away the least good stories and finally fashioned a script.

We took it to the studio, AIP [American International Pictures], which was doing movies like *Hell Up in Harlem, Sheba Baby, Beach Blanket Bingo* and all of that. But the guy who owned the company had a hunch that something this different would be a really good thing to do, but the rest of company said, "How do we sell this movie? It doesn't have any sex in it. It doesn't have any violence." It was not in the mold of *Sheba Baby.* They were at a loss as to what to do, but Sam Arkoff, the head of AIP, believed in it. So we'd bring it back to the executives, and they kept challenging us. They were really good at this. They would say, "Yeah, yeah, but we've seen this. Go back and rework this scene and try to come up with a way new of doing the same scene."

That was really good in terms of kind of forcing us to think out of the box. For example, Cochise [played by Lawrence Hilton Jacobs] has applied to colleges and he's waiting for his letter to come back to know whether he's gotten accepted or rejected, and so it was written: "He comes home and gets a letter and then finds out that he's accepted to school." My younger son at the time was a toddler, barely able to walk, and he had this habit of throwing things in the toilet. I said, "Wouldn't it be interesting if Cochise came home and found that his little brother had thrown his letter in the toilet?" So it was a combination of things that were happening in our lives combined with what had been written, so when we added those elements, it made what could be an ordinary scene into something real interesting, and the whole movie was fashioned that way.

GA: *While making Cooley High, did you have any idea that you were making such a classic?*

MS: Not really, but in that time period it was a constant fight with the studio [AIP] in trying to populate the film with real people and not Hollywood's idea of what Black people are. For example, when I hired Garrett Morris to be the teacher, the studio had a conniption. They said, "He's too short. Why can't you get someone like Sidney Poitier?" Sidney Poitier had played teachers in other movies [To Sir with Love], so that was their idea of what a teacher should be, and I said, "No, there are short teachers as well as tall, handsome teachers." The same argument occurred when I cast the light-skinned girl who Preach has "eyes" for. She was not an actor, but that was not a problem for the studio. What they had a fit about was that she was too light, and I said, "Well, look, what you don't understand is that Black people are the whole rainbow. There are Black people that you don't even know are Black." We can spot 'em in a second. [Laughs] And it was a constant battle to cast the people that I cast.

For example, like the two thugs who steal that car and go on a joyride: We were in Chicago, and we went to all of these casting agencies, and the people they'd come up with were people who were well-scrubbed—commercial Negroes. [Laughs] I said, "No, no, no, no. They have to be hardcore, ghetto thugs." So I was sitting with some young people from Chicago who owned a drugstore in Cabrini Green, which was one of the toughest ghettos in the country. I was telling them about my dilemma of not being able to find real actors who I believed were gangsters or that type. And they laughingly pointed out two guys across the street and said, "Why don't you cast those guys?" And I said, "Who are they?" They told me that they were the leaders of the Pea Stone Nation [a gang], so I said, "Well, call them over here." [Laughs] So they called them over, and I said, "Look, we're doing this movie about Cooley High, and if you can read I want you to come over to the hotel and take a look at the script and audition. You might get in the movie." So it was those two guys in the film, and they were serious gang bangers.

GA: You employ a lot of classic comedy tools in Cooley High, like the car chase and the incident in the party sequence when the girl's greatest fear is that she'll topple her mother's china cabinet. Did you study classic comedy in preparation for the film, or did your sense of comedy come from the way you look at the world?
MS: Part of my theater stuff dealt with all kinds of Shakespeare and Molière comedies, material that you would never associate with Black America, but material that demanded comedic timing.

GA: I also loved Glenn Turman's performance.
MS: Glenn was about twenty-seven years old, playing a teenager, and he played him brilliantly and I thought he should have been nominated for an Oscar, but at the time Black movies weren't considered Oscar-worthy. He was brilliant and brought so much to that role. There were only three professional actors in the film: Glenn, Garrett Morris and Lawrence Hilton Jacobs.

GA: Do you think your use of real people as opposed to professional actors allowed you to bring an authentic representation of young Black people to the screen that we rarely see in movies?

MS: One of the things that I thought was so great about the movie, even before it became a movie, was the script. I had never recalled seeing a Black film where I felt the characters really loved each other—where there was real joy and real love in the context of the story. What I wanted to bring to it was a kind of window on Black life that most people don't get a chance to see, where no matter what the surroundings are, how poor or how tough it is, there's still this joy and this love that very seldom winds up on Hollywood screens. I wanted to put that out there. I also wanted it to be as Black as it could be, with no concession to crossing over. I tried to keep white people out of the movie—not because I was prejudiced against white people, but because I didn't want it to be about Black and white. I wanted it to be about the human beings, and my theory was that if you played it true, the humanity would cross over any color line and that people would get caught up in the humanity and not the color of the character and not their race. It wasn't a movie about race; it was a movie about kids in a particular time in space.

GA: Why do you think that Black films with universal themes of friendship and love, like Cooley High, are largely absent from Black movies today? Mable Haddock, who's the CEO at the National Black Programming Consortium, asked me, "Why does Black/urban now mean violence?" Why don't we see more families, love and friendship on the screen?

MS: I think it's because the filmmakers haven't fought the same kind of battles. Because the pressure is always on the Black filmmaker or storyteller to tell the story through white eyes because they hold the purse strings. Every now and then one film breaks through, but I always see it as going through the white sieve. Because white people think that they can't relate to something unless it fits their idea of what that something is, and so they look for the expected or something that reaffirms their prejudiced state of mind. They've already decided what we are, and so having those images recur makes them feel good. It's as if they know, "Yeah, yeah, we know." But then if you throw Condoleezza Rice in there or Colin Powell, it kind of shakes them up because it doesn't fit their images.

GA: Yes, and sometimes those Black images that don't fit the images they have are then considered non-Black.

MS: It has to be because it doesn't fit, you know. It couldn't have been a Black civilization that created the artifacts of ancient Egypt, because that would blow their whole concept of who we are. It would be a whole lot easier to have it be men from out of space who came down and instructed some people of non-Black origin in how to do things than to say, "Oh, this was a Black culture. Man, these mothers were bad." It does not fit. It can't. The construct that has been built over the ages is so solid that when you start chopping away at it, it shakes up the foundation a little bit.

GA: *You use music so well in your films—Motown in* Cooley High, *an element of a musical in* Car Wash. *Music is actually used in* Car Wash *to advance the plot. Tell me about that.*
MS: I'll tell you a trade secret. Car Wash was brought to Universal by the producers, Art Linson and Gary Stromberg, who were young Jewish guys who found the material, and they thought it would be a great Broadway musical, so they went to Universal to try to get money to fund a musical. The guy who was president of Universal at the time said, "Musical? No, this is a great movie." So it became a movie, and they told me this story when they hired me. I said, "Well, let's make it a musical and not tell anybody; it'll be an underground musical," and they said, "Well, whattaya mean?" I said that at the beginning of the movie we'll do a Car Wash ballet, and they said, "What's that?" I said, "Well, we'll open up the car wash with all of the things that happen in opening up—the people coming, the machines starting up—and it'll all be set to music and it will be the start of the day. They said, "Oh, yeah. That's a great idea."

That was the kind of thinking that went into constructing the piece. When I first read the script, I turned it down actually. I was going to turn it down, and I was friendly with Suzanne de Passe and I told her. I said, "Universal's offering me this movie, but it's really popcorn; it's really just a series of jokes and I don't think I'll do it." Because I really wanted to do the story of George Jackson and Angela Davis based on a script called *Blood Brothers*. And Suzanne said, "Are you crazy, Negro? This is a major Hollywood movie. If it's not what you want, then just take it and make it what you want." She sounded like Booker T. Washington at Tuskegee: "If you ain't got what you want, take what you got and make what you want." I told her, "You know. You're absolutely right." So I accepted the job and started working on the script to inject in it the serious elements that were there kind of latent in the material, but the studio head had the writer Joel Schumacher just writing the comedy part of it. So what I did was I said, "Look, there's all of this really interesting stuff that you've written or indicated." They had the idea to hire Norman Whitfield, who had written all of this great music for Motown like the Temptations' "Papa Was a Rolling Stone," and I went to talk with him [Whitfield] and I said, "Look, if you want to do this, I need three songs written before we start shooting the movie, because I want to choreograph the action to the music, and so he said, "Great."

I got two weeks of rehearsal out of the studio before we started shooting, because the way I wanted to shoot it was very different. It was kind of an ode to *Nashville*, because I really admired what Robert Altman was trying to do with that movie, but he didn't succeed completely in doing it but the idea was great. He had these multiple stories going on in the foreground and in the background, and multiple characters, and I felt I could do that with *Car Wash*. So I said that the actors had to be there—all of them—every day of the shooting, which they all had problems with because actors don't like to be in the background. If they're not talking in the foreground, they don't want to be there. And so I said, "All of the actors have to be there every day, and I need to shoot the film in continuity from the opening to the closing, not normally the way movies are typically made. Movies are scheduled to shoot all of the scenes in the same location, and then you go to the next location and shoot everything there. It doesn't matter if you shoot the end of the movie first or whatever. So usually movies are shot out of continuity," and I said, "No, this one's gotta be in continuity, because the choreography of everything is so critical that I would never be able to keep it on track if we shot it out of continuity." But the real reason was that I was fighting with studio at the time about the ending of the movie. They didn't want any serious scenes in the film, and I kept saying that the serious stuff has got to be in the film because it'll make the comedy better.

Taking a page from the success of *Cooley High*, where that blend of comedy and serious drama worked so effectively, I was saying basically the same thing about *Car Wash*. I said, "If it's just a series of jokes, it's going to be really boring, I'm going to hate it, the audience is going to hate it. [Laughs] So I built up the Bill Duke character—the revolutionary—and there were other scenes that didn't make it in the movie, unfortunately. So in order to try to get what I wanted, I talked them into doing the movie in sequential order so that by the time we got to the end they would be so tired of arguing with me that maybe they would let me do what I wanted to do. And that's basically what happened, because we started going over schedule and I started getting calls like, "Are you ever going to finish this movie?" [Laughs] I said, "Yeah, if you let me do it the way I want."

GA: *The brilliant thing is that the mix of comedy and drama really worked and the ending is powerful. It would have been a totally different film had you not taken your approach.*
MS: Yeah, well, it's also what makes the film last through time—it wasn't all jokes. You could relate to these people on a human level because you saw all of their desires and hopes and dreams in this little car wash environment.

GA: *How did you develop the characters for the film? Were most of them already created from the musical version?*

MS: Yes. All of the characters were Joel Schumacher's creation. He's a very gifted writer. I just flushed it out.

GA: How did you cast the film? You got to work with Richard Pryor on Car Wash. What was that like?
MS: It was great. I happened to be talking with Richard about doing another film, so I knew him and he hadn't popped out yet. He was a brilliant standup comic who had done Piano Man in Lady Sings the Blues. I was working with him on a film that he had written. It was a cowboy film called The Black Stranger, but it scared Hollywood to death so he could never get it made. This was really a good western. [Laughs] So I tried to get Rev. Ike to play the reverend in Car Wash, because it was designed around his whole philosophy and his preaching at the time, which was "Money is not the root of all evil, the lack of money is the root of all evil." [Laughs]

GA: Right. If I had money, I wouldn't do these bad things. [Laughs]
MS: I had a meeting with him at the Universal commissary and I almost got him, but he realized that it was a little too close to what he was actually doing and then I talked Richard into doing a parody of Rev. Ike. And with the Pointer Sisters I said, "Let's go as far out as we can with this being a musical and do a musical number within the movie, and if people don't get that it's a musical then, I don't know." So we just decided to break the reality, have them all come out and sing a song, and the whole focus is on the preacher and the revolutionary and it has a dramatic context. It advances the film.

GA: Next came Greased Lightning with Richard Pryor. How did that come about?
MS: I actually rescued that film, because at the time I was developing Which Way Is Up for Pryor when Steve Krantz, who produced Cooley High, approached me about what movie I'd like to do next. I said that I didn't know but that there are so many gifted Black actors who no one is writing material for and that I'd like to find some material that would fit the talent that's out there. He said, "Who?" And I said, "Like Richard Pryor," and he didn't know who Richard Pryor was, so Steve came to me with this idea. He said, "Have you seen this film, The Seduction of Mimi?" I said, "I don't go to pornos." [Laughs] He said, "No, no, no. It's not that." So he took me to this Italian movie directed by Lena Wertmuller, who directed a series of movies with Giancarlo Giamini. The Seduction, Swept Away, Seven Beauties—just brilliant movies. The Seduction of Mimi was about the corruption of an innocent through political maneuvering and working in the system and all of that. I said, "Yeah, Richard Pryor could do that, easy. As a matter of fact, he could play all three of these parts."

So we made an Americanized version of this Italian film, and I wanted to set it in the grape fields at the time, because Cesar Chavez and the whole effort to unionize the grape pickers and stop exploiting the migrant workers was big at the time. But by the time we got a green light to do the movie, grapes were out of season, so I had to make it oranges. [Laughs] But we got El Teatro Compensino, the brilliant Latino theater company, used some of their actors and created this story called Which Way Is Up, which I think is one of Richard's funniest comedies.

While we were developing that, he chose to star in the movie Greased Lightning, which Warner Brothers was doing, and I said, "Richard, why are you doing this? Which Way Is Up is supposed to be your debut as a movie star." Melvin Van Peebles was directing Greased Lightning, but he had a creative falling-out with the producers and they fired him and asked me to take over the film, and I said, "Nooo, I don't think so." Then Richard asked me if I would do it as a favor to him. Actually, I didn't want him to be in a failure before he came out in my movie, so I agreed to take it over and Melvin was very gracious in talking to the crew. He introduced me, and I think most of his crew stayed on. The producers even redid what I shot, because they had a different idea of what the movie should be. It was far more pedestrian than what either Melvin or I had envisioned, but everything Richard is in is interesting, because he makes you pay attention.

GA: Sergeant Pepper's Lonely Hearts Club Band. How did that come about?
MS: Robert Stigwood offered me Grease because he had seen Car Wash and said anyone who directed that movie could do Grease or whatever. But I was still finishing postproduction work on Which Way Is Up and Travolta had a short window of availability because he had to go back to Welcome Back Kotter, so I had to turn it down and they gave me Sergeant Pepper's as a consolation prize.

That was a very interesting challenge, too, because it was precast. The Bee Gees were attached, Peter Frampton was attached and this British comedian, Frankie Howard, was attached when they brought it to me. Unlike a normal musical, where you can write the dramatic through line and then add music to it, here you had to work backward, because they had the music from the Beatles album and wrote a storyline from the lyrics of the songs. So it was like a backwards creation. We had all of these lyrics, now how do we make a story out of it? But it was interesting to me from a directing standpoint. Again, you could visualize it any way you wanted to. This film was like doing music video, but this was in the days before anybody thought about music video. It was like one giant music video where you could create any images you wanted to set to the music, and it was a pretty big film. It cost about $10 million or $11 million.

GA: That was a lot of money back then. A lot of Black directors can't get budgets of $11 million today.
MS: [Laughs]

GA: Did you feel creatively constrained with the film, given that it was precast and that you had to work backwards? Were there some things you wished you could have changed?

MS: Yeah. I got Billy Preston and Earth, Wind and Fire in the film to give some color. [Laughs] But trying to give it some flavor. As a matter of fact, I ended up doing a concert film for EW&F after that, and a couple of music videos, because music videos were just beginning.

GA: Tell me about your experience directing Krush Groove.

MS: Great fun. What makes working with music fun is that the music keeps you going no matter how tough the film might be. The energy of the music is constantly inspirational. Krush Groove was a very interesting challenge, because we made it in New York on a budget of $2.5 million with twelve musical numbers, no SAG [Screen Actors Guild] actors, in twenty-five days. And we had to do it that way because we didn't want to be encumbered by the union rules, since all of the rappers were going to be in the film anyway, so I didn't need actors.

GA: It's amazing that you have directed signature films that dealt with music—Cooley High really brought back to life Motown music, and The Big Chill really bit off of it six years later and everyone said, "Oh, Motown is so cool," and you had featured it six years before. Car Wash deals with the funky music of the seventies. Krush Groove was about hip-hop. Would you like to do another film that incorporates music in the manner your previous films have?

MS: Oh, yeah. I love what Baz Lurhman did with his musical Moulin Rouge. I found it to be very bold and very interesting; it overused the special effects, I thought, but I thought the use of music was very well done. I'd love to do something like that. I'd love to take Stevie Wonder's music and make a story out of it.

GA: So when it's all said and done, why are movies important?

MS: I think that when man discovered he could actually make pictures move and that you could duplicate life and capture it and make it seem almost real, or where you could fracture it and take it out of time and space, it gave you this incredible arsenal of communication. Movies are very close to the dream state. We all have our own movies in our heads anyway. And when you can take that same technology and be able to create a story out of fragments of images or emotions, put it up on the screen and have your whole society participate in that dream state, it's a very powerful method of communication and very influential and very persuasive. No matter what images you're putting up there, they have a tremendous impact on the psyche and the social mores of people.

GA: *So at the end of the day, movies are not just entertainment?*

MS: No, no. There's entertainment there. What I call entertainment is the ability to capture people's attention; it's not necessarily to make them laugh or make them tap their foot, but you've got to capture it. Under the comedy and under the tragedy is the communication of ideas, philosophy of how we behave, of how we should behave, they're all lessons. It's not much different from sitting down at the tribal campfire and having the griot take you and your imagination into a story that has significance about how you run through the jungle and how you survive. In that sense, it's very magical.

Spike Lee

In the summer of 1986, my Morehouse College buddy Jay Jackson, from Oakland, California, sent me a note (back when people still wrote letters to friends) about a must-see hilarious little film directed by a fellow Morehouse man. Always looking to support another Morehouse brother and quickly getting caught in the feverish buzz about this film, three friends and I descended on the Quad Cinema in New York's Greenwich Village to see *She's Gotta Have It*. It was a night to remember. We howled with laughter!

Little did I know that this riotously funny film about a young Black woman and her three lovers, cast with unknown actors and shot in Brooklyn in just twelve days, would transform Black cinema, independent cinema, music video and perhaps the world.

With his feature-film directorial debut, Spike Lee catalyzed a movement in cinema that would later help launch the film careers of countless African Americans in front of and behind the camera, including Academy Award winner Halle Berry. In fact, Lee has inspired an entire generation of young Blacks to aspire to cinematic genius, indisputably more than any other filmmaker in history.

Perhaps the most popular of all Black filmmakers, and with an astonishing number of feature films to his credit, including *Do the Right Thing* (1989), *Malcolm X* (1992), the documentary *4 Little Girls* (1997), and most recently, *The 25th Hour* (2002), along with two Oscar nominations,

Lee continues to add to his illustrious body of work, encouraging us to question, to probe and to listen more carefully to the world around us.

With a filmic voice that clearly exclaims the thoughts of a master artist with something profound to say to us, cineastes and audiences far and wide know when they've seen a Spike Lee Joint, for it is an experience they are sure to remember and enjoy for years to come.

— — — —

GA: *Tell me about Spike Lee.*

SL: I was born in Atlanta, Georgia, and lived in Chicago briefly until I was about three or four. Then we moved to Brooklyn, where I grew up. As you know, after high school I went to Morehouse, where I majored in mass communications. I really didn't know what I wanted to do, so at the end of my sophomore year when I had to declare a major, I chose mass communications—TV, radio, print journalism and film—and I took those classes at Clark College (now Clark Atlanta University). That was when you could be a mass communications major at Morehouse, but you can't do that anymore. I was fortunate to have a professor named Dr. Herb Ikelberger, who is actually still teaching there, who took an interest in me, giving me guidance and support. After graduation (1979), I really wanted to pursue a career in film but felt like I still needed to do some more wood shedding, so I did my research and applied to the graduate programs at the top three film schools—New York University [NYU], University of Southern California [USC] and UCLA. But to get into USC and UCLA you had to get an astronomical score on your GRE [Graduate Record Examinations], and I didn't get that. However, to get into NYU all you had to have was a creative portfolio, and I got in. Plus, I was ready to get back home to New York.

GA: *Why film, and what made you think you could be a successful filmmaker?*

SL: Well, I really didn't know if I could do it at first, but I was going to give it a try. I enjoyed films, I had always gone to see films, always loved them. But it wasn't until college that I began to think that maybe I could do this.

GA: *What was the turning point for you that made you say, "Wow, I can make movies"? Was there a film you saw that inspired you?*

SL: A lot of filmmakers say, depending upon how old they are, that they saw *Star Wars* or whatever movie it was, and that's when they decided they wanted to be a filmmaker.

GA: Or She's Gotta Have It.

SL: Maybe. But it wasn't that one film for me. It was just an accumulation of going to films through the years that motivated me to pursue film. But one of the pivotal moments in my thinking that I could actually make films was when Jim Jarmusch's film *Stranger than Paradise* became a hit. We all knew Jim in film school at NYU, because he was a couple of years ahead of us. So that was a really key moment. And for a lot of us filmmaking became doable. We felt we could do it also.

GA: *Did you always think you would have a creative career? Did you get a lot of parental support when you decided to pursue film?*

SL: Yes, my parents encouraged not just me, but my siblings as well, in our artistic endeavors. That's very important, because a lot of times parents crush their children's creative dreams more than anybody else. They want their children to have a better life than they had, so a lot of times they calculate that success to mean a steady job and steady income with a check every two weeks. But that doesn't necessarily make you happy. So when a child says that they want to be a painter or a ballerina or a singer or whatever, parents have a tendency to discourage those dreams, but my parents weren't like that.

GA: *Do you think that Black parents discourage their children from careers in the arts more than parents of other ethnic groups?*

SL: I think there's maybe something to that. I can especially speak about my days at Morehouse, where a lot of the guys I went to school with were the first person in their family to go to college, and their parents, grandparents and probably the whole family had made great sacrifices, like working two or three jobs, working their fingers down to the nub, so they could get into school and get an education at Morehouse. And they expect you to become a doctor or a lawyer, preacher or businessman or something like that after you graduate, and you come back and say you want to be a musician. That's like heresy. So a lot of people have succumbed to parental pressure, especially knowing the sacrifices they've [the parents] made. So I have a lot of classmates now who are old, fat, balding, divorced and miserable because they pursued careers that their hearts weren't in. And here we are twenty years later and they're not happy people. I can never thank my parents enough for encouraging me and never saying that being a successful Black filmmaker is a one-in-a-million shot. They never even thought it. I also have to give thanks to my grandmother, Zimmie Shelton. I'm her first grandchild, and she was very instrumental in my success too. She's a Spelman College graduate and put me through Morehouse and film school, and still lives in Atlanta at ninety-six.

GA: When you set out to make film a career, did you have any idea that you would become the famous person that you are? Did you set out to be famous, or did you just want to make movies?

SL: Fame was never in the equation. All I wanted to do was make films to show different aspects of the African American experience. I knew what I wanted to see on screen and wasn't seeing, and I knew there were other people like me who wanted the same thing.

GA: Are movies so important that we need to see different aspects of the African American experience, or are movies just entertainment?

SL: Movies can be anything you want them to be, but I just felt growing up that I just knew I could look out my window and see the vitality of African American culture, but a lot of times, more often than not, that culture was lacking in film and television.

GA: And in bringing this vitality of African American culture to the screen, you've said that it was always important for you to create a body of work. A lot of filmmakers do a great film and then five years pass before they do another film.

SL: Right, like Ted Witcher with love jones.

GA: I loved love jones.

SL: And he hasn't done a film since. I've spoken with Ted, and he just hasn't found the right script, and other people want to make films but it's hard to get financing for the subject matter. That's definitely the case with Charles Burnett.

GA: Do you think it helped you that you have written most of your own material?

SL: That really helps. If you can be a writer-director, you have a lot more control. You don't have to wait on a script being given to you or for the material to come your way—you generate your own material. So the fact that I'm a writer and a director really helped me build a body of work, and I was able to do a film a year for a long time.

GA: Do you think you had any unique perspective on the film business or any insight that positioned you to direct a film a year?

SL: I don't think I had any unique perspective on the business—my films didn't cost a lot. So the studios would give me creative control, knowing that these films weren't costing a lot and that I wasn't going to make a ton of money for them, but that they could make a profit.

GA: I've heard a lot of your fellow filmmakers marvel at your ability to make so many movies back-to-back. How have you been able to do it physically? Filmmaking is very demanding.

SL: Woody Allen does it and he's older than I am and he has a much more accelerated pace; he's shooting the film, he's editing the last one and he's writing the next one all at the same time. Woody Allen has it down.

GA: And like Woody Allen you have your own style, a very specific view of the world. Was that vision something that you consciously set out to create at the start of your career or was it something developed over time?

SL: Style is really something that I think you have to work on. She's Gotta Have It had a look right away but it's through the accumulation of doing the work that you develop a style. And I was very lucky to work with a great director of photography, Ernest Dickerson. We were classmates at NYU and he shot all of my films at NYU and he shot She's Gotta Have It, School Daze, Do the Right Thing, Mo' Better, Jungle Fever and Malcolm X. So I learned a whole lot from Ernest. Ernest was very important in the development of my visual sense of style.

GA: After She's Gotta Have It, you became an instant brand, a pop icon.

SL: The whole pop-icon thing was an accident. I never really wanted to play Mars Blackmon, but because of circumstances, not a lot of time to cast, having no money, I had to play the role and direct the film. But then it was a big hit. Plus, I got hooked up with Michael Jordan and the Nike campaign and that just blew it up. Everything is timing. Nineteen fifty-seven was a good time to be born, because I was right there when someone could slip through. So when people talk about the so-called renaissance when it comes to Black cinema, I feel that there were two films that did it: Robert Townsend's Hollywood Shuffle and She's Gotta Have It. Those are the two films that made Hollywood realize once again there's an audience for these films, and not just a Black audience but white audiences were going to them also.

GA: Speaking of that, many of the Blacks involved in filmmaking today looked at that period and were influenced to go into film. You actually gave them possibilities.

SL: A lot of people went through 40 Acres, and not just in front of the camera. Director Darnell Martin [director, I Like It Like That, Prison Song] was a camera assistant on Do the Right Thing, and there are many others. Some people come up to me and I don't even know them and say they worked on my films. That's something we've always been proud of. We've been a stepping-stone, a launching pad for African Americans, people of color, to break into this industry, because historically it's been racist and the way to keep it locked down is through the unions, the hardest to deal with being the Teamsters. With the exclusion of us from the unions, they can keep us out of a film. So it's always been our goal to go head-to-head, toe-to-toe with the unions, to open up the ranks, so we can get in there, and once there, do our job.

GA: *A makeup artist told me that you got her in the union. Despite passing the exams and having feature credits, they still wouldn't let her in. Why do you feel it's necessary that you go to bat for other Blacks when others in your position don't?*

SL: Because there are so many people who did a whole lot of stuff before I was here: Oscar Micheaux, Ossie Davis, Sidney Poitier, Melvin Van Peebles, Michael Schultz, so that farther down the line it would be easier. And just philosophically, I've always had the thinking that if the little power I had could be used to get qualified Black people some more jobs to get them in the unions that are lily white, then I have to do that. On Malcolm X there were no Black Teamsters, so we threatened to shoot the film without the Teamsters and we said that if you want to come down and mess with the Fruit [the Nation of Islam], you can, and they caved in. I just think it's very sad that a lot of African Americans who are in positions, who could make a call, who could insist, who could really help this thing, don't do it. It's very disappointing.

GA: *It is sad. Where did you get the wherewithal to help other African Americans? Was that taught at home?*

SL: It was instilled in all of my siblings and me. That's just the way we've always thought, and we'll continue to think that way. Another thing is that we don't realize and utilize the power that we have. You make people some money, you have a say.

GA: *And you shouldn't be afraid of exercising it?*

SL: Not at all.

GA: *Because of your strong opinions on Black issues, early on in your career some called you a spokesperson for Black America. What are your thoughts on that?*

SL: I never presented myself as a spokesperson for Black people. I never have and never will. All of the views I've stated in the past and present and will state in the future are Spike Lee's beliefs. I never said this is Spike Lee speaking on behalf of forty million African Americans. Anytime there is one visible Black person they get appointed the so-called leader, the so-called spokesperson.

GA: In your films, you've explored themes like sexuality, race, Black college life and basketball. What would you like to explore in the future?

SL: One day I'd like to do a film on Jackie Robinson, and I'd also like to do a film on Joe Louis.

GA: Would you like to do more documentaries like 4 Little Girls? That was a phenomenal film and earned you your first Oscar nomination for directing. What inspired the film?

SL: One of the keys of the success of 4 Little Girls was the editor, Sam Pollard, who's a very fine filmmaker period, and so he helped me a lot. When I was in film school I read this article about the four little girls by Harold Raines, an editor with The New York Times. So I called up information and got the address of one of the parents—Chris McNair, the father of Denise McNair. And I said in the letter that one day I'd like to do a movie about your daughter, but he never wrote me back. I couldn't have done it at the time anyway, because I wasn't a filmmaker; I was aspiring to be a filmmaker. Years later, that thought never went away, but it changed from being a dramatic film to being a documentary. Years later, I was to receive an award from an organization in Birmingham [Alabama], so I called Mr. McNair and told him I was going to be in Birmingham and that I'd like to meet him. So he met me at the hotel and he took me to meet his wife, Maxine, and I told them what I wanted to do. Because I figured, and I figured correctly, that if I didn't have the McNairs on board, forget about it, this project would not take off.

And so I won their trust and I went back to Sheila Nevins, who runs the documentary division at HBO, and she loved our ideas. She asked me how much it was going to cost, I gave her numbers and she said let's do it. With this film, we wanted the audience to understand who these girls could have been had they been able to realize their potential. And the only way to do that was to have the witnesses speak: the parents, the brothers, the sisters, the uncles, aunts, friends, neighbors. I wanted them to speak about these four girls who were murdered and re-create this turbulent time in American history in the mecca of segregation—Birmingham—in that state of Alabama with Governor George Wallace standing in the door at the University of Alabama, and the sheriff, excuse me, the safety commissioner, Bull Conner.

That's just a great story with Dr. King, Fred Shuttlesworth and Reverend Wyatt Tee Walker, all those people and all of that stuff going on. I just wanted to tell that story. The hardest decision I ever had to make in that film was whether or not I should include the postmortem photographs of the girls. And I prayed on it and prayed on it, and at the end I included them because I felt like the audience should see what those numerous sticks of dynamite did to the bodies of those four Black girls. The first time we had a screening in New York, we flew all of the parents in and I did not tell them about the photos. So I was very worried about how they'd react to seeing them, but ultimately they all agreed that they needed to be there no matter how painful it might have been for them to see them again. It's a very important film.

GA: *And you got an Oscar nomination. How did that feel?*

SL: Well, I felt bad for the parents, because they really wanted the film to win the Academy Award. HBO flew the parents out to the awards and they got to meet Denzel and they were all happy. But we went up against a Holocaust film, and every year—you know people do research, I'm not making this up—every year in the documentary section, feature-length, there is a film about the Holocaust. Every year. And I remember the day the nominations came out and I saw this other film and I saw what it was about, and I saw that one of the producers was a rabbi too. I said, "Forget it." [Laughs]. I said, "No way we'll win."

GA: *It was disappointing.*

SL: I wasn't disappointed. I knew what the deal was, but the parents were very disappointed, and I remember we had a dinner afterwards at Georgia on Melrose in L.A. and the parents were melancholy because they really wanted to win. But what I hope they got from it was the fact that— and this really goes for everything—you really can't allow some other people or some other group to validate your work, your art, or validate you as a human being. You can't give someone that power that says that unless you get their USDA stamp of approval you're not legit or have no worth. You can't do that.

GA: *In making 4 Little Girls, was it also an emotional experience for you, just as it was for the parents?*

SL: It was an emotional experience for everyone. I had just become a parent, so I didn't know how to relate to the loss of a child. I knew going in that I was going to have to ask some hard questions—questions that they [the parents] had probably never answered before, questions that were deep and personal and that would probably make them break down on camera. That wasn't the intention, but it was my job as a director to ask those questions so we could tell the story.

GA: *How did you prepare for that?*

SL: Anytime you do a film, you have to do research. But doing a documentary, in addition to doing the normal research you have to be a detective. A lot of people ended up in the film that before I went to Birmingham I didn't know, but people said, "You know what? You need to speak with that person. You need to speak with this person." Like the woman who lives across from the McNairs who tells the story about how she had a vision two weeks before the bombing, of the whole Sixteenth Street Baptist Church in blood. I believe that stuff. I think that's something we've really gotten out of touch with—our spirituality—because back in the day that stuff [visions] happened all the time. I remember my grandmother lived three blocks from campus when I was at Morehouse. I never stayed with her, but three blocks away, and you know how the food is, so I'd see her every day and get a meal. One day I got in a fight with this guy from Mississippi, and he hit me in the eye and broke my glasses. The very next day my grandmother said, "I had a dream. Is something wrong with your eye?" That's something we've lost touch with.

GA: I'm from Alabama. I hear old people talk that way all the time. [Laughs]
SL: Sure. That stuff is real. [Laughs]

GA: Tell me how you actually prepare for your films. I think many people don't realize just how much preparation goes into making a movie.
SL: Filmmaking is no joke. I think making a good film has to be one of the hardest endeavors known to mankind, because so many variables have to happen correctly for things to be pulled off. You have to have good acting, a good script, a good crew and good timing. You could make a great film, but if it comes out at the wrong time, depending on where the country is or whatever, you could fail. For example, almost no one knew about AIDS when She's Gotta Have It came out in 1986. Two years later, you would have a totally different view of Nola Darling.

GA: Yeah, we'd think she was irresponsible. But in terms of making all of those elements hang together, what should a good filmmaker be aware of in this process?
SL: Well, the director is the one who makes it go; it has to be his vision. At the same time, you have to be a good collaborator, but ultimately people are looking at you for guidance. I think a director gets asked a thousand questions a day on a set, and it's an accumulation of those decisions over the course of the shoot from pre-production, production and post-production that will determine whether a film is successful or not.

GA: What's the best preparation for a filmmaker?
SL: There's no one way to become a filmmaker.

GA: To what would you attribute your ability to be a successful filmmaker and to be so prolific?
SL: Luck, timing, hard work and talent. Luck had a lot to do with it, and timing.

GA: You are credited with starting a whole movement in Black cinema. What are your thoughts on Black cinema today?

SL: It's terrible. Look at the movies being made.

GA: When you came onto the scene in 1986 with the success of She's Gotta Have It, where did you think Black cinema would be today?

SL: A lot farther along than now. [Laughs]

GA: Why do you think Black cinema is not where you hoped it would be?

SL: Well, we don't have any power. There are no African Americans in executive positions at the television networks or the film studios who can green-light a picture. We have the romantic comedies, the hip-hop drug films, the shoot-'em up things. We're just limited to the types of films that are made. So African American directors know what's happening, and they're going to write scripts or pursue projects that everyone is making. The filmmakers are writing what they think can get sold.

GA: Do you think digital filmmaking will bring about better African American films?

SL: That is the hope, but I had hoped that we would have advanced farther.

GA: What are your thoughts on Black television?

SL: It's horrible.

GA: What do you think Black writers and directors need to do to bring a broader vision of Black people to film and TV? Some say our young people need to read more about our history to gain a greater understanding of who we are and to bring that insight to the screen. What do you think?

SL: Well, our young people have been told that if you're educated you're a white boy or a white girl, and if you're ignorant you're Black. It's that type of ignorant thinking that keeps us back across the field. It's not just in the arts, but that's across the broad. You have Black kids failing school on purpose because they do not want to be ostracized or be held out as an example of a corny white boy or white girl because they're educated. To me, that's criminal.

GA: You've pursued your own TV projects. What would be an ideal Spike Lee television show?

SL: I just think that there's a universe of material out there that would show attractive, funny, intelligent, complex African Americans and deal with them. But they're not feeling that yet.

GA: How can Black filmmakers influence the process and bring about more quality programming?

SL: We can't just talk about ABC, NBC and CBS, but what is Bob Johnson doing with BET?

GA: Do Black filmmakers have a moral responsibility to bring positive representations of African Americans to the screen?

SL: I think "truthful" would be a better word than "positive." I think you're truthful when you show that African Americans have bad qualities and good qualities. I have always found that to be more interesting—people who are flawed.

GA: Who are some of your favorite flawed characters that you've created?

SL: Denzel's character in He Got Game would be one, because here's someone who's trying to reconnect with his son but at the same time has killed his wife. I also like Denzel's character in Mo' Better Blues, where we have a musician who's really torn between his love life and his music.

GA: When you think all of the films you've done, what film says what you really intended it to say and what film falls the most short of what you wanted it to say?

SL: I wouldn't say it fell short, but a lot of times people's misinterpretations or their attempt to tell you what you were trying to do occurs. A perfect example of a successful film was Jungle Fever. In no way, shape or form were we condemning interracial marriages or relationships. We were just showing the kinds of pressure interracial relationships go through, especially if you're from the neighborhoods like Harlem and Bensonhurst [Brooklyn]. This is amplified even more so when these two people are drawn together by superficial differences. Wesley Snipes's character Flipper is drawn to this white woman because subconsciously he's been programmed to think that the white woman is the epitome of beauty, and Annabella Sciora's character has been brainwashed into thinking that the Black man is a sexual superman, a stud. But the main thrust of that film for me was the destruction that drugs have had on generations and generations of people, as shown through Samuel Jackson's character.

GA: Looking back over all of your films, is there anything you wish you would have done differently?

SL: If there is any scene that I could change out of everything that I've done, it would be the rape scene in She's Gotta Have It. That's the only scene that I still think about.

GA: Why?

SL: It was just unnecessary. There was no need for it.

GA: Did you say everything in Summer of Sam that you wanted to say?

SL: Actually it was that summer [1977] that I actually decided to become a filmmaker.

GA: What do you do to stay on the pulse of your own creativity?

SL: I've always listened to a lot of music; it's always been instrumental for me.

GA: How has being married and a father influenced your filmmaking or life?

SL: Well, I've gotten to see a lot more Disney films than I had ever seen in my life. [Laughs] There was a time when I said, "If I ever have kids I'm never taking them to see Disney films, but little did I know." [Laughs]

GA: Given that you're Spike Lee, has it gotten easier for you to make a film?

SL: It's really hard to make a film.

GA: You teach film school at New York University. What is that like?

SL: For the past five years, I've been teaching at the NYU Tisch School of the Arts. I teach the third-year directing students in the graduate film program. I try to help them out and give them guidance. But it really amazes me how lazy some of these students are. I teach a two-hour class from 1:00 P.M. to 3:00 P.M., and I'm available for advisement from 12:00 P.M. to 1:00 P.M. And two weeks ago nobody signed up for advisement, and these kids pay a lot of money to go to film school.

GA: You've done a lot of executive producing of films of young filmmakers like Lee Davis and Gina Prince-Bythewood. Do you plan to do more of that, and why is that important to you?

SL: As I said before, I just try to throw the little weight I have around and try to get some more viewpoints shown. And a lot of times there are films I don't necessarily want to direct myself but I still think that they should be made, and it's giving an opportunity to a lot of people who are first-time directors. I also act as a kind of buffer, so that the studios don't try to run them over.

GA: What attracts you to the projects you executive produce?

SL: The script and the director. A lot of the projects are written by the director.

GA: You've been involved in commercials since your Mars Blackmon Nike commercials with Michael Jordan. Why was it important for you to have your own advertising agency?

SL: I got kind of frustrated and bored with just being a director for hire, because when you're a director for hire your creativity is really limited. And I felt that if I ran my own agency that wouldn't happen, so I got a great offer from Keith Rhinehart at D.D.B. Needham and proposed a co-venture—I own 51 percent, they put up all of the money and own 49 percent. It's been a lot of fun, and we're continuing to grow.

GA: Do you think your living a balanced life—you're married with kids, you go to Knick games—helps you keep up with the pace of filmmaking?

SL: Well, I enjoy life and I enjoy making art. And also, I know I'm blessed. I'm very lucky. I'm able to make a very good living not only for myself but for my wife, Tonya, and my kids, doing what I love. And I will say that the majority of the people in this world go to their grave having been a slave to a job all their lives, hating it. So as far as that aspect goes I really can't complain, because I'm doing what I love. Not too many people in this world get paid to do what they love.

GA: What legacy would you like to leave behind?

SL: I would like to leave my body of work. And it's interesting because my kids—I can see it right now and my wife sees it too—they have definite interest in movies and the arts. It's something that they are exposed to a lot—they ask questions and they know a lot more about this stuff than other kids their age. It wouldn't surprise me if they ended up in film also.

The 80's Explosion

Ernest Dickerson

For years this Newark, New Jersey, native was best known as the brilliant cinematographer for such Spike Lee films as *She's Gotta Have It* (1986), *Do the Right Thing* (1989), *Jungle Fever* (1991) and *Malcolm X* (1992). *Do the Right Thing* earned Ernest Dickerson the New York Film Critics Circle Award for Best Cinematographer. Dickerson also photographed John Sayles's *Brother from Another Planet* (1984). With his wide acclaim as a director of photography, in 1992 Dickerson jumped into the director's chair and made his feature-film debut with the urban drama *Juice* (1992), starring Omar Epps and the late Tupac Shakur.

A graduate of Howard University, where he studied with director Haile Gerima, and New York University's Tisch School of the Arts, where he met Lee, Dickerson's other feature-film directing credits include New Line Cinema's *Surviving the Game* (1994), starring Ice-T, HBO's *Ambushed* (1998), starring Courtney B. Vance and Robert Patrick, and *Futuresport* (1998) for ABC, starring Dean Cain, Wesley Snipes and Vanessa L. Williams and *Strange Justice* (1999) for Showtime. Dickerson recently directed *Our America* (2002) for Showtime.

— — — —

GA: *When did you become interested in film?*
ED: I've always been interested in film, but there wasn't anything to really push me in that direction or say that this is a career alternative. I was looking at other things as a career, like

engineering or architecture. I eventually studied architecture as an undergraduate at Howard University, and I always drew and I was fascinated by movies. I appreciated them as a craft. I didn't know what it was that really hit me—it was a visual thing. First, I thought it was art direction, but then my uncle, who is a jazz musician, probably had a lot to do with my development. My father died when I was eight, but my uncle, my mother's brother, had a lot to do with the direction I took in my life. He's a master percussionist named El Hajj Daoud Abdurrahman Haroon and was an artist-in-residence at Wesleyan University and started doing some black-and-white photography. He'd come back home with prints he'd done and I would look at the prints, and I thought, "This is fabulous."

It really started focusing me on photography, and the story I love to tell is when it finally hit me—what it was about film that really fascinated me. I was about sixteen or seventeen and we were watching Oliver Twist (1948), and that's the movie that always hit me visually on some level. I never knew what it was. We were watching the opening scene of the movie and my uncle said to himself, "Gosh, beautiful." And it hit me that the moving images on the screen used basically the same principles that my uncle used in his still photography. I really started getting into understanding what lighting does, and I think not long after that I went to the movies to see In Cold Blood (1967), and that just blew me away. That started me on a journey to find out more about motion picture photography. Conrad Hall [the cinematographer on In Cold Blood] became one of my heroes. I was in high school and really started getting my hands on everything I could find about making films, reading every article I could get on cinematography. I remember going to a bookstore in New York that had a lot of film books, and it had a lot of back issues of American Cinematographer magazine. I just bought as many as I could afford. But even still, I thought I wanted to go to school for architecture.

GA: *Really? Why not film at that point?*

ED: There was nothing or anybody to lead me, to tell me that film was a valid career choice. At that point, I wasn't sure what I wanted to do with my life. After high school, I went part-time to Rutgers University and was working, and then I finally decided I wanted to study architecture at Howard in D.C. The great thing about living in D.C. is that it has a great repertoire of cinemas, like the American Film Institute [AFI], which showed classic films, and I got to see a lot of movies when I was in school. And even though I was majoring in architecture and took a minor in color photography, I audited some classes in cinematography just to learn the cameras. Eventually I did a lot of film work, and even though I was an architecture major, the part-time jobs that I wound up getting were photographic. First, I started working for Howard's campus newspaper, the Hilltop. The editor at that point was a guy named Zeke Mobley, and he wanted to turn the Hilltop into the Life magazine of college newspapers and was going to rely heavily upon photography. The photo editor was a guy named Larry, and I really learned a lot of photography under Larry, because his attitude was go out and shoot, come back and print. "You don't know how to print? Get in the darkroom and don't come out of there until you have a good picture." [Laughs]

It was great. I'd be in the dark room until three o'clock in the morning, and I was lucky because I'd gone to Rutgers part-time, I got most of my core courses out of the way. So at Howard I could concentrate on architectural design and photography. I really became an intensive five-year student, because architecture was a five-year course in design. Then, probably around my third year, I knew I wasn't going to be an architect. I could see that it wasn't me. However, I still wanted to get the degree, because the thing that architecture really prepared me for was problem-solving. Architecture is being faced with a set of problems and previsualizing the solution to the problem. It's the same process in a film. I find that architecture helps me when I'm doing a film.

GA: In addition to problem-solving, what other ways do you use architecture in your filmmaking process?
ED: Well, I sit down and really draw the movie out on paper. I do storyboards, and even though I might not stick to the storyboards religiously, at least they give me a guide. It's like therapy [Laughs] It's a way of working problems out like how I'm going to get into or out of a scene, and working out the visual patterns.

GA: And you eventually decided to go to NYU for film school, where you met Spike Lee and started your collaboration with him.
ED: When I graduated from Howard I started working for the Howard Medical School doing medical photography. I was in surgery two to three times a week. But I really had to face the fact of what I really wanted to do, which was film, even though all the odds were against me of ever succeeding. I had to give it a try. I never wanted to be on my deathbed saying, "I wonder what would have happened if . . ." So I applied to film schools and wound up going to NYU. Spike and I were the only Black kids in the school, so [Laughs] naturally he looks a little like me and we gravitated to each other. When I found out he went to Morehouse and I'd gone to Howard . . . Morehouse and Howard are rivals.

GA: Yeah, I went to Morehouse. [Laughs]
ED: Oh, you did? [Laughs] There it is. So we started ribbing each other and joking and everything else. But after we stopped that, we started talking about movies and what we wanted to do. Spike

was a film lover and he grew up seeing certain types of cinema, and we found that we had a common vocabulary. However, we weren't able to work together in the first year because we were in two separate class sections, but the first year of film at NYU is for weeding out students. Only about a third of the students are invited for the second year. So when we came back in the second year there was just one class section. The second year is when you start dealing with narrative [storytelling] and sound. I had already declared cinematography as my major, and cinematography for me was easy because I was a photographer. You also started gravitating towards the students who were really serious. The people who were the most successful in film school were the people who already considered themselves filmmakers but who were using the facilities at the school to make their films. Spike was one of those people.

GA: The rest is history. What were some of your influences? You talked about the fact that you and Spike shared a common film vocabulary. What were some of those films and who were some of the directors?
ED: My major influence has always been Orson Welles. I think anything by Welles is really interesting. I also like Martin Scorsese, Francis Ford Coppola, and there's Kurosawa, and Sammy Fuller [The Big Red One, I Shot Jesse James]. When I was in my first year at NYU, Fuller came in to guest lecture for two weeks at the film school, but I found that he was giving more intensive and insightful lectures to the upper classmen. So I would sneak into their classes just to hear him talk and he just blew me away. I had been a big fan of his having discovered him while living in D.C. Students at NYU at the time didn't know who Fuller was, but to me he was the greatest filmmaker. I was also a fan of Robert Aldrich, Kubrick, Fellini, David Lean, Don Siegel and Bernardo Bertolucci.

GA: So why does Ernest Dickerson make movies?
ED: I don't know, man, I guess you might as well ask why do I breathe? I know literally, figuratively and creatively that if I didn't make films I'd die. But you have to love film because it's an insane profession. It's crazy. You're dealing with different problems every single day. You know the saying, "Shit happens"? Well, when you're making a movie, shit happens every day—probably fifty to one hundred times a day.

GA: One of your first big breaks in film was working as the cinematographer on John Sayles's Brother from Another Planet with Joe Morton, which I loved. I remember giving a copy of it to my father for Father's Day one year.
ED: Oh, really, that's cool.

GA: *How did your collaboration with Sayles come about?*

ED: I guess it was being in the right place at the right time. I was thinking about going to get my cabdriver's license. I had recently gotten married and was doing occasional jobs here and there, but I didn't have the slightest idea how I was going to break into the industry. A phone call came out of the blue and it was from Peggy Rajki, who was the associate producer on the film, and she said, "I don't know if you know John Sayles?" I said, "Yeah! I know John Sayles." She said, "He's getting ready to do a movie—it's a science fiction film." I love science fiction, I grew up reading science fiction and looking at science fiction films, so BING! At that time it was called The Brother Who Fell to Earth. And Peggy said, "I would like you to come in for a meeting." So I went in and I met with John—really nice guy. The thing that blew me away was that John had not written one page of the script but he told me the entire story out of his head. I sat there and afterwards he said, "What do you think? Do you want to do it?" I said, "Yeah." He said, "Okay, well, have you ever shot 35mm?" I said, "Of course." I lied.

GA: *Would you advise aspiring directors to do the same thing?*

ED: Well, if you know you can do it. It's just a film size, exposure and lenses. All of the photographic principles are the same, and I was a photographer.

GA: *You weren't going to let that stop you from taking the job. [Laughs]*

ED: No way, and you know John had already done Return of the Secaucus 7, and so he was the independent filmmaker at that time. They called me about a week later—they had the script, and I read it. He wrote it in a week, but he had it in his head, so he just mechanically put it on paper. It was going to be a twenty-four-day shoot, but the great thing about NYU is that I was used to working with nothing. They give you two lights and you go out and shoot a movie, so it was a chance to put all of my reading of American Cinematographer to work [Laughs]. I did learn a lot from reading those articles about how films like Network were shot by supplementing existing household or office lights [at the actual locations] with movie lights. I knew Brother was going to be a film like that. Not long after that, John called me to do the Bruce Springsteen Born in the U.S.A. video.

GA: *Springsteen is so alive in that video. He's so committed, and you were able to capture that.*

ED: The concert stuff was a real show. The thing that he was trying to do at that point was live down Dancing In the Dark. I think Brian De Palma had directed that, but De Palma really scrubbed Springsteen, squeaky-cleaned his image. It was not Springsteen, so with Born in the

U.S.A. it was about going back to his roots, and we shot it documentary style. Then I did a TV series called *Tales from the Dark Side* that was being shot in New York and L.A. During the show's second season I got a feature called *Krush Groove* directed by Michael Schultz, and that same summer I shot *She's Gotta Have It*. The thing was that by this time I had a wife and a daughter, but I made enough money off of *Krush Groove* that I could do *She's Gotta Have It* for hardly any money, and we shot *She's Gotta Have It* in twelve days.

GA: When I interviewed Spike, he attributed much of his distinctive visual style to you.
ED: The thing is that Spike always wanted to let the camera help tell the story in his films. He always believed very strongly in that, and so did I.

GA: Do you think that also comes from your early exposure to photography?
ED: Yeah, but I think it's also the films we [Spike and I] loved, the films we watched. When we were preparing *Do the Right Thing* we looked at *The Third Man* [directed by Carol Reed] a lot, and when we were preparing *She's Gotta Have It* we looked at Francis Ford Coppola's *Rumble Fish*. I think *Rumble Fish* was playing on HBO at the time and we were talking about the film, and I've forgotten who came up with the idea, but it was from looking at *Rumble Fish* that we decided to shoot *She's Gotta Have It* in black-and-white. Actually, it was great, because we wanted the center section with the dance sequence—the color section—to feel like old Technicolor because Spike loved old Technicolor musicals. And it worked out, because when you see a black-and-white film, and your eyes get used to seeing only blacks and grays then Boom! You put color in the middle of that and it's going to explode right off the screen. We were blessed with a nice bright sunny day that day, which contributed to the look, and then Wynn Thomas, the production designer, put a lot of colorful elements into it. Spike and I have were in a great position where we were learning and getting paid for it. And we were always experimenting, trying to find a different way of getting a feeling across. It was the willingness to just try stuff out. It was really just that, and a lot of that comes from, I guess, just having seen a lot of movies and seeing what some filmmakers were able to do with the visual elements. We never really wanted to do talking-head films [Laughs]. Our dialogue was always, "Yo, man, what can we do to make things more interesting?"

GA: What I've always liked about your cinematography is your use of angles. You're always aware that you're telling a story with pictures. For example, with two people talking you always choose to use a low angle or a high angle to convey subtext.

ED: Well, a lot of times I believe the use of certain angles also helps to illustrate the psychological position of the character in the story. Sometimes to show someone at a disadvantage, I'll shoot from a higher angle looking down at them, making them look smaller.

GA: *Old Hollywood techniques. The divine one looking down.*
ED: Old Hollywood techniques, they always work.

GA: *Did you always plan to direct your own film?*
ED: It was always in the back of my mind that I would one day. When I was at NYU, I either shot other people's movies or I directed my own. I directed two shorts that I just never got the money to finish, but when I graduated from NYU I'd hoped that I would. Before I got *Brother from Another Planet*, I wasn't certain what I was going to do, and that's when my old friend Gerard Brown, who is a writer, screenwriter and playwright, and I started to write *Juice*. I'd known Gerard since Howard—we were best friends and we loved movies and just wanted to somehow break into the business. We wrote *Juice* around '82, '83 with the intention of doing a low-budget film noir.

GA: *Oh, really? All of those elements of betrayal and deceit that are common in film noir.*
ED: Yeah, yeah, and fate and destiny and whether or not somebody can take control of their destiny and do something about it. Gerard was living in Harlem, I was living in Queens, and it was about this time that we started seeing that guns were making their way into the hands of kids, and that bothered us, because that was so much different than when we were growing up when if you had a beef with somebody, you duked it out.

GA: *[Laughs] Yeah, right.*
ED: And now trying to duke it out with someone probably gets you killed, and we wanted to do something about that. We figured we could probably do it [make the movie] for a couple hundred thousand dollars. Gerard and I worked on the script for several months, and we got it right where we wanted it and we took it to my agent who basically said, "Nobody wants to see this, you're not going to make this movie and nobody's going to give you money to make this movie. Nobody wants to see this film about Black kids involved in crimes." So it sat on the shelf, and I was working—my career as a cinematographer was doing pretty good. When we wrote *Juice* we always intended it to be a premiere for Gerard as a writer and for me as a director, and at the time Gerard was a writer-in-residence at Joe Papp's Public Theater in Manhattan, and he had his play running there. So we wrote *Juice* and

it didn't get made. Gerard later started working at Manhattan Cable, then finally he got an agent who actually took the script to Richard Donner's company at Warner Brothers, and they wanted to buy it. Well, okay, it sounds pretty cool all right, and so they send us notes back on the script, and the notes said that the script was too dark and that they wanted to make *Juice* into a comedy.

GA: [*Laughs*] *A completely different film.*
ED: Yeah. "We want to make this into a comedy, we feel that this is just too dark, nobody wants to do this and can't you make this into a comedy?" And then they had a list of directors, about twenty people, and my name was at the bottom. So I said, "Fuck this," and Gerard and I talked about it and we said, "You know, they're going to ruin it, man." We said, "Thanks, but no thanks." We could have made money on it and walked away, but it sounded like they were going to turn it into something we didn't even want our names on. I was looking at movies that were pretty bad but that had a great central idea, and I'd look at them saying that I bet that somewhere along the development process they screwed the film up, and that's what I felt they were going to do with *Juice*.

Several weeks later I was contacted by a guy named David Heyman, who is now big—he produced *Harry Potter*, but at that point the guy who worked for Donner, named Peter, read *Juice*. They were looking for a project to strike out on their own as producer. David contacted me and said, "Yo, I really liked your script, I want to talk to you about it." So we met at The Pink Tea Cup, the soul food restaurant in Greenwich Village, and he said, "Tell me about the movie you want to make," and I said, "This has to be raw, on the streets, a realistic film with a cast of unknowns. There are no actors out there today who can play this. I know Warner Brothers is encouraging you to use some well-known, young TV actors, but none of them can play these characters . . ." That's the direction they were going. I said, "This has to be a slice of life and it's a film noir." And he said, "Well, you know that's the way I see it. Do you want me to try and get funding for it?" I said, "Yeah." And he got $3 million through Island Pictures, because his father, John Heyman, I think, was one of the owners. He had been partners with Chris Blackwell.

So they raised the money and we started going into production and started looking for unknown actors. I got a great casting director, Jaki Brown-Karman, and we started doing open casting calls at local high schools, local theater groups. Hundreds of kids came in, and Jaki narrowed it down to a few—it was an intensive casting process, but out of it we found Omar Epps. I thought he was the ideal person to play Q, but I had to convince the producers, because they weren't as convinced. We were having a tough time finding Bishop, then one day Treach from Naughty by Nature came in and auditioned and he did a pretty good job. But he had this other kid hanging out with him. After Treach finished we said, "Thank you," and speaking to Treach's friend, said, "What about you? What's your name?" He said "Tupac." I said, "Tupac?" [Laughs] "You wanna try out?" He said, "Yeah, sure." We gave him side lines [scenes from a script used in an audition] from the script, and first of all we gave him the sides to Q because Omar didn't have the role yet. Tupac went and came back and read Q, did a pretty good job, but something told me because we were having a hard time finding the right Bishop, I just had a feeling from this kid that there was something there. I said, "Do you mind staying longer and reading the Bishop part?" He said, "No, sure, why not?" So I said, "What do you do?" At the time he worked as a background singer and roadie for Digital Underground, and so he went away, studied the Bishop part, came back later and auditioned, and I said, "Thank you. Thank you very much. We got your address, okay, see ya." He walked out the door, and as soon as he closed the door, I said, "That's it!" He had it because it was very easy to play Bishop on the surface, but Tupac understood the character deep down and in many ways he was Bishop, and we said, "That's him."

Then came mixing and matching and finding the guys, because it wasn't just finding the actors we wanted. The intention was always to find the four kids who together could create a fifth person—they had to create the group mind, the group mentality. That chemistry had to be really strong. Khalil [Kain] came in, and he always felt like the older kid because he was older actually than the part, but he looked seventeen, and he came in and he just had the leadership abilities. And then Jermaine ["Huggy" Hopkins], who was the mascot, but actually he was written as this little skinny kid, but Jermaine came in and made us change our minds about that. Then Omar had the intensity, and I always felt that Omar had the hardest role to play because he had to be the hero, the conscience, but he couldn't be a punk. It was very important that he not be a punk because of our key audience. I did not want them to think of him as a punk.

GA: *Was it great working with Tupac, though? Was he a genius cut short?*
ED: Tupac, yeah, yeah. He really was. It was amazing, because in between setups he'd go in the corner, sit down and write in his notebook, and eventually he was writing what was going to be his first album. But Tupac was one of those guys who was so open. He was very open and maybe that was one of the things that got him in trouble—the fact that he was open to a lot of people. Sometimes when you're open like that you get open to the wrong people and they try to take advantage of you.

GA: *The producers were able to get Paramount to distribute Juice. Tell me about that.*
ED: Our producers shopped the film around and Paramount eventually became the distributor for the film, and I guess that was a mixed blessing, because then we started going through the

preview screening process. Well, it was my first time dealing with it and it was tough, because the film was antigun—the key prop in the movie was the gun, the source of all the problems was the gun. To me the key moment in the movie is when Omar goes to buy the gun from that lady Sweets, who's played by my mother.

GA: *Really?*
ED: Yeah, that's my mom, but he goes to buy the gun, and the key moment for me is when he realizes that he's just continuing down a never-ending spiral of violence and he throws the gun away. We show that to the kids, and they say, "No! No!" They just didn't buy it. They didn't go for it at that point, so the studio heard that and they were freaking out. The biggest problem we had was the ending, because as we scripted it, Q and Bishop are fighting on the rooftop. Bishop goes over, Q grabs him and is holding him, trying to pull him up, and it was really Tupac's best moment, because as he's trying to pull up, in the script he hears the police sirens in the background and Bishop goes into almost a Zen state. He looked at Q and said, "I'm not going to jail" and he lets go. So he elected to die, which went against the grain of all Hollywood filmmaking—the villain should not decide his death. But the point of the movie was that kids with this attitude are not punks, they're forces you must deal with. You must deal with them because it's a whole different mind-set.

GA: *Kids totally have to contend with a very different world.*
ED: You know what I'm saying? Just the fact that he was more willing to die than go to jail and be like his father. That was how hard-core he was and how entrenched into that mind-set he was. But we were forced to recut when those numbers came in and the audience said that they really wanted to see Q take a gun and shoot Bishop and knock him over the edge. They wanted Q to kill the villain or whom they considered to be the "villain." The message of the movie wasn't coming across at that point. And the audience was mostly Black teens. The studio made veiled threats like, "Well, you know if you don't cut this movie, we may not support the movie the way you want it to be supported." So I caved in. We re-cut it, and so now it looks like Bishop slips out of his hands.

I had always hoped that they would give us the money to put together an alternative version when it went to video but the weekend the film was released, it opened at number two and made $9 million [behind *The Hand That Rocks the Cradle*]. But there was a lot of controversy over the poster, because in the original poster it shows the four boys, and Bishop is up front and he's holding a gun in his hands. Someone started complaining that the poster incited violence, and a couple of days before the movie opened, the studio airbrushed all of the guns out of the posters, which to me was total bullshit, because at that same time there was a movie out called Stop! Or My Mom Will Shoot [with Sylvester Stallone], where this old lady is pointing a gun. Bishop wasn't even pointing the gun at the audience, but this old lady has a gun pointed right out at you as you're reading the ad. I think at the same time there was The Last Boy Scout, where Bruce Willis is pointing a gun and Damon Wayans is holding a football, but no one ever complained about those posters.

Then, during the opening weekend of Juice, there was a shooting in Philadelphia and apparently there were lines to see the film, there was some jostling, a kid went across the street to get a gun from his car and he shot it. He hadn't even seen the film yet, had not even seen the movie, but he shot at somebody, missed the person he was trying to shoot and hit someone who was coming out from seeing the film. I wasn't even in the country. I was in Cairo shooting Malcolm X. But at that time, word got that the film instigated violence and Paramount decided to totally distance itself from the movie. A similar thing happened when Boyz 'N the Hood came out, but Columbia Pictures took out full-page ads saying, "We support this movie and we don't think that a movie causes violence."

GA: *Some experts will argue that violence like that could have occurred anyway. It could have happened at the bowling alley, the shopping center, et cetera, but it just happened at Juice in Philly that night, but it had nothing to do with the film.*
ED: I mean, the guy hadn't even seen the movie. But then the press said that the movie caused the violence and Paramount took the position that the film was responsible, and by the Monday after the film opened, all of the advertising, all of the bus posters, the subway posters, the billboards, had been totally removed.

GA: *How do you feel about that?*
ED: Aw, man, I was pissed. I was pissed because the movie opened up at number two, the movie stayed in the theaters for a month and wound up grossing about $20 million on a $3 million budget.

GA: *Was it racism that caused the studio to pull the ads for Juice? Or was it just that they didn't understand the product?*
ED: Racism usually comes from the fact that people don't understand, but I mean, I've seen interesting things happen. I've gone to see Black films in theaters and looked at my ticket stub and the ticket stub is actually for another film that's playing. So the money that should be attributed to

that Black film is not going to that Black film. It's going to something else. Several theaters in Jersey—I've been to a couple and I've talked to other people and the same thing has happened. It's like they went to see *Juice* but the ticket stub says *Stop or My Momma'll Shoot*. So yeah, I sometimes really think that there's an element that really does not want African Americans to gain a significant foothold in making films, deciding what films are made, stretching the genre and stretching what Black films can do. I just had a similar situation with a film I did called *Bones*. *Bones* got great reviews from *The New York Times*, *The L.A. Times* and *Variety*, but the studio refused to capitalize on those good reviews. The common industry practice is to put blurbs from good reviews in the ads, but they refused to do that and they spent one-third of what everybody else was spending to advertise the movie. So the movie came out and had a great soundtrack that never got to the radio stations. How are you going to turn down a Snoop Dogg album?

GA: Especially with Black audiences. The market is so radio-driven.
ED: You know what I'm saying? So radio-driven, but weeks before the movie came out they were playing music from the movie *13 Ghosts* but nothing from *Bones*.

GA: Going back to the point you just raised about Hollywood's resistance when it comes to different types of stories about Blacks—why is that? Some filmmakers suggest that movies are simply entertainment and that maybe Black filmmakers haven't figured out what audiences want and if you write what audiences want and do certain types of movies, the films will get made and will make money. What do you think?
ED: Well, first of all, I think the Black experience is so varied and it's such an international experience that there are so many different stories that can be told out there, so many different types of stories, but they haven't been allowed to be told. In Hollywood, a Black film means a "hood" movie, but there are so many different types of stories that can be told. I just don't think we've been given a chance. I just don't think the powers that be understand; do they want to understand? They have this self-fulfilling prophecy that Black films are not going to sell overseas and Black films aren't going to make any money. As a result, with that kind of thinking in their minds, they're not going to put so much into advertising. C'mon, even with a Tom Cruise movie, if you assume that just knowing that Tom Cruise is in the film there's no need to advertise it . . . Look at *Vanilla Sky*. *Vanilla Sky* came out and there were posters all over the place, there were billboards all over the place. You still have to sell the fact that the film is out.

It's tough to go see movies, because now you have to pay about $9 per ticket, and if you go with someone else, it's about $20, then maybe you have to pay for a baby-sitter, maybe dinner. So you're talking some money, and you have to be told that you're going to get your money's worth when you go see the film. But if you don't see the advertising, if you don't see anyone saying that this is a movie that you have to go see, you're not going to see the movie. You're going to see the movie the media's plugging. The media is saying that this is the movie you have to see, and with so many Black films they're just not doing that. It's interesting, because if it's a film starring an African American but it's directed by a white director, they'll put the money out. Hurricane with Denzel—Norman Jewison was the director and they put the money out there. Ali with Will Smith, directed by Michael Mann—they put the money out there. I have a tendency to believe that if Spike had directed Ali [Laughs] they wouldn't have put the money out. I think it is a matter of control in Hollywood and, rightfully so, African American film can be perceived as a threat to the powers that be.

GA: Spike Lee came onto the film scene in 1986 with She's Gotta Have It, a low-budget picture with unknown actors, and the film was a hit. Has the industry changed so much now that to do a Black independent film you have to have recognizable stars before you have a chance of getting a distribution deal for the film?

ED: I still think you can have a successful film with unknown actors. I want to do it, but I just don't want it to be something like we've seen before. I'd love to see something that's exploring different genres. I think digital filmmaking is making filmmaking more accessible to people. There are festivals that can screen the film. I think the thing that we have to do as filmmakers is make more varied types of movies. Unfortunately, lately we see the same kind of sit-com type comedy, over and over and over again. I'd like to see more films and genres being made. The film that I loved last year—it wasn't directed by a Black director—was Ghost Dog [directed by Jim Jarmusch] starring Forest Whitaker. That was a very low-budget film that looked like it was all shot in the same neighborhood, but it had an interesting and different kinds of characters. I think it is the kind of film Black filmmakers should be making. There're a lot of comedies with kind of the same old story all over again, but people want to see different types of stuff, and I think if you show them that, then if you're able to get it to a festival, I think that you have a chance, but it's still going to be tough going.

GA: You've worked on a lot of different types of movies. How do you make the transition? Frequently directors stick to one genre, but you've been able to do many different types of things. What attracts you to a project?
ED: Well, it's the story, it's who the characters are, who those people are, it is something I can get a handle on? If it gets a fire going inside of me, then I go for it. In terms of genres, I am more attracted to unusual stories, something in the thriller mode. The story I'm doing now is a true

story about a college kid who became a bookie and started a very successful bookmaking operation at Arizona State University. It's called Big Shot: Confessions of a Campus Bookie. It's for television. Some of the most interesting scripts that I've recently received have been television scripts.

GA: *What's it like directing a film for TV versus doing a feature film?*
ED: Well, even though it's a television movie, I approach it as a feature film. The thing that you always have to deal with in TV is really fast shooting schedules—usually about twenty-five days max. Budget-wise, you're usually dealing in the $4 million range. An exception is something like my film Monday Night Mayhem, which cost $10 million dollars, which helped in shooting it in New York. But nowadays, there is a lot of shooting in Canada, because of the lower production costs. However, you're always faced with making Canada look like America [Laughs], you know—which is hard, it's difficult to do.

GA: *Do you feel that given your track record—you have done an enormous amount of work—that you're still offered only Black projects?*
ED: Yeah. And I'm still offered low-budget projects. I try to go for bigger-budget films—larger budget in the fact that the shooting schedule is more comfortable.

GA: *You'd think that with your track record, and having directed lots of movies and having worked with Spike Lee and John Sayles, that wouldn't be the case.*
ED: Yeah, but for some strange reason I'm still an unknown quantity. I know of a lot of books and treatises about African American film and my films aren't even mentioned.

GA: *Does that bother you?*
ED: I think it does, because I want my work to be recognized. I was amazed when my daughter told me one day that all of her friends had memorized Juice and I found out that Juice is a major film for a lot of kids growing up.

GA: *You directed and were the cinematographer on your recent film Our American. What was it like doing both?*
ED: It was crazy, it was changing hats, trying to concentrate on a performance and then the sun goes in the clouds and all of a sudden, man, I've got to run my light meter and make adjustments. It was fun, and maybe I'll do it again one day, but I do like collaborating with a cinematographer because then I don't have to worry about filling out equipment lists [Laughs] and planning equip-

ment, but I find it's crazy [to do both], especially on a twenty-five-day schedule. It'd be easier if it were a longer schedule. I know Steven Soderbergh's probably got ninety-day schedules.

GA: *Would you like to shoot films for other directors in the future?*
ED: I don't know. Sometimes I toy with the idea of saying, "Spike, let's do one more for old times' sake." It's tough, though, because unfortunately, at least in America, you get known for doing one thing. I know that after I did *Juice* I went and photographed *Malcolm X*, and I think that got in the way of my getting my next film. It was two years before I found another project to direct, because people were saying, "Well, is he a cameraman or is he a director? What is he?"

GA: *What advice do you have for aspiring directors?*
ED: Just know that the road's going to be tough. You have to love film, because you can't do it just because you're hoping you're going to make a lot of money. If you do something just for the money, it's not worth it. There are a lot of better ways to make a lot of money other than being a filmmaker. If you want to make money, do something else. But you have to love film. Film has to be part of your life, part of your being. You have to love the work. You find the best musicians are the ones who play because they have to. I make films because I've got to. For me, it's make films or die. And always be open to new ideas. Never think that you know everything—and part of the fun of it is that you will never know everything. Part of the fun of it is that I'll always be learning. Every film is a different experience. No two films are the same. I think that when you get to the point where you know it all, you're dead.

Robert Townsend

Robert Townsend has to be one of the friendliest, most recognizable faces in Hollywood. Dining with him at a Hollywood haunt is sure to bring onlookers and strangers over to your table to congratulate or to just say hello to one of the film industry's most versatile and entertaining talents. Working as an actor, director, producer, comedian and writer, Townsend has had a career that spans more than twenty-five years.

A Chicago native, Townsend made his directorial debut with the 1987 comedy film *Hollywood Shuffle*, which he cowrote with Keenen Ivory Wayans. The film is hailed, along with Spike Lee's *She's Gotta Have It* (1986), as having helped revolutionize African American cinema.

Townsend has continued to make contributions to the world of entertainment as a director, producer, actor and writer. For television, Townsend created and produced variety shows such as the Cable Ace Award–winning *Robert Townsend and His Partners in Crime* (1991) for HBO, and *Townsend Television* (1993) for Fox Television. He also created and starred in the WB Network's hit sitcom *The Parent Hood* (1995–1999).

He starred in and directed an ode to sixties music groups, *The Five Heartbeats* (1991), *B.A.P.S* (1997) with Halle Berry, *Love Songs* (1999), with Lou Gossett, Jr., and Andre Braugher and the Disney family film *Up, Up and Away* (2000), with Sherman Hemsley. Townsend also directed the *Little Richard Story* (2000), with Leon Robinson, *Holiday Heart* (2000), with Alfre Woodard, and *Livin' for Love: The Natalie Cole Story* (2000).

Townsend recently directed *Carmen: A Hip Hopera* (2001), with Destiny Child's lead singer, Beyoncé Knowles, for MTV Films, and Showtime's *Ten Thousand Black Men Named George* (2002), a period film about the Pullman porter strike, led by A. Phillip Randolph. The film starred Charles Dutton, Andre Braugher, Brock Peters and Mario Van Peebles.

— — — —

GA: *Tell me about your childhood. Were you creative?*

RT: Well, what really happened was that when I was a kid, I was very quiet. I grew up in a really rough neighborhood on the west side of Chicago. My mother and father weren't together, so my mother raised four kids on her own, and because there were gangs outside, my mother kept me in the house a lot, so all I did was watch TV. My nickname as a kid was "TV Guide," because I used to watch everything on TV and could perform all the characters from all the shows from Alfred Hitchcock to movies like *The Wizard of Oz.* So everybody would be saying, "TV Guide, what did we miss today?!"

GA: *What were some of your favorite television shows during that time? Do you remember?*

RT: Oh, shoot, Hitchcock was one, and I loved Jimmy Stewart movies, I Spy with Bill Cosby, *Tennessee Tuxedo* cartoons, Mr. McGoo, Humphrey Bogart films, you name it, I watched everything. It started there, then I won an award in fifth grade in 1968 for a speech contest for doing a poem by Carl Sandburg called "Me, Myself and I," so that's kind of where I first started to blossom in terms of being an artist and an actor. My mother told me that if I wanted to do it, she'd support me. Then I really began to pursue it full-time, and you jump ahead to high school, I was doing plays—not at my high school but at a community theater—I did plays in college, then kind of found my way into show business.

GA: *What were some of the memorable plays that you acted in in community theater or college?*

RT: The first play I ever did was by Ira Rogers, and Chuck Smith directed it. The second play I did was *Where Is the Pride, What Is the Joy?* and Chuck and I have been working together ever since. It's a connection I've had since I was in high school, but they were all new playwrights, new theater, plays with a voice about something, so I learned a lot. I was a member of the Black Actors Guild, on the south side of Chicago, and that's where I learned all my manners to this day in terms of show business and everything. It was a little sixty-seat theater—that's where I learned everything.

GA: *Did you consider a career in the theater at this point?*

RT: I thought about it, but I think I love it all, I really love it all, I really do. I still do it all. I love it all, please. I love it all.

GA: *That sounds exciting, so all that theater training has obviously helped. What did you study in college?*

RT: My minor was theater, my major was radio and television communications at Illinois State University.

GA: *You were in Cooley High (1975). I saw it again recently and I noticed you.*

RT: That was my first movie, I was in high school, and they came to see me in the play Where Is the Pride, What Is the Joy? Then afterwards Michael Schultz said, "Come and audition for the movie." I got the little part in it, and that was the beginning.

GA: *Was that the moment you said, "I want to make movies?"*

RT: Uh-huh. To tell you the truth, I had directed plays in college and created my own on-campus theater troupe, called On the Black Hand Side, because for the main stage productions you would audition for the token parts and I would say, "Why can't I be the lead? Why can't I try to do something different? Why I gotta be just the best friend?"

GA: *What were some of the productions your theater company produced?*

RT: We did more experimental stuff, we would do poetry by Amiri Baraka and we'd sing, we created our own stuff. So it was more avant-garde theater than anything else. It wasn't Raisin in the Sun or the traditional plays. It was really fresh, and I used all of my few credits at the time from being an extra in Mahogany and Cooley High to say, "Yes, I am an actor." That worked, and people knew those movies, they came and we did really well. I did that, but I became a filmmaker after I appeared in the film A Soldier's Story (1984), which was the best experience of my life, and my agent said, "Robert, they only do one Black movie a year and you may never, ever do one again."

But it was just fun working with my fellow actors: It was Denzel [Washington], David Alan Grier, Adolph Caesar, Larry Riley, Howard Rollins, David Harris and William Alan Young. We just had the best time for ten weeks, as opposed to just being the token Black in a movie. When it was over, I said, "This is how movies should be." There was just a sense of family and everybody was cool and you didn't feel like an alien, and so I said, "I want to do that again. I want to have that experience again." I auditioned for The Color Purple and I didn't get the part of Harpo, and I said,

"I didn't get my Black movie, so I'm in trouble." So I saved money from A Soldier's Story and money from Streets of Fire (1984), and people thought, "Hey, you gonna buy a Porsche, you gonna buy a Jag?" I said, "Naw, you know what? I'm gonna make a movie." That's when I decided to make Hollywood Shuffle, which was based on a lot of my experiences as an actor. Keenen [Ivory Wayans] and I wrote it together, and we just wrote a lot of funny material. We connected it with some serious scenes like the stuff about my grandmother and everything. That's how my grandmother really was. She didn't believe in my career. So we just started writing real stuff and the film just took off.

GA: *That was such a funny movie. Did you have any idea that it would take off in the way that it did ?*
RT: I had no idea. I had fun, I had a good time and I believed in what I was doing.

GA: *The story about your financing Hollywood Shuffle with credit cards is legendary at this point. Is it the God's honest truth?*
RT: It's all true. We [Keenan and I] basically ran out of money, went on the road to do standup comedy for two weeks, came back and there was a stack of mail. I'd asked God, "Hey, God. If I'm supposed to do this, give me a sign," and then there were all these applications for credit cards. And I said, "Wait a minute. I can finish the movie with credit cards. It just came to me. Some light went on, then I called banks for all these credit cards and started charging the movie, and the Samuel Goldwyn Company saw the film, loved the film and said, "We'll put that (credit card story) in the press" and I said, "Really?" I thought it would hurt the movie, and they said, "No, it'll help the movie," and it became legendary.

GA: *I'll never forget watching Hollywood Shuffle in Times Square as a student. It was riotous. Why do you like to do comedy?*
RT: I love making people laugh, I love being silly. I just love comedy. I'm a big kid. I mean, why do Meteor Man or Up, Up and Away? There is a side of me that's just pure kid, and I love it, I absolutely love it. And I think with comedy you can say some funny stuff and then you can say something that's real, but in a funny way, and make people think. Like Hollywood Shuffle is very funny, but there is some stuff that is really serious, thought-provoking and touching at the same time. But in comedy my idol is Richard Pryor. I come from that school where you can be funny but you can say some powerful things too.

GA: *Besides Richard Pryor, who are some of your other comedic influences?*
RT: A guy who's passed away now but I think was absolutely brilliant was a comedian named

Dick Shawn—he really used to make me laugh so hard. He was a comic's comic. He wasn't really known that well to the world, but he's known for movies, like *The Producers* (1968), and he played funny characters in movies, but his real stuff was his standup comedy. He was absolutely brilliant.

GA: *What I like about your comedy is that you tend to celebrate the human condition. You understand the world you've created so you're not mocking the people in your work. Where does that come from?*

RT: Well, see, I think with comedy you can say, "Laugh with me or laugh at me." So it's which side you choose to be on. I'd rather have an audience laugh with me than at me so that they can say, "Well, hey, your character did something silly or stupid, but we understand why." I grew up on classic comedy, so when I'd watch those shows on television, *The Andy Griffith Show* or *Red Skelton*, or just the different comedians, I learned that there's a certain structure to good comedy. There's a setup and there's a punch line. I don't like mean-spirited comedy, I don't like making fun of people unless there's a subject that everybody's unified in hating or disliking. That's where my comic sensibilities come from. It's about being really funny and having a respect for the audience.

GA: *Tell me about* The Five Heartbeats *and what inspired that film.*

RT: I grew up on the Temptations, and when they broke up I kind of took it personally, and I just wanted to know what happened. I thought everything was good, so when they broke up I thought, "That's an incredible story, because they sing love songs but do they really have love in their lives?" And that's kind of the germ of the idea for *The Five Heartbeats*. Initially, it was going to just be funny, and then Keenen (Ivory Wayans) and I were just thinking, "Hey, it can be a funny movie about singing groups." But as I started interviewing groups for real, I soon discovered that they didn't make any money, they were ripped off. I learned a lot. Then the movie started to shape itself and then it became *The Five Heartbeats*, a drama and a comedy; there's a lot of stuff in that movie, a lot of stuff.

GA: *What was your process for researching the story?*

RT: The main source were the Dells. They gave me a lot of information. I also talked to the Temptations, the O'Jays, the Chi-Lites, different singing groups, and just got their take on everything. And they were all willing to talk, and we just had a good time. Shooting the movie was really deep, because I had to do a lot of the directing from underneath the hair dryer because

I had to get my hair ready. It was a hell of a feat, a hell of a journey to do everything: act, direct and produce.

GA: You've directed and starred in a number of your films. How do you do it?

RT: What's funny is that as a standup comedian you direct yourself anyway, so I kind of just looked at it like that. When you go on stage you say, "Okay, I'm going to do this joke first, this joke in the middle and I'm going to end this way." Now, it's just you and the audience and you direct it, you create it. People don't want to look at it as directing, but it is, because it's your presentation. In my standup routines, I always did a lot of characters, so it was a natural extension. It's just being focused, as long as I know what the camera is doing and I say, "Hey, the camera's going to be over here on dolly tracks going back and forth as we talk"—so while I'm talking to you from my eye I can see the camera drifting back. It's just really being focused. I learned directing as an extra, too, when I started out in this business. When I got to New York I was an extra for five years, and so that's where I learned about directing. I'd always know where the camera was, because it would be the difference between making $66 dollars as an extra and $200 as a principal, because if I could say or do the right thing, I'd get an upgrade. I'd watch where the camera was and do something so that the director would notice me. Then the director would say, "Hey, let that guy say whatever he's saying or let that guy do whatever he's doing." Then you'd get more money. That's kind of how I learned about directing. When you're acting and directing, it's the natural extension, because then it's okay—"What is the camera doing? What do I need to do?" Your comic instincts kick in. And it's just gags. A comedian thinks through the repertoire and says, "How many gags can I get out of this situation?"

GA: Since you're an actor yourself, what's your approach to working with actors?

RT: My approach to working with actors is you make the soil on the set as creative as possible so the actors can be as creatively free as possible. I listen to the actors—I think actors have really great instincts, I think sometimes when directors go wrong, they cast an actor and then they don't let the actor do what they do. They try to tell them what to do and try to squash their magic. I always leave room for magic on the set. There's what the writer says, there's what I see and then there's what an actor can do that goes above and beyond what I can probably envision. Michael Wright in Five Heartbeats [who played Eddie King, Jr.], who is a wonderful actor, brought stuff to that role that I hadn't even seen. But you have to trust the actor, and then if the actor goes too far, you gotta be willing to step in and say, "Hey, hey, hey, come back a little bit." But a good director will push an actor to their fullest point inside of themselves. For example, working with Alfre Woodard on Holiday Heart, which I directed for Showtime, I pushed her really hard. She's a fine actress, and there were times where she'd say, "Robert, I don't want to look ugly on screen," or "Robert, I don't want to do this." And she was nominated for a Golden Globe. As a director, you feel really good when a person trusts you and at the end of the rainbow they do the work and they get a Golden Globe, NAACP Image Award or some other award. For me, the best compliment as a director came at the 2001 Image Awards, because I had three people from three different movies nominated—Leon for The Little Richard Story, Natalie Cole for The Natalie Cole Story and Alfre for Holiday Heart. Natalie won for the The Natalie Cole Story, but just the fact that no director, I mean—I work my butt off—but no director had actors nominated in three different categories at the level of Leon, Natalie, and Alfre.

GA: *What's the dynamic when you're working with someone like Alfre Woodard?*
RT: You know, the bottom line is that when you work with good people, there is no ego. Alfre is a sweetheart, we just flowed. Part of my job is to listen to her, what she's feeling. The worst thing a director can do is force an actor to do something they don't believe in or they don't want to do. So when you have really fine actors, you get out of their way, you let them do their thing, if they're going in the wrong direction, or they're giving too much you pull them, or if they're not giving enough, you push. She's a fine actress, so it's going to be a great performance, but I think, those little notches here, notches there, took it to the other level in terms of the Richter scale.

GA: *Do you rehearse a lot?*
RT: I like to rehearse, but more so than rehearsal, I like to really talk to the actors about their characters. I don't really believe in auditions, to tell you the truth.

GA: *Oh, really?*
RT: I really like just meeting actors and talking with them, because I can look at their résumé and see what they've done. That's how I did The Five Heartbeats. There was no audition. I just met with people and talked for a half an hour and said, "You got the part," and that was it. Everybody thought I was crazy, but I knew instinctively what people could do. I kind of got a sense of their energy. When you look at people's body of work, Black actors don't really have a lot unless they've worked with one of the five [Black] directors.

They send over their reel, and unless they've worked on one of the major films that the handful of Black filmmakers have made, or they get a breakout role in some other picture, there's not a whole lot. So why send an actor through that? It's not really their best work, it's just the only work they could get.

GA: *So to what do you attribute your ability to instinctively realize that an actor is good for a particular part?*

RT: Well, I don't know what that is. Elia Kazan, who worked with Marlon Brando, James Dean got some of the most incredible performances out of Brando. What it is, is that Kazan really gets to know who the person is as a person and not so much who the person is reading the lines. So when you talk to a person you can say, "Okay, tell me about yourself, dada, dada, dada." They might say, "I love my kids." I say, "That's interesting to know, or dada, dada." They say, "I got into this fight, blah, blah, blah. I love basketball." Later on, I'll use that a key when I'm really working, to say, "See your kid walking across the street get hit by the car. Now let's do the scene." And they think, "My kid!" So I learn more in the interview.

The other side of it, too, for me is that I don't need a great audition in the room, I need it on the screen. I need them to know that because I'm an actor as well, I'm going to give you the role. But because I did not make you jump through hoops, I'm expecting a little bit more when we go to work so everybody says, "Whoa, I ain't never been treated like this before. I thought . . ." Normally, because some people are uncomfortable just talking, they say, "Where's the script?" I say, "No, I just want to talk." They respond, "Uh, you mean just talk? About what?" My response is "You." Some people would just melt right there and some people would say, "I like show business, man, and I wanna be a star. I wanna buy my mama a house, dada, dada." Then you see something about them or they say, "Hey, I just wanna get paid, man. I didn't even read the script, I just want some money." And you say, "Okay, now you learn something about the characters." In my game you hope that they have a little bit of that in them, because it adds to the mixture.

GA: *Absolutely. How do you prepare for a shoot?*

RT: Sometimes I storyboard. I kind of map out the direction that I'm headed in. I do what I call movement patterns, which is how I feel the movement of the scene will take place, because you want to go into it kind of knowing what the movie's going to look like. But then when you get to the location, things will change. Like this tree will be here, and I say, "Oh, let's shoot him through the tree." So maybe in the script I just had a guy at a restaurant talking, and then he sees somebody outside now, and that's one phase. Now, when we get to the actual location, I may tell him to lean back into the tree and let one leaf hide his eye. Now, let's see what's scarier than the green leaf. So I'll see certain things. When I'm initially planning the shot I may just say, "Scene happens in a restaurant. Gentleman is interviewing subject. Water is on the table, we have tofu, broccoli and we have dada, dada. There's a plant, and within the plant he jokes and makes various movements near the plant." But if I don't see the plant initially when I'm writing, when I get to the location and see the plant and want to use it, I storyboard. You map it out and then you leave room for magic.

GA: *You leave room for the magic to happen.*
RT: You leave room for all that to happen and nothing is wrong or right, it's just actors taking chances, so for me I do my movement patterns, I do a shot list, I rehearse, I rush my actors through hair and makeup because usually on movies you don't have a lot of rehearsal time. So I create extra rehearsal time, I say, "Please come through hair and makeup really quickly." Because a lot of times the actors are in there with the hairdressers and they're, like, "Girl, did you see Oprah yesterday?" So while they're taking an hour to light the set we've got forty-five minutes to rehearse. By the time we walk up to the set, everybody's ready. Then we walk on the set, two takes, three takes, finished, I'm out because they're so well oiled, their energy is high as opposed to it's seven o'clock in the morning and we've gotta do this big yelling and screaming scene and I'm still waking up. We rehearse, run the lines, and by the time they get in front of the camera, they're tight. So I have little tricks to save time, because you know time is always the enemy.

GA: *How detailed are you as it relates to costuming, set design, and props?*
RT: In my scripts, I lay in wardrobe description and what the set looks like in advance. I talk through it and say what props, what are we going to be eating today, what kind of food? It depends, it's a character choice. If we're talking about restaurants, it's what kind of restaurant? Is it Thai food? Is it soul food? All of that little detailed stuff I get into. I get into colors—like in *Meteor Man* I sucked out all of the colors. I said that I only wanted green to be around the school in the principal's office and on Meteor Man, so the only part you see green in the whole movie are things that grow, things that give energy, that give life—teachers, principals, so it's subtle little things. In *Five Heartbeats*, in the first half of the movie when everything is going well, it's very warm, we use warm filters, warm tones, the colors are more vibrant.

When everything starts to fall apart, we take away all of the warm tones, the color scheme gets dark. So it's conscious things, where as an audience member watching, you don't know what's been happening that manipulates you, but then you feel like the group's not together now, and then early on when they're jamming and they're singing and it's [sings] "I got nothing but love for you baby." It's warm, it's vibrant, it's fun, aw, man. [sings] "I got nothing but love." You know you're loving it, but then later on it's "Hey, guys, remember, dang, we should get back together, man"—the scene feels cold, not quite, but we don't know what it is. Is it the framing? The composition? What? So it's different, subtle things like that, that when you watch it as a director, you're manipulating the audience. I always try to get into detail, movement, color schemes, wardrobe. For example, women walk differently in flat shoes than they do in pumps. A guy acts differently in a sweatshirt than in a suit—all of those things. As an actor myself, I've gotten into arguments before when people say, "Hey, what's the difference between a sweater and a jacket?" My response to that is "No, no, no, I feel more like business in a jacket because of the shoulders and everything." There's a certain kind of, "Hey, welcome to the business world." There's a certain attitude it gives you, as opposed to a casual sweater, where you're going, "Ah, man, what's up?" Little things like that, but that's why directors get into details, because it does affect the actors.

GA: You've done a lot of films obviously, and you're a working director, you have a body of work. Out of all of your films, what's your favorite?

RT: You know what's funny? All my movies and television projects are like my babies. It's like you can't pick a kid because they all represent different things. Because if you say, B.A.P.S—I loved doing B.A.P.S Halle [Berry] did a funny, touching performance in that. With Carmen, I just liked the camera work and I thought Beyonce [Knowles] and everybody were just really great, and it was different, it was cutting edge, there's never been a hip-hopera until now. So anytime you go into the unknown, it's a good feeling. With 10,000 Black Men Named George, about the Pullman porter strike, with Andre Braugher, Charles Dutton, Mario Van Peebles and the legendary one, Mr. Brock Peters, there are some monster performances in that piece, and I like that period, the history. So I mean all my work has been different.

GA: Any regrets about anything you've done in film? Is there anything you wish you'd done differently?

RT: Well, I think that's natural. You always say, "If I had more money or time, I would do something this way or that way." But I gotta tell you, I've been really blessed, I'm happy with all my babies. There's a piece that I acted in that I hated, that I didn't direct. If I had directed it I could have made a great movie, but I did this TV movie, Thick and Thin, that I hate and it's playing all over TV now. People say, "I saw you, Robert. What the fuck were you thinking in that bullshit ass movie?" A guy said that the other day.

GA: [Laughs]

RT: "I saw this bullshit ass movie because of you, man. I saw your name." That's probably the only movie that I hate. I don't want to dog anybody out. I think there was a lot more going on behind the camera than in front of the camera in terms of—I don't know who got into a fight with who, but the film didn't come out and my wife and I sat watching the movie and saying, "This is garbage." But the thing is that, that's why when people raise the argument about why do you want to direct [a film] and be in it you know that used to be an argument, and it was like, I know what I want to see and I know how to make people laugh and I can touch people—you know what I mean? But you can only trust so many people with that. So that's why when I'm in the hands of another director and I say, "I'm trusting you to make me look good and hook me up," but if they take the wrong takes, and they say, "Well, I think he's funnier in this take," where if I were choosing the takes I would say, "No, use half of this take and half of another take and put them together. That's the funny punch." However, the other director might say, "Oh, let's use the whole take," because they don't see what I see. I'll try to get five jokes out of one routine, if you work it right and the average, a lot of cats just go for one joke and I'm going, in great movies, or great television shows, they get fifteen jokes out of [a situation]. In B.A.P.S there's a thing where [a character] goes to the record store and he's supposed to come in saying, "I'm looking for Big Booty Cutie," and that's all he's supposed to do, and then I say, "Have the guy dance," because I knew Alex Thomas as a comedian and he does this great dance stuff so it's just another joke. In *Hollywood Shuffle*, there are so many gags that you don't see coming and you milk them and that's what comedy is all about. You try to get as much out of it and throw the audience off, and so for me I've been really happy because I've done a crazy dance with my career—I've done drama, comedy, comedy, drama, drama, sitcoms, variety shows, so I'm a smorgasbord in terms of everything I've done. Sometimes I'll look at my body of work and it's probably for an African American [director] the most versatile. Because you get certain cats that all they do is this or that, and I'm *TV Guide*. I like cartoons, I like drama, I like variety singers, so I've had a really interesting time, because I've pretty much done a lot of everything.

GA: *How do you make the transition from film to TV to standup to acting, et cetera?*

RT: It's so funny, because the other night I was sitting with a friend of mine, Dave Talbert, I'm directing one of his plays. It's a gospel whodunit, and we created it together, and it's really about this gangster who gets this second chance at life. We were sitting in a restaurant, and all these different people were coming over to say hi it to me, fans . . . there were these senior citizens who were sitting at a booth, the waitress had to be in her fifties, there was a Spanish family, a Black couple and some Koreans. It was this little diner that was open all night, so all these other people were coming over and Dave was saying, "Man." And I said, "My fans are all different shapes, sizes, colors because the work I've done has been on all different kinds of levels." So I got little kids because of *The Parent Hood*, *Up, Up and Away* and *Meteor Man*. Adults like *Five Heartbeats*, *Carmen*, you name it, teenagers. I have a cross section of a lot of people who have seen my work on some level or another. Then there are the diehards from *Hollywood Shuffle* and *Five Heartbeats*. So the thing for me is that I think because I have that ability it works for me, not against me, because at any given point, I could write something, direct something, act in something. Like hosting this event [for UNCF] with Patti Labelle—I started working on my jokes because I did it last year with Luther [Vandross] and I had a good time and I like doing it. I like playing, I like playing, that's the bottom line. And I've created a body of work that I'm really proud of. There's nothing that I can look at except for that one movie [*Thick and Thin*].

GA: [Laughs] That one.
RT: Lord help us all.

GA: Who are your favorite directors?
RT: My favorite director of all time is Elia Kazan. He directed *On the Waterfront*, *East of Eden*, *A Face in the Crowd*, *A Streetcar Named Desire*. I love all of those movies. There's something consistent with all those movies in terms of storytelling and a level of quality and [they're] really well cast, [and then there are] little jokes, little details—just wonderful, wonderful work.

GA: *A Face in the Crowd* is one of my favorites. I like all those, but *A Face in the Crowd* is incredible, with Andy Griffith in a dramatic role.
RT: I talked to Griffith one time about it, and he kind of looked at me like, yeah, because working with Kazan, boy, Kazan worked with the finest—Marlon Brando, James Dean. I also like Francis Ford Coppola, because I love the the *Godfather* movies. I love those movies, but I'd have to say those and Steven Spielberg, those are my favorite directors.

GA: Why Spielberg? He's great, and I know a lot of people like him, but why do you like him specifically?
RT: Because he's versatile and he's talented. All of his movies are different. Initially it was *ET*, *Jaws*, then *Schindler's List*, and he flipped the whole script and went into a whole deep, deep, deep well.

But the thing I really love about him, too, as a director and as a businessman, he goes from the *Animaniacs* to *Roger Rabbit*. I like the fact that he is a producing, directing, creative machine. I like that. That's what I want to be when I grow up.

GA: *Do you have a dream project—something that you're just dying to do?*
RT: You know what's funny? Everybody talks about living their dreams and dreaming. I'm living my dreams—anything I want I can get, I really can. If I do the right movie, I can be up for an Oscar. If I do the right movie, it can make $200, $300 million. The thing is that any story that I've wanted to tell, that I really wanted to tell, I've told. The thing for me is just thinking about new goals, because starting out it was if I could direct a movie, if I could star in a movie, if I could write a movie, if I could do a sitcom, if I could—and to tell you the truth, when I think about my life, I've always won. I've never ever really lost, even with *The Five Heartbeats*. That is one of the most popular video rentals to this day, and still runs on TV every three months. Even my first sitcom [*The Parent Hood*]ran five years and then went into syndication so I ain't mad, I ain't mad. The only thing that can stop me is me.

GA: *Why do you feel that way?*
RT: If you said, not being cocky, but if you said, what are your limitations? I would say none—whatever I focus on, I can do. I've still got a lot to learn, but I know a lot.

GA: *What would you like to learn?*
RT: I'll be a student for the rest of my life. There's always something, the new technical, digital technology. But now it's getting good, now it's getting good, so I don't know. That's why I'm saying that now whatever I want to do I can do. There're rules to the game, make no mistake about that, they're not going to spend $100 million on a Black period movie. [Acting] "I'd like to do *Sojourner Truth* the epic with newcomers, and I need $150 million or the deal is off." They'll say, "You know what, Robert? The deal's off."

GA: [Laughs]
RT: [Acting] Hollywood is racist because they would not let me make a $150 million movie about Sojourner Truth.

GA: *Three hours, too?*
RT: [Acting] Four hours.

GA: [Laughs]

RT: [Acting] It's new, I'm on the new shit.

GA: You ain't never seen this before. [Laughs] When someone tells you that, you know you'd better start running.

RT: [Acting] When Sojourner Truth reads the dictionary in the opening of the movie, we got this newcomer, you ain't never heard of her. "That's my boy's grandmother, because she looks like Sojourner Truth, and in the credits we say 'Willie Johnson's grandmother.' We don't even say her name. It's the new shit."

GA: There are people like that. What do you do outside of film that feeds you creatively?

RT: You know what I did recently? I climbed Mt. Kilimanjaro in Africa. I met people over there and I had just finished directing 10,000 Black Men Named George, and we switched editors because the executive producer wanted another editor whom he had worked with. The new editor we got was the editor on The Godfather part one and part two, so I said, "Hell yeah." So I had some time, I went to Africa and I climbed Mt. Kilimanjaro, and that changed my life.

GA: How did it change your life?

RT: You always hear about people saying life is peaks and valleys and yada, yada. We hear about mountains, valleys, peaks—in church, you know. [Acting like a preacher] "You gotta climb the mountain, and sometimes you gon' fall into the valley." What I learned is that anything in life that you want, you take your time, but there's a certain way to get it. It took me six days to climb [Mount Kilamanjaro], I had never climbed a mountain before in my life, and the first day was just seven hours in the mud going up the mountain. Seven hours in the mud, and when I got to the top, it was just as hard coming down to the bottom. To get to the top, I needed my guide to really help me. You can't make it anywhere in life after a certain point unless you have pros to help you brainstorm, so every step of the way there were life lessons in terms getting to the top of a mountain that I had to learn. I had to learn how to breathe, how to walk again, because you're walking a certain way. You've gotta take your time, you've gotta pace yourself, you've gotta stop, you've gotta sleep. I'd never climbed a mountain before in my life, but I made it. I was in a daze when I got to the top. We climbed in the middle of the night for seven hours, starting at 11:30 at night. And I got there at 7:15 in the morning, I was delirious, but it was truly what it's like to be on top, success and everything. When you're really on top, you've been working so hard that it's not like stuff has slowed down. Everybody says, [Mumbles], "Hey, that's what it's like to be on top." People think you're on top. If you want to really be on top and handle things, there's energy always swerving around you because you're on top. If you ask me my goals and if you ask me what do you want to do? And what can't you do? I can do anything. And it's no bullshit. I'm just being honest—there ain't nothing [I can't do]. [Laughs] That's the new shit.

Keenen Ivory Wayans

Mention the name Wayans and one might have a variety of responses, depending on your politics, sense of humor or overall view of the world.

Unquestionably, once you've seen a film by Keenen Ivory Wayans, the eldest of the celebrity clan that includes Damon, Marlon, Shawn and Kim, you will know that you've been on an imaginative, satirical ride with a filmmaker who continues to push the envelope, cross barriers and beckon us to uncharted waters regardless of how deep and how badly the sharks may bite.

I first heard Keenen's name when I saw the explosively funny *Hollywood Shuffle* (1987), which he cowrote with another rising star, director Robert Townsend. The hit film helped push the burgeoning stars toward cinema and TV fame. Meeting Wayans in person for lunch, one is certain to laugh incessantly, but to also find a thoughtful and critical mind that can quickly crack a joke, then switch to the serious issues of the day in a split second.

Born in humble surroundings in Manhattan's Chelsea neighborhood, Wayans got his start in show business as a standup comedian at New York's storied Improv Comedy Club. It was during this stint that he linked up with Townsend, a Chicagoan who also aspired to make it big in comedy.

In 1988, Wayans made his foray into directing with his blaxploitation satire *I'm Gonna Git You Sucka*. The success of that film led to Wayans's highly popular, tantalizing, hip-breakingly humorous, if at times controversial hit show *In Living Color*, which helped launch the careers of such Hollywood stars as Jim Carey, Rosie Perez, Jamie Fox and Jennifer Lopez.

But the year 2000 was Wayans's big year on the big screen. In that year, with *Scary Movie,* he became the highest-grossing Black director of all time. The film grossed $157 million domestically and $278 million worldwide—eclipsing Sidney Poitier's 1980 *Stir Crazy* [$101 million domestic]. *Scary Movie* also made Wayans the highest-grossing director in the history of Miramax. The film was followed by *Scary Movie 2,* which Wayans also helmed. His other directing credits include *A Low Down Dirty Shame* (1994) and screenwriting credit for Townsend's *Five Heartbeats.* Upcoming projects include *Scary Movie 3* and *The Incredible Shrinking Man.*

— — — —

GA: *You come from a big family, dd you have a creative childhood?*

KW: Our household was creative in many ways—the survival method was creative. My mother was a genius at putting food on the table. And not that my father wasn't there, but you figure my dad's best year was when he made $12,000. Now, $12,000 for twelve people is a thousand dollars each. You divide that up by 365 days a year, and that's not a lot of money. But my mother managed—we called her Harriet Tubman because she'd work the system; we watched our mom get her hustle on, so in that regard, that was one aspect of creativity. As kids, we were creative because we didn't have much, but we never let that be an obstacle to being able to do what we wanted to do. So while other kids got little fire engines with the pedals, we would take an old baby carriage and wood box and make a go-cart. [Laughs] No breaks, but we were doing our thing, and we did that with almost everything. If we couldn't buy it, we would make it, so I think that's some of where the creativity started. We learned how to do more with less, and I think that really transferred later on when I got into filmmaking.

GA: *During this time, did you ever see yourself having a creative career?*

KW: When I was about nine years old, I had my first life-changing experience. I had gotten chased home from school by this bully, and when I got home Richard Pryor was on TV on *The Dinah Shore Show,* and he was doing a routine about the bully in school and how they beat you up before you even get outside. [Demonstrates brandishing his fist] And I was laughing, but I really identified with him and his perspective on that. I found it funny, and the sweat was still fresh on my forehead from the chase home, and that's when I said that's what I wanted to do. I had no idea how you went about doing that. It was really just a dream.

GA: *But you understood the truth and pain of comedy.*

KW: Comedy is pain, just a different take on it. If you listen to a comedian's act, there's nothing funny about it. Everything he's talking about is a painful experience. It's either a worst nightmare or something humiliating. There's nothing funny about what they're talking about except the presentation and the familiarity. You can identify with what they're saying. That's the gift of comedy.

GA: *Did your parents encourage you a lot growing up?*

KW: Well, my mother was very encouraging when it came to anything good that we did. My mother really instilled self-confidence, pride and self-worth in all of us that said that we were good and better than the conditions that we lived in. She was really, really good about that. If you made some achievement, she'd put it up and act like you were Picasso. So, yeah, she was encouraging.

GA: *It's one thing to know what comedy is, but it's another thing to free yourself enough to perform publicly. How'd you develop that skill?*

KW: I don't know. I enjoyed making people laugh, but one day I walked up on my friends and they were talking about me. They were trying to get somebody to do something, and I heard one of them say, "Get Keenen. He's stupid, he'll do anything." And I'm thinking they thought I was funny, but he was actually thinking I was stupid. That made me chill out a little bit, and I stopped doing as much stuff out in public. But then I went away to college and it was a whole new environment; it's how journeys in life work. So I went to Tuskegee University to study engineering, and I was one of the few guys there from New York, so I used to tell these stories about New York, and I would do all the characters like the heroin addicts in the park and I'd have everybody rolling. It was showtime on the campus fountains. One day after doing my routine, a guy who was also from New York came up to me and said, "You should check out the Improv when you go home." And I said, "What's that?" And he told me that it was the comedy club in New York where Richard Pryor started, and that's all he had to say at that point. But the irony was that it took me going to Alabama to find out about a club on Forty-fourth Street that was literally a mile from where I grew up. When I went home for summer break, I went to the Improv, auditioned and bombed.

GA: *You bombed? How'd you feel when you bombed?*

KW: It didn't mean anything to me, because I was so high on the fact that I actually got up on the stage and had lights and an audience. I might have well been the funniest man in the world that night, because when you pursue a dream, you have flashes of that dream, and that was a flash. It was a moment that stood still, because I'd dreamed about doing it, and finally I experienced the reality of being on the stage and being in front of an audience and having a mike in my hand, and

I did it. So I was high as a kite and didn't even know I had bombed, because I was just so excited, I'd done it and I was very confident that I was funny. I knew I just had to learn how to do it on stage. I went back and studied and watched the other comics, and I learned that there's a whole science to comedy and that you have to know how to set up a punch line. It's like writing—you may be a great storyteller, but when it's time to put it on paper, there's an art to doing that.

GA: *You eventually left Tuskegee to pursue stand-up full time. How did that happen?*
KW: The catalyst for that was Chris Albrecht who is now chairman of HBO. He was the manager at the Improv at the time and Chris took me aside one night and he was a really funny guy. [Laughs] He told me, "First off, if you come in here wearing red pants and an Afro pick in your hair again, I'm not going to put you on stage." He was trying to tell me that you're in a different world now and you have to understand that when you come in front of an audience, the first thing they see is you.

GA: *They weren't red polyester pants, were they? [Laughs]*
KW: Yeah, they were the red polyester, bells, the whole joint. So he was schooling me, and he told me: "You know, you're a really funny guy and I think you can go all the way with this." He told me that he knew I was going to school, but that I might want to think about pursuing comedy full-time. He said, "I really think you've got it," and he told me that there was another guy out in California who was doing stand-up, and the way he phrased it was that there was room for only one sheriff in town and I shouldn't let this guy get the leg up on me. So I heard him, but I knew that if I quit school my family would be disappointed, so I went back to college and came home that summer and saw the guy he was talking about. It was Byron Allen. Byron was the youngest guy to ever do Johnny Carson and he killed [was very funny]. So that sort of stirred up my competitive spirit. That's when I quit college.

GA: *What did your parents say when you decided to leave college?*
KW: Well, my dad was cooler about it than my mom. My dad felt like if you start something in life you should finish it, and even if you're not going to use the degree you should get it, because you'll have something to fall back on. My philosophy on falling back was that it was planning for failure and I didn't plan to fail, and that's what I told him. He disagreed with me, but he didn't really press it. My mother, on the other hand, went off. She said, "You're a jackass. You're the first one [in the family] to go to college."

GA: [Laughs] She was not having it.

KW: But I said, "This is what I've been dreaming about my whole life, this is what I want to do." (Impersonating mother) "You ain't gonna do it! You ain't gon' do it!" [Laughs] She did what a mother's supposed to do. To her, walking away from an engineering degree to do comedy was like going to join the circus. These days entertainment is something that's kind of real to the Black community because we've seen so many people have success, but back then, we're talking twenty-something years ago, in the projects you didn't know anybody in showbiz. Showbiz was so far removed from us.

GA: *And you eventually made a transition to acting. How did that happen?*

KW: I moved to New York and was doing comedy full-time, and that's when I met Robert Townsend. He had come to New York from Chicago and was basically a mirror image of me—he's from a big family in Chicago, dreamed about being a comic, moved to New York to do his thing. And Rob's hustle was acting, and so I schooled him on stand-up and he schooled me on acting. [Laughs] He told me that I had to shave my mustache and stuff. There's a whole commercialization of Blackness that goes on in show business, and I'm a product of the projects. And today you can be a rough-looking nigger and it's okay, but back then white folks were scared to death. So I had the Afro, the mustache and sideburns, the whole nine, and Rob said, "Yo, you're gonna have to cut that down, you're gonna have to get your hair cut." And I said, "Yo, man, that's gonna have me looking soft." [Laughs]. And he said that that's how you gotta do it and you have to get your head shots, and he told me to observe what was on TV. So he schooled me on the business and I went and got groomed and took my pictures. Then I went looking for an agent. The first time I went to meet an agent in New York, I could've been put in jail that day. I went to this cat's office, and I'm sitting down meeting with him, and the guy says [Impersonating agent], "You're gonna be my nigger."

GA: *Those exact words?*

KW: Yeah, he used those exact words. Twenty ears ago there was no cross-cultural exchange. It was Black over here and white over there and for a white guy to use the word "nigger" with no sense of hesitation in New York City was like, "Oh, I'm a have to fuck you up." It was as if all the hair on my back stood up, and I said to myself, "Are you going to sell yourself out and let this man talk to you like this?" Because I felt if I knocked him out I would've been blackballed from show business, and he said the word one more time and I had to check him. I said, "Yo, I ain't gonna be nobody's nigger and we're not gonna have this conversation." And I just got up and I left.

GA: *Very deep.*

KW: It was the first time I've ever had to restrain myself, and it was almost painful to leave without doing something, and that was the first shock, and I sat with Rob [Townsend] later and I said, "Yo, man, is this common? They do this?" He said, "Naw, I don't know where that dude came from." But I thought, "Wow, this is showbiz. I ain't gonna be able to do this." Anyway, that's how I got into acting.

GA: *So you also had some bit parts on things like Chips and Cheers?*

KW: Exactly, so it'd be little stuff like that, but there was really no work out there. And I moved out to L.A., then went back to New York, and Rob said that he was ready to come out to L.A., so we drove cross country together. We packed up all of his shit and drove cross country, dreaming the whole way. And we finally got to L.A., and we realized that if we were going to make it out here, we were going to have to do our own thing or we were just going out there to audition for bullshit. We would go to auditions and laugh. We'd get the material and say, "Yo, we don't even talk like this." And then for me it was the discovery that I wasn't Black enough for Hollywood. So here I am from the projects, ten kids, Tuskegee, my whole world was Black, and I get out here and I'm not Black enough. And they weren't looking for anybody with leading-man potential, because most of the roles were kind of sidekick roles and I'm taller than ninety percent of the people in Hollywood, so I'm not going to be anybody's costar who's five-seven. So Robert wanted to do more. He said, "I'm tired of this. I studied acting, was in the Negro Ensemble Company in New York, and I don't want to do this." That's when we decided to write our own movie. We didn't know how to write, but we knew how to perform, so we set up a video camera, laid out a bunch of clothes to represent each character, and then improvised the scene, and as we came up with something for a particular character we would put on that character's clothing. Then we'd watch it back, and the stuff that we thought was good we'd write down, and that's how we wrote our first script.

GA: *Very clever. And what was the first script that you and Robert wrote together?*

KW: The first thing that we did was a horror parody about five Black kids who get stuck in a horror house. We would go in and talk to producers about doing something with Black folks, and you could literally watch them get dizzy as you were saying, "And then it's five Black"... they'd just get dizzy on you. No one was looking for that, and between that and meeting the brothers in the industry who'd been doing it for a while, some of the old heads, they'd sit down with us [Laughing] and they'd be so bitter. I don't want to say this brother's name, but he got to talking about show business and he was so angry. He said [Impersonating old Black man], "Let me tell ya'll something. Yo, ya'll brothers trying to get ya'll thing off the ground? These motherfuckers got it locked, you understand me? They got this shit locked up and they ain't letting a nigger get a motherfucking thing." He was going off, and we were young cats.

GA: *He was one of those brothers who'd been stomped on so many times.*

KW: Oh, man, he had just been beaten into the earth. So Robert and I said that we have to make a movie on our own. And we made a commitment that we were going to do it. By hook or by crook, we were going to make a movie, and Robert came up with the brilliant idea of making a movie by using credit cards. And that's how we made Hollywood Shuffle. But the plan wasn't to do Hollywood Shuffle as a movie, the plan was to do a few short movies so Robert could put a reel together as a director and show people that he could direct and then go back and try to get the money for the horror movie, thinking that we could show them that we knew what we were doing. So after about four or five of these short films, we realized we had a movie, and that's when we decided to write the story for Hollywood Shuffle, but we had written the vignettes first—the Black acting school and the homeboys in the theater and all that. Then we started to write the story. By that time, we were better writers and we were able to put the script together.

GA: *And did you have any idea that around the same time you were doing Hollywood Shuffle (1987), Spike was doing She's Gotta Have It (1986) and that you all were creating a Black movement in film?*

KW: Now, that's the other thing. It was like the thing with the comedian Byron Allen, and somebody said that there was a guy in New York named Spike Lee who'd kind of done the same thing that we did and so we wanted to see what his flick was about. And a few months before Hollywood Shuffle came out, She's Gotta Have It debuted and we went to see the movie and met Spike, and that was sort of the beginning of a new filmmaking movement.

GA: *Then you directed your first film, the blaxploitation parody I'm Gonna Get You Sucka. What inspired that film?*

KW: That came about because Hollywood Shuffle didn't really give me exposure—it gave Robert exposure, and rightly so. I didn't mind that he got the attention, I just didn't like the fact that I didn't get any.

GA: *Why did he end up directing Hollywood Shuffle?*

KW: He wanted to direct, and at that point directing was not a big deal for me, but then I realized that as a director that's where it's at. So I decided to do my own thing, and that's when I came up with I'm Gonna Get You Sucka, which was based on the movies from my generation that I loved, like Airplane. Airplane was one of my favorites, and when I decided to sit down to write a movie I said that I was going to write my version of Airplane. I came up with that, and how I got to direct the film was funny. I took it to a few places, and everyone thought the script was real funny and they said, "Well, who are we going to get to direct it?" And I said that I wanted to direct it, and they said, "Aw, you've never directed a film," and I asked them who were they going to get. And they just scratched their heads and they couldn't think of any white director they could trust. They mentioned Spike Lee and Robert, and I said, "Well, they've only done one movie." And they said, "Yeah, well, you've got a point there." [Laughs]

GA: [Laughs]

KW: So by default I got to direct, because there was no one else out there to do it. But I'm Gonna Get You Sucka is the movie that wasn't supposed to be. I didn't know this, but the only reason UA [MGM/UA today] made it was because they had another movie with Kevin Kline called January Man that they didn't want to give to Fox because Fox had the video rights. That was back in the day when theatrical and video rights were typically handled by separate companies. So they didn't want to give Fox that one, they were going to give Fox I'm Gonna Get You Sucka and they were going to keep January Man, so they figured they'd make this movie, give it just enough of a release so that they could say they put it out there and then give it to Fox. So it was never supposed to see the light of day, and I didn't know this, and what happened was, after the movie was made and I saw the campaign for it, it was the shittiest campaign I've ever seen in my life. The poster for I'm Gonna Get You Sucka was a drawing. I was sitting there thinking, "What are ya'll doing?" They showed me the trailer, and it was just mumbo jumbo, you couldn't understand it. It was just image after image of nothing. It was horrible, and they said, "Oh, no, no, we think it's great, we've tested it." And this shit sucks and I'm just livid and there's nothing I can do. Then I saw that they were going to release the movie in five markets, but not New York and not L.A. The first release was in Atlanta, D.C., Philly, Chicago and Detroit.

GA: The studio didn't plan to open the film in New York? That's insane.

KW: Not New York, so it was those five markets, and if they spent five hundred thousand dollars on publicity, that was a lot. I went on the road to every single one of those cities, did the press, and the movie opens at Christmas, of all times, and they're waiting for it to just go in the toilet. Well, in those five markets the film comes in second, right behind Arnold Schwarzenegger and Danny DeVito's movie Twins, and the shock at the studio is unreal, because now they're making money so they don't want to dump the film. They say, "Okay, we're going to try New York. Let's see what happens in New York." This movie January Man opened the same weekend, they were on about 800 screens and we were on about 200 screens, and they made $1.9 million and we made $6 million. So they gave Fox January Man and they kept I'm Gonna Get You Sucka. [Laughs] When I came back to L.A. the guy just looked at me and begrudgingly said, "Yeah, well, I guess you got a hit."

GA: *"Yeah, I have a hit and the rest is history." What was your approach to directing, given that you had never directed before?*
KW: My whole philosophy about everything in life, and I tell my kids this all the time, this ain't rocket science. I'll be intimidated if you ask me to design a spaceship. I gotta know some shit to do that. There are people who direct movies who have more experience than I do, so I need to learn what they know and that was my approach. I took some classes down at Los Angeles Community College [LACC] just to get an understanding, because I was comfortable with the performance aspect. I knew I could do that, I knew I could communicate to the actors in terms of what I wanted them to do. The only thing for me to learn was the camera.

GA: *Do you think it's important for aspiring directors to engage in some level of film study?*
KW: Oh, absolutely. I don't care what you do, you want to study. Learn your business—that's the first thing I tell people, learn your business—and my philosophy about learning is about acquiring knowledge. When I went to LACC, I wasn't worried about grades. I took no tests. I just went to class to learn. I didn't care what grade they gave me, I wasn't there for that, so I didn't stress myself with tests and all that. I went there specifically to acquire knowledge. And I would go to workshops specifically to acquire knowledge. That's the thing, always pursue knowledge. Even today, before I sit and write any movie, I watch every movie in that genre and I study to see what they did right and what they did wrong.

GA: *What films did you watch to prepare for I'm Gonna Get You Sucka?*
KW: Every Black exploitation movie ever made, as well as Airplane, Kentucky Fried Movie, all of the Mel Brooks films.

GA: *Blazing Saddles?*
KW: Yeah, I watched all of the good parodies, so I learned, and all the questions I had were answered by just studying. I'm a firm believer in studying.

GA: The thing about comedy is that it's the most difficult genre, because either we laugh . . .

KW: Or you don't.

GA: How do you know when your work is funny?

KW: Doing stand-up comedy was the best training, because in stand-up comedy the audience doesn't laugh at what you think is funny, they laugh at what they think is funny. Many times you write a joke and you think it's brilliant, but it goes like this: If they don't get it, it ain't funny. So you have to know what references are relatable. For example, if you go on stage and you say, "All mothers," or you just go, "Mothers are strange," or you say, "You know what mothers do? They do blah, blah, blah." When you do that, you make the audience sit there and think, "My mother don't do that, hmm." Now, if I go on stage and I say, "My mother did this and my mother did that," then people go, "Oh, yeah, my mother does that too." And it's because I haven't told them what their mother does. I'm talking about my mother, I'm being specific so they don't feel like their mother's in any jeopardy. They only include their mother when they want to. So that's audience psychology that you only learn having gone on stage and done those kind of jokes and knowing when I phrase it this way I can feel the audience rear back, whereas if I phrase it this way I see them do this [moves forward], and so having that as a training ground and doing that for ten years, I still go do stand-up—I go to Laugh Factory, Improv or Comedy Store—that's where I learned my fundamentals. My comedy has always been about an audience, not about me. What I think is funny is irrelevant. When I see filmmakers who get self-indulgent, I just scratch my head because I don't understand. If you don't make a movie for an audience, then you can't be mad if they don't go see it. Filmmakers get so upset if you don't go see their films, because they think they did such great work. Well, you didn't make it for the audience. You disregarded the audience throughout the whole film. It's like cars. If you make a car that doesn't address the needs of the consumer, they don't buy the car. It's the same thing with a movie.

GA: That's a great analogy. It just goes back to understanding the commerciality of your product.

KW: Exactly. Robert Townsend taught me that. He said, "You are the commodity you have to sell. That's what people are buying—you."

GA: What makes good comedy? Is it good jokes, parody, exaggeration?

KW: Wow, it's a lot of things, but if you have great characters and a decent story, you have a good movie. And again, when I first started making movies, I was never really concerned about camera movement and all that. I would tell people if the characters are great and the story is good, the movie could look like shit and it would still be a good movie. I can make the best-looking movie in the world, and if the characters suck and if the story sucks, the movie sucks. People don't care about the look of a film, they're worried about the human interaction in the film, the emotional experience, the realness of the characters and if it has a fresh element to it. Those are the things that make a good movie.

GA: *How do you get good performances out of your actors?*
KW: Well, I like fresher faces, that's who I prefer to work with, because they have no bad habits and I will help them create their character. I'll give them assignments. I give them a list of questions to answer about their character's background and who they are and what their favorite TV shows are and what they carry in their purse. When Jada [Pinkett Smith] and I did *A Low Down Dirty Shame*, we created the character Peaches. You could ask Jada anything about Peaches and she could give you an answer. Peaches was a real person, and during the shooting there'd be times I would have to tell her, "No, no, no, you're doing this as Jada—remember, this is Peaches." She created a great character.

GA: *Now tell me about* In Living Color, *which was such a major TV hit.*
KW: Well, after *I'm Gonna Get You Sucka* we had an industry screening of the movie and they said the people from Fox were coming down. They called the next day and said that they wanted to have a meeting, so I went into the meeting thinking that they wanted to do some more movies, and they said, "We want you to do a TV show." And I told them that I didn't want to do TV, and they said, "Well, before you say no, we want you to know that you can do whatever kind of show you want to do." I told them about a show like *In Living Color* that would be like *Saturday Night Live*, but a little edgier with more of an urban flavor to it, and they were down for that. So I started to work on the idea a little bit more, and they wanted to do a pilot. We did the pilot, they loved it, but they were scared. We knew we had something, because when we did certain sketches we heard laughter like we hadn't heard before. When Damon [Wayans] and David Alan Grier did their "Men On Film" skit, people were stomping their feet, howling, and we said, "Yo, we're onto something here." That same night I did Mike Tyson, and it was like a nuclear bomb had gone off in the room. The chairman sat down with me and said, "We're really worried about this, but what we want to do is that we want to go in easy." They wanted to take out "Men on Film" and some other sketches, like "The Homeboy Shopping Network." And I said, "Listen, if I'm gonna fail, I wanna go out like a trooper. Ain't no need in hemming and hawing. I want people to know what this is, and they're either going to like it or they're not." They finally gave in, aired the pilot and it was huge. The rest is history.

GA: Did you have any idea you were creating megastars like Jim Carey?

KW: When I put the show together, my plan was to find the most talented people that no one knew what to do with, and Jim Carey was one of those people. I'd seen Jim when he was an impressionist, which is how he started out, and he was brilliant, and then he gave that up and started doing comedy and you could tell this guy was talented. My brother Damon was the baddest stand-up out there, he was off the chain and they didn't know what to do with him. As a matter of fact, he and Jim did a horrible movie together called *Earth Girls Are Easy* (1989). And I wondered, "Is this what ya'll do with people with this kind of talent?" So I went after all the people that I knew were funny and who nobody was doing anything with, and that was Jim, Damon and David Alan Grier, who had worked with me on *I'm Gonna Get You Sucka*, plus my sister Kim, and a lot of them were family members. I went to Chicago and found T'Keyah "Crysta" Keymāh doing theater, and Kelly Coffield was also doing theater in Chicago, and so I put this little ensemble together and it rocked. These people were already stars; *In Living Color* was their showcase.

GA: Tell me all about Scary Movie and how you got involved in that.

KW: Well, *Scary Movie* came after *Don't Be a Menace to South Central While Drinkin' Your Juice in the Hood*.

GA: Menace is hilarious. Even my dad, who is in his seventies, found that movie funny.

KW: That's from the minds of the little ones—Marlon and Shawn. They came to me with the script, and I read their first draft and there was stuff in there that made me laugh really hard, and I sat down and I told them that they had something but I had to teach them how to write. It was like reading the script that Robert and I had written our first time. So I had to teach them how to write, and it took about ten drafts before they got it to where it was a real movie, and then we took it to Island Pictures and they made the film. And that was their *I'm Gonna Get You Sucka*. It was the right time, it was the right voice—I thought it was a very funny little movie.

GA: You demonstrate a strong understanding of parody in all of your films, whether it's parodying teen horror flicks with Scary Movie or hood films with Don't Be a Menace. What's the trick to good parody?

KW: You have to let parody come to you, you can't just say that you're going to do a parody of something. What happens in parody is, first there is a good movie, then there are fifty bad versions of that movie, and when the audience is tired of seeing those films, then that genre's right for parody. Like we had *Boyz 'N the Hood*, which was a great movie, then *Menace II Society* came and it was a good film, but took *Boyz 'N the Hood* one step further. Then there was *South Central*, and then they just kept coming and they had inundated the audience with one style of film over and over again, and they were sick of it. So it was ripe for parody, and Scary Movie was the same thing except it was the one that sort of broadened our audience because it allowed it to be cross-cultural. Everyone has seen horror movies, and these movies weren't just geared towards white kids or Black kids. Everybody has seen horror films, so it organically crossed us over without our trying.

You can't try to cross over, it'll just happen. Crossing over is a difficult thing to do as an African American filmmaker—not necessarily as a star, but as a filmmaker. It's hard. I remember when we were doing Low Down Dirty Shame and the studio head at the time asked me if I would consider casting a white girl in the role Salli Richardson played. And I said to him that I can't be on screen with a white woman, because if I do that, the sisters ain't coming. I can't do that, and his thing was that if you don't do that the white folks ain't coming, and he was right. So you're in a catch-22. You can't alienate your audience, but at the same time you can't alienate the mainstream audience, so you have to figure out ways to bring them both together, and what Scary Movie taught me more than anything was that if we as Black filmmakers do it right, we can have it all. You can't compromise telling a Black story, so if you're going to do that you understand the world that you work in. The frustration comes from our wanting to make our movies, but then wanting our movies to have the same level of success as a mainstream film, and the truth is that they're not mainstream. They aren't interested in stories about the Black experience. They don't care, they just don't care, and the sooner you understand that, the better.

GA: [Laughs] So no one really wants to really hear all the details about our experiences.
KW: Yeah, there's nothing you're gonna do to change that, and Hispanics and Asians have the same problem. We are not the dominant culture, and they do not care, so understand that and don't get frustrated when your movies don't perform the way the mainstream films do. Don't get frustrated when the studio system doesn't give your film the same support. You have to understand what you're doing and accept the consequences that come with that. Now, if you want to move into the mainstream, then what you have to do is start to make genre pictures—not Black, not white, but genre. And in doing that, it will allow you to have the best of both worlds.

GA: Such as Antoine Fuqua doing an action film like Training Day.
KW: Exactly. Training Day is a perfect example—it's a genre movie, and you're not caught up in what color this person or that person is, it's not about that. There's a white character and a Black character with equal status, and you don't feel like you're going into each individual world racially, it's only emotionally that you're traveling in the different worlds. So Antoine did a great job with that movie,

but if you cast that movie with two Black cops, it becomes a Black movie. So you have to learn to tell stories with Black people in them, not Black movies, but movies with Blacks in them.

GA: *Such as* Scary Movie. *How did that project come about? I know Marlon and Shawn wrote it, but tell me about the process.*
KW: Marlon and Shawn wrote it on spec and I developed it, and we took it to Miramax. Marlon and Shawn had a deal with Miramax after *Don't Be a Menace*, because the movie was made by Island but distributed by Miramax, and then Miramax liked that movie so much that they wanted to make another movie with them, and *Scary Movie* was that movie.

GA: *Did you have any idea that* Scary Movie *would be so successful?*
KW: Again, it was like one of those things where you knew you were sitting on something but you didn't know how big it was going to be. And it just felt good at the screenings. There was that same kind of laughter that just made you say, "Okay, we've got something here."

GA: *You really pushed the envelope with* Scary Movie *and with the sequel.*
KW: Well, the truth is that we saw *There's Something About Mary* and said, "Okay, so they're going there now." We felt like the Farrelly Brothers took what we did one step further, so we said that we're going to take it another step further, so we did.

GA: *With all of your success with* Scary Movie, *has it given you more power in Hollywood?*
KW: I think it does to some degree, but we're all powerless.

GA: *You really believe that?*
KW: Absolutely, and the frustration is that everyone else thinks that you're so powerful.

GA: *Who's powerless?*
KW: Everybody in Hollywood is powerless—the only people with the power are the people with the money. I don't care who the filmmaker is, if the studios want to shut you down tomorrow, you won't make another movie.

GA: *Black, white, whatever?*
KW: Black, white, green, blue, you don't have any power in this town because you don't own anything in this town, you're not financing anything. There are people who in the context of making

movies have more clout than other people, people who get the job first, people who get the best material, people who can get higher budgets, things of that nature.

GA: *Have you seen that to be the case for you now that you have demonstrated success with the Scary Movie franchise?*
KW: Yeah, yeah, I mean, I would be considered for jobs that they probably wouldn't have considered me for before. I'm getting ready to do this movie called *Bell Boy* with Jackie Chan, and that probably wouldn't have been the kind of movie I'd have done.

GA: *So doors open, but that doesn't mean they can't shut you out if they want to?*
KW: Exactly. Understand that for sure opportunities come and that's all positive, but the illusion that you can become powerful and can change the system is the thing that has haunted and damned Black filmmakers from day one.

GA: *How so?*
KW: For example, when it comes to the media, some people don't know the business and they write about it in this idealistic way in which you can only fail. You can only fail. Since day one, and I'm not the only person, but I've never, ever seen Black media be supportive, and those are the only ones you can expect to be supportive. I have not seen them support anybody. And it's mind-boggling to us as filmmakers, because you just sit and think, "Wow, I'm catching more hell from over here."

GA: *Can you talk about what you mean specifically? Because some Black publications are supportive.*
KW: What happens is that in their jobs nobody wants a fluff piece from the writers, they want controversy. So they're trying to appease their bosses, so we [Black filmmakers] become something to write about, but they don't understand the damage that's being done by them taking negative spins on everything that we do. I can give you a great example. Let's take a movie like *I'm Gonna Get You Sucka.* When you leave here, I want you to get on your computer and pull up the reviews on *I'm Gonna Get You Sucka,* and what you will see is a movie that is a parody—that's all it is, it's a parody—it's a Black *Airplane,* and it is so politicized in the Black press that you would have thought that I [Laughs] had done a movie about the revolution.

GA: *So do you think you're damned if you do and damned if you don't?*
KW: You're damned if you do and you're damned if you don't. That has been the ball and chain.

GA: *Why do you think that attitude seems to exist in the Black media?*

KW: Well, like I said, because these writers have jobs, they're not writing independently, they have jobs and they have to answer to someone, and it's part of the institution of racism. The media is one of those institutions that constantly reinforms, and so it becomes an opportunity to assign blame in the wrong places—so now you can blame Spike Lee for crack?

GA: *Because Sam Jackson's character was a crackhead in Jungle Fever?*

KW: Yeah, you gonna blame Spike Lee for that? It's like, wait a minute, what are you talking about? And it's only allowed with us. It's only allowed to be presented that way with us.

GA: *Do you think that the Black intelligentsia and the Black media sometimes don't understand the dynamics at play in the industry?*

KW: Know what it is? They naively have expectations of people because they don't know the business. I remember sitting on a panel with Stanley Crouch, and I could see a revelation happen with him when I was talking about the neutralization of race in movies. And I mean that we as Black filmmakers have to learn how to neutralize race if we ever expect to have the same level of success in this business as whites. We have to get out of making Black movies, because if we don't, you're damned to go back into nonexistence, because the market share just keeps shrinking, and you have to approach this as a business. What happens is everybody is pointing you in the wrong direction. They're telling you that you're going to change the world, and you're not. You're going to make a movie, that's all you're going to do, you're not going to change the world. If there were a movie that could change this world, it would have been made before. They've been making movies for a hundred years now. Everybody who comes into this, especially if they're Black, comes in because they tell you the same story over and over again, you're going to change it, and what happens is they don't make changes, they don't have success, and they go into oblivion and you never see them again, and if we don't neutralize this and start to approach this as the business that it is, we won't have success. And I said to Crouch what I said to you: "They don't care." See, everybody is acting on the premise that you actually have a room full of people that you can go to and say, "You know what? I need $50 million to make the quintessential Black epic."

GA: [Laughs]

KW: That will display us as the princely people that we are and that there is a white man who will say, "Yes, that's the movie that hasn't been made, that will change our world. Yes, you go do that." They don't care.

GA: That's not happening?

KW: It's never going to happen, and you're not going to get Bill Cosby and Oprah Winfrey and Spike Lee and Keenen Wayans and Eddie Murphy to put their money together and make that movie either.

GA: Why isn't that going to happen? That must be the number-one Black film panel question.

KW: Because they will go broke, because they're making a movie to change the world, they're not making a movie that's going to make some money.

GA: Which is why you're in the business in the first place.

KW: Exactly, so that ain't going to happen.

GA: And, of course, there's no guarantee that the Black audience is going to go see a Black epic anyway.

KW: Exactly, because we're not going to see it, and once you understand all this as a writer, then you understand the filmmaker has limitations. For example, if I'm given $2 million dollars to make a movie, let's put all of the $2 million movies on the table and then talk about my $2 million movie. Don't take my $2 million movie and compare it to a $120 million movie, because I didn't have $120 million. So the naïveté of the intellectual and all their hope and expectations of what can be achieved through art is wrong, and the moment they understand that and lift that ball and chain off of filmmakers' backs, then people will be allowed to go out and think like entrepreneurs. This is show business, it's not show politics, it's show business. Steven Spielberg can make *Schindler's List* because Steven Spielberg made *E.T., Jurassic Park, Jaws*, etc., you know what I mean? The man is the most prolific blockbuster-making filmmaker in the world, so if he wants to take a little rest and go make a movie that's important to him, that speaks to his culture, nobody's going to say anything. They're going to say, "Steve, if you made me $50 billion and you want to go spend $60 million, go 'head. Matter of fact, we're going to give you an Oscar for that."

GA: Are you saying that you have to look at things in the overall context of what's happening?

KW: Yeah, right, so that's the reality of my business, and if we start to think entrepreneurially and really start to study this business and start to make classic films that represent all of Americana and with our vision and talents behind them, that's when we will see prosperity from this business. We won't be sitting around bitter and angry and not enjoying what we do, because you can see it—the bitterness. I still go to all the Black filmmaker conferences, I stay in the mix and I can see it. I can see people with all of this on them. They can't figure out how to get out of that box, they can't figure it out because they're doing the wrong thing. But also show business is no different than any other facet of American society.

GA: *So in terms of the survival of Black film, do Black filmmakers have to start making films with more mass appeal?*

KW: You have to get in the business, and you know there will be people who'll disagree with me, call it selling out or whatever. Get in the business, you're in show business—if you're going to be in this business, be in it to win. That's how a Black studio becomes real. When Black movies make billions of dollars around the world, that's when the financing will come. It doesn't matter how many of these little slice-of-life movies we make that you think are going to help you purge your pain. That's not putting asses in seats, and it's not gonna build anything. We have to make a business out of it. That's why we're so dominant in the music business. Ain't nobody writing folk songs.

GA: *That's the reality.*

KW: That's not what's selling records, hip-hop is king of the world right now, and as a result you have hip-hop moguls. You have guys like Russell Simmons, Puffy and Master P, and guys who actually own record labels, who can launch stars and clothing lines, and that's an industry.

GA: *Do you see that happening in Black cinema at some point?*

KW: If we wake up. Yes, absolutely, if we take the chip off our shoulder and understand the business we're in and take advantage of it and utilize the skills and creativity that we have, absolutely, absolutely. Look, Spike Lee can stand on par with any other director in his world, there ain't nobody out there who Spike can't fuck with. So can it be done? Absolutely. I'm on top of my game. Give me the best comedy directors out there, I feel like I can hang with any of them.

GA: *You always want to stay in comedy? Have you thought about sci-fi, drama?*

KW: I want to do all of them, add a little flavor to them, you know what I mean?

GA: *And who are some of your greatest creative influences?*

KW: In the past I would have said Mel Brooks and the Zucker brothers. Richard Pryor was my primary comedic influence. Currently, I have great appreciation for Ridley Scott—I think he is a great filmmaker. Steven Spielberg, now that I've come to appreciate how blockbusters are made.

GA: How are they made?

KW: Well, it's simple. They appeal to classic Americana, that's across the board, that's not color, that's cultural. It's the culture we all live in, but there are classic elements in that culture, there are certain songs. If you look at a movie like Risky Business or you look at a movie like The Big Chill, listen to the music that's in those movies, not just the score, but if they choose to use a piece of music, it's always classic.

GA: Like source music—music that comes from a radio, a band or TV within a scene in the film.

KW: Right, but usually what they do is they have a little thing playing in a montage or somebody's singing along or whatever, but it's very calculated. What we do with the soundtrack is like some bumping shit. You're doing this [demonstrates bopping his head à la urban music videos]. But that's not classic, that's not a song that's here to stay, that's what's happening now. The music that they [mainstream filmmakers] use is evergreen, and the themes, the emotional chords, that are struck are calculated.

GA: That reminds me of The Royal Tennenbaums. They used the "Peanuts" Christmas song. It really affected me emotionally and reminded me of my childhood.

KW: Sure.

GA: Are movies magical?

KW: Movies are absolutely magical, they are a magical two-hour experience, it's a two-hour fantasy trip, but that's all they are. Movies don't change the world—I don't care how good a movie is or what your experience is when you see it, when you walk out of that theater, you walk back into the real world. That movie is gone. So they're magical, but only for two hours.

GA: Do you see movies as just entertainment?

KW: It's a ride at Disneyland, that's all it is.

GA: Some would argue that movies shape images, shape perceptions around the world of who we are as a people and culture.

KW: And I say to them that's not what they do, because people know the difference between reality and fantasy. News and information shape people's perception of you around the world, you understand? Not a movie. The reason that we have a fear of Black people in America is not based on a film, it's based on the fact that every time you watch the news that Black face is associated with something heinous. Every time you see a murder, that's the face you see, every time you see a robbery, that's the face you see, every time you see a rape, that's the face you see. That's why you lock your door when I walk past your window, not because you saw me in a movie. People know that a movie is make-believe, they know that a TV show is make-believe. Again, that's the intellectuals living in denial, because like I said, the key to it is denial. You see, when people want to place blame in the wrong place, they can't accept the reality. The reality is that these are not the things that shape the views of people around the world. They're just movies. So maybe before CNN was global and somebody saw a film from America, I can see you saying that, but that's not how people get their information anymore. Twenty-four hours a day they're watching CNN—that's how people get their information.

GA: *What about the Black images in music videos? There's lots of criticism there.*

KW: Here's what I think. I think that the more negative impact is on us and not people's perception of us. I look at a music video and I worry more about my little girls aspiring to be like the girls in the videos. I worry more about our kids accepting some of the negativity that is put out there as their reality. But then, whenever I get into that head space, I think back to when I was a kid and none of those things shaped who I was. I didn't go to movies and come out thinking I was going to be Superfly. My influences were my household, my family, my mother and my father, people in my community.

GA: *The Black community needs more parents like yours.*

KW: Yeah, but my mother and father are sort of that last generation, and what they did was nothing compared to what their parents did. We're talking about folks who came up from Alabama with the Jim Crow laws. Our generation, following my parents' generation, is the generation of privilege. We have some burdens, but we have nothing compared to what they had to deal with, especially in terms of forming our sense of self-identity. We have a greater sense of equality than at any other time in history, but we don't take advantage of it.

GA: *Good point.*

KW: And again, it's not movies, it ain't movies, it ain't television shows, it ain't music, it's really mothers and fathers, and if people focus on their home and their children, that's what's gonna shape them as people, and like I said, whenever I start to cringe while watching a music video or listening to a song or something like that, I just think back to when I was that age and I think, "Okay, did that stuff influence me?" It didn't. It didn't make me who I am.

GA: It goes back to what you said about family structure. That's really the big ingredient that's missing.

KW: Yes, that's true, it's the family. When the kids don't have a father, then they will turn to other things for that father image, whether it be a guy in the neighborhood or a screen idol. And I come from a school of hard knocks. It was no easy route, but I don't regret a day of it because I know the realities of everything, so when I talk about stuff, I'm speaking from experience.

GA: You like working with family obviously. Tell me about that.

KW: You know the African proverb "It takes a village to raise a child"? Well, it takes a family to build a dynasty, you know?

GA: You Wayanses are just amazing. The kind of genius that can come out of one family is incredible.

KW: But see, everybody can do it. It just requires that you be a family. What is family about? You're given a family for a reason. It's about trying to build something. My feeling is that if I do all this and the next generation or generation after that is back in the projects, then I haven't done anything. I want our success to be generational; I don't ever want my family to go back to that.

Warrington Hudlin

first met Warrington Hudlin in the early nineties at a Black Filmmaker Foundation Saturday-afternoon workshop at NYU. As a banker, I cherished the moments in those sessions in which people like the actors Sonia Braga and Dennis Green spoke, because they gave me a chance to interact with artists and other emerging filmmakers. And Warrington made it all possible.

A native of East St. Louis, Illinois, Warrington has been at the forefront of Black cinema for more than two decades. As the president and one of the founders of the Black Filmmaker Foundation (BFF), he has consistently helped bring a public awareness to the relevance and critical nature of Black film to the world, perhaps more than any other individual. Through BFF he has showcased some of the works of some of America's most successful Black filmmakers, including Spike Lee, Charles Lane, Julie Dash and Kasi Lemmons. As the curator and cofounder of the Acapulco Black Film Festival (1997–2001), Hudlin premiered feature films by the next generation of Black independent filmmakers.

In 1999 Hudlin launched dvRepublic.com as a project of BFF. The project is designed as an online community interested in more socially conscious yet entertaining film and television programming.

As a filmmaker, Warrington is best known as the producer of the hit films directed by his younger brother Reginald—House Party (1990), Boomerang (1992) and Bebe's Kids (1992). Warrington is a graduate of Yale University.

GA: *Tell me about Warrington and the genesis of you as a creative person.*

WH: Who I am as a creative artist is an absolute result of where I'm from and who I'm from. I'm from what I consider the Blackest city in the United States, East St. Louis , Illinois, and it's a place of very depressing economic and social statistics, but very rich culturally. People who I share the Greater East St. Louis area with range from Miles Davis, Chuck Berry, and Thomas Dorsey [who really took a new direction to Black Christian music by creating gospel], Ike and Tina Turner and my brother Reginald. So it's a place of tremendous cultural richness. It's a blues town, a jazz town, an R&B town and a gospel town, so all of that served as an incredible artistic incubator. So all that was really brought to another level when the dancer Katherine Dunham in the 1960s brought her performing arts training center to East St. Louis. A group of Black scholars and academics were funded by the state university to create an autonomous Black-controlled educational program. It covered the last two years of high school and first two years in college. In high school it was under the umbrella of Upward Bound, and in college it was called Experiment in Higher Education. And the people who put that program together were like the who's who of Black scholarship and intellectual work. People like the poet Eugene Redman, the social critic Shelby Steele, the author Henry Dumas, the poet Quincy Troup and the painter Oliver Jackson would lecture there, and of course Katherine Dunham ran the arts and culture curriculum.

What that meant for me as a teenager was that I was exposed to an understanding of the world larger than where I was living. I was learning Yoruba and Woolof, learning how to play Haitian and Senegalese drums, and understanding not only Black dance but the roots of Black dance, because Dunham was also an anthropologist. So if you learned a dance, if you learned the drums, you had an understanding of the anthropological roots of all that. Later, when I got to college at Yale and studied Afro-Am studies, I was already familiar with what they were teaching because I had this incredible privilege of being prepared by these extraordinary mentors. That is why when you understand the kind of education I had, it explains where I'm from and who I'm from.

GA: *Wasn't your great-grandfather someone who contributed to the race in a big way?*

WH: To fully explain who you are from it is important that you trace back as far as you can go. My father Warrington was an insurance broker [he was the first Black in the East St. Louis area to represent a major insurance company]. His father, Edward Hudlin, was first a jockey then a stone-mason and a contractor. He learned this particular type of masonry called rubble stone that was unique. No one else did it but him, and if you go around East St. Louis now and look around on the streets you'll see what he built—it's a very distinct style. Interestingly enough, my grandfather's brother went to the University of Chicago and ended up being one of Arthur Ashe's tennis mentors, and when Ashe left Virginia he lived with my grand uncle in St. Louis and finished high school there, so he could coach him in tennis. My great-grandfather, Richard Hudlin, Sr., was a journalist, a playwright, and based on recent research I've seen, was one of the first Black filmmakers ever, certainly among the first five or ten. And his father escaped from a slave plantation in Virginia in the 1830s, married into the Cherokee Nation and with two brothers became very active in the Underground Railroad.

GA: *As a child, did you know that you'd do something creative as a result of your early exposure to the arts?*
WH: No. By the time I got to Yale, it was at the end of the Black consciousness movement and all my aspirations were revolutionary. During my freshman year Bobby Seale was on trial two blocks from my dorm room, so I'm absolutely sure that in the same way that where I'm from and who I'm from produced me, the times also produced me. I was old enough to be aware of the revolution of the sixties, but too young to participate. So I couldn't join the Panthers, but I would see them, and that has totally shaped my conscience. I saw a period when Black men just stood up and were ready to set it off.

GA: *And why do you think that changed?*
WH: They were repressed by the government. We didn't change, we got beat up. There were a whole lot of bodies, a whole lot of conspiracies, the whole COINTELPRO program is now common knowledge; it was a government-funded program to destabilize these movements—to destroy them.

GA: *When did you decide that you wanted go into filmmaking?*
WH: Two things happened. When I was a senior in high school—you know in high school how you always take these field trips—well, they took us over to St. Louis to a preview screening of *Shaft*, and I thought, "Wow, this is great." As I was leaving the theater, there was a man in the lobby signing autographs. I looked at the guy, I didn't recognize him from the film, so I'm saying, "Why is he signing autographs? He's not a movie star." And our field trip leader said, "Oh, he's the director of the movie. That's Gordon Parks." I said, "Whoa, Black folks make movies?" It just never occurred to me. Then, a year later, when I was in college, I went to see this movie called *Sweet Sweetback's Badaaasss Song*. It so blew my mind that at the end of the movie I said, "Oh, not only

can we make movies, but we can change the content of the movies," because Mel Van Peebles completely just blew up Hollywood conventions both stylistically and in terms of content. So after seeing *Sweetback* was when I said, "I've gotta do this."

GA: *Once you decided to pursue film, who other than Van Peebles were your film inspirations and heroes at the time?*
WH: Once I resolved to become a filmmaker and began taking courses it was in one of those early courses that I first encountered films by Akira Kurosawa. I was perhaps a sophomore in college and looking at this Kurosawa film, *Ikiru*, and I said, "My God, I didn't know movies could do this." I was virtually speechless. Kurosawa is such a profound transcendental artist. If I could be half as good as he is, I would be happy.

GA: *He does amazing stuff, and his humanity comes across.*
WH: Exactly, which is the whole point of it.

GA: *I'd like to talk about the Black Filmmaker Foundation [BFF], which you founded in 1978 because BFF is such a leader and in a way put Black cinema on the map in an organized fashion. Can you talk about how and why you started the organization?*
WH: Sure, it became clear that there were institutional racist barriers limiting Black cinematic work, and I said that one way to combat institutional racism was with another institution. So we created an institution that would overcome those barriers, not with protest, but through self-reliance. I'd made two films that distributors wouldn't touch—*Street Corner Series* and *Black at Yale*, and I knew whenever I showed the films people loved them. But the distributors said that there was no market so I started my own distribution company for those two films, and I realized that the promotional work for two films, you could do for twenty films. So I went to all of my colleagues who were in the same boat and I said, "Why don't we form a cooperative and put all of our films in one catalogue and market them?" That was one of the first programs of the Black Filmmaker Foundation—this cooperative.

Simultaneously, we said that in order to bring attention to our films we needed a film festival, so in 1979 we started a program that ran for five years called "Dialogue for Black Filmmakers." It was a summer program in which we would show films in New York and have discussions. I got the idea to create this type of exhibition after seeing a Cuban film called *For the First Time*, in which the Cuban government sent filmmakers to the mountains to show films to people who didn't have access to cinemas. I said that in a way Black people don't have access to cinema—not because of geography, but it's more of an issue of content.

Following that same concept as the Cubans, I took my films into the streets. Literally, we went to 125th Street, put a sheet up on a wall and showed films. We showed films in church basements, discotheques, roller-skating rinks, karate dojos. We were totally grassroots, and we were able to organize all the filmmakers who were frustrated. We did that for five years, and it became an annual festival where people knew they could see the work of a new generation of Black filmmakers. This led to the BFF administering an educational film distribution service. That was the focus for the first ten years of operation, and then we decided to become less filmmaker focused and more audience focused, so we started a membership program. I think we had more than three thousand members, and that also became a way to support the organization—through membership—as opposed to always begging for grants, which was always political.

This latest incarnation of BFF was formed in 1999. As we move to face our third decade, we see new opportunities with the Internet, so we've created this new program called dvRepublic.com. This is where we will fight the latest round of the battle to bypass the gatekeepers by moving to cyberspace. BFF came into existence because we were locked out, so now twenty-five years later we've found another way to break those barriers.

GA: I'm excited to hear more about dvRepublic. So you're looking to do original work?
WH: Mmm-hmm. The intent is to run socially conscious and entertainment-driven content. That's the mandate.

GA: What do you mean when you say socially conscious?
WH: When I say socially conscious, I don't mean ideological. On our Web site we have a series called "The Breech," which is done by a dancer/choreographer-turned-filmmaker, and what she's done through dance is choreograph on real locations. She's created this narrative from the point of view of a child. We're working with comedy writer Stephan Dweck, best known for the book *Snaps*. He's working on an animated political sketch comedy series like *In Living Color*, but probably with more of a political edge. There's also a Latino drama trilogy we did called *Once Upon a Ride* that again is episodic, and it follows this livery cabdriver named Moses, who is Puerto Rican. Each episode he picks up a person, you get in the cab, you start talking and he gives some flashback about some story that has some social relevance. Those are three examples of the kind of things they're doing in the BFF DV Lab. BFF also produces an event called the BFF Summit, which is an exclusive, closed-door, off-the-record retreat for the highest-ranking filmmakers and executives of color and industry leaders. So the ball is constantly moving.

GA: *You've been a part of the Black film movement for some time now. What makes a film Black?*

WH: That came up because when we were first putting together the Acapulco Black Film Festival (1997–2001), I was challenged by saying, "Why can't this movie be in, and why can't that movie be in?" And I said that BFF has a long-standing working definition of what a Black movie is and it always centers around the concept and the importance of authorship. One of the problems that Black people have had is that we're always talked about, we're always defined, described and depicted by people outside of our community. So I said that to call it Black, it's not Black because it is about us, it has to be by us. And "us" means that either the director is Black or the writer and the producer in combination are Black—that's our criteria. And I think that that criteria is reasonable, because anytime you're trying to promote an industry you do that. Why do you think we have those "Made in America" tags in your clothes? It's a way every nation—and we're a nation within a nation—protects itself by promoting awareness of their product. So by using the definition we are doing just that. And most importantly, it means that we're no longer just the subject matter, one difference being [at] the Acapulco festival and other popular film festivals around the country was the film selection. They may have many more films on their schedule, but they feature white directors, and to be quite frank, I'm not interested in what white people think about my culture and my political situation. That's part of the problem.

GA: *So under your definition, a movie like* The Nutty Professor *or* Dr. Doolittle *wouldn't constitute a Black film even though there are Black stars in them?*

WH: Having Black people in them is completely irrelevant because the lines, the words they say, the direction they take are all under the control of white people. Ironically, an all-white movie that's directed by a Black director isn't Black, because it's all about control, and white people understand this very clearly. It's control, and that's what defines it.

GA: *I see. So why are movies important?*

WH: Movies are important, one, because they're very popular and two, because they affect people. Movies can affect your imagination, your dreams, your desires, your appetite and your ambition. It's a very powerful medium.

GA: *Do you think films can be used to control, manipulate and subjugate certain groups of people?*

WH: Only in the most subtle and insidious way. When cinema defines your appetite and your values, then financiers and marketers are aware that they are creating and shaping consumers for their products and ideology. So if you support a social policy, which regards certain people of a certain color as being inferior, then you make stories that reinforce that point of view. This was particularly effective during an earlier period of American social history when there was limited and very restricted interracial contact. When our contact and awareness is limited to the movies, we say, "Oh, it must be true." Then it's in the appetite. That's where it really gets you.

GA: *So your wants and desires as a person can be affected?*
WH: Yes, and the proof of that is advertising. Advertising is all based on the fact that a company wants you to buy this, to drink this, to eat this.

GA: *And sometimes we as consumers are not even aware of it. The average person is not even aware that they are being duped.*
WH: You're not supposed to be aware. You're not supposed to be.

GA: *Given that you say film is a powerful medium, do you think Black filmmakers have a responsibility to bring positive images of Black people to the screen?*
WH: First, we're not in a PR war over propaganda with white people. We're trying to use cinema to bring human complexity to the screen, which is more than positive or negative. Complete and complex human beings are always going to be more dramatically engaging than just stick figures. This notion of responsibility is legitimate, but it can only be practiced if a person has the political education to understand where they come from and where they are in the historical continuum.

GA: *There's a lot of discussion about the race and culture issue and about our lack of understanding of who we are, our history and its role in Black imagery film.*
WH: It's very simple. Prior to the 1960s, much of our history was based on misinformation. In the 1960s, our artists and scholars began to popularize an analysis of who we are, and that knowledge was later either crushed or discredited. But culture's only one finger on the hand; it's also understanding the function of white supremacy. It's as much political as it is cultural. To simply talk about the fact that we come from Africa, but not discuss the colonization of Africa and the exploitation of Africa, is incomplete. I want to know about Yoruban art and culture and religion. I also want to learn how Nigeria developed this tradition of political corruption and exploitation and tribal conflict and all those kind of things. Those things are equally important. So in the absence of that, a filmmaker is only going to be as helpful as their own understanding, and one of the problems that I find is that the filmmakers take on these big subjects

and they're absolutely clueless. They need to leave that alone or do some compensatory work before they do it.

GA: Can you give me some examples of that?
WH: Trying to get me in trouble?

GA: No, never.
WH: It would just be harsh. Instead, let me give you an example of a film that has some profound insights and gave the kind of human complexity I'm talking about Carl Franklin's *One False Move*. It's very profound, deeply profound.

GA: It's great, riveting, and every time I watch it, it spooks me.
WH: That's the best example of the level of complexity that I don't see. Walter Mosley's *Always Outnumbered* [directed by Michael Apted] is an unbelievably profound movie—just a stunning movie.

GA: Why don't we see more complexity in more Black movies?
WH: Put me in charge of HBO, put me in charge of Warner Brothers, and it'd be different. It's all about who's making decisions.

GA: Would you like to be a studio head?
WH: No. Absolutely not. Much of what I do, I really wish I didn't have to do. I wish I didn't have to create a Black Filmmaker Foundation. I wish I didn't have to do all of these things. I feel like, as an artist, I have been sacrificed.

GA: How so?
WH: My brother Reggie once called me the George Bailey of Black cinema [Jimmy Stewart's character in *It's a Wonderful Life*]. If you remember the story, George had to stay in his hometown and build the Bedford Falls Savings and Loan alone, and because he did that everybody else he grew up with accomplished these other things. He always felt like he'd lost his opportunity and wasted his life. Of course, at the end, we realize that he hadn't. So I have accepted my fate. At least what I think is my fate. My role has been to serve. I'm hoping that eventually I'll be able to tell my story and in my way, but in the meantime I feel like there are many people who have been empowered through my institutional efforts to empower them to do their thing. When

my brother said that, it hit me, it really hit me, but I think I'm on the verge of being able to come back and make my own artistic statement. Quite frankly, my intention is to really shake it up. There's a rap song by Eric B. and Rakim that says, "Let the others go first, so the brothers don't miss."

GA: *Life is strange like that—the timing of things and our journey—you never know where it's going to go. But you've definitely opened doors for lots of people.*

WH: I'm more optimistic now than I have been my whole entire life. I think that there's an opportunity that might come to pass where I'll be able to make a contribution that will be on par with what Melvin [Van Peebles] did. There are certain movies, *Sweetback, She's Gotta Have It*, that are demarcation points, and I might have an opportunity to do something on that level.

GA: *I can't wait to see it. So tell me about the Hudlin Brothers? You and Reggie were doing a lot of things together. What happened there, and are you looking to do more work together?*

WH: Yeah, we work together on an opportunity basis. Lately, studios have been coming to Reggie with assignments. They gave him *Great White Hype, Ladies' Man* and *Servicing Sara*. So it took him in that direction and took me in just the opposite. I just sped out of the orbit and went back to my BFF roots, essentially, both in terms of curating festivals and dvRepublic, which is totally outside—not only Hollywood, but outside the world in cyberspace. But we're in constant communication. Even though I'm doing cyberspace stuff, he gives me comments. He's doing Hollywood stuff and I give him comments, so we're just simply not working together in a formal credited basis, but otherwise we're still working together.

GA: *Let's talk about the nineties when House Party came out. There was a lot of energy, there was a Black film "renaissance," and you and other Black filmmakers were on the cover of* The New York Times Mag-*azine. What happened during that period? Do you think Black filmmakers were able to build on that momentum? Some would argue that they didn't.*

WH: I think you can do another cover right now—some of the faces would be the same, some of them would be different. But we haven't moved beyond that. There are about eight Black-directed Hollywood movies every year, on average. I've stopped counting. I only did it for ten years. In 1991 there were something like twelve, thirteen or fourteen—huge. It's never been matched. So we haven't gone backwards, that level of access still exists and there are new people coming in every year. George Tillman, Jr., for example, is a new addition. Kasi Lemmons, Gina Prince-

Bythewood, so it's good, but if you measure it—what started in the nineties—we haven't moved to another step. We're still part of that same continuum, which is fine.

GA: *Why haven't we moved to the next step?*
WH: I'm not sure what the next step is. It's always easy to find out in hindsight.

GA: *Some would argue that perhaps the next step is seeing a wider range of the types of Black films in the theaters.*
WH: The only way that next step is going to happen, and maybe this is the answer to your question, is that until we finance movies ourselves nothing's going to change. So why is there is no next step? Because we're still going to Hollywood and asking permission to make movies.

GA: *I see. Are you satisfied with Black movies today?*
WH: The last Black movie that just really blew me away was Boycott on HBO.

GA: *Jeffrey Wright was incredible.*
WH: And Clark Johnson directed. I thought that was just extraordinary. That impressed me.

GA: *As a producer, how do you approach a project?*
WH: The formula's very simple. A film rises and falls on, first, the story, and secondly, the cast. You have to have the right cast and the right story, and do it for the right budget. It's very straightforward. Now, notice that I said story and not script, because an actor will give you the lines, but you gotta give him the story. The actors I work with and I prefer to work with are gifted with improvisation. In our movies, almost all those guys—Robin Harris and Full Force in House Party—that's their dialogue. Watch House Party again and focus exclusively on Full Force. Those guys are doing some interesting things. They are really smart guys, but they're not the focus in the film. In terms of scripts, Boomerang was one of the worst—it was a piece of shit and Eddie Murphy and the rest of the cast improvised, and so that's an example of a script being totally worthless but the story was good.

GA: *Who wrote that script?*
WH: Two white writers who are on Hollywood welfare rolls who just keep getting money with no talent.

GA: Well, that's the whole thing about people saying that Hollywood is eighty percent relationships and twenty percent talent. Do you agree with that?

WH: It's ninety percent relationships.

GA: Now, given that scenario, do you feel it's important for African Americans to align themselves with people outside of the Black community in order to prosper in the industry?

WH: Of course it is. It's a war, and in a war you've got to make alliances.

GA: You start wondering why some people make it in the business while others don't, despite having done award-winning films or strong first feature films. Yet they don't seem to be able to get over that hump in terms of making a living from filmmaking.

WH: But, see, there are politics in there too. One of my limitations is that they smell me. And there's an element of allegiance and submission that's expected of Black filmmakers, particularly males, because they are empowering you. They're giving you millions of dollars to do your thing, and they want to know if you recognize their authority. I tried to hide, I tried to wear the mask, but I'm not good at it. It's like the poem "We Wear the Mask" by Paul Laurence Dunbar—you have to wear the mask, and the more successful you are at wearing the mask the more freedom you'll have. My inability to wear the mask is not out of principle. I'd like to wear the mask, but I'm not a good enough actor. They always find me out. I don't recognize their authority. I will never feel I'm successful as long as I have to ask for permission to make a movie.

GA: Do you have any regrets about not being able to wear the mask?

WH: No, the regrets I have are all hindsight stuff. The first studio deal I had was with Tri-Star back in 1990, right after House Party. Reggie and I had an incredible provision in our contract to do low-budget films, and if I'd known then what I know now, I would have focused exclusively on the low-budget films. We kept trying to make this big—not big, but reasonably budgeted P-Funk movie, which we still want to do. But we kept going down the path of resistance when we should've taken the path of least resistance.

GA: So you wish you had made some smaller movies?

WH: Yeah, tiny movies, no-brainer, low-budget movies.

GA: But you would have at least been in business with the studios.

WH: Yeah, and we also would have made a lot of money.

GA: So do you think that's a lesson for other filmmakers who are presented with such an opportunity?

WH: Yes, but I didn't know it at that early point in my career.

GA: It's only in hindsight that you see it so clearly?

WH: Yeah, and it's a deal that no one would ever get again, by the way. My lawyer Steven Barnes, who is a top, top lawyer, says he couldn't get that deal again for anybody, not even his top people. It was just a fluke. Reggie and I were so blazing hot, but it is unlikely that we could do that again.

GA: Is that the lesson? When you have that moment, you have to shine and take advantage of it?

WH: Absolutely. And the thing is to remember when you first jump into a place you've never been before, you don't know what's going on. I didn't know, I just didn't understand. That's where wisdom comes in, now I know, but oftentimes I've seen some filmmakers get into a similar situation and they hold out for a better offer and end up getting no offer. I've seen it happen more than once. I've seen filmmakers go to war unnecessarily. They see what is a kind of combative, arrogant behavior that someone who's more successful has, and they want to imitate them. That person's done a dozen films—how are you going to imitate that person when you've just made one?

GA: So how do people equip themselves to manage the process? Are mentors important?

WH: I've gone through a different phase in my life and had different mentors.

GA: Who have been some of your film mentors?

WH: I can start with Melvin Van Peebles, even though it was years later that I would actually meet him in person, but the path, the blueprint that Melvin Van Peebles laid out functioned as a mentor for me. Then I met him in 1979 and we became friends, and he became that kind of counselor. My current mentor is Harry Belafonte.

GA: Really?

WH: Absolutely. Yes, we're in regular contact. He's someone to talk to about what I'm doing. I like how he walks into a room. I like how he greets people—he's warm and attentive and doesn't have to be. His generosity stuns me. I like how he takes time and talks to people. Ossie Davis inspires me the same way. See, people think of mentoring as a teenager being able to talk to somebody who's between twenty-five and thirty. But when you're forty, you need to talk to somebody who's seventy. The need is still there. The question is, "How do you act, how do you get old?" I look at Harry Belafonte and I look at Ossie Davis and I say, "Okay, this is how you get old. This is how an elder is supposed to act at each phase of his life." You have to look ahead and say. "Now, how does this go?" I've never been here before. So I study these guys.

GA: *What advice do you have for aspiring filmmakers?*
WH: Don't give up—if you stay in the game, you'll eventually learn. You can learn the hard way or the easy way, but if you're reasonably intelligent you will learn that the only way you can lose is by giving up. It's a marathon, not a sprint.

GA: *This industry can beat you up if you're not careful.*
WH: Oh, yeah, it's supposed to beat you up. It's supposed to. The stakes are very high—this ain't no joke game, this is the real deal. They're supposed to take you out of here. Melvin said it best. There was that play he wrote, *Ain't Supposed to Die a Natural Death*. Once you step out there, you understand that they're trying to "kill" you. It's supposed to kill you, because if you can become potent in this particular medium you can destabilize the status quo. They gotta take you out. So, therefore, to get in the game, be ready to go to war. If you're someone trying to make a career, trying to make some money, okay fine, they'll welcome you in there, but if you're trying to say, "That's not how it goes. This is how it goes," then you are a destabilizing influence.

GA: *How do you walk that tightrope?*
WH: Ain't no tightrope. You take a side. James Mtume told me this proverb that says, "The man who stands in the middle of the road gets hit by traffic going in both ways." So, no, don't straddle nothing.

GA: *What are your favorite films?*
WH: You got to divide them into domestic and international. Domestically, I like some of John Ford's early work, like *How Green Is My Valley*. I like Frank Capra's *It's a Wonderful Life* and I like Francis Ford Coppola's saga, *The Godfather*. Scorsese, early Howard Hawkes, like *His Girl Friday*, that kind of stuff.

GA: *Smart stuff.*
WH: Very smart, very smart. Internationally, I love Kurosawa. My three favorite films of all time were made by the same director—Kurosawa: *Ikiru, Dodes'Ka-Den* and *Red Beard*. He's a supreme director.

GA: Why do you like Kurosawa so much?

WH: Because he deals with complexity and he really deals with the human condition and man's fate. His films leave you stunned and speechless, especially *Red Beard*. If there's any cinematic character that I would like to be like, it would be the character of Red Beard. He's compassionate, but tough.

GA: That's an amazing film. Three incredible hours. So what mark would you like to leave on the world?

WH: My friend James Mtume says the only way we're gonna win the struggle for freedom is to understand that it's a relay race—the only way you win is by passing the baton, and I want people to say that I passed the baton. I received it and will be able to pass it, because there are people before me, like Harry Belafonte, Ossie Davis and Melvin Van Peebles, who did their work. They're the old guard. Now I want to say, "Okay, they did this and I did my part, I passed the baton." That's all you can do.

Doug McHenry

It's been almost two decades since Doug McHenry entered the Hollywood ranks. Reared in Oakland and Danville, California, McHenry has produced and directed some of the film industry's most successful and popular urban films.

After earning a BA in Economics at Stanford in 1973 and receiving a JD/MBA at Harvard in 1977, Doug got his start in the business working as executive assistant to Peter Guber at Casablanca Records/Filmworks. In 1985, McHenry partnered with the late George Jackson to form Jackson/McHenry Entertainment, and the two went on to produce the groundbreaking rap-themed movie *Krush Groove*. McHenry and Jackson later formed Elephant Walk Entertainment and subsequently produced the glossy and highly entertaining gangster film *New Jack City* (1991), directed by Mario Van Peebles and starring Wesley Snipes. McHenry and Jackson also codirected *House Party II* (1991) and served as executive producers on *House Party III* (1994), the sequels to Reginald Hudlin's classic directorial debut film *House Party*. McHenry made his solo foray into directing with the critically acclaimed 1994 film *Jason's Lyric*. In 1996, McHenry produced and directed second unit on the Martin Lawrence directed film, *A Thin Line Between Love and Hate*.

McHenry has also used his talents on the little screen, in 1996 serving as executive producer on UPN's *Malcolm & Eddie* and the syndicated TV show *Motown Live*. Ever busy, in 2001, McHenry directed *Kingdom Come*, an ensemble film featuring Whoopi Goldberg, L.L. Cool J, Vivica A.

Fox, Anthony Anderson, Loretta Devine, Jada Pinkett, Cedric the Entertainer and Toni Braxton. He also executive produced *The Brothers* (2001), directed by Gary Hardwick, and recently directed *Keep the Faith* (2001) for Showtime/Paramount, which co-starred Harry J. Lennix and Vanessa L. Williams. Next up for McHenry is *Got Money?*, which he will direct for Warner Brothers.

McHenry's numerous awards and honors include a Time-Warner Executive Forum Award, a Cable ACE Award, an NAACP Image Award and a CEBA (Communications Excellence to Black Audiences Award) for Producing.

— — — —

GA: *Tell me about growing up in the Bay Area. Were you a creative child?*

DM: My dad was in the Army, so I was born in Fort Knox, Kentucky, and grew up in Fort Louis, Washington, until I was seven years old. Then we moved to Berkeley and Oakland. I was always very visual in the sense that I started painting in kindergarten and won several art prizes as a painter at a very young age. So in terms of visual stuff—design, composition, color palette—that's always interested me. There have been two sides to me. There's been that emotional artistic side that I've always had and that I exhibited by painting watercolor, acrylic and oil. Then the other side of me was always political. I don't know why that was, but I was always interested in politics. Plus, growing up, we were in the Bay Area in the 1960s, which was very integrated, both economically and racially at that time, and I went to an integrated school. My dad was a colonel, so my experience really wasn't one of living in the ghetto, the Black ghetto or any other kind of ghetto in particular, and telling that story. My story has always been a different type of story. I graduated from Stanford with a degree in economics and was the first Black student body president. But being exposed to all kinds of people was great, and I was very political. Filmmaking was nowhere on the horizon. It wasn't anything I really thought about.

GA: *After Stanford you went on to Harvard and got your JD/MBA. Where did you see yourself going at that point? Were you still interested in politics?*

DM: Yes, I thought I would go in and out of government, that I'd work for a law firm, and I envisioned working for domestic counsels. [The White House domestic counsel, under Jimmy Carter, was the organization that focused on domestic policy.] I got interested in the movies because I answered an ad for an interview at business school about a program at Casablanca Records/Filmworks. The chairman was interviewing for an assistant, and I went to work for Peter Guber. I met Peter and I was very excited, and I was so influenced by that meeting that I decided to forget Washington and politics.

GA: And just by responding to the ad everything changed?

DM: Yes, so I said, you know what? In movies, unlike politics, we never promise to make any-body's life better. No one's saying, "Vote for me, your life is going to change." You make a movie and people either go to see it or they don't. Politicians always promise what they can't deliver and that was disheartening to me. So the movies offered me a chance to communicate with people, which is what I always wanted to do. I can make a movie and a person who maybe doesn't want African Americans living next door to them or marrying their daughter may see the movie and not even know I made it, but accept it, laugh at it, react to it.

GA: What did you end up doing for Peter Guber's company?

DM: Basically, I focused on business affairs, how to run the business, how to look at a record com-pany or a film company, its deals, its sources and uses of income, cost variances, et cetera. It's a very small business—there are about three hundred, three hundred and fifty people who matter in this business. It was interesting getting to know those people, and it was an exciting place to work. I enjoyed it thoroughly, but it was very demanding in a sense that I had to learn a whole other skill.

GA: What film projects did you get a chance to work on?

DM: Foxes (1980) is the first film I ever worked on. I did mostly the deals. We began to explore a technique where we would raise money independently and sell distribution rights in foreign ter-ritories [foreign presales]. This was a new business at the time, people really hadn't done it. There was a guy named Mark Damon, who had a company called Producers Sales Organization, who was using this technique. So I learned that business and got us involved in it, and Foxes and some of these other pictures were the results of that new technique.

GA: Yes, and that became a common way of doing business in the industry.

DM: Correct. And I was one of the first people to learn how to do it, which was quite amazing, and then around that time I decided that I wanted to be more on the creative side versus the business affairs side, so then I left that company and joined a small studio called AVCO/Embassy Pictures, since I had known pretty much the producer side and began to learn the business from the cre-ative side. I was an executive there for a couple of years, and I started the television department.

GA: Really?

DM: I was essentially researching their library and understanding history. For example, I learned how Universal got into the television business was through their film library. All of these pictures they had made and based TV series on, like *The Big Valley*, were based on their movie library, so I decided to do the same thing. I researched the Embassy library and structured a TV deal based upon what existed in our library. One example was a Eugene O'Neill play called *Huey*. I did a cable version. Jason Robards actually reprised that role for Ted, who's really responsible for the Circle in the Square theater in New York.

GA: *Good theater.*

DM: Good theater. Anyway, to make a long story short, I did a number of those. I set up development deals for TV series for cable. There were other famous titles as well.

GA: *So you went and examined those titles to see what could be easily adapted.*

DM: From the rights standpoint. Then I hired a TV agent and went and sold the rights. I had then become familiar with Alan Horne and Glenn Padnick and all these guys who were working with Norman Lear's company. They eventually ended up buying a studio and then I went to work for producer Jerry Perenchi.

GA: *So you said you wanted to do the creative thing.*

DM: Yes, I needed to make pictures. So at that point I began to put together my first picture with the late George Jackson, and George was working with Richard Pryor at the time, but for some reason Richard Pryor's company wasn't going anywhere, they weren't doing anything, so we decided we would get this movie done together. It's funny how I met George. I had gone to a party. I've forgotten who's party it was. I was there, and suddenly this big Black guy comes up to me and says, "You're Doug McHenry." I turn around and I say, "Yeah." "I'm George Jackson, I'm from Harvard. Someone told me to look you up. Glad to meet you," he said. It's so funny, because he had been working at this new *Odd Couple* show and these two Black gorgeous twins were working on the show as well. So he didn't have an invitation to the party and he had a really junky car, so he parked the car around the block. He walked the girls up to the front door, people see them, let them in, and he comes in behind them.

GA: [Laughs]

DM: And that started a seventeen-year relationship. A guy I really miss.

GA: *Yeah, I'm sure.*

DM: So George and I decided to make a movie, and we decided we were going to make a movie [*Krush Groove*] about rap music. People had heard about rap and break dance and stuff a year ago. When everybody went to the Victory Tour at Dodger Stadium to see the Jacksons, we went down to the raggedy Long Beach Arena to watch this thing called "The Fresh Fest" where all these rap groups performed: Houdini, Run-DMC, Fat Boys, Kurtis Blow, L.L. Cool J. I was so impressed and knocked out about this stuff that we started to make a movie deal with Russell Simmons and all his guys right there on the spot.

GA: And you and George didn't know Russell at the time?
DM: No.

GA: And you just approached him right then?
DM: Yup. So we finally set up the film. We thought we'd do it at Columbia, and then Columbia backed down. Finally Mark Canton at Warner Brothers said that he'd do the picture, and we had twenty-four hours to get to New York because we had to get Russell on board. We also had to go through Morris Levy. I didn't even know who Morris Levy was. [Levy was a record industry heavy who died in jail in 1989 after being sentenced to federal racketeering and extortion charges.] And I'm pulling into New York, and I know I have to sign these rap groups to be exclusive to this film but I got no [tangible] money—I had one hundred grand that Warner had promised me to start preproduction, but they could still back out of the movie. And I had to sign these groups with pay-or-play so they wouldn't go to other projects. Then I'd meet Levy.

GA: [Laughs]
DM: [Laughs] Levy controls the artists and I sign a contract with him, but it's like a death warrant. I didn't know this guy was a big gangster. Afterward, I told Warner, and they said, "You did what? With who? Morris Levy? Are you out of your mind? You can't . . ." [Laughs]

GA: [Laughs]
DM: Morris Levy is the guy who Quincy Jones was standing next to when Levy's brother gets gunned down at a nightclub. Anyway, I made a deal with Levy. I say that I personally am going to come up with the money for these guys, but I give myself only ninety days to start production. But I still had to go out and get each individual artist signed. I remember going out to Queens in a gypsy cab—Russell Simmons, George and I. We're going out to Queens at about twelve, one in the morning, waking up Run-DMC. We had little Darrell Simmons in his pajamas with us.

GA: Wow.

DM: Jam Master J with all these pit bulls and stuff. I almost got eaten by dogs. I was jumping over fences trying to get these guys to sign these contracts.

GA: [Laughs]

DM: In the middle of the night in Queens.

GA: Did you ever think, "My God, what have I gotten myself into?"

DM: I had no idea—I didn't know, man. This was quite something, and then locating Kurtis Blow at the Disco Fever where you have all these thugs lined up and people literally are being disarmed at the door by metal detectors. This was dangerous. I was so stupid, I didn't know how dangerous it was.

GA: All you knew was that you wanted to make a movie.

DM: That's all I knew.

GA: That's a funny story. Now, how did Michael Schultz get involved? What was the process?

DM: Now, after we got the group, we had to get a director that Morris would accept, and Michael Schultz had done so many Black movies at that time, so we got him involved, which really completed the team because he was a real filmmaker.

GA: That's a book in and of itself, that's a story, the making of Krush Groove.

DM: So it was kind of funny, but really the music side was so good. And I think that all the groups who broke through, like The Beastie Boys, L.L. Cool J, Run-DMC—when I think about it today, "If I Ruled the World" was the first rap song where the rapper sang and rapped. Prince also came to the set, and Sheila E. was in the movie. Prince hung out on our set for a week and came up with this song for us called "Hollyrock" and another song called "Love Bizarre," both of which were in the movie.

GA: "Love Bizarre" was a hot song.

DM: So Prince gave us two great songs, one of which was the number-one song. He really liked the whole movie process, but he didn't say one word on the set. You had to talk to his bodyguard, this big old Nordic guy. Prince is an interesting cat.

GA: Did you have any idea when you were making Krush Groove that it would be so successful?

DM: I had no idea that little film would do anything. That little film sold a lot of records.

GA: It's a great film. It's done so well. And you have actors like a very young Blair Underwood and Lisa Gay Hamilton.

DM: Right. Lisa Gay Hamilton is such a great actress. Krush Groove got made by hook and a crook and a signature. I put my life on the line with Morris Levy and two or three other people that we would get their groups paid. Now, I don't know what would have happened if we couldn't pay them.

GA: But during that period 1984 to 1985, what was the climate for Black film?

DM: In the seventies, they had the whole blaxploitation era but in the early '80s there weren't any Black movies.

GA: That was before She's Gotta Have It in 1986.

DM: And then there was The Last Dragon [1985 film directed by Michael Schultz and executive-produced by Berry Gordy]. We really came at it from the music side more than from telling a Black story. Making Krush Groove was really something, because of the nightclub system. I met Jellybean [producer John "Jellybean" Benitez, who produced songs for Madonna] and Madonna at the club Funhouse, and right around the corner was the Roxy, and the Roxy was where the rappers were, right? Then you'd go down to Danceteria, where The Beastie Boys would be—that was their club. There were certain groups that would hang out at certain clubs and perform, and the New York club scene—at least that club scene at that particular time—really had a lot of great entertainers. The second film we did was back in New York—New Jack City (1991). We came back to New York to do that a year later or two years later.

GA: What inspired New Jack City?

DM: George Jackson and I always wanted to make a smart gangster picture. The Nino Brown character [played by Wesley Snipes] was a composite of three people, including a notorious Harlem organized crime figure found guilty in 1977 of drug trafficking because a member of George's family knew him very well. We also used a guy in Oakland who was reported to have applied MBA techniques to dope dealing and was big. The third guy was a young drug dealer in Washington, D.C., who was busted with $2 million on him. And since there hadn't been a dark-skinned leading man in a long time, we were looking for one. And we found Wesley Snipes in Michael Jackson's "Bad" video (1987) and took him to the Empire Diner in New York. We said, "We're going to design a movie for you"—that's what we did, we designed it for him. We wanted to work with Wesley Snipes, and no one had ever heard of him. He was a great dancer, and Wesley's girlfriend at that time was Halle Berry.

GA: *Oh, really?*

DM: Yeah. [Laughs] And that was great. So we promised Wesley this role, and we asked him if he would do it and he said yes. We went on and designed the Nino Brown character for him.

GA: *Did you and George Jackson hire a writer at this point to write the script?*

DM: We had a script for a different movie, but we took the outline of that script and had it rewritten by a Brooklyn writer named Barry Michael Cooper, who was really a poet. George [Jackson] and I really directed the story and everything pretty much from our heads; that was really a producer-driven movie. We looked at *The Conformist* [1970 film by Bernando Bertolucci] and other movies to get our Dutch angles and to see how we wanted to do the picture, what the color palette was going to be, et cetera. And I told the film's director, Mario Van Peebles, what we wanted. We knew exactly what we wanted.

GA: *In addition to the The Conformist, what other movies did you study in preparing for New Jack City?*

DM: *The Public Enemy* with James Cagney (1931), *The Third Man* (1949)—all those movies with those Dutch angles MTV had started to use.

GA: *One thing about New Jack City I really like is that it's gritty, but the people look good—it's glossy and hip.*

DM: We wanted all our people to look glamorous and good—put good-looking women in it and good-looking guys.

GA: *Vanessa Williams [Soul Food series star, not the former Miss America] was brilliant.*

DM: The only thing I regret in the film is Wesley's haircut. That haircut was a little whacko.

GA: *Loyalty and family seem to be recurring themes in your movies. In New Jack City, Gee Money, the Allen Payne character, asks Nino [the Snipes character], "Are you my brother's keeper?" Payne really nailed that* character. In Krush Groove also, loyalty is important. Is that something you consciously seek to put in your films? Do you have a brother?

DM: I don't have a brother, but George and I were as close to brothers as we could have been, and loyalty was always very important to us. Our friendship influenced us creatively. When I think about the set of brothers in Jason's Lyric, the Allen Payne/Wesley Snipes relationship in New Jack City, the relationship between the Russell Simmons character and Run in Krush Groove, and as you go through a lot of these films, I wasn't even aware of it. But there are a lot of similarities between them.

GA: Absolutely. Do you get a lot of flack from actors about giving roles to rappers as opposed to traditionally trained actors?

DM: Well, there are certain people who can act and there are certain people who can't. I've always believed in L.L. Cool J—I cast him in his first movie, Krush Groove. I cast him in his last big leading role, Kingdom Come, which I directed. That's a tough decision. A lot of actors wanted that role [in Kingdom Come]. I won't name who, but several of them have been nominated for an Academy Award and that role of Bud was a much-sought-after role. I made the whole cast ten years younger than was stated in the screenplay. I felt that that was important and I felt that L.L. could pull it off. When I see him deliver that last speech in church, I know I'm right. You could have had a lot of people do that, but he was the right guy to do it whether he was a rapper or athlete. If the acting is believable, if his face is believable, that's what matters.

GA: Is that what you typically look for in all the people you cast—can they bring truth to the role?

DM: Yes, can they bring truth to the role. Is the scene real to me.

GA: What I liked about Kingdom Come was that I got a chance to see Blacks in a setting in which I hadn't really seen Blacks in a film before. You dealt with death from a comedic standpoint as opposed to the traditional, stereotypical way. Tell me about that.

DM: The movie was originally about a white Kentucky family and the script required very little changing, because when you think about it, country white people and country Black people, the difference between the two is very small. That's why—you take a Jason's Lyric, you take a Kingdom Come, to me to some extent I love working with African American characters, but really these characters are very transparent in the sense that Jason's Lyric could have been a story about a boy and a girl in Bosnia or an Arab boy and Jewish girl on the West Bank. The same thing with Kingdom Come. That could have been any family—it could have been a rich white family, it could have been the Rockefellers.

GA: And you're really drawn to these universal themes?
DM: Yeah, I'm drawn to that. I'm drawn to that kind of truth.

GA: When and why did you decide that you wanted to actually direct movies?
DM: I got bored being a producer.

GA: What was it like to do a sequel to House Party, which had been such a successful film?
DM: Very tough, because there's a different sensibility that we had. It was almost over for that movie.

GA: Then you independently directed Jason's Lyric. What was that transition like, and how did you prepare for that? Or did you feel you were already prepared?
DM: I don't know. You know what it was? I think it's important that every three or four years I do something that I get scared shitless about that I just don't know how to do. I had never gone to film school. I just read the script for Jason's Lyric and I said, I'm doing this script and I'm directing, and I just decided I'd do it.

GA: How did the project come to you?
DM: A script came to me that was "Romeo and Juliet" of the ghetto, and that appealed to me because, again, it was a universal story.

GA: Wow. I really connected with Jason's Lyric because I knew you understood relationships for brothers especially. Something about the way Allen Payne plays Bokem Woodbine's brother was very real.
DM: Right.

GA: How did you go from being a producer working with actors to working with actors as a director? Do you rehearse a lot, or how did you make that transition?
DM: Even as a producer I rehearsed the actors a lot. For example, with Chris Rock in New Jack City, George and I worked with him. He brought his little girlfriend with him and we worked the entire weekend on his Pooky role, which was a character I invented. George and I created the character and put it in the screenplay. He wasn't in the original script. Chris wasn't sure he could

do it, and we worked with him that whole weekend. He's a brilliant performer—he easily could do it, he just didn't know it.

GA: Interesting. And your director [Mario Van Peebles] wasn't involved in that process?
DM: Not really.

GA: And you guys—again, the partnership between you and George Jackson seemed so special—for seventeen years you kind of shared a vision. How did you guys work together?
DM: We laughed a lot. A lot of laughter.

GA: You've done some good comedies, you've had some success producing some recent comedies: Two Can Play That Game, The Brothers. Kingdom Come made some great money for Fox. And Screen Gems [Sony specialty division] has been successful because of your films largely. So what's the secret?
DM: You know what it is? It's an instinct. It's an instinct. I know what works on a certain level. Obviously, not on a level that I'd say Keenen and those great guys know, but if it's a relationship picture I think I know who to cast, who not to cast; it's just an instinct. I've been very, very lucky, but it's something that I know how to do. But I've been lucky in a sense that I've done a lot in the motion picture business.

GA: What are some of the biggest lessons you've learned in your film career?
DM: When I started in the film business there were two skills I had to learn. In the merit system in school, whether people like you or not, you're going to get an A, B, C, D. It's not dependent upon how popular you are. In business, popularity is a big deal in terms of how successful you'll be. It's not always the smartest and most creative person who succeeds in our business. It's the person who gets along with other people to get things done. If you're crazy, you're not going to get anything done unless you're independently rich.

The second thing I had to learn was a different type of courage. And that is, when I graduated from Harvard, I thought I'd be in the domestic counsel, then join a law firm, become a partner for the rest of my life and that's that. In other words, I would probably never be out of a job or have to make a leap of faith other than to go to law school and pass the bar. But in show business it's different. There is no guarantee that I get to do another picture tomorrow unless I'm independently wealthy. At some point I had to leave the corporate environment and go out on my own. So if I wanted to be a producer, I had to go out and figure out how to get money and make a picture. And during that year of making Krush Groove, I couldn't do anything else. It was like walking the plank.

Will I be successful or won't I be successful? Many other people take that risk in other businesses as well, but it's not one I really expected to take. And that was to leave the womb of a weekly paycheck so to speak and say, "Forget about it. I'm going to somehow by hook or crook go make a movie." If your phone gets turned off and your car gets repossessed, it doesn't matter. Whatever it takes to get the movie made, I've got no other choice, I've just got to get it done. That's another skill that I had to learn, that I was going to be all right. Because if I could learn to take care of myself and come up with my own movie deal, I'm safer than the guy who sits around in a corporation because that guy's subject to getting fired or downsized. I learned to become the wheel myself.

GA: *How did you prepare yourself mentally to take that leap of faith?*
DM: I didn't. It was just something that I had to do and I was scared to death. I just did it and I've not worked for anyone for fifteen years.

GA: *Good for you.*
DM: Good for me or am I nuts? But few people in entertainment avoid taking such a leap of faith. You think, "Okay, I have a year's worth of money, and if I don't get this movie made, I'm not going to have any money." Or "I've got a week's worth of money. I've gone through my change in my big jar. I've gone through all the quarters. I've gone through all the dimes. I'm going to have to start rolling these pennies up in here unless this project comes through." That was me in trying to get *Krush Groove* made. And when you go to Harvard, you don't really expect to go through that experience. Can I tell you something? It's one of the most valuable things you can learn. Failure and being scared and being able to walk through it anyway and being able to keep your focus on the ball and say, "I'm doing this. I don't care." When someone tells you, "No," you tell them, "Well, maybe I didn't explain it right." That's a totally different mindset from joining a corporation and being a corporate lawyer. That's show business.

Give Me That Old Indie Spirit

Charles Burnett

When you first meet Charles Burnett you might never guess that he is one of the most respected names in American cinema. Easygoing in a very Southern California way, this native of Vicksburg, Mississippi, has won some of the of the most prestigious awards in the arts: a Guggenheim Fellowship, a tribute at Lincoln Center, a Rockefeller grant and the MacArthur Fellowship.

An independent filmmaker who has a legacy of examining the complexity of the human condition as it relates to African Americans, Burnett is heralded by many of his fellow filmmakers as being one of film's most important and creative minds.

Burnett studied film at UCLA in the 1970's along with the noted filmmakers Haile Gerima, Larry Clark and Billy Woodberry. This revolutionary group of filmmakers earned the name the L.A. Rebellion by New York University Professor Clyde Taylor.

In 1990, Burnett's first feature film, *Killer of Sheep* (1977), a seminal work that explores the everyday challenges of a hardworking meatpacker in Watts, was chosen by the Library of Congress for the 1990 National Film Registry. Though never commercially released, the film was awarded top honors at the Berlin and Sundance film festivals in 1981.

Burnett's other motion picture directing credits include *Bless Their Little Hearts* (1984), *My Brother's Wedding* (1984), *To Sleep with Anger* (1990), *America Becoming* (1991), *The Glass Shield* (1995), *Annihilation of Fish* (1999). For television his directing credits include *Night John* (1996), *The Wedding* (1998), *Selma, Lord, Selma* (1998) and *The Blues* (2001), a PBS documentary.

GA: I know you were born in Vicksburg, Mississippi, but actually grew up in southern California. What was it like growing up here?

CB: Where I grew up [California], everyone was from Mississippi and Texas and Arkansas. That sort of southern culture was removed, relocated here, except picking cotton and the heat and mosquitoes and things like that. There was still racism here, but it wasn't blatant. It was clear where you couldn't go and could go. Like Inglewood.

GA: Really?

CB: Yeah.

GA: Black folks weren't living in Inglewood at the time?

CB: Heck no—early sixties, uh-uh. In fact, there were laws restricting where you could buy a house. My deed on my house where I live now was restricted. If you go back and look at it, it says that you couldn't sell it to non-Caucasians.

GA: Wow.

CB: Yeah, I didn't want to buy the house because of that. The house had nothing to do with it, but there were a lot of communities after the war [World War II], particularly after the war, that were built for veterans and that excluded Blacks. This is here in California. It was all over basically, but California's very racist.

GA: Were you exposed to a lot of creative things as a child? What did you do to express your creativity?

CB: I used to draw, and I used to play the trumpet.

GA: Growing up, did you think you'd have a creative career? What did you think you wanted to be?

CB: As a musician, a horn player I thought I'd be something like that. But I think the sorry part of it was this fatalistic attitude about life somehow or another that was adopted by kids in my neighborhood. There was a belief among young people that they weren't going to live to be twenty-one.

GA: Even when you were growing up?

CB: Oh, yeah. It was very clear.

GA: And from where do you think that attitude arose?

CB: It's from a very confused attitude about life. People seemed to live for the moment and you witnessed a lot of violence. It was almost like, why bother? It was that sort of attitude, there wasn't a sense of the future because so many kids were getting killed. And your parents were always telling you horror stories about if you don't do this and that. It was violent, but not nearly on the level that it was in the eighties, nineties.

But I think there was a class thing as well. The kids were mostly from a single parent household and were more of the working poor more or less. Having a future was never stressed. College wasn't encouraged. The biggest thing people would say was for you to get your high school diploma. If you didn't screw up, if you just stayed in school and if you're dumb enough, they'd give you one. Someone in your family had to fight against the school's "You'll never be anything" attitude. I remember this teacher going down the classroom telling everyone, "You're not going to be anything, you're not going to be anything."

GA: So how did you break out of those conditions to become a great filmmaker?

CB: I just sort of stumbled my way into it, really. I had no plans to be a filmmaker until I got out of junior college at Los Angeles Community College [LACC]. I thought I wanted to be an engineer. I was trying to avoid the draft, so I started taking some creative writing classes. I was going to the movies a lot and became interested in the image the camera recorded. I wanted to become a cameraman, because I always wanted to do something with photography.

GA: Oh, you did? Did you have a camera?

CB: No, I never had the opportunity. I needed a push, some kind of guidance. I wasn't ambitious at all. I didn't have a clue.

GA: [Laughs]

CB: I didn't have a clue what was going on, and it was awful. I think, largely, I got discouraged early. At one time I wanted to be a pilot, but I have this speech impediment, so someone said, "You can't be a pilot, you have a speech impediment." That killed that.

GA: How did you finally break through in community college? You were always taking writing classes, you were saying? I understand that you worked in a library as well.

CB: Yes, in the main library in downtown L.A. That was a part-time job. What I was basically doing was putting magazines away back into the stacks.

GA: What was that like?

CB: Awful. The reason I say that is because it wasn't the people that were awful, it's just the fact that you were upstairs in the stacks and there were no windows, and you ran around with a little cart and people would send requests up in a tube and you would communicate by another little tube. But we got the chance to read all of these obscure magazines and things.

GA: Was that helpful?

CB: Actually, it was because I started reading film reviews and writer's journals. And there was a film magazine called *Critique* or something like that, and it was one of the best magazines for film reviews in the sixties.

GA: When you left community college and went to UCLA, is that when you thought you'd be a filmmaker?

CB: No, but I knew I wanted to tell stories. It wasn't like it is now, where you can expect to get a job in the industry. I never thought I could make a living out of it because it didn't exist, the idea didn't exist then.

GA: There were no role models for you at the time?

CB: Not successful ones. You had directors Spencer Williams and Oscar Micheaux and people who had worked outside the system many many years earlier. This whole thing of Black filmmakers never really became an idea really until the late seventies, when festivals in Europe started to showcase Black independent filmmakers. It was recognized in Europe that there was a voice in America that was missing.

GA: Did you always see yourself as operating outside of the system when you thought about going into film?

CB: I never thought I would make it in Hollywood because the film industry was pretty much closed to people of color.

GA: What was it like going to UCLA?

CB: One of the good things about UCLA was that it was sort of anti-Hollywood. It had this anarchistic flavor to it and it encouraged the individual and the rebel. UCLA was where you went if you were interested in film as an art form and you wanted to make film outside of Hollywood. What was also great was that at UCLA you were exposed to political cinema, third world film and Black awareness. Black students started to enroll in the film department which further changed the atmosphere. And there was Elysee Taylor, one of the first Black teachers in the film department in the early 70s.

GA: *Who were some of your influences then? What did you look to for inspiration—literature, other films?*

CB: Everything. In the sixties and seventies there was a real film culture. For example, if Federico Fellini made a film, it was like someone next door made a film. It wasn't considered a foreign language film. It was part of world cinema. You waited with expectation for a new film from classic filmmakers like Robert Besson, Fellini and the likes. Earlier Hollywood films under the studio system also had some really good-quality films, some artistic films that were incredible.

GA: *Can you give some examples of films that you saw during that time, early Hollywood films that spoke to you?*

CB: I remember Jean Renoir did a film called *The Southerner*, which I admired greatly as a kid. When I got to film school, they were talking about Europeans not being able to make movies about the South and used *The Southerner* as an example. I said, "They must be crazy," because I thought it was one of the best films because it didn't take a typical plot or structure or American view of either romanticizing the victim, nor did it show white people coming to save the day. Renoir treated both a Black family and a white family equally. In one of Renoir's movies, either *Rules of the Game* or *Grand Illusion*, you see French Africans in bars with French troops having a good time singing and dancing with white women which is something you'd never see in American movies.

GA: *Just being human.*

CB: They weren't making jokes or anything like that. They were giggling and having a good time—a white girl dancing, and all these guys, they're all drinking, right? You'd never find that in an American film at that time. Only when Europeans direct a movie would you see that humanness.

GA: *And why do you think that was the case?*

CB: Racism. Hollywood has serious problems when it comes to dealing with racism, some serious problems. They don't want to deal with it. Look at Hollywood today and you have this issue about there being no directors of color on the top TV shows [Directors Guild of America Report dated January 30, 2002]. They don't deal with that. I mean, you say something [about racism] and they get mad and call you difficult. They kill the messenger and think they know all the facts, they're just arrogant.

GA: *So some of those films, like the Renoir films, started shaping what you wanted to do in cinema?*

CB: Renoir had a big impact. It was mostly foreign films that had an impact on me, particularly when Third World cinema came about and you had all of the political films, films from Africa, films from Chile, Colombia, Brazil. Seeing these wonderful films encouraged me, and I'm sure others at UCLA, to really think about what our purpose as a filmmaker was or might be.

GA: *How did the political atmosphere at UCLA affect your work? Do you think that environment shaped you in a positive way as a director?*
CB: Yeah. It was charged. Everyone had a vision. It was exciting; those years were about developing your sensibilities as a filmmaker.

GA: *Who were some of the other Blacks there with you at the time?*
CB: Robert Grant, Don Blackwell, a guy by the name of John Henry, Lillian Drew, Dave Garcia, and Betty Chan in the early sixties. Then a few other Blacks, one was in animation—I've forgotten his name, but there weren't very many. Larry Clark, Haile Gerima, and Walter Gordon. We got into filmmaking to speak to the community in particular and the world in general. The political atmosphere at the time really matured us.

GA: *In 1977 at UCLA you did you first feature film,* Killer of Sheep. *What inspired that film?*
CB: The community. The people I grew up with. I was trying to tell their story without imposing my values, plotting a situation of if you do A, B and C then this will happen, because it wasn't like that. It wasn't like we could go to school and do this, that and that, and come out and be a doctor or whatever. There are certain things you couldn't communicate to people. There was the immediate concern that what we need be filled, and so you couldn't talk about the future unless you saw all these issues that were there then. For example, you needed an infusion of money and it's like if you see a kid and he's homeless, you don't give him a couple of dollars and say, "Well, this is it. I'll give you the rest of it if you go to school." And then tell him to go to school and get an education. For those things you have to have support, you have to provide him with an environment and make it possible for him to understand what you're talking about. So unless you do that you can't make a story for him to follow and say, "Well, if you do this and that, then this will happen." You couldn't do a story like that and be honest and try to show how people lived. The film was never intended to be shown theatrically. It sort of got around by word of mouth and started being shown here and there, and from that there was a response to these middle-class kids, white kids at the time making films about and romanticizing workers and things like that and using this sort of social realistic kind of method of telling stories, which I found inappropriate for what I was doing.

GA: The film was supposed to be your thesis film at UCLA, right?

CB: Actually, yeah, but I was just doing it because I was trying to make movies at the time.

GA: And how did you get the money to do it?

CB: It didn't cost too much to make. All in all, it may have cost about $10,000, maybe less. I took it to different labs—that was the biggest cost, trying to get a negative.

GA: You say something interesting about the film in terms of dealing with working-class people and letting their story unfold without trying to manipulate; it seems very European. I've heard Europeans say, "We tell stories that don't always have to have a happy ending, because life doesn't always end that way." Whereas the Hollywood sensibility has a happy ending, because that's our worldview.

CB: It's a cultural thing. I think there's always been a debate on whether the industry is an art or an industry, and I think Europeans have leaned more towards an art form. And I think there was this sort of different admiration for film, and I think there was always more debate about film in Europe than there was here. Some of the early magazines that came out about film were more about serious art and cinema. Pauline Kael wrote some good reviews of film early on, but in general I think the marketplace really dominated, and Hollywood's so interested in not losing an audience and they would do tests where the audience would dictate how the film would end or not, who was popular and stuff like that. And on one hand, at the same time they feed them all this other junk. Like Black films, for example, Hollywood would just create the same old stereotypical images, and I think they feel that since Black people will go see those movies that must be what they want. At the same time, that's how they believe we are. I think here we try to go for mass appeal, and I think that waters things down. A lot of it has to do with that, and a lot of it has to do with the studio executives. A lot of people at the studios don't have experience in anything, they don't interact with anybody.

GA: In terms of filmmaking?

CB: In terms of life in general. The diversity issue, they just don't have time to see you as a human being.

GA: With Killer of Sheep, did you have any idea that it would become a film that people revered so much when you were creating it?

CB: No, no, no.

GA: It even made it into the National Film Register.

CB: Yes.

GA: So tell me about My Brother's Wedding and how that project came about.

CB: I got some money to do another film, and I wanted to do one that talked about the late seventies, eighties, about where people were. Could you be responsible for someone else? What does it take to be a brother's keeper? That's the reason why I wanted to make the film, but it never really got finished. A whole bunch of problems happened, and we had a rough cut, and that's what it is now. People see a rough cut of it and I keep telling them I'm going to go back. But the farther you get away from it, the harder it is to go back and recut more of the film, but people at Pacific Archives have made a dupe negative now, so maybe I can do it on video if nothing else.

GA: Then you became a MacArthur Fellow. How did that come about?

CB: I don't know. Someone nominated me.

GA: What did you work on during that period? What did you do with the money?

CB: I was broke, I wasn't doing anything. I was struggling. [Laughs] When they called me, I really thought it was a joke.

GA: [Laughs] How much money was it?

CB: $250,000.

GA: Let's talk about To Sleep with Anger [1990], which I liked a lot, having grown up in Alabama. The film incorporates so many things, folklore and mysticism, that I was familiar with growing up. Did it surprise you that Black people didn't embrace it as an audience as much as you would have thought?

CB: Why do you say that?

GA: Well, because I think people liked it, but I remember going to see it in New York. Actually, the New York Times wrote an article about it—I think it was a Tuesday, I have a good memory—it was cold as heck, and there was an article that there was a new Black movie, but that the audience finding the film was mainly white at New York's Angelika Film Center. I saw the film that night and there were only a few Blacks in the audience. It seemed to be embraced more by whites.

CB: Well, you know why?

GA: Why is that?

CB: I'm just curious—why do you think?

GA: My thought is that it wasn't like the other Black films that were coming out at the time. And then I don't know if it really was marketed to Blacks.

CB: You're getting there. I'm going to tell you something very funny about this whole business. I'm going to tell you what happened, and it makes one have to get a bit defensive. They say, "Well, the film didn't do well in the Black community." You ask, "Well, how much were the distribution and print and advertising costs on it? How many theaters was it in?" It was in a total of 18 theaters. Some movies run in 2,000 theaters or 500 or 100. When you only have 18 theaters, how can a movie like that do anything? They [Samuel Goldwyn] didn't market it. We screened the film at the Baldwin Theater in Los Angeles for a Black audience and it went over well. If a marketing person would have been there they'd have said that we had a sure hit. There were Black people in the theater. Goldwyn didn't market it and they didn't take advice. We said, "Put a $50 ad in this *Black Baptist* magazine, a church magazine sold all over the world," but they wouldn't do it. They didn't want us to have anything. They spent all of their money in Atlanta on one theater. They spent $700,000 on one opening, and that was the end of the money. They didn't want to put money in it, they wanted there to be some kind of controversy. And so we had a thing in IFP [Independent Feature Project] where we tracked why the film didn't do well.

Now, two things: You don't want to get into this thing of arguing with the Goldwyns and Disneys, but in reality everyone knew at that particular moment what had happened. You can't expect the film to do anything in 18 theaters, and you can't expect it to perform with no advertising. You can't expect it to do anything when you put it in the wrong theater. In Washington, D.C., a friend of mine said, "Charles, they have the film in a theater where you have to go around the corner to an alley to enter, there are no posters or anything. The [theater owner] was mad at Goldwyn, so what they did was take the movie down for a couple of days, then they put it back up. So we had all this disruption with the film. Now, had it been a gang movie, they would have known what to do with it, what theaters to put it in. First of all, Goldwyn didn't know what kind of a film it was. There are problems with the film, but give it a chance to get to that point where we can discuss it rather than saying, "Well, it didn't do well in the Black community." See, this is why they say the Black community doesn't like these kinds of films. Well, how would they when they ain't even seen it? It's taken them little by little by little by little to get some kind of awareness of the movie.

GA: To Sleep with Anger could do the same business that Eve's Bayou did later, I think.

CB: It could have done at least that.

GA: Anger was fantastic, scary and haunting.

CB: But they did not market the film. That was part of it. Now you say, "How come Black people didn't rush out to see it?" Part of it is that they didn't know about it. For the Haile Gerima film *Sankofa*, people came all the way from Diamond Bar, California, and all these places out there because he had promoted the film and it had no stars in it or anything. We had Danny Glover.

GA: Mary Alice, Sheryl Lee Ralph, Carl Lumbly.

CB: Yeah, Mary Alice, Paul Butler, Vonetta McGee, all these people like that. We had marquee names. Goldwyn did not market the film.

GA: And those names were people that our community really identified with?

CB: I saw the film in Atlanta at a special screening where people asked, "What happened? Why didn't this film come out?" I said, "Well, it did come out." They'd say, "I ain't seen it!" Well, they didn't put it in the theaters. When the film was in Texas, a guy sent me a paper of a review of the film. It said, "The theater had the good sense to put the film far away from the Black community," and he said, "Even a white woman said, 'You have to make a U-turn on the freeway to get to it, if anything.' It was just that ridiculous where they put it." And all these things like that. Goldwyn sat there with their hands in the air, saying, "We don't know what to do."

GA: You needed someone at Goldwyn who believed in the film and who was willing to push it.

CB: Gets the film, but it has to be a situation where you just don't one day wake up and say, "Oh, we gotta get Ebony, we gotta get Jet, and the magazines respond, "Look, you guys never called us."

GA: I've heard other people complain about the same issue. Sometimes publicists don't pitch films and the actors to Ebony and Jet, when those publications could be key in reaching the target audience. Those magazines have been around for over fifty years for a reason. Folks read them. Every Black beauty salon and barbershop has copies of those magazines.

CB: Yeah. But you see these guys, they have to reinvent the wheel every time. It's the same thing you have to inform them and tell them.

GA: You wonder if they want to succeed.

CB: No, they just want certain kinds of films to succeed.

GA: I have a friend who manages a Black celebrity, and my friend told the star's publicist that she should try to get the star on the cover of Ebony for the star's next movie. She said, "Oh, no, we just want to do mainstream magazines." She does not understand that the Black folks are his main fans.

CB: Yeah.

GA: Ebony's big, but a person can be in that position as a publicist for a Black actor and discount a magazine that's been around for over fifty years as not being important. Whether you like it editorially or not, it travels. How dumb is that?

CB: It's arrogance. That's the whole thing, is exactly what you're saying. There's a battle, you go in all the time trying to fight. And so when you say, "Well, how come the film didn't do well?" you have to look at all these other things that were going on and things that didn't go on at the time. And then we can talk about how the Black community did or didn't respond to it.

GA: Absolutely. It's not an apples-to-apples comparison to other films—you didn't market it, the audience didn't respond, they didn't know about it.

CB: No. It's like when you have a chance to spend $800,000 or $500,000 and that's the max—we don't know where the money went, to tell you the truth. They said, "We spent it all in Atlanta." We said, "What? On what?" We couldn't figure out what they'd spent it on.

GA: And you're not a part of the audit process—they may not have even spent it.

CB: No, and then it turns out that we owed them money. That was the big catch. We thought, "Well, it must've made something," and we get this thing that said, "You still owe us money."

GA: How was your deal structured which left you owing Goldwyn money?

CB: I have no idea. I have no idea. You're supposed to start getting money when this movie starts raking in. It was a back-end deal.

GA: So what was the big lesson learned from that experience?

CB: We just had the same thing with Annihilation of Fish with James Earl Jones. A distributor [Regent Entertainment] picked it up and didn't do anything. Now, we're trying to get the film back, and we tried to tell them how to market the film. But it's stupid and so arrogant, arrogant.

GA: There are a lot of egos to manage in this business.

CB: I can't say how many.

GA: And then you've also done some TV work. You did Night John, The Wedding and Selma, Lord, Selma. What's it like working in TV versus feature films?

CB: Night John was very good. There was producer David Manson on it, who knows how to work with directors. On Selma, Lord, Selma I had a great experience, because I had Leah Keith, a Black woman who was an executive over at Disney Television. She's since moved on to Dreamworks. She's great to work with and just made that whole experience, which can be very difficult, just tremendous.

GA: What advice do you have for aspiring directors?

CB: I would say that whatever you do in film school, learn your craft as an art form. Craft is one thing, but art and craft are two different things. Learn filmmaking. It's not so much the mechanics of it, but know about story and what it takes to make a story, to develop characters, to make something live. Develop a vision as a filmmaker that is particularly yours. I think each individual has something special to say, but if he gets trapped in all of the commercialism and everyone else's opinion, you don't have anything special. If you're looking at what's special and your special interpretation of the world, then I think you'd get some really interesting films. Lots of writers had their own particular point of view, his/her own particular stamp. You could recognize Faulkner, Baldwin, Richard Wright because they all had their own particular stamp, their viewpoint.

GA: Do you think things have become more homogenized?

CB: It's not even about that. In film now, it's about who can be the stupidest. One of the things that I liked about the Black blues musicians was the fact that they created music in a rural environment away from everything, and it happened in the South right after Reconstruction, where Black people suffered the most, and the songs are the most liberating songs in all respects. And then it became commercialized with records and they started standardizing, codifying. What is blues? And what isn't blues? Who should be marketable? All this kind of junk. During the early part of the blues, the musicians did their thing and were able to create what is rock and roll today. I give a lot of credit to these guys who really invented, took the guitar and made it their own, or took the harmonica and made it speak and took lyrics and played with them. They just sort of manipulated the instrument.

GA: Do you think the same sort of creativity could happen in Black cinema?

CB: No, we're not brave enough to do that kind of stuff because we're so locked into the rest of this madness and trying to sell things as opposed to expressing our deep feelings.

GA: What legacy would you like to leave in the cinema?

CB: Leave a body of work that's significant and that bridges the past and the future and the present. Leave work that gives people strength.

Haile Gerima

When you have had the privilege of a conversation with Haile Gerima, there is no question you have encountered an independent mind that challenges us to think and grasp for an understanding of the world perhaps beyond our comfortable, indoctrinated boundaries. He is an independent filmmaker in the truest sense.

Originally from Gondar, Ethiopia, Gerima came to the States in the 1960s, where he studied at the Goodman School of Drama in Chicago. He later earned a B.A. and an MFA at UCLA, where he, along with Larry Clark, Charles Burnett, Jama Fanaka, Billy Woodberry, Julie Dash and others, was a part of a signature movement in independent Black cinema in the 1970s.

Gerima's most popular film, 1993's *Sankofa*, which examines slavery through the eyes of a twentieth-century Black fashion model, is a model itself of the spirit of the ancestors in bringing a story to the silver screen and to audiences with self-determination. Reminiscent of Oscar Micheaux, Gerima self-distributed the film by renting movie theaters all across the country. Gerima is a tenured professor in film at Howard University. His other film credits include Hour Glass (1971), *Child of Resistance* (1972), *Harvest 3000 Years* (1976), *Bush Mama* (1976), *Ashes and Embers* (1982) and *Adwa* (1999). Gerima is dedicated to bringing the voices of Black filmmakers to the world and continues to create and distribute African and African American films through his company, Mypheduh Films, Inc. He is the recipient of numerous honors worldwide, including the Paul Robeson Award at the first FESPACO Pan African Film Festival in Burkina Faso, the 1984 Tribute to Haile Gerima at the Festival De La Rochelle in France and the Critics Choice Award at the 1983 Cannes Film Festival.

GA: *Tell me about growing up in Ethiopia and how your family's involvement in the theater influenced your creativity.*

HG: My father and mother were both teachers, and my father was also a playwright. Traditionally, in Ethiopia theater is not for living, it's for teaching. In high school I began to direct my own plays and was recruited at the Haile Selassie University, where I staged plays and studied theater. That's how I ended up coming to Chicago to study theater at the Goodman School of Drama. And it is really in the theater that you find the workings of white supremacy; everybody else is an appendage. All the plays are about white people, and for an actor to aspire to audition for parts is a very real awakening that makes you see that your life, what you are about, the kind of image you have of the kind of community that you want to reincarnate, is not the work or in the interest of the power structure. So the power structure in the theater evokes its own traditions without being loud and aggressive. It silently calls to Shakespeare, then to Ibsen, then to Chekhov. The whole Indo-European culture is the daily diet, and it's the law of culture and nature. So in the process, those of us who do not see ourselves in this image aspire to become part of that. You go through years of disorientation. I just left the school. I realized that in this theater I wasn't going to do anything meaningful about myself. Most of the Black people who were there were sidekicks to white dramas, and you get fed up. Most Black people are fed up and self-destroy, some go to drugs.

So I decided to just start all over again and left for the UCLA School of Drama. Even there again, I was faced by the same racism, but it's not like the racism you couldn't march over. White people are just exercising their power. They do plays and you're the one who is transgressing their world. They can't write a part for you, and you don't look like Hamlet or whatever they want to audition. Even if they do *Othello*, they have to have a painted white man play Othello.

So all this crisis starts to teach you. For me racism is the crux of the matter of my even finding myself in the motion picture department at UCLA. I never even thought that I'd make films, it was not on my agenda. I accidentally stumbled into the film department and there I found Larry Clark, who was an independent filmmaker who encouraged me. I saw a screening of student films and I said, "Whoa! This is powerful." And so all the Black students—including Charles Burnett, who was there—really encouraged me to go into film. So my life in film is really accidental. I wasn't born to be a filmmaker.

GA: What inspired your stories in your initial films?

HG: Most of them came from my coming to America. My orientation of America was that I was coming to a white country. And to discover African descendants who were demonized as Negro Americans in movies literally threw me through a loop of identity crisis, because African Americans were always demonized in films and I grew up knowing that African Americans were thieves, murderers, killers and buffoons. And so this to me was a shamed race that I didn't want to have anything to do with. So coming to Chicago and seeing Black people was very traumatic for me. Then for the white system to slap the hell out of me, to line me up with all the segregated people that I didn't think I was a part of, was a big psychological struggle for me.

The whole initial part of it for me was really making films out of guilt of the very people I betrayed—the African Americans. Therefore, whether it is *Hour Glass*, the first Super 8 film I made, or *Child of Resistance*, or *Bush Mama*—those three early films I did were like rage and anger that were coming into my life as a result of white betrayal, white racism. And because of the fact that, yes, the African descendants were badgered and brutalized by my people, it is almost like I was writing a letter to repent. Each film was like *Dear Friend* almost, but it had rage and anger in it. That is the background of the early films that were really buttressed or saddled by the racial turmoil of my own journey, from coming to a country feeling very peculiarly different—at least I'm different, I'm not them, I'm afraid to be a part of them. Then when you start to do films and you start to see politically the very Black people I disassociated from began to resurrect my militance. I started to wear my Afro, to be literally nurtured, to accept myself and become the person I wanted to be instead of the person I was being packaged to be by forces beyond me.

So within that struggle itself, I found African American visionaries and warriors who fought back whom we don't see in movies. It was the nameless, faceless militants, and then you see it come into the fold. Malcolm X and Paul Robeson come to mind. Then the whole Black Panther Party movement was on the surge. Kwame Toure, known as Stokely Carmichael then, all these forces made me study slavery, because I felt almost the same kind of parallel that Black people have. As I discovered not only Nat Turner, Denmark Vessey's uprisings and rebellion without white management, it was Eureka! My God, Black people also did things, because you only knew Black people as first from Africa.

You look at Black people, they are called Negro Americans, and that itself just decapitates them out of origin coming from nowhere. It's a very dangerous thing that is even perpetuated by Black people—oftentimes. The disconnecting of Africans here from Africa is a very, very dangerous plan of those who are the architects of slavery. This I'm telling you now, knowing what I know now. Then I didn't know. All I knew was Negro Americans are those people who were cloned by white people—they didn't come from Africa. If you really broke it down, every African betrays African Americans or doesn't accept that they're from Africa. And it is because it's a shamed population, and the reason it's a shamed population is because its emotions and intellects have not been recorded culturally. All you see is white America's concoction of what Black people are. Who are those Black people? Those Black people are Black people who do not have the human enzymes to even desire freedom without it being reawakened by a white man who comes from the north, a Quaker, a Lincolnite. Now, that's a very dangerous propaganda, but you don't know it. Many Black people don't know it. Many Black filmmakers don't know it, because you see them perpetuate the same arrangements that are fundamentally white supremacist, meaning white people are human, they are good and bad, and Black people are the casualties of this good and bad force and yet they do nothing to free themselves.

Up to *Amistad*, this is the narrative of Black cinema. The way Blacks are portrayed is rationalized by new spectacles, by new technical effects, but the formula of white supremacy is that Black people did not participate like any human beings towards their freedom. They were freed by good white people, and that information decapitates everything because it makes you indebted to a white person. That's the relationship we see every day manifesting in boardrooms in Hollywood or in Congress—that Black people have to be grateful for being freed. So now for me to find how Black people fought, organized—Denmark Vessey, Touissant L'Overture, nameless, faceless Black people. When you slowly find these maroons, these fighters who fought in spite of white people not being aware of the oppressive system they unleashed, Black people knew it from the jump as the very victims of slavery to fight back. Now, that fighting back is a very important information that white American supremacists' cultural expressionists always negate in films. Either it could be a courtroom drama, like *To Kill a Mockingbird*, or its descendants. You could almost have a family of kittens of these types of film. I'm sure you've seen films where a Black man is in court accused of something and they show do-good and do-bad white people and Black people are just at the mercy of these forces. At the end, society is relieved because the good white people want to free Black people. Then, oftentimes in fact, Black people should also know that they sold each other, they created the slave market before the white man came to the African shores. All those kinds of marginal stories are also thrown around, so who wouldn't be ashamed?

So from my own shame of Black people, I said, "Why are they so ashamed of their past also? And why are they being ashamed about having a complex about being African?" Africa has negative connotations. I asked, "Why am I ashamed of Black people?" Because I saw them in movies like *Tarzan*, I saw Black people in every movie and I hated them, I didn't want to be part of them because they were losers. Who wouldn't develop a complex watching them in movies, so I said, "Ha! I should do a film on slavery," and that's how *Sankofa* [Akan word that means that one must return to the past in order to move forward] comes into the picture. Though initially *Sankofa* itself has all these stereotypes, because I'm reading white books and referencing white books as my resources. The same plantation owners' children divided on good and bad are now giving me the history. Of course, at a certain time when I began to walk the slavery landscapes, when you start to see those nuances, you see a very glorious people. Then you say, "Well, let me make other people aware of what I am aware of, whether it's elementary or not." *Sankofa* came about as an early exploration of trying to come to grips with my own guilt of being ashamed of my own people.

GA: Based on your comments thus far, film is clearly a critical medium to you. Why are movies so important?

HG: The best people to articulate what a film is about are the Latin American filmmakers. They call it the new hydrogen bomb. I think if you are in the craft other than as an enslaved person, by the command center that dictates what cultures is, you have to parrot the master's propaganda whether consciously or unconsciously. Consciously defending white supremacy is a fact of life. White supremacy was about to die until it created Black people to carry the virus of white supremacy. In most cases now, most Black films advance white supremacy without white intervention.

GA: Can you give me examples of that?

HG: The *Booty Calls* and all those movies, *Mo' Money*, *Rosewood*. *Rosewood* advances white supremacy in narrative as far as I am concerned, because the protagonist didn't free himself. The film needed a mature approach to handle it. Even a film like *Do the Right Thing* is a very white supremacist film. Yet, I know Spike is a nationalist. Spike, I'm sure, cares more about Black people than me. But caring is not enough. You can care and kill your lover. You have to understand the workings of white supremacy and how it manifests in our nerve endings as artists.

GA: Please explain how Do the Right Thing is an example of a white supremacist film.

HG: It has a fundamentally flawed premise to start from. One is that Black people who are often depicted in Hollywood as irredeemable creatures would come into a working man's family trying to pursue the American Dream selling pizza. So if you're sitting in Tunisia or Russia or anywhere, you're looking at a human story. It's as if you're coming in my office here. This is my liberated zone that I have earned and created. This is my building with all its implications of the mortgage and all that—this is my liberated territory. I will not let anybody come here and put posters on my wall. I put up posters I believe in, I make films I believe in. Nobody comes and says, "You'd better have a poster of my people on the wall because I buy pizza here." That's a very unjustifiable argument, it's a very flawed argument. It's as if Black people have no case to set in motion.

GA: *You're relying on the character Sal in* Do the Right Thing *to give you credibility, you're saying?*
HG: Yeah! Yeah! You're saying, "White man, I buy pizza here, instead of your people on the poster, put my Black people on your wall." Now, no white man would come and put any posters in my house. Nobody does that. So the argument itself is what I call a "negrotic" argument that has no place in the human story.

GA: *[Laughs] Explain to me what negrotic means.*
HG: Black folks have gone crazy. [Laughs] Negrotic is something that is loud and wrong by premise. It is loud and wrong, and it's provided in the international marketplace as a normal argument, as if Black people run out of stories. If anybody runs out of stories, it's white people.

GA: *Based on your argument, do you think the white power structure knows we are being negrotic and sits back and watches?*
HG: Oh yeah! For example, to protest against the United States, if you look at Denmark Vessey who started a revolution and said, "We die silently, we don't repent." None of the rebellions, Nat Turner's, nobody said, "I am innocent. I didn't do anything." They all said, "Yes, I wanted to change you. I'm a revolutionary." But if you look at later in the 1960s and '70s, people declared revolution against the system and then they'd go to court to be innocent. And so in the world people would ask me, "Why is it that Black people will attack the system and then want to be innocent in the eye of the system?" That is what I call a negrotic argument, where it doesn't make a historical statement. When you stand against the system for it being unjust, you stand by it all the way. That's why the Black community gets confused. This whole thesis we advance is not grounded on human argument. And so you look at that pizza man who wants to sell pizza, anybody will know a hardworking, family man trying to sell pizza and here come the crazy people. Who comes? The irredeemable people come. When the irredeemable people come and are disposed of there is no human association. We don't feel emotionally attached to these characters because they do not do anything human. When in fact, Black people are daily abused in America for just being human.

And as if there's no story like that, we saddle it with Hollywood-influenced devices that we think are dramatic devices, which in the end are really not. So to me, while I respect what some Black filmmakers are trying to do, the narrative they advance, the device they concoct still falls within the idea of white supremacy. For me, I feel that if we continue to push the idea that Black people can come into a scene and then be abnormal, when in fact, what we see daily in the Black community is Black people dying for being normal—going to work they are intercepted, going to visit a girl-friend they are intercepted, going to a party a Black kid may never come back—normal things. So why would I concoct an abnormal dramatic device [like Black characters demanding that photos be placed on the wall in Do the Right Thing] to set a story in motion when in the end it doesn't hold for me? That's the problem I have with a lot of Black films.

GA: *You make very strong points. I must say that I've never looked at Do the Right Thing that way.*
HG: Film for me, for example, if you travel and you say you're a Black American you will find peo-ple claiming to know who you are before they have known any of your group, because of the movies they have seen. In the first place, even white America never believed film was entertain-ment. It only told its slaves that it's entertainment and to not take it seriously. But look at Con-gress. Congress is always at the business of Hollywood, even now with the 9/11 case. They called them all in and said, "This is the kind of play we want to see now." They are almost literally direct-ing movies now—the State Department, the Pentagon and the United States Congress—and so to me, Black people, if they come and tell me, "It's entertainment," either you are advancing your livelihood or you're upholding the white supremacist idea because you don't know the danger of it or you don't pay attention to your own instincts as such. For example, how many Black women have gone through changes hating their hair? Where does it come from? From the standard of beauty. Where does it come from? The mass media—film, television—always abuses Black peo-ple's noses, Black people's lips, Black people's faces, Black people's skin, Black people's hair. How many Black women are daily abused by television by the dictatorship of straight, white, blond hair and blue-eyed people's stories? And then how does it manifest in our desires? Why would a Black man make a film where he is attracted to a lighter-skinned woman and not the woman who looks like his momma? He's horrified when a woman who looks like his mother shows up. But then when he sees this light skin he's pursuing, how did we get into this kind of thing? How many Black men make movies about their desire for a white woman, in an artificially inseminated desire of a white woman? They don't desire a particular white human being, just WHITE. I know many Black men who are obsessed with whiteness. We should do a movie about that to see what movies have done to our desires. Our aesthetic of love and hate is contaminated, our notion of

what's beautiful, what is ugly is contaminated. Where did it come from? It didn't have this much colonial space before the cinema. It is cinema that brought about the standard of Eurocentric culture to be almost the standard of the world. Cinema pushed it, nobody else. Before film, every village, every peasant, every country had their own good and bad, their own ugly and beautiful until the whites brought Marilyn Monroe and Farrah Fawcett into the middle of the village and said that they're the model of white women—all those blond-haired women. In certain societies in Africa to be light-skinned is ugly, and now all of a sudden Black people in Africa, Jamaica and the U.S. are bleaching themselves to be lighter. Time magazine ran a story on it a few months ago. A Black girl was saying, "I feel incomplete because I'm Black. I'm not desired, I'm not wanted." It's very torturous and on the magnitude of a cultural holocaust and genocide with which Black people inner-torture themselves. Where does it come from? Films, images.

GA: *Can you give examples of films which you think defy the very white supremacist ideals you've been mentioning?*

HG: I would say all of Charlie Burnett's films, Julie Dash's *Daughters of the Dust* and Kasi Lemmon's *Eve's Bayou*. There are people scuffling to tell a normal story but we are inundated by making stereotyped characters in new circumstances to perpetuate colonial ideas of white supremacy. By and large these are the movies that come out. For me, most of the films I see, 90 percent of anything that has anything to do with Black people are about Black people as irredeemable creatures, or triggering points to white stories like Steven Biko in *Cry Freedom*. He dies thirty minutes into the story and the story is about white people. Emotionally it jerks Black people off into abnormality. What it does is dehumanize Black people and it orphans Black people. You take a film like *Hurricane* with a fantastic actor [Denzel Washington]. You have a very interesting movie going along, we see him in a family context—he has a wife and a daughter—then suddenly the system takes him captive, imprisons him and now he's orphaned. No more do we see the painful experience that results from taking this Black man from Black people. So he becomes nobody connected to the Black community. Then white missionaries from Canada come to rescue him. Hurricane is then foster-homed. And this is a typical classic case: a Black man is hurt and the Black community feels no impact. It's the white community that takes him from then on, adopts him, foster-homes him and he's gone from the Black community and we don't see the residual emotional and economic effect it leaves on Black people, so it dehumanizes the same character again. So even if the movie is made more sophisticated by a good actor like Denzel Washington, the story still perpetuates orphaning the Black man. Whatever happened to his family, his wife and daughter? It doesn't matter, now white people have taken his cause. And I think about what

I know living in the Black community, a young Black guy dies, the grandmother who's been working her whole life is hurt and she no longer walks normally. The real things I see in the Black community from here to North Carolina to Louisiana, Black people are like all human beings, hurt when a member of their family is taken captive by this system as a prisoner out of just or unjust situations. And the repercussions to the family are equally important for Black people. In fact, my film *Ashes and Embers* was inspired by my seeing four brothers in California on their knees being held by the police with their hands up; it was as if half of me left. We went to see *Sunset Boulevard* after that and I couldn't even enjoy the movie. So I said, "Hah! I have to intervene now." When the police have the brother and his friends on their knees, I have to cut to the grandmother, I have to make a logical cinematic cut to associate the brother with a woman who dreams about his coming to visit her. But the system always disconnects Black people from human origin. Slavery, as I was saying, disconnected Blacks from Africa, the umbilical cord, making you nonhuman. This gives people license to abuse Blacks, because the repercussions of human life are not visible. In Hollywood movies Black humanity is not important, you have to go with the gimmick. Laugh at me at the expense of our humanity. And to me it's unacceptable. I'd prefer not to ever make a movie.

GA: Do you think this is intentional?

HG: Subconscious most of the time. Particularly when you don't do your homework as a filmmaker. To me no Black person should just be a filmmaker. Every Black filmmaker should know that he or she has just picked up a very dangerous weapon that has a virus or nerve gun that could decimate the whole psyche of young people growing up in this country. So when you make a story, you'd better take the responsibility of studying the history of how many Black people before you tried to make a movie, how were movies treating Black people? and then how is your story going to avoid all of the booby traps of racism? That is historical responsibility. You avoid that responsibility, you will perpetuate what we've seen in the past, the virus of racism.

GA: Do you think there's a Black aesthetic in cinema?

HG: Well, I hope so. I hope it will emerge. To me, every village, all humanity has their own evil and good based on their own historical, social and psychological circumstances. Of course, ours is intervened, interrupted, intercepted. As Black people, we're trying to find our psyche, etc. But I think if jazz musicians withstood all the racism to create a musical form that they made the world recognize, so could Black filmmakers. However, the problem is that most Black filmmakers are unprepared, untrained, unhistorical and oftentimes most of them are hooligans, pimps and those who would have shot people in the community if they were let loose because now they're just using the camera as a gun to kill people.

GA: *Why do you say that is the case?*

HG: A lot of times, film gives those of us who are hungry for the limelight an opportunity for posturing. Most producers are old white men who don't care about film's repercussions for Black people. They just want to make money. The cycle of Hollywood is that filmmakers will come into Hollywood, they suffer for years and then they eventually stop making films. A new hooligan is brought in to do what they want them to do—curse, shoot, fornicate. For most white people, I think they get off on producing these kinds of films. But when you look at mature, simmering Black filmmakers, they're always rejected after they dare to say, "Let me do something serious here." I don't want to say names, but most of them will tell you. One of these Hollywood guys was asked at a conference what he regrets and he said, "The fact that I never made a film that shows the resilience and courage of my people." Most serious Black people in Hollywood someday want to do serious films and they do all kinds of stupid films to get there, and by the time they get there they never get to do the serious work. That's where I come in, and I say, "Hey, do low-budget films of what you feel you should do. You don't have to think in terms of Hollywood. You could begin to look and create an art of low- budget cinema the way African Americans did in the 1920s, '30s and '40s." The low-budget idea is something that people need to resurrect now to just express ourselves. We don't have to make the same spectacles. You have to look at your reality and do it. And so to me, there are filmmakers I know—I'm not trying to say I'm the only guy—I know these filmmakers and most of them are frustrated to the point of suicide and the reason is because white people tell them what to do.

They do not do the stories they want to do. Instead, they do the story that they feel can fly, and oftentimes the story that can fly is concocted out of that Aristotelian formula—the three-act, the two-act, whatever and so they can never come to do a story about their grandmother from Louisiana that they want to do one day. I mean, *Eve's Bayou* is like an escapee, it's a runaway. I don't know if it can be repeated, because I haven't seen much from the industry that I can compare to that film. It was a very serious film. Though there are things that for debate, I have apprehensions about, but it's a very decent film to present. Without the sister [director Kasi Lemmons] compromising her whole self, she told a very fantastic story with very fantastic acting. So to me, there are people who know what I say is true. They can't say it because the punishment, I think, is enormous. They may never do a movie again, etc. But in that industry, all I know is that they could not do the story that they wanted to do because the juries who greenlight films are white people and they're governed by a white supremacist paradigm of what a movie is. They are manipulated for the key positions to be taken by white professionals—in the process the story is hijacked to be what it becomes. It's a big problem, and I know most Black filmmakers would take the opportunity to do films outside the system if they could conjure that up. But most of the time, most of them have no guts. You're always wondering, "What the hell, why don't you do something, you've got a good name?"

GA: *I find also that many of the films that Black filmmakers are doing independently are poor derivative versions of Black films coming out of Hollywood. Why do you think that is the case?*

HG: The best thing about Spike is that he really encouraged a lot of young people to want to be filmmakers. He's a good symbol for young people and I've seen them come to Howard. Now they'll say, "I want to be a filmmaker like Spike," and then they'll go to the bookstore or read stupid books by Spike himself. But they'll usually go buy a manual like How to Write a Script, How to Make a Movie, by white folks who are waiting for a film gig. The kid starts to study the formula. And then every plot device that a screenwriter gives you is contaminated. The step-by-step manual which says that for a good story you should have a or b, the kid studies the manual, but nobody stops them to say, "What is the story you want to tell? Form will come next, but what is the story?" And I've done exactly what I'm telling you. I teach at Howard, I've gone to South Africa and done lectures, I do workshops all over.

Oftentimes people come to you with formula scripts and oftentimes those formulas do not accommodate the true story they have because the true story they have has its own form, but no one spends the time to say, "Okay, cultivate that story." No, which film did they say is great? Oh, soap operas are now coming into film classes across America. Kids are writing those things now as if they are original. Some of them even write stories they've already seen in a movie and they're writing it thinking it's theirs. So you can see now the dead and the living coming together and the confusion created as to where the real you starts and the false you begins and everything else; it all comes together. And you start to perpetuate what you see as the only thing out, and oftentimes you do so by suppressing a great deal of what is uniquely original about you. So people come out, they write, but they're writing what they've heard is acceptable, what they think can fly, that can get greenlit from a producer. I think you should do a book about not the ones who makes movies, but the people who really go around Hollywood with script ideas. I met so many young people when we opened Sankofa, lined up, waiting to be fabricated by the system and daily losing the very good thing their parents sent them away from. You leave Louisiana, Alabama, Mississippi or North Carolina and there are so many good stories that the world would be riveted by, but when you get to the world that story is in the back. To get by you start something new, and the new thing starts to eat you up and make you feel that it is the real world. By the time you're really maybe in a position to do something, the real you is so distant you can't even evoke it anymore, you can't resurrect it. In the process, you see so many stories dying by the dictation of what white supremacy says is a good movie. At the same time, white supremacy accommodates its own rebels in its own rank and file.

So the things you were thinking of rebelling, a white kid begins it, so now it's a new phenomenon of a new white director who's changing the world. Oftentimes, when you look at a Charles Burnett film, a Larry Clark film or my film Bush Mama, when we were at UCLA we were in the forefront of any cinema movement in America. With all of our imperfections, with all of our problems, we were making an impact on cinema, yet we were a group of Black people. Had we been white people, we would be all over the place, history makers. But it's not the case. White kids could even come and imitate us and be recognized for those flaws. This stupid notion of Dogma. We were doing that. When I did Bush Mama I was trying to do a film without lights, creating with many windows. Everything they are claiming, we've done in our rebelliousness against the white supremacist cinematic narrative, and yet no benefit that often readily comes to white filmmakers was endowed to us. So the innovation we did that should be in a normal situation, there should be a young cadre of Black filmmakers coming from behind to resurrect those movies, bypass what we did and advance its own language—this kind of generational transaction is totally unheard of. A Black kid will even recultivate. As far as I'm concerned, most of the Black filmmakers like the Spike Lees were created by our movement. Now I don't say this for arrogant purposes, I say this for what they said to me when they were young. They came to me and said, "Oh, you are our mentor. We believe in you, my brother. Bush Mama is my movie. I hope to make a film like you, my brother. Yet when they make films and they're being interviewed they talk about Scorsese, Spielberg and Orson Welles. Why? They want to be validated by the film aficionados. Yet the whole cycle of the group that I came with, that I was engulfed by—after 1948—like St. Clair Bourne, Bill Greaves, the Charles Burnetts, the Larry Clarks. All of these movements gave birth to Black filmmakers being able to take their films to Hollywood to sell them.

In fact, in our rank and group, we didn't even care to go to Hollywood. So that cycle itself kills the organic process because we are dishonest because we can't say a Black film movement influenced us; it's not validated by the system. Then, too, you have an ego and you are insecure about admitting that the historical process unleashed by a Black movement could have taught you a lesson. This kind of complex of negrotic culture takes you where? To place of lack of continuity. We can't sustain it. That's why I like independent filmmaking now. The fact of the matter is that we should go towards independent as well as the major studios. We should serve there and still take money. To me the best metaphor is Noble Johnson, one of the early independent Black film-makers. The most educational thing about him was that he worked in Hollywood acting and all.

GA: *Well, you continue to work outside of Hollywood. Tell me about how Sankofa came together.*

HG: My wife and I and the line producer, Ada Babino, worked on the project for nine years. It took us that long to raise the money and we kept raising money as we shot. The money for the film came from Burkina Faso and Ghana, then a German television company WDR and Channel Four London. This is where the co-production partnership was forged. Underneath that is the history of all the other films I've done. It is the early films that brought us some revenues from European television sales. Within the U.S. meaningful funds never really came through for us. By and large the whole idea of a film on slavery did not sit well with the power structure, so most everybody like American Playhouse and PBS would have preferred that I do another kind of film. My wife, who's also a filmmaker, and I have always agreed not to use film money for anything other than a film. If you gave me $10 for a film, it would go into the pot for whatever film that is to be shot next. Even with what we brought to the table, without the European television presale relationship forged, without the two African countries, the film would not have happened. But in terms of looking to make a film on slavery and taking nine years to make it, the process gave me time to shape the script. Before, all slavery movies were about victims and Blacks did not make history. I wanted to make a film where Black people fought back. In making the film, I discovered the landscape before the nice white people were aware of the oppression of Black people—the oppressed people knew they were oppressed. To make this film work, I walked the landscape from the southern part of the United States, from North Carolina to Louisiana, to Florida, to Jamaica. The film in the end was this journey I made, smoking the souls and experiences of Black people out and letting the landscape of slavery whisper to help me renovate the script. That is what I think made *Sankofa* successful. The environment started to give me stories. The psyche of places like the slave ports started to give input. My humble ability to give in to the story and in to the power of the spirit of the ancestors who have passed made me only a vessel for what they wanted to say. This is really what shaped the film.

GA: *How does one allow oneself to get out of the way and become a vessel?*

HG: Surrendering your ego is very important. Filmmaking itself, out of context, sometimes makes people grotesque. It starts to make you feel that you can walk all over people. And you perpetuate this false importance of being a filmmaker when in fact you should be grateful and humble that people line up to see your film. In my case, I was in Louisiana and I saw this preserved slave shack and I saw the mortar tool to pound grain they kept outside their houses; it comes from Africa. And I thought, "Why would I be a slave and then have a mortar in front of my house, a broom, a flower?" And I said, "Damn, that is a declaration of one's humanity, because slavery says you're not human." And so Black people are saying, "I am human." That alone is a form of resistance.

GA: *Let's talk about your whole relationship with time in producing a project, in terms of the length of the project and the actual time used to produce it. You seem to see the film as a living thing.*

HG: Oh, yeah. The story's shaping. I did a documentary for the BBC and I wouldn't accept their request that it come in at ninety minutes, and I told them that I did not know how long it would be and that I would not discuss it, or I would not make the film. Then they said that they wanted it in a year. I said, "I'm not going to say a year. I'm going to delve in now and the whole process will determine when I will finish and how long it is going to be, but I'm not going to have a deadline." They said, "Haile Gerima, you've got to be pragmatic, this is how the world works." I said, "This is the way your world is, and then my narrative automatically changes if I submit to your clocking of ninety minutes in three months or six months. No. I'm not going to get into that." Because they wanted me to do the film, I got hired anyway, and you can't get this kind of deal anywhere. That's why for most of the films I do, I go to Europe or Africa and I say, "Let's do a co-production based on my past films, not on what this film is going to be." In most cases, they don't even get into my business of the script unless I want their feedback because he is a European, they bring money to now, what, change my story? Then why make a movie? Why me? Why is Gerima making your film when in fact you could make the same film? So we have to be born outside their boxes of what all the rules and regulations of what a movie is, how a movie should come out and the process of a movie itself, because the cultural aspects that you bring into the process of filmmaking itself are legitimate and inseparably linked to the form of the film and the end process of the film.

For example, if you notice in *Sankofa* there is a woman who does not listen to the divine drummer—the sankofa—she has no antenna to receive his message. She's literally cut off her communication line; the drum was supposed to be decoded by Africans. But that's what they destroyed. The drum is the enemy of white civilization. Here, we're saying that the drummer is trying to talk to her, but he can't. Then she has to go through the mental journey of rape that is coded in her memory. After we got permission to shoot in Ghana, they told us that to shoot in the dungeon, we had to get permission from the high priest. And we went there thinking that they wanted payment and they said, "No. We have to pour libation to the filmmaker and the actress before they shoot there." So they poured libation on us to give us permission to shoot. Now, there are more things in the workings here. So for her to be branded there in the shrine invokes the collective memory of all people, and all the characters have to come onboard. When I asked the woman to play the part for me she said, "I do this all the time. When people come from across the ocean [from America to Africa] they go through changes and I always embrace them and help them calm down." So who's casting this woman, how did I get this woman to come? Somehow the story of a people never dies. It embodies ripe vessels, and what is ripe?

First, if you want to be a storyteller, ripeness means to be very humble and to be known for what you believe in. You can't be a politician lying to everybody. In the storytelling, I would say that I don't have a special gift but I know one thing: this film humbled me to not be that professional filmmaker who must make a film by any means necessary. No, I will not kill my mother's story to make a movie. I will never compromise any racial group, including white people, to make a movie. Because once some Nigerian producers came to me and said, "Since white people make fun of us, we want to make films making fun of them." I said, "What a civilized plan. Just because they laugh at us, we have to laugh at them? Shouldn't we make and tell our stories? Why do we have to react to their program?" And the guys dropped me, and I'm happy I never became a part of that. People are not thinking about the historical mission of being a vessel to millions and trillions of untold stories that our ancestors are trying to find a living body to put them through, and that is the structure and narrative of *Sankofa*. When you write, there will be souls and spirits that would like to come to correct the world.

GA: *Film ultimately is a part of culture. Overall, how important is culture to a people?*
HG: Very important. If you notice, white capitalism understands the importance of culture. You see whites involved at all levels—as CEOs, producers, government dictators. They tell the system to coalesce in the state of mind. You can see the white capitalists being so visionary about the benefits of culture, the benefits of subsidizing culture, but if you take the Black capitalist—whether he's the farmer in Georgia or the urban capitalist or the Congressman or NAACP or the highly intellectual activist like Jesse Jackson—all they understand is the script that the system has been given them and they do not understand the implications of cultural evolution. They do not understand how that cultural struggle quantifies into economic property. We do not see the relationship between cultural identity ownership and money. To me there is no automatic economic change for our people without cultural transformation. They are inseparably linked. Economic does not come without cultural. You look at white people. For example, Shakespeare, Goya, Picasso and Spielberg, they are all an integral part of the banking world order. Money sometimes comes in the form of dead presidents, but money also comes sometimes in the form of paint-

ings, music—the Beatles, Michael Jackson, motion picture properties. All of the films we make are intellectual properties, and it could be that the forces that were unfriendly towards us may actually be the beneficiaries of those properties. This is a concept our generation doesn't understand. To me, all of the Black intellectuals—in the U.S. and in Africa—are divested, miseducated to not understand the significance of culture and the fact that people who are not culturally empowered do not have economic power. The Europeans and Americans have economic power because of their cultural assets. Shakespeare brings in the biggest income for England. They don't go to India anymore to get resources.

GA: *Some argue that we tend to export our cultural resources without receiving the benefits of it.*
HG: This is the whole problem with even the hip-hop culture. Members of the hip-hop culture are publicity shouters and criers for Nike, Reebok, Starbucks. They are like the town criers for capitalism. They say that they sell shit all the way to Singapore. I agree. They even brag, "Man, hip hop is big all the way to Japan, man." You say to them, "Yeah, your voice is all the way to Japan but your bank account doesn't show me all the properties disseminated all the way to Japan for all that money that a white kid is going to inherit from his grandfather and father for owning the copyright to your voice on the song that you sang." We're quick to dance, but we don't say, "Hey, it's copyrighted. I'm going to make some moves here, but I own the copyright." No. We're quick to show off and white kids take it and own it. The most frightening part of it is the fact that Black folks produce the biggest intellectual property and own less of it. If you are a capitalist, bourgeois Black yet have no cultural investment in your children, they have low self-esteem, they've never seen anything like them represented in the media, they are full of complexes, they are hostages to white culture and they're fragile and erratic and negrotic. Then you have all of this money in the bank. What happens when you die? They'll wastefully throw it around because they have no landscape for them to have been nurtured to understand your vision. It's a disastrous prospect to not be aware of the implications of culture to the well-being of a people. So to me, I don't care how good your singing is. It's the way Black people brag about how hip-hop is famous all over the world. I say, "Yeah, the queen never drank tea without sugar." Enslaved people don't say, "Man, I may not own the goddamn sugar, but goddamnit the queen don't wake up without having a sip of my shit!" So what? That's negrotic. Just loud and wrong. Economically you can't go to the bank with it, and that's the tragedy.

Euzhan Palcy

When it comes to examining the multilayered beauty and complexity of the human condition, internationally acclaimed writer, director and producer Euzhan Palcy ranks with the best creative minds. Born on the Carribean island of Martinique in 1958, Palcy has for over twenty years brought her cinematic brilliance and study of the social and political ills and triumphs of our world to the screen.

Palcy's career began in 1975 with a short film entitled *The Messenger*, which she directed while still a teenager. She made her feature film debut with the heartwarming and loving *Sugar Cane Alley* (1983), the spiritually uplifting story about the relationship between a little boy and his grandmother who envisions a life for him far beyond the oftentimes inescapable rows of the nearby sugarcane fields. The film won over seventeen international prizes, including the Silver Lion and the Best Lead Actress Award at the Venice Film Festival, and the Cesar Award for Best First Feature Film. So impressed with her work, Robert Redford handpicked Palcy to attend the 1984 Sundance Directors Lab.

Committed to social change and the impact film can have on our society, Palcy earned the admiration of actor Marlon Brando, who agreed to star in her second feature film, *A Dry White Season* (1989), for free. With that film, which dealt with apartheid in South Africa, Palcy became the first Black female director to be produced by a major Hollywood studio [MGM] and received the Orson Welles Prize for Cinematic Achievement for her work on the film.

Palcy most recently directed for Paramount/Showtime Pictures *The Killing Yard* (2001), about the 1971 Attica prison uprising, and which starred Alan Alda and Morris Chestnut. Her other credits include *Ruby Bridges* (1998) for *The Wonderful World of Disney* about school desegregation in the 1960s, and *Siméon* (1992), a musical fairy tale set in Paris and Martinique.

A graduate of the Sorbonne and the renowned Louis Lumiere School of Cinema in Paris, she was honored in 1997 by having a movie theater named Cinema Euzhan Palcy in Amiens, France. In 2000 she was honored by having Martinique's first film study high school named after her.

▬ ▬ ▬ ▬

GA: *Tell me about your childhood in Martinique.*

EP: When I was a little girl I was a dreamer, and I'm still a big dreamer and somehow the little girl is still inside of me. That's why every time I make a movie there is always a child who pops out and says, "Okay, what about me?" In the end the child ends up being one of the film's main protagonists. I always loved music and I loved stories. I would spend a lot of time with older people because I found kids my age boring and my paternal grandmother was such a wonderful storyteller. She was the matriarch, as you say, and she loved to tell stories. In fact, every Sunday my parents would take us out to visit her, and that was our gift if we behaved. The grandmother in *Sugar Cane Alley* has the same name as my grandmother—Amantine. I was born in a family of artists and my father loved painting, sculpture and music. I had a cousin who wrote poetry. I was born into this kind of environment and I was certainly influenced by them. I started writing stories when I was ten. Four years later, I embraced suspense story writing while in high school and wrote suspense stories every month for *Martinique* magazine. I wrote suspense because I loved Alfred Hitchcock.

GA: *When did you decide to pursue film as a career?*

EP: I went to the movies a lot when I was growing up. Every Sunday my parents would give us money, we'd go to church and after the service, we kids would go to see a matinee. There were a lot of American films. Very early I was fascinated by Hitchcock, but I was never fascinated by the actors—I admired them, but most of my questions would be about how the movies were made, the techniques. Like the Indians: They would kill the Indians and the guy who was killed in a movie today would appear in another movie playing someone else, and I'd say, "But he died. What happened?" That was when I was ten. Very early I knew that I wanted to make films and tell stories. Everyone wanted to put me on the other side of the camera, and I said, "No, I don't want to be an actress, I want to direct, I want to make the movie," and I was ten when I said that. As a child, I'd always question things and challenge the adults, and I would get punished sometimes. I wanted everything the adults had. For example, my family would have dinner together at home, and my parents would tell us that they were going to the movies and put us to bed. I'd pretend that I was having my shower, but I'd hide and put on my dress and my shoes and let my parents leave the house. It was a little village and they would walk to the movies. As usual, they'd walk and stop by the woman who sells peanuts and then they'd go to the movie. I'd look at my watch and say, "Okay, now they're near the market, now they are walking near the cemetery, and now it's time for me to go." I'd run and catch them. They'd be furious and they'd say, "Oh, my God, what are you doing here?! You're supposed to be in bed. This is not a movie for kids." I'd say, "But I want to go to the movie with you." My father would tell my mother that if they took me back home they'd miss the beginning. So they would tell me that I'd be punished later. The man who worked the door was tough but my father knew him very well. He would see me and although he knew that the film was for adults, he'd let me in. I'd sit between my parents, and every time there was a love scene, my mother would put her hand over my eyes so I wouldn't see. [Laughs]

GA: [Laughs] That's classic.

EP: Then when we'd go back home after the movie, they'd be so happy about the movie that they'd forget about the punishment. I'd wait a little while and I'd do that over and over from time to time. That's how I was able to see films like Dr. Zhivago, which they'd never show to kids for the matinee. I saw films like Hitchcock's Rear Window and discovered people like Francois Truffaut and his film L'Enfant Sauvage. I started to see all of his movies, and I love him. I could relate to him. He was a character-driven director and cared about good stories. He loved his characters, what was happening to them and how things affected them. When I discovered him I also discovered people like Costa-Gavras with Z, and State of Siege and later Music Box. On the American side, I discovered Orson Welles. I loved his movie technique, how he'd shoot his films, the framing and the way he used the lenses to express emotions and tell the stories. On the comedy side, I liked Billy Wilder, whom I first discovered when I saw Some Like It Hot. That's someone who just made me laugh when I was younger.

GA: You made a film called The Messenger while you were in high school.

EP: Yes, I was a youngster and it was my very first movie. I was working at a radio station to make a little money on the side. They gave me some radio shows to run, but there were no movies there. I said, "All the movies come from France and that's not right. I write stories; I need to do something." I went to see the station director, who was a very nice French guy, and I said, "I'm working here, I'm saving my money, I want to go to France to study film, and I want to make a movie. Why can't we do a drama here? I have a story." I showed him my story [The Messenger], and he said, "This is amazing." So he proposed to me that he work the camera because he'd had some camera training in Africa, and when he came to Martinique he bought a 16mm camera; I would direct. Every weekend we shot, and I put all my family in the movie because I needed people who could be free when I needed them. So we did that film in a very amateurish way, but it was very professional actually and I shot for six months. We cut the movie secretly, because the head of the station didn't care that there were no movies with Black people in them, so we couldn't tell him that we were doing the film until it was finished. They presented the film and people started to call and write because they wanted more. You bet they did. It was an event for them to see themselves on screen. The film was shown everywhere, in France, in the Caribbean, everywhere. But I said, "No, no, no, I don't want to do that." I'd done it. I learned how to make a film, I was self-taught because I ordered books from Paris and I knew how to write a script, how to do my shots—wide shot or tight shot, close-up, traveling and pan. I had learned all of the techniques, but I knew that if I wanted to be a real professional I had to master the techniques, I had to go to France to study properly. So I decided to leave for Paris to study film.

GA: *Tell me about studying film in Paris.*
EP: When I left Martinique I was the first one to go study film, and my father told me that it was good to study film because he knew that I really wanted to be a filmmaker. I had to do it and he proposed to help me, to pay for my studies, but he gave me a good piece of advice. He said, "You never know what can happen. This seems to be a very tough world. Maybe you should study literature as well at the Sorbonne, because if you fail in filmmaking, at least you can teach to feed yourself." My father was the first feminist I ever met. I think he gave me a good piece of advice and also at the time the French government was giving grants to people who were studying literature and things like that. So I studied at both the Sorbonne and at the Louis Lumiere Film School in Paris. At the time, studying film was considered a luxury. Rich people paid to become filmmakers, because when you are from a country like Martinique you study to become a doctor, a professor or an engineer. That's why there are so many lawyers, doctors, intellectuals and scientists in Martinique. They go back to work there. They study hard, and that was the story in *Sugar Cane Alley*. No one wants to go back to the sugarcane plantation because they've come from slavery and they know their grandparents paid the price for them. The grandmother in *Sugar Cane Alley* wanted the little boy to be somebody. She didn't want him to have the same life she had.

That's every single parent in the Caribbean. You might be poor, but you have to be educated. The good thing about French colonization, among the bad stuff, is that they wanted to make you a good French person, a good French brain, and that means that they educate you, which is a good thing. So you can study for free even at the Sorbonne, and they will give you a grant. When I went to study film [at the Louis Lumiere Film School], that was the first year that they opened the school to women and there were maybe six females there, and I was the only Black out of a total of thirty-two students.

GA: *Did you experience any problems being the only Black and by being a woman?*
EP: No problems at all.

GA: *How did you manage attending both the Sorbonne and film school?*
EP: It was hard but I have no regrets, because I was able to study literature, theater and opera. I love opera. I also studied theater, because I love theater and I wanted to really study everything about directing theater, the stage, the meaning of the stage, how to adapt a story for the stage and how to divide the space on a stage. I studied *cineographie* as we call it in French, which means lighting and how to use lighting and space. I was very curious about these things. There's a relationship between the characters on stage, the story and the space and how the characters relate to the space and how the characters move within the space. It's very interesting. So I studied all this at the Sorbonne and I also studied art and archeology. At the film school I studied film and got my degree in cinematography.

GA: *Sugar Cane Alley is a beautiful story. What inspired you to do that film?*
EP: I first discovered the book *Sugar Cane Alley*, by Joseph Fobel, when I was fourteen. I said, "Oh, my God, I want to make a movie out of this." So I started to write my screenplay. Actually, when I went to Paris I had maybe four versions of the script for *Sugar Cane Alley*, but they were not great because the script was more difficult than *The Messenger*. But I studied film and was able to improve my writing. That's how I met Francois Truffaut's daughter, Laura, who was a good friend of my roommate's. Laura Truffaut read the script and said, "This is great! Let me give it to my father." I said, "Oh, no, I love your father, he is one of my spiritual mentors, I cannot give this script to him. It's not good enough." She said, "C'mon, Euzhan, this is good, and if it's not good he will tell you. You have nothing to lose." So I agreed and she took the script to her father, and maybe two weeks later I received a call that Mr. Truffaut wanted to meet with me. Oh, my God, I was shaking. I said, "Oh, my God, I will meet my spiritual mentor. Master Truffaut wants to see

me." I went there and I remember meeting a little man with very bright and piercing eyes. You would think that he could see through you because of his eyes. He told me that he loved the script, the story and the characters, and he gave me some ideas. He made a lot of notes on the script and said, "Let's keep in touch because really, this is amazing that you wrote such a beautiful piece and it's so original. You know we've never seen a story like this here. If you need anything, come to me." That's how he became my godfather, and when I did *Sugar Cane Alley* he put my whole crew together for me.

GA: *That's amazing. And you shot it all in Martinique. Who financed the film?*
EP: I received a grant from the French government. There is what they call the National Center of Cinema in Paris, which helped filmmakers a lot. You submit your script to the center, and there is a competition. They receive maybe one hundred to one hundred and fifty scripts every two months. There's a committee of about twelve professional people—editors, producers, directors and actors. They read the script and select three or four screenplays and give you one-third of the film's budget. When you receive the grant, it's a mark of quality, so you are able to get a television deal and a distributor immediately.

GA: *Your films seem to draw on all your experiences—theater, music, the arts. There's a scene in Sugar Cane Alley when they go looking for Mr. Roc. It is almost like looking at a Van Gogh painting. Do you know what I mean?*
EP: Oh yes, I do. The torches of light.

GA: *You knew what I was thinking. You actually paint with the lights. It looks like a painting.*
EP: I paint with the light, it's very important to me. Lighting is absolutely important, and there's just so much you can do with light to express so many things and the sound is also important. But I was gifted because I was born in a country full of sound and color, so I had that in me when I opened my eyes as a baby. What did I see? Colors. I heard birds, the wind, the river, all kinds of things. So in my movies you find all these things and the soundtrack is very important. The sound in the movie for me is important, and sometimes I create the visual with the sound. For example, I didn't have time to shoot a helicopter in the sky in *Dry White Season*. I had the time, it was scheduled, but I had two scenes with the helicopter and I wasted so much time with the first that I told my producer that I didn't want to waste time with the second one during the riot scene. I told her not to worry, that I had an idea and to trust me. I told her to give me the money for more extras, more kids in the street, and that I would surprise her with a solution for the heli-

copter. I knew in my head what I was going to do. In the cutting room, what did I do? I played with the sound of the helicopter [makes helicopter sound] and I played with it for a long time, but at different levels. When we are outside, we hear the noise, but we don't see the helicopter. There is the action going on, and we have the noise. Then we cut inside the house, but we hear the same noise from inside. When he shuts the door, the noise is still there but in the distance. So I play like that and I swear to you when people talk about that piece of the movie, they actually saw the helicopter and I love that. People say, "And with the helicopter dropping the tear gas and the people running . . ."

GA: *The sound frightens you because it's still very ominous, even though you don't see the helicopter but you think you do. When did you develop your appreciation for sound?*

EP: As I said earlier, I was born in a country full of sound and colors. I'm sensitive to sound. What I used to do every time I went to Martinique was record sound. I would go to the beach, and I would record the sea, the sound of the waves. I was born with that sound, and that's why I'm very picky about the sound in my films. When I want to, for example, transition from one scene to the next, you can do it with the image—the way you cut it—but I do it with sound a lot also. I go, "Boom!"

GA: *One thing I love about Sugar Cane is that despite being poor, your characters display a lot of dignity and pride.*

EP: During slavery in the Caribbean, and I'm sure it was like that everywhere in the world where there was slavery, my people would be put on display naked. They would open their mouths like horses to show their teeth to see if they were in good health, then sell them like animals. The first thing the people did when they got their freedom was to cover themselves the best way they could. They dressed because at that time everything beautiful was for the white woman, the white man. The slaves would get the rags. But as soon as they were able to get their freedom, they were able to be their own man, their own woman, they decided that that would never happen again. They would have to get their dignity back by working hard, educating their kids and being dressed. Even if their clothes are not fancy, they will always be clean and pressed. They taught us since we were little, "Yes, we are poor, but we are queens and we are kings."

GA: *And you draw upon the concept of dignity a lot in your work and it's important to you.*

EP: It is important to me.

GA: I see it, and it's something that I think is frequently missing in African American cinema, and I would like to talk about this because you weren't born in this country.

EP: No. I can see the difference. I see the difference.

GA: The poor people in all of your films have dignity.

EP: They're very dignified.

GA: So why do you think the difference exists? Do you think that African American directors are jaded by the Hollywood system?

EP: I think so, oh, absolutely, because I think the problem is that the African American community, has lost that [dignity]. They had it, but they lost it, because there is less respect for the elders here [in the States]. I will say something, which is very sad, I hate to say it, but I have to say it. I realize that after all the years I've spent here that Black people were more advanced and had more solidarity with each other during segregation. I saw it and I see it every day, because they had dignity, integrity, self-esteem, love. They didn't lose it all, but they lost a lot of it. There are still people out there who are struggling to keep those values. There are still families who are working hard to keep that, but there are fewer of them, because now they have integrated and so that means that they are American, period. Becoming integrated meant losing all of those values, and they embraced the only one value which is important in this country—money. That's so sad, because I experience that when I talk to kids at schools. A kid said to me, "I want to be rich, I want to be famous." That's what they promote. The values that they promote to every little American kid, Black or white, are that you have to be rich and famous, but they don't promote education and they don't promote education because education is not free in this country. You have to pay to be educated the same way you have to pay to have good health care.

GA: But we say this is the land of the free.

EP: And that's the problem, and every time I hear that I feel like asking, "For whom? Free, but for whom?" I realize that all the time with my American friends, white or Black, and I discuss with them and I am so sad to see how narrow minded they are. They don't know anything besides a dollar and that's it. Very few of them know about Europe, Africa, the Caribbean. They don't know and sometimes they don't give a damn. "We don't give a heck because we have the dollar and we are the masters of the planet."

GA: And you think it affects how Black filmmakers express themselves?

EP: Oh, absolutely, and I think that's because that's what has been promoted. For example, kids say to me, "Why is education so important for you in your world? We don't care about education here."

GA: Do you think movies are important or are movies just entertainment?

EP: Oh, my God, that's what I say all the time. I am a filmmaker, an educator, an entertainer. I am all these things. I want to entertain, to tell stories. I also want to educate, and I'm saying to educate without being pretentious. I don't want to lecture anybody, but if I believe that with my films I can contribute to the education of a child or an adult, or open someone's eyes to something different, something that they didn't know, another world, another way of thinking, another way of being, my God, I would have achieved my goal as a filmmaker. Even if I do only four movies and die, if these four movies can do that? Gee, I'm happy. That's why it's so important for me to not be in a hurry to make movies, but to pick the right ones. I've done political movies, and I hate when they call them political movies. They are political, yes, because life is political. Life is political; it's a struggle, meaning the poor against the rich. A fight to survive. A fight for love, a struggle against evil people. But what is important for me as a filmmaker is whatever so-called political movie I've done, if you look at my movies, they're all about people, relationships, emotions. They're about the so-called political situation and how it affects these characters.

GA: And you like the social implications. Why?

EP: I love that, absolutely. That's very important to me. Because I come from a world that suffered a lot. I come from a land of violence, that was very tough. I'm talking about slavery, people fighting, killing people. The past, the history, slavery, it was awful, so when you come from that, you know the price, the price for dignity, the price for integrity, the price for freedom. As a filmmaker, it's important to me. I care about people, I care about freedom, I care about social issues.

GA: What was it like making the transition from Sugar Cane Alley (1983) to a big studio film like A Dry White Season (1989)?

EP: It was difficult in that on A Dry White Season I had a bigger budget, it was a bigger story, everything was bigger, bigger, bigger. The budget was something between $15 million and $17 million, but I love challenges, I'm always well prepared. I take care of myself physically—I eat well, I try to sleep well, I have a lot of massages and I meditate a lot just to spiritually stay in synch with my body and not be sick on the set. Then I exercise a lot, and when I work on my script, I take a lot of notes. I work with my director of photography and my main technicians, I go on location, I make photos, I take models from every location. The production designer knows that they have to give me a model for each location, and I work, I do my shot list.

GA: Are the models like those an architect would make?
EP: Yes, they're made out of cardboard. I work from that, and then I do my homework and then I call my director of photography and I say, "Okay, let's go on location," and I start with him. I tell him what I want. I want the camera to move like this and I want this and I want that, and then the third step is with the actors. When I walk through with the actors I leave room for them, but I have my basic idea.

GA: So when you show up on set you know the shots in detail?
EP: I'm telling you, when I show up everybody has a shot list, everybody. Every department has a thick pile of papers from me, so they know exactly what I will shoot. The people in makeup will say, "Oh, she'll do a tight shot here." When I hand the stack to the first assistant director, his work is done. He knows everything—how many cars I want, if I want a dog, if it's black or white, whatever I need. He has everything written down.

GA: Even the costuming?
EP: Everything. And for Sugar Cane Alley all the clothes were brand new. We developed a technique to age them. I gave the clothes to the kids a month before the shooting and I asked them to wear them after school and to sleep in the clothes, so the clothes would take the shape of their bodies, develop holes and stuff. I did the same thing on the Sugar Cane set. We did the shoot in the middle of a sugarcane plantation, we built that set, so I asked all the people around, the sugarcane workers, to bring their pigs, their cattle, to bring everything there, and I asked people to live in the house on the plantation. So for two months in advance they were there every day. They were there having fun barbecuing, playing.

GA: It's obvious why cinema verité works in Sugar Cane Alley. The plantation scenes look very authentic.
EP: Yes, because the people in the film are real workers from the sugarcane fields.

GA: Wow. It must have been just as incredible on A Dry White Season.

EP: In South Africa, what I did, I rehearsed with the kids and I talked and I had to do lessons also with them, because apartheid was their real life.

GA: They'd had experience.

EP: They knew the song, the marching, they were doing that all the time. The people I had to train were the white guys who were playing the policemen beating the kids and killing them. There was a rugby team from Zimbabwe and one guy was very sweet, I'd never seen that. I always thought that rugby men were rough, tough and mean, but they were the sweetest guys and they were afraid of beating the kids. But I told them not to worry because the kids were protected with stuff in their backs. It was very hard and I had to stop [filming] many times because of them.

GA: In A Dry White Season, you focus on relationships, and it's obvious that they're very important to you. Donald Sutherland's character's relationship with his son, his wife and Stanley, his gardener. Relationships are really tested in the film, there is a level of complexity.

EP: Exactly, they're tested all the time. In the relationship between Ben du Toit [Sutherland] and the gardener, Stanley answers, "Yes, master, yes master." But when Stanley's in his home he's a man of dignity, he's the man of the house, and his kids say, "Daddy, look, you are smart, you could be a lawyer. Here everybody treats you like a king, they respect you, but in that world, who are you? Nothing, you are just a gardener for them." This is a tough thing to tell your father, and that's not in the book the film is based on. I put it there. It was important to show. You know what made me write that scene? Too many times I heard people saying, "Why are the Black kids being beaten up by the police?" When they would see that on television [news], some people would say, "Oh, they deserve it because they are troublemakers. They are breaking everything, they are troublemakers." I said, "They are not troublemakers. They are trying to call attention to the fact that they want to teach them in Afrikaans instead of English. Who the hell speaks Afrikaans besides the Afrikaners? They're already enslaved, and forcing them would totally destroy the children. So that's why they are protesting in the streets." It was important for me, making a movie to make that point clear.

GA: How did you feel about doing a film that on some level showed sympathy for the white Donald Sutherland character? Were you criticized?

EP: There was no sympathy, because you know what some people say, well, "She made a movie with a white lead." I said, "Who cares. South Africa is Black and white. My problem, my concern was to make a movie to show both sides. To me it's not a white man's story, it's the story of two families, one Black, one white, and I wanted to show what happens in a white family when one member of that family saw the light. That family member said, "Okay, this [apartheid] is not right. I can not in the name of my human dignity, I cannot close my eyes anymore, I cannot pretend that I do not know anymore. I saw it, I learned the truth, I've got to take a stand against what is wrong." So what happens to that person when that person takes a stand? That's what I wanted to show. And to also show that if they treat him [the white man] like that, guess how they'd treat a Black person, and I showed that, so I showed both sides. It's not a question of sympathy about the white character, because there are some good white men like there are some bastards. But after I did A Dry White Season, I was so disturbed because I spent maybe a total of five years after Sugar Cane Alley trying to get that movie off the ground. The studio was behind it, but I spent two and a half years developing the script and then Warner Bros. said, "Well, there is another movie about South Africa called Cry Freedom coming out. That's enough." But I said, "How many movies about Vietnam have we had and you keep making them, but two movies about South Africa, apartheid, and it's too much." Anyway, five years in total and then having to deal with real tough things like people being tortured and kids being shot, it was tough. That really got to me, because I went to South Africa underground under a pseudonym, so they gave me a visa and I was able to get in. I interviewed people, and everything I put in the movie is real. There is no fiction there. I was shaken by that and I would overreact emotionally. Sometimes I'd put the TV on, and if I saw somebody, a black face, an old woman, an old man or a child, I'd cry and there would be all these questions in my head: What did we do? Why do we deserve this? Why us? Why? Why? Why?

GA: How did you deal with it while you were actually shooting in South Africa?
EP: Actually, when you are shooting, you're in a "second state," as we say in French, so you don't think about it, you just do it. But I didn't shoot in South Africa, I shot in Zimbabwe, which is next door to South Africa, but we closed the set. We couldn't let any journalists get in because of all the South African actors we had, we had to make them go to England, take them from England, bring them back to Zimbabwe, because the Black South Africans didn't have the right to have a passport, so in order to get your passport you had to be an artist. You'd go do your job in England, but when you came back, they'd keep the passport, so there was no way out. You couldn't get out. So in order to get the actors in you have to say that there is a group of people doing theater in England. They said that they had a deal to be in a play, so that was how they got their passports. They went all the way to England, and from England we send them back to Zimbabwe to be in the

movie. The fact that I had these very people who were experiencing apartheid every day—all of these actors—they knew the story by heart because they went through it, they lived it, they had a tortured brother or father, they had to go to the morgue with a friend, and find their relative or stuff like that. So when you are in it with them you don't think, you just do it, get it done, and that's what I did. But when you carry these things for so long and then it's over and you start to have some rest, your brain starts to work and says, "Okay, I did that," and then you have flashes of images going through your head and I realized how fragile I'd become from this long experience—this long time of working and digging and dealing with this material. And so that's why that made me so sad, so depressed, so sick, and in fact, I needed music. I used music as a therapy to cure me, to bring me back to life, normal life and to joy. I decided to do Simeon (1992), a comedy with music as the backbone. It's a mixture of genres. And you have special effects because it's also a fantasy of sorts. You have the music, you have the comedy and there is a love story, so it's a mixture. I was looking for something, and I said, "I need a comedy, I need to laugh, I need to have music." I love all this, and it's is based on our culture. To me Simeon is a celebration of life, a celebration of music, a celebration of the Afro-Caribbean culture.

GA: And there's so much life in it. The performances are excellent.
EP: You know what? I love that in all my movies. I love to find people who are untrained actors and mix them with the professionals, and of course it's tough for me because I have to work with them so hard to bring them to the same level, but I love the challenge. I love that, and every time people say, "Oh, my God, your actors . . ." They believe that they are all professional actors, and that's the best compliment for me. In Sugar Cane Alley it was the same thing. I had maybe three professional actors, the grandmother, the old African man, and one of the military guys. Everybody else was a nonprofessional.

GA: That's amazing, and you audition the nonprofessionals?
EP: I audition them, I choose them and I say, "Okay, good, now we have to work." So I work more with them. I start to work with them ahead of time. As soon as I cast them, we work. We do very simple things and I develop techniques to work with these nonprofessionals. I have tricks that I use.

GA: Can you share some of your tricks? [Laughs]
EP: It's very personal. It's not a recipe that someone else could follow. I can share it, it's not a secret, but if I say it, somebody else might try it and it might not work. Like the kids, for example, they live with me. Their parents give them to me, and they come to know me, trust me. It's like

when you do a marinade, every lemon has to take. So I work with them and we talk and laugh and joke. And during such time I observe them. I say, "Oh, my God, this one is a very sensitive kid. I notice that he has a way of blinking his eyes or swallowing his saliva when he's emotional or he has this kind of little thing that he does, a nervous tic." I observe them and I take notes and I use that information to express the emotional bit.

GA: *And how long do the children live with you?*
EP: I usually keep them for fifteen days. They come, I cook for them, I eat with them, we work, we go out, we have fun. With the adults, it's different. They come to my place on the weekend and we work, we talk about the characters and I show them films and I explain to them everything about their characters and I make them feel so comfortable that they forget about the camera. They just do. I think that it's purely a question of relationship and trust. They have to trust you.

GA: *I just love the way you deal with your characters. The kids seem so alive. They really don't seem like they're acting. The little girl in Siméon is a doll.*
EP: And also, talking about dolls, did you see my message with the Black doll in Siméon?

GA: *Yes, it was powerful, very powerful.*
EP: That's why I'm saying that as a filmmaker, I'm trying to use my art to help people open their eyes and make them think.

GA: *But you didn't hit us over the head with your message about the doll.*
EP: That's the point, because when you do a comedy, you have to do it but with a smile. You see, you do it in a very subtle way. The kid wanted a doll, but she didn't want the Black doll, so she threw it on the floor. She is shocked because if it's supposed to be a doll she should be white with blond hair and blue eyes, because it was a part of colonialism that all the dolls in the countries were white. There were very few Black dolls in Martinique. If you looked for a Black doll before I made Siméon, they would tell you, "Oh, no, we don't have Black dolls." And you would have a lot of white dolls, blue eyes, all kind of stuff. The only Black doll you would find was Barbie. In the collection of Barbies there is a Black girl, there is an Indian girl, and that's it.

So I was sick of seeing all my little girls in Martinique playing with white dolls. I'm not racist, that's not the point. But I'm saying, imagine if every kid in this country, the first minute they were born, the first gift they would receive was a Black doll or a Japanese doll. How would that affect their psyche? You see, so the little girls saw themselves as white girls, and I was sick of it. I said,

"Okay, I cannot go and write about it. I cannot go and be on the radio and ask the mothers to be more responsible and to change it. I have to put it in a movie." That's the power of images, and I played it subtly. I made it funny, because the kid says, "I don't want the doll because she's Black." Simeon is laughing like hell. He should be shocked, but he's laughing like hell because he knows exactly what that means. But then the big sister takes the little girl and says to her, "Come, look at her. She's beautiful." The little girl says, "No she's not!" The big sister says, "Yeah, she' s just like you. Look at her little mouth, just like yours. She's pretty." Then she says, "The white people, why do you think they are lying out in the sun? Just to be tan like us," and the little girl says, "Oh, really? I thought it was to become red." So you make a joke with it, but then the little girl is happy with her little Black baby.

When the movie came out, that changed the whole thing. Oh, my God, people stopped me to say, "Wow, every kid wants a Black doll now." You see the power of movies. That's why I say when you are a filmmaker, you have to be responsible because you can, you can set fire in a country, revolution, and you can make progress, make people change to become better, think, take a stand for what is right. You can do that too.

GA: *Do you think that is why it's so difficult for people of color or Black people to get control of their images, because film is such a powerful medium?*

EP: I do believe so. The white people want to be in charge of our images because they want to perpetuate the ones that they have been selling for centuries, which means that Black is not commercial, you cannot sell Black, they don't know how to market Black because if it's not funny, they do not know how to market it all of a sudden. When Black is smart, Black is intelligent, Black is beautiful, they do not know how to market it. That's why my relationship with the studio is fantastic, because I've got no problem with ego. And when I walk in and they give me a project and it's all white, I say, "Okay, it's up to me to sneak some Blackness into it, some color," and very simply I say, "What about making this character Black, Latino or Asian?" I'm working on a comedy and today I asked what if the dentist, instead of being a man, were a Black woman. Would you have a problem with that? Do you have a specific reason why he's a man?" The executive said, "No." I said, "Okay, fine, thank you. I'll change it."

GA: [Laughs]

EP: It's good because the studio is open. The executives listen to me and we discuss it. So it's up to us as creators to take them on that ride.

GA: Very powerful. Tell me about The Killing Yard, the Attica film, which you did for Showtime. How did you get involved in that project?

EP: I was developing some action comedies, and I got a call that there was a movie called The Killing Yard being produced by Paramount for Showtime—the most expensive film that Paramount has produced for Showtime—and that Alan Alda was attached and that he would like me to direct. The studio also wanted me to direct. So I read the script and I said, "Okay, this is a great story." We just needed to fix some stuff in the script. The writer Benita Garvin was fantastic, and she was very open to all the changes, because in fact, Warner Brothers had developed the project for eight years and after that dropped it. Does that ring a bell? A Dry White Season. They dropped it and MGM picked it up. So they dropped The Killing Yard after eight years, after they asked Benita to write and rewrite the script, and when I got the script, it was a mess, but the story was great. You could feel that there was a lot of stuff that they cut.

For example, Shango [played by Morris Chestnut] didn't have a mother, didn't have a family, you didn't know where he came from. All you knew was that he was in jail. But Benita was such a great woman. When I told her that the script was good, but that she had to do some more rewriting because I didn't know who Shango was, she said, "I'll tell you something. I had all this in the script, but they made me cut that, but I can bring it back. I'm so happy that you are asking me to bring that back, because of course I know this is needed." We started to work and she brought everything back. So it's important that I tell you that, because in another article the writer didn't put everything that I said in the story and it came out a little bit nasty about Benita because I was saying that the script wasn't in good shape. But she has no ego problem and she knew the script needed work because Warner Brothers made her cut out important scenes during the rewrite, which happens all the time. They make you do a lot of rewrites and then you lose focus. Then they go so far in the rewrite process that they go away from the very reason they loved the script in the first place. The result at the end is terrible, and then they say, "Well, we don't like it anymore," and they dump it. So that's what happened with Benita, poor girl.

GA: In a story like that where they decide to focus on . . .

EP: One character or two, yeah, and guess who's the first person that they cut? The Black people. So I read it [the script] and I loved it and I said, "Okay, so let's fix that and it will be fine," and even Alan Alda had some problems as well, because he said, "Well, I don't want to be the great white hope here." He wanted me to direct the movie for the same reason, because he knew that if somebody else directed the film, the focus would be put much more on the white guy, but with me he was sure that I would find the right balance.

GA: Morris Chestnut was great in the film. I hadn't seen him in a dramatic role in a long time.

EP: And the studio didn't want him. Paramount and Showtime felt like they needed somebody stronger and more dramatic.

GA: Who did they want?

EP: Oh, they went all over the place for the big obvious guys, but they were not available and I said, "Look, I need Morris Chestnut for two reasons. I know this guy has the potential and second of all, I'm used to working with non-professionals." Morris is a professional, but he'd never done this type of role before and I knew that I could take him to that level. I said, "You have to trust me on that, and also he's very handsome, and, so what that he's done romantic comedies, but there are many, many handsome brothers in jail, so that doesn't hurt. That's a plus." They said, "Okay, fine, fine, fine." The whole relationship I had with the studio was good, because they would argue about something, and I would say, "No, no, no, wait a minute." And it was up to me to convince them. That's how Morris got the part. And I shot outside the real Attica. The studio allowed me to do it. I said, "I cannot accept the idea of making a movie in 2002 about Attica today and not be able to show the real face of Attica, c'mon." So they said, "You're right, we'll try, we'll do our best." And they said yes. They gave me what I needed to make the movie.

GA: What's your advice to aspiring directors?

EP: There is something I'd like to tell you, because it's very important. You are maybe the second person I've mentioned it to in some years. When I did A Dry White Season I worked with Marlon Brando, who played an anti-apartheid lawyer. The movie went very well, everything was great, but I shot a scene with him when he insults the magistrate, and the magistrate asks the bailiff to drag him out and expel him from the courtroom. So I shot that, I did maybe five takes, and every time Brando's robe would open it would expose his belly. He would be out of breath [demonstrates by panting] because he hadn't worked in ten years, and we were so scared, my producer Paula Weinstein and I.

She would say, "Okay, Euzhan, you know what? Every time you do that [scene], it's the same problem. I don't want him to have a heart attack on the set, so leave it alone, okay?" I said that I'd have to work around it in the cutting room. When I re-stitched the scene, I put all the pieces together and it was so funny. It was hilarious, and I couldn't leave the scene in the movie with big Brando being dragged out screaming, kicking with his belly out in the middle of a dramatic piece. But because I didn't have final cut on the film, I called the head of the studio about it. My producer had already said, "Oh, my God, this has to go." So the head of the studio said that I had to cut it. So out of respect for Marlon because he did the movie for free, I sent a tape to him with the scene and without the scene so he could compare and see why I cut it, but he wanted it to be in the movie. To make a long story short, Marlon gave me hell. He called and begged me to leave it in. I told him that the scene was bad and that it would hurt him and the film. I said, "People won't recover, they won't go back into the movie after they see that scene." Brando later contacted the head of the studio and argued with him on the phone. He said, "I want to come to the cutting room, and I want to force her to put my scene back."

The studio head said, "Look, this is her movie, she doesn't want the scene there and the scene won't be there, and I will not allow you to come to the cutting room to substitute yourself as the director." Marlon felt insulted. Up until then, he was in love with me, but the minute the studio head said that and I said, "No, I don't want to put it [the scene] back," he hated me and he said, "She's a woman, you realize she's a woman, a young director, and I am Marlon Brando!"

So Marlon was very mad at me and he said, "If you don't put my scene back you are playing hardball with me. I will make sure that you never work in Hollywood again." He went on and on and on.

GA: Oh, wow.
EP: Yes, and that was very hard for me, because then we hung up.

GA: How did you deal with it at the time?
EP: It was very hard for me. I was so sad, I was crying and I was very hurt. Then the movie came out and he went on TV and he lied and he said that the studio made a money decision and cut off the movie—a very important moment that would definitely bring America to take a stand and nail apartheid in their minds and just make them say, "No, no, no to apartheid." But he never explained what the scene was that we cut.

And he went out and he wrote the book *Songs My Mother Taught Me*, and at the end of the chapter about *A Dry White Season* he wrote that I was a neophyte and out of my depth and didn't know anything and that I cut the movie poorly—everything I told you, he said it in the book. And if I'm not right, tell me, this is the first time ever in American history that a head of a huge studio like MGM backed up a young filmmaker against a star. That had never happened before, because if I had been a shitty director, Marlon Brando could have gotten me fired in a minute.

But the situation with Marlon was very hard for me, and I called my friend Ed Bradley from 60 Minutes. He's a good friend and I needed to talk to somebody. I needed to know what to do because I hate injustice, I hate lies. I'm Caribbean and I'm African, and I'm European, so people here [in the U.S.], when you put dirt on them or you write about them, they are hurt, but they don't do anything, but I said, "I cannot do that. This is not the truth. I cannot let that happen."

I wanted to do something about it. I wanted people to know that this was not true. So I flew to New York, and I spent hours at Ed's house and asked him his advice. He said, "Euzhan, you came all the way to get some advice from a friend. I'll give you my best advice on that—forget it. Dump it. Don't do anything, because the most important thing is the movie. You don't want to bring attention to Marlon Brando, because people know Marlon, they know Marlon. Every time he makes a movie, there is a big scandal.

"So don't worry, so don't worry. Wait for your moment and when people ask you about it, the truth will come out, even if it's ten years later, the truth will come out. Don't do anything, just leave it alone and focus on the promotion of your movie."

And when I did all the promotion, people would ask me what happened with Brando because nobody could understand what the hell was going on, and I'd say, "I don't know, why don't you ask him?" I never answered the question. So now years later, a few months ago, I was in a meeting with some people and the creative producer told me, "Euzhan, I have a story for you. I cannot believe how small the world is, because the day that Marlon called the head of the studio to tell him that he wanted to come to the cutting room to force you to put the scene back, we were in that room hearing Marlon cursing and screaming because he was on speakerphone." I said, "Can you believe this?" Twelve years later I have someone telling me that he was in that room, he heard everything Marlon Brando said.

GA: Wow.

EP: And he said , "I was sitting there, and we were laughing. It was hilarious."

GA: [Laughs] That's amazing.

EP: You see how everything comes full circle? And I've never published that story because it took me time to heal because it was very painful for me. Here is a man [Brando] who did a movie for free, we had the most fantastic relationship, and then he became evil because he wanted his bad scene back in the movie and I protected the film.

GA: That's brilliant.

EP: So to answer your question, if I have another piece of advice to give to filmmakers today—it's that you have to keep your integrity. Try to stick to that. Keep your integrity, sell your art, not your ego. Don't let people make you do what you believe is wrong, because sooner or later, you'll pay for it. That's the best advice I can give. Stick to what you believe is the truth, what is right. Don't let people make you take another road, because you'll pay for it—any compromise, you'll pay for it.

Julie Dash

Any cinema lover who has witnessed the panoramic beauty and African American pageantry of Julie Dash's 1992 *Daughters of the Dust* knows they've tasted an eye's feast of that which is special, original, honest and fresh about African American storytelling on these shores.

Her first feature film and the film for which she is best known, *Daughters* made Dash the first African American female director to have a full-length general theatrical release. *Filmmaker* magazine named *Daughters* one of the fifty most important independent films ever made. In 1999, the 25th Annual Newark Black Film Festival honored Dash and *Daughters* as one the most important cinematic achievements in Black cinema in the twentieth century.

More recently, Dash has directed *The Rosa Parks Story* (2002) for CBS starring Angela Bassett, *Love Song* (2000) for MTV with singer Monica and *Funny Valentines* (1999) for BET/Encore/Starz3 with Alfre Woodard, Loretta Devine and C.C.H. Pounder. Dash's music video work includes videos for Tony, Toni, Tone's *Thinking of You* and Tracy Chapman's *Give Me One Reason*, for which she was nominated for MTV's Best Video for a Female Vocalist in 1996.

With her awarding-winning Web site, www.geechee.tv, Dash has entered the world of new technologies. She is presently working on an interactive CD ROM/Internet project called "Digital Diva" for the Wexner Center for the Arts and her company Geechee Girl Media.

A native of New York City, Dash got her start in film at the Studio Museum in Harlem in 1969. She went on to study film at the City College of New York. Following her undergraduate studies, Dash attended the Center for Advanced International Studies at the American Film Institute, where she studied under the tutelage of such renowned filmmakers as William Friedken, Jan Kadar and Slavko Vorkapich and later earned an MFA in film and television production at UCLA.

■ ■ ■ ■

GA: Tell me about growing up in New York City. Were you creative as a child?

JD: No, not at all. I grew up in the Long Island City Queens Bridge projects right underneath the 59th Street bridge. I don't think I was very creative at all, and in my last year of high school a friend said, "There's a film workshop in Harlem at the Studio Museum in Harlem. You wanna go?" So we started going, and we were there for two weeks before we realized that it wasn't still photography, it was motion pictures. We were so stupid.

GA: [Laughs]

JD: [Laughs] And that's how I got into filmmaking.

GA: I love the Studio Museum. That sounds like a great program.

JD: They don't have the program anymore. It ended in '71, I think.

GA: But you learned a lot about filmmaking?

JD: Oh, yes. I saw my first foreign films. I saw my first subtitled films, Eisenstein's, The Battleship Potemkin. We were hardcore.

GA: So did you have to apply to the Studio Museum program, and was it expensive?

JD: The program was free, and you just showed up. Whoever showed up, they'd give you a 16mm Bolex camera and some film and tell you to go shoot. And they had people coming in explaining the whole editing process. The teacher would talk about the films, and he would show us foreign films and we'd watch. The Eisenstein films were the most memorable because they had subtitles. I thought, "Are we expected to sit here and read this? We have to read it?" We were so immature as I look back, but then I feel in love with storytelling and especially the foreign films, because you'd go in there and it was like a clean slate, you don't know the culture, you don't know the characters, they don't necessarily work from a Hollywood formula, and it's total immersion into a story and that's what I like. I don't like to know what's going to happen. But of course we're at a disadvantage now, because we've all taken all these screenplay courses and we know how to structure a film now, but it's quite refreshing not to quite know what's going to happen and be able to go along with the magic.

GA: *Tell me about the magic of cinema. Are films magical?*
JD: It's all smoke and mirrors, and I like that. It's so hard to control the real world, but I always like the notion of being able to control what's inside of my frame to re-create the world—we define it, create magic. It's just a wonderful thing to be able to have an idea playing inside your head and then be able to make it a reality, make it into something you could not only physically see in real time in the real world, but that other people could see and comment upon. So I just think as storytellers and filmmakers we're all blessed.

GA: *Did you decide to be a filmmaker while you were at the Studio Museum?*
JD: No, because I was young, and I didn't think of filmmaking as something that I'd do to support myself. I did it for the joy. It was my hobby. It was what I did. We were being artists.

GA: *When you were in high school, what career path did you plan to take?*
JD: My mother and father were going to take care of me. I thought the revolution was going to take care of that. This was during the '70s. [Laughs]

GA: [Laughs] *That's funny.*
JD: [Laughs] We'd find out later. So then it was time for me to go to college, I went to the City College of New York, and I was studying psychology. Then, after my second year, they were going to create a program—the David Picker Institute for Arts and the Picker Film Institute—and I said, "Mmmm. Well, if I switch over to film from psychology I'll get an A because I've already been doing this." That was my reason for majoring in film, because still at the time it was just something that I did. I went to the Studio Museum. I hung out at night. I'd walk or take a cab home. By that time, my family had moved up to Harlem, 138th Street. And it was just cool. But then I graduated with an undergraduate degree in film, and by that time I was really hooked and I had gotten all these fliers from L.A. about filmmakers like Haile Gerima and Larry Clark and Charles Burnett. They were doing dramatic narratives and we were doing mostly documentaries, because we were telling the people's story and doing newsreels, a little bit of experimental stuff with animation, but these guys out in L.A. were doing dramatic narratives.

I thought, "Uuuuu, so let me go to UCLA for graduate school." So I applied and I came out here, and for some reason all of my paperwork wasn't in so I didn't get into UCLA, but I got into

AFI [American Film Institute], which was a two-year conservatory of intensive film study, and for the first time threw me back into a situation where I was dealing with a lot of foreign students, a lot of foreign film, and it was very good for me at that time. After I finished AFI, I went to UCLA for four years for my MFA. I actually did six years of postgraduate work. At UCLA I was able to work with people like Larry Clark and Haile.

GA: *How important is film school for filmmakers?*
JD: It's always nice to know the history and to know the language of film, but you don't have to. I would not say that you cannot be a filmmaker if you don't go to film school, because some people don't have access to it but they still have the passion to tell stories. So you don't have to, you can come into it from another discipline. But what you should know is that there is a definite language, a grammar of film, and you must know the history of film. Otherwise you will start repeating things like . . . Who wants to be negative? I won't go there.

GA: *Well, just give an example without naming names.*
JD: Well, people often make suggestions to directors of things that they've seen before or something that impressed them. But you may not know that it comes from a very biased notion of our history. I mean, I've seen contemporary movies with scenes re-created from *Birth of a Nation* [D. W. Griffith] in Black films, like in the Senate hall when Black people take it over and they're eating chicken with their feet up on the desks. I don't know if that's supposed to be funny or not, but it's not. Is that supposed to be a postmodernist's version of the D. W. Griffith's *Klansmen* [the original title of *Birth of a Nation*] or what? But I think the filmmakers don't even know, but the producers above them or the people making suggestions do, and I don't think it's a heinous plot or anything. I just think that at some place you just have to draw the line.

GA: *You celebrate women a lot in your films. You have lots of very strong female characters in your work. What's the genesis of your storytelling?*
JD: I come from a family of lots of women and I know what we do and what we talk about. Also, I came up and was educated in a time during the second wave of feminism. So I'm very much aware of issues, womanist issues, and now we're living in a time where people are trying to not be politically correct. But what they're doing is reversing things by trying to not be politically correct.

GA: *Give me an example of what you mean by not politically correct in the context of women's issues.*
JD: Not being politically correct is when a studio decides to not hire a woman to direct a woman's

story because people expect a woman to be hired. It might be expected, but it's not usually done. We're still in the infancy of producing our own movies and telling our stories.

GA: *Would* Waiting to Exhale *be an example of that for you, where a man, Forest Whitaker, directed a woman's story?*
JD: Uh-huh. Yeah. I think he did a fine job, but it would have made a big difference had a woman directed it, and it didn't have to be me. I mean, at the time you had Neema Barnett, Euzahn Palcy and now you've got Kasi Lemmons, Gina Prince-Bythewood, you've got all these women who would have brought something more to it. One of the most sensitive male filmmakers I know is Charles Burnett. When I first saw his *Killer of Sheep,* I thought, "Who did that?" For a man, he's a very sensitive filmmaker. So I think it is doable for a man to be sensitive.

GA: *When you started out, was it always your intent to make independent films?*
JD: That was my intent, to do independent filmmaking.

GA: *Why?*
JD: Because I make films first to please me, and of course there is always a situation of art versus commerce and the pleasing me part is the art part and the commerce part is the audience. You have to make films that people want to come out and see, in addition to films on subject matter that you enjoy yourself. The films have to be entertaining, enlightening in some kind of way. Now, things are very competitive in terms of independent films that even get picked up, because there are plenty of them being made that are not being picked up by distributors, which is the commerce part. But in general, the independent film that they're talking about now is not really independent unless it's from a single mind or independent voice or thought. The director can't have a group of people, a committee, telling her what to do, then turn around and call it independent, but that's the new spin of a lot of these new independent films.

GA: *So companies like Lions Gate and . . .*
JD: And Miramax, that's not independent. It's not independent thought. It's not a filmmaker's vision. They're not signature films, no. The independent film movement is on a slippery slope going down, because even that term, that moniker, has been co-opted by Hollywood. It's independent at Sundance, right. They have very few real independent films at the Sundance Film Festival [the country's most prominent independent film festival].

GA: When you did Daughters of the Dust, did you have any idea you were creating something that would have such impact and would be considered a masterpiece?

JD: No, because once again it was more of a collaborative effort between myself and the cinematographer, Arthur Jafa, and the production designer, Kerry Marshall. We had so many meetings about it. We wanted to do an authentic African American film that was truly a foreign film to the eyes of Americans because it was so not like Hollywood in terms of the story structure. It was very African in the way the story is revealed and unfolds slowly, like the way an African griot would tell a story and recount tales.

And then there were the two narrative voices: the voice of the unborn child and the voice of the great-grandmother. Because I remember at AFI, they would say, "You could never have two people . . . !" I thought "Oh, well, that's what I'm gonna do." And it wasn't just to be contrary, it was that we come from a whole different vibe. We [African Americans] come from the vibe that created jazz, voices speak to us and it is not like something spooky. We deal with ancestral relationships in a whole different way than Western society. We see them as protectors. Like in the novel Beloved [by Toni Morrison] when the baby was coming.

GA: The "crawling already baby." I love that. The mysticism and ancestral relationships, do you think this is something we as African Americans have gotten away from as a culture? Spike Lee was saying the same thing, that we have gotten away from some of it. He mentioned his grandmother and dreams.

JD: We don't incorporate that in our work anymore. When I say "we" I mean the larger "we." One of the most endearing things that I remember from Spike's She's Gotta Have It was when his character's girlfriend was combing and greasing his scalp. On one hand, my sister was saying that embarrassed her in the theater, and for me it was, "Oh, yeah. We always do that." It's just the little things, the tiny specifics of our lives are becoming very homogenized. And in working in Hollywood, I notice that there's such resistance to it because some people assume because they've never seen or heard of something before then no one has. I remember when I was doing Funny Valentines, I wanted to include these Baptist church ushers in the story. Well, there were some people who had never heard of an usher. And I said, "Well, I was an usher. I was a junior usher." They'd never heard of an usher, so they couldn't understand how anyone in the television viewing audience could appreciate it or would want to see one because they'd never seen an usher.

GA: So as far as they're concerned, it's not valid.

JD: Yeah, it doesn't exist. It's zero, not. You don't exist. I said, "Wait a minute. Don't you see on Sunday all of the ushers." They said, "No, I've never seen one of those." And the thought is "If I don't know, no one else will know, so you can't put it in there." So, little things like that in our lives just don't exist. It's not that we don't exist, the tiny specifics of our lives don't matter in many instances. And you have to be very careful to make sure that they do remain in the story and that they do matter, because they really do matter.

GA: *And how does one do that—make sure the details stay in the film?*
JD: You write it in and then you fight for it. And the fighting goes on from the time you first insert it in to the time you shoot. They try to make sure that there's not enough time during the day to shoot that scene. When you're editing they try to say that due to time constraints you can't edit that segment. So you're battling, battling, battling until the very end, until the film is locked. It just goes on for months and months and months. It's exhausting, and sometimes the battle is about a second and a half or three seconds of information. Three seconds of information.

GA: *And this happened on Funny Valentines.*
JD: Funny Valentines, The Rosa Parks Story.

GA: *Give me some examples in Rosa where you had to push to keep relevant details in the film.*
JD: In Rosa it was with the hanging of the NAACP flag, the silent protest that said, "A Man was Lynched Today." I just shot that. I didn't even put it in the script. I didn't even try to get it in the script because I didn't want to argue it, so I just shot it. So the arguments began during post-production, because the producers had never seen it or heard of it before. I said, "Well, I have never witnessed it, but I've seen pictures of it—the hanging of flags in Harlem. That was their silent protest." I felt they would shoot the tracing of the shoes at the shoe store. Black people weren't allowed to try on shoes or anything at the store, and why have a situation with a store being there and you're right there and you're shooting it and you have the opportunity to tell more, why not? And they said that it was too much off the main story. No, it's right on story. It's deeper into the story. We could not try on shoes. I was raised by a mother who could not try on shoes, and so I'm growing up in the fifties and she's still tracing my foot. I said, "Mommy, why are you doing this? You don't have to do this." Because she grew up in the South, I was reared by a woman who this happened to.

GA: *Why do you think producers don't want to include information that should, in fact, make for a richer and truer story?*
JD: I think it's a combination of things. Most television producers don't know our culture at all. They don't know the tiny specifics, the nuances, the depths of our culture. It's a lot of new infor-

mation, because most only know the broad strokes of history and culture. It can take them weeks to process something new before they can say, "Yeah." One producer told me—I was suggesting including Septima Clark [Black civil rights worker] in the story—they said that they had to check because they didn't know if Septima Clark was white or Black. I said, "Well, she's Black, because she was down home talking to my grandmother when I was growing up." He said, "Well, we're going to have to check." I said, "I just told you. Do you want me to pull down the books with her picture in it?" Basically, what they're saying to you is that you don't have the facts until they find the time to legitimize and approve the information you're giving them.

GA: *Do you think a white director would be challenged in the same way?*
JD: No. No. And I think that when you have a whole lot of information that you start sharing, it starts to become scary to some folks and they say, "No, no, no. It's getting off story." I'm not just talking about *Rosa* or *Funny Valentines*, it's across the board. One of the things that really upset me, and it was the network—but that person is no longer at the network—but she sent a memo during post-production saying that she wanted a line of dialogue written in for Rosa to say, "Well, I just didn't get up because my feet hurt." That was the prevailing myth at the time. Why would I do something like that when every Black person on the face of the planet knows that was not true? These network executives and producers were asking me to commit cultural suicide, just because they had no idea of what the impact could be within the Black community. And furthermore, they did not care. Months later, we did a tour of the states promoting the film, and just before each and every screening, an African American representative of the community would stand up and say, "We no longer have to live with the myth that Mrs. Parks refused to give up her seat just because her feet hurt or that she was tired." I'm paraphrasing what was said, but my point is, what if I had allowed that statement to be made in the movie? And we're sitting there with everyone who knows it was not true. They never acknowledged that they were wrong or off track, they just played it off like it never happened. Of course, this was before the *Barbershop* controversy.

GA: *Right, but it was as if Rosa didn't have any political motivations.*
JD: The rationale was that they wanted her to be liked. I said, "That's undermining the truth with rumor. Why would you do something like that? Isn't film supposed to clear up those kinds of misconceptions?" They said, "Just do it." I said, "No, I'm not going to do it."

GA: *How did you get involved with Rosa from the beginning?*
JD: Angela [Bassett] asked me to direct and do something more with the script. Willis Edwards

and Yvonne Chotzen approached Les Moonves, president and CEO at CBS, about doing the movie and he said, "Yes, if you get someone the caliber of an Angela Bassett to play Rosa, yes." So they went to Angela, she said yes and she became a producer, and thank God that she did, because there were so many times during our short nineteen-day shoot when they pulled the plug on me and Angela unpulled it. [Some]times a wrap was called, people started to scuttle for a wrap and she said, "What about this scene?" I said, "The plug was pulled on us." She said, "No, we're going to do it." I was shocked. The wrapped crew was unwrapped.

GA: *What was it like working with Angela Basset as an artist?*

JD: I was impressed. She is a consummate professional. She does her homework, does her research. There's a sequence that takes place over time with the hanging of an NAACP flag, "A Man Was Lynched Today," and since it wasn't in the script, costumes, cars, were not scheduled. But we did it anyway, and Angela was willing to change costumes right there on the street in order to make it happen. She nailed the way Rosa spoke, which was very difficult. We used to call it the "I Dream of Jeannie" speak, because Mrs. Parks to this day doesn't use conjunctions. She doesn't say "I won't" or "I didn't." It's "I will not, I did not." To speak like that is very difficult. She only says "I won't" once, because it was too difficult when she and Mr. Parks were arguing about going to the church that night and she said, "But you are my husband, and if you do not want me to go, I won't."

GA: *Interesting. I didn't think about that as I watched the film.*

JD: It's the subtleties of it, but it's very authentic in the way she's speaking. I even had people question the way Angela speaks in the film. They would say things like, "Well, she doesn't have a southern accent. Why not?" I'd say, "Well, Ms. Rosa Parks didn't have a southern accent. What you've been seeing on television with everyone drawling their voice isn't the truth." I heard the same thing with *Daughters of the Dust*. They were saying, "What are they speaking?" They were speaking Gullah dialect, but it's not a southern drawl. Both of my parents came from South Carolina and neither one of them had a southern drawl. And Mississippi accents are different, Alabama, but everything is like Scarlett O'Hara, "Oh, hi, darlin'." This kind of drawn-out antebellum stuff. It's not real.

GA: *And Black people definitely don't speak that way. Like Whitley on A Different World, it's funny but we don't speak that way down South.*

JD: I know, but they like to lump us together, we're this big monolith. The urban "Yo, yo, yo." All the people I know who talk like that, they don't talk like that when they get into their homes. They talk like that on the street. They don't talk to their mother like that, but in some of these films it's "Yo, mom."

GA: And it's not true. I also like your music videos. The Tracy Chapman video was great.
JD: And Tony, Toni, Tone's *Thinking of You* was good.

GA: That's a hot song. I like that one.
JD: What about Keb 'Mo? I did him too. I'm going to do a Robert Johnson movie and he's going to do him. He looks just like Robert Johnson.

GA: The blues man. Do you think we as Blacks value our history and the front-liners of the Civil Rights Movement?
JD: I think prior to *Boycott* and *Sins of the Fathers*, this new kind of telling of our civil rights icons, prior to Clark Johnson's *Boycott*, I never really considered Martin Luther King the man, the family man. I saw him as this larger-than-life figure who died for his people, and there's this wonderful humanity that Clark was able to bring out in his story. It had such resonance. I just cried and cried and cried at the end. And I knew that I wanted to do something like that with Rosa. I wanted to make her Rosa the woman, not Rosa the icon, who's sitting there stiff and prim with her little hat on and the glasses. But she was a woman too, she was a wife and she was the mother of many. She was the mother of the Civil Rights Movement but they were not able to have children of their own, which is really the irony.

GA: How did you research for the Rosa project?
JD: I did interviews, I spoke with Mrs. Parks, went on the Internet and read books, books, books written about women who were around her, because I was determined to get a more womanist vision, a female version of what was going on, because it was a very male-centered script. Rosa was just kind of floating in the background.

GA: So you wanted to present her as a strong woman?
JD: Not so much as a strong woman, but human. She was strong in her determination. But she was a seamstress, and she was and still is a deeply religious person with a firm commitment to her community and to her work. And when things just stopped making sense all around she just refused to continue on with it. But she was a very private person and still is, and if she had known that all of this publicity would come from it, I don't know if she'd have done it.

GA: Daughters of the Dust has such a specific style and voice. How do you bring your style and voice to your other work like your music videos, Rosa, and the MTV film you did with Monica, Love Song?

JD: That's a great question because it's a difficult one. I'm very interested in the culture of women, how women see things, how I see things, how the women I've known have seen things, what they talk about, how they do it, the tiny specifics and all the nuances of what it is to be a woman of the African diaspora, living, working, thriving, functioning.

I want to see authenticity. That's what I strive for, because I think authenticity provides us with just as much flavor, interest and spice. It's wonderful for me watching a foreign film, because there are so many unknown elements that keep rising to the surface. With more films being made by African Americans, we're starting to see a wider variety of things that are authentic and that really hit the spot. So in my films that's been a task; I try to create something new, something original, something authentic, something that makes people say, "Hmmm," something more like music—jazz. It's complex, quickly changing and it takes you places.

GA: Hitchcock liked to get involved with the minute details of costuming. You like to get involved in a lot of things. Are you meticulous in that way? Were you very involved in the costuming of Daughters?

JD: Yes. I love to go through the colors, because colors, in each culture mean different things, and so since I'm doing things mostly for Western culture I tend to lean toward the whole theory of color in Western society.

GA: So you study lots of books and photos?

JD: Yes, there are journals about what colors mean when they're combined together. For example, if you have red and blue together that's supposed to make you angry and anxious. There are books by Johannes Itten, about the psychology and aesthetics of color, one of them being The Art of Color. I go through those books and things like that. So there's color, design and movement. If there's a scene with constant movement or if the scene is static, how do you lay these emotions? It's scene by scene, sequence by sequence. And you get on the set and it's totally something else.

GA: Given your love of foreign film, who are some of the directors who've influenced you?

JD: I love the Hong Kong films, like Chunkung Express and the early works of John Woo. From India, Sajyit Ray—his Pather Panchali, and the Apu Trilogy, Ozu's poetic work from Japan, and the work of Russian directors like Tarkovsky, a lot of the French directors and Mira Nair, the contemporary Indian American director who made Monsoon Wedding. You know when you go into the theater and you come out and you've had a different experience. You come out of the theater feeling like you've been taken somewhere—on a delightful ride or you've had an experience or you've met someone you didn't know; I get excited even thinking about it. When walking into an American movie, you see the movie and on the way out you can't even remember what the movie was about because you've seen it, it's a tale that's been told a thousand times before; it's the tall tale, the American western way of storytelling: Once upon a time . . . You know the formula. But then sometimes you get a nice roller-coaster ride. I love the American filmmakers like M. Night Shyamalan, but he's Indian American. His Unbreakable, I loved that. To see Sam Jackson walking around with that afro askew, loved that!

GA: What are your hopes for Black women behind the camera?
JD: We have a lot of different stories to tell and we've been seeing some of them. I mean, Gina's [Prince-Bythewood] film Love and Basketball was great. [Laughs] There are all different levels. It doesn't have to be something that's wildly romantic and lyrical. It could just be straight-up good. And I thought that her film was that. But I have hopes for authenticity, something new, something exciting.

GA: What legacy would Julie Dash like to leave?
JD: Oh, killing me off already?

GA: No, no way.
JD: That I had fun creating worlds within a frame. I had fun living and learning and doing.

GA: What advice do you have for aspiring directors?
JD: I would tell them that it's going to be a long journey and along the way people will tell you that you're crazy, that it's not working. But you have to understand that they're looking at it through their eyes and you have to do work that's honest for you. You have to tell your truth, and everyone won't recognize what you're saying, but unless you want to be a traffic cop, you have to do work that pleases you. You have to look for your own truth in each situation and try to work towards that. And always try to do the best that you can do. Just do your best, create the reality you know is real even if it's only a moment of grace from within that you share with your audience.

Lee Daniels

To make it in Hollywood requires guts and tenacity. Lee Daniels has demonstrated that he has what it takes. Daniels started his career in the entertainment industry as a casting director, and then launched his own management company, Lee Daniels Entertainment. Daniels's client list over the years has included such popular Hollywood actors as Marianne Jean-Baptiste (*Secrets & Lies*), Morgan Freeman, Loretta Devine, Michael Biehn, Wes Bentley (*American Beauty*), supermodel, and up-and-coming film star Amber Valletta.

But it was his vision and confidence in the script for the movie *Monster's Ball* (2001) that catapulted Daniels to the ranks of feature-film producer. The critically acclaimed, but risky and controversial, film earned actress Halle Berry the 2002 Academy Award for Best Actress, the first ever for an African American woman.

With an eye that ignites the mind and with the confidence and spirit to accomplish the overwhelming, along with an earthiness and humility seldom seen alongside film-industry glory, Lee Daniels could be a force to reckon with in cinema—Black and otherwise—for years to come.

—   —   —   —

GA: *Growing up in Philadelphia, did you ever envision yourself having a career in show business?*
LD: Yes, I did. I knew I didn't want to act, but I knew I wanted to be in the entertainment field

in some way, shape or form. But there were no outlets. There was the CPA [Creative and Performing Arts] high school in Philadelphia at the time—I'm not sure if it still exists—but it was an outlet for kids in the urban environment to express themselves. However, I couldn't even afford to take the bus to get there, so I think I kept my dreams in the closet and just pursued school. Philadelphia really didn't shape the creative side of me at all. And that's a good point to bring up, because there really should be more creative outlets for minority kids in the ghetto.

GA: *After your father passed away you actually worked on an AIDS project. Tell me about that.*

LD: What happened was that I went to a liberal arts college, Lindenwood, in Missouri and after two years I was burned out on school. I didn't think that I was learning anything and it wasn't really helping me. I said, "I'm outta here." I only had $7 and a plane ticket, and I went to L.A. and stayed with a friend in Hollywood. I wanted to be a writer, but I went to work for a nursing agency. I sold nurses to sick people who were homebound. I knew nothing about nursing. I started as a receptionist and then became a sales rep. It was good because the hours were great, and I could focus on writing. I wasn't really talented as a writer, but I didn't know that yet. And so, before I knew it, I was the manager of the agency. I got burned out on that. I get burned out very quickly on things. A year into it I said, "I might as well open my own agency." So I did, and I started out with five nurses working from my home. By the end of the year, I had five hundred nurses working for me. It was the beginning of the AIDS epidemic and I worked with wonderful women who were fantastic caregivers. I grossed a million dollars at the age of twenty-one. It was insane. It was the easiest money I ever made. One client was a producer's mother. Her son said, "You should really be in the entertainment business." I told him that's what I had started out wanting to do. He was working on a music video for Prince, and I worked on the project and got the bug. One would think that it was etched in stone. You make a million dollars your first year in business and obviously that's the business you're supposed to be in, but at the end of that year, I sold the agency and went to work as an assistant at a casting company.

It's strange. I was wearing an Armani suit and driving a Porsche as an assistant. I learned the business from that perspective and then grew in that arena—limited as it was—because there weren't many casting jobs for Black people at that time. This was the post-blaxploitation era, pre–Spike Lee. They assumed that if you were Black that all you could cast were Black films. There really wasn't much work. So I started managing, and my first client was Morgan Freeman. I realized that I wanted to manage because there was more money in that end of the business.

GA: How did you sign Morgan Freeman?

LD: Well, he wasn't famous, as famous as he is now. But when you're Black in this business you sort of know all of the up-and-coming people. I had seen him in the movie *Street Smart* (1987). He was brilliant, I thought he was going to get an Academy Award. He got the nomination and the rest is sort of history for me. I've been blessed to work with so many great actors. But I didn't like working from Los Angeles, I felt that it was sort of stifling. A lot of the people there are so caught up in trying to be something that they're not. You lose sight of who you are, of the things which make you special. So I had to move to New York, and I've been there for the past seven years; I enjoy it better out there. I come out to L.A. for business, but I find that I'm not caught up like everybody else who lives here because they're so focused on who's doing what. When you live in New York and one next-door neighbor works on Wall Street and the other is a plumber—they don't care about the movie business at all.

GA: You'd been a successful manager, but then you decided to produce and got involved with Monster's Ball, which was actually written in 1995. How did that come about?

LD: I represent an actor named Wes Bentley from *American Beauty*, and the script for Monster's Ball came to me several years ago for him to play the young guy in the film. I thought it was brilliant; it was wonderful. I read three scripts a day, so you know when that special thing is there. About that time, it was with Marlon Brando and Robert De Niro. Sean Penn was directing and they wanted Wes, but they didn't have the money. It was disappointing because I really wanted to see this story made. I said, "Oh, well." Then a year later I got a phone call from Oliver Stone. He was directing it with Tommy Lee Jones playing the now famous Billy Bob Thornton character. We were ready to rock 'n' roll again and it didn't happen. I said, "Ahh, c'mon, I'm not going to live through this again," because when you represent talent they become very attached to a role, to the story. And I said, "You know what? I want to produce this movie." It was time for me, because I was really tired of going down that road—I had taken four clients to the Oscars. I had picked up the phone personally and gotten them that job. As I told you, I get bored very quickly, and I was surprised that I had actually stayed doing what I did for such a long time. So I said that I'd produce it, but the writers of course couldn't understand. They said, "We've had Robert De Niro and Sean Penn, you name it, they've been involved with the film in one way, shape or the other." And I hadn't produced anything. I wasn't a proven producer. I said, "Give me three months and I bet you we can get this greenlit." Because when you're dealing with stars, you're dealing with money and my take on it was that the material spoke for itself. And I saw people every day. It was just a matter of selling the right stars to get the right package together to get it to the right financier. And then it meant finding the right visionary to helm the piece. So they gave it to me and three months to the day—when my option was up—it was greenlit.

GA: *What was your strategy to pull the film together in three months, given that it can take years to put together a project?*

LD: God, I've been asked that often and I have to give it to God, because I just did it. I just made it happen. I was new to the process. I had spent my life on sets for fifteen years. This was my first film, so I wasn't taking NO from anybody. It was incomprehensible for me to assume that I wouldn't get my way. And so, yeah, it was hard. Finding a director was the hardest thing, because we had a lot of big directors who wanted to direct it. I really wanted to find someone fresh, someone who looked at the racism from a naive standpoint. I've been given some flack from the Black community for not hiring a Black director, but I didn't want to hire an American director. I really wanted to hire a foreign director [the director Marc Forster is from Switzerland]. He could have been from anywhere. Just not America. I wanted to find someone who wasn't from this culture and didn't have an American approach to looking at and interpreting the race issue. Black Americans know the deal and white Americans know the deal. So I felt that if we had someone who really did not have a clue to this experience that we would see it from a child's eyes, and they would give us a fresh perspective on interracial relationships.

GA: *How did you get comfortable yourself with the race dynamics in the film?*

LD: I like to choose projects that make people think. And I want America to understand, not just Hollywood, but America to understand that Black people THINK.

GA: *How did Halle Berry get involved in the film?*

LD: She read the script, she liked it and she came in to meet me. I didn't want her for the part; I thought she was too pretty. She said, "Who do you think you are that you can tell me that I'm too beautiful for this and can't play a woman who is downtrodden? Don't you have relatives you perceive to be good-looking? Don't you know somebody in the hood who looks like me? Her words hit me, because I know I have relatives who are strung out on crack, evicted from their homes and who are good-looking. And it made me really think to myself, "I'm practicing reverse discrimination." I had this stereotypical sort of MAMA in mind. She was right. We come in all different packages. That's deep. You know what? I'm really happy that she did it, because she brought a naïveté, an innocence, to the character that maybe the other people would not have brought.

GA: You make an excellent point, and I was thinking of the very same thing today. We as a culture have been so prejudiced by the media that we think that beautiful people are only in magazines or on TV, but in fact there are many beautiful people on welfare rolls, in jail, all over.
LD: Absolutely. Even I had been brainwashed.

GA: I could've given Halle the Oscar just for describing the curtains in her living room in the film.
LD: Utter brilliance.

GA: When it came down to Oscar time, what were your thoughts?
LD: It was an out-of-body experience for me. I don't remember her name being called.

GA: [Laughs]
LD: I knew she was going to win. I knew it! Because it was time. And I knew that from the way God had looked after me on this piece, there was no way that the Oscar wouldn't be the icing on the cake. We had so much love on that set. Everyone worked so hard and put themselves out there to make it happen.

GA: As a producer, what did you do to motivate people on the film?
LD: I was just myself. It was great because the asset that I brought to the project was my experience of working with actors. So when there was minuscule drama, just being able to relate to actors and speak their language helped.

GA: How did you get the cast to come onboard with the project?
LD: They wanted to do it. Everyone in town wanted to do our movie.

GA: Has Halle Berry's Oscar win affected your career?
LD: Yes. I get offers to do movies that I would absolutely never go see.

GA: So you're very selective about the types of projects you want to do?
LD: Yes, I'm selective for my actors and I'm selective for me, so I'll probably starve through the process. But the types of movies I've been offered are embarrassing. That's to be expected. I could

scream racism. But I guess I'm just going to have to educate these people and let them know that this is not what I'm going to do. I'm proud of what I did. I take pride in what I do because I totally commit myself. I could have made a quick million on a couple of projects, but I want to continue to do the types of films that Monster's Ball was, and it's difficult. It's a difficult act to follow. So I want to focus on what I like, and they're not going to be only Monster's Ball–type stories. They're going to appeal to different audiences, but there will always be a Black element involved because I'm Black.

GA: *It appears to me that you have this independent, renegade spirit. You're working within the system, but outside of the system at the same time, and you're working on risky, daunting projects. How do you pull all of the elements together? What's your strategy?*

LD: People say that I'm some overnight success when really it's been years of doing what I do in terms of reading material, etc. I find that it's just the way the cards play out. I have to find stories where there is a Black character or two in the film. A lot of the submissions that I receive are not written with dynamic roles for us. So most times I find myself making a character more dynamic for a Black actor. From there I surround those Black actors with white stars and a few unknowns and then new directors—that's the hard part. Finding material is really easy for me because I read a lot, but really finding that genius of an eye [the director] is the hardest part. Also, I really want to work with Black people. I really want to find films for Black directors, I'm searching desperately to find a discovery in the ghetto. That's really hard to do, but I'm going to find him or her. Because she's there. She's up in the projects someplace waiting for Big Daddy.

GA: *[Laughs] Do you think your approach is perhaps the future of Black film—different stories, unique stories—or are you just doing what Lee Daniels has to do to keep his thing going?*

LD: I don't know how other Black people do their thing. I can just speak for me. I think that the problem is that there's no unity in Black entertainment, and in fact it makes me sad, because without unity we have nothing. I can't even say what I want to say, but I'll speak generically about it and say that whites are definitely unified and we're not. It has nothing to do with Hollywood, it's just Blacks in general. It has to do with slavery and how they separated us. So I don't have an answer for that. I can only be responsible for myself and try to make sure that most of my crew is Black. Sometimes that gets difficult because of the union thing. I understand and respect that a union film has to have a union crew, but getting into the union, which comes via contacts and work experience, is not always so easy for people of color to accomplish. It's important for me to continue to make Hollywood think about Blacks in this business because they see and know us from the films that we've done. And I didn't know this—that's what's so deep about it—and I'm forty-two, I'll be forty-three in December, and I did not know that there was racism in Hollywood. I mean, many of the friends who have helped me are white.

GA: *Are people conscious of their racism or are they unaware of it?*
LD: It's the way they think about us, and I didn't know that. And that saddened me too; it's a sad state of affairs. But I don't have time to worry about all of those politics, I've got movies to make. However, I can say that they don't want us in that house—producing. They want us to sing for them, to dance, play ball, maybe direct, write, act, but they don't want ME [a producer]. They don't want Black decision makers. There aren't many me's out there and I'm aware of that. It took me a minute to get the significance of what it was that I did. I just wanted to make a movie. I figured, Halle Berry, Billy Bob Thornton would hit the video box. I didn't know that it was going to be the sensation it's been. It took me a minute to really grasp the magnitude of what happened.

GA: *Have there been any negative reactions to your success?*
LD: Some. "How did you get this?" But for every player hater there's been a little old lady who grabs my arm and says, "Didn't I see you in Ebony? Honey, I loved your movie!"

GA: *[Laughs] I loved the film, but why the sex scene? To me, you could've removed the sex scene and the film would've worked and Halle Berry still would've deserved the Oscar.*
LD: I felt that the sex scene was instrumental because I wanted to depict life as we know it and I don't like your stereotypical sex scenes. I don't like what Hollywood gives us for sex scenes. I told Marc Forster, my director, that I wanted to feel that we were sneaking in, that we shouldn't be there. I wanted it raw and I wanted it to feel like we shouldn't be in that room, and that's exactly what we got.

GA: *So that came from you? That was your vision?*
LD: No, it was the director's vision, but I told him what I envisioned before I hired him, to make sure we were on the same page.

GA: *How did you get Halle comfortable with the sex scene?*
LD: Lots of smiles. No, she knew what it was beforehand and I told her that I didn't want any problems.

GA: [Laughs]

LD: No, she's the best. She's the best. What we did to make her and Billy Bob happy was, we said, "Listen, we want you naked, we want you doing your thing, fancy free. But we won't show anything unless—and we'll put it in your contract—unless you approve it." I felt that gave them the liberty and the freedom to go on and do their thing.

GA: That's very smart.

LD: I am. When I want to be.

GA: I've heard positive and negative responses to Halle's Oscar speech. What are your thoughts on that?

LD: I thought it was brilliant. She's so, so wonderful. I can't speak highly enough of her.

GA: Why do you think there was some negative commentary?

LD: You figure it out. This is what I think. You make history. You get up there and you start stuttering. Halle is one of the most articulate women I've ever met. She's baad. We were at the Berlin Film Festival. She was nominated and won. Once again the Philly boy came out of me and I lost it. At the Oscars, she was like me. She lost it. She spoke from her heart and her soul. For the people who don't get it, that's their problem. I got where she was coming from because she didn't think she was going to win. I thought she was going to win. Right before they announced her name I looked at her and I could see her acting sort of nervous—her knees were buckling, et cetera. I said, "Are you good?" And she said to me, "We're not going to win this. And it has nothing to do with me or you now, Lee. It's about our people." She genuinely felt that it was bigger than she. It's nice to have a trophy, but it was really bigger than Halle, and she felt the enormity of it all.

GA: It seems that people are more comfortable with manufactured responses as opposed to true human responses. We're not used to honesty.

LD: All I can say is that her speech was beautiful. When you look at the Oscar broadcast tape scanning the audience with all those stars, you see that everyone was visibly moved.

GA: Give me your thoughts on the whole Angela Bassett situation and her comments likening the Halle Berry role in Monster's Ball to prostitution.

LD. I think that Halle's character, Leticia, is a survivor who rises above the pain and finds a way out in a similar mode as Tina Turner's character [which Ms. Bassett played in What's Love Got to Do with It?]. Isn't that ironic?

GA: Do you think the comments were taken out of context? I find it hard to believe that she would say such a thing.

LD: I don't know. I love Angela's work, but she was never offered the role. I think her representatives must have misrepresented something to her. I was saddened.

GA: Have you or Halle received apologies from Ms. Bassett?

LD: No, and let's not add fuel to the fire.

GA: It's unfortunate. Now tell me about your next project.

LD: One is "The Narrative of Arthur Gordon Pym" by Edgar Allan Poe. A gothic, horror tale. It's starring Wes Bentley from American Beauty and will be directed by Oliver Hirschbiegel [Das Experiment]. And then we have The Woodsman, about a pedophile and his attempt to return to his community. The writer/director of this piece has written a really gripping and moving story.

GA: What's your dream project?

LD: My dream project is to make a classic fairy tale, and I want to put Macy Gray in it. I want to give sister some lovin'. I want Hollywood to get her as the beauty she is. Yes, Macy Gray in a fairy tale.

Kasi Lemmons

I first recall briefly meeting director Kasi Lemmons in the summer of 1998 at the closing night party of the Acapulco Black Film Festival. I told her how much I loved Eve's Bayou, how I'd organized a group of about ten of my friends in New York to see the film on opening night and how we gathered for dinner afterwards to talk about the film in a restaurant in Manhattan's Union Square. "I loved the film and actually saw it twice in the theater [a rarity for me]," I told her. "Bless you," she said softly and genuinely as she thanked me.

From the opening sequence of Eve's Bayou, I knew I was in for a very special experience of African Americana, one that we rarely see come to life in the movie theater. Set in the bayous of Louisiana among mossy oak trees, swamps and the tenets of voodoo, the film, which starred Samuel L. Jackson, Lynn Whitfield, Diahann Carroll and Jurnee Smollet as Eve, became the highest-grossing independent film of 1997, grossing $14.8 million domestically. Eve's Bayou won the Independent Feature Project's Independent Spirit Award for Best First Feature and received seven NAACP Image Award nominations, including Best Picture. Lemmons also received a special first-time award, created just for her, from the National Board of Review and she also won the Director's Achievement Award at the Ninth Annual Nortel Palm Springs Film Festival.

Lemmons followed Eve's Bayou with The Caveman's Valentine (2001), which also starred Samuel L. Jackson. She will next direct The Battle of Cloverfield, for Columbia Pictures. The film is from a script she wrote about a fictitious Southern town where ghosts of the past conspire to change the future. She was also a talented actress before getting in the director's chair; her acting roles included Jonathan Demme's Silence of the Lambs (1991) opposite Jodie Foster, John Woo's first American film, Hard Target (1993), and Fear of a Black Hat (1994) by Rusty Cundieff.

— — — —

GA: You were a very creative child and started acting as a child. Tell me about that.

KL: I guess I was about nine. My parents had just divorced and my mother moved us to Boston. My father was still in St. Louis, and my mother wanted to give me things to do, so she put me in Boston Children's Theater and instantly, I mean instantly, I was smitten. I was completely, totally stagestruck and wanted to be an actress. Acting became my life. I knew I wanted to be an artist. I knew I wanted to be involved in that "thing" since I was nine.

GA: Do you have any favorite roles from that period?

KL: Through the Boston Children's Theater I got my first role on TV, which was on a local soap opera I believe called You Got a Right, a civil rights, courtroom drama. I auditioned with hundreds of kids and I got the part to play a little girl named Catherine Cooper, who was the first Black girl to integrate an all-white school.

GA: Was your mother very encouraging at this point? She was working on her Ph.D., right?

KL: Yes, she was getting her Ph.D. at Harvard, and she neither encouraged me nor discouraged me, because I loved it. She went along with it, but I think that at a certain point I think it started to make her anxious, but that was later. [Laughs]

GA: [Laughs]

KL: Then she had a lot of anxiety for years about it.

GA: What was she studying?

KL: Clinical psychology. Her thesis was on child motivation, which is interesting, you know.

GA: Sometimes parents encourage children to pursue the arts and sometimes they don't. She put you in theater. That's a good thing for a child.

KL: Well, she put me in a theater, but that was . . .

GA: Not for life.

KL: That was not for life. I think if she'd known [I'd stick it out] I'm not sure . . . I'm not sure.

GA: And then you did the popular children's show on Public Television called Zoom.

KL: I did Zoom.

GA: So when did you decide to pursue film? You went to the New School?

KL: Yes, I went to the New School. First, I pursued acting, so I was already acting professionally for a long time. The New School came at a time when I began to realize how much time I had on my hands. You know, being a Black actress. And I had a lot of friends who were singers and dancers, so they could stay in dance class or keep their voice lessons up, but that wasn't really my thing. I danced, but it wasn't really my deep love. After a while I started writing plays and scenes. I've always been a writer, fooled around with writing. But at this time there had been the whole Nicaraguan situation, and there was some interesting stuff going on politically in the world, and I thought I'd maybe pursue documentary filmmaking. I wanted to do something more meaningful than going to auditions, waiting for auditions or waiting for the phone to ring. I thought that maybe I should really learn to make films. In the building where I lived, The Brewster, in New York on Eighty-sixth Street, D. A. Pennebaker had his office downstairs. So I don't know, I was always just really interested in documentaries and documentary filmmakers and I just said, "Okay, I want to learn to do that kind of photography." So I went to film school, really to learn cinematography, and I made two documentaries while I was at film school.

GA: Was this after your role in Silence of the Lambs?

KL: No, this all kind of happened at once.

GA: And what were these documentaries about?

KL: Well, the first one, which is by far my favorite, was about homeless people, and it was called Fall from Grace. It was actually quite good. It was one of those periods in your life where the first thing that you do turns to gold, you know what I mean? [Laughs]

GA: [Laughs]

KL: It was a great thing for me because it festivaled. This was my first assignment at film school.

Reggie and Warrington Hudlin saw the film and had a big BFF [Black Filmmaker Foundation] screening for me. They kind of took me under their wing.

GA: *They're great guys.*

KL: We were the first BFF screening that HBO sponsored. Then a whole bunch of things happened. I did a screenplay with a theater group I belonged to called Naked Angels, and Naked Angels was doing a play called *Avenue Boys*. I also got *Silence of the Lambs*.

GA: *At that time, did you see yourself continuing with theater as a career?*

KL: Mm, hm. It's still a possibility. [Laughs]

GA: *That's the beautiful thing.*

KL: That's still a possibility. I was just talking to George Wolfe about it—coming back to New York and directing theater, man.

GA: *How were you able to bring all of your training together? Did you find that your acting helped your filmmaking?*

KL: It's hard for me to say, because I always figured I'm just in it, doing the best I can. I watched the EPK [electronic press kit] on *Caveman's Valentine* and the question was: "What makes Kasi special as a director?" They asked everybody in the cast that question and every single person said, "Well, because she was an actor." It never occurred to me that I was special because I was an actor.

GA: *But the actors realized it.*

KL: Yes, every single person said it, and I said, "Wow." I guess it's different working with an actor than it is working with someone who's not an actor. But until then, I had certainly been asked the question, but I couldn't really say if I was any better or any different because I had been an actor. I'm just trying to hang on to the movie and get the best performances I can. But there are all kinds of ways to get a performance.

GA: *But do you think the Caveman actors were saying that you understood?*

KL: Yes, she understands actors. I love actors. I guess I'd assume most directors do, but that's probably not the case. But I love actors, and I love the filmmaking part of it alot. We get way into it—storyboarding, picking the lens package, how we're going to shoot certain things. My director of photography, Amy Vincent, and I, we always had this "wait 'til the actors come, the actors are coming" attitude. Then the whole thing's going to come to life. I guess I appreciate how tenuous and fragile that moment of inspiration is. I really, really love actors. I have a greater appreciation for actors as a director than I did as an actor.

GA: *Explain why that's so.*

KL: I never do things that I hated [having] done to me. I hated being directed from across the set—screamed at in front of the whole crew. So I go up and make it a very private conversation between me and the actor, and I feel that even the other person in the scene might not need to hear what I'm telling you. It might be a secret, and I think that people tend to respond to that. Of course, there's always going to be a time when you're going to be like, "Okay, that was great. Do it again!"

GA: *[Laughs]*

KL: "Take it a little slower this time." But if it's something that is in any way delicate, and even if it's not, I prefer to go up and have a very private conversation with the actor.

GA: *Tell me about Eve's Bayou and what inspired that wonderful film.*

KL: I wrote the script. It was in my head for a very long time before I wrote the whole thing down. The first draft was like a novel, and the drafts became progressively less literary. So eventually I had my final draft. Now, in that process I went from being an actor to being a screenwriter. [Laughs] Because the first draft that I showed my agent—my acting agent at Innovative who was also my friend—he was incredible.

He gave the script to Frank Willinger, in the literary department at Innovative, who's still my agent but he's now with Gersh. Frank said, "You are a writer. You really are a writer. Do you have any interest in this?" I said, "I don't know." I also think one of the reasons I had written the script to begin with was because I'd written a script for Bill Cosby with two other women, and I was in the Writers Guild. But I really was trying to write that jewel that I would one day either star in or direct, and it was kind of insurance against a rainy day. I thought I was going to be Mozelle [played by Debbi Morgan] maybe, but I needed to get a little older. I needed more world experience. When we started casting, we had a screenplay reading early on and the girl who played Cisely, Meagan Good, played Eve in the reading and she was fine, she was wonderful. Then years pass and of course this girl got older. So when we were looking for Cisely, I said, "We should call Meagan." All of a sudden there she was—this little lady. It's scary, just at that scary age, which is exactly what we wanted, of course, from that character. She was one of the first people I cast and she sat in on the Eve auditions and we could not find this girl [Eve]. I mean, we could not find her. A lot of beautiful, wonderful little children came in and they were just precocious or just not, they just didn't breathe it. They played it and I would say, "I don't want that kid. I want an authentic feeling child." And I couldn't find her and all of a sudden we had gotten the money and we were in preproduction in Louisiana, I've dragged a crew down, and I didn't have my star.

Now I'm auditioning in Louisiana and all over the South, and they're having talent contests. [Laughs] Searching in five cities and I couldn't find this girl. My casting director called me one day and said, "You've got to come back to L.A. and see this girl." She said, [Snaps] "This is the girl." I came back and I had these children working. They were reading half the script and this girl [Jurnee Smollet] read two scenes and I thought . . . Then Meagan looked at me, I looked at Meagan, Sam Jackson was in the room and we all looked at each other and we knew that she was the kid.

I went downstairs to ask her mother if she could stay and read some more pages, and her brother was sitting there. I said, "Are you an actor?" He said, "Yeah." I said, "Come upstairs." I had them improvise together and I cast them both. She was a blessing, and her mother said to me later, "I know what you were looking for all that time. You were looking for yourself."

GA: Mm, interesting.

KL: And, in a way, I think I was. I was looking for the kid who reminded me of me—of the Eve part of me. If you wanted to go to white, classic literature, Eve was my Scout character from *To Kill a Mockingbird*. And Mozelle was my Blanche Dubois. Jurnee was great. She was a very sophisticated, urban, modern, little girl, but I could see that she could go there and, within the rehearsal process, really within three days, she became a kid from 1962, the year that I'd chosen.

GA: *Did you use any special tools to get her to go back to 1962 and to become Eve?*

KL: Dealing with children is really easy [Laughs] because you can tell them what to do. It's harder to tell Sam Jackson what to do. You have to kind of negotiate your point of view, but with a child you kind of tell them to try this—try folding your arms, which she does during the whole movie. One of the first things we had to do was quiet her body movements down. But not just the kids. The adults don't move their hands around either, and it's probably the last time I'll ever get away with it, but it was like painting to me. So it was very specific where the actors stood and how they used their bodies. I was very, very bossy about it.

GA: I was going to ask you about that, because it's funny that you said painting. I saw the film again this week; I've seen it several times. But this time it reminded me of a Monet painting.

KL: Mm, hm.

GA: I mean, I actually saw a painting. I saw these lily pads or marsh.

KL: Yes, we were painting and it was a real pain in the ass for the actors. I tried to be as open and inviting as I could within the confines of that, but I really wanted them to be still [Laughs] and stand exactly in relation to the window [Laughs] or whatever. I made a conscious directly opposing decision on *Caveman's Valentine*. It was a different kind of painting, but I absolutely did everything around the actors' blocking and gave them a lot of freedom.

GA: Your costuming for *Eve's Bayou* was also very intriguing to me. I've heard you say that you didn't want your characters walking around the bayou in rags and sweating.

KL: [Laughs] I've seen that.

GA: And I'm from the Gulf Coast. It's not always humid in the bayou. It's humid a lot, but it could very well not be.

KL: Mm, hm. And first of all '62 is before my time. I picked a time mostly for the aesthetics, mostly for the old-fashioned setting. It was more the reality of my memory than the reality of the time. My memory as a child of my family. If I were to pull out pictures of my parents, you would say, "Oh, my God. They look like movie stars."

They were glamorous and beautiful and all their friends were glamorous and beautiful, that's true. That's not me imposing that on the cast. And they had fabulous clothes and fabulous parties, and I wanted to capture that the way I remembered it at the time—they were just luminous. Come to a party filled with adults and they were just gorgeous, gorgeous, gorgeous people and I just thought, "I haven't seen that, but it's a lot of people's experience with their parents."

GA: Absolutely.

KL: And yet, we're seeing the rag on the head and the sweats and the noble Black woman.

GA: Sojourner.

KL: Mm, hm, and I'm talking Dorothy Dandridge. That's what I wanted. I wanted deep southern glamour because I just hadn't seen it in a movie. So it's funny looking at *Eve's Bayou*, because when I first came out as a filmmaker, and it was separate from my acting, everybody was surprised at how young I was. I think in its own way it's old-fashioned, but it was very radical at the time. It was very, very radical.

GA: What do you mean the film was radical, how so?

KL: Everybody thought it was very radical. Most white people in the industry had gravitated towards an aesthetic of Black filmmaking that was gritty and in your face and, I mean, it's *Boyz 'N the Hood* and, wow, the Black experience. We're getting closer to the Black experience. So this was a whole different Black experience and nobody in the film mentioned white people, which was radical, and I got more radical progressively. For example, there was one mention of white people in one of the earlier drafts, but as people started to tell me, "Well, can't you have a white character even if it's a white racist character?" I said, "No." Then finally I said, "Ain't no white people in *Eve's Bayou*."

GA: [Laughs]

KL: By the time we got to shooting, all the extras were Black, there were no white people in the movie, and that was radical.

GA: Yes, when you express it like that, you're right.

KL: But it became a statement of mine. Then there's another thing that's going on in filmmaking right now and always. It's tricky talking about this too much, but ageism exists. I mean, it was, "Can Lela Rochon play Mozelle?" "Well, no. I love Lela, but she's not old enough," I said. So the fact that I had two children under fifteen as the stars and all the women, let's say, were over thirty was radical. There were no hot twenty-five-year-olds in the movie.

GA: It goes against the grain.

KL: And I'm saying, "You don't understand; these women [Lynn Whitfield, Debbi Morgan, Diahann Carroll] are fabulous."

GA: Oh, absolutely, and I know those women. As soon as the movie started, that party, I said, "Oh, this is going to be a good movie." Because I, too, hadn't seen it before on the screen and this world exists.

KL: Mm, hm.

GA: Where'd you come up with the line "The summer I killed my father, I was ten years old"? It was very powerful. It was deep. [Laughs]

KL: It wasn't my original starting line. I started always with memories of selections of images, some printed indelibly on the brain. I felt very passionate about it. I thought it was very beautiful, but I didn't have the line that says, "The summer I killed my father . . ." for a long time. Actually, I was talking to a girlfriend of mine who is a writer and she said, "You've got to start with something strong to really grab you." Another friend said, "You've got to start really strong" because it had started softer and a friend of mine, British, said, [Whispers] "Can you have them fucking on the first page? Now, if you can put them fucking on the first page . . ."

GA: [Laughs]

KL: And my girlfriend's kind of saying the same thing, but she's saying that if you can indicate that there's a murder on the first page it would be strong. So it was really a process of talking to people about it early on. That got me to Eve seeing her father fucking [Snaps] on the first page [Laughs] and I put in the word fucking. I said, "This is not lovemaking. It's hard, thrilling, fucking, okay?" Before I had a lulled and kind of intellectual, lyrical, literary piece that told this story and now I said, "Okay, we're going to fuck. . . ." [Laughs]

GA: [Laughs]

KL: ". . . on the first page." It was helpful. At least it got people to finish the script.

GA: *They were drawn in.*

KL: They were drawn in and also by having a child say, "The summer I killed my father . . ." And then having that not being exactly what happened. I mean, it's an interpretation.

GA: *But the fact that a ten-year-old could even think such a thing is deep. I've heard you talk about how you shopped the script around Hollywood and everyone loved the script but didn't want to make it. Tell me about that.*

KL: The people who ended up making the movie, the film was exactly what they wanted. They wanted a prestigious movie with a big star attached that didn't cost any money. They weren't thinking race, so it was perfect for them. But years before when we were shopping it, I think everybody liked the script because it was beautiful but I think that the main question was "Who is going to be the audience for this?" And see, my being foolish and not knowing shit I would say, "African American college graduates." The room would go still and I'd be asked to leave shortly thereafter. [Laughs]

GA: [Laughs]

KL: And I'd never hear from them again. So it wasn't really until I talked about the *Waiting to Exhale* audience that I finally got a positive response. Because people would say, "What does this movie remind you of?" I'd say, "Well, *Daughters of the Dust*." Then the room would go silent and I would be asked to leave shortly afterwards, never to hear from them again.

Once you can say *Waiting to Exhale*, you know, *Waiting to Exhale* did a lot for me because my movie is nothing like *Waiting to Exhale*. It's the opposite of *Waiting to Exhale*, but at the same time I could make them go "cha-ching" by mentioning that movie, and it was often the same audience.

GA: *What was the audience breakdown in terms of race of Eve's Bayou?*

KL: Half and half.

GA: *Why do you think your audience was 50/50 split, Black and white? Was it the universal themes you explored?*

KL: Yes. Mm, hm. I always thought that was the case. When people first asked me who did I think the audience was, I'd say, "Well, people like you. You responded to the script, why wouldn't you respond to the movie?" It was naive, but actually Ray Price did the marketing. He was at Trimark then. He was one of the people who brought the script in to the company.

Who knows where Ray is now, but the man is one of the smartest people I've ever met, not just on that mental level, but he can market an art film. He just knows what he's doing, and they really made two campaigns—a Black film campaign and an art film campaign. Before they released the movie, Mark Amin [former chairman and CEO of Trimark] was threatening not to release it.

GA: *Really. Why?*

KL: And I don't blame him, because it didn't test well and we didn't get into any major festivals. Cannes, Venice and New York turned me down. I had said to them, "I'm giving you this art film." Then I was turned down by the classiest festivals. We were also taking the film to Magic Johnson theaters to test it, and it wasn't testing well.

GA: *How did you feel during this period? What was going on in your mind?*

KL: My editor, Teri Shropshire, and I were absolutely certain that we'd made something special. I mean absolutely special. We had faith in it. We thought, "Well, don't they see what we see in it? Are we crazy?" I always said to people that I didn't expect it to test well. How do you test a film that has an ambiguous ending and that's asking for a new audience? So I don't blame Mark. His point of view was, "You haven't given me a commercial film, you haven't given me an art film, why should I release it? You're going to have to make it more conventional in some way." Of course, that was something that I desperately didn't want to do. But I really didn't have to make any changes. We had a rather bloody fight, but, in the end, Mark was a gambler and in the end he gambled. It was as simple as that. He gambled on the film. I was doing press on the road, I was in San Francisco and I remember him calling me up and saying, "I'm not sleeping. Are you sleeping?" He was afraid. You know, he put more money into it, and after the movie came out and I would go to Hollywood parties, all of a sudden, it changed my life. People came up to me who had passed on the project and said, "I'm so glad I passed on it, because I would never have put so much money into marketing it as Mark did." He was a renegade and I have a lot of respect for him.

GA: And it was the highest-grossing independent film of 1997.
KL: It did really well for a small film, and it did better than any African American art film had really ever done. There was no precedent.

GA: I read once where you told the L.A. Times that you don't think commercially. What do you mean by that?
KL: Well, I want to. I have some commercial ideas, but those aren't the ideas I'm driven to [Laughs] write through to completion. [Laughs] One day I really believe I'm going to inadvertently make a commercial movie. One day I'm going to just happen upon it and it's just going to converge with my tastes. But I tend to be literary.

GA: I see. Who are some of your favorite authors?
KL: Wow. I read everything. But I'd say, if you were looking at Eve's Bayou I would definitely say Toni Morrison and Gabriel Garcia Marquez were big influences. And I'm a movie buff.

GA: You like Hitchcock, I've heard you say that.
KL: Fuck yeah.

GA: And you've got some Hitchcockian stuff going on in Eve's Bayou and in Caveman's Valentine.
KL: I love Hitchcock, I love Hitchcock. Truffaut, Kurosawa, Polanski, Scorsese. The great ones.

GA: Now, before you did Eve's you did the short Dr. Hugo, which actually positioned you to direct Eve's, correct?

KL: Yes, I was trying to show what I was going to do to a certain extent.

GA: And there's a good little story behind Dr. Hugo and how you financed it with the help of your agent. Tell me about that.

KL: The story was that I had entered into a handshake agreement option with producer Cotty Chubb to produce Eve's Bayou. We went down that path, looking at directors, taking meetings, and I woke up one day with an epiphany that I was going to direct it myself. When I told Cotty he said, "Okay, but forget those little films you did in film school." [Laughs] He said, "You've got to show me that you can direct a big 35mm film with a big crew. Why don't you write a short film and we'll do it together?" He financed half of it and my agent lent me the other half against screen-writing jobs I had. So we produced it ourselves. And it was like a pilot for Eve's Bayou.

GA: So then people bought into the fact that this woman can direct and this is a good story.

KL: Well, also it was the glamour thing. I was going for something that I wanted to demonstrate. I was going for a certain look.

GA: So with the short film, people could buy into the visual.

KL: People could buy into the visual.

GA: Tell me about Caveman's Valentine, which followed Eve's Bayou. What attracted you to that project?

KL: I think the character of Romulus Ledbetter [played by Samuel L. Jackson] is a fantastic character. You just don't see this character and I got really, really excited about it. I thought a lot of things. I thought that if I don't make this movie, I don't know who's going to make it and I believe in this guy. I believe in this character and I want to show him, I want to get into his head. It was very important to me, and who's to say why things resonate with you? One reason was that I had done this film on homeless people before and I come from a family of psychotherapists and psychiatrists. It's a family profession. My mother and my sister are both in the field and schizophrenics are in the family. It was something that I was interested and grew up interested in, and here's this guy [Romulus]. It meant a lot to me. It still means a lot to me. I'm very, very happy I did it. It was a painful experience. [Laughs] But I'm very happy I did it—great producers, great cast, not enough money and not enough support ultimately. It was a very hard film, it was hard. I knew it was hard when I went in. When I read the script, I said, "This is impossible. Who could do this?"

GA: *Were you disappointed you didn't have the same level of success, at least commercially, as Eve's Bayou?*
KL: I intentionally chose something so different and so complicated that I wouldn't compare the two. I intentionally chose something very hard. I could've had a second film that was as successful as Eve's Bayou, but I intentionally chose something else, because for one thing I didn't want to be the lyrical-little-homey-southern filmmaker. Eve's Bayou was one part of what I had to say.

GA: *You don't like being put in a box, do you?*
KL: No.

GA: *[Laughs] You're the rebel, aren't you?*
KL: Yeah, so it [Caveman] was kind of a rebellious movie and to me it will always be a power move, because it's just different and it has more masculinity. I loved it. It was really, really artistically fun. I got off.

GA: *You and Amy Vincent had a lot of fun again with the visuals?*
KL: We had a lot of fun, we had a lot of fun. Phyllis Detrich, who was in the prop department, gave us a card when we were working on Eve's Bayou. It was a picture of a woman's face, and at the top of her head is a door and there's another woman peering out and she says this is you and Amy. It was really like that. Amy was inside my head and I can look at her across the set and she'll say, "Oh, we should go tighter on that, right?" [Snaps] We absolutely understand each other. She's been a really good collaborator. We have a very interesting dynamic, but artistically we totally vibe and we're really good friends as well.

GA: *At the end of the day the relationship between the director and the director of photography is so important.*
KL: And the director and the editor.

GA: *Absolutely, and tell me about that.*
KL: I've been working with two of my really dear friends and I know that it can't necessarily go on

forever, but it's been incredible and I'd work with them again whenever I could. Teri [Shropshire] has been incredible. When you think about somebody that you're going to sit next to thirteen hours a day. I mean, on the last film it was just sick how many hours we worked. It was sick. We pulled something like six twenty-seven-hour days. It was just out of control. But who's the person you can share this with, and you know how Teri and I met? Did she tell you?

GA: Yes.

KL: She wrote me a letter. I was in preproduction, I was in Louisiana and my fabulous assistant laid a letter on top of my desk and said, "You should read this letter." I read it and it was a plea to work on the movie. She had read the script, but the interesting thing about it was that she never said that she was African-American. It was Terilyn A. Shropshire. She started the letter saying, "By reading my resume you might not know that I'm born to work on this movie [Laughs], but I am." It was a very passionate letter and it was also very, very formal. It was both formal and passionate and it just haunted me. I just thought about it and on her resume was 9 1/2 Weeks II. God, must I watch this? And I watched it and that shit's edited. [Laughs]

GA: [Laughs]

KL: You know, really. It wasn't until I said that I really wanted to hire her that Cotty told me. He said, "I've got a surprise for you. She's a Black woman." And he hadn't told me. There was another editor he was really pushing on me. He was a fabulous editor, a fabulous editor, but I really wanted to go with Teri—the other editor was a friend of his—but the day I said that I definitely wanted to go with Teri he said, "Well, she's a Black woman." And I said, "Wow." So the whole time we were shooting I never met her. We just talked on the phone. Teri, the way she speaks on the phone, and you two know each other, she has a conservativeness that I don't have, you know? I mean, I just don't have it. [Laughs]

GA: [Laughs]

KL: And I thought, "Wow, how's this going to be?" But we slammed instantly. We got along famously. I'd say within the first hour it was like being with someone I can be friends with forever.

GA: She's such a good spirit.

KL: Oh, she's fabulous, Teri's fabulous.

GA: Your characters in Eve's Bayou are so rich. I loved the way the kids interacted with the adults. What was your process for creating your characters?

KL: A lot of it was based on people I knew. I come from a colorful Southern family. Like, "I had a dream last night and I don't think you should go outside." That's totally my family.

GA: [Laughs]

KL: There is a language, there's the way that different cultures, not just African American, but the way that French people talk to their children and the way politically correct Americans talk to children and the way Italians talk to children, all very different. There was a way that Black people talked to children that I had seen in the context of some movies but I had never seen in the context of a movie like this—this loving outrageous use of language. Like Mozelle's line to Eve, "I'm a smack you blind." And, "I'm gonna kill you." [Laughs]

GA: *"I'm a smack you blind"* is one of my favorite lines. [Laughs]

KL: [Laughs] And Mozelle loves her [Eve] and I just thought it was hilarious. I thought it was very, very beautiful, and also Eve's Bayou has such a complicated story. It's an experiment with a use of language. There were several things I was trying to do at once. I was trying to write poetry as prose, I was trying to write a libretto, like it could be sung or spoken, and I wanted to use authentic language, an authentic way of talking, authentic rhythm, but yet it was very stylized. So it was kind of an experiment in the use of the language. It became very, very, very precious to me—besides making the actors stand on marks and not move, I was also very specific about the language.

GA: It comes across.

KL: Mozelle says, "You must've been thinking something before you was thinking that." It's very important to me that she says it that way. It was just the way I heard it. It sounded beautiful to me that way.

GA: *Lynn Whitfield's character Roslyn says things in a manner that is very Southern, especially specific parts of the South like the Gulf Coast of Alabama, where I'm from.*

KL: Mm, hm.

GA: *She doesn't say, "He wasn't." She says, "He whatn't," and I caught it. Was it Lynn Whitfield, did she say that or was it scripted?*

KL: No, Lynn knows that shit inside out. Lynn comes from that world. She comes from Baton Rouge with all those doctors, she comes from that world. She's totally from that world.

GA: She played it to a T.

KL: She played it to a T. Fabulous.

GA: There's a scene where she's cursing the Sam Jackson character and she's off-screen, but we hear her say, "Damn doctor!" It's loaded.

KL: Mm, hm.

GA: And it's very powerful. You were conscious of it, right? To be married to a doctor was the highest thing a Black woman could do at the time, but yet it's a double-edged sword and there's another part of it that she has to deal with.

KL: Louis Batiste had his own baggage. The most beautiful thing to me that Roz says is "When she married him, she thought he could fix everything. She leaves her family and comes to the swamps and finds out that he's just a man." Yeah, my favorite script. [Laughs]

GA: The relationships between the children and the adults are also incredible. In Eve's relationship with Mozelle, Mozelle communicates with her as if they're the same age. Were you influenced by other films or books?

KL: Yes.

GA: Euzhan Palcy's Sugar Cane Alley has the same thing in terms of relationships between adults and children.

KL: First of all, Sugar Cane Alley is one of my favorite films and I love Euzhan. Eve and Mozelle are myself and my Aunt Muriel, I mean absolutely, totally. It's really funny because when people look at it, they think certain things are autobiographical that are totally made up. Like the Louis, Cisely stuff. There are reasons why I told the story that way, because I was interested in how two different people can look at their past and see two different things. But the part that was the most authentic was the relationship between the two sisters which was me and my sister, and the relationship between the little girl and the relationship between children and adults in general—besides the incest, [everything else] was very much part of my youth. In terms of the characters, I wrote a bunch of short stories. The first Eve's Bayou short story I wrote was about Eve and Poe and how they'd go up to their grandmother's room. She's got all these medicines on her table, and it's impressionistic about how they had the doily hanging on the table and the way the bottles looked to the kids. Then I think it may have been the second Eve's Bayou story I wrote was about Mozelle and her dead husbands and that was my Aunt Muriel. My Aunt Muriel had five husbands to die.

GA: *This is very Southern stuff, people don't know.*
KL: Very, very Southern.

GA: *Mobile has a lot of stories like this.*
KL: And you know people in the South are always shooting each other. My mother and my Aunt Muriel were extremely close. One time they went to a fortune-teller and the fortune-teller at a fair told my mother something she can't remember but looked at my aunt's hand and said, some things are better left unsaid, so that was just an outrageous part of the story. It's taken from my family history.

GA: *What was it like working with the legendary Diahann Carroll?*
KL: I saw her in *Agnes of God* and I just wanted to stand next to her. It became clear to me that they wanted a bit of stunt casting for that part and they were talking about all kinds of people and I said, "Well, I really want to work with Diahann Carroll." So I called her up and she had a lot of questions. But she's fantastic. I could not love her more. She had worked with Jurnee when Jurnee was a child. She said, [Whispers] "She's a spooky little girl." And Jurnee is my dear friend, but there is an otherworldly quality about her. Diahann said she'd do it, I started shooting her and I was instantly in trouble with my producers. They said, "Okay, we've got a big problem. She's just so beautiful. She's not scary at all. She's gorgeous. [Whispers] I saw this book of Yoruban ceremonial makeup and I took it to her and I said, "Diahann, I want you to look at something, everybody's complaining because you're so beautiful." She says, "Oh, God, these bones." [Laughs]

GA: [Laughs]
KL: I said, "Would you look at this," and she looked and I walked away because I was scared. A little while later she called me and says [imitates], "I don't know, I don't know." I said, "Well, just think about it. Maybe it's something she does because she likes to get attention. It's not authentic, it is a show, it is a side show, it's her own little schtick." Anyway by the time she got into it, she put that Black marker on her face herself. [Laughs]

GA: [Laughs]

KL: And she got way into it. I had a lot of fun with her, I love her. I have to say on both movies, my affection for the actors goes incredibly deep. I can't say enough about all of them in both movies. I mean, I love Diahann, I love Diahann.

GA: *Is there something that someone that seasoned brings to the whole set? I mean, you're dealing with Sam Jackson, too, but something about her seems to be almost goddesslike.*

KL: She was a goddess, but it was a little bit of a panic because she's in the swamp, you know, the swamp, it's funky.

GA: *You're married to a director, you're married to an actor. What's that like?*

KL: My husband Vondie Curtis Hall is immensely supportive. We usually are not together when we're shooting, but I find him immensely supportive. Vondie is a completely different animal than I am, we're completely different people. He's easygoing. Vondie can be on a cell phone right before he calls action, whereas before I call action, I'm all intense. I'm a more intense person than he is, he's a more relaxed person. Less fazes him. He likes production better. I love it in my own love/hate way. I love the moments of inspiration and working with the actors and, in that wicked masochistic way, I like the pressure.

GA: *What's motherhood like in terms of your career?*

KL: Well, for one thing it gives you perspective. I think it's really easy as a director to get caught up in the life and deathness of making your day, and do I have a movie that's good, is it great? Do I suck? That whole artist thing, and I think that having children gives you perspective in life. It gives you something that's really important, and if your child has a cold or a problem or even a big hug, it's completely grounding. So I've been very grateful for it. On the other hand, it'll be really nice and interesting for me to shoot a film not postpartum, because things happen. Like, you get to the end of the shoot and you're getting doctors coming up to the house to give you vitamin shots in the butt and you're hoping you're going to live through it. I remember this doctor coming to my house and looking at my baby and saying, "You're postpartum. You're probably going through a postpartum depression as well," and I thought, "Wow, I could be and I just haven't even had time to think about that." When I finished, my daughter was only six months old. When I started she was three months old.

GA: I recall your saying that you don't put off living to be an artist. Explain what you mean by that.

KL: Well, I would say that the things that are most important in my life are my family and art, so I don't put off being an artist. I don't wake up every day saying I'm a Black woman because it's too given, but I wake up every day feeling like an artist and I feel I'm an artist. I've been an artist since I was a child and yet I have an appreciation for it on a day-to-day basis, but I think living your life makes you a better artist. I think living your life, going places, meeting different people, having experiences makes you a better artist and so there's not a way to qualify and quantify it.

Bearers of the Race

THE DOCUMENTARIANS

St. Clair Bourne

Producer/director/writer St. Clair Bourne has been a part of the vanguard of documentary filmmaking for over thirty years. He began his career in American public television and was the youngest staff producer for the public affairs series *Black Journal*, for which William Greaves served as executive producer and cohost.

In February 2002, at the invitation of my Morehouse College classmate Charles Reese, I had the privilege of interviewing Saint, as I can now call him, before a standing-room-only crowd at the Museum of Natural History in New York. The discussion followed a screening of my favorite Bourne film, *Langston Hughes: The Dream Keeper* (1988). The screening and discussion were in celebration of Hughes's 100th birthday.

Like Greaves's, Bourne's work centers on cultural and political themes through his depictions on film of the lives of some of the most important African Americans of our time. Through his production company Chamba Mediaworks, Inc., Bourne has made more than forty-two films. For HBO Bourne produced *Half Past Autumn: The Life and Works of Gordon Parks* (2001), about the photojournalist, filmmaker, novelist and composer. He directed *Paul Robeson: Here I Stand!* (1999) for the PBS series *American Masters*. He also directed *John Henrik Clarke: A Great and Mighty Walk* (1996), a feature-length documentary executive produced and narrated by Wesley Snipes about the historian and Pan-African activist. Bourne also executive-produced Kathe Sandler's *A Ques-*

tion of Color (1992). He is presently at work on a documentary on the history of Cuba through baseball.

Bourne's other significant works include Making "Do the Right Thing" (1989), a documentary about the making of director Spike Lee's acclaimed film In Motion: Amiri Baraka; Langston Hughes: The Dream Keeper (1988) and Let the Church Say Amen! (1973).

In dramatic film, Bourne served as coproducer on the independent feature The Long Night (1976) and on the HBO film Rebound: The Legend of Earl "The Goat" Manigault (1996), a real-life playground basketball legend.

Bourne is a native of Brooklyn, New York.

GA: *Tell me about your childhood.*
SB: I was born in Brooklyn of West Indian immigrant parents who were very ambitious, very striving. My father was actually born here, but he's from Barbados. My mother is from Antigua and they met here. I went to Catholic schools all the way up, but at age ten I decided not to be a Catholic.

GA: *Really?*
SB: Yeah, absolutely, the whole faith thing I just couldn't buy.

GA: *It didn't make sense to you?*
SB: Didn't make sense, but the initial influence was probably my father. He was a journalist, lived in Harlem and worked on all the Black papers, so that was the first influence, because I noticed that he could look at television and write a story at the same time. He was really smart, but they weren't prepared for him at that time, you know, a smart Black man. So he went into the civil service, but in the community and middle-class Bed-Stuy he was known as the person, if you needed a press release written or if you needed some kind of journalistic connection, he was the person. So people were always coming to my house asking, "Mr. Bourne, could you write this?" And I would see him write and I probably picked that up, the whole writing, service through journalism thing.

GA: *What did your mom do?*
SB: She was a nurse, and she became a social worker and later a social service administrator. There was a big battle in my family. They didn't want me to go into journalism or film because basically, as with most immigrant families, they wanted me to do better than they and my father was a journalist. Journalism was a field that he left in order to make more money to take care of his family, and here I was saying that I wanted to be a journalist. In their head it was like going

back to an environment where I wasn't going to make that much money. The thing that they didn't anticipate and I didn't anticipate was that in the sixties Black people began to get into mainstream journalism. And because of the threat of violence, white publications couldn't send white reporters to cover certain stories, so they sent Black reporters. Then in public television the *Black Journal* series was created essentially out of a sense of desperation to answer the question "What do these people want?" That's what white people were asking. So the idea was to create a monthly documentary television show that would be produced by, for and about Black people. But they didn't really do that until we decided to strike. There were thirty-two people on staff and only ten were Black. So three months in we worked under those conditions and then we began to realize that this was jive. We went on strike and we were able to shame them into giving up control, and switching their white producers to other shows and installing a Black executive producer, a Black story editor and we became the producers.

GA: *That was with William Greaves.*

SB: William Greaves was the executive producer, right, and Lou Potter was the story editor. My connection to that was sort of a pivotal situation for me, because I had gone to Georgetown University foreign service school because I was going to be a diplomat, but in my third year I was arrested for a student sit-in right across the river in Arlington, Virginia, which at the time was legally segregated. So obviously I said, "Why am I going to represent a country that won't allow me to eat in a place?" Stokely Carmichael was one of the people who taught me how to do the sit-in.

GA: *You got expelled from school after that? How did that work?*

SB: Well, it was a combination of my having stopped studying, I became disenchanted and they threatened to throw me out anyhow. I'd had it and we parted company. Then I went into the Peace Corps, because it was touted that if you were a renegade you could go overseas, be on your own, help people and be supportive, and Harry Belafonte was on the board and it was the Kennedy period. I ended up running a newspaper in an urban community outside of Lima, Peru, for two years beginning in 1964.

GA: *What was it like running the newspaper?*

SB: Well, for me it was great because I was on my own in Peru. I sharpened my journalism skills, and I took a lot of photographs. Another volunteer named Jack and I were the editors, but our purpose for being there was really to get the indigenous people to run the paper. I learned how things worked. I sharpened my communication skills and began to understand the story and how to write, how to get news and it probably showed me how news could be political and get people to act because we would have these newspaper crusades—get the mayor to clean up a garbage area or put in fresh water or pipes and that kind of stuff. So we did that and, in fact, we were so successful that some U.S. government agents visited me. They came to my house, put me in a car, took me to the embassy and told me, "Look, you're interfering too much into the affairs of the people." I said, "Oh, no, no, you don't understand. I'm in the Peace Corps, this is what we're supposed to do. We're supposed to change the lives of the people." I parroted the line I was given. I sort of believed that, and the guy said, "Look, we control the government. You tell us what you want done and we'll make it happen." They never said who they were, but they were agents and they took me to the intelligence section of the embassy.

GA: What was that like? Were you afraid?

SB: Yeah, it was very scary. I didn't think they'd kill me, but at the time I was fairly naïve. I just thought they were misguided white Americans who were overly missionary. Then I began to see on Peruvian television, and when I got back to the States, documentaries about the Civil Rights Movement. This was about 1965. I was in Peru from '64 to '66 and I'd see these documentaries, but it was clear that the filmmakers didn't have a clue. Plus there was a white on-camera reporter talking about these people who were Black to an audience he assumed was white. We were not in the equation at all except as subjects, and that used to piss me off. Then here I was working as a journalist in Peru telling stories about oppressed people and speaking on their behalf, and I began to make the connection. I said, "Wait a minute. I'm one of the people he's talking about. I want to make films." That's when I decided that I wanted to be a CBS documentary producer. That's what I wanted to do originally, because CBS had the best coverage at the time. So when I got back from Peru I finished undergraduate school at Syracuse University and I decided to go into film production. After Syracuse I went to Columbia University for film school, but I didn't finish there either, because I started in September of '67 and in March of '68, as you may remember, there was a student takeover and I was one of the people who took over Hamilton Hall. I was arrested and sent to jail. Then the film school kicked me out. But Arthur Barron, who taught me documentary film, said, "Look, you know what you need to know now even though you're a month shy of graduation. There's a new series being created, and they're looking for young Black people. I recommend that you go down and talk to these people." That's when I met Bill Greaves and Lou Potter and I was hired as an associate producer. I was told that I was one of the worst associate producers ever because I was always forgetting things. You're supposed to take care of the producer's details, but I would never do that. I would always start forgetting stuff and I'd always start saying, "We shouldn't do that. We should do this." So Kent Garrett went to Bill Greaves and said, "Look, this guy is an awful associate producer, but he seems to have a good idea of what he wants to do, so look, forget about this, just make him a producer, then I don't think he'll have any problems." So that's how I got to be a producer in just three months!

GA: *Excellent. So tell me about your personality and why you think you were always getting involved in protests and putting yourself on the line.*

SB: I've thought about this and essentially I think I was rebelling against a traditional West Indian upbringing, which essentially is designed to get you to fit in. The British conquered the West Indies, so if you were successful under that system that means you were successful at fitting in to their style. Well, this is America. I didn't like fitting into something that was very stiff and formal at least from my American point of view. Then when the '60s came it gave a political and cultural context for my impulses and I could say, "Oh, I see, what they really want me to be is European, and I'm not that. I'm African." So then I think you can question everything. Plus at the same time the SNCC [Student Non-violent Coordinating Committee] kids were protesting and then the white kids began and the women began to question, so I was right in the groove. Essentially, that's what the '60s gave me. There used to be a phrase called "Question authority." Well that stayed with me, and over the years I have not let up on that. You have to question authority. Bill Greaves, who was the executive producer of *Black Journal*, made this speech to the young producers. He said, "Look, this is not going to last forever, so you've got to do three things," and I'll always remember this, he said, "If you're going to make a film about Black people you have to capture Black reality. Don't start with the way white people say capture the reality. And if you do that you're going to find some form of oppression or problems. Number two would be to identify the problem, because usually that's the subject of the film. There is some situation that is oppressing Black people, and if you're going to make a real film you have to capture that, because that's the core of our existence in America—constantly struggling against the denomination of other cultural and political forces. The third thing is, suggest a solution." He said, "In many instances, what people try to do may not occur. It may not be successful, but if you can show the attempt at making a solution then the film will act as a road map for future generations." He gave me a structure for a kind of energy I was trying to rebel with. I've never really forgotten that, and he's right. The fourth thing he said was, "Always try to make the films about Black people with the interior voice." In other words, don't be like the white people and just say this is what so-and-so said. Instead, try to get the Black people to say it. That's what made *Black Journal* different than 60 Minutes.

GA: I see, you're really giving a voice to these people who are oppressed.

SB: And letting them say what they wanted to say and how they felt and not having one of the news correspondents serve as the stars who interview the subjects. In our films, the subjects were the stars.

GA: What were some of your more memorable subjects during that time?

SB: In '69 or '70 I got to do a film about the Nation of Islam from the inside with an interview with Elijah Muhammed. We went to Chicago, to his factories, his newspaper. It was cool. Everybody was real cool and I got an interview with him, who in fact was a bit senile at the time. So it was hard getting a straight answer, but every once in a while his genius would pop out and you could see that he was this organizing guy who had charisma and motivated all these people. I also did a two-part series on Black student movements. Now if you looked at it like the prototype of what the Black students were thinking of as Black studies came into being because it didn't just [snaps fingers] pop up like Black studies at first. It was, "Well we want these white organizations to teach us who we are." Then other people said, "Wait a minute. They don't know. They're going to make you hip slaves." Then the next step would be, they said, "We have to be taught skills for nation building." That was the big phrase then, and you could kind of get away with saying that because those are in fact not racial characteristics. Nation building is nation building. Anybody can do that. But then Black studies came into being and it evolved into what it is now, although from what I understand, it's mellowed and it's softened. It was reinterpreting history from an Afro-centric point of view, but in these two films I did, you could see the thought process evolving. It was a great time, because I get out of jail and a week later I'm an associate producer for a national documentary television show and I'm being paid to go around the country making films about Black people. Now true, they only aired one evening a month.

GA: That was significant for Black people at the time, though, wouldn't you say?

SB: Very, and so in Harlem where I lived I was a celeb, because I could walk down the street and people would say, "Hey, he made that film." It was that kind of environment. Basically it gave me a feeling of appreciation, but it also gave me a feeling that I had to be committed, because if I did something jive, they would let me know. So why I make the films I make comes out of that experience guided by Bill Greaves's advice, but with service and artistic expression. Back then my expression essentially was journalistic and what I've been trying to do over the years is to customize the journalistic style into a more personal film style. The first time I began to do that was with Let the Church Say Amen, which allowed me to tell a story. I didn't use any voice-overs, which is a journalistic approach. It has a beginning, middle and end and a cast of characters. It's very powerful.

GA: *Very cinema verité.*

SB: Yeah, that's right. That's when I said, "Ah, this is what I really want to do." So this is basically what I've been playing with over these years.

GA: *And Black Journal was your foundation, your launching pad for who you are today for the most part?*

SB: Very much, yes.

GA: *Getting into the journalistic part of your job, it's a journalist's job to find the truth and tell the truth. What are your thoughts on that?*

SB: I think when people say that the obligation of the filmmaker is to tell the truth, what that means to me is that there really isn't any objectivity in telling the truth. What you can do is tell as clearly and as articulately as you can what this person thinks, how they see the world, how they view the forces that affect them. If you can do that, it will be a vision of the world people can react to and discuss and agree and disagree with. That's how I approach it. This short film I'm doing now is essentially the reaction of a segment of the Black community to the World Trade Center bombing, and I know what's going to happen. People are going to say, "Well, do all Black people feel this?" I say, "Well, all Black people don't feel anything. I've chosen people who don't get a chance to talk and I'm going to give them a chance to have a voice." So in your understanding of the world and Black people's roles and place in it, if you look at my films you will get a deeper idea of how they see it. That's about as far as you can go, I think, in terms of the truth.

GA: *So in other words there is no one truth?*

SB: No, I don't think so, and the problem with the treatment of Black people in this country in general, in almost any media, has been that the people who have the tools—I'm not saying anything startlingly new—to tell the story, when they get to the African American participation in America, they tell that story for their own psychological reasons and not to get to the truth of the Black experience. In other words, they know that there have been some injustices done to Black people, they know that the conditions that started with slavery have not entirely disappeared. There's still bias in all aspects of the institutions of American life. They know that there's this prejudice and bias in the structure and they don't really want to move to change that, because then their position in the world—Black, white people's position—would have to change.

GA: So it's for their psychological comfort, you're saying.

SB: Exactly, so my job is to say to the white people, "No, no, this is the way other people see that. And because of their position in this culture, you're going to have to deal with it, so you should get to know this kind of work." To the Black people I say, "Here is stuff you say about yourself that you don't often get a chance to hear and see." Here's a classic example. I lived in Los Angeles from 1975 to 1980 and one of the films I made for public television there was a film about Val Verde. Val Verde was a community that essentially was the Black Palm Springs of the '30s and '40s. There was segregation in L.A. and rich people went to Palm Springs, but the Black middle class and some of the Black stars went to a section of Los Angeles County called Val Verde, where there was a lake. They built cabins there, had horses and barbecue pits. So I made this film about it. It was created for and by this white developer, but I met a guy who was one of his salesmen, and he showed me pictures and described it and then by the time I made the film, which was '78, it had come back in sort of pseudofashion. Church groups would take buses and go out there. So I made a film about this, and in the process there was another white developer who was living there who actually had been going around buying land out from under the people. He would give them money, but he would also go to the tax rolls of the county, find out who was behind, pay the taxes unbeknownst to the people who owned the property, and take the land. For some reason, though, he agreed to be interviewed by me and show me his property. So in my film he's walking around saying, "This land is the cheapest dirt in Los Angeles County and I'm going to make a killing." When I put that in the film it was on the air, but the Black people in Val Verde couldn't see it because it was outside the TV viewing area. But I went back to screen it for them and they had a big dinner and they had a big screening of it in the high school auditorium, and when they saw that section, they got all upset, jumped up and ran down to the guy's house. I had to go back, but I heard about it two days later. They confronted him and threatened him. He had to give back some of the property that he had purchased just straight without any skulduggery, and he agreed to have the people from the community work to develop and build the houses. So that's one of the ways that filmmaking can serve the Black community. Now, interestingly enough, that function is not just what the Black filmmakers can do, white filmmakers, some of them do that, too, especially the documentarians. People like Pam Yates and Bill Jersey do that too, but for us it's hard because we have to justify the validity of the culture every time we ask for money, which is really a problem.

GA: Which goes back to who controls the process. But you're speaking of film not just as entertainment but as a catalyst . . .

SB: For action, and the thing now is documentaries because it's interesting. You know who's had a profound influence on the development of Black documentaries although he doesn't realize it? Spike.

GA: Why?

SB: Because, previous to She's Gotta Have It documentaries and Black documentaries had essentially true street credibility. It was the most real thing that you could find on film for Black people, but it was on public television. That's where Black filmmakers were for a long time. What Spike did was take a version of reality and put it up on the big screen. That's what really made him distinct—he kept it real before "keeping it real" was the thing. So what happened was that much of our thunder, much of our claim to being exceptional or special, was reduced because Spike's films were verité, not in technique but in the conceptualization. Before, a person like Buggin' Out in Do the Right Thing, you'd only find him in a documentary. But here was a character who was written and acted. Spike changed that, and so for a long time much of the documentary audience was reduced because the reality that people wanted to see with documentaries they could now see on the big screen. Ultimately, they were fooled because Hollywood—with the exception of Spike, Melvin Van Peebles and maybe Bill Duke—can sort of restructure reality and make you think you're getting it, but they're not really giving it to you. At the same time, people wanted to be more entertained than educated.

GA: Why do you think that was the case?

SB: Because in a weird kind of way it was always the case. It's just that with Black documentaries we said things and treated important subjects in a way in which they hadn't been treated with the interior voice—our own people talking as opposed to a white expert. We captured their attention, and if you look at the Black Journal stuff, we had jazz music as themes, African drums. You have to put in some entertainment elements, but when Spike and that crew came in, if you look at Do the Right Thing and you have Rosie Perez dancing in the front, that's not real but psychologically it's real and right. It touches a nerve.

GA: You're there.

SB: You're there and people said, "I'm for that." Even though if you really looked at it in the cold light of day, you say, "Wait a minute. Here is a good-looking girl with boxing gloves on and she's dancing. What is that about?" It captures the mood, so the entertainment thing just clicked in, and once the audience buys that you can't ask them to go back. That's one of the reasons why in my films I've upped the ante for using music, for telling a story making sure that the characters not only have to be educational, but they really have to be entertaining, provocative. It's sort of what Cornel West does. Cornel's message without a messenger is kind of flat. But he performs it, and so with the documentaries we've kind of had to do that. Otherwise, the audience, they just won't stay without that.

GA: *Especially now in this generation when everyone is throwing something in your face 24/7 and everything is in sound bites.*

SB: Yeah, that's right, bites of MTV. For me with the film I did called *John Henrik Clark* about Clark, a white editor did that, but I chose him because he had done a lot of MTV editing and he was very good at it. He had his own personal style, but I'd seen a documentary film about an important subject matter about jail that he'd done with Larry Fishburne. So he understood the use of a main Black male character telling good information, but the editing style pops and makes it kind of interesting. That essentially is what we ended up with on *John Henrik Clark*. So he could do that, and it's sort of like Miles Davis using Dave Holland, the white bass player. People would say, "Well, how can you use this guy?" Miles would respond, "Well, he brings something to it that I want." That's why I chose Chris Fiore. The same kind of thing.

GA: *Very interesting. I want to go back to Spike. You were reading something into Spike, and I want to bring it all together and that's Spike's ability to bring us characters. People started going to the cinema saying, "I'm going to see the real deal. These are real Black folks." Is that what you think was happening for a time in the 1980s?*

SB: I think so, and also it was a deeply modern take on Black life. Say what you will, to me *Do the Right Thing* and *She's Gotta Have It* are creative, but really the key thing is that they captured that moment so well and in a pop way. But the key to them is that they were new and modern and spoke to Spike's generation. Now, the only person who actually has had more of an impact but is less recognized than Spike is Melvin [Van Peebles]. Melvin is the Charlie Parker of cinema. He's out there. His style is sort of fractured, but it comes together and it stays with you, but it's not immediate like Spike's things. Spike's films are basically not as deep as Melvin's, but they're more flash. That's his generation and that's why I'm a big Melvin fan, because essentially without Melvin there would be no Spike.

GA: *I like your Charlie Parker analogy.*

SB: That's who Melvin is. I mean, I would like to think of myself as sort of a Cannonball Adderley.

Sort of. Because I'm working towards that essentially. I always liked Cannonball. He could really play, he had very creative licks but he had a populist stance, and I think if you took all my films that's where they are.

GA: *Since we're on music, do you look to music to inspire you?*
SB: I listen to Black music all the time. So when I look at scenes or look at people I'm influenced by the internal rhythm of what they're saying. In fact, when we did *Baraka*, when we filmed him doing poetry we would tape just the poetry. We'd re-record it and we'd make it loop. While we were editing we would just play his poetry for eight hours on end. We'd just listen to it, and after a while it got to be where it wasn't someone reciting poetry, it was like a singer singing. Baraka could really do that. He still does it now. He could really do that, and the words began to morph into sounds. It was almost like scat singing. If you heard it over and over again you could go [Hums], and if you thought about it you'd say, "Oh, wait a minute. These are sentences." But we began to think of them as tunes in songs, so yeah.

GA: *Post–September 11 people seem to be more concerned with hard-core news. Tell me about the film you're doing about the attack, and do you think people will be more interested in the truth or the perceived truth through the documentary format as a result of the attack?*
SB: When I started the film—and it's basically been proven that essentially Black people have their own take on American life, so when people say things like, "Oh, I was shaken. My innocence is lost." Well, Black people, ever since we got here we know that there is a double standard and that we've been terrorized through slavery and even with the Diallo murder. If that's not terrorism, tell me what is—so what I wanted to do, I wanted to start with a leftist, a cultural and political leftist view of Black America, and so the people I chose were an activist minister at House of the Lord Baptist Church in Brooklyn, which has a long history of activism. I also spoke with a sixties activist who's still active. For another view I got a bunch of Black firefighters. And I followed them in a meeting and they also had a big memorial service in Brooklyn, which we covered.

GA: *What did you find?*
SB: There's a range. The most moderate were the firefighters. They basically liked being on the receiving end of new respect from the Black community and the white community of firefighters, but in the midst of that, while they were planning this memorial they took posters and put them in firehouses around the city to let the other white firefighters know about the service. In one of the firehouses, somebody wrote racist slogans on the poster and this came up in the meet-

ing I was filming. So the Black firefighters, too, have a double consciousness about service, pride and being a good firefighter. But realizing that in a city of 55 to 60 percent people of color only 3 percent of the firefighters are of color. In the three hundred who were promoted to replace the three hundred who died, none were Black, and twelve firefighters of color died in the World Trade Center attack. Six weeks after the attack one Black guy was mentioned, and that's because he was a popular singer at weddings and used to perform for benefits for the fire department and community groups. So they know there's a double consciousness, and when you're making documentaries about a Black subject it has to have that cultural authenticity. It must be culturally authentic. Even for the white people, even though they may object to it in the beginning because they might not like that take.

GA: *And what exactly do you mean by cultural authenticity?*
SB: In other words, most documentaries have a certain premise that the subject is based on. For instance, if you're making a film on housing you can take the premise that even though there are problems, the dream, the aspiration, the hope of housing in this city is being accomplished even though there are some problems. But a Black point of view would say, "Well, when the design for housing was created we were not included. So it can never be okay until the design of housing includes the style and the preferences of the previously left out people." That's why when I say culturally authentic that's supposition. If you're making a film from that second set of assumptions, it's culturally authentic. So many of the films I've done are usually based on prominent Black people who have achieved but have struggled in reaching their achievement. Robeson, Langston Hughes, John Henrik Clarke, Baraka, Spike to a certain extent and even the National Geographic films, which are mainstream films like *Heritage of the South Carolina Sea Islands*, or the film about the brass bands in New Orleans. To be culturally authentic is to, number one, document their achievements, but also document the times in which they achieved.

GA: *You have to contextualize things, then, you're saying?*
SB: Exactly, because usually what white people do is they say, "Here's a guy who did this, isn't he wonderful?" You can take it for that, but if you want to show that person in a more profound way you have to show the society in which he lived, and that's when the interior voice kicks in, that's when the cultural authenticity kicks in. That's what I meant. And that's the hardest one, but I'm usually the producer of my own films. I raise my own money, so that issue, once I get the money, doesn't come up. But part of the problem of being a producer is—I'm running into this more now than ever—the subject and the cultural authenticity that he or she brings is sometimes dis-

puted by the people who ordinarily put up the money for films. Like STARZ Encore, which is a cable station. I suggested they do a film about Dick Gregory, an older comedian, contemporary of Lenny Bruce, breakthrough guy, pioneer, activist. They didn't know who he was. This was a young white guy in his early thirties. Even when his Black staff told him who Dick Gregory was, he didn't want to do it. I suspect he just didn't see how this critic of the culture was either legitimate or funny, where, in fact, Dick Gregory made his name by being both a legitimate critic of the society and being funny. As a producer I run into that a lot and people tell me, "Well, choose somebody who's not so anti-establishment." But they don't interest me.

GA: *Why are you attracted to people whom mainstream society would call controversial?*
SB: I'm not attracted to controversy, I'm interested in people who achieve within the society and whose activities project a search for truth from the African-American viewpoint. What I've been interested in more lately is, what is the cost for this effort? What does it cost them? What I'm discovering is that they have families. That's where the first wound is. He's not around to be a father to his kids as much. That's what Gordon Parks's daughter says about him. Robeson's son says that his father wasn't the greatest dad. He admits there were problems. With Langston, he was gay, but in my film I don't say that, which is probably a major mistake. That was deliberate. For that series we wanted the person's life to come out of their work, their poetry, and Langston never addressed a gay subject in his poetry, except there is one piece where he talks about a guy on a ship but it's veiled in all kinds of subtleties. So you don't really know what the relationship was. With Baraka he just fights all the time and everybody around him sort of knows that's how he is so they just go with it. With Spike, I caught him early, because the film I made was when he was doing Do The Right Thing and also I was interested more in the process of production rather than Spike as an artist, so the film really was what the title says, Making "Do the Right Thing" and that's what it is.

GA: *What is your process for getting and achieving cultural authenticity in your work?*
SB: I always try to find out how the subject feels about what he's doing. Why did you do it? Do you think that if you hadn't had this resistance would you have done it another way? Why did you do it in the first place? With Langston, "Why didn't you become an engineer like your father said?" He says, "Well, I couldn't get it, I got into words and poetry." Now cultural authenticity is something that white documentarians should work at too. The women do, but the men tend not to, because they sort of assume the world is what you see because that's how they live. There was a whole wave in the late '70s, early '80s of films by white women, mostly Jewish, like Amalie

Rothchild, who did a film called Nana, Mom and Me (1975), which paralleled the rise of white feminism. They were going back to their roots in a way—their mothers—and examining why their mothers taught them to be the obedient wife. They were rebelling against that, so they made films about it. So that was culturally authentic. It's not just Black. Then there was a wave of gay exploration, too, like Before Stonewall (1984).

GA: How do you approach each project in terms of your process?

SB: There are three phases in my career, I think. First is my TV journalist career, that essentially was Black Journal. I hate to admit it, but that's kind of what it was. I kind of jazzed it up, but it was essentially TV journalism. Then in the second wave I did what I call cheerleader films. These were films that up until maybe five years ago were pretty much the same. My approach was the same, but I would get a researcher and I'd gather a lot of facts and I'd also gather a lot of names of people who were connected to or knew about this person or the subject. I would then go and interview people, sometimes with a camera if they were old or if I wouldn't get a chance to see them again. Then I'd distill all of that information. I'd get the interviews transcribed. Now I always work with a writer, mostly Lou Potter. In the beginning I wrote my own stuff. So we get all the information, these facts, we create time lines of what was happening when the subject was born, his first poetry or his first demonstration or whatever happened and the events that occurred that may or may not have affected him. I then transcribe the interviews, put them into a computer, then cut and paste so that in the end I basically have a narrative, which is told mostly by people talking. That's what I did during that phase which was the cheerleader phase. My film on Baraka is an example of a cheerleader film, and all of my films after Black Journal, except what happened with John Henrik Clarke, with Paul Robeson, and less so Gordon Parks because I didn't direct that, I just produced it. But even that, I would say that I kind of influenced it, so that's more of a swan song than I would like it to be, but it is what it is. Now I'm trying to make more complex renderings of history and personal histories so that you'll still understand what he or she did, but you'll understand why, the cause as well as some of the wrong decisions and the fallout. Now I'm thinking of subjects that aren't hallmarks of Black nobility. Like I want to do something on the Republic of New Africa. These were groups of Black guys who bought land to start their own state and they had shoot-outs with the government. This was in '65 or something like that, and there's footage too because of the shoot-out in Detroit. It's a complex story. There are heroes, but some of them were not heroes—some of them were fools. It broke up because the people who organized it fell out amongst themselves. I didn't feel comfortable enough to do it when Black achievement was under attack or even questioned, and Black people themselves didn't feel comfortable about themselves.

But now they've been told enough, you have a history, you're an African—they know that, that's cool, all right, so now what does that mean? How does that help us live now?

GA: More analysis.

SB: More analysis and class. How does class come into it? Also, it's going to be less journalistic and more interpretive. That's about as much as I can say. I'm even going to examine myself. I want to have a project called *The Search* where I want go back and find this guy I worked with in Peru as a Peace Corps volunteer, because I still have photographs of that time. Also, the history of Shining Path [the Maoist guerrilla group] comes up during that time, and I want to go back and shoot and interview some of the old Peace Corps volunteers I was with.

GA: And how would you angle this piece? Looking at your own life?

SB: Yeah, basically, yeah, what lessons can one learn. I'm going to play myself, but conceptually I have to pretend as if somebody is making the film about me. What can you learn from a guy who was smart but got into trouble with the existing social mores of the time, renegaded to the Peace Corp and decided that's what made him want to be a filmmaker? So that's social history, personal investigation and hopefully artistry all in one if I can do it, if I can get the money now. Somebody will say, well, why should we make a film about you making a film about yourself, which is valid. But you see, with digital video I can do that, I can shoot it all.

GA: You employ very classic documentary techniques—interviews and archival footage in your work. Tell me about that.

SB: Yes. That came out of the *Black Journal* experience. That's what they taught us and that was the easiest to do, and also given the time we didn't really have time to really hang with people. We had about four days to shoot. Once I left *Black Journal* I did *Let the Church Say Amen*, which was verité, and I also did some other films.

GA: You've been able to work in documentary successfully for thirty years. To what would you attribute your ability to continue to work?

SB: I work very, very hard. I work all the time. I'm always writing something, always thinking about something, always on the phone, and the reason is that it's not work for me.

GA: What's been your most important work, you think, of all the films you've done?

SB: Well, there are different generations. I'd say the one that people even now still remember is *Let *the Church Say Amen*. People still remember that because it was the first narrative documentary with an interior voice that was well produced and was filmed in three different cities. I started in Atlanta, went to Mount Bayou, Mississippi, a little country town, and then we followed this one guy and ended up in Chicago, then back to Atlanta. And the Whitney Museum [in New York] put on a big premiere for it. The year after I did *Baraka* I did a film called *The Black and the Green* and that made a lot of noise. Because it was Black people going abroad to Ireland and that was the point of analysis of a white subject, which was essentially the IRA. So that was interesting, but it was banned. It was supposed be on public television. It premiered at the Kennedy Center at a public television conference and got a rave review in the *Washington Post* the next day. Then they had a private screening for the Congressional Black Caucus that night, oh, people were into it. And then they scheduled it for broadcast, then I got a letter saying that they were not going to air it.

GA: *Did that feel like censorship to you?*

SB: It was censorship. Because what happened was a write-in protest was orchestrated by a lot of the Irish organizations. They called me and said, "Look, the English Intelligence Service does not want this film on American public television. It's as simple as that—you've got Black people saying, justifying, legitimizing violence against the English by the Irish."

GA: *So how do you feel about that?*

SB: Well, I was pissed, but what happened was they had screenings around the city and then I sent copies over to England. Then one of the guys who was in the film was a folksinger. He went on tour and I gave him a couple copies and he showed it all over Europe. It's still sort of my least seen biggest secret. Afterwards I would say *Clarke* and *Robeson* have been the big films for me. *Langston* too was kind of big because it was on public TV, but basically there were five that were the ones that made big splashes: *Robeson, John Henrik Clarke, Let the Church Say Amen, Baraka* and *Langston*. *Let the Church Say Amen* gets the church, *Langston* gets the artistic sort of old-style cultural people. *Baraka* gets the '60s people. *Robeson* gets the Black Marxists and *John Henrik Clarke* gets the Afro-centric scholars. And *Gordon Parks* [*Half Past Autumn*] gets the Black middle class. The next wave will be personalized, like the film that we started shooting about the La Pelota, baseball in Cuba. That's going to be interesting because it's foreign. We're going to have a story, but there's going to be some history in it.

GA: *What makes a good documentarian and what makes a good documentary film?*

SB: What makes a good documentary is the answer to a documentarian's curiosity.

GA: Tell me what you mean by that.

SB: A good documentarian is curious. That's why you go through the process of asking, why is this? How did this happen? That's interesting. Why did he say that? That's what spurs you. Now, that initial impulse can come from several different aesthetics. One can be the curiosity of the eclectic. For example, here's a funny guy. Why is he like that? I'm going to capture that. It's like the guy who did the film on Crumb. That's an eclectic cat, weird, he just made a film about himself. Or it can be analytical. How does society work? Why do people act like this? Then you try to answer that, and with my films it started off with these Black people are not as they've been portrayed by the general media. Let me go and demonstrate what they really are like. That started me on a lifelong journey of different types of people, much of which reacts to the same negative impulses of the Eurocentric society, but it comes out differently sometimes, and that's what makes the films different.

GA: So the good documentary filmmaker is curious?

SB: Curious, persistent, you really have to be persistent. If the curiosity isn't organic, heartfelt, then the persistence won't be there, because in many instances the reason why you're persistent is because you really don't have the answer yet and you have to keep going after the money or going after the person or putting up with this or putting up with that. Then I would say the third thing in a weird kind of way—I know some will say it's not true— but you want to be of service. So it's curiosity, persistence and service.

GA: Does service mean you're looking to educate people?

SB: Yes, in some ways you think that their lives are going to be better. People don't want to cop to that a lot, but that's really why you're doing it. If you look at this film, it will give you one more bit of information about the life you live and the way the world is and how it operates, and maybe you'll learn something about it. It'll empower you to make your life better. That's kind of what it is.

GA: Outside of your own films, what films have been most influential on you as a filmmaker?

SB: There's a white guy, the first one whose film knocked me out, a guy named William Jersey. It's called A Time for Burning (1967). It's a classic verité about this white minister in Kansas in the midst of the Civil Rights Movement who says, "Wait a minute. We should integrate the church." Then I saw Bill Greaves's film called Still a Brother: Inside the Black Middle Class (1968), and so that was an interior voice film—the first interior voice film that I ever saw and it's ninety minutes. It's all this really interesting stuff I'd never really seen before, like a successful Black middle-class man questioning his integrated life. Those are the two films that really influenced me. They started me off.

GA: You knew then that you wanted to be a documentary filmmaker.
SB: Yes, like that.

GA: And how old were you at this time when you decided this is it, "I'm going to be a documentary film-maker"?
SB: I was in film school, so I was about twenty-four or twenty-three, something like that.

GA: Do you ever want to do any narrative work? You talked about some narrative work.
SB: I have, but they're all based on real people or real incidents. There are three actually, one is called Deacons for Defense and Justice. It's a group of Black church men who in 1963–1964 they formed armed patrols in Bougaloosa, Louisiana, to protect the kids who came down for voter registration. When they came down, Klan activity increased, so these guys said, "All right, we got something for them," so they patrolled their communities and had shoot-outs and everything, but what happened was Martin Luther King condemned them. He said, "No, no, no, no, no violence. We're nonviolent." And they said, "Hey, look, we're not buying that. You don't live here, we do." I have a script but I haven't been able to get it funded.

GA: Do you tend to like history, given the films you've done?
SB: It's not so much history. I like that there are characters who do things. I mean what I would really like to do is to find contemporary people and then shoot that.

GA: Who are some contemporary people that strike you as being potentially good material?
SB: Tupac. I was supposed to do that for HBO, but it fell apart because of a negotiation thing with his mother and HBO.

GA: He'd be fascinating.
SB: Yeah, and I'm preparing a doc on Stokely Carmichael, which is becoming history, though. I just got a treatment and I'm just applying for money to do some research. It'd be nice to get that done, but ideas are not the problem. It's trying to shape the ideas, develop-

ing them and getting them to a position where people can judge them and give me money for them.

GA: *What are your hopes for Black documentary filmmaking going forward?*

SB: I'd hope that it would recapture the fervor of advocacy and that it becomes more pointed in its concerns, and number two, which is even more important, I hope that the level of craft improves. One of the deep secrets of the Black documentary world is that much of it has good intentions, good material, but less than good craft.

GA: *Why do you think that's the case?*

SB: We don't get a chance to practice a lot. I've been doing it for thirty years so I know what I'm doing, but I can see my work with the Black Documentary Collective, which was formed two years ago—we have eighty-eight people on our roster—and we've done different projects and the level of craft is not that good. It could be better, and I'm hoping that with this new equipment like DVD that people are beginning to shoot more and begin to perfect the craft because the craft of making a documentary is very distinct from features. Cinema verité's a very demanding set of exercises and craft, and you only learn if you do it. Usually people get only a chance to do it if somebody puts up the money, but if you have a DVD camera you can just shoot, shoot, shoot, and you can shoot for hours without going to process it. You can look at it right away and reshoot it if it doesn't work. So those two things I'd like to see: an increase in advocacy, point of view and advocacy, better craft, and I think if that happens then the third thing would be an increase in the audience. I think that would come, but those first two things would have to happen before the audience, because the audience is now used to quality stuff. The features, most of them, are pretty decent in terms of quality.

GA: *So documentaries have to go back to the basics of the craft?*

SB: I think so, and what's also happened is that documentary white and Black tends to be the stepchild of media.

GA: *Does that bother you?*

SB: Oh, very much. In 1988, I had a twentieth-year retrospective at the Whitney Museum and this was a major, a major accomplishment for me. I was amazed. I also had these gallery talks. I thought there would be fifty people, but there were plenty of people, packed all in the aisles. It was just amazing to me, and one of the first questions was: "When are you going to make real films?"

GA: *That was like a slap in the face, huh?*

SB: It was, and I said, "Look, my films are more real than most fiction films, and the fact that I've been able to continue to make these films and people relate to them." I said, "They're not Hollywood films, but the documentary carries a noble tradition of empowerment and giving knowledge, and so in that sense they're more real than the Hollywood films."

GA: *So it's almost an educational process for audiences, you think. You have to educate.*

SB: At this point I can't do that. What I can do basically is make the best film I can and get it out there and move on to the next one. What I'm considering is maybe doing some speaking engagements with films now to kind of keep in touch. Ossie Davis told me when I was doing *The Making of "Do the Right Thing,"* "You have to prevent yourself from being consigned to the dust bin, to the history bin. You have to always reinvent yourself every four years, because it's every four years that there's a new generation of people who come out of school, they don't know things." It made me realize that he's right. I used to do speaking engagements, but then I got tired of it. But in order to keep current and find out what people are thinking you have to go out, and in addition to making the films, you have to show them with groups to see what they think. So I'm probably going to do some speaking.

Stanley Nelson

Born in 1954, New York City native Stanley Nelson is a 2002 recipient of the coveted MacArthur Foundation Fellowship. Anyone who knows Nelson can witness that he is a living testament that nice guys don't always finish last. He has been making his mark on the world of cinema for over twenty years as a producer, director, and writer of documentary films and videos. His most recent film, *The Murder of Emmett Till*, on the horrific lynching in Mississippi in 1955, aired on PBS in January 2003.

Nelson's film *Marcus Garvey: Look for Me in the Whirlwind*, about the life of the controversial Black leader who created a Black nationalist movement in the first half of the twentieth century, was featured at the 2001 Sundance Film Festival and aired on PBS in February 2001.

In 1999 Nelson won the Freedom of Expression Award at Sundance for *The Black Press: Soldiers Without Swords*, a documentary that explores the history of African American newspapers. Nelson's credits also include his first documentary, *Two Dollars and a Dream: The Story of Madame C. J. Walker* (1989), on the life of the African American businesswoman who became America's first self-made female millionaire, which earned him the CINE Golden Eagle award and which was cited as the Best Production of the Decade by the Black Filmmaker Foundation. Nelson also served as producer on such PBS programs as *Listening to America* and *What Can We Do about Violence?* with Bill Moyers, and *Election '93*, for which he was nominated for an Emmy Award. He was also a producer for the acclaimed Fox-TV series *TV Nation*.

An alumnus of the Leonard Davis Film School at the City University of New York, Nelson has taught film production at Howard University in Washington, D.C., and has been a fellow of the American Film Institute, the New York Foundation for the Arts, the Washington, D.C., Commission for the Arts, and a Revson Fellow at Columbia University. Nelson served on the selection panel for the Fulbright fellowship in film for three years, and in the spring of 1997 was named a University Regents Lecturer at the University of California, San Diego.

GA: How did you get into film? Were you a creative child?

SN: I was a normal kid who liked sports and that kind of stuff and I never looked at myself as being particularly artistic. But I always had an interest in film. Another thing was that growing up in New York City, I saw endless possibilities. There were actors, musicians and filmmakers. All of these people exist in your city and there are possibilities for you to do that. I think those things were great in opening my horizons.

GA: When did you decide to commit to filmmaking?

SN: When I started college in 1969 I didn't know what I wanted to do, so I kind of bounced around, and the more I thought about it the more I knew I did not want to sit behind a desk and carry a briefcase. Instead, I wanted to do something I thought would be rewarding to me for the rest of my life, I thought I wanted to do something artistic. So at that point, looking around for something artistic, I saw the blaxploitation era and I found that the idea of making films was much more real, because Black people were making films and I thought I could get into it, and that there was a lot of room to make the films better.

GA: During the blaxploitation era was there a particular film that really sparked your interest and motivated you to pursue film as a career?

SN: No, it wasn't that I liked any particular film, but more so that I didn't like any of the films that were being made.

GA: What didn't you like about the films?

SN: I just thought the content was bad and that they were badly made, and it was very clear that they were not technically as good as the Hollywood [mainstream] films. But you would go to the movies and Black people would be packed in the theater hollering and screaming at the screen, and I thought that if we got into the business and controlled the content we would make better films that maybe had a little more to say, a little more truthfulness, and a little less of the shoot-

'em-up type films, and that you could bring in a Black audience. That sort of pushed me into filmmaking and into saying that this idea is real and possible. Before that, what a lot of young people may not see and understand is that there were no role models when I was growing up. Very rarely would you see a Black actor in a film, and generally, there were no Black people behind the camera, so no one really thought of breaking through and how to go about doing it.

GA: *Do you believe that the success of the blaxploitation era as a whole is attributable to the fact we were hungry for our own images on the screen?*
SN: Yes, I can remember the shock of going to see Black people in a film—the stars with a kind of a Black attitude. It wasn't a Sidney Poitier film or the third-string cowboy buddy in a couple of scenes, but these were films made for Black people, about Black people, but the problem with them by and large was that a lot of these films were not being made by Black people. And I thought that if that component could be added, that could really make the films better, and if you made good films people would come and you could make money.

GA: *You come from a very comfortable background—your father was a successful dentist. Many artists or would-be artists forgo their artistic dreams in order to meet family and societal expectations. Did you get family support when you decided to pursue film?*
SN: My father was a dentist, but I think for him that was the best he could do for his era. But he was in some ways an artist underneath and had the attitude and soul of an artist. My father said early on that he worked really hard as a dentist so that we wouldn't have to be dentists, and so my parents were fine with what I did. At some point, when I was struggling in my younger years, they said, "Maybe you should try something else," but they never hit the roof and said, "What are you going to do?" They were very supportive and I bounced around school for a few years; I was twenty-four or so before I really took up filmmaking in school, so they were happy that I took up something.

GA: *Do you suggest film school for aspiring directors?*
SN: I went to film school and I found it to be a great experience; it was a way in. I saw a lot of films, talked to a lot of people, and started thinking about film in a different way. It also helped me to have an eye on a different prize when I worked for the documentarian Bill Greaves and at United Methodist Communications, the communications arm of the Methodist Church. It made me always know that I wanted to be a filmmaker. Film school talks to you about being a filmmaker; it

plants that in you. My life was not going to be a producer for United Methodist Communications, there was something more. I could use the tools that I learned there and use them to do something where I had more freedom. That's my model, but you can do it however you want.

GA: *What made you think you could succeed in the film business?*

SN: Part of it was just being young and stupid, and being very naïve, I thought things worked pretty much on merit. And I knew that I could make a better film than a lot of the films being made. I felt you could have more to say, more originality, and that the films could be done technically so much better than the films that were around then.

GA: *When you started out, were there any mainstream Hollywood films you saw that you wanted to emulate in terms of Black cinema?*

SN: No, once I started studying films I saw directors that I liked, but in the beginning it was more just the idea of making films and the fact that we too could make films, and that there was now a proven audience for our films. Early on I had the feeling, as did some of my classmates, that if you make a good film you could find a market for it, because it will make money, and the idea that it will make money will drive it no matter what the message. The message could be the most revolutionary message in the world, but if Hollywood or whomever feels they can make money on it, they will put that film out.

GA: *When you started studying film, did you know that you wanted to make documentaries?*

SN: No, in fact, the documentarian D. A. Pennebaker was a teacher of mine in school and I used to argue with him because I never wanted to do documentaries. I thought of the documentary as an out-of-date form and just going nowhere, so my senior thesis was a fiction piece, not a documentary. But after school I got a job working with Bill Greaves as an apprentice and kind of got into documentary filmmaking. And by that time the blaxploitation era, which was very short-lived, was over, so I just stayed in documentary, because there was a long period of time, from the blaxploitation era to the mid-eighties when *She's Gotta Have It* came out, when there were no Black films being made. And I came to love it [documentaries].

GA: *How did you meet filmmaker Bill Greaves and what was it like working with him?*

SN: After graduating from film school, I actually took a production guide book of production houses in New York and just went door-to-door trying to find a job. I had done about three or four days of that but couldn't find any work. I had also found out about a program as a part of the

Comprehensive Education Training Act [CETA] by which the government paid you for six months in an apprenticeship program. So at the end of a day of pounding the pavement, I called my mother for some reason, like maybe to get a free dinner, and she told me she had just been reading a profile on a Black filmmaker named Bill Greaves in the *Daily News*, and that I should go talk to him. So I looked up his number and it just so happened that his office was a block away. I went up there, knocked on his door and started talking to him, and he said, "No, no, no, I can't hire you. I don't have any money. Forget it. Forget it." And I told him he could hire me through the CETA program and that he would not have to pay me, but that he would have to hire me at the end of six months. He told me that he couldn't agree to hire me because he didn't know where he'd be, and I told him that all he had to do was agree to do the program, and at the end of six months if he wasn't happy with my work he could just fire me, we shake hands and walk away. He said, "Great. Fine. You're on. We're shooting a film, you can go with my son David tomorrow to pick up some equipment." I actually ended up living with him in the country in Sheffield, Massachusetts, for about a year.

GA: Wow. Great story. What did you do for Greaves?
SN: I was hired as an apprentice film editor. I did that for a few months, then the editor quit, so then he made me the editor. So I was the film editor on some of the documentaries. I also production-managed for him and I ended up producing and directing documentaries for him.

GA: What films did you work on with Greaves?
SN: We worked on a bunch of documentary films, including one about Black barbershops called *Just Doin' It: A Tale of Two Barbershops*, and a couple of films for the Marines. Bill was doing a lot of government documentaries at that point, so I worked on those. Bill was great to work with, but Bill was cheap. [Laughs] And once he saw that I was willing and able to do stuff—I remember when we were in the car going to the shoot on the barbershops and he said, "You're going to come on this shoot with us," and I said, "Oh, great." I had never really been on a professional shoot, and he said, "Oh, yeah, and you're going to be doing sound," and I said, "I don't know how to do sound." He said, "Well, you took sound in school," and I said, "Yeah." "Well, go to the sound house and have the guy check you out on the equipment, make sure you know how to use it because you're going to be doing sound," he said.

GA: Trial by fire, huh? [Laughs]
SN: Yes.

GA: Your documentaries have mainly dealt with historical figures and events. Were you always interested in history?

SN: No, but I was interested in telling our story; that's what I was really interested in doing. *Two Dollars and a Dream: The Story of Madame C. J. Walker* was the first historical story I did, and I did that story because my mother's father was general manager of Walker's company as well as her lawyer and he actually inherited a good piece of the company.

GA: So did you grow up hearing stories about Walker?

SN: Yes, I did, and the company was based out in Indiana and my mother had five brothers who still lived there and they were still associated with the company. One of my uncles was still general manager of the company, so as a young filmmaker starting out it was the sort of story that I thought was natural for me.

GA: Tell me about making Two Dollars and a Dream.

SN: I went out to Indiana and my uncle gave me the key to the Walker building and let my cousins and I look around, and we found boxes and boxes of pictures and letters from the 1910s and some other great things: a movie the company did in the 1920s and some other stuff that nobody had seen, like some hand-painted glass slides that the company used for promotion in the 1920s, incredible stuff. And at that point it became obvious to me that there was enough material to do a film. At the same time, when I was out there I kind of did some pre-interviews, talked with some people who were involved in the company and who could remember Madame Walker and A'lelia Walker, her daughter, and it became real.

GA: I enjoyed it quite a bit but had no idea there was a family connection. I know that documentaries, like all films, can be difficult to finance. How long did it take you to make Two Dollars and a Dream?

SN: I started the film in 1980 and it took me about seven years to complete it because it was a struggle to raise money. I did the research, I directed and produced it, I did ninety percent of the sound and I edited it. The cost was probably somewhere around $100,000.

GA: How did you raise funds to make the film?

SN: I financed the film with grants from the Eli Lilly Endowment in Indianapolis, Indiana, as well as with grants from the Indiana Arts Commission and the Indiana Historical Society. Finally, we sent out letters to individual donors around Indiana and raised about $10,000.

GA: Over the seven years it took you to make the film, did you ever question yourself on why you were pursuing film at all?

SN: Yes, there were those times, but what happens is that at some point you go so far down the road that you can't do anything else. It's what you do. And I was fairly successful and I've always been able to work. While doing the film I actually had the job at United Methodist Communications where I learned a hell of a lot about filmmaking. We made films all of the time, it was a job basically making films and I also did a couple of radio pieces there. I was able to pursue money for Two Dollars and a Dream, but I was also able to work and continue to get better and learn about making films, and do that day-to-day.

GA: Do you recommend that aspiring filmmakers work on others' films as they try to make their own films?

SN: Yeah, I think you have to try to do anything you possibly can to stay as close to making films as you possibly can—that's volunteering for other people's films, cutting films—somehow you have to be involved so that you get better. I also spent some time working on fiction films and in trying to do fiction films. I had a fellowship at American Film Institute in Los Angeles. And one thing I found hard for me as a filmmaker in terms of doing fiction films was that it's kind of either feast or famine. You spend a lot of time dreaming and planning and not making films, and I don't know how much better you get doing that. I like making films so much, that's how I learn. I do a lot of stuff. For example, we do industrials here at my company, Firelight Media and I love doing them. That's not all we do, but I love doing them.

GA: As far as documentaries go, do you prefer historical films?

SN: Even though the last few films I've done have been historical, I try to go back and forth and not just do historical films. I love doing historical films, but I just think they're hard to do and it's hard to keep them exciting and fresh. The tendency is to do the same thing over and over. I mean, you have a style and so if you're doing a film on Booker T. Washington or Madame C. J. Walker or Marcus Garvey, how do you do it differently? Obviously, they're different stories, but how does the way of telling the story differ? And that's one of the things you have to try to get to. That's why in some ways I try to go back and forth between historical films and contemporary pieces. Like now we have a proposal out to do a film on domestic violence—a very contemporary film. A couple of years ago I did a film called Shattering the Silences, which was about minority academics and their trials and tribulations.

GA: Why did you do a film about the Black press?

SN: [Laughs] That's funny. My mother again. She was my muse. She was a librarian and always had a real interest in Black newspapers and said to me, "You should do a story on Black newspapers." That was one of the ways I got into it, and in doing the research for other documentaries like *Two Dollars and a Dream* I was always looking at the old Black papers and I found them to be really fascinating. This was a world that had been forgotten.

GA: *What did you find that was so intriguing about the Black newspapers that made you want to do an entire film on them?*

SN: When we hear about Black people in the 1920s or 1930s there is a certain image that pops into our minds from popular culture, but we don't think about these newspapers that were being put out in every city in the country pretty much. So if you had a Black newspaper, then there were people earning a living from it: publishers, photographers, cartoonists, writers, all of these people. This is something that had gotten lost in our culture. We weren't all janitors and maids and redcaps, and I became really interested in that world and thought it was a great story and a way of looking at American history.

GA: *After* The Black Press *you did* Marcus Garvey: Meet Me in the Whirlwind, *about the Black nationalist leader. Why Marcus Garvey?*

SN: I first became interested in Garvey's paper, *The Negro World*, which at one point had the widest circulation of any Black newspaper in the country, but we really weren't able to give it its due in *The Black Press*. And while we were still working on *Black Press* we were talking about *The Negro World* and were looking at some front pages we had copied and we said, "This paper is so amazing." Because one of the things about *The Negro World* was that it was very revolutionary but it also looked at the Black diaspora. On the front page there might be an article about the United States, next to an article about Jamaica, next to an article about Liberia, next to an article about Nicaragua. It was an interesting take not only on the diaspora but on Third World people, as there might also be an article about China, all on the front page. And we were looking at it one day and I asked three or four people working on the *Black Press* production if they had seen a film on Garvey, and no one had. One of the PAs [production assistants] went to the library and did a search to try to find out if there were any films on Garvey and found that there really weren't any except for one half-hour piece for teenagers as a part of a series on great "Negroes." So I started reading a bit more on Garvey and became fascinated by the story. It was a story I had always heard but didn't know much about. It's a story that your parents tell you but you don't know a lot about it.

GA: What do you hope audiences come away with when they see your films?

SN: First, I hope they come away entertained, because that's what I really like. I think when you're seeing a historical documentary you're going to learn something. People come up and say to me, "I really learned a lot." Well, yeah, of course you did. [Laughs] You know what I mean? You should learn something, that's a given, but I hope that you're entertained and I hope that you start to look at American history and history a little bit differently. I think there's a lot of text and subtext to the films hopefully, and some of the subtext is that you start to question the way history has been taught. People come away from the The Black Press and Garvey and say, "Well, I never knew any of that. How did I not know that?" Well, you didn't know that because history is taught in a certain way; it is taught by certain people in a certain way. And hopefully, it'll help you to question the history that you're taught and to open your mind a little bit and see that maybe there's more than one history in this country and that Black people aren't the ones that are still portrayed in the movies: the maids, the sidekicks, the helpers, the second fiddles. But that these were people who had hopes, lives, dreams and realities that were just as valid as anybody else's.

GA: In this increasingly visual age, do you see documentaries as a way to perhaps educate people about history through entertainment?

SN: I hope so. Hopefully as you're entertained you get some kind of education, but first you have to entertain.

GA: I have heard you say that on any given night a documentary on PBS will have to compete with MTV, HBO or a sporting event. Given the competition, what techniques do you try to employ in your films to keep them entertaining?

SN: I try to use anything I can think of. I try to use background music, which is one of the things I'm good at, and I try to find music from the period concerning the subject. In The Black Press we actually found a couple songs that actually talk about the Chicago Defender. I also try to use music to push the story along that maybe has nothing to do with the story. For example, we used a song in Marcus Garvey called "I Saw the Light," which talked about the rise of the Garvey Movement. It's a religious song saying I saw the light of Jesus, but we cut out the Jesus.

GA: How do you find the background music you use?

SN: I first try to find out what the themes of the story are and I have a woman I work with who is a music researcher. Part of the story of Two Dollars and a Dream is about women and the empowerment of women, and there was a woman who had put out a series of blues records about women being empowered. One's called "Mean Women Blues," one's called "I Ain't Got No Man Blues" and there are CDs and albums with different songs on them. I called her record company and I told her about the film and that in addition to empowerment the film was also about hair and that I was looking for any songs about hair. She told me about a song called "Nappy Headed Blues" that she had not heard herself. So as I'm doing this film, which took seven or eight years as I told you, I tried to find this song and I hooked up with these music collectors. There are a lot of people who collect old music, and now with the Internet it's probably easy to find them. Well, finally I hooked up with this guy in Canada, in Vancouver or somewhere, and I called him on the phone and he said, "Oh yeah, 'Nappy Headed Blues.' Yeah, I have that. Send me $10 and I'll make a tape for you, and I'll send you the tape." So I listened to the song and the last verse comes on and it's: "Write to Madame Walker. Send her a $50 bill. Gonna get Madame Walker, send her a $50 bill. Tell her to come help a young girl if you will." I was sitting there with the associate producer and we were looking at the tape recorder and said like, "What? Did you hear that?" And so that song starts the film.

GA: That's amazing. How did you find music for Garvey?

SN: On Garvey we called a couple of record companies. We called Rounder Records and told them what we were doing and had them send us a bunch of CDs of music of the period. They had one CD of nursery rhymes from the Caribbean, which are actually very great and very haunting, so we used those when Garvey was a little boy and when Garvey goes back to the Caribbean, when he is deported. So I try to use period music as much as possible.

GA: That's always good, especially when the piece is historical.

SN: Yes, it adds to it, and sometimes we try to use music to let the story be pushed forward. In documentaries you have interviews and narration and you're always trying to find a way to get a break any way you can. One of the things we're always trying to do is figure out a way to use music so we can get away from people talking.

GA: How did you finance the The Black Press and Garvey? Did you get grant money?

SN: For The Black Press we ended up with fifteen different funders and for Garvey we got grant money for the research and to write the script, but American Experience [PBS] came in and basically funded the production.

GA: Was it difficult getting PBS onboard?

SN: Yes, I had been talking to them off and on about stuff since Two Dollars and a Dream.

GA: What ultimately persuaded them?

SN: The Black Press was considered to be a really big success among everybody and this was a film I couldn't sell to anybody. But there was a little bit more of a tendency to say, "Maybe he knows what he's doing. Let's take a chance." Another thing is that I believe Garvey is a great story. If you told someone the story of Marcus Garvey they wouldn't believe you. The straight text is an incredible, dramatic rise-and-fall story, but so many people know nothing at all about Garvey. Some of the people I talk too, especially white folks, are like, "Who?" But they feel like they should know him and are embarrassed.

GA: What is your greatest accomplishment as a filmmaker?

SN: I love the The Black Press because when I see it there's not too much I want to change, and I like Garvey. I'm very proud of both of those films. And I like Two Dollars and a Dream, because that was something I did totally in the dark, by myself pretty much, without a lot of help, and to have it air on PBS nationally as a special was just an incredible experience for me.

GA: Have you had any major disappointments in your career?

SN: A major disappointment for me was a film I did on methadone treatment called Methadone: Curse or Cure. I did it five or six years ago and I'm still trying to get it aired. I'm not sure if that is because of my failure, but it's a difficult subject matter and it's not the film I wanted to make in some ways. I don't know how to explain it except that filmmaking is not easy; it's a very hard thing to do, and I'm not sure if we made the people we profiled sympathetic. And I think there is a film to be made there, but maybe the film is not the film it should be. But it's an important subject, it's a very important subject and it needs to be aired.

GA: Who are your film heroes and who are your creative influences outside of film?

SN: Miles Davis. I don't really know if I have heroes in film in that way, but Bill Greaves was kind of a mentor and I saw that it was possible for a Black man to work as an independent filmmaker, control his own films and his destiny, have a film company and make a living doing that. By seeing Bill early on in my career that was very, very influential.

GA: Why Miles Davis?

SN: I love Miles. I just think Miles is great and creative, and when we talk about people being able to change their chops, well, here's a guy who could go from bebop, to the "Birth of the Cool," to the Miles Davis Quintet, to the kind of new music "In a Silent Way"–type stuff with Herbie

Hancock, into the complete fusion stuff, and do that stuff at the end of his life when he had that go-go drummer. That's just incredible to be that creative. I remember when we started the The Black Press I was listening to some music like "Kind of Blue" and I called the editor in and we were just listening to it, and I said to the editor that I just want, at some time in my life, to do something as beautiful as any one of these songs on this album. I don't care, just one. Just once. That's all I wanna do and I'd be happy.

GA: And you're right. Miles evolved despite what people or critics might have wanted.
SN: Right. You have a sense that he's doing what he wants to do. He's creative and he is totally in control of his instrument.

GA: You said at some point you would like to do feature films. What types of films would you like to do?
SN: I'd like to do feature films, like films that I'd like to see. I'd like to do films that are for me; films for people who are reasonably intelligent. That's what I'm missing in the Black films I see. I like suspense films, and there is a way to do suspense films that are intelligent, but most of the films that I see for Black people are geared toward kids.

GA: Some argue that things for Blacks will not change until we own our own studios.
SN: Yeah, but we have to find ways to make movies in the meantime. Saying we need to wait until we have our own studios is like saying we need a revolution. [Laughs] I think there are a lot of conspiracies going on, but the conspiracy of wanting to make money is greater than any of those conspiracies. If you can figure out a way to make some money, then your film will get out there.

GA: Why do you think some talented people succeed in film and others don't?
SN: I think a lot of it is timing and perseverance, a lot of it is not getting bitter, a lot is choosing what your next project will be, and who knows? A lot of it depends on what your circumstances are so you can hang in there. If you have a wife and kids and you're twenty-five years old, you may not be able to hang through it. I don't think there's any formula, but a lot of it is perseverance and a lot of it is trying to continue to get better.

GA: And how do you do that?
SN: I think that's what you want out of it. What I want out of it is to be able to make the next film;

that's all I'm gunning for. I'm not gunning to get rich, I'm not gunning to hit the jackpot and I'm not gunning to get on stage and win an award. All I want to do is be able to make the next film.

GA: Everything else is a by-product of that?
SN: Yep. If you tell me, "Okay, Stanley, Marcus Garvey was okay, now you can do another one," that's fine. Or you could tell me that Marcus Garvey was crummy, do another one, that's fine. [Laughs] Because that's what I'm trying to do.

GA: Stay in the game.
SN: Stay in the game and continue to learn and grow.

GA: Many say that a good story must be universal. Do you agree?
SN: I think that good stories are good stories, you just have to figure out how to tell them. That's how I have felt about Two Dollars and a Dream, The Black Press and Garvey. All I was trying to do was do the story justice, and if I can do that I'll be happy because these are great stories. All I have to do is tell them and try to keep you relatively entertained, sitting in your seats. And tell them in a way that's interesting and shows some kind of creativity, and at times throws you back so you can go, "Oh! That's a different way to do that." If you have a good story you've got to figure out a way to tell it, and I think people anywhere will be appreciative and sit there and love what you have to say.

GA: What's your dream project?
SN: I want to do a documentary on James Brown. That's the one I want to do the most.

GA: That's a story to be told.
SN: And I'm the one to do it. I love James Brown. You can't imagine what music would have been without James Brown. His music is incredible, and I think that somehow African Americans have a very personal connection to James Brown. When you say James Brown to an African American you get this feeling inside, this little smile. There's a special place that we have. In some weird way he's central to what our culture is here; there's something about him that is central to who we are. If you tried to describe what's African American, you could say a lot of things. You could just jump up and yell, "James Brown!" And everybody would know just the hell what you meant. [Laughs]

GA: He needs no explanation.

SN: Not to us. [Laughs]

GA: *What advice do you have for aspiring Black filmmakers?*

SN: Black filmmakers need to make films, because only by completing films do you actually become a filmmaker. Also, see as many films as possible—Japanese films, Italian films, African films, etc. If we don't see different types of films, we're doomed to repeat the stereotypical Hollywood film. Try to find a job in the film industry either answering phones at a production company, working in an editing room or volunteering on productions. Be in the business somehow.

Camille Billops

Gregarious, warm, humorous, a divine conversationalist, filmmaker, sculptor, potter and archivist, Camille Billops and her producing and directing partner and husband, James V. Hatch, first came on my radar when their film *Finding Christa* (1991) was shown at the Museum of Modern Art's New Directors, New Films series in New York. The extraordinarily bold film follows the reunion of Billops and her daughter, Christa Victoria, whom Billops, to be an artist, gave up for adoption at the age of four. The film won the Grand Jury Prize for documentaries at the 1992 Sundance Film Festival and aired on the PBS series P.O.V. on Channel 13 New York public television and was screened at the 1993 Whitney Biennial at the Whitney Museum of Art.

Finding Christa is the second film in a trilogy of projects in which Billops examines her family history. The first installment was *Suzanne Suzanne* (1982), which explores Billops's niece Suzanne's battle with drug addiction. In her most recent film, *A String of Pearls* (2002), Billops shows four generations of men in her family and ponders why the men die so young.

Her other film credits include *Take Your Bags* (1998), *The KKK Boutique Ain't Just Rednecks* (1994) and *Older Women and Love* (1987). Along with Hatch, Billops runs the Manhattan-based Hatch-Billops Collection, an archive collection of African American books, documents, recordings, art, film and video.

- - - -

GA: Tell me about the role creativity played in your childhood. Did you always think you'd be an artist?

CB: I was an artist then. My husband Jim and I come from very similar backgrounds, and when our parents met we knew they were the same except for race. My mother had one white friend, and when she visited her it was "my white friend." Jim's parents hadn't had much experience with Black people. I mean, they knew people in the town, but they had no Black friends. But my parents were blue-collar worker people, so they didn't really have the time to dote on me about having any talent. What they wanted was to make sure I was safe, that I had a job, that I went to school, because as soon as they got out of the South they tried to better themselves. The first thing they did was try to lose the South Carolina accent. I never heard it until I went to South Carolina. Our language was always corrected by my parents. They always dressed in lovely clothes when they went to a Baptist church, where they sang anthems and not gospel. [Laughs] Even though they'd come from poverty, they were more broke than truly poor. There were two of us— my sister was seven and half years older than I.

As a child, I did little drawings and I played with toys, but I didn't have a whole lot of stuff. My mother was a dressmaker, so I knew that every Christmas and every Easter I would be dressed to the nines. She would make my hat and my cape out of beautiful fabric—silk, taffeta, and wool. I knew how to test for pure wool. My mother taught me that. I didn't make dresses or gowns or coats. I made drawings, but the images come from her. I see it in my sculpture. My parents were talented too. My father was a very fine cook. He worked for the railroad, as did his father. Those were the good jobs at that time. In grammar school I had average grades. When I went to Catholic school I was held back because I couldn't read: Catholic school in 1948 was a good education, except for the religion, which was toxic. But I could draw. See that picture of Hernando Cortez on the wall? I drew that in the fourth grade.

GA: So you always had an artist's eye.

CB: Oh, yeah. I could draw. There's a photo I have of me, my sister Billie, Frank "Sonny" Braxton, and Lucion "Sonny" Collins, which I included in a short autobiography. It's about the children of the maids and the butlers. And all four of us were artists. Sonny Braxton, who was my godbrother, became the first Black animator to work for Warner Brothers. He died at forty. My mother and his mother were all in a club called the Thrifty Housewives. My godmother, Camille, was also a member of it. I incorporated all of these people in my work. Later, I did a sculpture about my godmother which I called The Story of Mom, from which I did four drawings, which were concerned with essence because she loved perfumes and luxury. That's where I learned about things. My godmother worked for rich white people who owned beautiful things, which she would emulate in her own life. I learned from my mother and her sister, Phine, not to have a lot of children. That was the pact that she and her sister had made. They said that a whole lot of children would make you poor.

GA: When did you start taking art seriously?

CB: I always took it seriously! When I was about ten or eleven, my mother gave me an oil set. I didn't paint any painting; I took it and painted my shoes. I had dolls and puppets, and some books, but we weren't great readers. My father had comic books—we called them funny books back then—which he would hide under the seat of his favorite chair.

GA: I understand your family made a lot of home movies.

CB: Yes, my stepfather, Walter Dodson, and my mother made home movies, and I have thirty cans of their films. My birth father died when I was fourteen.

GA: What did they shoot?

CB: Celebrations, birthday parties and traveling in Africa and across the U.S. and Canada.

GA: How did you meet your husband and collaborator Jim?

CB: I met Jim because Josie, my stepsister, was his student at UCLA. That changed my life. Later I tried out for his play Fly Blackbird, which Jim wrote with C. Bernard Jackson. George Takei was in the play—he later became Capt. Hikaru Sulu on Star Trek—and the guy who did the lighting and carpentry was Francis Ford Coppola.

GA: Wow.

CB: He [Coppola] was a drag, and everyone would ditch him to go to parties because he was dull. Well, we sure blew that one.

GA: Yeah. [Laughs]

CB: Well, we did that play Fly Blackbird, which was about integration and civil rights. It was very radical for its time.

GA: One of the biggest decisions in your life was to give up your daughter Christa for adoption when she was four. That's a very radical decision. Tell me about that.

CB: It was very scary. If one knew the whole thing, maybe I wouldn't have done it. But I knew that

I did not want to be a mother. I think because the daddy was gone. I wanted to play house, but I didn't want to do it by myself. I didn't want to be alone, and the daddy wasn't there. The daddy left. And everyone around you just told you to cope. I couldn't figure out why I needed to cope, because I had now met Jim and Josie and Jackson and they had very radical ways of looking at the world. Josie, my friend in Finding Christa, introduced me to Jim. Someone said to me, "You can give Christa up," and Jackson said, "That would be a very good thing." Jackson was one of the brightest persons I ever met in my life, and the most radical.

GA: *How did you feel when you gave her up?*
CB: It was sad. Very, very sad. Because I wasn't able to give her up when she was a baby. I kept thinking her father was going to come back, but I never knew where he lived. One day before I gave Christa up, he wrote me a note from New York with his address on it. Barbara Cochran, who was my friend [who became Johnnie Cochran's first wife], and I got on a plane and went to see him. That sure was a surprise for him. Everything fell apart, and l left. I cut off my hair and went to Egypt with Jim, who was on a Fulbright. I had wanted to become somebody else. I went to school in Cairo at the Leonardo da Vinci Institute of Art. I was introduced to contemporary Egyptian artists by Virginia Simon, wife of the cultural attaché. My whole world changed. Forever it changed.

GA: *Did you feel liberated at this point?*
CB: Yes, but see, when I had Christa, I had no idea what it meant to have a child. I felt shackled.

GA: *In many of your films, you tend to focus on the women in your life. Was that because your father died at the early age of forty-eight?*
CB: I was considered Daddy's baby. He had two girls, but he wasn't the one who disciplined me. I also think that women were the ones who seemed to have had the power as far as I was concerned. The women lived longer than the men. At that time when I was growing up, my parents were domestics, and sometimes they lived where they worked. I had an older sister who kind of watched out for me and signed my report cards. I had a large extended family of older people. I was fourteen when my father died. I've seen the pictures of the women in my South Carolina side of the family, but I don't have pictures of the men. I have a photo of my great-great-great- great-grandmother in 1875, I have her daughter, I have her grandchildren, but no men. They didn't have their pictures taken. I didn't realize why the men were so absent until I had a gathering of my cousins from South Carolina and the men were watching sports on TV. They didn't care about

pictures. You had to drag them into the photographs. Everything that was handed down to me was handed down through women. I think we have that kind of family.

GA: I've heard you say that you want everything the men have.

CB: I want access to those things that, because of gender, are given to men, but it doesn't mean that it's male. It just means that access to walk and go and come and be safe and do whatever you want.

GA: You say in Finding Christa that men leave their children all the time but we cast aspersions on women when they make that choice.

CB: Sure. In those days when I would make remarks about Christa's father abandoning me, my friends would say, "Don't be so hard on the brother." I'm looking at them thinking, "I had to incur these images of me being morally compromised because of having a child out of wedlock at that time." And they say, "Don't be so hard on him"? And they continue to be hard on women if you do what I did. That is a no-no. Julia Lesage the film critic wrote a piece about Finding Christa, and in it she said that the decision I made was usually reserved for white males—deciding that you are going to do this without consulting with God. The tribe does not grant that decision to women.

GA: You're able to get your subjects in your films to really share intimate details of their lives and their thoughts with you. How do you do that?

CB: Well, maybe they feel comfortable with me. When I did the film Suzanne, Suzanne, and my sister breaks down in the middle of a scene with her daughter, she was so exposed and vulnerable. And I think I said in the back of my mind, "When I do this film on finding Christa, I won't give up emotions like that. I'm going to control this film." The older women in Finding Christa play the role of my mother. They had the attitude of my mother, who was dead, so I had to let them say what might have been my mother's opinion. Once I did that, I experienced a whirlwind. When I asked my cousin Bertha in the film why I had given up Christa, she said, "Do you want me to say this?" I didn't really want to hear what she had to say, but I had to let people say what they wanted to say. When making a documentary, you tell your subjects what you're going to ask them, but there is no rehearsal. I knew I had put myself in the mouth of the dragon. Also, the subjects of our films are my relatives, but the technicians are all white. My husband and my stepson, and now a stepgrandson, who shot some footage on our last film.

GA: In your films you use still photos, home movies, interviews and drama. Would you say that some of your work is experimental in nature?

CB: The process of art is experimental. You look at stuff that you made five years or ten years ago which you thought was fabulous; later you can't make sense of it. But sometimes you look at it and say, "Look at the composition of that. That's working." The film that we just finished, *A String of Pearls*, is a little different from doing *Suzanne, Suzanne*, because we're more sophisticated. We know more, but we still use the same approach. Our movies are not refined. You use the tools that are available to you. The theatrics in our films I learned from Jim, who is a theater scholar. Our films tend to be a little theatrical anyway. They're not chasing up and down the street, walking through the door, coming up the steps, as in other films. They're more "Sit down and tell the story." But I know how to tell a story a little bit better, I think. And I find film is good for me because it requires a long process, which is a reflective time for me. Your process helps you. When we were doing the video transfer, the technician said, "I can tell that you were working on a Steambeck [editing machine]." I said, "How?" He said, "Because the shots are longer. They would have been shorter using an Avid because of the speed of the machine." And so that process and time has an effect on me, whether I'm doing film, drawings, prints or sculpture. The sale of the prints and sculpture helped pay for the film. We shot *A String of Pearls* at the same time we did *KKK Boutique* (1995), in order to save production. Then we had to set it on the shelf for seven years, because we didn't have any postproduction money. *KKK* cost $208,000 and *String of Pearls* (2002) cost $101,000.

GA: *What are your thoughts on Black women in cinema today?*
CB: Black women are perceived as being at the back of the line. I don't think there is a line. I think it's a circle. The suggestion that there is a line comes from the people who oppress you. I was at the "back of the line" when I started a library and learned how to be a filmmaker. You learn all these things because there are no gates with a sign saying you couldn't do that. And I would like to see Black women not stand behind the Medici, the gatekeepers at the gate and that they trust going down the road and finding the footpath across the meadow, and that's what I did. I stood behind the gatekeepers. You could stand behind those people and you'd be standing straight, then one day you'd be bent over a little bit, and by the time they let your ass through you're on a walker.

GA: *[Laughs]*
CB: You always hear people say "*They* won't let me." Well, in some cases it is true that there really is a barrier. They think that they have the barrier down tight, but the way we come is way too complicated. They can't stop me. They cannot stop me, because they don't know how I walk. Why

would they look at a little picture of me when I was ten years old on the grass with a sucker and pretty little skirt—how would they know that I would become a filmmaker? Would you kill me then and make sure that I wouldn't get that? How would you know that? How would you know in Oelwein, Iowa, when you look at Jim in his overalls, at his Crowfoot school, how would you know that he would become the cofounder of an African American library and become a Black theater scholar? How would you know to kill him? How would you know to stop him? What way would you go? You can't. It's like trying to stop the galaxy. Yes, it can kill you, but it doesn't mean that we're all dead. It doesn't get everybody. So I think about that. Black women, say, "Those people, they, they . . ." I say, "Well, what do you want to do? Do you have a dream book? Do you have a project book? What is it? You want to do a project about yourself?" They say, "Well, I don't know." I say, "Well, why don't you learn?" You can learn that. You can learn how to raise money. You can learn how to save money. You can learn how to get yourself free from debt. Why would you use credit cards unless you just need it for the month and then paid it off? Why would you get addicted to that? Why would you spend money that wasn't yours? During that "Black revolution" in the seventies, we were riled up at Howard University at a National Conference of Artists. One person said that they were going to get rid of all of the light-skinned artists in the organization. You know, that went across the room for a split second. I said, "Well, I've got an idea for a workshop. Let's cut up all of these credit cards. Let's get the scissors out. Let's be free. We're going to be financially free. Cut these cards up!" Honey, there was much incomprehension as to what I was saying. I said, "No, we're all talking about freedom here."

GA: Who's really free?

CB: Who's really free? Cut the [credit] cards up. But Black women need to empower themselves. They're not half a person because they don't have a man. They're not half because they don't have a Black American man. If you must have something Black, why don't you go to south India? They're so Black there, they're blue. You can go get something pretty and drag it back. You're an American woman with the eagle as a passport and a credit card. You have a lot of power in the world as an American. Why don't you think about yourselves as powerful? Yes, "they" are out there to stop you, and sometimes people don't want to listen to that coming from a Black female face. No matter how oppressed people feel, if somebody who looks like Jim [white] tells them that, they'd listen, but if somebody like me tells it, they don't listen. I may be their oracle, but they don't know who the oracle is. Others made it safe for me to think this way, to feel free, especially the progressive Black people like the activists Esther and James Jackson, and Louise and William Patterson. They're fabulous, all those progressive people who made it possible for me to understand what I could do to just be a part of an historical landscape, and film is one part of it. The most powerful thing I have is my art, and hopefully, it will stay around. Hopefully, people will appreciate it and understand what I'm trying to do.

GA: *Tell me what inspired A String of Pearls.*
CB: The need to celebrate the men in my family.

GA: *Who are your creative influences?*
CB: My husband, James Hatch, and my parents and my community of artists. James was the first one I knew who officially admired my work. He said, "You are a wonderful artist."

GA: *What legacy does Camille Billops want to leave behind?*
CB: The Hatch-Billops collection, my films, my art.

Kathe Sandler

I first met Kathe Sandler in the early 1990's at the incomparable Frederick Douglass Creative Arts Center in New York City where we both studied writing. I was first introduced to the her work at the Film Forum in New York during the run of her film, A Question of Color.

A Guggenheim Award winner, Sandler is best known for her documentary film A Question of Color (1993), an intimate and provocative examination of the issue of "color consciousness" and internalized racism within the African American community. The film makes the viewer self-assess one's own behavior as it relates to a phenomenon that is believed to be outdated but is omnipresent nonetheless.

A Question of Color was the first film ITVS (Independent Television Service) program to air nationally on PBS prime time in 1994. The film is studied at hundreds of universities, colleges and high schools across the country.

For her dramatic adaptation of writer Rosa Guy's novel The Friends (1996), Sandler received First Prize in the Cross Cultural Category from the Black Filmmakers Hall of Fame. Her other documentaries include her first film, Remembering Thelma (1982), which was screened at the New York Film Festival; Finding a Way: New Initiatives in Justice For Children (1997); and A Tale of Two Schools (2002).

Sandler is working on a one-hour documentary that explores the impact of race, gender and class on African American women through a Black feminist lens. She is a graduate of New York University.

GA: Why did you decide to pursue filmmaking?

KS: My upbringing was culturally and artistically rich, but somewhat schizophrenic. My mom is African American, Harlem born and raised, and my dad is Jewish, from Brooklyn. My parents were artists involved in left-wing politics and civil rights. My dad was and is a painter, my mom was an artist and clothing designer who later became an arts administrator very much involved in the Black Arts Movement. Artists always visited our home. So I was always influenced by this artistic and political activist sensibility. I was nine years old when Dr. King was killed in 1968, and I believe that was the year my parents separated.

GA: Who are some of the people you recall coming to your home?

KS: My mother's close friends were often writers. My godmothers are Rosa Guy and Louise Meriwether. Maya Angelou is a part of this circle, and my mother had grown up with the late Audrey Lorde. So Audre and her husband and her kids, who were younger than my sister Eve and I, were in our house a lot. Both of my parents are interesting, but my mother was perhaps my central role model. Later when we moved down to the upper west side, there was an even more intense interaction with artists, who lived in or spent a good deal of time in the West 90s. There were a whole bunch of artists and folks who congregated there, because it was one of the first places that opened up to Black folks to live in in the early 1970s outside of Harlem and some other areas.

Some of the people who visited and were a part of my mom's scene were Vertamae Grosvenor, James Baldwin, Romare and Nanette Bearden, and Rod Rodgers, whom I later worked for while I was in college. I had a bunch of terrific godfathers too like Roger Furman, the Founder of the New Heritage Theatre in Harlem, arts administrator Harold Youngblood and the poet and scholar Wilfred Cartey. Sadly all these men have passed on. I'm not saying this to name drop, but I was influenced by these folks.

GA: I don't see it as name dropping, exposure does influence and shape us.

KS: My mother was doing the Black theater movement work and all these theater people from all across the country, and from the Carribbean, Europe and Africa would stay at our house. Errol John, the Trinidadian playwright, would visit from England, my sister and I adored him. There were folks from Unesco and the UN as well. It was always like this big center. Oh yes, and St. Clair Bourne used to visit us when I was a kid. Little did I know that some ten or twelve odd years later he would become my mentor and executive producer for my documentary A Question of Color.

There was also a more working class dimension to my upbringing. My mother's family lived in the building I grew up in on the second floor and I was very close to my grandmother, my young aunts and uncle and all my cousins who lived there.

But, there was always this tension between what my mother was trying to do and what was going on in my grandmother's house and there was this sort of resentment and admiration for my mother at the same time because she had broken out of the fold and done different kinds of things. But also there was this perception that my mother was uppity or trying to be white, or pretentious. So I often felt I was navigating or trying to be a negotiator between those two different but very interconnected worlds.

I also had this other experience of having a white father and looking white, but being very socialized in the Black community and always feeling a certain sense of outsiderness. It was a source of a great deal of pain for me. Like you're accepted as long as people know who you are, but if people don't know who you are. . . . And one of my biggest concerns was always about rendering myself visible as a Black person to other Black people. My sister is a little browner-skinned than I and looks like a light-skinned Black woman, so we always grew up with these different kinds of experiences. Even though my dad lived nearby and remained a part of my life growing up, I rejected him in fundamental ways, and distanced myself from him. There were some understandable and justifiable reasons for that but a lot of it also came down to a strong rejection of myself—something I am still working through.

Some of the schizophrenia, or dueling consciousness, came into play in my grandmother's house with my African American cousins, some of whom came from the South. They didn't relate to Black consciousness at that point. For instance, if they saw Black people on TV one of my cousins might say, "How did they get that Black man on TV?" or "He's too Black . . . ," or "Look at her with her nappy hair." There was a lot about color that flew in the face of the Black Arts Movement which was part of my upbringing upstairs. I would say, "Black is beautiful," and then my cousins and I would argue and inevitably someone would cut me up by calling me Casper [the "Friendly Ghost"] or whitey. I wasn't so good at the dozens and I would always be very self-righteous, but I never could win any of these arguments. Plus all of us were still just moving from Negro to Black. Some of my relatives believed that dark-skinned people shouldn't wear red, things like that.

GA: *That had been planted in their heads, obviously.*
KS: It was really the mainstream thinking in the Black community and it was just being challenged at that time. Muhammad Ali was becoming very popular. "Say it loud, I'm Black and I'm proud" was coming out. I'm talking '67 to '70. So even though we think of that as being such a rev-

olutionary period, it was gradual process in a lot of people's minds. I remember for our junior high graduation there were parents on the PTA who didn't want girls to wear afros to the graduation and this is New York.

GA: *In New York?*

KS: Yes. I think that part of what happened to me was it made me want to create a sustained dialogue about the issues, so that I could communicate better with my own family members and friends. So I think that's what I try to do with my work. And I was trying to be very clear about my own identity as a Black and proud person, who looked white.

GA: *So what was it that triggered your desire to work in film?*

KS: When I went to college in 1977 at NYU, I was designing my own major called Arts Communications. I was studying dance with this great woman named Thelma Hill who died in a tragic accident, a fire. I was very stunned by it all and everyone started telling me all the stories about how important Thelma was and how she had been the first "Umbrella Lady" in Alvin Ailey's "Revelations." So I started doing research on her and I proposed for independent study to do a research credit and start a documentary. I started it in film school and it took two years to make the film *Remembering Thelma*. I wanted to help place Thelma Hill for people who'd never known her, but show what an important person she was—teacher/performer. I wanted people to feel like they had met her and understood her. That was my way of dealing with loss, but it was also my way of dealing with having grown up in the cultural arts scene. By the time I finished, I realized that I had become a filmmaker. So I sort of stumbled into filmmaking that way in an attempt to do something to commemorate my teacher.

GA: *That's a great way to pay tribute to someone. You worked on the film at the film school at NYU?*

KS: I was taking classes at the NYU film school. I wasn't in the film school, I was in the Gallatin Division, the independent studies division, but I started taking a lot of classes in the film school. The film became my senior summer workshop project. Actually, I found it hard to get across to my teachers at that time why this was an important project to do. My film instructor told me that it was too ambitious and that I should just forget about it. Of course I went ahead with it anyway and he actually gave me the second-lowest grade in the class, which stunned me. I had a rough cut of the film and to my view it was better than so much of the stuff that was there. It took me two more years to finish the film, but even with the rough cut it was a strong work. Then I found an editor because I learned that I can make a film and I can put things together but I'm not a great editor, and I found a wonderful young woman editor in the program, Anne-Marie McNeil from Jamaica. Everyone was talking about what a great editor she was—there were very few Black folks, by the way, in the school at that time. She came on and started editing and I paid her $400 for the whole job. At that time, I was working as a waitress, but I said, "If you edit the film, I will pay you $400 over time. She said, "Well, you're the first person who's ever offered me money." She was pleased to do it and we started cutting at what was then called Young Filmmakers, which later became Film Video Arts. I had a lot of people looking at the film. We went to a photo animation house and this award-winning photo animator named Frances Lee gave us a great break on the prices and showed us how to work with the animation stand. And we found out that we had to reshoot all of our stills—they were sort of clumsy.

GA: *How did you go about researching the project?*

KS: It was one of these things that grew on me. After Thelma Hill's death I started seeing all of these articles. All her students would gather together and talk about what a great teacher she was and some of the articles would mention that she had been a dancer in "Revelations." Everybody would say that they called her Ma Hill because she was like everybody's mother. They'd say, "You know, she taught Alvin Ailey. Arthur Mitchell depended on her. All these people, they wouldn't have had their companies without Thelma training everybody. . . ." So I did summer abroad in France, and when I was there one day the idea came to me. I said, "I want to make this my senior project." I came back and I had names of people who had worked with Thelma, her former students and I knew these folks from having studied with her at Clark Center for the Performing Arts. I started interviewing them and borrowing their photographs and shooting them. We would get these little shoots together. I shot most of the things over one summer, and the stills I would borrow and shoot. That's how we came up with the first rough cut. Then I had to go back and re-borrow a lot of the stills

GA: *Were people really willing to lend you material?*

KS: It was mostly Thelma Hill's fellow dancers from when she was a performer and they would look in their archives and give me photos. I was very careful and would leave them a note and would keep a copy. I got everyone their photographs back. As a consequence, I ended up becoming a photo editor and taking a job at *Essence* magazine because I got so skilled at researching photographs and then started working with photographic historian Deborah Willis, who was then at the Schomburg Center. She's been a tremendous mentor and influence on me. But to get people to share their archives with me, that's one of my favorite parts of documentary filmmaking—when you actually sit down with somebody who knew somebody or has a piece of history and they start telling you about it and they start pulling out their photographs or whatever they have like "Playbills." That's one of my favorite parts of the filmmaking process. The other part is the editing room. I love research and I got such a sense of dance history, Black dance history, from Thelma Hill. I thought I knew Black dance history, but when you start sitting down you hear about these segregated companies that traveled around Europe and were little known in the States like The New York Negro Ballet, and you learn that Thelma had been there, had worked in a bank at night and all these things and had been the company's ballet mistress. And I just wanted to distill that and somehow place her. Who is this wonderful teacher woman? What produced her? What influences produced her?

GA: *How did you finance the film?*

KS: It was made on very little money. I had all of my equipment at school and most of my people worked for free except my editor, the one person I paid. But when I finished school, NYU let me keep editing there. That's one of the reasons film school can be a good thing if people want to make films. You can at least get your first works out of it. Then I started taking out loans. I used a student loan and I got some personal contributions from the dance community. I started raising money. That's something I grew up in because my mother was also a fund-raiser. So I started writing letters to Thelma Hill's friends. I guess the whole project must have cost about $8,000. I also got a couple of small grants along the way. When I was trying to finish the film, I had to have a big benefit at Clark Center for the Performing Arts where Thelma used to be an important force—and the dance community came out. They actually helped me finish the film. That's another part of the filmmaking process; having benefits, raising money, contacting Thelma's friends, we had rough cut screenings. I also received a lot of help at the Frederick Douglass Creative Arts Center. They were my nonprofit sponsor. Overall, Frederick Douglass was a very helpful place to me in developing as an artist because I was a member of their writing workshops from the time I was a teenager.

GA: *Founder and director Fred Hudson's great. He's helped so many folks including myself.*

KS: Fred is extraordinary. I was in his workshops as a teenager, and I worked for the Center since on and off for many years. It's home to me. It's a really economical place to get some great training in writing. . . . When *Remembering Thelma* was selected for the New York Film Festival in 1982 that was the greatest thing that had happened to me professionally. It was my big comeuppance. It was shown opening night with *Say Amen Somebody* by George Nierenberg, a documentary about gospel music. A few days before the screening, I called up NYU—I told you about my former film professor, who will remain unnamed, who said that the project was too ambitious and gave me the low grade. Anyway, he was then heading the department. I said, "I just want to let you know that my senior project from your class is screening opening night at the New York Film Festival. I can invite any NYU faculty or students to the press screening as a guest." I was very excited to extend that invitation. He said, "Of course. We knew you could do it."

GA: *Gosh, that's what he said.*
KS: That was the big joke.

GA: *That just goes to show you that academia and the real world frequently have nothing to do with one another. But nevertheless, you found your film studies at NYU to be helpful in your development?*
KS: Yes. Then there was the Black Filmmaker Foundation [BFF]. Warrington Hudlin had started BFF and some people had been involved early on with it. I just got a chance in my early twenties to interact with Black filmmakers who were doing documentary. I remember Warrington coming to NYU and looking at a rough cut of *Remembering Thelma*. I was trying to see if BFF could help me get some money, and I think they helped me with my benefit. It was a very interesting period because all of these people were making films and I was a college student and I was hooking up with Black professional filmmakers because there were no Black filmmakers or instructors at NYU I could talk to. BFF was very helpful. It was a supplement to my NYU education. At that time, it was a very important institution. There was also the Third World Newsreel, all these places.

GA: *Tell me about* A Question of Color. *I know you had issues of color in your family, but more specifically, how did this project came about?*
KS: A Question of Color was something that had been percolating around in my head for a long time, which was my interest in trying to come to terms with issues that affected me personally, but also knowing all this stuff about color as it affected other Black people from my family, and my friends. I wanted to create a whole dialogue around that. It took me a long time in the process of making the film to realize that my own voice and personal experience was a key to helping tell the story. Finally, after six years of making the film I decided to let myself be a character, and that's when the film sort of came together. I had been doing all of this research and traveling and talking to all these folks and raising money—producing and directing. And I just wanted to be able to have this sustained, deeply transformative conversation about color. That was my interest in it. So people begin to put this whole thing together and realize that a job had been done on

us as a community, and that we needed to incorporate our own understanding of ourselves and transcend it.

GA: *Was it an emotional experience for you to approach such a sensitive topic?*
KS: Yeah, it was, very much so.

GA: *How did you deal with the sensitive nature of it?*
KS: I remember a friend and colleague of mine named Karen was helping me do research and she said, "I know you're doing research for your film, but I was thinking about it. I'm getting ready to get my extension braids and when I went to buy the hair I saw all of the Black women buying the hair and I was thinking that it's like an inferiority complex. I feel that I want to have longer hair and that I haven't accepted my hair. You know it's African, at some level it's European." She was just talking to me and I said, "Oh, my God. Could you talk about that?" She said, "Yeah." I said, "Would you talk about it on camera?" She said, "Yeah." So I shot her getting her hair braided over nine hours and interviewed her intermittently through the process. She was so honest and in the midst of the interview she said, "I have an inferiority complex about my hair and I know it's messed up," and she was sitting across from me and I said, "I have an inferiority complex about my hair. I really do." I sat there looking at her and was looking in a mirror.

GA: *She had an inferiority complex about her hair being kinky or what?*
KS: Yeah, she was saying, "My hair is kinky and I'm not comfortable with its natural state. I wanted to move away from straightening, so this is my way of dealing. But I feel like in some way it's a way of having long hair like white women." It was a very contradictory kind of a statement, but when you do think about braids and the implications you think, "Braids are great. Remember, Black women had to fight to be able to wear braids, right? And they're African and they're beautiful." But in some ways this hair extension thing also becomes a way of having long, white textured hair too when you think about it. She was just putting her finger on it. That was the most beautiful thing, but I remember when she was talking about this inferiority complex she was wide open, we had a camera crew, everybody was shooting her and she said, "What about you, Kathe? I bet you've got a story." I said, "Oh, yeah. I do. I do." But when she was sitting there and she was saying that I said, "This is my experience too. It's a different experience, but it's also my experience." Then there was a time when the elderly woman, Mrs. Caldwell I was interviewing in Tuskegee, Alabama—I was trying to always stay out of the frame, but she kept referencing me in her interview, saying, "You're real light. I'm real dark. We didn't care a thing about mixing with

people who were your complexion." She says, "You no better than me, because you are mixed." So she was continually doing this in her interview and I said, "This is a good interview, but we've got to cut all of that out because I'm not in the film." But that was part of the process of my becoming a part of the film. The woman getting her hair braided, Karen, asked me, "What about your stories? What about you?" And Keith and Keyonn—the two teenage boys in the film asked me, "Just what was your experience with color with you and your sister?" My sister was on that shoot and Keyonn said, "You two look different, what about your experience?" I said, "Oh, that's some story." But these were questions, people were asking me along the way as I was asking people to share with me. They were also saying, "You have something to say. Share with me." Sometimes it wasn't as friendly as all of that. Sometimes it was confrontational and so that was the thing that helped me to make the piece more honest.

GA: *How did you get people to open up to you about something as sensitive as color consciousness in the Black community?*
KS: I had a lot of help and guidance. My ideas and thinking about the work was always filtered through my husband, Luke Harris, who is a race relations scholar, and who helped me think through all the issues. He was the co-writer of the film as well. So he helped me think through the whole process.

I also had a lot of team help and creative input from two associate producers, my sister Evie Sandler and Wayne Middleton. There were some interviews that I was having difficulty with so I had my sister Evie do some of them.

GA: *Really, which ones?*
KS: I think for me it was painful to hear certain things. There are a lot feelings of anger and resentment sometimes toward light-skinned women and toward very white skinned looking Black people and I didn't necessarily want to hear it. But I knew it had to be heard. I knew it had to be in the film.

GA: *So would you give her questions to ask the subjects?*
KS: We worked on it together, but she brought her own experience and asked certain questions. Just like the dynamic with two teens in the film, it was very parallel to some dynamics between my sister and I, and they saw that right away. I mean, they saw it. And they're kids and they always say what they think.

GA: What were some of the experiences you and your sister had around color growing up?

KS: Well, I always felt that we were treated differently both in our family, on the Black and white side, and in school and all over. I can't speak for my sister's experience. But I can speak for my own, and I know that if there was a way I could have been born a visibly Black woman like my sister, would I have been her color? Yes, I can speak for myself and say I would have preferred to be her color and have her hair too.

GA: Why do you think people had a tough time seeing your vision for A Question of Color and how long did it ultimately take you to make it? I've heard you talk about the fact that along the way some people had a hard time understanding the color issue, particularly whites.

KS: A Question of Color was an eight year project and I had to educate the funders about the issue. For some, like the scholarly funders, it meant proving the scholarship so I gave them a list of books on the subject. But the topic hadn't been covered in visual media. There was one piece, which Warrington Hudlin had done with Denise Oliver, called "Color." But he doesn't show it anymore. They had finished that film while I was working on A Question of Color. Also, Spike Lee had started School Daze in 1986 and I was still shooting my film. School Daze actually had an impact because all of a sudden people were talking about the color issue. They [the mainstream media] didn't really understand it, but then there was all this press about School Daze, and you can argue whether or not Spike did a good job of covering the issue. People argued that he made it a women's issue and that he missed some points. But then some of the funders started to get it. School Daze was helpful to me. I already had a trailer for my film, and I had to create other trailers to show the drama of it, people talking about color. People would say, "This is fascinating." It still happens quite often that white people who see the film say, "I never knew anything about this, but it reminded me of something I experienced as a woman. . . ." There are people who can relate to it on different levels saying, "You know, in the Chinese community people do this surgery and Italian women dye their hair blond." It was an educational process and there was a resistance to the idea that it wasn't good for the community to see this and we don't want white people to know that we have this division. And there was that discomfort sometimes with Black folks about airing our dirty laundry.

GA: Since documentary filmmakers have to rely mostly on foundations or grants for funding, there's usually a panel of people who have to approve your project. One hopes that there's a Black person on the panel who understands your vision, but depending on that person's politics or view of the world, that Black panelist could either be an asset or a liability.

KS: That's the problem with trying to do something that hasn't been done before. People do say that and you do hope you get good people on the panel, but this was an uncomfortable issue. Sometimes when I screen the film for a Black audience there's such a different response than if it's an integrated audience.

GA: *How so?*

KS: If I show the movie to a Black audience, a Black student union at a college or when it ran at the Film Forum in New York and the audience would be almost all Black folks, people felt very comfortable to respond to everything on a very visceral level. If the audience was integrated, there were moments when people felt a certain uptightness, and I found that integrated college audiences would participate. Sometimes the Black students would feel weird and they'd wait until the white students left to talk about the film. Or there would be a discussion and very few Black hands, but then when it was over they'd come over and talk. I can understand some of that inhibition because you feel like you're representing the race and you're trying to further our conversation. But there are topics that are uncomfortable and there are topics that are difficult to talk about. That's one of the things with the Black feminism film I'm doing. I'm looking at the gender issue within the Black community, and many people feel like it's not helpful to talk about it, that it divides us.

GA: *Do you think Black filmmakers have fewer freedoms or have to face greater scrutiny for the stories they want to tell that perhaps white filmmakers don't have to face? Do Black filmmakers have this extra burden?*

KS: Yeah. There's the burden of being Black, but it's a great gift too. Oppression makes us open and sensitive to different things. Sometimes a Black artist or an artist of color can see and read things that mainstream artists can't see. Artists of color have experiences that can make us more open to a wider range of things. Just by virtue of the fact of being considered to be outside of the norm, you're an outsider. This is one of the things I was talking about, this outsider vision.

I felt like an outsider in many ways while I was growing up and I think that it's often people who are on the outside who are able to have the vision to see what the limitations are of the mainstream. It's the outsiders who can offer a critique or an interpretation, who don't buy the lie. Mainstream people can do it too sometimes in different ways. You have people bringing a range of experiences, but there is a burden to being outside of the mainstream and there is a burden to being discriminated against. So as a Black filmmaker you carry certain baggage. There's baggage that you carry for the community and sometimes yes, you do have to drop the baggage and breakout. I know there's sort of a raging question about whether there is censorship of Black artists internally, and I think there are things that we do experience because of the fact that our community has been underrepresented and distorted in the media.

As Black filmmakers, one of our jobs is that we are reconstructing the images of our community and we're also making films as an intervention, an alternative to the mainstream. We're creating interpretations of our community that don't really exist because beauty is in the eye of the beholder. And sometimes the mainstream just cannot see us. They walk into the same room and they don't see the same thing. They walk down the street and they don't see the same people. Woody Allen's New York does not look like our New York. The question of censorship has been debated for many generations. What images are important to project, what images are good to project. Are we sometimes cashing in on stereotypes of our community in our films? Are we perpetuating them? Do we ourselves have to transcend stereotypes that we have? Sometimes it's interesting when we look at some of the earlier Black narrative films. I was recently looking at Cooley High (1975), which is always a fun film to watch. But there are messages about color in there. The way the director Michael Schultz portrays the woman who's undesirable and the woman who's desirable is based on color, and I don't know that he meant to do that.

GA: Interesting. Talk about that because Cooley High's one of my favorite films.

KS: If you look at it again, the light-skinned girl who works in the coffee shop is the ideal in the movie. She's portrayed as the hottest thing in the universe. But the girl who Preacher [Glynn Turman] is dating—whom he's not really that interested in—is dark-skinned and portrayed as not being glamorous or pretty. And this is a projection of what desirable is. Now, in some ways he's reflecting what's going on in the heads of these young men, but he could also be reflecting a transcendental understanding of beauty—he could also be giving us another message about that. At that moment in time, that's where Michael Schultz was. I think that if you look at that film again and look at the gender, color thing and who's the desirable woman and who's the object of affection and why, and what makes her so important—I remember people laughing at the darker-skinned girl. This is partly what the audience brings, but this is also partly what the filmmaker brings. So I think that when you have Julie Dash creating the film Daughters of the Dust (1991) and she says I'm going to fill in every frame with Black women and most of them are going to be dark skinned Black women and their hair is going to be natural and the whole movie is about Black women and the film celebrates Black women, I think that's partly what Daughters of the Dust is doing. It's a subversive movie about Black women and our history, and Julie's taking the standard and really opening it up and exposing it in a whole different way. This is a Black woman with a certain kind of consciousness, making transformative media. Cooley High is a wonderful men's story, but in that context there is a problem in that story that certainly in 2002 we should be able to look at and critique, and I think you'll find those same issues in a number of Black films. He's not the only director who does that.

GA: Well, I'll definitely see it again with a more enlightened eye. You've given me much to think about, which brings me to your Black feminism project. What inspired that and where are you in the process?

KS: The Black feminism documentary I am working on is a natural follow-up to A Question of Color, because the gender issue combined with the race issue, has made internalized racism and Eurocentric standards of beauty even more salient for many Black women. People would always ask me, why is this more of an issue for Black women, and I would talk about transcending internalized sexism as well as internalized racism. But how can one truly do that, without at least addressing male privilege and patriarchy, including Black male privilege and patriarchy. Then too, it has always been the most forward-thinking Black women who have pushed the envelope on these issues. So that led me to thinking about the Black feminist movement as a powerful and important intervention in looking at the history of Black feminist activism.

GA: What are some of your favorite documentaries?

KS: The Eyes on the Prize (1987), parts 1–6, is just phenomenal. I just remember being hooked and glued to the TV every week that it came on. My husband and I would call friends and family and say, "Are you watching, are you watching?" The Times of Harvey Milk (1984) by Richard Schmiechen and Rob Epstein is a film that had a big impact on me and I studied the evolution of that work by reading many articles and interviews with its filmmakers. I am a big fan of Haile Gerima's documentary work, as well as the late Jackie Shearer, Marlon Riggs, J. T. Takagi, and St. Clair Bourne. Two films that have had a great impact and influence on me in recent years are Iris Morales's documentary Palante, Siempre Palante! the Young Lords (1996) and Thomas Alan Harris' That's My Face (2001).

GA: What advice do you have for aspiring documentary filmmakers?

KS: Do as much work as you can in a school-based program if you are in school or thinking about it. There's a great deal of resources and you should focus on graduating with a strong first work, which can and should become your calling card for future work and funding. Take advantage of internships and use them as a way to hook up with professional filmmakers or companies you admire. If you can work for free for them and they are in production, chances are you can get on board and develop a working relationship with them.

Supplement your institutional learning with professional organizations. Remember that no matter how strong you are in one area, you need to diversify to pay your bills. Develop and home in on a marketable skill such as vidoegraphy or cinematography, editing, and/or sound recording. You can more readily get production work, or become part of a small production company, if you can perform more than one significant role. Be prepared more and more to be a one person crew, and embrace the digital. And learn the Web and Internet because film and videomaking will be increasingly more interactive in the future.

Study documentaries. The best of them usually have a strong narrative line. Read about the medium and find out how the filmmakers made these works. Trust yourself and start from the places you know and need to explore. Your best work will come from there. Also always think about your audience, how to reach them, what is the minimum you want them to know having seen your film, what do you want them to feel having watched it and what you would like them to do as a result.

Orlando Bagwell

Orlando Bagwell's films take one on a visually stunning and deeply engaging ride through the annals of American history. As a producer, director and cinematographer, his expansive list of award-winning film and internationally acclaimed film credits includes the PBS documentaries *Africans in America: America's Journey through Slavery* (1998), *Frederick Douglass: When the Lion Wrote History* (1995) and *Malcolm X: Make It Plain,* (1994). He also produced two films, *Mississippi: Is This America?* and *Ain't Scared of Your Jails,* for Henry Hampton's groundbreaking PBS series *Eyes on the Prize* (1987).

A Baltimore, Maryland, native, Bagwell has won numerous awards for his films. His 1999 film *A Hymn for Alvin Ailey,* premiered on PBS's *Great Performances* and received an Emmy Award. He has also received three Peabody Awards, two Columbia School of Journalism DuPont Awards, eleven Emmy nominations, a Golden Rose from the Montreaux Film Festival, Grand Prize at the New York International Film Festival, the National Association Grand Prize, Five Prize Pieces Awards, and a Gabriel Award.

Currently, Bagwell is working on a four-part series for PBS called *Matters of Race* and is also developing a four-part biography of Dr. Martin Luther King, Jr., as well as an *American Masters* program on the Pulitzer Prize–winning playwright August Wilson.

Bagwell founded Harlem-based ROJA Productions, an independent film and television production company, in 1989. He holds undergraduate and graduate degrees from Boston University.

GA: What was it like growing up in Baltimore?

OB: I had a fortunate childhood. I was the middle child of five children of really young parents who had five children by the time they were 28. My parents started having kids in their teens and they hadn't finished school, so while I was growing up I saw them finish college, go on to graduate school with five children. In many ways they were my real examples of what was possible. When I was growing up Baltimore was still segregated, so I was living in this world where my parents would tell me what I could do, and the outside world, school and places like that—I went to Catholic school and a private high school—were very clearly trying to tell me what I couldn't do. I never thought of myself as being artistic when I was young. I was inquisitive, very outgoing and opinionated about what I felt and what I thought, and I had a lot to say all the time. But that was something that was nurtured by my parents' sitting around the table and challenging us to talk on Sundays and to engage us in current events. They would have conversations and bring us into them and ask for our opinions. My parents were, in my mind, pretty exceptional in terms of how they reared us and the things they gave us. We weren't well off. In going back to college, my parents were holding second jobs and going to school at night or going to school during the day and working at night, so we [children] kind of reared ourselves and lived a pretty modest life. But my parents were driven. My mother's a Ph.D. now and my father is an engineer, and I have a lot of respect for them and the things they did for us. I was into sports; my brother and I played sports from the time I was eight years old all the way through, so that was my world. My parents really didn't allow us to watch TV and I didn't go to lots of movies as a kid, but my mother would take me to movies sometimes. It would be our separate time. When there are five kids in a family, those few times you're with your parents by themselves is such a special time, and my mom would take me to the movies maybe, because when we all went together we'd go to drive-ins, and I was the one who would usually stay up and watch everything. When she wanted to go see a movie on her own, she would take me along with her and talk with me about it. At that time, I never took it to mean anything. The idea was to become an engineer or a doctor, a lawyer, and my parents were steering us into professions like that as a way of moving beyond their achievements. I think my parents may have been the first in our family of that generation to graduate from college. We were the next generation, and we were expected to do better; it's the story of our community. So when I went to college at Boston University, I went into the sciences with an idea that I would move into the medical profession. One good thing was that at BU they require you to work in a hospital one semester, and I realized then that my temperament was not going to work in a hospital. I came home from work very depressed every night. It wasn't what I wanted to do. I liked science, but I didn't want to work in a hospital. [Laughs] So I left for a semester and a summer school, because there was a lot of student activism going on at the time, and I was growing into my own sense of politics and I was figuring out what's it all about . . . ? What am I doing? Why am I here?—all of the relevant questions.

During that time, I decided that I wanted to get into something that gave me an opportunity to say things and to express some of things I was feeling. I had always worked with film, because in high school I was in leadership training and I always used documentaries in the training sessions with the kids and adults, but never thought of it as something I would make myself. I happened to do a presentation in school using documentaries, and I remember my roommate saying, "Why aren't you thinking about getting into movies?" I had never even thought about it. At that point, I decided to buy a still camera and started taking pictures, and in my search for relevance I started working at a community center and was running an after-school program, and I also started a dark room and turned that into a small business with another guy to do posters. I also started teaching kids photography and bought some video equipment and started teaching video.

When I came back to school, I studied film. But I wasn't very good. I realized I wasn't. I had passion, but I didn't have any skills. The comments on a lot of my work was that it had strong content but my film grammar was not there at all. Therefore, I was never recommended for any of the advanced classes in the department. I don't think they really saw me as someone who had potential. But I was driven and started to do my community work and making contact with other Black filmmakers in the community who were working either in television or documentary, then started trying to find ways that I could work with them. I was really into jazz, and one of my roommates was a jazz deejay, and I used to go to clubs all the time, and I found someone who was doing films of musicians in the clubs. So I started working with them doing lighting, and I slowly started getting into the work that way. While I was in college I started working as an assistant camera person. That's when I started making my own independent films, and as crude as they might have been, I kept making films of my own.

GA: Who were some of your creative influences at the time?
OB: I wasn't drawn in by other filmmakers or a knowledge of who was doing what. I would watch movies, but I wasn't really trying to be a Hollywood filmmaker. I was really drawn to documentaries, but I didn't know any Black documentary filmmakers—I wasn't speaking with them then, or seeing their work. When I think back, the people who had influence on me at the time were people like Gordon Parks and his photography, and the fact that he had then moved into mak-

ing movies. Because I was a photographer first, his journey and his work were really inspiring—his journey was inspiring, but his work was kind of challenging, and I paid a lot of attention to it. I saw it and it spoke to me, and it conveyed things that I was trying to reach in my own life, in my own soul, but also in terms of what I was trying to say about the world that I knew, which was me and the Black community—my place in a larger America. And I saw that's what Parks was trying to do through his work.

Interestingly enough, the other person who at that time had a real influence on me, whose voice was speaking, trying to say some of the things that I was saying, was Alvin Ailey, and looking at his dances and how they connected to you on a certain real kind of visceral level. But they conveyed things in a very large way through a very compact story or a representation of Black life—things I felt. And the person who came later and who became a great influence was August Wilson, and what he was doing in terms of his writing and how he was able to represent Black life in this amazingly particular but available way. His characters and his stories are just big, and I felt that in film that's what I always wanted to do.

You could take a small story that in fact spoke very large in terms of the things you would talk about and connected to—not just Black viewers, but everyone. In fact, the things that we were about, the things that were essential in terms of our own lives, were realities and ideas which were important to everybody, they spoke to everyone. I think that you grow up in a certain time period, and Black life was this kind of separate space, and there was also this effort to define it in very narrow terms, and we all along are growing up knowing that it's much bigger than that. Everything we felt and knew anything about was much larger than that—we had much more to offer. No one was really letting us out of the box, and whether you were feeling that in schools or feeling that in terms of how you were being represented in terms of the images you saw. I wanted to make movies, and so I went to California with my mom, who had moved to California, and she wanted me to stay out there and go to graduate school, but I wanted to be involved in making movies. I realized that's what I wanted to do next. It wasn't about going to graduate school to study movies anymore. I needed to get the experience of making them, I needed to learn how to make movies. So I started freelancing in public television. I got on a show which came out in '75 about teenagers. They were ten-minute films that made up a half hour. The great thing about it is that I could work as an assistant camera person. And for the first time it allowed me to travel outside the United States, making these films. Then I'd come back and I'd work with the assistant editor, and while I worked in public television they'd allow me to use their facilities to do my own films. At night I'd edit my own films I'd shoot, using their equipment. So it was a great learning experience because so much of filmmaking is really learned in the editing process.

In 1976, I won an AFI (American Film Institute) grant for one of my own films that I'd shot and edited, and that was the beginning of a kind of recognition of my path as an independent filmmaker. Other people started seeing my work and encouraged me to do more. So it was a great thing for me to get that opportunity. I was working at WBGH, and they had a film department there with lots of edit rooms, a big room with lights and cameras where I could work. I bought my first film camera back then, and I was single and I spent all of my money processing my film, buying equipment, and that's how I was living. My life was making movies. The complicated thing is that the year I got the AFI grant, I also decided to go back to graduate school in journalism school at Boston University, to get married and have my first child. Writing is the first step in any film, and I felt that one of the skills that I wasn't really strong in—it's still not my ultimate strength—was my writing. So I wanted to go back and be a bit more disciplined and develop my writing skills. I felt that the graduate program would help me do that.

Because I'd gotten the AFI grant, I had a film that I was working on, and I felt that would be my project. It was about a street storyteller. It's a tragic story for me, because I spent a lot of time working on this film and traveled all over the country shooting it and carried it back and forth across the country when I moved from Boston to L.A. and back. I cut it a number of different ways and learned some very strong lessons about working by yourself on a project and never finished the film. That's the one film I never finished. Unfortunately, I kept going back and forth from L.A. to Boston and I left the film somewhere. I went to go back to try to retrieve it and it wasn't there. All of the outs, all the rushes, all the negatives were gone. Hopefully, it'll show up somewhere, because in those boxes were also some of my earliest films.

But moving to L.A. was another big step, because that's when I first started working with Henry Hampton at Blackside. At that time, Blackside was a company that did a lot of government contracts, and it was another great place for me to work, because they allowed me to be a producer, a writer, a director, a camera person and an editor, to do everything on my films or on other people's films. I learned from that AFI film that you shouldn't shoot and edit your own films. You allow someone else to do one of those jobs. And I did a lot of work for Blackside in a short period of time. When I was there, in the late seventies, it was the beginning of the Eyes on the Prize series. I was shooting a lot of it and producing a couple of the segments. Some of the stuff we shot for that early piece ended up being the elements that Henry used to revive and to raise money to bring it to PBS.

GA: *Did you have any idea that Eyes on the Prize would be such a phenomenal success?*
OB: Well, I'd moved to California, because I really wanted to pursue dramatic films at that time.

Not so much pursue the films, but I wanted to learn how they were made. I worked as director of photography [D.P.] on a number of dramatic films for PBS, and then out of that I started doing music videos and started to working for Shelly Duvall's company shooting dramas for them, and I started developing a reputation in L.A. as a D.P. But in the course of doing that I thought about going back to documentary. I bought a new camera, and I started shooting for National Geographic and for other programs, and Portraits of America for WTBS. I was supporting two children at the time, so I was trying to work as much as possible. I wasn't making a lot of money, but I wanted to grow and was doing freebies whenever possible in order to work with other directors. And then Henry (Hampton) called me about Eyes and I thought he was calling me to shoot, but he asked if I would produce and direct.

I remember when we went back to Blackside, we held a school where they brought in scholars and people from the civil rights movement to talk with us for a week about the history to help us get a jump start into the history. I can remember that being a really incredible experience for all of us as filmmakers just to be in the company of people like Bob Moses, Vincent Harding, Bernice Johnson Reagon and C. T. Vivian, and other people from the movement. The experience was pretty overwhelming; it was amazing. I was in touch with people I'd only read about. At the same time, we were overwhelmed with this sense of responsibility. Their presence and their presentations forced you to consider what you were getting into. At the same time, I walked out feeling like I was incredibly stupid. [Laughs] I thought, "How am I going to do this? I've got so much to learn." But coming out of it, I think that we realized we were into something, and I think the three producing teams felt that we were involved in something that was quite demanding. We felt the weight of the responsibility. We had no idea how it was going to turn out. I'd never produced any national PBS programming before, and the sense of responsibility I felt was pretty overwhelming. I had to leave my family, move to Boston, and that was hard. First Henry pitched the idea, saying that I would be able to go back to California every two weeks. The first time was two weeks, then a month, two months, three months. Then I was bringing them out to see me, and it was hard. It was very hard, and I was living above the offices in a little apartment, but it was a great opportunity, it was good work.

I don't think we realized how strong the films were and the potential of the series until we had our first rough-cut screening and we invited the world, and that was overwhelming too. But the response let us know that we had something that was unique and special and really could move people. Still, I don't think we realized the overwhelming response to the film until it went on the air. When it went on the air I was in China shooting a film for the industrialist Armand Hammer, and I remember calling home and—I'm divorced now, but I remember my wife then saying, "Oh, man. All of these people are calling the house. Your film is on and they're saying all of these interesting things on the machine about thanking you." So I was really proud.

GA: *The way in which the civil rights movement was chronicled, you really took us right there to the center of the action. We went back to the Movement frame by frame. It was very moving and still is.*

OB: It was also a real learning experience in terms of how films are made and the idea of how collaborative they really are and how you create environments where everyone supports the other person to do their best work. That support can sometimes be in the form of a challenge, it can be competition, all these things. But how do you harness all of that and make it a positive element in the production? That's something Henry created, and it's not a simple thing, it's not always successful, but you realize it's all a part of what is going on, the dynamics of the process. The dynamics of production are something you have to think about on different levels so it works for everyone, so that everyone works hard and makes their best film and is ready to make another film. A filmmaking experience is such a difficult experience and you put so much into it.

I don't think the worst thing is to make a bad film. I think the worst thing is to never make another film. The idea is that each film should be a step to make the next film. Because if you're committed to making movies, you're a filmmaker, and that's why you have to keep making movies. You don't ever want a film to be something that stops you from doing other films. It's such a difficult process that it can do that if you don't walk out feeling whole. Filmmaking can be a very isolating and very solitary endeavor if you allow it to be, and I think that's a problem. It's part of the dynamic between filmmaking being very technical and scholarly, especially documentary, and at the same time being art. And as an artistic expression, it becomes very personal, and we have a sense of real propriety over the idea and what it's going to be. At the same time we feel very vulnerable, because you know that until the film is finished almost, all of your mistakes are showing, and it's hard to let others know that you're struggling and that it is hard. You don't have this beautiful thing, and we tend to kind of close ourselves off from others, and if you stay in that mode and you go through the whole thing by yourself, it can be very unsatisfying and at the same time, very lonely.

For me, one of the best things about movie making is the collaborative process and the relationships you establish in it and the process you engage in with other people to make it happen. Oftentimes they help you get past those stages, and not just portions of the film, but they also help you get past those moments when you're really doubting yourself and doubting your work and doubting your potential. And when you doubt, it's hard to get yourself off the mat and start fighting again. I think a lot of us fall victim to that and find it difficult to realize that it doesn't necessarily have to be a solitary endeavor; it can be something that you can share, and begin to develop a community of people whom you will continue to work with and enjoy.

GA: *Tell me about Malcolm X: Make It Plain. I know you had some challenges, given that Spike Lee was doing his film on Malcolm X around the same time.*

OB: Yeah, it was a tough time to do a film like that. Part of it was the fact that there are people in your life who have major influence on you, and Malcolm was one of those people. I think I'm of that generation where it was the voice of Malcolm and Stokely [Carmichael] and H. Rap Brown in many ways who defined who I was as a young Black man coming into my own. So when Spike started doing his film on Malcolm X, it kind of made the possibility of doing a documentary much more possible, and Judy Crichton at PBS's *American Experience* approached me and said that it was a film that they really wanted to do, so we started to pursue it. But once Spike started making his movie it made the whole world of Malcolm a difficult place to negotiate in terms of materials, people, voices. Everybody was very concerned about how Malcolm was going to be interpreted. The politics of interpreting Malcolm were unbelievably complicated.

GA: *How did you deal with that?*

OB: Well, there were a lot of negotiations with different people in lots of different camps. I had to sell them on the fact that my interest in this was strictly about Malcolm and my own particular interest in him, and that I wanted to tell the story well. But at the same time, I wasn't wedded to any particular camp. I was interested in everybody's voice and everybody's voice was going to be a part of it, and if they were going to deny me access to them, then they were going to be a voice that wasn't going to be a part of the film. That always gets everyone at the end. So it's about negotiating one at a time and thinking from the very beginning about which voices are most important and most critical in getting to the next group.

GA: *And frequently people don't want to be left out.*

OB: That's right.

GA: *The fascinating thing about your film is that you focus on Malcolm's inner circle: his wife, brother, daughters. How did that come about?*

OB: Well, when you start talking to people about someone like Malcolm, everyone has an opinion of him, everyone has something to say. I realized that when you're making a film like that, you have to decide, "How am I going to cast this and what standards and criteria am I going to use?"

And I decided that I could talk to anyone, and anyone would have something to say about Malcolm and that wasn't going to be enough. I wanted to do a film that I felt was authentic in its own way and offered you something that you could rarely get, that you wouldn't get just anywhere, and that would offer something new to the whole discussion about Malcolm. I wanted people who actually knew him. I didn't want someone who was on the periphery talking about him. I wanted people who actually had experiences with him. I didn't want the historian or the journalist or the government official who had an opinion. I wanted people who actually knew this man to be a part of this film, and the closer you were to him I felt the more you'd give me, the more you'd help us see him beyond the kind of public presentation, which Malcolm was a part of constructing, as were those around him. I thought we had to penetrate that some way and find out what was at the core of who Malcolm was and what were the things that were most important to him. I felt that if we wanted a larger audience to invest in this life and get beyond their own personal feelings about who and what he was based on the limited information they might have had or the things they might have read or what they might have heard, they needed someone who could say, "Well, no, this is the real deal. This is what he really cared about." I think in the end you realize that so much of what he's about is something that we all share as human beings, therefore we can all be engaged in the story because he spoke to all of us about just living and being alive and pursuing life.

GA: *Once you decided on your cast, how did you get them to open up to you to discuss their feelings honestly with you? Sometimes when your subject is someone with a strong public persona there can be a tendency for the interviewees to present only that well-known persona as opposed to a more personalized, intimate observation.*

OB: Each person was different, but of all the films I've been involved in, this film required the most time and patience—with particular individuals especially, his family. I made endless visits to Lansing, Michigan, to Detroit.

GA: *Didn't his brother cancel on you several times?*

OB: The story of the interview with his brother is amazing, because we were actually ready to shoot his brother, and three times he was supposed to show up and three times I called and three times he told me that he just couldn't come. And he finally came, only to tell me that he can't do the interview, and I again spent a long time talking. What was scheduled to be an interview at nine in the morning, we don't start shooting until about two, three, four in the afternoon. But I finally got him to sit in the chair for almost six straight hours, and it was an amazing interview. You see only a small bit of it in the film, but he starts from the beginning to the end. I remember him getting up, and he's not totally comfortable at the very end. He realizes what he's done and he realizes what he's given me, and I try to say something to make sure he's okay. And he's not sure, but he kind of looks at me as if to say, "It's in your hands now," and walks away. What I find is that, you're asking people for things that are probably the most valuable—the memories, the stories, the moments in their lives that are probably the most important moments that they've ever lived—and that was one of the things I learned in doing *Eyes on the Prize*. I learned that I was talking to people and I was asking them to give me stories that really for them represent the most important moment in their life, and they're very concerned about what you're going to do with it. It's not that what they're saying is going to hurt anybody or blow people away—in *Malcolm* some of it was—but you're asking them for things that you can't put a price on and they want to know what you're going to do with it. They want to know that you're going to be honest and fair with it and not distort it.

GA: *Especially if you're the first person with whom they've ever shared something.*
OB: Yes, that's what was happening on *Eyes* and almost the case on *Malcolm*. You have to also realize that a lot of people don't have a lot of confidence in television, in movies, in how those things are interpreted in those media, and you can understand where that's coming from. Most times you're looking at the lowest common denominator represented on television and in film, and people are disturbed—especially people of color—about how we're represented in the news media. That's only changed recently to a certain degree. It's only changed to a certain degree in the past twenty, twenty-five years. Before that it was really horrific in terms of how people of color were represented or included or a part of those media. And only in rare cases did you see examples of yourself that you could identify with, so their concern with some little skinny young kid coming in saying that he wants to take your story and do something with it and that you can trust him is not enough. You've got to give them more. You've got to be willing to spend the time to give them more assurance, that you're going to be honest with what they say and not distort it.

GA: *Do you think documentary as a whole is a very important tool in which to convey Black stories?*
OB: I think it has been an important tool in the past for conveying our stories. I think the interesting thing about documentaries right now is that if you look at feature films you can count on one hand—and you don't even need one hand—those directors or producers who are really in control of their content, and that's one person: Spike Lee, a Black man who's working in feature films. Everyone wants to talk about the things they do, but Spike is the only independent person who produces films and has editorial control over what he does in the end. He has final cut, and

he's fought for that. In documentaries—and it bothers me that as a community that we don't pay more attention to documentaries—when it comes to public television you have a whole group of Black directors who have editorial control over what they say. They don't tell Stanley Nelson how to interpret his films or Sam Pollard or Jacqui Jones or myself. We are responsible for what's there. Now, we might miss something, we might make a mistake, but we have to answer for it, because no one is standing over our shoulder saying, "No, it's gotta be this way," or "No, you've got to take that out." That's a rare thing on television. You definitely don't see that in commercial TV.

GA: *In commercial TV, filmmakers have told me that they've had to fight for the inclusion of historical facts. Do you find that you ever have to fight for historical fact in your work?*
OB: No, I don't have to fight for the inclusion of certain historical facts. We include the facts and we have the ability to interpret those facts, and that's an important thing. That's one of the big problems I think in historical documentary filmmaking right now. There's so much potential in historical documentary form for a real democratic kind of involvement in the process. I use this example all the time that history is about facts. We can all agree on certain facts: a certain time and place that something happened, the order of events and things like that. But we can both be standing on a corner and watch an event take place, and because of who we are, what we've been before that moment, it could be the police arresting somebody, we could see the event totally differently. We can interpret it totally differently. Now, it doesn't mean that your interpretation is wrong and mine is right. They're both valid, because they both come from our experience: how we are positioned in the society to see a certain point. And the valuable thing about it is that both views are important to our study of history or our understanding of that moment. Yes, we may bring the same facts to our interpretation, but we bring a perspective that's very different, and there needs to be, I think, in our work as historical documentary filmmakers, the opportunity for everyone to be actively involved in this interpretation.

What we find, even on PBS, is that people of color only do stories about themselves. But white people do all of our stories and are interpreting us all the time, and there's a sense that we bring some sort of bias or subjectivity that is different from white filmmakers. White filmmakers are just as subjective as we are. We look at how they interpret us. We see that if you're going to do the Scottsboro boys, suddenly the core of the story is about the white attorney who goes down to Alabama, and that's going to make it available to a white audience. And suddenly the NAACP is not a critical element in this ongoing anti-lynching fight, and they were in the fight long ago.

How do we see a moment and see the important story to be told? Well, it depends on who we are. It doesn't mean that the other story is not valid, but there's room for so much more, and I think that those who write and study and do scholarship around history are very much aware that it's important to bring these multiple perspectives to the work. As filmmakers, there's room for alternative interpretations of Thomas Jefferson or the Civil War or different things that represent, at the core, these essential moments in American history, because I think in all those moments we were all there and we all have a perspective, and it has to do with our continuing existence in this country.

GA: *Why do you think that double standard exists in terms of white directors and producers being able to interpret the stories of people of color but not the reverse?*

OB: Some of it is readiness and some of it is ratings. In the ratings game, certain communities are not a large portion of how those ratings are determined. So they represent the viewing habits of white America. At the same time, the ratings drive commercial support and dollars, even in public TV. Public TV is viewer-sponsored, and a lot of those viewers are people who have disposable income.

GA: *Your films are very cinematic, and nature seems to be very much a part of your storytelling. In many of your films, you focus on swamps, the forest and the land to help move the story along visually.*

OB: I think as a people we are deeply tied to the land we come from. As Black people in America, our roots are in the land, and in an interesting way my film Roots of Resistance made me pay a lot more attention. Roots was kind of a life-changing experience, because I realized that so much of our souls are in the land—especially in the South, especially in the swamps. The interesting thing about the swamps and everything that I learned when I was there was that a lot of the canals that are a part of those swamps are on land that was owned by George Washington. And the early landowners at that time believed the swampland could really be fertile land—you could drain the water off. That's in the film—those canals. What you realize when you travel those canals is that at the bottom are souls of Black people. If you were down there you realize how much pestilence exists all around. Mosquitoes just cover you, they're all over you. Snakes are everywhere. I think there are about six to eight different species of poisonous snakes in the place. And you have slaves at that time building canals big enough for barges. They dug these things with baskets in bare skin, so you know that people died in these swamps, and when they died they were left there. They didn't drag those bodies out, so at the bottom of these canals and swamps are bodies.

I started thinking that it's not just the land that we're connected to, because we come from the land or we developed the land, but we're in the land. Our souls are in that land, and I wanted that to be very much a part of the story. Also, the thing that you begin to recognize in this country is that the whole memory of slavery is being washed away from the landscape. In doing *Roots of Resistance* we were constantly looking for examples of slave communities. We'd find some here and there. We found these deteriorating buildings in North Carolina out in the forest. But when I went back years later to do *Africans in America* (1998), the same place was an industrial park. This is only one example of the many examples of the physical relics of slavery and slave communities that don't exist anymore; they're just gone. And so it was important that if even if you couldn't see those places, we needed to be on the land, we needed to be there where they existed. You need to represent it, at least.

GA: *I think it's very important, because a swamp paints a picture of just how badly someone wanted to escape.*

OB: And some lived in the swamps permanently, and that was better than living this other existence [as a slave]. We're not talking about it being better in terms of a physical reality; it's better because of the whole notion of freedom, the idea of being your own person, and this was a very important concept that was essential to anybody, and to them and it was understood on many different levels. What's so exciting about *Roots of Resistance* is—I remember when I decided to do the story, it was really a story about the Underground Railroad. Again, I remember Judy Crichton at *American Experience* taking me to the press junket in L.A. and I hadn't even started the film. There were some other filmmakers there showing their films, and she was so proud to talk about my film: "Here's this film from Orlando Bagwell about slavery and he had no archival footage, no photos, nothing to use." [Laughs] That was the big thing. What is this film going to be? How are you going to tell this story? At first I thought it was so exciting, then I thought, "Oh, shit, what am I getting myself into?" [Laughs] But that's why you get into movies. I'm in this business, I love history, I love dance, but I like making movies. One of the best things about working in L.A. is that you come directly, fundamentally affected by the idea that movies are all about make-believe. They really are about creating this relationship between the audience and what's happening on the screen, and really at the core of it all is the ordering of images one next to the other, and those images have to transport the audience someplace in some way. If the film is only talking to you (as opposed to using images) and teaching you, then it's not a movie. You're making radio. If I can go in a room and turn up the sound and do other things while the movie is on and feel like I know what the movie is all about then, I should make radio. We're making movies, and movies are really something else. At the core of it—it really is turning off the lights and sitting down and watching something, and for the time it's on you've been someplace that you've never been before.

GA: Your experience with narrative filmmaking in L.A. is clear in the way you shoot. You use pan shots, zooms, dissolves, fades to black. These are techniques that in my opinion not many documentary filmmakers use. You really have a grasp of those tools, and it makes for a very visually appetizing experience versus just talking heads, which is a conventional tool in documentary work.

OB: Each film has its own language to bring to it. That's the whole part of the early stage of writing a script. We have a form that we follow in terms of making movies. It really makes you go through certain steps to get to the place where you're ready to start shooting, and I think that you have to first figure out what your film's about then begin to start figuring out how you're going to tell your story. There are some filmmakers who will use the same approach with every film and in a certain kind of way their films are really saying that the same filmmaking approach works each time as if you can just fit every subject matter into one style of filmmaking.

GA: What tends to be your approach?

OB: I try to spend a lot of time figuring out what my film is about. Like with Malcolm X, it's about a person, it's about a life. We're all people, we all have a life, but it doesn't mean our story can be a movie. What is his story about? So I try to get down to that very particular idea of what the film is about. Malcolm for me was about becoming and constantly changing. *Eyes on the Prize* was about power. So you go through each film and you get these clear ideas of what the film is about. Once you're there, you decide on how you're going to convey that and what you're going to use. What do I have to work with? We have this idea that if you're making historical documentaries you can only use certain things because you have to have the confidence of the audience. You can't create these other things. Well, we're making movies. The audience will accept anything as long as there is a sense that it is appropriate, you've introduced them to the language you're going to use and given a reason why this language is appropriate for this film and it's not something perverse or ridiculous. You have an obligation to the audience to make sure that they never feel lost in the story or the storytelling. Anytime there's something that is confusing, the audience is stopped. No matter what it is, it could be a sound or something, and suddenly you've lost them for a moment. You have a responsibility to constantly keep them in the story. Then, at the same time, depending on what you're trying to say and what your film is about, it begins in some way to dictate the form that it takes. What are the elements that you're going to work with to tell the story?

Some of my choices and sense of openness about making movies and what's available, what's the language, does come from my work in dramatic films. Even in *Eyes on the Prize*, we could only use archival footage of the moment, that was authentic to the moment. We could only use music that came out of the material we were shooting, meaning that it had to be sung or played within the material [not a score]. But I'm glad we got away from that one. And there's one scene in part five that I had to fight for, and it's a contemporary shot, a constructed shot that is not archival. It's a shot of the Tallahatchie River, because it's the river that is critical to this larger story of Mississippi. And Malcolm X opens with a kind of very stylized image of the microphone. In Roots of Resistance in re-creating the existence of slaves we used shadows. By the time we got to Africans in America we were using shadow figures; it's suggestive and allows you to see the whole image in your head, you complete the image in your mind. But now we don't want to use this technique anymore. Everyone is doing it now, and some are doing it well and some are doing it badly.

GA: How did you get involved with Africans in America?

OB: It kind of came out of Roots of Resistance. I've had this great relationship with Judy Crichton and thought that maybe we could do a series on slavery. So almost ten years later it turned into a series.

GA: What is your preproduction process like for your films?

OB: Sometimes we get a lot of flack about this, because some people think we're overindulgent because we spend a lot of time doing preproduction. We will hire producers, we will hire associate producers, we will have a team on staff and we're not shooting anything. We spend months on research, writing and rewriting. We do this on all of our projects.

GA: What advice do you have for aspiring filmmakers?

OB: There's a sense of filmmaking as this kind of glamorous, wonderful lifestyle, and I encounter that a lot when I talk to students. And filmmaking is extremely hard work. It is hard not only because of the amount of hours and the amount of time and effort you put into it, it's hard because throughout the entire process you're constantly in a state of doubt. You're not only doubting the material, but you're doubting yourself no matter how many films you've done. Every film is exactly the same. On each film I have these feelings of inadequacy. So if you're going to get into filmmaking, make sure it's really what you want to do. You have to really be into making movies. It's not about having something to say. That's not enough. We all have something to say. You have to want to make movies, because it becomes all-consuming. There's a period of time on a film when you're not just living it all day, but you're sleeping it all night if you sleep at all. It's all-consuming. I've seen filmmakers who've gotten involved and they realize how hard it is and they don't want to ever do it again. That's fine. I'm glad the experience taught you that; I don't want you to be unhappy the rest of your life.

Black Wave
Cinema

George Tillman, Jr.

I was so deeply moved when I first saw the movie Soul Food, in August of 1997 at the Urbanworld Film Festival in New York, that I organized a soul food dinner party at my Harlem apartment for thirty friends on the film's opening weekend. I told everyone to go see the film first and to then come to my place. As with the movie, the party was a celebration of the joys of family, love and good southern cooking, and no one could stop talking about that wonderful presentation of African American life so seldom seen on the big screen. And I knew that film had to make money, and that it did. The film, starring Vanessa L. Williams, Vivica A. Fox, Nia Long and Brandon Hammond, opened at number two at the box office in September 1997 and went on to gross $43 million domestically.

It just so happens that Milwaukee, Wisconsin, is the hometown of writer/director/producer George Tillman, Jr. It's also the hometown of director Michael Schultz. And it was Schultz's 1975 classic film Cooley High, which first inspired Tillman to pursue filmmaking himself. Like the elder statesman Schultz, Tillman has a loving grasp of the peculiarities, the nuances, the complexities, the social mores, along with the hopes and dreams of African Americans. And he lovingly brings all those elements to the screen.

A graduate of Chicago's Columbia College, it was there that Tillman met his longtime producing partner, Bob Teitel. The two now house their partnership under the State Street Pictures label at Twentieth Century Fox in Los Angeles.

Following Soul Food, Tillman also directed Men of Honor (2000), an epic story inspired by the life of Carl Brashear, who became the United States Navy's first African American Master deep-sea diver. The $32 million film, which starred Cuba Gooding, Jr., and Robert De Niro grossed $50 million domestically and $35 million overseas.

Tillman and Teitel most recently produced the MGM hit film Barbershop (2002), directed by Tim Story, which starred Ice Cube, Anthony Anderson, Sean Patrick Thomas, Eve and Cedric the Entertainer. The film which opened at $21 million, had one of the highest opening weekends for a Black-directed film and went on to gross $75 million domestically, making it one of the most successful films directed by a Black director ever. Looking ahead, Tillman will produce Barbershop 2 and Avenue A, a story about four twentysomethings from Spanish Harlem who seek success and love on their own terms in New York City. Tillman is next set to direct for Fox 2000 Criminal Minded, a character study of a criminal mastermind from South Boston.

— — — —

GA: You grew up in Milwaukee. When did you realize you were creative?

GT: I think for me it started kind of early, when I was about eight years old. My father worked at the American Motors plant out in Kenohsa [Wisconsin] and my mom was a secretary. So after school I pretty much had to take care of my sister and my brother, so I couldn't leave the house. So all of the time I would sit up and watch daytime television. The only things on television during the daytime were soap operas, so I'd watch All My Children all the time. I remember watching the show and at the end of the show they had the addresses where you could send letters. So I sent a letter to All My Children and I told them about a certain plot change that I wanted that I thought could help the characters out. And they sent me a letter back that said no thank you, we're going to do this and this with this character. I actually sent the letter back to them and asked for a script, and they sent me a script. That was the first time I saw an actual television script, and at eight years old I pretty much wrote my own soap opera and I did a five-minute show, created characters. My father still has that letter. That was the beginning for me, the writing.

GA: You said you were inspired to make movies after seeing Cooley High. Tell me about that experience.

GT: That was around 1975 when I saw Cooley High in the movie theaters, and for me that film spoke to the African American audience. I felt that I wanted to somehow be involved with that. I was in the theater, and the theater was packed. People were laughing, people were crying, people cheered, and I just felt like I wanted to be involved in the medium. I didn't know if I wanted to be an actor, a director or a writer, but it was just that I wanted to be involved in film. And then later I saw a film called *Five on the Black Hand Side* (1973), and then I saw *Claudine* (1974). I felt like these were important films that I wanted to be involved with, and after leaving the theater after seeing *Claudine* I knew then that I wanted to be a filmmaker. That's the reason I have Glenn Turman in *Men of Honor*. Those were the films that made me realize that African American films—this is before they started calling some films of that era Black exploitation films—spoke for us, and I wanted to be involved in that.

GA: *Then you decided to go to film school?*

GT: It was interesting, because at an early age I started writing and my father had an 8mm camera that I started shooting things with. And Milwaukee had a public access channel, so I started doing things with public access. So that's how I started actually becoming a filmmaker at an early age (eight).

GA: *And how did you end up in Chicago?*

GT: It was tough, because in Milwaukee I never knew too many filmmakers. There aren't any filmmakers, but I found out later that the Zucker brothers, who did *Airplane*, are from Milwaukee. But most of the things that were happening creatively in the midwest were in Chicago, where they shot *Cooley High*. There is a lot of theater there, and there are a lot of things happening in Chicago that I wanted to be a part of, so that's where I went to film school.

GA: *Some people say film school is the best way to learn, and some people say "take that money, go make a feature and you're a filmmaker." What's your position on that?*

GT: I had a love for learning about film, so I went to film school. I got accepted to the School of Visual Arts in New York, and I wanted to go there, because around 1987 when I graduated [from high school] and Spike [Lee] had already done *She's Gotta Have It*, and there was a big independent film scene in New York at the time and I really wanted to be there and kind of be involved in independent film. I got accepted [SVA], but I couldn't afford it. I was actually the first person in my family to go to college, and my father couldn't afford for me to get an education. But Columbia College actually starts school on September 28, and it was open admissions. And after seeing everybody go to school I was able to get in, and they actually had a great film program. But I had a love for film. But now when I travel I meet people who haven't gone to film school, and these guys are making great films; they have great scripts. So it all depends on what you want to do. For me film school worked because I wanted to know everything about film. Even Denzel Washington has directed, Antwone Fisher (2002), and when I was mixing Men of Honor, he came down and saw the actual mixing of my film because he hadn't been involved in that process. It all depends. If you want to know everything about film, I think film school is the way to go.

GA: *Tell me about* Scenes for the Soul, *the feature film you directed before* Soul Food.
GT: That was a long process. After 1991, when I graduated from Columbia College, I really wanted to direct. At that time I was a production assistant [PA] working on commercials, and I felt like, how am I going to direct if I'm just working as a production assistant? Usually, I was the first guy on the set and the last guy to leave—eighteen hours of hard work. And I just felt like if I want to direct, why am I doing this? I had the privilege of working on a film called Mo' Money. Damon Wayans came in to shoot the film in Chicago, and the only reason I got to work on the film was because Damon told the unions to let more African Americans on the crew. So I got a chance to be a set dresser and to actually see how they made that film. But besides that, that was my only experience, and I felt that if I wanted to direct I should write my own script and make it happen. It was going to be a long road from being a PA to a director.

So I wrote this script, and initially what happened was, I sent the script off to New Line and they immediately passed on it. And our budget was a million dollars for the film, and my partner and I couldn't raise a million dollars. All we could raise was $150,000. We raised that over a period of about two years with forty-five investors, and the investors that we found were not investors who were lawyers and doctors. They were investors like plumbers and guys who did regular jobs. And I had shot a film short called Paula, a thirty-minute film, and I had a screening. I'd bring in these investors, and we pretty much begged guys for about $500 to about $5,000. Our largest investment was only $10,000. So with that we got to $150,000. Actually, we got to $130,000 and we started shooting.

There were three stories set in one film with a lot of actors who had never acted before, and we shot the film in about thirty days. I felt it was a film that I could at least sell to video. I never expected the film to go to theaters, but I thought it would be my calling card. So I took about a year to edit the film, and I made a deal with this production company that did music videos, so I got to cut it on weekends and at night. And then my partner and I drove to Los Angeles. All I had was $400 in my pocket, and we moved into this hotel on Vermont and Third. [Laughs] I still remember that place. I was here for about a week and knew somebody who knew somebody at William Morris. So we took a meeting, we gave them a tape of the film and they called us back. They were very impressed with the directing of the film, and wanted to represent me right away as a director.

GA: *That's great.*

GT: So we were sitting in this office and they introduced us to one of the agents, and we came into one particular guy's office whose name was Sheinberg, whose father was Sid Sheinberg, who got Spielberg started. We're sitting there and a call comes over the phone and it was George Jackson, Doug McHenry's partner. And Sheinberg had never seen our film, and he said, "I've got this great film. I love these guys. Come over and check out the film. I think you should buy this." [Laughs] At that time, Jackson and McHenry had a deal over at Savoy Pictures where they could green-light any film under $10 million. So he [Jackson] said okay, let me see the film. So we gave the film over to George Jackson, and he called us about two days later and said he loved the film and to come over to his house so we could talk. So my partner and I went over to his house, and at the time he lived on Kings Road in Hollywood. I went into this house—and this was after Milwaukee, seeing this house. It was incredible. It overlooked all of Hollywood, all of Sunset. He saw the film and said, "I want to represent you guys. I want to buy your film and get it into theaters."

At that point my whole life completely changed, because the next day we went back to William Morris and they asked my partner and I, "How much do you want Savoy Pictures to pay for your picture?" So my partner, just making a joke, said $1.5 million. And the film only cost $150,000. The next thing you know, they said, "No, we're not going to spend $1.5 million, we'll spend $1 million." [Laughs] And they never bothered to ask us if the film was on print. The film was only on video, and they never bothered to ask any of that.

What ended up happening was we spent about five or six months trying to get that film ready to go into the theaters. This was an independent film, and at the time they called it a hip-hop art film or something. That was the title they put on the film, and they actually put it out in Beverly Hills for test screenings. They really wanted to put this film in about nine hundred theaters. So I went back to Chicago—and when you go back to Chicago when you've sold a film for a million dollars, a lot of people look up to you. [Laughs]

GA: *I bet.*

GT: And I'm back in Chicago writing my next film, and my partner calls me and asks, "Did you read the paper today?" I said no. He said that Savoy Pictures went out of business. Nobody ever saw that film [*Scenes from the Soul*]. And that was the worst time for me. I got married right after that incident, so that was a tough time for me.

GA: *Did you think you'd ever make it in Hollywood after that experience?*

GT: It was tough. I met everyone in town, and everyone thinks you're the best guy in town; you're the greatest filmmaker around because you've just done one film. And eventually, when you take that away, it's a tough process. So I went back to Chicago and I just said forget about Hollywood. I said I'm going to write something personal. I think that's the most healing thing to do, write something personal from your own experiences. And I started thinking about all of my experiences with my uncles and my aunties. I grew up around my mom and seven women, and I thought about my uncles, and I thought about the soul food dinners that we used to have with my grandmother. So I looked for a way that I could put all of this in a script. My first script was actually four hundred pages. And immediately George [Jackson] and Doug [McHenry] really wanted to make Soul Food.

GA: Four hundred pages [Typical screenplay is one hundred and twenty pages.]. Wow. Tell me about the entire process to make Soul Food.
GT: That was a tough process, because I had to keep coming out to L.A. to straighten out the first film. I was now living in Park La Brea over on Third and Fairfax [in Los Angeles].

GA: Moving on up a little bit.
GT: [Laughs] Yeah, moving on up. It was kind of tough, because I really didn't know anybody, and I used to walk from Park La Brea to the Beverly Center to watch movies. I would watch movies until about ten or eleven at night and come back and start writing, and pretty much did that all day. About that time, I was forgotten. Savoy Pictures wasn't calling me and they weren't returning my phone calls. I was just trying to get the script right, because I feel I'm a director who can write instead of a writer. It takes me a good year just to get a script down that I like to show someone. I know some guys who can do it much faster. I know some guys who can knock it out in two weeks and it'll be great. That's just not my process. I actually went back to the way I originally wrote—on paper. A lot of writers do that. I spend a lot of time talking to actors who are close to me. Sometimes I will throw out dialogue and they improvise and I'll find the right words. So it took about a year for me to get it where I wanted it. I came back out to Los Angeles with the script, but I couldn't show it to anyone for about two or three months because it was all tangled up in the Savoy Pictures situation.

GA: Describe your rewrite process and how you reduced those four hundred pages. How many drafts did you go through?
GT: Yeah, I had several drafts. I think I did about five or six before anybody saw it. Then I would get six or seven actors together. I did that in Chicago, because I didn't know anybody in Los Ange-

les. And I would have the actors read my material and have them speak about it, tell me what they thought. Then I would go back and do the same thing again. That is actually the process I just found out that Robert De Niro does. He just really trusts what people are saying off the page, hearing the words. And I think that's a good process for a writer, to just get a few friends around and just see how the script is reading. So I'll do about five or six drafts, go through that process and do another rewrite.

GA: How did Babyface get involved with Soul Food? What was it like working with him?

GT: When we were tangled up with Savoy Pictures, William Morris told us not to show the script to any other studios until we could get out of that legal situation. But my partner and I couldn't wait. I just felt like I have to do it right now. So without William Morris knowing, I showed the script to October Films, Paramount and Warner Brothers, but everybody passed on it. When my agents found out everybody had passed on it, they didn't really want to touch it anymore. And I didn't quite understand, because I felt that it was the best work that I had done. We needed something to back us up, and there was one company that was interested in making the film, a company called First Look Pictures. They do a lot of small independent films. The only problem they had with the script was that the lady who owned the company was an animal activist and there was a scene where I had someone cooking bacon or something, so they had me take that out of the script. And we needed somebody to boost us up, we needed a soundtrack, and that's where Babyface got involved. It was initially given to them just to do the soundtrack. Next thing you know, I get a call that everybody at William Morris was talking about Babyface wanting to make the movie, so that's when I had my first meeting with Tracey Edmonds, Babyface and my partner.

GA: Describe the transition from a much smaller film like Scenes, to the larger Soul Food, which had Babyface and a studio attached.

GT: [Soul Food] was different, because they didn't really want me to direct the film because I hadn't really done anything. They were giving me names like Forest Whitaker and Carl Franklin. And I told them that this was my script, this was my family. I told them that if I don't direct, you don't get the script. And I knew there were going to be some complications, because Babyface and his wife Tracey were taking their films and their business to a whole other level, and I knew it could be a situation where the filmmakers could be overshadowed. At the same time, I had another deal at First Look Pictures for a million dollars. I had the choice to do the film for $1 million and get it into twenty theaters or to do it with Babyface for $7 million and probably get it in a thousand theaters. So I kept using my First Look Pictures offer. "If I don't get to direct, I go somewhere else." And that was my power to get to direct. I really believe in the power of your being able to control your own destiny if you write your own material. I had that power, and that's how they gave me an opportunity to direct the film. But working with Babyface was not the hard part. The hard part was working with the actors. Before, I was working with first-time actors, and with Soul Food Tracey Edmonds had an idea to put who's who in African American media in the film, and they were calling Vanessa [L. Williams] and I really wanted to work with Vanessa. And they chose Vivica [Fox], and I wanted Mekhi [Phifer]. It was kind of like a give-and-take and they wanted everybody who was a big face at the time to be in the film. As a first-time director it can be overwhelming to talk to an actor, but that was a process that worked out, and I think it worked out best for the film.

GA: *What is your process for working with actors, given that many come from different schools of acting? How do you get the performance you want?*

GT: I think that's one of the things I love doing the best—getting the performance out of individuals and working with actors. It all goes with directing. It's really about communication, how you communicate with an actor. I really try to find who I want in the casting process. I try to find actors who can really go behind the words and really find the subtext of the scene. I'm looking for an actor who can improvise. I don't really believe in the words. I believe in having the right idea and just taking them away and trying to find really what you're trying to say in the scene. I'm looking for an actor who can collaborate, and once I find that in the casting room you've got so many places you can go. I had two weeks of rehearsal with the actors for Soul Food, and was able to get a unit, a family unit, together.

Men of Honor was totally different. Robert De Niro was just coming off of a movie, Cuba Gooding, Jr., was just coming off of a movie and I had a lot of supporting actors. The only person who had script notes for me in a week's time was Robert De Niro, and he and I would just sit around and talk. He's the kind of actor who will call you at two o'clock in the morning and talk about a character. He's a guy who will take that process, just little things I like about an actor. I like an actor to call me to talk about a character. I like an actor who can say if I'm going to have an action in this scene maybe I can find six or seven different actions and maybe the director can choose. I'm looking for people who are able to glean things from me, and I think finding the performance is really finding a variety of different performances. I try to do a performance two or three different times but really find that subtext of the scene—and leaving that subtext there but trying different things. I like an actor who can give me that, and I think that's how I get good performances.

GA: Was it intimidating with Oscar winners like Robert De Niro and Cuba Gooding, Jr.?

GT: Robert De Niro is one of my favorite actors of all time and I really wanted to work with him, but the studio really wanted me to go with Sylvester Stallone, then they wanted me to go with Kurt Russell, because of their draw overseas. It's interesting being an African American director working in a white film world. It's a whole other world, a whole other agenda. In the beginning with Robert De Niro, I knew from other directors that he can sometimes do up to fifty takes. I knew from his preparation that he looks for a director to have all of the answers. So I started doing my research very early on just to prepare for him. It was intimidation. I remember I called him one day and I said, "Bob, I wanna know how you like to work on a set because I wanna make it easy for you." And he told me, "I like what you did with *Soul Food*, you won't have any problems from me. [Laughs] That made me feel completely comfortable. Just his work process can be kind of scary. I mean, in the film he has this pipe, and it took us about five weeks just to figure out which kind of pipe he wanted. It's just little things like that. With Cuba I was a little concerned, because I loved what he did on his first film, *Boyz 'N the Hood*, and I really wanted to get back to that. I feel that he is a mainstream actor, and I really wanted to have him connect with the person I felt as a filmmaker I was speaking to. Cuba's the kind of actor who comes in, he talks and I give him the back story. He likes motivational speaking, but that's okay for an actor, because I need it too sometimes. Robert De Niro at the same time just wants the facts: "What are the facts of the scene? What do you need me to do? Where do you wanna go? How was that?" It all depends on a person, on an actor, and it's my job to figure those things out.

GA: What's your role in Soul Food the TV series?

GT: I'm an executive producer.

GA: What are your feelings about the series?

GT: In the beginning, I have to say, I didn't really want to do the show, because all of my heroes— Spike Lee, Martin Scorsese, all of these guys—have never had one of their movies made into a TV show. I just felt like among a lot of my peers in the filmmakers' world that's considered almost a sellout, and I looked at that and I talked to my wife about it. And one of the things I started realizing is there aren't many African American shows on the air. There aren't many African American directors working. There are no hour-long dramas. We tried to do the show as a drama on network TV, but we couldn't get it done. That made me realize that it's not all about what I think or what I feel and how I feel I am perceived. It should be about what am I doing to take us to the next level. I feel that in most of my films what I try to do is take us to the next level. And I felt like with the show, it was my responsibility to make that happen. I took the script and made notes and I knew all the actors. The great thing is that the actors are not playing Vivica and Vanessa [L. Williams]. They're making the roles their own. The director's not doing what I'm doing. I'm proud of it, though.

GA: What inspired you to do Men of Honor?

GT: What inspired me was seeing F. Gary Gray do The Negotiator (1998) and not seeing enough opportunities for African American directors to work with bigger stars. I actually met Carl Brashear and I read the script. The script was sent to me while I was editing Soul Food, and I was totally blown away by it. I didn't totally understand the world that the character was in. I think a great script is when you have a great other world—a world that other people can explore and other people don't know about—and that script had that. At the time I was afraid of water and actually I couldn't swim, and I knew that I had to get down in there and get involved. I feel like as a director sometimes you have to get down in there and prove to your cast that you can do it. So I went down to Norfolk, Virginia to see Carl Brashear. We met at this small diner, and he gets out of his Cadillac and he walks, and he was in the best shape I've ever seen any man in, and he was sixty-two years old. I couldn't tell that he had one leg. And then he told me his entire story and how Bill Cosby got involved in the project, and how the film never got made. I just felt it was my duty to do a film about an African American hero. And I was totally inspired, and I just felt like, if he can do it, why am I afraid to get in the water and swim? Why am I afraid to deal with problems that I know I'll have being a director in a white community, in a white world? Because once you do a film where the entire cast is white, you're going to get into a whole different world. So I had to accept the whole competitiveness of it, and I wanted to do the film.

GA: African American dramatic films typically have a tough time getting through the studio system, and because of that you said you had some reservations about doing Men of Honor. Tell me about that.

GT: At the time the only recent Black drama Hollywood had done was Malcolm X (1992), almost ten years prior to that. So I felt it was time for it to happen. But the budget was $32 million, which was a big budget for me. I had just finished doing a $7 million Soul Food. But they had certain reservations. They didn't really believe African American films could make money overseas, so at the time it meant who is the biggest white actor who can be sold in Europe. That's why they thought of Sylvester Stallone, because he's a big box-office draw overseas. And Kurt Russell is huge overseas. They didn't really want to pursue Robert De Niro for the film, because they didn't think he was going to do the film. They were telling me that Robert De Niro was buying a lot of real estate in New York and that he ain't gonna do a movie for less than $15 million. So as soon as I met Robert De Niro and he said he'd do it for $5 million, that made it real to me.

At that point they said, "Okay, well, you gotta go for Will Smith." I think Will Smith was never in, though, because he was prepping for Ali and he didn't want to do two period pieces back-to-back. But I went down that road, and the next guy in line was Cuba. Chris Tucker, then Cuba. And seeing Cuba—he looked exactly like Carl Brashear. I knew Chris Tucker couldn't do it—I don't see him being a diver. [Laughs] I just felt that Cuba was the role. He was Carl Brashear. He had the build to definitely be an athlete, a diver. The problem with Cuba getting involved was that with all of the films he had done he was asking for a certain price, and Fox did not want to pay him that certain price. So the next guy in line for me was Mekhi Phifer, who I worked with on Soul Food. He looked nothing like Carl Brashear, but I felt we would have a problem aging him thirty years. He came in and read and he did a great job, but aging him through those years was a problem. We worked it out and got Cuba, but the studio gave me certain restrictions. We couldn't go over $32 million. If we went over, it was going to come out of my pocket.

GA: *What was the transition from* Soul Food *to a project like* Men of Honor *like?*
GT: It was a tough transition. In Men of Honor you had effects, visual effects, which I did not know anything about. And then you had the different actors. I definitely had help from guys like Glenn Turman, Lonette McKee. De Niro was great. Everybody loved what I did on my first film; they were very supportive. The problem was just dealing with the crew. I try to have as many African Americans on the crew as possible, but when they see a young African American director coming in on a $32 million movie it becomes problematic, because you find yourself having to prove yourself. And along with that you get, "Oh, he doesn't know what he's doing. Well, this is how I'll do it." Right away you have to let everyone know that you know what you're doing. That has to be done right away.

The second part was trying to do all of this stuff with a certain amount of days. There were times when I was shooting four and five scenes a day, and it's really hard to get a scene right when you have four other scenes to shoot that day, because they try to put so much in the schedule. It was only $32 million, so there was a lot to be done. Then you had the water—under water and on top of water. And on top of water was the hardest, because we were shooting out in San Pedro and we would have to actually ride out two hours just to get away, just to see Long Beach. That was in November, and we were trying to make it look like summer. And a lot of people were getting seasick. It was the toughest thing I've ever done, and I'm really proud of the film.

GA: Tell me about Bill Cosby and his involvement with Men of Honor. What resources did he bring to the project?

GT: He actually found the script. He found Carl Brashear and wrote the script with his writer in 1995. He sent it over to Paramount, but Paramount wasn't going to make the movie. They sometimes give vanity deals to a lot of people. That means I give you a production deal, then you send me a script, but if they won't make your script . . . I think that happened to Bill Cosby. They couldn't get the film off the ground. It just sat there. I read it and I got Twentieth Century Fox to buy it from Paramount, but they wouldn't give it to us right away. They made a trade. Like they gave Fox Men of Honor and then Fox gave them Fat Albert. They [Paramount] wanted to do a remake of Fat Albert. So there was a trade just because Cosby was involved. But he actually got the script and got it together.

GA: A constant argument in Hollywood is that Black films don't perform well overseas, but Men of Honor made $35 million in foreign markets. How did that happen?

GT: The white critics always say that Black films don't do well overseas, but Fox sent me to Tokyo to promote the film and Carl Brashear went to seven countries. Even though we had a white actor, Robert De Niro, in the movie, Fox actually promoted the movie as a movie about a Black man and it made money. I'm trying to let people know that Black films have the ability to make money overseas if the studio pushes the film.

GA: What was it specifically about Fox's marketing campaign for Men of Honor that helped make the film a success overseas?

GT: I think it helped that the film was a film with universal themes. The film is about an African American character, but it has universal themes. It's about courage and never giving up. You can accomplish anything you set your heart to. I think that's the theme they sold overseas. Another universal theme they sold was racism. With everything going on in the world today, that's a universal theme that people can understand and I think that helped. It also helped that we had Cuba Gooding, Jr. and Robert De Niro who are Oscar winners. With that in mind, Fox actually went out and spent money on marketing the film. I had a chance to go overseas for the first time. In Tokyo I met people who knew of the films I did in college. I went to Paris last spring and met people who knew about Barbershop before it even came out. I was very happy that Men of Honor did $85 million; it did it very quietly. However, the white reporters didn't really report the film's overseas performance, especially given that the film dealt with racism and that it was a period piece set in the fifties and sixties. So the critics want to keep saying that Black movies don't do well overseas, but the films do perform well if the studios push them.

GA: How did you get involved with Barbershop?

GT: When I was editing Men of Honor, my producing partner Bob Teitel came across the script by Mark Brown and he liked the premise. I remembered my experiences in the barbershop—-I go twice a week—-and I thought, "This is going to be a great vehicle." We knew from the start that Barbershop was a movie that could be very commercial but also strike an emotional chord with audiences at the same time. So we took the script to Twentieth Century Fox, our home studio, where we have a deal and did our last two movies, but they also passed on it. We were shocked. We went to Fox 2000, they passed and to Fox Searchlight and they passed. We then went to MGM. One of the executives on the film, Alex Gardner, who was actually an executive on Men of Honor, brought the script over to MGM. At that time we got involved with the final two writers on the script, Marshall Todd and Don Scott.

GA: Why did Fox pass on the script?

GT: They weren't happy with the script. Even now when I talk to the guys at Fox they say, "Hey, next time get in our faces about something like that. Let us know that you have the solutions to the script's problems. When they passed, we just let it go. We didn't push. We should have been in their faces more, letting them know that we could make changes to the script to make the characters stronger and the script more viable. But we didn't and I think it worked out because MGM marketed the movie like it was a Tom Cruise film. They put a lot of money into marketing the film, which tells you that if a studio gets behind an African American film, which has universal themes, and markets it like any other movie, you can make a lot of money.

GA: How much did MGM spend marketing the film?

GT: Those figures aren't disclosed to me, but when I spoke with MGM's president, Michael Nathanson, before the release of the film, he said that they were going to treat Barbershop like any other [mainstream] film by going hard on TV campaigns. And I saw advertising spots on TV every day, every fifteen minutes. We also had radio ads and billboards and posters on city buses in major cities. On our previous films, we only had TV ads. So MGM probably spent as much marketing the film as they did making it—$12 million.

GA: Do you get involved in the marketing process of your films?

GT: Bob and I get very much involved in the marketing. We learned that with Soul Food. The executive Bob Harper at Fox always got us involved very early on in the marketing. We wanted to make sure that we sold the film as an all-around comedy. We also tried very hard to make sure that it was heartfelt and dramatic and that it was an ensemble piece.

It's not just an Ice Cube movie. Ice Cube is the major character in the film, but we wanted to emphasize in the campaign that there are other important characters in the film. Unlike other Ice Cube films like Friday, we wanted to play up that he was part of an ensemble cast, so we pushed to have everyone in the film on the poster. We really tried to market it like Soul Food. But the difference between Barbershop and Soul Food was that with Barbershop we added a little bit more comedy and we consciously made it a PG-13 movie, which made the difference at the box office.

GA: Did you ever consider directing Barbershop yourself?

GT: Very early on I did. But after directing Men of Honor I felt that I wanted to keep challenging myself by doing something different. To me, Barbershop explored the same themes as Soul Food did. I thought this was a great opportunity for Bob and me to bring in another director to produce. That's what we've wanted to do from the beginning—produce other filmmakers. We thought Barbershop was the best film to do this with and Tim Story was the best director for the project.

GA: What was it like producing someone else's work?

GT: It was tough. I kept thinking I was going to get there and just produce, say a few things and do work on my next project. But as it turns out, I was working on the set every day. But it was just a fun shoot. Out of the three movies we've done, this was the most fun because everyone had a good time.

GA: Working as the producer, did you find yourself having an urge to direct?

GT: Every day, man. Every day. It was hard to be there every day as a director and not direct. But the main thing is producing is another extension of what I want to do, it's part of a bigger plan. Not only am I a director, I'm a producer now. You sit back and you learn as you go along. You watch and you learn because this is the first time we've ever done a comedy. Comedy is much harder than drama.

GA: How so?

GT: It's all about the timing. Off the back, you know it's not funny if it's not working on the set, and you have to find very quick fixes to make it work. We had a great team, working with writer Don Scott. I always like to bring my writers to the set; it's very helpful for a director in case you get in trouble.

GA: But it's unusual to bring the writer on the set.

GT: I do it every time. On Men of Honor, I had the writer Scott Marshall Smith with me 80 percent of the time because something always comes up where the script is not working. And you want to have someone on the set who can write very quickly and keep the film on track. Don Scott was there on Barbershop, and for a first-time director, that was great for Tim. I think it's a plus to have your writer on the set.

GA: Let's talk about the controversy with the civil rights leaders surrounding Barbershop. What's your reaction to that?

GT: I was very shocked when I first heard that after making $21 million our first weekend. First, I wasn't expecting the film to make that amount of money its opening weekend and then to get a call from Jesse Jackson, who of course demanded to speak with me. We had shown the film to 5,000 people before it was released. We did test screenings, we showed it at the National Association of Black Journalists convention in Milwaukee, the cosmetology convention in Atlanta and no one had a problem with the film. Then all of a sudden the controversy came out of nowhere.

We made it very clear that there was only one character [Eddie] in the film who says something about Rosa Parks, Jesse Jackson or Martin Luther King. It was just one character's opinion. And the way Eddie [played by Cedric the Entertainer] speaks, the way he comes off, you know the guy is ridiculous in what he's saying. He's like the Sweet Dick Willie character [played by the late Robin Harris] in Do the Right Thing. We all know those characters, we all know these people in real life. The Barbershop character's not making sense in what he's saying, it's just his opinion. And we consciously had the character played by Sean Patrick Thomas tell Eddie that what he was saying was disrespectful. So this one guy—Eddie—has an opinion about the civil rights leaders. I was never expecting this controversy to happen. However, once Rev. Jackson came out with his comments and Al Sharpton jumped on the program, it didn't hurt our box office at all. The majority of the people totally disagreed with what these guys were saying.

GA: What did Rev. Jackson say when he called you, and what was your response?

GT: Well, he first said that he wasn't upset about the comments about him but he was upset about what the character of Eddie says about Rosa Parks and Martin Luther King. We told him that it was just a movie and that Eddie is a character; we don't agree with what Eddie was saying. Rev. Jackson said that it's something that you don't joke or laugh about. He then said that he was going to speak with Cube and Cedric about it. I don't think he ever reached them, but I told him to look at my movies and that I always do positive films about African Americans. I sold my rights to the movie Soul Food so that I could do the TV show Soul Food to get other African American directors, actors and actresses working. I feel that over the past five years, I've made a contribution to African Americans by showing positive African Americans on the screen. I was a little hurt by Rev. Jackson's comments, but at the same time, I refused to go out and debate him.

GA: *But what do you say to those in the African American community who feel that there are some things about us that are just sacred and should be taken very seriously?*
GT: I say that people speak this way in a barbershop in real life, so why can't I say these things in a very positive African American movie? Each of the conversations we heard in the film has been said. It's not like we just made it up. And now we're getting ready to do *Barbershop 2*.

GA: *Are you going to push the comedy a little harder this time?*
GT: We're not going to push harder but we can talk about the war, we can talk about Bush. I mean, we aren't going to talk about the same issues we discussed in the first *Barbershop*, but we're gonna talk. That's what we do in a barbershop.

GA: *How did you respond to Rev. Jackson's request that MGM should edit out the scene with Eddie's comments for the DVD?*
GT: We never responded. However, we did send out letters saying that we apologize if we offended Rosa Parks and Martin Luther King's family. We did not apologize for the movie and we're not going to change the film for the DVD version. The scenes are going to stay in the film.

GA: *How do you prepare for each production? Do you study related films, photography?*
GT: The best thing is watching films and studying other artists. I try to study other filmmakers.

GA: *Who are your favorites?*
GT: I really love what Spike is doing, and he's the kind of guy who wants you to do a film a year. He's the kind of guy who can work every year. I have a hard time keeping up with his schedule, but I love what he's doing. Everything he does is thought-provoking, and he's taking it from a filmmaker's point of view. Sometimes not necessarily from an audience's point of view, but he tells it how he wants to say it, and I give it up to someone like that. I also like Michael Maan [Ali, Heat] a lot because he is committed to his vision. I had a chance to speak with him and to ask him about his process and he's committed all the way. And I love all of his films. He has a vision, he maintains it, and he sticks to it until he gets it. And I watch a lot of younger filmmakers. A lot of

young guys right now are doing things on digital. A lot of guys are doing stuff on 16mm, and those are some of the best works, I think.

GA: What suggestions do you have for directors who want to make it in Hollywood?

GT: I tell all aspiring filmmakers to create their own material. If you're a director with writing ability, write your own screenplay. That's the best way to create a directing opportunity. And if you don't consider yourself a writer, find material that you're passionate about—a script, a short story, a scene from a play—and then shoot it in any medium available to you, film or video. The way to get people interested in you as a director is to get them familiar with your work.

Malcolm D. Lee

I first had the opportunity to meet Malcolm D. Lee at a SoHo cocktail party given by independent filmmaker Bridgett Davis (Naked Acts) and her now-husband, Rob Fields, during the 1997 Independent Film Market in New York. I introduced myself and we briefly chatted, along with producer Taj Paxton, about screenwriting and the business. I told him I was working on a romantic comedy about young Black newlyweds and he said he, too, was working on a romantic comedy.

But little did I know that this Brooklyn, New York, native and cousin to Spike Lee would be the genius behind the brilliant, sexy, smart and handsome debut feature film The Best Man (1999). It was the film that African American audiences had been dying to see. A story of love, commitment, friendship, romance, marriage—all neatly packaged with the classiness and sophistication of the Harlem Renaissance. I so loved the film that I wanted to run up and jump in the screen, I felt I knew the characters in the film. They were my Morehouse College buddies, friends from Spelman and Clark, childhood friends. Lee made Black folks look good, and that is what I had been trying to do. And as it goes in Hollywood, he beat me to the punch. The Best Man opened to rave reviews and took the number-one spot at the box office its opening weekend.

After The Best Man, Lee entered the world of animation, developing the series My Babies' Mamas for UrbanEntertainment.com. UrbanEntertainment then signed Lee to direct Undercover Brother (2002), a smart, funny, politically savvy, live-action film based on the animated series by celebrated writer/producer John Ridley and released by Universal Pictures. *Undercover Brother* was the first-ever Internet-based series to be converted to a live-action film by a major studio.

Other credits include his film short *Morningside Prep*, which won several festival awards, including two from the Black Filmmakers Hall of Fame, and was featured on Showtime's Black Filmmakers Showcase.

Lee is presently developing several screenplays, including an ensemble comedy about Black male exotic dancers for Miramax pictures titled *Buckwild!*

He is a graduate of Georgetown University and New York University's Tisch School of the Arts, and was a participant in the Disney Screenwriting Fellowhip.

— — — —

GA: *Tell me about your upbringing. Were you a creative child?*

ML: I was born in Queens, and in 1975, when I was five years old, we moved to Crown Heights, Brooklyn, into a house my parents still own today. The majority of my life I went to predominantly white schools. I was the only Black male in my high school class at Packer, a private school in Brooklyn Heights. I can't necessarily say it was culture shock, because I wasn't shocked into it, but my parents always cautioned me against acting like the white kids act because there are certain things you can't get away with as a Black person. I didn't understand that at first, but it became clearer to me as the years went by. From an early age I was exposed to film- and video-making, and I think it was a result of being at the schools I attended. As early as fifth grade there were elective courses that allowed you to play around with video cameras and do stupid skits on video. Plus, I was always involved in the theater—I was an actor in school plays all the way through school. I played the Big Bad Wolf when I was in kindergarten. I was Max from *Where the Wild Things Are*. In fifth grade I was Oliver Twist's grandfather, and it was a white kid who was Oliver Twist. And I was the bad guy in *Oklahoma!* in eighth grade.

GA: *(Laugh) Did your parents encourage your creative pursuits?*

ML: Well, they didn't discourage me at all.

GA: *Were your parents creative people?*

ML: My father is a musician. He plays trumpet. My mother is a retired hospital administrator and college professor. All of my father's brothers and sisters had to play an instrument. My grandmother was a classically trained pianist. My great-grandfather went to Harvard, then started a school, the Snow Hill Institute in Alabama. He graduated from Morehouse, then went to

Harvard and was a contemporary of Booker T. Washington. I come from a family of—I guess you could call them overachievers. I like the term "high achievers" rather than "overachiever," because it's as if you're an overachiever, it's not expected of you. I tried the trumpet for a little while, I played the cello when I was in the fourth grade, then I tried the saxophone for about a year and a half, but it wasn't in me. I did a lot of things. I also wrote short stories, and I would draw a lot. Before writing any short stories I played with action figures and always created little scenarios. I was also acting. I liked it and I thought maybe I'd become an actor, but it seemed impractical. I remember seeing *Entertainment Tonight* in high school. There was a casting call and they showed a long line of people. It just really hit me—"Holy cow, everybody's trying to act." Plus, Spike lived with us the three years he was in film school from 1980 to 1983, so I saw him leave early and come back late. He had a Steambeck [editing machine] in his room.

GA: *Did you work on any of Spike's films?*
ML: I was in Spike's second-year student film entitled *Sarah*. It was a little scene that he shot, and then I did the slate. But I always wanted to be in his movies rather than behind the scenes. I remember asking him why he was in school for filmmaking. And he said, "I'm gonna be making movies." I said, "For the theater?" He said, "Yeah. I said, "Get out of here." But when he made *She's Gotta Have It* and it was such a critical and financial success, I thought, "Wow. This is serious."

GA: *Did you know you were going to have a creative career at that point?*
ML: I didn't know I'd have a creative career at that point. I thought I wanted to go to a school that at the least had a communications program and maybe some theater. I did an animated film in eighth grade. It was called *Battle with the Swamp Monsters*, or something like that. It was shot on Super 8mm film. That was eighth grade, and then I didn't really take on any more filmmaking for a while. There was a filmmaking course offered at my high school, which I took my senior year, and I would see these films that people were making and I said, "What is this?" People would make these self-referential films that no one understood, or at least I didn't. So I made a couple of short films that semester as well. I felt good about what I could do in film.

GA: *What was the trigger that made you know that you wanted to be a filmmaker?*
ML: I worked with Spike on a number of films. Between my junior and senior years of high school he'd just shot *School Daze*. I was going to work at a summer camp that summer, and Spike told me that he thought he could get me a job. He said, "I can probably get you a job with this guy I know who is a manager at this sporting goods store, Paragon, in Manhattan." I said, "Yeah, cool,

free, discounted sneakers." Then Spike said, "Or, if I can work it out in my budget, you could come and work with me." I thought: "I want free sneakers." My parents said, "You'd better go ahead and work with Spike." I said, "What about the free sneakers?" So I got to PA (production assist) for him, running errands and stuff around the city that summer while he was editing School Daze.

GA: *Is working as a PA something that you'd recommend for young aspiring filmmakers?*
ML: Absolutely. You get to work your way from the bottom up, and you get to learn that you never want to be in that position again. You need to be humble. A lot of people come into this business and think they know everything, and a lot of kids in film school think that they know everything without having any set or behind-the-scenes experience answering phones and running errands or whatever. I didn't know what the hell was going on, to tell you the truth. I knew they were editing the film, I knew I couldn't go in that room. It was "Go here, get this, go here, get that." Hey, all I knew was that I was getting paid $250 a week—and that was good money in 1987 in high school.

GA: *After that you still wanted to be a filmmaker?*
ML: I took that filmmaking course my senior year of high school and worked with Spike again during preproduction on Do the Right Thing. Then I had to go to a summer program at Georgetown for three weeks just as Spike was beginning to shoot the film. I came back, worked on the film again and ended up being an extra in the movie. That's what I wanted to do anyway, because I was still on the whole acting thing. I'm actually in Do the Right Thing. I walk by the pizza parlor and actually had to audition for that part.

GA: *No family preferences, huh?*
ML: Uh-huh. And it's probably a good thing, because Spike would always encourage me. When he gave me copies of his companion books to his movies, he would always write inside, "Make film." There were a number of people who were around those days, like Monty Ross, who was one of Spike's producers for a long time. Monty said, "Man, you should write a script. You should do this, you should do that." I thought, "Eh, well, maybe."

GA: *You thought, "Look, guys, I want to act. I'm about to move Denzel out of the way."*
ML: Right, and Denzel wasn't Denzel at that point either. But I had so many interests. I saw during my freshman year at Georgetown that there are so many aspects of filmmaking. It involves business, law, writing, acting, technical know-how and politics, and I was interested in all of those

fields. It was all encompassed in film. I felt that I didn't need to transfer to another college to learn filmmaking. At Georgetown I felt I could major in English, brush up on my writing skills, then possibly gather stories from my college experience as an undergrad who's just living life and not just pursuing film. I also did some acting at Georgetown and had two roles in a campus production of George C. Wolfe's play *The Colored Museum* during my sophomore year. The following summer, I heard about a summer filmmaking course at New York University and I really wanted to take it, but it was really expensive. It was $3,500 or something like that, and Spike paid for it. At the time, Spike was so hot. Spike said that Black people can make movies and he was my cousin. And there was something about cinema as opposed to theater for me. You were much more able to suspend your disbelief and fantasize with cinema than with theater—at least that was my thinking. And there was so much to learn about filmmaking. I had done a number of plays all my life, but film was just the thing to do at that particular time. And music videos were hot, and Spike was a huge influence on that.

GA: Do you think that the suspension of disbelief is the part that makes filmmaking magical?
ML: Yeah, absolutely. Spike always said that film is the most powerful medium in the world because its energy is coming at you on this sixty-foot screen with the power to change thought and affect change, and that was one of the reasons why I thought I was meant to do this. Film has the magic to shape thought and behavior. As much as Hollywood wants to try to deny it, film does influence thought and behavior.

GA: Do you think because of that Black filmmakers have more of a responsibility to bring certain images to the screen?
ML: I know I feel I have a certain responsibility as a Black person, as a Black filmmaker, and it's a battle. We're the only people who I feel need to be concerned with that—or we seem to have that moral burden. A lot of filmmakers just say, "Fuck that, I'm gonna make movies. I'm making the money." Surely, I could have written a *Friday* or a *Booty Call* before I wrote *Morningside Prep* while I was trying to get *Best Man* going, but I'd never want to make a movie like that. I didn't enjoy those films. That's not my kind of thing. I thought a lot of them were full of sight gags, easy jokes with nothing cerebral about them. It's just not for me, and I think in some ways those movies were just stereotypical, so I didn't dig it.

GA: Why do you think African American filmmakers and consumers tend to identify sometimes with low-brow comedies and violence?

ML: We almost believe that we have to be that way because that's how we are portrayed. It's like one feeding on the other—it's cyclical. It's like what came first, the chicken or the egg? But I was arguing with a friend of mine about Menace II Society, which I think is a brilliant piece of filmmaking. I told him that when I went to see the film there were kids in the audience who were cheering when the Korean man got shot and they were laughing when the Larenz Tate character stomped this guy. But that wasn't funny. It was very serious. The same thing happened with Baby Boy. I was watching that movie with a bunch of knuckleheads who believe for some reason that violence is cool or funny. And when questioned about their behavior off screen, a lot of these hip-hop artists say that they're just acting, it's their persona and not really who they are, and they ask, "Why don't you get mad when Arnold Schwarznegger shoots up thousands of people in his movies?" But Arnold Schwarzenegger is playing a character, and when he's not playing that character, when he's out with his wife and kids, he's Arnold Schwarzenegger. He's not trying to project that image 24/7. He's not The Terminator all the time. I think it's a weak argument for a lot of artists to make.

GA: What's also interesting is that it seems that even with Black independent productions we still see violent gangsta films. What's motivating that?

ML: I think there are a number of things. Number one, those people who are making the violent movies are doing it because it might be an experience they want to tell, it might be because they think they're going to get picked up by a distributor because whoever raised the money for them wanted to make that type of film. That's the only thing the investors would finance. I was reading an article in The Hollywood Reporter, and they were basically saying that a lot of people were influenced by John Singleton's and the Hughes brothers' early films and that we're seeing the babies of those films now and who needs it? I see enough of that crap [violence] on the news and they're not going to bring anything new to it. I've seen this story a thousand times, and you're not telling me anything different. Tell me something new. If you're not going to tell me something new, shoot it a different way.

GA: You received a Disney writing fellowship. Tell me about that.

ML: Well, I heard about the program when I had just returned for my senior year at Georgetown. I'd taken the first semester off to work on Malcolm X as a production assistant (PA). I came back to Georgetown the second semester of senior year and I heard about the Disney program. You had to write a feature-length screenplay, and I wrote my first screenplay, Morningside Prep, which I had first written as a one-act play. So I applied to the program and was accepted. I flew out to L.A. that October and they liked the idea of Morningside Prep and thought that maybe it could be the Black Dead Poets Society. I was young—I was twenty-two or twenty-three—and really didn't think I knew how to write. I had some good ideas, but writing screenplays is a discipline, a real skill, it's hard and it's a lonely business. Being in L.A. is even lonelier because everything is so isolated there. I had plenty of friends in L.A., but it was a tough year. The amazing part was that I got to make $30,000 that year writing for a major studio right out of college.

GA: *So what was the program like day to day?*

ML: Maybe once a week we'd meet with our executive, maybe once every two weeks we'd meet as a whole group and listen to an established writer, director or producer tell us what it was like in the business. The rest of the time I was writing at home. I wrote two screenplays that year— *Morningside Prep* and *North vs. South*, which was about these two college kids who were the brightest kids in school. It was a fish-out-of-water comedy. We had a reading of it, and Allen Payne, Malcolm Jamal Warner, Jenifer Lewis, Richard Gant and Robert Gossett were the readers. It was well-received. I thought it was a perfect vehicle for Disney at that time, and they felt *Morningside Prep* could be the thing for them, and they actually optioned it. I said, "Wow, they're optioning my work. Holy cow, my first screenplay." But the option ran out before the movie was made, and I had already gone back to New York—I left the Disney program early in order to go back home to NYU for film school. I had applied while I was a senior at Georgetown, but deferred. They don't allow you to defer, but I deferred because Spike stepped up.

GA: *Tell me about* The Best Man, *which is one of my favorite movies in recent years. The film portrays a segment of Black life seldom seen in popular culture. I saw myself in the film. What inspired you to make* The Best Man *and why was it such a success?*

ML: Thank you. I was tired of seeing us portrayed as one monolithic group that's violent, fatherless, selling drugs, living in despair, in poverty, and I knew that wasn't everyone's reality. It certainly wasn't my reality. I always felt early on, "Why can't there be a Black *Big Chill* or *Superman?* I was trying to raise money for another screenplay I had written, and I said that I was going to write a commercial screenplay that I thought could sell. I was planning on selling *The Best Man*. I remember reading in *Premiere* magazine that a movie called *Soul Food* was coming out, and I said, "Now, there's an ensemble cast of some really good Black actors, and I think this movie is going to make money." I just had a feeling. Wedding pictures always do well at the box office, and a Black wedding picture hadn't been done. I took that as a formula, and I wanted to have old friends come together, like in *The Big Chill* and in *Diner*. In *The Big Chill* it was a funeral, and in

Diner it was a wedding. I wanted to center it around four very different guys—layered characters. That's what I set out to do.

I wrote it and I came up from my parents' basement after I'd finished a draft that I was ready to show, and I said, "Mommy and Daddy, if this ain't it I don't know what I'm doing. I'll go on to do something else." Because it was my sixth screenplay, and I said, "If this ain't it, then I'm lost, I'm at a loss." So it got going, and I think people responded to it because it's different. I think it gives us hope. It's almost a wish for a filmmaker—we like seeing ourselves in that light and we don't get to see it often. Everyone gets to see themselves on screen. White people get to see themselves in film and on television in a number of different ways. The Cosby Show was the most popular show in America in its tenure, and it had nothing to do with being Black. They were just people. We rarely get to see ourselves as people. It always has something to do with being Black.

I didn't want to strip away our Blackness in the movie, and although the characters could be of any race, they're clearly Black. It's a story about love, trust, friendship and old friends. People just relate to that, because we all have experiences with old friends we haven't seen in a long time. So I don't want to take credit for it, but my wife told me that after the movie people were making songs about getting married. Like that Jagged Edge song, "Let's Get Married" and the Next song "Wifey." Before that people were saying, "I'm not getting married, dada, dada, da." It wasn't cool. And I think also the dudes especially weren't expecting The Best Man to be a guy's movie or a movie that a guy could relate to. I knew that people would like it. I felt like the characters were people that we can all relate to. We are some of these people, and if we're not these people, we want to be these people—they're good-looking people, and people want to see good-looking people on screen and they want to see weddings. For some odd reason, people want to see people getting married. I remember having an argument with the studio about the wedding scene because they wanted me to cut down the wedding ceremony, saying that we've seen weddings in movies before, and I said, "No way. We've seen weddings in My Best Friend's Wedding and in this movie and that movie, but Black people haven't, and they need to see a wedding and they want to see it. So I'm going to fight with you to keep it in there."

GA: *In writing the script, what was it about you and the way you live your life that allowed you to create these full-bodied characters that we relate to so well?*

ML: I took plenty of examples from my own experiences, not actual events, but I listen to people talk. I just wanted to create characters that were layered and developed. If you say someone is a lawyer in a movie, I think a lot of times that doesn't define who they are—your profession doesn't define you. There are so many more things that make you up, more than just what you do.

GA: *And what is your approach to that? Do you start with characters first?*

ML: Most of the time I do. But with *The Best Man* I knew I wanted an ensemble piece, but I had the story structure and it had to take place in one weekend. There's only so much you can do in a weekend. A lot of the stories I was telling happened over a semester or over three years or over whatever amount of time. But it's better if you just give yourself a time and place an event. Like with a wedding there are so many things that are built-in—the rehearsal, shopping for a gift, friends coming back together. And I loved giving my characters intros. A lot of people felt that it was long giving each character an introduction and in some respects it was, but I wanted to make sure that we got a sense of each character when we first met them. I start with character and try to give them depth, a history and the history includes their behavior.

GA: *The Best Man explores issues of trust, commitment.*

ML: Absolutely, all of us go through those, it's a universal thing. Black people have psychological issues, they have hang ups and quirks. You take a character like Murch, people think there's not a black guy like that but sure there is. The vulnerabilities, the not standing up to his woman and that kind of stuff. Those things are important to me and everyone can relate to it, it's universal.

GA: *How did you go about casting* The Best Man?

ML: When we got the greenlight we were asked, "Who do you see in this movie?" So you go with the list of possible people for the roles and you chose maybe five people for each and then you get a casting director involved. There were people like Sanaa and Morris who I didn't think of at all. I had Terrence Howard and Nia Long in mind, but I didn't know who Taye Diggs was at the time. The studio brought him in because *How Stella Got Her Groove Back* came out around the time we were casting and there was a lot of buzz about Taye. I said, "This guy has a lot of screen presence and charisma and he has a cerebral quality about him. He'd be good to play Harper." For the Robin character I had about eight actresses in mind to play that role and Sanaa wasn't one of them. I didn't know who Sanaa was. I'd had heard of her, I'd seen her photo spread in "Vibe," then she came in and I knew right away she was Robin. She brought a bubbliness, vivacity and vulnerability that the character needed—a sweetness and absentmindedness that was believable. She's just a great actress. You've got to have good actors—people who can do something besides these little tricks like cursing and stuff like that. A lot of the Quentins who came in played it very stereotypically with the waving of the hands and sucking on lollipops. When I met Terrence Howard [who played Quentin] he told me, "I am Quentin. You gotta cast me in this."

GA: *He's hilarious. He stole the show. In prepping the film, did you story board?*
ML: I didn't do any story boards. It's not really a story board movie. I discussed a long time with my director of photography, the kind of look I wanted and the shots for each scene and said, "Okay, this is how I want to shoot this, this is how I want to shoot that."

GA: *Do you recommend that directors study acting?*
ML: Absolutely. It can only help because acting is hard. It's some hard shit and people think acting is getting in front of the camera, being you or spouting off lines. But there are a lot of emotions, real layering that goes on and some people can get it and some people can't.

GA: *How do you go about getting the performances you need?*
ML: You talk about the character, you talk about the script, you talk about how you see it, you do line readings and stuff like that. We rehearsed for about two weeks all together. It was very important and I encouraged the actors to hang out together because the characters are a crew of friends who've known each other for a long time and they naturally bonded.

GA: *With your second feature film, Undercover Brother, Urban Entertainment [L.A.-based black owned production company] became the first company ever, to convert a Web-based series to the big screen. Why do you think they were successful?*
ML: I think it's the idea of an undercover brother. From the mind of writer John Ridley comes this blaxploitation hero modeled after Jim Kelly who's thrust into 2000 but who lives by the mores of 70's Black people. It was a time when people were no longer assimilating and were proud to be Black and expressing oneself and what it means to be Black. And it has nothing to do with being a gangster or being a thug or being a bitch or a ho and all that kind of stuff. Undercover Brother doesn't let anybody off the hook, Black people or white people. So I think it's a unique premise or a unique character and I think that's what drove people to want to get involved with it; the whole idea of a secret organization, a brotherhood that exists in the bottom of a barbershop, a James Bond-type organization. It's about smart Black people using technology and creating things and leveling the playing field for African Americans. So you know, it's great.

GA: What was the budget for The Best Man?

ML: Nine million.

GA: What was it like moving to a much higher budget of over $30 million for Undercover Brother? Did you lose any sleep? Tell me about that.

ML: I didn't lose any sleep over it. It is what it is. A certain movie requires a certain budget. I try not to think about money. I think that Undercover Brother deserved its budget and I thought I could direct the movie. So they had faith in me. I do have a responsibility to deliver so there is that pressure and plus when you're dealing with that much money there are a lot more people who have a lot more things to say. There's a lot more collaborating, especially with a script that you didn't write and there's a lot more compromising that you have to do.

GA: How did you approach the film given that there was above average collaboration and compromising?

ML: Telling myself that I'm the director and that's it. I knew that The Best Man was mine and that no one could tell me how to do it. I was the best person for it, not only because I wrote it, but also because I knew the characters and I knew what the life was like. On The Best Man a lot of time my producers at the studio would say, "This is a comedy you've got to pick up the pace." I'd say, "No, it's a romantic comedy." I always felt the film was a drama with comedic moments—a romantic comedy. So it's not the same pace as let's say an Undercover Brother, which has to be rapid fire. For example, I felt very confident about their taking their time with the card game scene in The Best Man. It's one of my favorite scenes in the movie. With Undercover Brother there were a lot more cooks in the kitchen, we were dealing with a bigger budget and bigger egos.

GA: People see themselves perhaps as stars as opposed to actors.

ML: Right, there was that and after having that experience I never really want to work with stars again or people who think they're stars. I want to work with actors who are about the work. To me it's all about the work and having fun while you're doing it. It's a challenge, so it's going to be hard. If it wasn't hard everybody would be acting, but I like working with actors and it's good when people are all on the same page.

GA: Did you find yourself in battles?

ML: Not battles.

GA: Creative disputes?

ML: Creative disputes, certainly, certainly.

GA: A lot more than on The Best Man?

ML: Oh, without question. But it'd be great to work with stars as long as they're about the work. Everybody has their process, a certain way they like to work and certain things they're accustomed to and I'm learning as I go. I give my opinion and I say, "I'd like to see it done this way." Hopefully they give me what I want and if they don't I say, "Okay, fine. I'm not going to stand there and argue with you while we're wasting valuable time to shoot." Because I can always say, "Okay, well fine, do it how you want. I'm going to stick with the best of what's there and cut out the shit that I don't want."

GA: Was there much more studio involvement on Undercover Brother?

ML: There was heavier studio involvement and heavier producer involvement. Imagine Entertainment [Brian Grazer and Ron Howard] is a very powerful company in Hollywood. They have done some of the biggest hits in Hollywood history—The Nutty Professor, Liar, Liar, especially comedies and you know—Brian Grazer. In some ways it was intimidating and in other ways it was kind of cool that they wanted me to direct the film. So they had a lot of opinions about what needed to be shot, but I always had to tell myself, "Look, if they knew how to do it, they'd do it themselves, they wouldn't have hired you so obviously you must be bringing something to the table." But too much studio and production company involvement can stymie your confidence and make you doubt yourself and second-guess your instinct.

GA: George Tillman, Jr. told me that on Men of Honor he had to show right away that he was confident because he was new to some of the technical aspects of the film. Did you find that you had to do that as well—establish yourself more clearly up front?

ML: No, no and it's funny that you talk about George like that because when he went ahead and made Men of Honor I thought, "What the fuck is he doing? That is such a huge leap. Why would he want to do that?" That was before I got involved with Undercover Brother and now I see. It can easily be done and if people have the confidence in you and you feel passionately about a project why not do it? For me, I was honest enough to say, "I don't know this technology. How is this going to be done? I need help when it comes to doing this car chase scene. I'm going to look at a bunch of movies and this is what I think I want and you guys have got to help me." That's why I say this movie was a more collaborative process than The Best Man.

GA: So you did story board Undercover Brother?

ML: Oh, yeah, oh, yeah.

GA: What movies did you study to prepare for the film?

ML: The French Connection, Bullitt, Black Belt Jones, In Like Flint and some "Matt Helm" films. I was completely unfamiliar with Dean Martin in the role of Matt Helm in films like The Ambushers (1967). I also watched some blaxploitation movies like Black Boat Jones and Truck Turner. I looked at Shaft again. Because Undercover Brother involved a lot of different genres—blaxploitation, spy and the whole seventies Quinn Martin production type stuff like Get Smart and Austin Powers, as well as recent films like The Matrix because it has some karate in it. The thing about Undercover Brother is that it was rushed into production because of the impending strike. There wasn't adequate time to prep. The thing is that if the strike hadn't been expected they wouldn't have rushed the film into production and I probably would've been working on something else because I was writing something else at Universal at the time.

GA: So are you grateful for Undercover Brother?

ML: I am, I am. I don't know if I will be doing too many more movies like this, or maybe I will, I don't know yet. But it's told me a lot about what I like to do and what I don't like to do.

GA: What are some of those things?

ML: I like emotional stories, I like things that are going to tickle the funny bone, things that I know are definitely going to be funny and that I think people are going to laugh at. With a broad comedy you just don't know what little Timmy in Kansas City is going find funny. You have to be mindful of that because with such a big budget you've got to be able to promote that or produce that for the studio that's shelling out the dough. I also like doing things that I've written. And I never really got an opportunity to put my stamp on Undercover Brother and that's frustrating. It tells me that I'm going to have to write my own shit or at least have a lot more control and say over how something's going to turn out, but this is not to say that I didn't have control and say over the film.

GA: But you're going to have less if you don't write the script.

ML: Exactly.

GA: Why do you think you were chosen to direct Undercover Brother? I mean, given that you like to write your own stuff and it's very different from The Best Man. Why you? There are other people who've done action movies?

ML: That's what I was trying to tell them too. I tried not to get this job to tell you the truth. I didn't think I was ready for it. I was a little scared of failure, special effects, visual effects and the stunts.

GA: *So they approached you anyway and offered you the film.*

ML: Oh, yeah, mind you when I saw the animated Web series I thought it was hysterical and I said, "I've got be involved." I told my executive that when they got up and running with it, I wanted to be considered and come to find out they were thinking of me anyway so, I don't know, why am I the person? Because I think that "Undercover Brother" is a character that has a lot of dignity and I think I've proven that I give Black characters dignity in movies, I give them dimensionality. All the action stuff, the explosions and what not, a lot of that is not in your control anyway as a director. You tell them what you want and they can produce it for you and I'm a lot less intimidated now than I was before. I think that's what they really wanted—somebody who would work well with actors and who was communicative, not a control nut and who had a strong vision for the film. When I made my pitch for it, I felt like I was "Undercover Brother" because I had been around plenty of white people who had told me, "I don't think of you as Black." So I know what this is like and I know what it's like to want to make a change and bust out as this hero and say, "You jive turkey motherfucker."

GA: *[Laughs] What are your favorite films?*

ML: I have a bunch of them like *The Godfather*. *Parenthood* is one of my favorite films of all time. *When Harry Met Sally* is one of my favorite films of all time. *The Big Chill*. Spike is one of my favorite directors—*Do the Right Thing* and I've got to say *Bamboozled*. It's brilliant. Norman Jewison is also one of my favorite directors. Steven Soderbergh and Ang Lee are two filmmakers I'm really trying to pattern my career after right now. Because he's a great filmmaker, a great storyteller and he does a number of different things. You don't know what the hell he's coming out with next. It could be a big budget movie or it could be small. He can do it all and I really respect that. I'm digging him right now.

GA: *What advice do you have for people who want to direct?*

ML: You have to study the craft, you have to watch a lot of movies. You don't have to go to film school. I needed to go to film school because I like a structured environment.

GA: *But if you don't study the craft in school, watch a lot of movies.*

ML: Study and watch a lot of movies. Write, write, write, write, write, write, write what you know, write from your heart. Don't start off writing what you think is going to sell. You have to write for the love of filmmaking, for the love of wanting to work with people. You have to be open to ideas, you have to be collaborative. Directing is hard work and success is not going to come over night. And you have to recognize whether or not you can do it. Whether or not you have talent in that area or ability in that area. Filmmaking is a long process, it's a difficult process and it's a harsh process and you may not be a good writer, you may not be a good director. You've got to be organized and you've got to be able to think on your feet. There are so many things you have to know and learn. It's a hard craft.

Gina Prince-Bythewood

I first interviewed Gina Prince-Bythewood along with her talented director husband, Reggie Rock Bythewood (*Dancing in September* for HBO, 2000) for *Savoy* magazine in December of 2000. Warm, focused and unassuming, the Pacific Grove, California, native is doing her part to broaden the canvas of story fare for African American cinema.

In the winter of 2000, Prince-Bythewood made her feature-film directorial debut with her original screenplay *Love and Basketball*, which starred Sanaa Lathan, Omar Epps, Alfre Woodard and Harry J. Lennix. The New Line Cinema release won the Humanitas Prize and an Independent Spirit Award for Best First Screenplay. She next directed Wesley Snipes and Lathan in the HBO original movie, *Disappearing Acts* (2000), a film based on the novel by best-selling author Terry McMillan.

Prince-Bythewood got her start in the entertainment industry on the small screen. After completing film school at UCLA in 1991, she joined the staff of the popular sitcom, *A Different World*, as an apprentice writer. She became a staff writer after one season. Later she worked on the critically acclaimed Fox dramatic series *South Central* (1994) and also wrote and directed the CBS Schoolbreak Special *What About Your Friends* (1995), winning an NAACP Image Award for Best Children's Special and two Emmy nominations for writing and directing. She's also written for the television shows *Sweet Justice* (1994), *Courthouse* (1995) and *Felicity* (1998).

She is presently a producer on her husband's second film, *Biker Boyz* (2003), and writing her next screenplay.

— — —

GA: Tell me about growing up in Pacific Grove, California. Were you a creative child?

GP: I was adopted by a white father and Salvadoran mother, and I have an adopted brother who's also Black. In terms of creativity, I wrote a lot of stories growing up—I was always told that I had an overactive imagination. What's amazing is that when my parents came to the premiere of Love and Basketball they brought one of my stories I'd written when I was about ten—they'd framed it—and gave it to me. Writing stories is where I think my creativity began.

GA: Having been adopted—and by mixed parents—did that feed your creativity?

GP: Growing up, you don't realize that things are that different or it's not that big a deal. It's when you get older and people start commenting on it that you suddenly realize that things are different. I've definitely drawn on a lot of stuff as I've gotten older in terms of writing. As a child, I also loved to watch TV. TV was an escape for me. I remember my family used to watch The Donny and Marie Show, and one a day while flipping through the channels we came across Different Strokes, and that was it. It was "This is our family," and from that day on we'd watch Different Strokes. One of the other defining things, I believe, for me was when our TV broke and my parents decided not to buy another one. I then started reading a lot and I'd go to the library every week and check out about fifteen books. I read a lot of teenage books. I really liked the S. E. Hinton books and read all of them. I must've read The Outsiders fifteen times. I also liked Judy Blume, who wrote Are You There God? It's Me, Margaret.

GA: When did you decide that you wanted to be a writer?

GP: When I started getting into soap operas during my junior or senior year of high school, I started seriously thinking about writing. I used to watch about five soaps a day, and I'd read Soap Opera Digest. One day I read an article about how much money soap writers made and I thought, "Wow, shoot, that's what I'm going to do." It's actually funny, too, because I remember reading in Soap Opera Digest a long time ago about a character named R. J. on Another World. I think the title was something like "Why is R. J. Sexless?" He was a Black character and he was sexless because Black characters weren't allowed to have relationships and sex, and it was back to the whole racial issue. Come to find out years later that my husband Reggie was R. J.

GA: Oh, get out of here! [Laughs]

GP: Oh, no, it was very funny. I always bring that up to him.

GA: [Laughs] That's hilarious. Now, for college you went to UCLA. Tell me about that.

GP: I was an athlete back then and I'd been recruited by a couple of schools to play basketball, but UCLA had not recruited me. By that time, however, I'd decided that I wanted to go to film school, but none of the other schools that recruited me had film programs, so I decided to go to UCLA despite not being recruited to play basketball. I still had my goal of writing soap operas, but at UCLA you can't officially enroll in the film school until you're a junior, but I used to hang out there all the time and I'd volunteer on some of the student films. One day when I was working on one of these student films, carrying a bunch of film equipment on a set, I had an epiphany and suddenly it hit me that this was what I was supposed to do with my life—not carry equipment, but making films and being on sets. That's when I suddenly wanted to be a director as opposed to a writer.

GA: You later enrolled in the film program, but I understand that UCLA's film school didn't accept you at first. Tell me about that.

GP: Yeah, they only took about twenty out of seven hundred people, but I was just sure I was going to get in. Again, I'd been hanging out at the film school for two years, I knew a lot of the professors and it was the only thing that I knew I wanted to do. I just knew I was going to get in, and the day I got rejected was one of the worst days of my life. I was pretty lost for a couple of days, then I just decided that I would appeal the decision. I went to talk to an advisor at the film school, and he of course said that no one had ever appealed and not to bother. But I wrote a letter anyway, and at the time I was an intern on Bill Cosby's movie *Ghost Dad*, which was basically just hanging out on the set, talking to different people every day—a kind of an unofficial intern. So Bill allowed me to put his name on the letter, along with the exec producer and a professor of education at UCLA, Gordon Berry. I sent the letter to the head of the film department, and in a couple of days she called and told me I got in.

GA: Nothing like having Bill Cosby to recommend you. How did you meet him?

GP: I met him when he came to a track meet, and for some reason we just hit it off. So on weekends we would train on the track, then I'd watch football at his house with his wife and kids.

GA: What was film school like, and would you recommend it?

GP: I highly recommend it, because it gives you a chance to grow and make mistakes. You have all this access to free equipment, free film and free food, because when you're shooting a student film, merchants around town give you stuff, and again, it's a chance to make mistakes and a chance to learn from people in the business. You also get to make films you can use as your calling card. You're surrounded by people who are interested in the same things that you're interested in—you just talk about film and debate film, and I learned a lot. Granted, writing-wise I learned more actually writing on A Different World and listening to Reggie's [Rock Bythewood] advice. But in terms of directing, I came out of film school with a good student film called Stitches, and was all set to be a director. There was hype around my film and it got me some good meetings around town, but I had nothing to talk about because I had no screenplay. All of the meetings ended with, "As soon as you write something, let us read it." I had nothing, so all of those great contacts were just wasted.

GA: And you ended up writing for TV on A Different World. How did that happen?
GP: I was so lucky to get that first job on A Different World, because it was my favorite show at the time and it's probably the only show I could've written for because I was only twenty-two years old—it's just amazing how little you know at that age. I told Bill Cosby what I was interested in doing, and he introduced me to Yvette Lee Bowser, who was a story editor on A Different World at the time. I met with Yvette, showed her my student film script, and she got me a meeting with the executive producer of the show, Susan Fales-Hill, and it was a horrible meeting. I was so unprepared, because I'd expected to meet with only one person—instead, there were about four or five producers in the room. There I was trying to sell myself but not knowing how to do so. I was basically giving them monosyllabic answers when they asked me questions, and I know I was doing badly, because Yvette wasn't even looking at me anymore.

GA: That must have been rough. What did learn from that experience?
GP: You have to be prepared and ready with just a ton of ideas, energy and enthusiasm. Because, one, in TV they're looking at you as someone they're going to spend twelve to fourteen hours a day with and they need to know that they want to be in the room that long with you. With film, they're paying you a lot of money and want to know if you're worth it: Can you come through? Can I trust millions of dollars with you? But about two months after that meeting, I got a call from the show because the intern they ended up hiring was messing up and spending more time at the craft services table than working.

GA: Incredible twist for you. You did some additional TV. Tell me about that.
GP: Yes, after A Different World I worked on South Central and that was one of my best experiences, because it was essentially all Black writers except for one of the show's cocreators, Michael Weithorn. The show was pretty much a drama with jokes, which I was so excited about, and I felt like

we were doing something important. I had a great time on that show, but unfortunately it was canceled due to controversy. Every week we'd get a bunch of phone calls from Black folks saying that we were misrepresenting them. From there I really wanted to move into drama, and was lucky enough to get on a drama show called Sweet Justice starring Cicely Tyson and Melissa Gilbert. I learned a lot there, but that was also when I started getting the itch to direct, because I found it hard to spend a month on a script only to have to turn it over to a hired director who wasn't reading my stage direction and who was more concerned about staying on the shooting schedule than having something to say. So it was getting more and more frustrating with my having to sneak around and talk to the actors myself about the script, which you're not supposed to do. I felt like ninety percent of my time was spent arguing to save every little word in my script. I was tired of fighting and felt that if I were directing I wouldn't have to fight.

GA: How did you get the confidence to just leave a TV career to pursue film? It's easy to talk about switching careers, but it takes guts to actually do it.

GP: It was hard, because after Sweet Justice I had planned to take off some time so that I could write a screenplay, but I got nervous and then Court House came up, and on paper it was a really good show and I was excited about it. I thought, "Well, I'll do one more season of TV, then I'll take the year off." Fortunately, the show only lasted for nine episodes. I couldn't be scared after that, because I was so frustrated after Court House. I had to control my own stuff, and from there I took time off to write the screenplay. I thought it was only going to be a year, but that year quickly turned into two years. But the great thing about TV is the pay—they pay you so much money, you can afford to take time off.

GA: What was your approach to writing a feature-length screenplay versus writing for TV?

GP: It's funny, because I kept saying that I was going to write a screenplay while I was in TV. I said, "How hard can it be? It's just two-hour-long TV scripts put together." It's obviously a different animal. I read books like How to Write a Movie in 21 Days by Viki King, which Reg recommended, as well as Making a Good Script Great and Creating Unforgettable Characters, both by Linda Seger. I also read Syd Field's book, but the structure of my screenplay Love and Basketball was different than the three-act structure that Syd Field preaches, so I knew I couldn't really follow that. The thing about How to Write a Movie in 21 Days is that it forces you to write, because my biggest problem was that I'd write for a couple of hours and then spend days rewriting what I had written in those two hours. I honestly must have rewritten the first scene in Love and Basketball for a week, and it never even made it into the final script.

GA: It's hard to build momentum that way.

GP: Oh, definitely, but it's so much easier to continue rewriting something, because it's something concrete and it's on the page. The best thing How to Write a movie in 21 Days taught me was to just keep writing and do what Reg and I call a "bullshit draft," where you just keep writing no matter what. The dialogue can be horrible, it may not make sense, but it's down on paper.

GA: Everyone in Hollywood seems to be writing a script on spec. How did you keep yourself motivated when it came to writing and rewriting the script?

GP: It was really, really hard, because writing a spec script is so difficult because there's no guarantee that anyone is ever going to make it, and pushing yourself to keep writing and rewriting and rewriting is very, very hard. You just have to keep telling yourself that someone's going to want this. Out of all the thousands of screenplays that are written, someone is going to want this one, and it's very hard to keep reminding yourself of that, and truthfully the way I got through it was by sitting, fantasizing about my cast and the premiere. I worked on the script for about a year and a half and completed about fifteen drafts of the script before I finally went out and tried to sell it, and everybody turned it down. The biggest note that I got from most people was that it was too soft.

GA: Do you think some of those responses were due to the fact that they weren't used to seeing Black people in those settings?

GP: I think so. I went out with the script just as Soul Food [the movie directed by George Tillman, Jr.] was doing so well in the theaters. I thought that Love and Basketball would be an easy sell, and it was really shocking to me that no one wanted it. Production companies like Magic Johnson's were interested, but once we got to the studio level they weren't feeling it, and that was a hard thing, because I feel like we keep having to prove ourselves despite the success of films like Waiting to Exhale and Soul Food. We still get the same argument that Black dramas don't sell. I also went to 40 Acres and a Mule and met with producer Sam Kitt—he gave me a bunch of notes that I totally disagreed with and I told him, "Thanks, but no thanks." After having everyone turn it down, there was nowhere else to go. We thought about trying to attach some actors and trying to generate interest that way, but that's difficult when the script is not set up at a studio. So it got to the point where it was just dead, I didn't know what to do—it was very depressing.

GA: Then came the Sundance Institute and everything changed. Tell me about that.

GP: Two people on two different days had meetings with the heads of Sundance and mentioned my name and my script. Sundance called me, which was great because the Sundance Writers Lab was a program I had wanted to be involved with. So I submitted my script and got an interview, and I had one of my best meetings and I got in the program. That was such a great moment, because I felt like they gave my script another life. We had these amazing advisors there and to hear that writers like Scott Frank [Get Shorty, Minority Report] and Paul Attanasio [Donne Brasco, Sphere, Quiz Show] liked my script—it was validation. I got a lot of good notes on the script, and one of the best comments came from Scott, who was my last advisor. He told me that after the program I should take a break and not work on the script, but instead just write about the characters, which is what I did. Later, Lynn Auerbach and Michelle Satter at Sundance called and told me about Sundance's staged reading program and wanted to know if I wanted my script read, and I of course said that I did. It was about mid-March, and they asked me if the script would be ready by May. I said that it would, but I hadn't done one damn thing on it since the lab, but I promised them that it would be done.

At the same time, I was applying for the Sundance Director's Lab, and to do that while rewriting an entire script [Laughs]—that was a hellish time, boy. I remember one week when I didn't sleep at all, but it was a great diet—I lost so much weight because I was writing all day and all night. It started to be surreal, like the movie Groundhog Day—I kept finding myself up at three and four in the morning working on the same exact problem in the script, and then I'd hear the newspaper hit the door. It was so weird. I was literally not sleeping at all. But I was looking at the script and knowing that it was going to be read by actors, and suddenly I became aware of every word. I thought that what I was saying had to actually mean something, and the people at Sundance laughed because every day they would get new pages of the script from me up to the day of the reading. It was just ridiculous. But I did the reading and it just went so well. I had such a great cast—Sanaa Lathan played Monica and Mekhi Phifer played Quincy and Brandon Hammond from Soul Food and Jurnee Smollett from Eve's Bayou played the young Quincy and Monica, and it was such a great night.

GA: But there's an interesting story behind Sanaa doing the reading right?

GP: Yeah, well, Tamala Jones was originally supposed to do the reading, but got sick the night before, and I was in a huge panic and Reggie suggested Sanaa, who he'd seen audition when he was working on NY Undercover. So I called her father, director/producer Stan Lathan, whom I knew very well, and asked him if Sanaa was available, and he called me back and said that she was supposed to do a staged reading for her theater company but had canceled to do my reading. I said, "Stan, I've never met her, I've never even seen her. I asked if she was AVAILABLE." Now I'm kind of stuck, so I called Sanaa and told her that I needed her to audition, and in my mind it was perfectly legitimate because I'd never seen her and didn't know what she looked like. But in her mind, and we laugh about it now, she thought, "Is this girl crazy? I just blew my relationship with this theater company to do a reading, and now she wants me to audition?"

So we finally met and she read a couple of scenes and she was good—not great, but I felt she could do it. However, there was still one other woman I wanted to audition. But as Reg and I were driving I tried to contact the other woman and she wasn't home, so I thought, "I guess it'll be Sanaa." I drove back to Sanaa, and again, to me I was giving her this gift, my screenplay, my baby, and to her it was just a reading of something that might be fun. When we had the rehearsal the day of the reading, Sanaa was awful, and so I was going to fire her that night. I called Reggie in a panic, then I talked to one of the actors who was a very good friend of mine and I asked her how to fire Sanaa because I'd never fired anybody before.

Finally, I just said that I'm going to have to just go for it and I gave her this big impassioned speech the night of the reading—which she says meant nothing to her—but I'd like to think it did a little something. I was sitting with Reg in the audience and with the first five words out of Sanaa's mouth she was this totally different person, and I just relaxed. Afterwards, I couldn't stop hugging her—she was so great. If Tamala hadn't gotten sick I never would've had Sanaa do the reading. Had she not done the reading, I wouldn't have had her great performance in my head. Sanaa had never played basketball before, so she'd never even had a chance to audition for the film, but it was only because I'd seen her work at the reading that she was considered, and everyone else who auditioned had to compete with that.

GA: *Spike Lee's company 40 Acres was at the reading. What happened?*
GP: The audience thought the cast was great, and hearing it come alive was a big moment. Afterwards, Sam Kitt from 40 Acres came up to my agent and said, "I want to buy this." But it was funny, because at that point I actually pulled back and said that I wanted to take the time to make sure it was perfect, because in my mind I didn't want the script to have to go through a development process. I didn't want to have to take a bunch of notes. I told him that I wanted to submit the script so that when they took it to a studio it would be in the best shape possible and a done deal—they'd buy the script and then we'd shoot it. I also knew that I had gotten in the Sundance Director's Lab and had that coming up, so I told them that I'd give them the script after I completed the lab.

GA: *Tell me about the Sundance Director's Lab and how it played a part in the development of the project.*
GP: The Director's Lab is great. It gives you a chance to shoot three to four scenes of your screenplay, and you cast it as well, so you can have two or three actors come to Utah. But Sanaa and

Mekhi, who had done the reading in L.A., were unavailable, so Richard T. Jones and Tamala Jones did it, along with Tina Lifford. And the Director's Lab is also great because you have these great advisors. I had Kathy Bates, Blythe Danner, John Toll, who is a great cinematographer, and Michael Ritchie. These people watch your work, give you notes and teach you about directing, cinematography and editing. It just doesn't get any better than that. Getting your script on film just makes your screenplay real—you're a director, you're creating and it's just a great feeling. At the end of the week, you sit there with all of the other people at Sundance, you show your scenes and look at what everyone else is doing. It's just so much fun; it's such a supportive and nurturing environment.

GA: In terms of casting the film, Spike Lee, who was an executive producer, wanted a real basketball player to play Monica, but you didn't. Tell me about that.

GP: Spike was adamant. This is the guy who cast NBA star Ray Allen in He Got Game, so he felt that you had to cast a ballplayer, and truthfully, I felt the exact same way—I'll hire an actor with a name, like Omar Epps, then hire an unknown ballplayer who can act. And I looked and looked, and it really came down to two people—ballplayer Neisha Butler and Sanaa. Neisha had an acting coach, while Sanaa had a basketball coach, and they were competing against each other for the part.

GA: And the good old craft of acting won out after all.

GP: Yeah, it finally did, you know.

GA: I can't imagine not having Sanaa in that movie now.

GP: And yes, I had to adjust some of the basketball sequences, but I never had to adjust any of the emotional moments, which would ultimately carry the film. Sanna worked her ass off, and as a director she's the type of actor you dream about working with. You want someone who's willing to fight for a part in your movie and who believes in it that much. There was trust that had to build between us, and now we have that. I had to trust that she would work her ass off and train and become a ballplayer, and she practiced six days a week for three months. I didn't even play that much when I was playing ball.

GA: What was your process of working with actors? Had you studied acting?

GP: Well, a great thing about the Director's Lab at Sundance is that for one whole day you have to be an actor and actually perform a scene in front of everybody. But it also freaked me out. I kept thinking of ways to fake an illness or how I could fake something and get out of it, because acting in front of people is probably one of the biggest fears I had. I learned so much in that day in terms of being an actor. You're so naked up there, and you don't know it until you're suddenly doing a scene in front of a bunch of people—it's so nerve-racking. So I learned a lot about being more sensitive, about giving the actor time to get ready and to get in the moment before doing a scene. In film school, I felt an actor was wasting time when they said that they needed a moment.

GA: What was it like working with the great Alfre Woodard?

GP: Alfre is amazing. She's so meticulous with props—down to the food she's working with in a scene. She gave us the menu of what she was cooking, and it had to be the real food. At first glance you could say, "Isn't this excessive?" But it really is all about the details, and she taught me that.

GA: Overall, you had a great cast. How important is casting in a film?

GP: Oh, it's eighty-five percent of the movie. Viewers can forgive a lot of things—low light, a bad camera angle, crossing the line—but they won't forgive bad acting. At the end of the day, if I've totally messed up the shooting of something, at least I know I have the acting and I could play it all in the master shot. I know it's on the page, but I also know I have the actors to give life to the words.

GA: What do you look for in actors in the audition? What is that thing that tells you that this person has it to make my movie work?

GP: It's pretty easy to tell a really good actor. It's like watching Sanaa's auditions for the film [not the Sundance reading mentioned earlier]. She was just at a level above everyone else. For the role of Monica's sister, played by Regina Hall, it was between Regina and Tisha Campbell, and both were really good. It just would have been a different relationship with Tisha and Sanaa. It was a choice. Sometimes someone just walks in the room and you know it. With Kyla Pratt, the first couple of words out of her mouth and there was no question—this is little Monica, and there is no one else who would be as good, it was so immediate. It took a little more time with little Quincy, but you could tell when Glendon Chatman walked in the room that there was something about him. Some people just have it—the thing where you want to watch them. It's exciting when you just know it immediately, but it's harder when you have to decide between two or three people. Then it's just about which direction you want to go, and you always wonder if you made the right choice or not.

GA: And what do actors need to be prepared to bring into the room?

GP: Be prepared and on time. An actress came in, and she was fumbling over the lines and she kept laughing and apologizing; "I'm sorry—I'm just a little out of it today." You know what, then? Bye. I see thirty, forty people a day. If you don't have it together, don't waste my time. Be professional. Some people come in and do a little small talk before the audition, and I don't mind that at all, because it gives me a little sense of who you are. My biggest thing is being on time. If I can make it on time with all the stuff I'm focusing on, then you can be on time. That's my biggest pet peeve. And being prepared doesn't mean knowing the script lines by memory, because actors have multiple auditions a day with a slim chance of getting a role, so who am I to say that you have to know it? I think that's a bit much to ask, but be able to show me some different things. Don't memorize the lines and perform them by rote so that you only know one way to do them. I may ask you to try it another way, that tells me if you can act or not. Can you go off of what your preconceived notion of what this scene was? Can you play it a totally different way? Can you take direction? Be ready for that as well, and if you make a mistake, just go for it. If you've made a choice, go with that choice and if the choice, is completely wrong, commit to it. I can always say that what you did was wrong and tell you to try it another way. Just don't come in passive. Go for it and own it.

GA: What was the budget for Love and Basketball?

GP: The budget was $14 million. Initially, I thought we needed $10 million, and that's what we said in the meeting with Mike DeLuca at New Line, and he said, "No, you're going to need a little more." Then it was going to be about $12 million, but casting Alfre, Omar and Dennis Haysbert pushed the cost up a little more. New Line was so great, especially Mike DeLuca. That's still so amazing to me. That it was my first film, they didn't know if I could direct, they didn't know me at all, and they gave me this money and trusted me with it. That's another thing to balance when you do a studio movie. A lot of people bad-mouth the studio. I got some notes on the script that I didn't agree with, and I fought those to the death. Then there were a couple things that I ultimately compromised on because I didn't think it would negatively affect the film. I had to remember again they're giving me $14 million, so who am I to suddenly say, "Fuck you guys," and shut them out of the process? That's just wrong. You have to compromise. Don't ever go against your vision, and don't ever do something you'll always regret. On the other hand, at least listen to the folks who are giving you the money, because they may have something good to say and you have a responsibility—you have to make the money back.

GA: *Was shooting in Spain expensive?*

GP: That was a shock, too, but when we actually broke it down was the same amount to shoot in the back lot at Universal as it was to shoot in Spain. That's because Tyra Banks plays a flight attendant in the film and we had her wear a Virgin Airlines uniform. For that we got about eight free first-class Virgin tickets to Spain. That helped the budget a lot. Budget-wise, a good chunk went to the cast. We had a good number of shooting days at forty-five days, which is a lot, and a lot of cameras because of the basketball sequences and the extras. Getting all those extras there was the hardest thing, because you kind of had to shoot all of the basketball stuff in the arena in one day. We had twenty-five hundred extras for one day, so I shot everything I needed. And I storyboarded all of the basketball sequences, and I also storyboarded probably the first two days of work, because the first couple of days—the crew, producers, studio, actors—they're all looking at me saying, "Does this chick know what she's talking about?" And you don't want to lose people the first day. You don't want to look a mess. So I had it all storyboarded. I knew exactly what I wanted going into that day, and after the first day we actually ended up a day ahead of schedule.

So that sets the tone. It's very, very important to be prepared your first couple of days. It helps your confidence as well, because you know exactly what you want. So as it went on I didn't have to storyboard everything. I'd always be the first person on set. The director of photography [DP] and I would meet an hour before everyone else was supposed to be there, we'd relax, have breakfast and then walk the set and talk about my shot list. And that just helped a lot. Also, arriving an hour early gives you a chance to be quiet and get your thoughts together for that day. It gives you a chance to eat because after that you're not really eating and it gives you and the DP a chance to hang and talk and possibly watch dailies.

GA: *How did you handle twenty-five hundred extras? In the movie they really seemed like true basketball fans.*

GP: I let the first assistant director handle that most of the time—the first assistant director handles the background. You really have to watch, though. I was watching a shot and I noticed this guy sitting there like a deaf mute in one of the big basketball sequences.

GA: *[Laughs] And it's a one-point game now.*

GP: Or you have the idiots who are leaning into camera and waving, which kills an entire take. Extras have the worst job in the world. They're treated like crap. I definitely talk to the assistant directors about showing respect to them, because they do have the worst job. They're there all day long, they are last in the food line, they sit outside when it's cold or they sit outside when it's hot, and then in an instant they have to, in our case, scream their heads off or that kind of thing. But again, you're there for that job, and if you're not going to do it right then you're going to be replaced.

GA: *Talk about the transition from* Love and Basketball *to* Disappearing Acts.
GP: It was hard, because that was my first time directing something that I hadn't written. I loved the book *Disappearing Acts*. It was one of my favorite books, and still is actually, and I was excited to direct it. If I had to choose anything to follow up *Love and Basketball* with, it would have been *Disappearing Acts*. However, I wish I had taken a break between films. I started *Disappearing Acts* when I was in postproduction on *Love and Basketball*, and I'll never do that again. I needed a break and didn't realize it. I was just riding the high, and I decided to do it. I was a fan of the actors involved and I liked the screenwriter, Lisa Jones, but the script still needed some work and I felt I'd have time to work with her on it. But it's just not the same directing something you haven't written, because it's almost as if it's not yours. When you've written it, no one knows the story better than you do, and that's just a great and comfortable feeling. In this case, it was Terry McMillan's vision first and then Lisa's vision. It just wasn't the same—you feel more like a direc- tor for hire than a filmmaker. Again, I'm not saying that the film doesn't have my stamp on it, because I love the look of the film. I had a great DP, Tammy Reicher, a great production crew, and there are a lot of things I like about it. I don't love it like *Love and Basketball*, even though I can't watch that anymore because it just bores me to death—I've watched it over a hundred times. [Laughs] But still, when I watch *Disappearing Acts* it doesn't feel a hundred percent, mine and there were a lot of negative things to the experience.

GA: *What were some of your negative experiences?*
GP: Well, it was difficult because the process is very important to me—showing up on time, respecting everyone involved. That's all I really ask for, and I mean, let's have fun. Filmmaking is a hard enough process as it is, so let's have fun doing it. I love doing it, and to not have fun is a very disheartening thing. It drags the process down if you're not having fun. God, you're working so long and so hard, you need some levity and you need a nice, light comfortable set, and when someone brings that down, it brings everyone down, and ultimately it's the director's job to not let that happen. There are things I would do differently now, but it's a learning process, and one of the big things I learned is why some directors work with the same actors a lot, like Paul Thomas Anderson and the Farrelly Brothers. They work with the same people because

you surround yourself with people who love the process and people you can have fun with. It's exciting to put these people in different roles, but you always know you're going to get a great performance, and have a great time and I really see why that's important now and why people do it.

GA: *What are you favorite movies?*

GP: Martin Scorsese's *Goodfellas* (1990) to me is almost a perfect movie. I like the camera work; it's creative, yet it's not showy. The camera tells so much of the story, yet as a viewer, you're not so focused on it. But if you sit and break it down you can see how this high-angle shot tells the viewer something, even subconsciously. When Scorsese follows the characters all the way through the restaurant in the opening sequence, it's not just about a cool shot, it's actually furthering the story. The voice-over, the freeze-frames, the lighting, the music, I just love that movie. All the elements seem to come together. It's like a visual feast, and it's a great story. For the storytelling and the performances, I love *Broadcast News* by James L. Brooks (1987). That is one of my top five favorite films. I could watch that over and over and over again. I just watched it yesterday. *The Graduate* (1967) is a film that I saw in film school, and that's the first time I realized the importance of music and the soundtrack in a film and the feelings that a song can evoke. That's another case where music is pushing the story forward. A scene could be giving you something but the music that you put behind it can totally change the tone. *Central Station* (1998) and *Life Is Beautiful* (1997) are up there for me too, although I can't technically say that they're up there with my favorites, but before I saw those films I'd really lost faith in Hollywood films for a while. I'd just seen Con Air (1997) and that film was so empty, and I was so angry when I left the theater because I had wasted two hours of my life—the money didn't even matter. I just walked out of there empty, because it was writing by numbers and you could dictate every supposed turning point. It was just so disappointing, and I said that I was not going to see action films again because there's nothing new you can do with the genre because this is what we're getting. So I didn't see movies for a while, and then I saw *Life Is Beautiful* and *Central Station*, and that just restored my faith in what film could be—film as art and what it could evoke from a viewer. I cried at the end of *Central Station*, and I rarely cry at movies. And I didn't see movies after that for a while, because I didn't want to let go of the feeling those movies gave me.

GA: *How did The Graduate influence your selection of music for Love and Basketball?*

GP: I paid attention to it a lot more and realized what I loved in movies and what I disliked in movies. I don't like it when music is arbitrary and you can tell it's about putting in a cool song in at that moment. I think the song should have a purpose and it should be there to evoke an emotion. Even if it's just a song playing on the radio, there has to be something about it. So it was really fun putting together the soundtrack for *Love and Basketball* because it was going back to high school and college and saying, "What were we listening to at the time," putting on many different songs against different scenes and seeing what you're feeling while watching it. I remember the scene at the high school spring dance. I had originally wanted to use Keith Sweat's *Make It Last Forever*. It seemed like the perfect song for that moment. But the day of shooting I had Roger's *I Wanna Be Your Man*. That song pulls something out of that scene. I feel something every time I watch it. And I didn't get that with other songs that I thought would have been perfect, like *Make it Last Forever*.

GA: *How has motherhood affected you creatively?*

GP: You know what it is? It makes you more conscious about what you are putting out into the world. It's also another experience that I draw on. Like on *Disappearing Acts*, the character was pregnant, and if I knew then what I know now about pregnancy, that would have totally shaded some of the rewrite that we did about her character and even some of her behavior, because I would have known how deep having a child is. And especially in her case, ending up a single mother.

GA: *And what's it like being married to a director?*

GP: Writing is so hard and a lot of times you just get miserable because you're not flowing right or you're not happy with what you're writing and you kind of go inside yourself a little bit until you can fight your way out of it. I know I go through that and Reggie goes through that, and it's good to know that's what's going on—as opposed to thinking that the person's mad at you because they're so quiet or not really talking, you know what's going on. It's also great having someone, whose opinion you respect more than anyone else's, read your script, give you notes and their thoughts, and just someone who supports you.

GA: *It must be awesome being married to someone who understands the rhythm of writing and creating art, because most people just don't get it.*

GP: They think it's easy.

GA: *[Laughs] Yes. They equate writing a screenplay with writing a high school term paper. What's it like being a woman in Hollywood?*

GP: I've been fortunate in that I don't think it has hindered me in any way, and maybe it's actually helped me, because there are so few female directors—that there are some projects where people feel this should have a female voice to it. I get those offers, so I think it's a good thing.

GA: *What advice do you have for aspiring directors?*
GP: My first piece of advice is to write a screenplay, and the second piece of advice is that the first thing you come out with says so much about you, so choose wisely.

Crossing Over

FROM THE BLACK EXPERIENCE

AND BEYOND

Bill Duke

Bill Duke is known for being in front of the camera as much as he is known for working behind it. As a director, actor, producer and writer, he has over forty credits to his name.

Born in Poughkeepsie, New York, Duke made his theatrical directing debut with the 1991 *Rage in Harlem*, based on the Chester Himes novel. The film starred Forest Whitaker, Gregory Hines, Danny Glover and Robin Givens. Duke went on to direct the feature films *The Cemetery Club* (1993), *Sister Act 2: Back in the Habit* (1993) and the $35 million budgeted Harlem crime drama *Hoodlum* (1997), which he also executive-produced.

Duke also brandishes his directing talents on the small screen, where his impressive list of credits includes the film *America's Dream: The Boy Who Painted Christ Black* (1996), for which he received a CableAce Award, and the pilot for the 1990s Fox series *New York Undercover*. He also directed award-winning segments for such 1980s hit shows as *Cagney and Lacey*, *Hill Street Blues*, *Knot's Landing*, *Dallas*, *Falcon Crest* and *Miami Vice*.

His teleplay *The Killing Floor* (1984), which he directed for *American Playhouse*, earned ten film festival awards and was chosen to compete in the Critic's Week of judging at the 1985 Cannes Film Festival.

Duke is a graduate of Boston University and New York University's Tisch School of the Arts and completed two years of study at the American Film Institute.

– – – –

GA: *Tell me about growing up and how creativity played a role in your life and your family's life.*

BD: Well, my mother had a beautiful voice as a singer; my father along with uncles were a gospel singing group. They gave it up because they couldn't make a living at it, but they did try, and I think that rubbed off on me somehow. We were a pretty poor family, lower-middle working class, blue-collar Black people. My parents had grade school educations and insisted that my sister and I have higher educations, because they did not want us to suffer through the same things that they'd gone through. My father could not afford to take us to the movies when I was young, maybe from the ages of five or six to eight or nine—we went to the movies very seldom. His way of taking us to the movies was to have my mother pop a large bag of popcorn, and we'd go down to Main St. in Poughkeepsie, New York, where I was born, and sit in the car. My mother and father would sit in the front and we would sit in the back seat, and we'd watch people and eat popcorn. It's like the world was a movie for us. My father used to say, "Now, what do you think that old man does for a living?" And we would guess, then my father would say, "Well, how can you tell? How do you know?" We'd say, "We just kind of feel . . . ." Then he'd say, "Look at his shoes and look at his hands. See his hands? Look at his face. Look at his tattered coat." He was a great observer of human behavior and human nature. I didn't know at the time, but he was teaching me about character, he was teaching me how to observe character, and about what creates a character from actually using life as an experience itself. Then I was kind of goofy and tall.

When I was fourteen I was around six feet tall, really awkward, not popular, introverted, and I started writing my thoughts down. I used to write my ideas and stories down on paper, and I'd keep a little journal. One day when I was junior in high school—I was always daydreaming, not paying attention—and I was writing in my journal and my English teacher took my journal away from me. She snatched it and said, "I'm taking this. Pay attention from now on." I really hated her. I really, really hated her for an entire semester, and I was rebellious. I did the work, but I never spoke to her. At the end of the semester she came to me with this package. She put it on my little desk, and I looked at her and she said, "Open it." I opened the package and it was the *American Poetry Journal*. She had entered my poetry, and I'd won first prize.

GA: *That's an incredible story.*

BD: True story. It was the first time that I had received a reaffirmation that what I felt in my head had value to anybody else outside of me. My English teacher was a major force, in addition to my father, in terms of validating my creative instincts. Last but not least were the stories my family told. We used to sit around, and my mother, father and uncles and aunts would tell ghost stories and we'd be terrified. We'd be terrified!

GA: *Sounds like they had imaginations.*

BD: [Laughs] Yeah. They would scare us, then they'd put us to bed and we'd be shaking. It was a very rich, rich childhood of folklore and observation from my father and reaffirmations by people who were strangers who God sent my way. But all that would disappear, because my family were pragmatists. In those days you didn't choose what you were going to do, you were told. My father said, "You're going to be a doctor," because doctors made money. So I went to junior college and took some anatomy and physiology courses, cutting up frogs and cats, and it was the most miserable experience. I don't really even think I can describe it, I just hated it so much. And I used to look at these kids who had this greed in their eyes, they'd take veins out and pop them and cut the cats open and enjoy the mystery of the insides. Anyway, I failed anatomy and physiology with a lower grade each time. My father said, "You're not really a doctor—you're still interested in writing, you're going to be a teacher. At least you're assured a living." So I got a scholarship to Boston University. I enjoyed writing creatively, but it's a different thing writing what you want to write than being forced to write something in a genre—we were studying old English, and Chaucer, and Beowulf—I had fallen asleep for the third time in my Chaucer class and the teacher kicked me out. My friend and roommate Ezra Hood said, "You've been talking all this time about being interested in drama. Why don't you try that?" So I went and auditioned with a piece I'd done in junior college. I was Emperor Jones for one show. That was the only acting I'd done, and I did a monologue from that and Lloyd Richards, who was the first Black director on Broadway, became my mentor. Lloyd was at BU at the time, and he brought me in his class.

GA: *Wow, Lloyd Richards as a mentor! You can't get much better than that.*

BD: I just talked to him two weeks ago. So the next semester at BU, I was dancing across Joe Gifford's ballet class in tights. Not a beautiful sight.

GA: [Laughs]

BD: Then I was in my element, because the same googly eyes I'd seen on the kids who were in my anatomy and physiology class I saw in myself, because I hit that part of myself that was real reaffirming in terms of my existence, and I understood that I had something to say and I wanted to find the ways to say it and perfect my craft. I then followed Lloyd to NYU because he went there after BU and he got me to NYU. He also got me my first professional job. I was at the Negro Ensemble Company with Douglass Turner Ward. I was in . . .

GA: Day of Absence?

BD: Day of Absence, yes.

GA: Great play. What character did you play?

BD: Rastas.

GA: Rastas. Funny character.

BD: And I was one of the white citizens with whiteface on. It was a great start, a great beginning. Then for many, many years in New York City I wrote and directed and produced my own plays and worked with Woodie King and Jean Franco Theater, Joe Papp, and at other places in New York. I worked all the time, but I couldn't make a living. You worked, but there was no money in the theater in those days. Lloyd again, he saw that I was floundering and said, "Bill, why are you wasting your time here? I'm going out to L.A. and I'm going to direct a thing called Gold Watch (1976) for PBS [part of a series called Visions], and I need an assistant." He didn't really need an assistant, but he saw that I needed something. I love him to this day, because without him I don't know what I'd be doing. But he brought me out here, and I was his assistant on two shows, then I got an agent out here. I started acting, and shortly after that I got a TV movie of the week or something and I was on a couple of other shows, like Charlie's Angels, Starsky and Hutch, little bit parts.

GA: Those were very popular shows.

BD: Yeah, they were popular, and I made more money on one show than I made in a whole year almost in New York. Then I got the film Car Wash (1976) with Michael Schultz. He's a great human being.

GA: I love your character in the film.

BD: Thank you. After Car Wash (1976), I did American Gigolo (1980) and some other things, like Santiago's Arc, I still wasn't directing theater a lot. At the time, I wasn't directing movies, I was directing theater. Then I had my own TV series called Palmerstown, U.S.A. and I was costarring in it and I thought I'd made it. I was making a lot of money and dada, dada, dada. But after the series was over I didn't work for two years. After that I decided that I'd better make use of my time and not just be an actor but be a businessperson. So I always wanted to direct films, but I was totally terrified of the equipment. Stage is different. It's like a static pilot, but with film you have the cameras and the cables and the crew and the lights. I said, "You'd better get over this thing." So I applied to the American Film Institute. I got in and stayed there for two years, dropped out of the business and made a film there called The Hero. I then tried to get into the television business, and what I found was that everyone would tell me that they'd give me a second job [directing], but not a first job.

That went on for a couple of years, and I was just so depressed and discouraged that I went to a meditation retreat. My agent called me after about two or three weeks—I was there and he said, "Bill, I've got a job. David Jacobs wants you to come and direct Knot's Landing [on CBS]." I said, "Get outta here!" So I rode down from Napa Valley, started preproduction and I was in my last day of preproduction when Joe Wildstein, the producer of the show, came up to me and said, "You know, Bill, I know that you're going to be a good addition to our directing team, because I can tell by your directing reel." I said, "What are you talking about?" He said, "Your directing reel you sent over." I said, "I never sent you a directing reel. I've only done this one little film called The Hero. Joe said, "Oh, my God." We went to Joe's office, and they had mixed my reel up with somebody else's reel. They wanted to fire me right there, because I had never directed anything other than my small film, The Hero. But we were shooting the next day, and they couldn't find a replacement quickly enough.

GA: That's incredible. Talk about serendipity.
BD: True story. True story. So they said, "Okay, okay. Be here at 6:30 in the morning." They were on my shoulder for the entire day—every shot I called they would go with the decision, but they were nervous. At the end of the day, though, they saw that I knew what I was doing and they let me shoot the whole show and they hired me back. I directed multiple episodes of Knot's Landing, and Falcon Crest. For Falcon Crest I used to go up to Napa Valley to shoot seven or eight shows with Holly Harris, another mentor of mine.

GA: What was it like making the transition from acting to directing?
BD: I had gone back and forth from directing and acting in theater, so I knew what that was about. But getting in front of a camera, when I first started, I was all over the place. The camera lens is small, so a lot happens in your eyes and your face. If you move too much, you'll move out of the frame of the camera. So I did a lot of that. I was very large, you know, "Ahh, yes! To be or not to be!"

GA: [Laughs]
BD: But I learned, and I was able to have a little success as an actor. Then years of television, directing all types of shows—pilots, movies of the week, different kinds of things—I wanted to

enter the feature world, so I wrote for PBS and I directed A Raisin in the Sun, with Danny Glover, and The Meeting, about a fictitious meeting between Malcolm X and Martin Luther King, Jr. That went really well, then from that Elsa Rassbach saw those things and there was a film called The Killing Floor that PBS was doing as a feature on American Playhouse. So she hired me to do that about the stockyards in Chicago being unionized in the early 1900s. I did that and New Line saw it and they gave me A Rage in Harlem, then from that to Deepcover, from that I did Cemetery Club, Sister Act 2, to Hoodlum and a number of things.

GA: I've noticed that many of your films are period pieces. Are you attracted to the past? What exactly attracts you to period films—there so many details involved?
BD: I think I'm a kind of a really detailed, planner-type person. I really get off in terms of the details of things. When you're doing a period piece, everything has to be changed. It's not only the process of creating reality out of thought, but if you're doing a period piece you're also putting it within the context of the past. So it offers the challenge of creating a believable past because everything has to be changed, from the plants, the fencing, the lines in the street, the cars, the gate, the clothing. When you see it change before your eyes, it's a powerful thing, because you're moving back in time. And the more convincing it is for you, the more convincing it becomes for your audience. History teaches you a great deal if you pay attention to it. History has a way of bringing its lessons to us in the fabric of stories that you may not think are directly related to today, but if you've got a universal story, it's applicable forever. So I enjoy the past, because the past has something that we can learn a great deal from. I love going back and digging and finding out what's universal that I can use today and that is still applicable tomorrow. That's why I like period pieces.

GA: What's your typical research process for a period piece?
BD: I have a researcher I've worked with for years, Gilbert Brownhart, and he's a master researcher. I've worked with other people, too, and what happens is that if it's a Black piece we'll go to the Schomburg Center [for Research in Black Culture in New York City] or we go to the library, the Internet and museums, and we bring forth a pictorial point first. We look at what the buildings, the clothing and the architecture were. What was the music of the period? What would the newspaper look like? What were they reporting? What was world news like? What was national news about? What was the news of that state about? What was the news of that city about? And most specifically, what was the news of that town about at that particular time?

GA: Very thorough.

BD: It's a very thorough research job, and by the time I'm finished with my research, I know pretty much every nuance of that period. I know the music, the photography, the philosophers, who the stage actors were, the film actors. I know who the directors were of that time. And we come up with a book that is almost as thick as a phone book. It's divided in terms of historical context. It gives you the world view, city view, national view, et cetera. Then we do wardrobe, makeup, cars, street signs, architecture, museums, music. And we get tapes of the music of the time, of the news broadcast of the time, and we hand out these books and these packets of tapes to every actor, every department head, so that we're all on the same page. In our production meetings we open our books and I say, "I want this to look like that." So they're not guessing. Their creativity works within the vision that I've created for the film from my research.

GA: *Having been a trained actor, as a director working with actors from different schools of training or no training, in addition to your book, what's the process of working with them in the context of a period piece, given that perhaps people behaved differently in the early 1900s or in the 1950s than they do today?*
BD: Well, I try to walk actors through the truth of the moment, whether they're trained or not trained. What's inescapable is that the writer has given me the director and you the actor a job to perform at that particular time in the script. Your mother just died and you loved her more than life itself, and you come into the funeral parlor for the wake and everybody else leaves the room and you're standing there with her body. The writer has said to you that I want you to tell her all of the things that you never said.

GA: *That's pretty heavy.*
BD: Now, as long as you give me that moment, you'll have no problem. And it's not the character's mother who's dead in that coffin, it's your mother who's dead in that coffin. So tell me how that feels.

GA: [Laughs] *Wow. Heavy.*
BD: Ain't no place else to go! No place else to go! Hell, where are you going to go?! [Laughs] It makes it very simple, you know. So wherever you come from, as long as you can do that job, and it is a job—it's not make-believe. It's a job. Actors are probably the most underestimated people in the world.

GA: *And writers are right behind them.*
BD: You know what I'm saying? It's very true. If the average person goes to a therapist to forget, writers and actors have to use those things every day to create reality. That's why I think many

actors are the way they are and many writers are the way they are—because we're doing things on a daily basis that the average person shuts away someplace. That's why I think it's important that actors and other creative people find another centering ability—the ability to center oneself. A lot of them try to do it through drugs and alcohol to feel better, but you have to find something much deeper and much more reliable that's not destructive to your very essence as a person.

GA: *What are some of the things that you do to stay centered?*
BD: I've been doing transcendental meditation since 1975, and I don't miss a day. I meditate every single day. I do yoga, tai chi and chi gong. Those are the four things that keep me centered, keep me going. I'm not suggesting on any level that I don't have my very, very difficult times—I'm a human being—but it's the resilience of your deep spirit that's important. Where does your elasticity come from? Where does your resilience come from, and it comes from, a commitment to something much larger than just the material realities of things, going deeper in oneself and cultivating that reality as deeply and as thoroughly as you possibly can.

GA: *Why are movies important to Bill Duke? Why does he continue to make them?*
BD: A friend of mine who is a reporter was asked this question by a student dissatisfied with a column he had written: "Do you report the news, or do you create the news?"

GA: *That's a pretty loaded question.*
BD: It gave him pause. [Laughs]

GA: *[Laughs] I'll have to write that one down.*
BD: [Laughs] Pretty interesting question, you know. And it made me think about myself and movies. Are we in the process of replicating reality or creating reality? I think it's a little bit of both. I think, particularly in the minds of children, that both music and film have a severe impact in terms of how people perceive themselves in the world around them. When you don't see your values depicted very clearly or people who've influenced you—your heroes—then you want to add your note to the chorus, so to speak, because your note is by no means no more important than anyone else's, but it is most certainly no less important than anyone else's. And for me, I just want to be able to add my creative voice and my perspective or reality, and my perspective of what's important to a rising tide of things that are antithetical to what I value. So that's why I continue to make movies. Movies, to me, are messages. There's a message in every movie, no matter what it is. They're saying something and they're very powerful. Some messages are subliminal and

some messages are overtly out there. I do believe that there should be room for many divergent kinds of opinions and ways of thinking about reality. And I think that many of the issues reflect the beauty of who we are, particularly as a people and a culture. By that I mean Black people, but I also mean people who have a different view of our society that is not necessarily in lockstep with everybody else, but is a little out-of-the-box thinking.

GA: *Could you give me an example of what you mean by that?*

BD: Well, I don't necessarily believe, for example, that Black directors should just direct Black movies. Because if we do that, we allow ourselves to be limited by our ethnicity and not our ability. The only limit that we should have on ourselves as creative people is our ability. I can't direct *Star Wars* because I'm Blaaaaack. I can't direct *Godfather* III because I'm Blaaaaack. Well, then you can't direct *The Color Purple* [directed by Steven Spielberg] because you're not Black or you can't direct *A Soldier's Story* [directed by Norman Jewison] because you're not Black. Those are two wonderful films that had nothing to do with the color of the director. It had to do with his ability. I just want the same standard applied, and I think that a very important consideration as a creative person when you go into the world of film is that you're already a Black person with certain experiences. But do not be locked by merely that, because I think our humanity transcends our Blackness. And maybe because we get buried in our Blackness, the humanity is overshadowed by that. I think that if you lock into your humanity, you can lock into any human experience. The human experiences you can lock into are limitless.

GA: *But you haven't locked yourself into the "Black" box. Is that how you've always seen it? You did Cemetery Club.*

BD: You know, I got a lot of flack for that.

GA: *From Black people?*

BD: From both, because Hollywood is a box town. You direct *these* things. You don't direct *those* things. And so, when I'd say to someone that I want to direct everything, people would say that they were confused, it's hard to sell me as a director, it's difficult. But I like directing things that I feel something about and that catch my fancy as a creative person, and say something through the medium of this particular tale.

GA: *As a great actor yourself, what was it like working with other actors?*

BD: I've been very, very fortunate. If you're a director, you know, you can work with Rolls-Royces or Pintos. I've been very fortunate to work with Rolls-Royces, and they kind of drive themselves. It comes equipped with so much and gives you so many choices that you're not bogged down or trying to ignite something. The engine's started, it's going. You just say, "Slide over to the left or to the right." That's all. You're not telling it how to create, because it comes ready. It comes to the set totally knowing more about the character than you do. And your job is really to create an objective eye that enables it to move as effectively and efficiently with impact without self-indulgence. That's really focusing the actor with what he or she is bringing. Working with a good actor is like . . . You sit there and say, "Wow." People like Cicely Tyson, Lawrence Fishburne, Andy Garcia, Jeff Goldblum, Wesley Snipes, Forest Whitaker, Ellen Burstyn, Danny Aiello, Whoopi Goldberg, the list goes on, just wonderful people. I also worked with Ava Gardner on *Falcon Crest*.

GA: I did not know that. Great.
BD: I worked with Jane Wyman [also *Falcon Crest*].

GA: Was it intimidating to work with an icon like Ava Gardner?
BD: [Laughs] Yes.

GA: That's Hollywood royalty at its best.
BD: I also worked with Lana Turner.

GA: Wow. What's your approach to working with such actors?
 BD: That's a tough situation. You have a job to do as a director, and once you get them to the set it's amazing. Lana Turner, Ava Gardner and Jane Wyman come from the old school Hollywood of acting.

GA: And how would you describe old school Hollywood?
BD: The studio system. A friend of mine who's a second assistant director [second A.D.] worked with Jimmy Stewart when he [Stewart] was older. It was this kid's third film, and his job was to make sure that whatever Jimmy Stewart wanted he got. And in the old days if you [the actor] left the set, you reported to the second A.D. where you were going, so that the cast and the crew, particularly the director and first A.D., would know where you were. You didn't just leave the set without reporting to one of the A.D. crew. So one day Jimmy Stewart was sitting in his chair watching a scene and my friend was standing next to him, and Jimmy Stewart said, "Excuse me, sir." He said this to this kid—this kid is around nineteen years old. He says, "Is it okay if I go to the bathroom

now?" And the kid says, "Yes, sir. Do you want me to go with you?" Stewart says, "No, that's okay. I'll be back in five minutes." If you can imagine the impact on him when Jimmy Stewart asked him if he could go to the bathroom.

GA: That's amazing. [Laughs]
BD: That's the way Jimmy Stewart was trained, you see? You don't go anyplace unless you tell the second or third A.D. We own you, you sit here and you go there. That's it. Okay?

GA: We'll make you a star. [Laughs]
BD: That's right, we'll make you a star. Right? No drama, no drama, no drama. [Big laugh] Can I go to the bathroom? That's real. [Laughs]

GA: Today a star might say they're going to the bathroom and not return for hours.
BD: No, not in old Hollywood. There's a certain respect, a certain decorum, a certain class about all of those people of old Hollywood. I was very fortunate to work with them. They came to the set prepared. These are the people with class. They had gotten all of the accolades they could get, they had the money, they had the Academy Awards, they had everything, so there was nothing to prove. They didn't have to prove to you, "I'm Jimmy Stewart." He just is. He comes into a room and people bow because of what he's accomplished. He ain't gotta say, "I'm the king." And people out there now, the young Turks, say, "I'm the king!" No one pays any attention. If you're the king, you don't have to say that you're the king. When you get to the room, people bow. It's a different time. I'll tell you a story. I was directing Lana Turner on the set of *Falcon Crest* and I would say, "Action!" and you would hear this rattling, this noise. The sound guy would say, "Cut, cut!" We'd look around. "Is there something in the mike?" No. "Action!" We'd hear some noise, this rattling. "Cut! What's going on? Try it again. Action!" Rattling again. I looked around and I looked down at Lana's Turner's arm, and she had these bracelets on—and she hadn't acted in fifteen years—and she was so nervous that her arms were shaking. And so I looked at Jane Wyman, and Jane Wyman saw it. I said, "Cut," and Jane Wyman took her over in the corner and talked to her. She said, "It's okay. You're beautiful." She came back and made the shot. True story. So I was fortunate to have these kinds of experiences with some great people. It keeps you humble, because you're not—you ain't all that!

GA: Who are your creative influences in film?
BD: Frank Capra and Orson Welles continue to be my creative influences. My favorite Capra films

are Mr. Smith Goes to Washington and It's a Wonderful Life. With Orson Welles, it's of course, *Citizen Kane*. They're not my only influences, there's also Antonioni, Fellini, Truffaut, Ingmar Bergman, a lot of European directors, as well as Kurosawa. I also had great pleasure working with Sam Fuller. He's really important to my career. My film *The Killing Floor* was entered into the Antwerpen, Belgium, Film Festival, and I went to Belgium and I met Sam Fuller. He said, "Young man, I like the film. You're a decent filmmaker." I said, "Thank you very much." He said, "I have some friends at the Cannes Film Festival, you mind if I take your film?" I said, "Yeah." He said, "Come to Paris in a week." So I went to Paris and it was director's fortnight for new directors. He got my film submitted and we became friends after that. He invited me to Portugal five weeks after that to be in a film. So I'm observing Sam Fuller direct. The great Sam Fuller, man. I'm on the set and he's directing this scene, and I'm in the scene and I'm sitting on the edge of a desk talking to Keith Carter. And Sam had the top of the desk cut off and put a plastic top on the desk and is shooting through the top of the desk. It was driving me crazy, because at AFI we were classically trained. After the master shot, the camera is always placed from some character in the scene's point of view. You were never allowed just to arbitrarily put it in the wrong place. If the camera's placed in the wrong place, it's me talking to you or you talking to me or a two shot from an objective point of view or from a master. And I'm looking at him put the camera under the desk, and then he moves around the desk and a dolly and comes over my shoulder and over the top, he's moving all around. I'm saying, "This is my god I look up to. He doesn't know anything about . . ."

GA: [Laughs]

BD: [Laughs] I've got to tell him that he can't put the camera . . . [Laughs] I said, "Mr. Fuller, sir." He said, "Yes, yes . . ." I said, "Please don't take this as disrespect. But you know, you have the camera starting underneath the desk on my feet, and it comes up and it shoots through the plexiglass and goes around our heads. At AFI, where I graduated from, we were always taught that the camera accept for the master and a two shot has to always be from someone's point of view. And there's no one down there under the desk, so there's no point of view. He said, "Young man." I said, "Yes, sir." He said, "Yes, you're right that the camera must always be placed from somebody's point of view." I said, "Yes, sir." He said, "And you know whose point of view that is under the desk?" I said, "No, sir." He said, "My point of view! It's my goddamn point of view! It's my point of view!" [Laughs]

GA: That's classic. [Laughs]

BD: But you know what's great about that moment? It changed me as a filmmaker. Because before that I had no point of view. My creativity, my use of camera was simply very stoic, but once I saw that, and he explained to me that filmmaking is more than a technical exercise in the story-telling of the script on the page, but that it's the director's perspective of that story in a larger context—it was BOOM! It was like an explosion out of a box for me.

GA: *There are rules, but you can adjust those rules.*
BD: Once you know them. See, I knew all the rules because I'm meticulous. I know the rules. But what Sam was saying was that once you know the rules, then you can break them. But know the rules first, because you've paid your dues in knowing them. We stayed friends until he died. He was a great man. His wife and I are still friends.

GA: *You've been fortunate to have tremendous training throughout your career with some of the industry's best. Are mentors very important in this business?*
BD: They're imperative. First of all, you're in a business, and when you're a neophyte you think that you're a filmmaker if you're not a businessperson. But as a filmmaker you have to under-stand the context within which you are working, and a good mentor will point that out to you and make you understand that it's okay to be an artist but don't get lost in the mythology of the auteur theory of moviemaking.

GA: *Is it a mythology, the auteur theory?*
BD: It is a mythology. You're an auteur? Okay, come to the set one day and the craft service guy had the coffee cold. See how much work you the auteur gets out of the crew that first five hours. If you're not dependent upon anybody else except your own great vision, if it's not a collaboration of people who you see as seemingly insignificant, let the coffee be cold one day or have the guy who's the camera assistant change the film and a little light gets on the film in the changing drive one day. Or have the dolly grip not be able to quite hit the mark each time.

So it's all a lot of crap, this auteur theory. It's an ego trip and a good mentor will tell you that your responsibility is to come to the creative people whom you've hired with a clear vision of what you want—a clear vision of the film, to bring the actors a clear vision of how you see that character, to bring your set designer a clear vision of how you see the set, colorwise and every-thing else. Once you have done your job in terms of the vision of what you see—the message of the film, the vision of what it is—you've hired them because of their creative contribution, and they add to that vision by bringing in their expertise and their creative process, and you create what we so fondly know as a film. It's not about you, it's about your ability to manage. See, directors are managers, and there are two parts to that. One is the creative process, your vision. The second job, which is equally or more important, is your management skills. And you're managing three things: time, people and money.

GA: *Could you elaborate on those three things?*

BD: The management of time is basically, I have to shoot this many scenes in this many days. Those days are broken down into hours, minutes and seconds. How has progress been on this scene, so that I can get this scene done? And how do I wait out that process? In the afternoon, I'm going to do a scene where the actor uses her mother, and I'm going to need a lot of time because she cries. If we do ten takes, she's got to get that emotion up ten times, and I can't rush her. I know that's in the afternoon, so I'm going to spend three hours on that. For the scene where she walks out of her house to get into her car, she's been told that her mother is dead, she runs out of her house. That's an hour. There's no dialogue, she understands how she's supposed to walk to the car, BOOM, take off. And what's more important, I have to determine what to do if it rains. I still have thirty days to do the filming. They don't give me another day if it rains, so what happens? Do I shoot in the rain or do I work with the scenes inside? That's time.

People—the management of people is a skill that is probably more difficult than any of the other two, because you have personalities, and everybody in the film business has some great modicum of ego, and sometimes you have to bite your lip. Managing people comes down to distinguishing between losing a battle to win the war. As a director, your job is always to win the war. So if you're an actor and we disagree on how this character would maneuver in the scene, I may not get my way in this scene. I may let you have your way, because I want you to work with me as the actor in the whole movie. I'll get my way in another scene down the road. But hey, you want to be right this time, cool, man, let's do it this way. Because I have an obligation to the studio to get this thing finished. So I've got to manage you in such a way where I pay you respect with the vision of my film in the can. At the same time, I must make sure that you and I are cool on working together. Even though I think that was a totally ridiculous decision you just made, I can manage you as a person.

Then there's money. There's never enough money to do the film. There's never enough money ever to do the film. Film is a game of compromise. Things always happen. For example, you were supposed to shoot this particular set this day and it rained. Or the camera broke or the dolly does not work, or the actor is pissed off at his girlfriend. He comes to the set and can't remember his lines. So for a scene that should have taken twenty minutes to shoot, now you're in the third hour. And guess what? We can count that now at the cost of every second. Every second in a film that goes by that's not productive costs money. Because what you do is take the script and break it down in terms of shooting days. If it's thirty days, this is how much it costs each day to shoot. That's twenty-four hours. Then you say twenty-four consumes this number, each hour is costing us this much. Then, sixty minutes a hour—this is how much it's costing per minute. There are sixty seconds in a minute—this is how much it costs per second. In the final analysis, the studio doesn't care, because they're not giving you any more money or any more time. So you've got to find ways as a director to manage your time, the people and the money so that in the final analysis it comes in on budget and on time. If you can do that, for the most part, you'll get work.

GA: *You work a lot with young people through your work with your Actor's Boot Camp [as part of the American Black Film Festival] and other things. What are your thoughts on these young people entering the world of cinema today?*

BD: First, I always tell them that you have to approach this as a business, as an art form, because the paradigm is changing so quickly—we've moved from the analog to the digital age. The bad news is that we've become very corporate and sometimes individual ingenuity is not appreciated as much as replicate behavior. If this one works, make ten of those. The good news is that with the move from analog to digital you can make a movie. A friend of mine is making a feature film for $10,000. He's getting the actors for free and he has a great concept. I mean, there's no excuse, if you've got talent, to not make a movie right now. You have Final Cut Pro or the Avid systems, if you have $15,000 to $30,000 you could have your own little studio set up in your garage or spare room. You could make movies. When I came along, no one could do that. You had 16mm camera or Super 8 or some video, but now a digital tape costs $9 or $10, so it's a totally different day.

But we have to research and understand the technology, and many of us are not. We're sleeping on that. We are doing some independent filmmaking with a sixties mentality. A lot of people do not understand the impact of digital filmmaking and how much you can do with a digital camera. They don't even know the equipment. They're still using film. Film is okay, but if you're a filmmaker and you say, "I can't make my film because I can't afford the film"—you don't have to wait to afford the film before you make the film. With digital you can shoot the film and then take it into postproduction and give it a film look. But at least you're taking advantage of the technology, so you're not waiting. We're still in a reactive pose as minority filmmakers, rather than being proactive and taking advantage of the equipment. We're still waiting for Godot. Godot done come and gone.

GA: *[Laughs] And you're walking around with your script.*

BD: You're waiting for your ship to come in and you're at the airport. [Laughs] The ship is here, right? And you're at the airport saying, "I don't see no boats!" That's 'cause it's gone! You know what I'm saying?

GA: [Laughs] And mad, right?
BD: Pissed off! LAX, pissed off waiting for a boat to come in!

GA: Gonna protest now!
BD: [Claps] Racism! Racism! The white man . . . ! [Laughs]

GA: [Laughs]
BD: You know how we are now.

GA: We're gonna complain now, and all the Black folks who've made it are "caught up." That's what we say. They've gone Hollywood. [Laughs]
BD: That's right. [Laughs] It kills me, man. It kills me. What can I tell you.

GA: Funny. What are your thoughts on Black film today?
BD: It's very limited. We're not thinking outside the box. The films I look at and enjoy are films like Run, Lola Run, Amelie, Amores Peros, a number of films where the thought about the movie, the way of dealing with images and sound and music, is so totally amazing.

GA: Why don't we see those types of films coming out of our community? Why don't we see those unique views of the world coming from our filmmakers?
BD: As a people and as filmmakers, based upon almost a slave mythos, we're attaching ourselves to our ethnicity and not to our humanity, and we're attaching ourselves to old myths that have been constantly perpetuated that we cling on to.

GA: Could you give me an example of what you mean?
BD: I'll give you a joke, which a friend of mind told me. A friend of mine said that this guy he knew was riding up in an elevator and this brother was standing across from him and he said "Hey, man, how you doing?" The guy responded [stuttering], "Ummm . . . I'm fine." The first guy said, "What are you doing here?" The guy said, "I'm g-g-g-going to the fifteenth floor." He said, "Really, what are you going to do up there?" He said, "W-w-well, I'm going to a-a-a-a-apply for a job." The first guy said, "So what kind of job are you applying for?" He says, "I'm, I'mem a go up

there. I-I-I'm gone b-b-be a radio announcer." The first guy said, "You're going to be a radio announcer?" He said "Yeah, I-I'm gon' be a radio announcer." It turns out later, the first guy is coming down the elevator and the same guy is coming down the elevator and he's crying. The first guy says, "You okay?" He says, "Y-y-yeah." He says, "Well, what happened?" "I d-d-didn't get the job." The first guy says, "Well, why didn't you get the job?" "W-w-w-well, they wouldn't hire me because I'm colored." [Laughs]

GA: [Laughs] *That's terrible. It's good, though. He's completely unaware, right?*
BD: [Laughs] But you know what I'm saying, though? He is hooked into that. He is committed to that. That's where his commitment is. Now, there's sunshine over here, man, there's food on the table, there's nirvana over here, man. We're not saying that, that [racism] does not exist. But if I have a choice of taking my life energy and putting it into that or moving toward the sunshine, the unknown, the uncharted, the un-experimented with, the learning of, the evolution of, the new-ness of, the challenging of, the growth of—for me there is no choice. I understand that, I can [claps], "Ungawa, Black Power!" I get it, okay, but this [the sunshine] is an opportunity for me to grow, to unshackle myself from that which limits me ethnically only while ignoring my ability. And what's worse is that if you do decide to go over here and look at some sunshine, you are asked, "Hey, man. What you doing with that sunshine? You got a problem? What you doing in the sunshine? You're supposed to be over here with us dealing with the darkness of the past and the police beatings and the urban setting and Black history and blah, blah, blah, blah, blah." And it's not enough that you make one of those—only make those. You do those and you're a [claps] Black man, you're a Black filmmaker, you are with your people. No other group of people requires that of themselves. Steven Spielberg makes Schindler's List (1993), he makes The Color Purple (1985), Jaws (1975). He said, "Cool, I'm with Black people. Here's my Black people thing. I'm going to do Schindler's List." But he was making E.T.

GA: *Do you think there is a fear in our community which limits us?*
BD: It's the mentality. It's fear. Fear. Fear! We have dogma for it. We have justifications for it. We have language for it. We have rationales for it. We have all kinds of things for it. It's fear. And suppose Melvin Van Peebles had just said, "Well, I gotta make a film about . . . " He didn't say that. He made Sweet Sweetback's Badaaasss Song, just BOOM, out of the box.

GA: *Way out. That's a bold film.*
BD: But he just jumped out the box. That's what you gotta do. Here's what reminds me of Black

people generally and Black filmmakers, most of us. Do you know how they train elephants in India?

GA: No, I don't.

BD: When the elephant is a little baby, to break his spirit they take a piece of barbed wire and tie it around the back leg of the elephant and they put a stake in the ground. And they put the elephant's food just out of the reach of the elephant, so when he goes after the food, it goes to the length of the barbed wire so that it cuts into the flesh of the little elephant and he screams, "Ahhh!" When he stops going for the food, they give it to him. After a year, when the elephant is very big, they take the barbed wire off and take a thin piece of silk, a strand, and they put it in the same place as the barbed wire was when it was attached to the stake, and when the elephant is hungry they put the food out of reach of the elephant, and when the elephant works for the food, he feels the tug on that same spot and he screams, "Ahhh! Ahhh!" and he stops going for the food. This is an elephant that is almost fully grown. Then they rip the stake out, the silk out, but his memory is that this hurts. And once the elephant no longer goes for the food with the silk strand around his leg, they put the food there for it to eat and they take the strand off and they consider the elephant trained. That's us. They give us limits, we're given limits that we reinforce ourselves.

GA: *To the acknowledgment of the fact that they do limit us, some Black filmmakers might argue that they have tried to do different types of films but they're not offered diverse projects.*

BD: Yeah, but the thing is, what I've said to you is, I'm not suggesting that this isn't a rough business for any filmmaker at all. We have to deal with the restrictions on distribution within the industry in which we're in. All that I told you about. That's all that.

GA: *That already exists. That's a given.*

BD: But we have the ability now with digital technology to look over here. And we can now create a feature film for $10,000. We can create images now for almost nothing, stories of our own, and there are places to see them and show them. Get paid here [Hollywood], but there are distribution channels that are just blossoming now that have no content. We should be exploring those new channels of distribution and exhibition. Get paid. I'm not saying that you shouldn't get paid. But if you were given no limits, what would you make? Let's see some of that. And if I can get a digital camera for $1,500 and a sound system for another $1,000 and shoot anything I want, what's stopping us from doing it?

GA: Our great actors say that there are no roles, but I don't see them collaborating with our directors and great writers to create roles and perhaps making these $10,000 films.

BD: I think you're seeing it done now, but I think that there's a disease that is rolling out in epidemic proportions in terms of Black culture. You know what that disease is? Amnesia.

GA: Why do you say that?

BD: We're the society and the culture of "I got mine, you get yours." We forget where we came from. If you forget where you came from, if you forget the people who paved the way for you to get there, it's very hard to know where you're going except to the bank. I'm not putting that down, I'm just saying that it's difficult if you don't know how you got there and who bled for you to get there. And the fact that we can sit in this room and speak today as freely as we want to and not have to go to a segregated bathroom—someone paid for that, some with their lives. If you have no recognition of that, if you don't understand it, or if it's not relevant or if it's passé, then it's very difficult for you to think of collaboration, because it's all about you—until you're reminded by someone that in their opinion you're just a nigger. And that day always comes. Not everybody is going to admit it to you. Whether it's in subtle or overt ways, you're a nigger. You're a nigger with money.

GA: [Laughs] I never knew that you were so funny.

BD: [Laughs] I'm just being honest. I'm being honest. That thing that Chris Rock said on stage in his concert, he said, "I'm here today, standing on this stage and I'm rich, and the white janitor who's in the bathroom in this concert hall right now would not trade places with me." He says, "Cool, Chris. You keep yours. I'll take my chances."

GA: That's a very profound statement.

BD: Don't you think that's true?

GA: It's very true. I think so. I think it's very profound and very scary.

BD: It's totally frightening. So that's why our amnesia culture is very, very, very, very, very disheartening to me. Because with an amnesiac malaise around us, it's impossible to have what my father talked about, which is generational responsibility in that it's not just us. We have to make a way for the future. It's not enough for us to have ours, but we have to lay some groundwork for the people coming after us and they've got to lay groundwork for the people coming after them. Most of us are void of that vision, and as a result, we may very well reach our demise.

GA: *How do we fix it?*

BD: One storm at a time. One storm at a time. I can't save the world, you can't save the world, but I can put my stone in the pond. I have three Howard students working for me right now. Other people have students working for them, and they're teaching them the ropes and passing information on.

GA: *In terms of training, you've done quite a bit. How important is formal training?*

BD: Yes, because I'm old-fashioned. My belief is that you break the rules after you learn them. Break the rules because that's what you want to do? No. I believe in film migration and certain filmic techniques. That's what I believe in, and I believe you have to adhere to certain aesthetics principles. I believe in understanding what a master shot, a medium shot, and a close-up and an extreme shot, and what those shots are and what they're used for and the use of lenses and angles. It's a study. The texture of film, what is that about. Depth of field. The core vision of colors in a scene. No, you've got to have the wardrobe lady and the set designer and yourself and the cameraman sit down and determine why she's wearing that dress and what color that dress should be, because there's certain wallpaper on the wall and where you're putting certain filters in the film. Now, if you can't go to school and you don't know any other way of making films except to do it by yourself, then cool. But don't put some crap up on the screen say, "I done made a film," and expect me to say, "That's a great film." No. It's adequate. It's not excellent. It's adequate. And adequacy and excellence are not the same thing.

GA: *We've hit on this some, but more specifically, what is the most important piece of advice you have for aspiring directors?*

BD: Business. Learn the business of the industry. What is the studio system? What is distribution and exhibition? What are the film festivals? What are the film markets? What are the funding sources? What banks should you use? What is the festival system? What is digital versus analog? What is the newest technology coming out? Learn the business.

Carl Franklin

I first discovered director Carl Franklin after seeing his skillfully directed but haunting, blood-churning independent film *One False Move* (1992). The thriller about three criminals on the run, starring Billy Bob Thornton, Michael Beach, Bill Paxton and Cynda Williams, earned Franklin the Independent Feature Project's 1993 Independent Spirit Award for Best Director. Hungry for more fare from Franklin, I found his 1986 film short *Punk* on PBS one evening and was blown away by his sophisticated and riveting treatment of the story of a latchkey kid who must navigate his own survival in a neighborhood of child predators.

With his clever eye for making audiences experience the pain and emotions of his subjects, connecting them with universal truths of the human experience, Franklin is arguably one of the film industry's most erudite master craftspeople.

In 1996 Franklin helmed the beautifully shot film noir film *Devil in a Blue Dress*, which starred Denzel Washington and was based on the Walter Mosley novel. His other credits include *One True Thing* (1998) with Meryl Streep, Renee Zellweger and William Hurt, the 1993 HBO film *Laurel Avenue*, and, most recently *High Crimes* (2002), with Ashley Judd and Morgan Freeman. For his next release, he reunites with Denzel Washington in *Out of Time* (2003).

Franklin got his start in the film business as an actor working on such TV shows and films as *The A-Team* and *The Fantastic Journey*. He later directed films for producer Roger Corman.

Born in Richmond, California, in 1949, Franklin received his B.A. from the University of California at Berkeley and received an M.F.A. degree from the American Film Institute.

■ ■ ■ ■

GA: *Tell me about your childhood and your first memory of movies.*

CF: My first memory of movies in a theater—and I don't know how we did this, but somehow my brother and I and another kid sneaked into a Brigitte Bardot movie back then. I think I was around seven or eight. It was something with Jack Palance and Bardot. That's the first recollection, and of course it was steamy and very sexual and all that, and that was twisting me up in some direction.

GA: *It may have been* Contempt.

CF: Yeah. I guess. I haven't seen it in a long time. But, man, I was smitten with her. [Laughs] But the first time I was ever inspired by a film—and I can't actually tell you what inspired me—but I remember seeing On the Waterfront somehow in my living room, and that had to be sometime in the mid- to late fifties. It was bizarre, because it came out in 1954 and I guess it came to television in '58 or something like that, and I remember walking through the living room and it was black and white—everything was black and white for us, because we didn't have a color TV. But I remember Brando in one of the scenes where Karl Malden got beaten up. I remember that and I remember Brando in the car in the scene with Rod Steiger. That actually inspired me later to want to be an actor. It was interesting—I always go back to that for some reason. And really, it wasn't my type of movie at that time. I didn't understand it, I had no idea what was going on. There was just something about that scene that drew me in and kept playing over and over in my head later in life.

GA: *Wow. Yes, that's a powerful film. And you actually pursued acting and were very successful.*

CF: Yes, I did that for a while. I studied at UC Berkeley, dramatic arts. Actually, first I was a history major and then, in a kind of serendipitous way, I kept being asked to do plays, first by my TA. I took a Dramatic Art 1A class because it was a literature class and because English seemed too drab and Comparative Lit didn't sound that interesting. But Dramatic Art 1A, where you read plays sounded interesting, and the only Black TA there was a woman named Margaret Wilkerson, who later became the head of the department. She was doing her thesis play and she cast me as Jean in Miss Julie. That was my first theater experience at Berkeley.

GA: Wow. Some Strindberg, huh?

CF: Yeah, Strindberg, right. Then another dude, a guy named John Reyes, had me do an original play called *Master Clay* and I was actually in that play with Philip Michael Thomas. He was doing *Hair* in San Francisco, and we did that together and that kind of got me interested. Then the head of the dramatic art department saw the play and started encouraging me, of all things, to get into acting, which is really something [Laughs]—not really a good piece of advice, actually [Laughs], in a lot of ways. But I did, I took classes and I liked acting. I didn't really like studying theater that much, but I liked doing the plays. Then a guy who was a stage manager at the Zellerbach Theater, a guy named Rusty McGraf, had worked with Joseph Papp—and somehow the head of the department, Travis Bogard, and another man named William Oliver got together and got him to arrange an audition for me for Joseph Papp's Public Theater. So I went to New York and did that, and I guess it was a token role, and when I say token, I don't mean racial but I'm sure they did it as a favor to the head of the department. I had a little speech in *Timon of Athens* and *Cymbeline*, two plays, in 1971 in Central Park. And I really didn't want to go to New York, but I felt it was an opportunity, so I took it. Everybody was telling me what a great opportunity it was and I didn't really want to leave Berkeley, because Berkeley was a great place to be at that time. I was having a ball, but I didn't like New York. New York scared me.

GA: Really?

CF: Yes. New York in the seventies was kind of a dangerous place in a way—a lot of drugs on the street, junkies, muggings and all of that, and drab. I had never been in a place where I couldn't see outside the city. That depressed me, but there I was.

GA: You said earlier that it's bad advice to suggest to someone to pursue acting. Why do you say that?

CF: Well, it wasn't ultimately bad advice because it worked out for me, but I would certainly never recommend that anybody pursue acting. [Laughs]

GA: [Laughs] And why not?

CF: It's one of those professions that's a bit like a crapshoot. I shouldn't say that, because really I think that the people who actually work at acting and who look at it as a career and who go out and do plays and who act in whatever venues are available find themselves fulfilled—and I was certainly of that ilk until I was introduced to television. I didn't even know there was a connection between film and stage when I first started acting, but I just find that it's one of those fields where there's nothing to fall back on. You have to go for broke. It's not like when you get a degree in teaching or degree in law or something like that and you do something else with it. The only thing you can do with a degree in dramatic art is either teach or act, and really the degree has nothing to do with that.

I've never advised anybody to get in any aspect of this business. My feeling is that if you have this passion, it's a jones that you can't get over, and you know it and you can't be talked out of it. And that's something that rears its head whether you like it or not. So I never suggest that anybody do this. I just feel that if it is that passionate a thing then they'll gravitate toward it, because the rejection is just incredible. It's one thing to go out and to lose a job when you want to be an accountant or you're interviewing for any other kind of gig where you have a skill that you bring and they judge you on that skill. But in acting you are your skill, and the disapproval that you face is oftentimes a disapproval of you or you certainly perceive it as such.

GA: *If you're passionate about it, it's worthwhile?*
CF: I think if you're passionate about it, you don't have a choice then. It's like a hunger that has to be satisfied and you're filled with some kind of inspiration that has to spill out.

GA: *Right. Then you decided to get behind the camera. Tell me about that and how you made the transition.*
CF: I had been acting in television, and I was one of those guys who was actually fairly fortunate. I was one of those less than two percent who was able to make a living. There was a time when I was able to stay busy with three regular TV series roles. They never ran any length of time, and I had a couple of recurring roles on series and then guest-star roles. But if you could get all of the roles, you could make a good living as a Black actor—but you're not going to get all of them, and it was just simple math, the dearth of stuff just wasn't enough to look at and feel comfortable that you could support a family in that way. And think about it, in the seventies the only bankable Black star at that time was Richard Pryor. Even people like Billy Dee [Williams], people like James Earl [Jones] and Sidney Poitier, who had been a big star in the sixties—you couldn't really get a movie made on their names at that time. Sidney was doing all of the comedies with Harry Belafonte and Bill Cosby, and Billy Dee apart from *Lady Sings the Blues* and a couple of others, really was not a major star, even though he was quite a talent and he was a heartthrob, certainly coming out of *Lady Sings the Blues*. But you weren't able to get a film bankrolled on Billy—James Earl either. And that baton was passed to Eddie Murphy, and again, you're talking a comedian. So the skills that you painstakingly developed in classical theater or in any kind of theater—I did a lot of workshops and did plays, I tried to do a play a year—those skills weren't necessary for you to succeed or not succeed in the film business. They just weren't required.

I characterize the seventies and the outlook for Black actors with a movie called *The Klansman* where you had Lee Marvin, who was an Oscar winner, you had Richard Burton, who was an Oscar nominee, and you had O. J. Simpson, who was a football player. Black football players and comedians at that time—Fred Williamson, Jim Brown, a few other folks—were able to get work, but there were all those actors out there. Basically I started to look to gain more control of my own destiny and started to write and had some degree of success with both of the first two scripts I wrote. PBS was interested in one and I optioned the other, a suspense terror thing, and I thought I'd make myself the second lead. I realized I couldn't be the top lead, because that had been explained to me by a man from a major law firm. I don't know if I should mention his name, but at any rate he was kind enough to explain to me how it all broke down in terms of Black films. He said that a Black lead makes the film a Black film, and that Black films had a limited number of bookings because most of the theaters were located in malls in white communities [late seventies]. And for the most part, the store owners did not want a large influx of Black people coming into those malls because they said it promoted crime. I said, "Man, I don't even see any reason to continue to do this." And he said, "But if people like you quit, there will be nobody to change it." That stuck in my mind. Think about it. In 1973 there were 110 Black movies made—"blaxploitation films." In 1977 there were ten, and by 1979, there were about three Black movies—*Penitentiary* by Jamaa Fanaka, *Richard Pryor Live* [directed by Jeff Margolis] [Michael Schultz directed *Sgt. Pepper's Lonely Hearts Club Band* in 1979].

So it was just not a very encouraging landscape. And so I started writing in order to try to free myself from that and to try to create some roles for myself. I actually ended up trying to get a movie done in 1983, but I had a bad relationship with someone I had relied on to direct the film. We both wrote the script together, I was putting up the money, we were producing it together and I was going to play the lead. But it was not a good relationship and I lost the money, and at the end of 1985 I decided that I would try to enroll at the American Film Institute [AFI]. People like Bill Duke, Bob Delegall, and a woman by the name of Myrna White had gone to the AFI and seemed to be able to change their careers a little bit. So I went to the AFI, and I remember I had a meeting with Irv Kirshner because I said I had directed a play and I hadn't directed anything.

GA: [Laughs]

CF: I had scripts I had written and they had been optioned, so that looked good in my package, but I didn't have any experience in directing anything, and I certainly didn't have a movie. So I met with Irv Kirshner [director of *The Empire Strikes Back*] for a second interview, and I found out that was a bad sign because it meant they weren't convinced. I remember his asking me who my favorite directors were, and I told him. I was thinking that this is an American—most of my inspirations at the time were European, South American or from a country other than America. I named some people, I named Kurosawa, Ozu and Fassbinder. I mentioned those names, and when I said Kurosawa he got up from his desk and went over and got an eight-by-ten of he and his son on the set of *Ran* and said, "I'll see you in September."

GA: [Laughs]

CF: [Laughs] I was in, right? So now I'm in—okay, what do I do? Things worked out.

GA: *That's incredible. And at AFI you did a film short called Punk. Tell me about that.*

CF: Actually, it was a compilation of things. I grew up in northern California in Richmond, California, and it had a reputation—and I guess it still has that reputation—of being a fairly rough town. Close to the elementary school and junior high schools I went to, there was a continuation school called Samuel Gompers, and there would be these guys who were about twenty, twenty-one, who would get out at noon and basically come down and kind of terrorize you. And there were these guys who were kind of demented. They would hang out in the park, and there were infamous guys who you knew would rob you for money or crash a party or rape somebody—mostly girls, I hadn't heard about anything happening to a boy. But then, when we were about seven, eight years old—nine, something like that—this other kid told us that a boy our age had been accosted by one of those older dudes and had been given the choice of either giving this guy head or getting beaten up by the other guy who was with him. Evidently nothing happened, but they tormented this kid that way and it stuck with me, because we were all afraid and we were all speculating on what we would do in that situation, and we tried to band together, saying that we'd be tough and all of that. Nothing ever happened, but it stuck in my mind—the street survival-of-the-fittest kind of attitude you grow up with when you grow up in a rough area. Your parents can't be with you all the time, and plus you got your rep to hold up, and just the terror of knowing that there are certain areas of the town that you could go to and you could get in a lot of trouble—and I'm talking about Black areas. I'm not even talking about the white areas.

And it stuck with me, and it was the formative thing in my own mind in terms of keeping me occupied with fear and trying to overcome that and playing sports to try to overcome it [fear] and all kinds of different things you adopted to try to deal with the potential encounter with that phantom thing that was out there. It could always possibly consume you and it stuck with me, and it's kind of what it grew into.

The other thing that was at work also was that a lot of the dudes I grew up with, my buddies, would later get in trouble. It's like you're with this person and you know him as your friend and maybe you're gone for a week or something like that, or maybe he's gone for a week or whatever, and you come back and that dude is in jail and you never saw any indication that he could get in trouble. And he had done the crime. So I often wonder what the motivation, what the genesis of the criminal, and Punk sort of deals with that—the evolution of a criminal.

GA: What I like about the film is your ability to build tension. You build tension well in all or your films, and Punk, especially. How do you do it?

CF: Well, it was in the script, and maybe some of that inspiration came from something far more stylized than what I do, and that would be the Sergio Leone westerns and how they extend those moments by double-cutting, triple-cutting it, and somehow it helps to sustain the action as opposed to the quick action that you get in an action film. It's a different approach, and it's something I did I think more instinctively in Punk, but I consciously went into that when I did One False Move. It wasn't an action movie. A lot of people would call it that for some reason, but it clearly was not that. And I just felt that again, because my interest has so much to do with relationships between people and oftentimes what we know of—and going back to my background—what creates the tension in a situation is not the actual event itself, but it's the buildup to it. It's the psychological adjustment to it. Generally, your fear of something is usually much greater than the thing itself.

GA: The guy in Punk who lurks behind the kid is very ominous. You actually feel the tension. You also use the camera very well in the film, and dialogue is used very economically. It's quite clear that you're telling a story with pictures.

CF: Thank you. Well, you know, it's interesting—of all places to learn an important lesson, I was doing an episode of Barnaby Jones [Laughs] and Buddy Ebsen was talking to me about film. I don't remember our full conversation—it's been a long time, it was sometime in the seventies—and the final thing he said was "Remember that it's called motion pictures." And that stuck with me. That was something that capsulized something that I was already buzzing around. By that time I had been exposed to the Sergio Leone westerns. There was such a sparse amount of dialogue used in those films and I liked that style—and I liked what he was able to do with telling a story with just pictures.

GA: How did you find the children who acted in Punk? They were brilliant.

CF: None of them was a child actor. The kid who played the friend actually had a little bit of a career as an actor, and he was just very natural and strong. I always kind of liked the rawness that you get from people who have not become so self-conscious. So we went out and put the word out in various places and tried to got to workshops in some of these places where they taught kids to act and all of that, but basically the kid who played the lead was a performer but not an actor. He was pretty raw and was basically a little Michael Jackson clone who sang, danced—and he was a performer who could moonwalk and all of that. He had an interesting little quality to him. There were a lot of kids that I saw, and a lot of it was finding a kid who was well-adjusted enough not to act—well-adjusted and comfortable within himself enough not to feel the need to show off or pull a lot of focus his way.

GA: *Let's talk about One False Move. When I first saw the film, I thought the opening was very disturbing. It was just haunting. We've seen violence in films a million times, but you drew us into the characters—they were very familiar to us and then they were brutally murdered.*

CF: My intention was to, first off, treat violence in a way that I felt was respectful, which was to treat it in all of its seriousness, in the invasion of humanity that it is. And I wanted to do that not only with the people in the party who were killed, but also the killers themselves. I wanted you to get the sense that these people could be standing next to you in a convenience store—people who are not extraordinary. Because, again, I don't believe that people are born with guns in their hands—they could be any one of us. I was basically chosen to direct this film in February of 1990, but it wasn't until October that we began shooting, because we had a difficult time casting.

During that time, especially during the summer that year, I saw a lot of big blockbuster movies that showed all kinds of violence, and I remember seeing *Total Recall* (1990) and seeing all of these people being killed in these spectacular ways, then seeing the audience's only human response to this violence being when a goldfish bowl broke and the goldfish were on the ground gasping for air. And I thought, "Something's wrong with this." I don't want people to go into this *One False Move* and to look at the violence this way. I want them to be affected by it. I want it to frighten them. I want them to identify with a horror as opposed to getting excited about it and getting thrilled. There are two ways to treat it: to drive people away or to draw them into it. My feeling has always been to drive them away from it somehow, to let you know that this hurts. So after having seen that it kind of influenced me in a way, and I knew that there were six people who had to die in the beginning because all the action was predicated on that, there was no getting around the need to have it. And again, because it is motion pictures you have to show it. It's not powerful if you don't see it. So I thought, "How can I do this?" And I didn't actually know until the day that I shot it.

I went in, I was in a rush and I basically covered it in three shot—the scene where he's stabbing the woman. First you see him on the phone. He walks out of that shot, goes and gets the pillowcases, and you stay on the girl lying down on the floor. You're waiting for him, but you can barely see him in the background. Then he comes in and stabs the victims [people in house]—that's another shot. There were three shots, and I had to do it economically. I also felt that, again, it's not really graphic because you don't see any blood or anything and the wound is actually upstage—you don't see anything going into anybody. You think you do, because it's a wide shot and you can see the people in the room. I had actually watched The Godfather and respected the violence I had seen in that, and I found that most of the time when they wanted to really affect you on an emotional level they went wide [shot] as opposed to going tight. And so I realized that gave you the opportunity to see the effects of the violence on the other people. That is also a perspective for those of us who've seen violence. Under Fire (1983) also had a scene in it where Gene Hackman is murdered from a distance, and that affected me, and I'd seen the start of a shooting across the street where a guy got shot here in L.A. eight times in the head down on La Brea and Twenty-first Street. That also influenced me.

GA: The opening scene in One False Move is so well done and so haunting that it makes you think, "This is what violence is really like."
CF: And you don't want any part of it when you see that. One thing that I feel is true is that I don't think that you ever leave One False Move exhilarated about going out and killing anybody. Another movie that had impressed me was Henry: Portrait of a Serial Killer (1986). I thought that was a very strong film.

GA: How did you get involved in One False Move?
CF: My wife, Jesse Beaton, was the producer on the film and she was looking for a director. She had been in sales and acquisitions at Island Pictures and had bought and marketed films like Baghdad Café (1988), Mona Lisa (1986), River's Edge (1986), Trip to Bountiful (1986), She's Gotta Have It (1986), Kiss of the Spider Woman (1985)—all those movies. So she was going into her first producing foray. It was her first opportunity to produce something, and she was being careful. She felt that it was the kind of piece that could go either way. It could be just standard cops and robbers or something very special. She contacted several people, and one of the people she contacted was a woman named Anna Roth, who had hired me when I worked for Roger Corman, and she recommended me and Roman Coppola to Jesse. Jesse interviewed us both, and something in what I had to say inspired her. Then she saw Punk, and that sealed it. She said, "This is my direc-

tor." When I met her, I met her with Billy Bob [Thornton]. I didn't know what to expect from these people—I actually didn't like Jesse when I first met her, because she said something I didn't understand. She mentioned that a particular movie was slow, and she meant that the movie was bad, and I got this totally wrong impression of who she was. I thought, "Oh, she's another one of these people who's into this whiz, bang, Hollywood, quick-cutting films," and that was totally not who she was. I ended up finding out that she was a lot deeper than that. And Billy Bob, it was cool working with Billy Bob. He said something very interesting. I thought of him as the writer, and there had been some resistance by his partner to rewriting. In reality, there was no money to pay for the rewrite. They were busy with other projects because they had other stuff happening. And Billy Bob being the actor—I thought, "Okay, he's the writer. We're going to be on the set, there's going to be trouble." So I asked him about that and he said, "I'm an actor now, man. I wrote the script, so hey, now I'm in my acting mode. Whatever you need to do, do it."

GA: How did you bring such complexity out of the Michael Beach character Pluto? Beach was brilliant and scary.

CF: I felt that the "brilliant" thing that I did in terms of Michael Beach was just choosing him as the actor. I didn't have to coach him a whole lot. Michael brought it with him. I just felt that he was the guy. The role actually called for a big guy to play Pluto, and I felt that would be a little bit obvious and not as interesting as someone who was less imposing, someone who really did rely more on their brain than they did on their body. Even though Michael is all rocked out and everything—he's still not a big guy. And the glasses were something else we wanted to add to bring the intellectual quality to him, because he was supposed to have a genius I.Q. So there was the incredible mix of intelligence with psychosis or whatever that was an interesting blend for any kind of a villain. Michael was one of those guys I was worried had done such a good job that he would not work again. That had happened to Andy Robinson, who was a friend of mine and who was the Scorpio Killer in *Dirty Harry*. He had a hard time getting work after he did that role, he's so convincing. And Steve Railsback, too, in *Helter Skelter*. I was afraid that was going to happen to Michael, because it was very interesting to me that everybody who contacted me would say, "Man, what a great film. We loved the movie. Who's the Black guy with the glasses?" But no nominations for anything, Independent Spirit Award or otherwise. I think they were afraid that was just the way he was, not realizing that he was Juilliard-trained. He dances, taps, all that kind of thing.

GA: He was a very scary person in the film, because he could live next door to you.

CF: Yeah, exactly.

GA: Laurel Avenue, which you did for HBO, was also very good. What was it like doing a film for cable TV versus a film for theatrical release?

CF: Really the only difference in that case, because it is cable and because the format was so different from what you normally get an opportunity to do on television, was the time in which I had to shoot it. I actually did things in Laurel Avenue that I would never probably be able to do in film, certainly not in a studio motion picture.

GA: What were some of those things you were able to do?

CF: One of them was the oral sex scene with the Dan Martin character and the Gay Thomas character, where he's going down on his wife. But we simulated that. I thought it was very tastefully done myself. No pun intended.

GA: It worked. [Laughs]

CF: But I'm sure it was something I would never be able to do unless it was in an independent film. That's really the case in many ways with cable. Cable allows you to tell intimate stories that are really much more meaningful than you would ever be able to do in a feature film.

GA: It's amazing and it's incredible what HBO and Showtime continue to do.

CF: Yeah.

GA: I loved Devil in a Blue Dress. How did you get involved in that?

CF: We were in preproduction on One False Move and as I said, we had a lot of time before we made that movie and Jesse was out there looking at stuff and she came across this book in a bookstore—Devil in a Blue Dress by Walter Mosley and just loved the cover, read the book and said, "You've gotta read this." So I read it, and I thought, "This is great." Then we found out that it had been optioned a few times and had been at Universal, and I think Warner Brothers and some other places, and was way beyond anything that we could have afforded to do. So I felt that I'd never get a chance to make this movie. So Donna Gigliotti, who had worked with Walter Mosley, had been trying to produce the film. I think the script had gone into turnaround [script owned by studio but project inactive]. We were in St. Paul and found out that Walter had done a book signing in Minneapolis, was due to do one in St. Paul, and Jesse said that we had an hour to get there. We raced over there, and she had her books and she was standing in the front of the line to get her book signed, and we really didn't know how to approach him, and I said to him, "Let me ask you. Why did you kill Mouse? Why did you get rid of Mouse? There was no Mouse in that script." Walter said, "How did you know? How did you read my script?" He didn't know me or anything. So that was our introduction.

Then Jesse contacted Donna and we had a meeting with Walter in Los Angeles, and the more I talked with Walter the more comfortable he got. Then, around that time, *One False Move* came out in May. A couple of months later Jonathan Demme, contacted me and said, "Look, I'd like to produce something with you under our banner. What is it that you want to do?" I told him that I wanted to do *Devil in a Blue Dress*. He was interested in that series of books, too, and so he said, "Cool." The project was at Tri-Star, he was at Tri-Star, Denzel was at Tri-Star and he was already interested in Mosley's book *White Butterfly*. So I got together with Denzel and we talked about that, and he was very excited to do it. It just all came together. Jesse had worked behind the scenes to get it out of turnaround at Universal and on the open market again.

GA: *What was it like doing a period piece and re-creating Los Angeles's famed Central Avenue? Was that challenging, and what was your process?*

CF: It was quite challenging, because as you know, in Los Angeles there's not much here that is any earlier than 1980. They tear down everything here, like the Brown Derby and other places. They don't save anything. I didn't want it to be like a lot of period films that I'd seen where you have a static shot and see a car pull up in front and you cut and you're inside and you know you're on a movie set. I wanted the ambience to totally envelop you, because one of the strongest elements in the book *Devil in a Blue Dress* was the ambience, that vibe, and trying to re-create the 1940s. The challenges were in trying to put together enough of 1948 Los Angeles, and pre-1948 Los Angeles was something that we really had to focus on a lot.

For research I went out and spoke with the first Black fireman in Los Angeles, and he gave me a lot of information. I talked to some of the artists who had been musicians on Central Avenue, like Ora Bryant and Roy Porter. I talked to a lot of those people. The L.A. Library had burned down and they were reopening it. And they were reopening it with a collection called *Shades of L.A.*, put together by Carolyn Kozo Cole, who is an author and the curator of photographs for the library. The collection was celebrating people of color in Los Angeles, starting from right before the turn of the century up until the sixties. So I went to her house, and she was gracious enough to let me pull about five hundred photos from her collection of Black people in Los Angeles starting from the twenties through the fifties. And then I honed it down so that I could get a sense of what it was like.

What kept coming back to me was Oakland, California—that L.A. was like Oakland was in a lot of ways. I remembered Oakland in the fifties because I was five in 1954 and I used to go to my aunt's house, and it was very much like the street that I re-created. I remember the open-air markets, people on the street dressed up in suits and all of that, interesting blues coming out of the bars. And probably because the culture didn't change as quickly in those days as it does now, I felt that some of it I could draw from my own experiences, my own recollections. In some ways it was a bit of a nostalgic kind of thing, maybe romanticized. But it was strong enough of an inspiration that I felt that I could delve deeper into it and hinge the kind of reality on that. I wanted to make sure I read books on Los Angeles, like City of Quartz by Mike Davis, the Raymond Chandler books, and I read some Chester Himes just to get a sense of a writer who wrote during the time. Then I started to go through the sociological elements in the story: What would it look like? People's houses would probably be houses that had come all the way from the turn of the century. Very few houses would be new. We had just come out of wartime, there wouldn't be a whole lot of new cars on the street—most people's cars would be from the thirties or earlier. Because it was a humble time, most people's clothes would not be new, because people had just come back from being in a war for four years. But there was a sense of prosperity. My own family was part of that exodus that came from Texas, Oklahoma and Louisiana out to the shipyards to work in World War II for the war effort. My family went north, Walter's went to L.A. It was basically the same migration. So there was family experience to draw from.

I grew up in the projects, and that was a transplanted southern community, and a lot of that vibe was there and a lot of the promise that people felt when they came to L.A. and came to northern California—Richmond, Oakland and places like that where they felt like they would be able to get a better life. They were trying to escape Jim Crow in the South. Segregation was still the law, and lynchings were still very actively going on.

GA: *I also felt that the costuming was very specific and so was the music. I really loved the Jimmy Witherspoon music—it provided a real sense of place.*

CF: One of the things that was real important to me—Gary Goetzman produced with my wife, Jesse Beaton, on the film, and Gary is a music guy who had produced The Pointer Sisters and Smokey Robinson at different times. He got me a lot of albums, and what I'd do was if there was a song that stuck out, I'd just mark that song for future reference. And it was not only an inspiration in helping to create the environment that I surrounded myself with as I wrote, but also suggestions as to source music [music which emanates from radio, stereo, or singer in a scene in a film, not the film score] that I would ultimately use.

In terms of the wardrobe, I looked at The Godfather again and I thought, "Now, what period piece is convincing in terms of its re-creation of an era but at the same time does not lose any of the urgency in terms of the story? You still feel the jeopardy for the characters, and yet at the same time you still buy that it happened several years ago. Oftentimes people do it with sepia tones and heavy filters, and what The Godfather did and what we selected to do was to choose the colors that we actually shot so that it would still have that clear immediacy and not that separation, not that generation removed that you get when you really load it up with too many filters and make it a memoir. That distances it. Most of the clothes were earth tones, were beaten down. We had Sharon Davis who was my wardrober and whom I worked with first on Laurel Avenue and who has done pretty much every film with me except for One True Thing because there was a post-sixties residual clause that wouldn't let me take her back to New York. But on Devil she did a lot of research. We worked together and she beat down the clothes, and really the only primary color we used was the blue dress [worn by Jennifer Beals], and even that was muted because we didn't want anything to pop, we didn't want any real saturated colors. We wanted it to have a worn kind of a feeling, but at the same time we didn't want the whole film to have an overcast of sepia, because that tends to distance you from it.

GA: Nevertheless, critics compared it a lot to Roman Polanski's Chinatown (1974).

CF: Yes, I think people compared it to Chinatown because they're making a general comparison in terms of the genre—they're both film noir. But really it's much more in look—and we weren't copying this, because one of the things I didn't want to do was be a derivative of a film—it's much more like Howard Hawke's The Big Sleep (1946) in terms of look. I wanted it to have a feeling of black and white but be in color. And Chinatown if you'll notice, is very washed out. Their whole theme was water and the lack of water, the aridness of Los Angeles at that time. It's a very well-constructed movie—very, very well thought out in terms of its theme. But that demanded another kind of a look than what we were able to get and what we wanted to get. That's a much more washed-out kind of a feel where you get the searing sun. Devil is much darker, with darker shadows, like The Big Sleep with Bogart. So I didn't want to copy a film style, because I felt that would separate us—you remove yourself and a generation from it. It's like making a copy of a videotape and making another videotape. It just gets weaker. I wanted to start from the source itself. I had a lot of conversations with Tak Fujimoto, my cinematographer, as to how to realize that, and he, I thought, just did a brilliant job of lighting that film. That movie is almost edible in terms of the look to me. I thought it was just one of the most beautiful films that I'd seen. I thought he did an incredible job.

GA: Definitely. And the critics really liked it. I remember reading Joe Morganstern's review of Devil in a Blue Dress in The Wall Street Journal the Friday that it opened. He described the film as being "elegant."

But despite the strong reviews the film people didn't flock out to see the film, and I was very disappointed about that. Why do you think that was the case?

CF: I think there were several things. There was the fact that we were making that film at a time when there was a shift in regimes at Sony. The people who green-lit the movie were no longer there by the time the movie came out. It was not handled well, it was not promoted well. I don't think they knew quite what niche to put it in. I've even heard that it was actually dropped, dumped. It certainly felt like that. I just don't think they knew how to market the film. The other thing is that movies of that genre, including even something like L.A. Confidential traditionally don't make a lot of money. L.A. Confidential began to make money after it got the Oscar nominations. That as well as Chinatown. That wasn't a big box-office film. But for the most part it's not a genre, whether it's a Black film or otherwise that people are accustomed to going out and seeing. It plays much better in video. People like to see those kinds of things at home, it seems, because it's been a very popular rental. But I think that coupled with the fact that the Black audience needs a little education in terms of going out and celebrating their own culture. I think that we oftentimes respond to very, very obvious and very stereotypical presentations, as opposed to something that's a little more complex even if it deals with our own culture. I just don't think that they necessarily were following the film. Also, I don't think Denzel was as big a star as he is now, but I don't know. It was a confluence of reasons.

GA: I think the O. J. Simpson verdict, which came that week, didn't help the film either. That's my theory. The film should have crossed over.

CF: In fact, a lot of whites told me that they felt that was the case.

GA: Yeah, the verdict had an impact.

CF: I think it did have an impact. I think it was an unfortunate thing—the timing was bad. I agree with you.

GA: But who knew the O. J. Simpson trial would ever happen. So you can't worry about that. Would you like to do another period piece? Had it been more successful, I know there would have been more adaptations of Walter Mosley's books, correct?

CF: Well, that was the plan. My heart was broken when we couldn't do more of them. We had such a good time making that film [Devil]—not just me and writing and directing, but the actors, man. I can remember one morning driving down and actually I just remember seeing the set, the look of the street, the cars, and forgetting for a second that I was actually going to work. It took me back. And people coming up in the dance scenes where we went to John's Bar, and just the enthusiasm of those extras working in a very hot room—we didn't have a lot of air-conditioning and people were just having a ball.

GA: *Well, you can tell. The extras don't seem like extras. They're in the moment. It's obvious that they've bought into your vision and understand the world they're inhabiting. Brilliant.*

CF: Everybody was so willing to go there. All of the extras were just so willing to go there. I mean, I can't express to you. It almost makes me start to cry.

GA: *And that's a good thing. Going back to the Black audience thing—in terms of the need to educate, how do you go about educating the Black audience in terms of being receptive to different images of Black people and a broader canvas of Black life?*

CF: I don't know. I know that I got into this because when I was at the AFI [American Film Institute] I had no dreams whatsoever of being able to work in the studio system. I just had not seen any Black directors do it. I mean, Spike had broken in and that was cool, but actually I was already at the AFI when *She's Gotta Have It* came out. So when I made the decision to go into that, I didn't have any examples of people who had actually gone out and been really successful at it. Michael Schultz had experienced a bit of success, and there had been a few others—Gordon Parks earlier. But I was thinking, I had this whole scheme of wanting—because Black people are configured in the major urban centers of the United States, I had this whole thing of trying to go out and distribute movies at community centers, city colleges and junior colleges, because a lot of them were third-world, low-income people. My thought was that you could distribute in those places, and too, it could also serve as a source of income, as a syndicate of funding. I was very naïve and didn't realize that it was a whole lot of work and that so much of what inspires people has nothing to do with the substance at all.

We have been victimized by this whole commercialization. This is a market culture, and it's been a culture that has conditioned everybody in this United States to be consumers and to respond to packaging and to respond to brand names. And people do respond to that kind of thing. It can be a generic product or Bayer, and they'll go for the name every time. It's the same problem that you have with film and that I'm sure I would have had if I had tried to do some of those regionally distributed movies. I'm sure that I probably could not have gotten people to come to see them, because there would not have been any names associated with them. So much of it is just packaging and oftentimes something like *Cry Freedom* (1987)—when Denzel was in *Cry Freedom* or when he was in *Crimson Tide* (1995), that's perceived as a different movie than when he did *Devil in a Blue Dress* with a Black cast or with nonrecognizable white names. And I think that the perception was such—we are victims of that ourselves, are guilty of that ourselves—we respond to the headline. We go with the brand name. We are notoriously uneducated consumers, pretty much like the rest of this country is. We rely on the same Madison Avenue whiz bang pitch.

GA: *What was it like adapting a book for the big screen?*

CF: It was interesting. It was deceptive. When I first read *Devil in a Blue Dress* I thought, "This will be such an easy adaptation," because it was so visual. It just seemed to me that it would just translate so easily. And then, when you get into it and start to take ideas that are in your head and put them on the page where you're going to have three-dimensional characters now, you're actually going to have a real person play the role who has a specific sound, where you're actually now taking locations that are suggested in the book and where you are kind of halfway participating in imagining them, now you have go out and find or build that location, and it has to be a real place. That kind of a translation is very difficult. Also, because with a book you've got the issue of conflicts being within the character, as opposed to in film, where it's between characters. And in a book, that's an art form where you (the reader) control the pace. You can pick it up, read a chapter today and not pick it again up until two weeks later. You can finish it at your leisure. Ideally, a movie is supposed to be seen in one sitting and has finite parameters that it exits within, so every line, every word, every shot means more than just the word or the shot; it's emblematic of something bigger always, it's symbolic of something larger. The structure is a much more contained, rigid kind of a thing—you are trying to communicate the spirit of something that has already been successful or has already delivered itself in some form that has been appreciated in literature. So certain changes had to take place. There were certain things in the book that we couldn't do in film.

GA: *Could you give me some examples?*

CF: Well, for instance, the Daphne Monet character. In the book she had already decided to leave Todd Carter at the beginning of the book, which really doesn't give her much of a motivation to stay in town. You can explain her reticence for leaving, because human behavior is oftentimes very different than cinematic behavior, so there are those complexities. But when you put it all on the screen you need a specific reason for her to be active and to still be there. Otherwise, you say, "Why doesn't that chick just split? There's danger brewing around her." So I had to make that conflict—the mayoral race, which was a foregone conclusion that Matthew Teran, as he was called in the book—we called him Terell—because Teran sounded too much like a Middle Eastern name and he would never get a chance to run for mayor in 1940 in L.A. But we had to make that whole mayoral issue, instead of it being something that had already taken place and where Terell was out of the race, we needed to make that active, to make that something that ultimately is going to play out. And so suddenly now she had to have a reason for her being there, and that's where the whole thing about his pedophilia comes in. We decided we needed to find a way to somehow make that active in his demise. Then that's what was underneath everything, because in fact it was in the book, but in the book it didn't have to be active because again, your imagination does that.

GA: *You hit on something key regarding the way images play in real life and how they play in film. That's a very important point.*

CF: Well, even in documentary film you select the images, and even though it appears to be reality it's still a syntax—you still have created some kind of a visual syntax that ultimately delivers the message based upon the selected images that you put together. And it's of course even a more exaggerated form in a theatrical format. That meant that if the whole idea was that Todd Carter could not be with her because she was a Black woman posing as a white woman, then we needed for her to really be in love with him in order for that to actually have any resonance. That needed to be the issue, which meant that if she were in love with him she couldn't have a dalliance with our lead character. That would mean Easy was doing Todd a favor by sleeping with his old lady and letting him know, "Hey, man you don't need to be with this chick." That was a major story point that had to change in order to make everything cohesive. Whereas in a book she already had decided she was going to break up with Todd—that was not a problem. She had already set in motion problems, so Easy was off and running on something and she didn't have to be there that much, because she could be kept alive by what he thought about her. Because you can't really get inside of a guy's mind and continue to use voice over, over and over again to talk about somebody—again, it's motion pictures. For instance, I invented the character in the film, *The Tree Man*—the guy who's cutting down the trees—because in the book there's a lot made of Easy taking that assignment from Albright, takes that hundred dollars, goes out, basically makes a pact with the devil, loses the innocence that he had when he lived in this little simple neighborhood with all of these migrants who tended their yards and homes and who were very proud. In the book Walter is able to accomplish that by the flowers dying. His garden that he had so meticulously nurtured was suddenly dying. That was metaphorical, and it was also showing you that he was no longer a part of that innocent world anymore. He was now a part of that subterranean world where the real American dream exists—behind the facade where the cogs and pulleys are and the back-room deals are made. Yet I needed to somehow show when he was victorious and when he emerged from the underground back into the light, that swell you got from the end of the book that almost makes you cry when you see him back with all of those people he knew, with his friends, with all of those people with their dreams, and now he's changed. But he's back in the element that he loves so much, which is his little house. So I couldn't just shoot flowers dying throughout, I needed something that would be active, something that would not stop the action and movement of the story, but at the same time could serve as a representation of the community.

When I was speaking with the man who integrated the fire department, he showed me this picture of this very handsome young man and then showed me a picture of the same man ten years later where his hair was all straggly and he was pruning trees. He had gone a little mad and was in the community actually making things beautiful. But I thought, "Interesting character, but he needs to be someone who creates some conflict. Let him be that lovable eccentric everyone in the neighborhood is pissed off with, but if anything ever happened to him would be very upset about because he's the signature of the neighborhood. So at the end of it, when Easy comes back and he's over there trying to cut that tree down and you see Easy run across the street and then watch him with his wheelbarrow go up the street and then see him as part of all those people out there—the people with the pony ride, the people with the lemonade stands and people on their porches—which is the way I remember the neighborhoods in Black communities in the fifties, because it's a southern thing. You'd sit out on your porch and you knew everybody. There was a whole social scene—the kids playing in the street and the parents out there gossiping, playing cards and whatever. Then it would give you that swell of emotion that you had in the book. My mandate, I felt, was to try to somehow deliver the spirit of the book in the same way that I felt great films like Grapes of Wrath had done, where John Ford in two hours was able to deliver the spirit of the novel. Even though it's not to the letter exactly, you got the feel of the book. And that's what I wanted to do. I wanted to do what Walter had already done with the book.

GA: *Next up was* One True Thing. *What was it like working with someone like Meryl Streep on that?*
CF: That was incredible. She is one of those people who lives up to everything you expect of her. She's so elegant, she's so smart. It true. I'm not just saying this. She's someone who lives up to all of that, and you want to make sure that you're on your game when you work with her, because she's someone who does a lot of research and comes very well prepared and whose bullshit barometer is very keen. She's very serious, and I don't mean humorless or anything like that, but she's there to work and I am, too, and so I felt it was a good marriage. But it was a piece that my wife and I did because—my mom died of cancer in 1986.

GA: Oh, I'm so sorry.

CF: And I to some extent had seen some of that [pain] and I was not as fortunate as Ellen [the main character in the film played by Renee Zellweger] and able to discover who my mother really was while she was alive. It was after she died that I realized how much she had sacrificed—I mean, I knew how much she had sacrificed, but I didn't fully appreciate all that she had done until she was no longer there. And so really that was my reason for getting involved in it. My wife had the same feeling. She had actually read *One True Thing* the book [by Anna Quinlan] and had not wanted to show it to me a couple years before. She had shown it to an assistant who worked with us at the time who didn't respond to it, and Jesse was nervous that it was too personal and felt that it was something that she would only appreciate. So we didn't option it, because the woman who was our assistant said that she didn't get it. [Laughs] Jesse was kind of being quiet. She didn't know how much to trust her own judgment on this, because it felt so personal. It felt like the story was her and her own mother. Her mother did not have cancer, but she was someone who she took for granted because she had always gravitated toward her dad, who did the much more obviously important work. "She's just the housewife, just the housewife," as we always say, not realizing what that means and the importance of that.

GA: *The mother is the center.*

CF: The center of the society, man. That's why society is falling apart now. It was something that we all did—Meryl did it for that reason, Casey Silver green-lighted it for that reason, Stacy Snider wanted to make it for that reason. She said, "Yes, let's make it" for that reason. Casey Silver was her boss, but she's the one who basically shepherded it. We all got into it for that reason, every one of us.

GA: *What's it like being an actor working with actors?*

CF: I think mainly I speak their language. I've acted, and I know what is difficult to do and I know what's possible. And I also have some degree of insight into how you get there, even though I think that the best thing I do is I'm able to get people to go much deeper than I've ever gone. Actors are interesting in this respect. This whole society is made up of people who have difficulty expressing their innermost feelings to those people who are closest to them. People go to see analysts and whomever to talk about issues that concern husbands, wives and daughters, et cetera. Actors are expected to delve into those personal feelings on a daily basis and to expose those feelings—a lot of time you are dredging up stuff that is very personal to you—and to put it on display for potentially millions of people.

So they have to be protected a little bit to do that, they have to be encouraged to do that, and exhibitionism isn't enough because exhibitionism oftentimes gives a show and is not honest, is not authentic, is not genuine.

So what you want to do is to get someone to bare their soul in front of millions of people so you have to arm those people, in a way that they feel protected. That means participating with them in that subtext world, participating with them and making them comfortable that you're there with them and making them comfortable with their emotions as they get to that. Actors get up in front of folks and do stuff like make love on camera, and people can say, "Hey, that's not the way I, you know . . . " They open themselves up to that kind of criticism all the time to re-create what we are accustomed to doing in our everyday life, and so they need ammunition. They need an environment, fertile ground that allows them to do that unmolested. When I say unmolested, I mean where they don't feel impaired by fear. Fear is the biggest enemy that an actor can have. It is that hesitation that will make you not make that freaky choice. Just that split second of hesitation that will make you do something safe as opposed to really going for it when it occurs to you. And I like to try to create that arena for them and let them know I'm with them. They've got me there to support them, I've got their back. Basically what I try to do is to bring those kinds of things out of people and to encourage them to be private in a public situation.

GA: *How do you know when a performance is honest?*
CF: I don't know if I can quantify that. I just feel it. That's one of those instinctive things, I believe. I think it may have something to do with my own preoccupation with history and the truth. I have a tendency to want to get to the real underbelly of something, whether it's revisionist history or whatever—oftentimes because history is fable that's agreed upon. It generally is just what everybody decides that it is. That was Napoleon's quote, and he was one of the most famous history makers there ever was, so I'm sure he knows how it comes about. But I think it's a preoccupation that I have with truth, with somehow trying to get to some fundamental principle. And oftentimes up until—I guess even until this last work—I've pretty much always tried to just go for something—and even in the last work, High Crimes (2002), it's popcorn, but I thought it was good popcorn but we tried to root it with a political backdrop that gave it a little resonance.

GA: *What was it like working with Morgan Freeman on your recent film* High Crimes?
CF: He's a consummate professional. Morgan brings it with him. He's always on time—Morgan is cool. Morgan is a gentleman, people like him and he's very easy to work with. It's one of those

situations like with Denzel. There's not a lot you have to do there. They bring a whole lot of that with them. You may coach something here or there, but for the most part they're bringing it. They have a very strong sense of who they are and where they are at all times.

GA: *Who are your creative influences inside and outside of film?*

CF: In terms of literature—Gabriel García Marquez, I like his writing. I like John A. Williams—I love his work. Chester Himes—I love his stuff as a writer. In film I like John Huston, John Ford, Scorsese, Coppola, Jean Renoir I like a lot. I like Ozu, Kurosawa of course, Hector Babenco. Ozu is one of the most emotional directors I've ever seen. I don't mean that the scenes themselves are that emotional for the most part but I find that he works you. A couple of his movies, *Tokyo Story* and *Late Spring*, man, you just bawl in his movies, and it's a very interesting and mesmeric quality that he has. The camera is always on sticks, it never moves, there are hardly any close-ups. I don't even know if there are any close-ups. Certainly at max you may get a medium shot once or twice in a film that I just find what he's doing in film to be incredible. Louie Malle is another I liked a lot too.

GA: *What are your favorite films?*

CF: *Late Spring, Tokyo Story, Rules of the Game, Les Enfants du paradis, Godfather I and II, Apocalypse Now, Grapes of Wrath, The Maltese Falcon, Chinatown,* Scorsese's *Goodfellas, Raging Bull, Moon Over Parador, Get Shorty,* and *Bowfinger.* Another one of my favorites is *Fear of a Black Hat* by Rusty Cundieff. I'm crazy about that film.

GA: *Oh, that's a cult favorite. What advice do you have for aspiring filmmakers?*

CF: I feel that you gotta. If you look at people like Paul Bartel, who did *Eating Raoul* (1982) for $30,000, Spike Lee with *She's Gotta Have It* (1986), Robert Rodriguez who did *El Marriachi* (1992) for $7,500 for the first piece before the post came in, Robert Townsend, $100,000 with *Hollywood Shuffle* (1987), Wayne Wang $20,000 *Chana Is Missing* (1982), John Sayles, $60–$65,000 with *The Return of the Secaucus 7* (1980). I find that those people come in the strongest. They didn't wait to appeal to the industry. I mean, that's what I tried to do, in fact, and you can lose that way. But the problem was that I was overstretched myself. I think that you shoot with whatever you have. If you've got a Super 8 camera, then that's what you shoot with. If you've got a video camera, that's what you shoot with. If you have a still camera that's what you shoot with. The thing that Terry Gilliam's *Twelve Monkeys* (1995) was based on was originally a brilliant montage of stills that created that narrative. It was a French film, and I don't remember the name but I saw it, and I think you just start shooting with what you've got and you begin to assemble the components that you need to get bigger and bigger and to begin to express more and more of whatever that inspiration is that you have inside.

I think the mistake is to think that you arrive at some place or that there is some goal that you have to reach or that you have to go out and try to appeal to somebody. You have to declare yourself already a filmmaker and do it with whatever you have. And now with all the venues, all the film festivals that are cropping up all over the country, there are a lot of places where you can show your work. And with digital video now you can do things very inexpensively. I just think that people ought to—if you have that passion—exercise it. I don't think that anybody who needs to ask somebody if it's a business for them should be in this business, because I do believe that it is a jones, it's an illness. You can't get over it. It bites you and you gotta do it.

Reginald Hudlin

Following in the footsteps of his talented elder brother Warrington, director Reginald Hudlin first gained prominence in 1990 with his hit film House Party. Based on a short film Hudlin directed while an undergraduate student at Harvard University, the fun, exhilarating, innocent and music-infused House Party won the prestigious Filmmakers Trophy and the Best Cinematography Award at the Sundance Film Festival. The film was also awarded the Clarence Muse Youth Award and a New Visions, New Voices Award from the Black Filmmakers Hall of Fame. The success of House Party has created a profitable franchise, resulting in three sequels, a Saturday-morning animated series and a comic book.

Hudlin followed his directorial debut with the sexy romantic comedy Boomerang (1992) starring Eddie Murphy, Robin Givens, Martin Lawrence, Halle Berry and Chris Rock. An evergreen favorite among African Americans, the film earned $120 million worldwide and presented Murphy as a classy leading romantic lead. While making Boomerang, Hudlin simultaneously wrote and executive-produced Bebe's Kids (1992), based on the comic routines of the late comic genius Robin Harris. The film was the first African American animated feature film.

Hudlin's other credits include The Great White Hype (1996), with Samuel L. Jackson and Jeff Goldblum, The Ladies Man (2000), based on the popular Saturday Night Live character Leon Phelps, played by Tim Meadows, and his latest work, Serving Sara (2002), with Matthew Perry and Elizabeth Hurley.

With a knack for comedy that is smart, hip and entertaining, Hudlin is currently partnered with Aaron McGruder, the creator of the controversial comic strip *The Boondocks*, to develop an animated series based on the popular strip.

— — —

GA: *You grew up in East St. Louis. Were you a creative child?*

RH: East St. Louis is a very inspiring place, and my family always encouraged me to be very creative. I remember my mom would bring home a movie projector from the school she taught at and she'd check out movies from the local library. After watching those movies about a million times, we'd start standing in front of the projector beam and start making up our own shows. I guess that was a sign of things to come. When I was in high school, my dad got me a job writing vignettes on the history of East St. Louis for the local radio station that ended up getting nominated for a national award. So they really supported my creative endeavors.

Not only was education always important in our family, we actually knew our family history going back many generations. I come from a long line of iconoclasts, so when my brother and I decided to become filmmakers, while it was sort of a shock to our parents, it wasn't like, "What in the hell are you doing, boy?!" [Laughs] It was more like, "Have you thought this through? What's your plan here? You know it's going to be hard." They were amazingly supportive, considering the ridiculousness of that career choice. [Laughs] It's a ridiculous career choice now, but back in the day when there was little to no Black presence in Hollywood, and no one knew what independent films were—they were more so called underground films—the whole thing just seems really audacious. My brother started making films while he was in college and was successful right off the bat, with incredible reviews in *The New York Times* and with his films showing at film festivals all around the world. So even though he wasn't making a lot of money, he was having critical and artistic success and making a living. So I knew it could be done if he could do it. [Laughs]

GA: *[Laughs] In-house inspiration.*

RH: Exactly, so I was very fortunate. Most people don't get to see independent films until they're at least young adults, but I got to see Hollywood films *and* independents when I was a kid. I remember going to go visit Warrington in New York, and we'd go to the Carnegie Cinema. We'd see a Costa-Gavras double feature: *Z* and *State of Siege*, which is some heavy stuff. Before we'd go, he would warn me, "This is a foreign film and it's going to have subtitles, it's not going to have a lot of action sequences—can you handle that?" And of course I'd say, "I can hang!" It became an act of machismo, to appreciate a sophisticated film. Those "high art" experiences affected my perceptions of the cultural influences I was absorbing in East St. Louis, which was so raw and funky. It's the kind of place where alongside Earth, Wind & Fire and Parliament-Funkadelic on the radio you would hear Bobby Blue Bland, Tyrone Davis, Johnny Taylor and other old, old school music—the blues. So growing up in a place with that kind of intense cultural retention and then being able to visit a place like New York and get all of that worldliness that my brother was experiencing was great.

GA: *And in pursuing film you decided to go to Harvard. Tell me about that.*

RH: It was a great experience. Harvard's film program is very documentary oriented, but for some reason our class was very fiction oriented. But even so, I think it's really healthy to train in the documentary approach, because you get grounded in real life as opposed to artifice. Even when you're going to make fiction, you focus on how realistic it can be. That really shaped my sensibility in terms of filmmaking. During the second year of the film program, the class splits in half to make group documentary projects. One group decided to make a documentary about people who work at night—policemen, janitors or guys who make the donuts. I thought, "Uh-uh!" Then this other group of guys said, "Let's go down to Daytona Beach during spring break and make a movie about that." I said, "I'm down with the spring break people, not the stay-up-all-night-in-cold-ass Boston people." [Laughs] And almost all of that crew were members of the *Harvard Lampoon*, and I had a tendency towards that kind of humor anyway.

As a kid, I was a huge Monty Python fan, a huge Woody Allen fan. I remember when Chris Rock came to visit my house out here, he was looking through my bookshelves and he saw my copy of Woody Allen's *Without Feathers*, and he said, "Man, that's a really old copy. I didn't get mine until years later." He was impressed, because only true fans read Woody Allen's books. Everybody loves *Annie Hall* or *Manhattan*, but for me to have bought the book while still in high school, Chris said, "Hmm. You're hardcore." All that to say I was into that sensibility already, but hanging out with the *Lampoon* guys permanently warped my sense of humor. We drove down from Boston to Daytona Beach nonstop in somebody's mom's station wagon with film equipment in the back, doing hours and hours of bad jokes like "how to give the finger in the most creative way." I got immersed in that kind of humor. Most of the people in that car have gone on to be very successful in Hollywood—Jonathan Mostow, who directed *Breakdown*, *U-571*, and is now directing T3 was with us; Mike Ferris, who has written features for Mostow and others, was there; and John Payson who directed *Joe's Apartment*. I'm the voice of "Rodney Roach" in that film, because John acted in one of my student films, so I had to pay him back.

GA: What inspired House Party, which you first did as a short film at Harvard?

RH: That was very funny. Between my junior and senior year, I was working in New York to make enough money to finance my thesis film. I'd been working all summer on a screenplay, and by the end of the summer I had it pretty much in shape and I had the money to do it. As I was packing to go back to school, the radio was on and Luther Vandross's Bad Boy Having a Party came on and I thought, "Man, that's a badass song." At the time I was doing this exercise where I would imagine the music video version of a song—this was before Black artists were really doing music videos. I thought, "If I were going to do a video to that, how would I do it?" Actually, I've been doing that since I was a kid. I never understood why they never had little movies to go along with the records. So listening to Bad Boy Having a Party I imagined this cool video. Then I thought, "That's actually a movie." So after spending all summer writing one short script, I wrote the short script for House Party in three days. So I had two short scripts and ultimately decided to go with House Party.

GA: The feature is such a fun movie. The comedy reminded me of Cooley High in some ways. Did you study a lot of classic comedy to prepare for it, because you had a real good grasp of comedy as a film art form?

RH: Well, no, not in preparation for shooting that movie specifically, but I had been "preparing" for that moment by watching classic comedies all my life.

GA: What comedies specifically?

RH: The two movies that had the biggest influence on House Party were American Graffiti and Animal House. I remember when I saw Animal House I thought, "This is the revolution. Comedy will never be the same after this movie," and it wasn't. That really did change the game. The characters were more fully rounded in American Graffiti and the humor was more bawdy in Animal House, but somewhere between the two was the movie I wanted to make about my life, the same way those movies were about the experiences of those filmmakers. But I was always serious about my comedy. There was this late-night film series on one of the local stations in St. Louis called Comedy Theater, and they would show films by the Marx Brothers, W. C. Fields and other classic old comedians, and my brother and I would stay up late and watch. I always took a very academic approach to film, even back then. There was a series on PBS called The Japanese Film, with Edward O. Rhineshour, that I watched faithfully every week. That's how I first saw Kurosawa and Ozu when I was . . . I don't think I was even in high school yet.

GA: Kurosawa and Ozu? That's some pretty intense and highbrow stuff.

RH: Very intense films, man, very intense films, but for some reason I was young Mr. Hardcore.

GA: On the surface, House Party appears to be just a hip-hop teen comedy, but you tend to integrate the issues of class, gender and sex in a subtle way. Was this conscious or subconscious?

RH: Well, it started out being a movie about safe sex, but I hate preachy movies, so I wanted to make a movie that had so much misdirection that you wouldn't even feel a "message" when it hit you. The nicest compliment I got in that regard was after the film came out when we got an award from this group called The Center for Population Options. At the awards ceremony I was sitting at this table with this brother who ran an AIDS clinic in Jersey, and I said, "You're really on the front line. It's nice that we're getting this award, but does it really make a difference?" And he said, "Oh, absolutely. When I talk to these kids who come in the clinic, they wear condoms because they saw it in your movie, and they mention it by name." I said, "Wow!" As a filmmaker you emboss your movie with "positive" ideas because it's the right thing to do, but when you actually hear that it works, it's very exciting.

In terms of the class stuff, it's one of the secrets of my success . . . and I don't even keep it a secret. I always tell people, because no one ever believes me. I just say that Black people hate being shown as a monolithic group. Black folks hate being ghettoized and criminalized, but then turn around and complain about the upscale lifestyles in The Cosby Show. But when you show a diversity of Black life—poor people in the projects, middle-class people living in a house with a white picket fence, working-class folks—and you show them all hanging out, which is how I grew up and how most Black folks grew up—Black people see that and it feels the most real to them. After all, we're all one sneeze away from one class to another [Laughs]—none of us are that financially secure wherever we are. And all of us have family or friends who are in a different class bracket than us. When I was a kid I walked five or six blocks to visit my friends in the projects and rode my bike to visit some other friends who lived in a big house. But we all went to the same school and we all hung out and we all went to the same parties, and that's the Black reality that is the hardest to get on screen.

GA: House Party also has the elements of a musical. Music actually advances the story. Was that intentional?

RH: Yeah, at the time the only kind of rap movies around were bad ones, like Rappin', Breakin' and Breakin' 2. I wanted to make a hip-hop movie about the kids who actually listened to hip-hop. The plot wouldn't revolve around trying to get a record deal—just regular kids being themselves. Even once we put rappers—Kid 'N' Play—in the roles, I still wanted it to be realistic. But I felt that we would have so much music in it that at a certain point we could cross the line and get away with it. By the time we get to the scene where Kid's in jail, he just breaks into song and no one complains. It's a complete violation of the rules, but no one notices because there have been enough motivated musical numbers throughout the picture that the audience just flows with it.

GA: *And it works. It's actually a device.*
RH: That was my greatest magic trick, because it's just wrong, and I remember Bob Shaye, the head of New Line, saying, "He just broke into song. You can't do that." But I told him that we did it, it's okay and no one's freaking out. We'd pulled the audience in enough that they accepted it when we finally crossed the line.

GA: *Were you surprised that this film did so well and then became a franchise?*
RH: Well, it was very interesting. When we first did the deal with New Line, they said that the film would make about $10 million, and we felt that it would make $14 million because that was pretty much what the perceived ceiling for Black films was at the time. When it made $27 million, we thought, "Oh, my God!" None of us expected it to be that big of a hit, and we were all really excited about it. During the first week of production we all said that you could do one of these every year: *House Party, Dorm Party, Rent Party* and *Old Age Home Party*—you could just keep banging them out. I really loved the characters and the actors, but I didn't want to necessarily do that as my next project. I didn't want to just be the teen movie guy for my career.

New Line, however, wanted to make a sequel immediately, and basically pay me the same thing they paid me on the first one. That kind of ended the conversation. Every other studio in town was offering me big money, but New Line couldn't come up with a way to compensate us in other ways, so New Line and I parted. I don't think they were motivated, because they felt they knew how to make the sequel without us. They had a really cocky attitude that I didn't think was warranted. We had tremendous disagreements about how to develop the script initially, then eventually went with my approach and really helped me structure the material. But I still knew there was a set of rules in my head that are not obvious but are the key to the movie's success. But they felt they had the formula. I didn't see *House Party 2* until it came on cable. Doug McHenry and George Jackson directed it, and I remember the actors called me after they saw the finished product and they said, "Reg, we saw *House Party 2*. It's bad. [Laughs] It's really bad, we just wanted to call to let you know." [Laughs] So I didn't want to see it, and then when I saw the film, I was really stunned because it was so much worse than I had imagined it to be. They violated almost every rule I had in my head about how House Party works.

GA: *What were the rules?*

RH: Well, in the original film the point is that Play, the player, doesn't get women and Kid, the nice but uncool kid, does. I remember Play joking around that on the next movie he'd get all of the ass, and sure enough in the next movie he's just sleeping around with all these women, which violates the sense of justice the first film delivered. The reality is there are more guys not getting any than there are cool guys getting over, so the first film was designed to appeal to who the audience really was. Another big comedy rule I have is no undercranked shots—like someone's running, then the film goes into high speed. Never do that. Once I saw people running at high speed, I was out of there.

GA: *Have you ever spoken with the directors about House Party 2?*

RH: I remember talking to Doug before I saw the film but after he'd finished it, and he said, "You know, people don't appreciate the first film. Trying to reproduce that film is really hard—that touch that you had," which I really appreciated. When I saw the film, I really understood his frustration. And I really like Doug, liked George, God bless his soul. So I never confronted them saying, "You fucked up my franchise. That's shitty." They did the best they could do. The fact is that every time New Line makes a sequel, I get a check, so I'm making money without doing anything. The only downside is that people blame me for the sequels. People come up to me and say, "Hey, man, House Party 2 sucked!" I'll tell them that I had nothing to do with it, and they'll say, "But I saw your name on it! [Yells] Your name was on it!" [Laughs] The fact that the sequel says only "Based on characters by Reginald Hudlin" means nothing to them. I've never seen House Party 3, but I recently saw in the store the video box for House Party 4, which ironically stars the rapper Immature. And one of the guys in that group was one of the voice actors in Bebe's Kids, the animated movie that I did. Their first single was on that soundtrack. So when I saw the House Party 4 box, I thought, "Oh, my God, my worlds are colliding effortlessly."

GA: *[Laughs] That's funny, and talking about Bebe's Kids, what was it like working with Robin Harris on House Party? I thought he was incredible.*

RH: He was just amazing. The thing about Robin is that you just felt like he was some Jurassic Park re-creation of a comic from the Pigmeat Markham days. . . . We were like, "Damn, I thought brothers like you were an endangered species." Them kind of old, old, old school comics—he was that cat. He felt like a contemporary of Red Foxx or something. You just had to go back beyond Eddie Murphy, beyond Richard Pryor to some earlier comedic time. [Laughs]

GA: [Laughs] In House Party he really sounded like someone's father. It was believable.

RH: Oh, yeah. He was great to work with, obviously a genius. I remember when we were shooting this scene where he was going through the party insulting different kids, and the director of photography, Peter Deming—who's a total pro—had the camera on his shoulder and one shot was ruined because he started laughing. You could see his shoulders bobbing. Robin got him. [Laughs]

GA: And it was so real. It reminded me of growing up. Someone's mother or father was going to show up at the party. [Laughs] It's a favorite. Let's talk about Boomerang. How did you get involved with that film?

RH: I never imagined working with a star of the magnitude of Eddie Murphy, but he really liked House Party, and he met with me and he said, "I like you guys. You go for the joke. I like guys who go for the joke." So we decided to do something together and we talked back and forth for a year pitching different ideas to one another, and he finally said, "I got it! I got the script!" He sent the script over and the script needed a lot of work, but the premise was incredible. It was just a classic Rock Hudson, Doris Day kind of romantic comedy. So I thought, "Great! This is perfect!" It was an incredible experience, because Eddie and I really got along creatively and we got to put together a dream cast with Martin Lawrence, David Alan Grier, Chris Rock, Halle Berry, Robin Givens, Eartha Kitt, Geoffrey Holder, and Grace Jones. Literally, everyone we wanted we got, because it was an Eddie Murphy movie. I remember talking to one of the producers—I said, "You know, five, ten years from now no one will believe all of these people were in the same movie." They looked at me like, "What are you talking about?" But now so many of those people are bankable independently.

However, Paramount was very nervous about handing over their big franchise star, their big summer movie, to these Black guys who'd done one little low-budget movie. But since Eddie had made up his mind to get behind us, they fell in with the program. But the studio was very nervous, and one outgoing executive said, "Well, I don't know how you're going to make this movie work. A romantic comedy with Eddie Murphy? He's got that broad nose and thick lips."

GA: They said that?

RH: Yes. It was like a scene out of that sci-fi TV series V, where the aliens take off their masks and eat a rat. I thought, "Damn! We are in the room with Satan." The stakes were so high, the veneer of white liberalism went away and they came out with their real shit.

GA: *It's one thing to think that people believe this, but it's another thing to hear them say it.*
RH: And it was an interesting moment, because we realized that the guy was saying this because he wanted us to beat his ass so he could fire us. But you realize that the point is not to whip this guy's ass but to make the movie.

GA: *That kind of psychology was really going on?*
RH: Yes. That level of game, you have to have your wits about you. "Whew, okay, okay, what are we here for? What's really going on in this room?" And we went forth and made it.

GA: *Deep stuff. One thing that came up when the film was released was the white audience reaction to it. Some thought it was an unrealistic portrayal of Blacks.*
RH: Oh yeah, oh yeah. There was a big review in *The Hollywood Reporter* (June 29, 1992) where they said that the film was some kind of science-fiction movie. Some white people would much rather be depicted as the evil white man who is repressing Black people than be rendered irrelevant. A world where Black people are living really great, comfortable lives and where white people don't make a difference in their lives one way or the other is something they cannot abide.

GA: *And why is that? Is this still the case, then, years later?*
RH: Sure, because Hollywood is very segregated—both the city in general and the film industry specifically.

GA: *And why do say that?*
RH: Geographically, I think its sprawling size makes it easier to maintain racial and class separation. As far as the industry goes, the art world in general gets away with discrimination in hiring, because they say, "Well, it's about cultural tastes." And because they define what cultural tastes are, it's a self-fulfilling prophecy. You look at the music business and you obviously have tons of white people who love Black music. They have no problems expressing their love for Black music and Black artists who make Black music, as well as white artists who make Black music, but for some reason that's not true in the movie-business, yet we're talking about the same consumers. So it's not the consumer, it's the attitude of the studios.

GA: Does it seem like this is the last place where Blacks are largely excluded?

RH: Oh, yeah, because again it comes down to jobs. These jobs pay very well and there are very few of them, and anytime you give someone you don't know a job, you're not giving a job to someone you do know. So if you didn't go to college with Black people, don't have any Black people in your family, and if your close circle of friends doesn't have any Black people, you're not hooking your friends up. You're giving it to some stranger, and why would you do that? We're talking about food on the table, putting kids through college, let alone shaping the minds of the world, so it just gets down to very real issues.

GA: Speaking of Los Angeles, do you think it's necessary to live there if you want to be a filmmaker or a screenwriter?

RH: It depends on what you want to do. You can make films independently anywhere. You can even be a Hollywood player and live outside of Hollywood. I think it's easier to be here, but not necessary. Obviously, Spike has a great career and he lives in New York.

GA: And Woody Allen. There are exceptions. What's your fantasy project?

RH: There's one that I've been fantasizing about for most of my life—the movie that I went into movies to make is a musical based on the concepts of George Clinton and Parliament Funkadelic.

GA: That would be hot!

RH: That's one of those movies that when you talk to regular people, they're like, "Oh, damn! Man, you got to do that!" Everyone gets really excited, and you talk to Hollywood executives and they're like, "What? What are you talking about again?"

GA: Why do you think it's difficult for them to see it? Is it because they didn't live through some of that music? That music was pre-crossover.

RH: Right, but the irony is that if you go to a P-Funk show today it's all of these thirty- and forty-year-old Black folks and all these twenty-year-old white folks. The white people know all of the lyrics too, but the studio executives don't belong in either of those demographics, so there's an information gap.

GA: Why are movies important?

RH: I think they are important for a lot of reasons. One, from a kind of cultural, sociopolitical point of view, they literally represent our collective unconscious as a culture. When they call Hollywood the dream factory, I think that's really true. We have to put our dreams out there. You have to imagine it first before you can do it. Movies are probably our number-one export, and now more than ever it shapes thinking and opinion on a global basis. When Woodrow Wilson saw *Birth of a Nation* he said, "This is history written in lightning." I think that's one of the best descriptions of movies ever, and it's perfectly ironic that he was talking about *Birth of a Nation*, which is a completely fictionalized version of Reconstruction, but he's right. Film is electrified and electrifying, and becomes people's dominant source of information. Its emotional power is more persuasive than the written word.

So for better or for worse, that's how we're defining what the world is and how things happened. It's like, "We lost the war in Vietnam—that's okay, Rambo can win it." "Ali's the champ, yeah, but so is Rocky." You can literally change time and space and change our collective consciousness through movies. I thought about the impact of movies as an art form when I was very young, because I liked to draw, liked to write, did theater, all that stuff, but then realized movies contain all of the seven arts: theater, painting, literature, music, dance, sculpture and architecture. Film also pays the most and is seen by the most number of people, so it just seemed like the smart move. By doing film I could do everything. Originally, my goal was to either work in the comic book business or make movies, and I'd still like to do comic books. I still have an interest in doing theater at some point—I'd like to do a big Broadway show—and I have an interest in television and publishing, all of those things.

GA: *Why a musical?*
RH: I think all filmmakers want to do musicals because great musicals are such movie movies. Oliver Stone, Woody Allen, Spike . . . John Woo wants to do musicals, and one could argue that John Woo does musicals—to the rhythm of the machine gun. Baz Luhrmann's *Moulin Rouge* just flipped me out, because when you see that film you see a guy who just loves movies, loves music and you can see all of that love on the screen, just pushing out of every frame. I watch it all the time, and I never see movies twice.

GA: *It's pretty amazing visually. Musicals are great.*
RH: I just feel like doing all those things that gave me so much when I was a kid. I feel like you should give that back, pass it down to the next generation. However it hit you, you need to do that again. That's what George Clinton was for me. George Clinton is my favorite artist of any medium, because he said, "Yes, I'm Black and I'm intellectual and political and raw and *funky*, AND I have a sense of humor about the whole thing." He really had his cake and ate it too. He balanced

it all out and he did not treat audiences like they were stupid. He presumed that people were as smart as he was while making it art that you could enjoy on any level. If you wanted a funky beat you could dance to, it was there. If you wanted to listen to the lyrics and laugh, that was cool. If you wanted to listen to the lyrics and say, "Wow, that's kind of deep." Whether it's from a political or cultural point of view, however you want to take it, it was there. It was holographic.

GA: *At the same time, it had commerciality.*
RH: Exactly, exactly, so to me I'm like, "Yes!" That's the goal—if you can do it all simultaneously, then you are making successful art.

GA: *Do you listen to George Clinton to inspire you? What's your favorite cut?*
RH: I've listened to so much P-Funk in my life, I can't even play the hits anymore. I listen to the really obscure album tracks and B-sides and stuff from early in his career.

GA: *Is moviemaking magical, and why?*
RH: Oh, yeah, because getting a movie made, whether independent, Hollywood or whatever, is an accident. The system has so much entropy in it that it's just not designed to produce things. It's designed to stop things from happening.

GA: *Give me some examples.*
RH: Well, it's so expensive. If you want to write a book, you just sit down and write it—on toilet paper if you have to. If you want to make a record, you can make a smash record for $500 in your bedroom. But movies just cost on average millions of dollars. Even a no-budget movie like *She's Gotta Have It* costs hundreds of thousand of dollars. Some people don't make that much in their lifetime.

GA: *There are huge barriers to entry.*
RH: The entry costs are so high and you need to get a good script, good actors—and anything can ruin your movie. Like the wrong lamp in a scene could ruin everything. Any little thing can undercut the power of what you're doing. So on one hand you have access to music, light, dance and all of these other art forms, but they all have to be done at a certain high level of expertise to make it all worthwhile or else you've wasted a bunch of money. It's just a very tough medium to work in, and then to add race on top of that makes it tougher. Whether the subject matter of the film is racial or not, if you're talking about putting Black people's lives in a film, then certainly the level of difficulty gets so much harder.

GA: From the perspective of the craft of filmmaking, how do you make sure you have the right people behind the scenes to help bring all of the elements together?

RH: I believe in being the dumbest person in the room: surround yourself with people who are smarter than yourself. A lot of people don't work that way—they want to be in control, to feel powerful, so they don't share information or they're not collaborative. Not me. I just think you have really smart people around you, let them know, if they have an opinion or they see something going wrong, to speak up. I always tell everyone who works with me that I will listen to anything you have to say if you don't mind my saying no. People really appreciate that, because then they're invested—it's not just a job. At the same time, no one wants anarchy. Everyone wants to know that there is someone in charge, there's someone saying yes or no, there's someone who has a vision and who's going to move the thing forward, because if it's just a committee, then the movie doesn't get made. Particularly at four in the morning—everyone's tired, no one wants to think. There needs to be someone with a plan of where we're going and how we're going to get there—that's the director.

GA: Do you want to write more work of your own?

RH: The tough thing about writing is that if I'm writing I can't do anything else. I'm really good at multitasking and working on more than two things at once, but if I'm writing, I really have to shut down everything else. So it's really not necessarily very time-efficient, because you just shut down for three or four months, and once you're finished maybe it gets made, maybe it doesn't. But I work with writing partners. I can lay out a conceptual framework and contribute tremendously, but someone else is helping and doing all of the legwork. That's what I find the most satisfying and efficient. Right now, I'm working with Aaron McGruder, who writes the The Boondocks comic strip, and he's hilarious.

GA: He's on the pulse, right?

RH: He's way on the pulse. So I'm developing two or three projects with him and a couple of other new writers. And some veterans, too. Again, all that experience they bring helps me.

GA: What has been your most rewarding directing experience?

RH: House Party, because it was my script and we were completely free. It was so low-budget that the studio wasn't really sweating us. It had no stars, the actors were all glad to be there and we just did our thing. It was just a lot of fun.

GA: What's been your least favorite and why?

RH: Ladies' Man was a very tough project, because I had the least amount of freedom in terms of the material. Saturday Night Live has this set way of making their films, and we talked about that up front. We both knew there would be sort of a dynamic tension, and they welcomed that. At the same time it was frustrating, because you're arguing with people who have discovered so many great comics, created so many classic characters, but only made one great movie.

It's important to maintain your own standards, because no matter how bad a movie flops, how distasteful the final product is to you, there will be people who'll tell you how much they loved it. And you look at them like, "What's wrong with you?" [Laughs] But there are things about Ladies' Man that I like. Especially the musical number. Anytime I can do a musical number, I'm really happy.

GA: What are your thoughts on Black film today?

RH: What's frustrating is that Black movies have just settled into this terrible kind of mediocrity. Part of it is a reflection of where we are in terms of Black culture, but it's also the effect of Hollywood on the Black film movement. In some ways Hollywood's initial hostility to Black film was good, because we made films based on what we wanted to see, with little to no studio input, or even with any real idea of the commercial marketplace. The only previously existing models for Black film were Eddie Murphy or Sidney Poitier vehicles, which didn't really apply to us, or blaxploitation movies, which didn't really apply to us either. So what we were doing was literally cutting a path in the woods—there was no template. But now that middle path has been abandoned and now films fall into the same previously existing categories. There are mainstream vehicles for Eddie Murphy, Denzel, Will Smith, Morgan Freeman, et cetera . . . and there are these low-budget Black films that are inexpensive—which is okay—but they have no originality in theme or style. They aren't even as well made as white films made for the same budget. The studios really just have a contemptuous attitude toward the audience, and it shows in the product. They're all very bad knock-offs in either bad gangster films or bad romantic comedies. They're embarrassing, and I just don't see the white equivalents of those films being made. Maybe they exist, but I just don't see them.

GA: Is the problem with the writers and directors or with the studios, which are not spending the necessary time in the development process with some of these Black projects?

RH: I think it's both. The way the system works, innovation is discouraged. No one wants to be first, everyone wants to be second. They'll pay twice as much to be second. After all, if it's a new idea, how much will it make? How should it be marketed? How much should you spend on making it? Too much risk involved. So very mediocre, very derivative products get made.

GA: *You once told me that things wouldn't change until we started our own studios, but some directors liken that to waiting for the revolution. What's to be done in the meantime?*

RH: Learn your craft, don't waste time on bullshit projects and keep growing as an artist. It frustrates me that people don't study what they do. They haven't seen Fellini and Kurosawa's films, they don't know who Preston Sturges is and they don't know the films of Howard Hawks. There's a similar problem in Black comedy now. Black comedians used to be on the same comedic circuit as Jerry Seinfeld and Tim Allen, and now Black comedy has its own circuit.

GA: *That's not a good thing?*

RH: It's a good and a bad thing. Economically, it's a good thing that it's a vibrant enough industry that it can support its own, but if Black comedians are only influenced by other Black comedians and they only do derivative routines, it gets very, very reductive. And I worry about the same thing with Black filmmakers who judge their films only in comparison to other Black films. No, no, no, think of your movie opposite The Matrix, opposite Erin Brockovich. This is the world we have to compete in—we have to look at it on the biggest scale. Some Black movie stars are very uncomfortable with working with Black directors.

Now, I don't want to frame this as purely a racial issue. Not all directors are created equal, and just because someone is Black doesn't mean they are not a hack. But when you see Black movie stars work with hack white directors, you wonder why. At least a Black hack recycles Black dollars! There are some people who just believe "the white man's ice is colder." But it's usually not that simple. They feel that if the project is too "Black" they won't have the same budget for the film, they won't get their salary and they won't get the same promotional push. They might also feel that if they work with a white person they can have more control of the project by "mau mauing" the studio and the director as the "Black expert." Sometimes it just comes down to who you like. You may not like or get along with certain people. Or you want a director with a certain expertise, like in heavy special-effects pictures. Or one of a certain age group. There are plenty of factors that go into the decision besides race. But I think cultural affinity to the material is underrated. So many great white directors meet their Waterloo—or maybe Little Big Horn—doing a film with Black subject matter. Their otherwise great instincts fail them. Anyway, these choices are only available to a small number of actors, although thankfully that list of Black stars with clout is growing.

GA: *Like the Will Smiths of the world?*

RH: Exactly. Will Smith, Denzel and Chris Tucker and so on, and thank God they're actually getting the money and the clout they deserve. They've paid for it in blood, there's no doubt about it. Obviously, the system can "improve," but it only improves by pressure. The success of *She's Gotta Have It* as an independent film outside of Hollywood created a form of pressure, because here was a film that was making money and it had an authenticity that made Hollywood representations of Black life look pale in comparison. Therefore, Hollywood needed to co-opt and integrate Black directors into their system. So when we say, "Jeez, we're looking for the next big leap in terms of the depiction of Black people," it's going to take an outside event to create pressure on the system to make radical change. The big problem is in the permanent "government" of Hollywood—the studio executives, the agents, the managers. As long as those ranks remain virtually all white, we're not going to have substantial change, and you can certainly look at waiting for that to change like waiting on Heaven or the revolution, whichever comes first. It certainly feels that way sometimes. At the same time, there are those sudden breakthroughs. In the music business, you had Motown, which for a long time was the greatest example of Black institutional building in the entertainment field. Now you have several joint-venture deals with multinational conglomerates, like Def Jam, Bad Boy, LaFace, and Master P. Sometimes those deals are very profitable ventures for all concerned; sometimes they're just rhinestone sharecropping situations where the smaller partner takes all the risk and ends up in debt so the parent company ends up with the hard assets at the end of the day. Whether it's a stand-alone company or a joint venture with an existing multinational, there is a need for that type of home for Black film. The challenge is that the film business, unlike the music business, requires a certain amount of literacy. [Laughs] Now, you don't necessarily have to read scripts in order to run the company, but you do have to work with people who do read. Bringing together the MBA types, the bohemian hipsters and street hustlers and having them all work together is an ambitious goal. But if we can't overcome class and cultural hang-ups and work together, we cannot win.

GA: *Earlier you mentioned that Black writers and directors often settle for mediocrity. Why do you think that's the case? Is it subconscious?*

RH: Oh yeah, I think it's part of our profound psychological dilemma as a people. What Black people need today are SWAT teams of psychiatrists just flooding into our neighborhoods and helping us deal with all the mental illness that stops us from going to the next level. [Laughs] So part of that is the legacy of self-hate and overcoming that. As Chris Rock once said, "There's no Black on Black crime, there's just crime. Crime is bad." There is so much positive reinforcement of negativity in the era we're living in right now. When I was a kid, I hated when they said "Stay in school, don't use drugs," because I resented the assumption that I wasn't going to stay in school and that I needed to be told not to use drugs. That same negative reinforcement extends itself to the current cultural marketplace. The reality is that if you want to cross over, one surefire way to go is social pathology, because that's exciting and exotic to the white audience and there's a greater appetite for it than being normal. Public Enemy is a greater crossover artist than Luther Vandross. If white people want to fall in love, they listen to Shania Twain or Jon Bon Jovi. But if they want to be angry and powerful, then that's when they want to assume the guise of a Black man.

GA: *That's kind of scary. Getting back to your craft, how do you prepare for a film shoot?*
RH: If it's a script that I have not written, first of all, can I read it straight through? So often you hit page twenty and you go, "Whew! Let me take a little break, go get a glass of water, see what's on TV." You go check your e-mail, then realize "Man, I ain't got back to that script yet." So that's a bad sign. And sometimes if it's really bad, I'll read the first twenty and then I'll read the last ten, and if I feel like I haven't missed anything in between, then that one goes into the garbage. If you read it straight through and you get caught up in it like it's a movie, then that's a good script, that's something you should do. Even then the script usually isn't perfect. The second question is "What don't I like and do I know how to fix it?" So you make notes that are just script notes. Finally, you look at it from a directing point of view in terms of how do you visualize this, how do you visualize that, how do you make it as cinematic as possible. Comedy can be very tough, because it's just people talking. It's easy to do something very visually dynamic if there is a fight scene or chase, but if it's just people talking, even though they're telling funny jokes, the challenge is to find visual metaphors that enhance the theme, or give subtext through lighting, locations, costumes, camera placement. Can you eliminate words by saying it some other way?

GA: *Who are some of your favorite influences in film?*
RH: There are so many. It's weird—as incredible as Spielberg's credits are, in a certain way he's underrated, because movies that are pure entertainment are always underrated. I have a range of influences. Howard Hawks, who made *His Girl Friday*, which I think is the funniest movie ever made, then *Red River*, a great western. Then you look at Preston Sturges, who just defined what romantic comedy is—we're just all trying to rip him off and not doing it as well. Then you have international influences—Kurosawa, Fellini . . . and, of course, there are new school cats. The Coen brothers, Baz Lurhmann, Oliver Stone, the Washorksi brothers, Beat Takashi . . . I could just keep going.

GA: What are your favorite films?

RH: Everything from Charles Burnett's *Killer of Sheep* (1977), George Miller's *The Road Warrior* (1981), a Cuban film called *Memories of Underdevelopment* (1968) by Tomás Gutiérrez Alea, *The Wedding Singer* (1998), *The Man Who Shot Liberty Valance* by John Ford (1962), *Spartacus* (1961), *Evil Dead II* (1987), *Lumumba* by Raoul Peck (2000) . . . I could go on literally all day in every kind of genre.

GA: What's your advice for aspiring filmmakers?

RH: If you're going to get in the game, come humble and come with it, because there's no time for lemon heads. It's a tough business, but there are tremendous opportunities. If we had five more great African-American screenwriters, they'd work all the time. People who can balance the raw funk of Black culture with cinematic sophistication. There's a tremendous need for that.

GA: What legacy does Reginald Hudlin want to leave on this earth?

RH: I'd like to leave a body of work that stands the test of time. But it's really hard for comedy to get any critical respect—at least initially. A really bullshit melodrama will get critical acclaim, while the well-executed comedy gets overlooked. But eventually the great comedy gets the love it deserves. I can look back on George Clinton's music and see how deep it all is. I'd like to have a body of work like that. If I can do that and eventually have children that take whatever I've done and go two or three times as far as I did, then I'd be happy beyond imagination. The great choreographer and social activist Katherine Dunham was a big influence on me. On several occasions she's remarked that she wants "She tried" on her tombstone. Maybe I should put "Me too" on mine. [Laughs]

John Singleton

Few films knock me out of my seat and haunt me for days. But John Singleton's first feature film, Boyz 'N the Hood (1991), was one of those films. The riveting, largely autobiographical, coming-of-age film about boys growing up in South Central Los Angeles brought me closer to young boys I knew from growing up but perhaps thought I didn't know so well but did nonetheless. Singleton's simple, honest portrayal of human life ignited a plethora of derivative urban films to follow, with few carrying the emotional intensity and integrity of Boyz 'N the Hood.

Boyz 'N the Hood garnered Singleton a place among the Hollywood elite, making him the first Black and the youngest person ever to be nominated for the Academy Award for directing in 1992. He also received an Oscar nomination for Best Screenplay.

A native of Inglewood, California, and a graduate of the University of Southern California School of Cinema, Singleton followed Boyz up with Poetic Justice, with Janet Jackson and Tupac Shakur; Higher Learning with Ice Cube; and Rosewood, with Ving Rhames. In 2000 came Shaft, with Samuel L. Jackson, which became Singleton's biggest box office success to date, grossing $70 million domestically. In 2001 came Baby Boy, starring Tyrese. The film is the final work of a trilogy of films dealing with urban Black young men, which started with Boyz and was followed up with Poetic Justice (1993). He is currently at work on Fast and the Furious 2 (2003) for Universal.

- - - -

GA: *You grew up in Inglewood, California. Tell me about your childhood and the role movies played.*

JS: I was a latchkey kid, and I think I broke into movies because of that. My mother and father never married, but I was always close to both of them. My mother's apartment was adjacent to a drive-in theater called the Century Drive-in, which was an L.A. landmark, and I used to watch movies, including the slasher films, out of the back window of the apartment. And growing up, my father and mother would always take me to the movies. My mother actually took me to my first movie—*Rosemary's Baby*, but I was too young to remember. My father and I would always go to Hollywood to see the big films at Grauman's Chinese Theater or the Egyptian. In the summer of 1977, when I was nine, he took me to see a film, but he didn't tell me what we were going to see, he just said that I'd like it. And the movie starts, the Twentieth Century Fox logo comes up, you hear the Fox theme song, then BOOM, it's the beginning of *Star Wars*, the opening of Episode IV. I remember the star cruiser coming down chasing a smaller ship and firing at it, and that was the defining moment for me. That's when I decided I wanted to be a filmmaker. I saw *Star Wars* about a dozen times over that next three years, and because I saw the movie again and again and again, I began to break down how a film was made. I learned that a film had to be written, shot and edited.

Another defining moment was watching Steven Spielberg on a late-night news program. I think he was discussing *Close Encounters of the Third Kind*, and I said, "Hmm, that's what a director is." At the time, I knew nothing about Black pioneers like Gordon Parks, Melvin Van Peebles or Michael Schultz, whom I admire as a pioneer in studio filmmaking. I only knew about George Lucas and Spielberg. In elementary school I would take a notepad and draw slightly different images on each page and make these little animatics—little animated films on paper. My friend Aaron Spears and I would do this all the time from elementary school to junior high. But when I got to junior high I had problems because I wore glasses and I was picked on, but I wasn't about to be no punk. So I carried a box cutter to school, because this kid kept asking me for my money and my comic books. My dad worked at Thrifty's (the drugstore) as a manager, and they used box cutters at the store and I brought one from home. One day when this kid picked on me I slashed his jacket with the box cutter and I got suspended. When I came back to school they had a rule against bringing metal combs—cake cutters—to school, because they could be used as weapons, so this time I didn't bring a box cutter, it was just a comb to pick out my little afro. And this teacher saw me with the metal comb and he said, "Singleton, don't you realize you can't bring metal combs to school? Aren't you halfway intelligent enough to understand the rules?" So he took my comb and embarrassed me in front of the whole class and I threw it in his face and said, "Fuck you, motherfucker," and ran out of the school.

The next day I went from living with my mother to living with my father up the street on Century Boulevard. My friends in that neighborhood got up at 6:30 or 7:00 in the morning to take a school bus out to the San Fernando Valley where they went to school with all of these Jewish kids. My friend said, "They got all the white boys out there, you know, it's more fun and you don't have to worry about anything." So I got up early with my friend across the street and I walked to the bus stop with him, got on the bus, rolled out to the Valley and enrolled myself into that school. Janet Jackson also went to that school for a time, but I don't think she was there while I was there, but she came to visit. At my new school there were last names like Shapiro and Abramowitz, and that was my first time interacting socially with kids who weren't Black or Mexican. Actually, it was all very refreshing, because we all had the same interests—comic books and movies. A lot of the parents of the kids who went to this little public school, worked in the film business. The father of one of the kids in my class was a casting director who cast a lot of the movies in the seventies. So this kid would get to go to premieres for films like *Raiders of the Lost Ark* and E.T.

GA: *Lucky kid. Did he come back to school and tell you all about it?*

JS: Yeah, yeah. Because, see, in my neighborhood when we sat around talking about what we wanted to be when we grew up, everyone would say that they wanted to be a basketball player or a football player. When I'd say that I wanted to be a film director, they'd say, "Film director? What's that?" I'd tell them and they'd say, "Ain't no white people gonna let no Black people make no damn movies." I would get dashed, but at my school in the Valley, I could be a film geek, I could love movies, I could love comic books. We'd go to all types of movies. In my neighborhood Kung Fu movies were popular, and I had a very good friend named Carl Austin—Carl was significant, because in eighth grade when *Blade Runner* (1982) came out, he bought the Phillip K. Dick novelization of the film, which was called *Road Warrior*, and gave it to me to read. These cheap novelizations were basically just the screenplay transposed into novel form, and Carl would always read the novels quickly, then let me borrow them. He also gave me Syd Field's *The Screenwriter's Workbook*.

GA: *So you were exposed to Syd Field very early.*

JS: Yeah, *Screenplay* by Syd Field and *The Screenwriter's Workbook*, and all Carl and I would talk about was making movies. He'd get these books about the making of *Star Wars* and we would read about *Raiders of the Lost Ark* and how Spielberg used storyboards and everything. I had no film equipment but the kids in the Valley all had 8mm cameras and were shooting shit. I didn't have any of that shit; all I had were my animatic storyboards. So I went to that school for a year, then my father suggested that we move in with my grandmother out in La Puente, and I cried like a baby. I really wanted to go back to that school, because all of those cats who went to the school in the Valley were from different cultures, and one thing I learned from them was to be proud of where you're from. On weekends the Jewish kids studied Hebrew and the Japanese kids studied Japanese, and for African Americans it's important to be proud of our music, our heritage and our culture. That's why I want my kids to be proud of being Black and to know that we built this country.

GA: When did you start taking your filmmaking dreams seriously?

JS: At Eisenhower High in California, I really began to get serious about my future, and whether or not I was going to go to college and I ended up writing film criticism for the school newspaper and I'd get preview passes to movies. I wrote reviews of The Breakfast Club (1985), Ladyhawke (1985), Mask (1985) and Sixteen Candles (1984). I also remember complaining to my mother during this time. I said, "I'm bored, I don't have nothing to do. I need some money." She said, "You're bored, why don't you take your ass over to South Pasadena and go to that old theater? They show old movies." So I started hanging out at this theater called the Rialto, and the first thing I saw there was Woody Allen's Bananas (1971), then Annie Hall (1977), and then I saw A Clockwork Orange (1971).

GA: Kubrick, huh? That's heavy stuff.

JS: Yeah, films were an escape from delinquency for me. Like François Truffaut, who said that films saved him from being a delinquent, films saved me from being a delinquent. The great epiphany for me was when I realized that all of the films that I went to see were basically big Hollywood movies. But in high school I got interested in art films and different forms, different types of cinema, when I realized that I could bring a lot of my own culture to my work and that's what would make me unique. During the summer between eleventh and twelfth grades, I took an 8mm cinematography class at Pasadena City College, and this was my first time using film equipment, and I learned about exposures and lenses and started shooting stuff.

GA: And you eventually decided to go to film school at USC. How did your parents feel about your wanting to be a filmmaker?

JS: My mother and father didn't really want me to go into film, they wanted me to go into business. My father said, "Go into real estate or go to business school." My mother's response was "Oh, shit!" Because in any family one generation works hard and the next generation wants to be artists. I don't know where you're from, but when you say that you want to be a writer most parents say, "Aw, man, how are you going to eat off of that? You're going to be coming and opening up my refrigerator and letting the cold out."

GA: [Laughs] *Of course, no one really encourages it.*

JS: Yeah, but before I went to film school, my mother had become friends with a woman in Pasadena named Tracy Willard, who had gone to Spelman College. Tracy was in charge of this NAACP film program, and I entered one of my 8mm films that I'd made at Pasadena City College to the program. My films were always controversial, even then. This film was about a Black dude who's so bent out on this blond girl that he kills himself over her. I don't think that went over too well with the NAACP. [Laughs]

GA: [Laughs] *I wonder why.*

JS: So I didn't get an award for it, but Tracy said that she liked my work and that I reminded her of a friend named Spike who went to Morehouse when she was at Spelman. She told me that he'd just made a movie, he'd be coming to L.A. and that I should meet him. And she gave me a flier for a *She's Gotta Have It* preview screening, and I asked my mom if I could borrow the car to go and hang out and meet this guy, but she wouldn't let me borrow the car. She figured it was an adult movie and she didn't want me going out there, hanging out with all of these suspicious Hollywood types. I later found out that the film had gone to Cannes, got an award and was coming out in August. It was the summer of 1986, and I went to see Kurosawa's *Ran* at a theater in Santa Monica, and a trailer came on that played the beat to the rap song *Set It Off*, and here was Spike Lee on the screen saying, "Tube socks, tube socks, tube socks. Wanna buy tube socks? I wanna tell you about my new movie, *She's Gotta Have It*. And I said, "That's the guy Tracy was talking about!" When the film came out, they showed it in a theater in Santa Monica and there were all these Black people going to see it on opening day, and I went out there, and who was in the front of the theater passing out buttons and talking to people? Spike. I said, "Hey, you know Tracy Willard? My name is John Singleton and I'm going to film school in two weeks, Tracy was trying to hook us up. I'm really looking forward to seeing your movie." I go in to see the movie, and I thought, "Wow! Black people on the screen acting like real Black people." I'm blown away, loving it, and so I came out of the theater afterwards—I'll never forget this. People always say that Spike is ornery and antisocial sometimes, whatever, but I'll always give him love for this. After the movie, all of these Hollywood types were surrounding him, and I walked out of the theater and was trying to get to him in the crowd, and he moved everyone aside and came to me and said, "What'd you think of the movie?" And I told him that I really liked it and was happy he'd made it, and I said, "I'm going to film school, watch out for me." [Laughs] It's a classic story.

GA: Definitely a classic.

JS: And so every year for the next four years, from *She's Gotta Have It* to *School Daze* to *Do the Right Thing*, I'd see Spike on his promotional tours, I'd go to his book signings and say hello and he'd ask me what was going on with me and how I was doing in school. And I was like, "Damn, I want to be like this guy, right?" But then something keyed into me because all the white boys at USC wanted to be like Spielberg and Lucas and they were telling me that they (the industry) were only going to let one Black person in the film business, and I used to be like, "Fuck all ya'll!"

GA: You also later met actor Lawrence Fishburne. Tell me about that?

JS: Well, I got my first paying job in the business as a production assistant/security guard on a television show called *Pee Wee's Playhouse*, and I was cheese grinning because I was on a studio lot. My first day, this guy walked up to me and spoke, and we introduced ourselves and he said, "You can call me Fish." And we ended up grabbing coffee and donuts. And I said, "Wow, you're Larry Fishburne." Man! Larry, coffee, donuts? And so he came out to the stage periodically and we'd talk, and I'd tell him that I was going to be a filmmaker one day and that I might write something for him. And he said, "How old are you?" I told him that I was nineteen, and he said, "Go on, brother." And he gave me his number and everything and I went to school and I kept going to school and I kept looking at movies, and I really realized that the cheapest way to make a movie was to write a movie. If you don't have a pot to piss in, you can get paper and pen and you can write a movie. I also read a lot of screenplays, and I realized that your screenplay can't be boring to the reader. You have to write the screenplay so it's enjoyable to read. If you write your own movie, then you're not at the mercy of getting or finding a script. You can write your own script. That's the most powerful thing to have in this business—the ability to generate new ideas—I tell my kids that all the time. So I wrote a screenplay called *Twilight Time*, about these five women who get together for their mother's funeral and in cleaning up her house, discover that she wasn't such a good person at all. She was a real ornery chick. For it, I won the Jack Nicholson and the Robert Riskin Awards at USC. After that, I started making the rounds to agencies, but no one wanted to sign me and I was getting frustrated because I wanted to quit school for a while and go to Brooklyn to work on *Do the Right Thing*, but Spike's company 40 Acres didn't hire me. Thank God they didn't, right?

GA: *Yeah. Why did you want to quit school?*

JS: Because at the time, which was 1989, I was feeling a little resentful because I really wanted to make it happen. It was the best time. It was the golden age of hip-hop music—you had everyone from KRS-One, Eric B and Rakim, and Public Enemy was coming out. In L.A. the hottest group on the streets was NWA (Niggaz with Attitudes), and Ice-T was out here, the whole gangsta style was coming in. And as adverse as I was to growing up in gang-ridden streets and having to deal with all that bullshit, and the stress from real life, I saw what was happening and I said, "I'm gonna write about my experiences." And I got the title for my script *Boyz 'N the Hood* from the song off of Eazy-E's album, "Eazy Duz It," which was written by Ice Cube.

And that summer I went to a preview screening of *Do the Right Thing* and I came out of the theater and said, "I'm gonna make my fucking movie, watch this." That was June, and I started making my notes for the screenplay, and that fall I wrote *Boyz 'N the Hood*. I sat in the computer room at USC and I just started writing the script. I was basically doing what they said in film school that we should do—write what you know. I wanted to put L.A. on the fucking map. Spike was doing it in Brooklyn and I was going to do it in L.A. That was my whole mantra, and I would sit and listen to NWA and Eazy and write. When I pitched the script in class, I got up and said, "My script is called *Boyz 'N the Hood*. It's about South Central L.A. where you hear automatic gun fire and helicopters in the distance, it's about three boys growing up. It's my magnum opus. This is the movie I was born to make."

That year, I won the Jack Nicholson Award for a second time and started to get some notice. At the time I was interning at Columbia Pictures reading these stupid scripts, and I told Karen Teicher, who was in charge of the internship program, that I was a writer and she asked to see some of my work. So I gave her a copy of *Twilight Time*, and she liked it and I told her that she had to read *Boyz*. She read it, loved it and asked me what I wanted to do with it, and I told her that I was going to direct it. She gave it to her boss, who said that he didn't think they could let me direct it. But Karen had some friends who were agents, and she gave them the script and set up some meetings, including meetings at CAA [Creative Artists Agency] and William Morris. I went to the CAA meeting, and a guy named Brad Smith was there and some other agents, and they said that they wanted to sign me. And I had adopted this kind of cool reserve about anything I was excited about and said, "Okay." But then the excitement hit me and I said, "I'm in film school and I got an agent! The top agency in Hollywood. CAA?! Mike Ovitz?!" So you can't tell me shit now. I'm a senior at USC, I'm represented by CAA, I'm Black, and they all hate me anyway because I'm the one on campus who plays loud music in the middle of campus, and thought: "Fuck all ya'll. I have something to talk about." That was my attitude, and I guess what got me through USC—that predominantly white university—was the fact that I had something to prove. I had to prove that our stories were worth something and that was a combination of what was going on in hip-hop at the time and the fact that we were into it, because not a lot of white kids were listening to hip-hop then, or watching Spike and Robert Townsend's films. Eddie Murphy was at the height of his fame and stuff, but it was still small in comparison to what was happening in the mainstream. There was no real Black Hollywood.

GA: *What happened after you signed with CAA? Did you start taking meetings in Hollywood?*
JS: Yeah, my first meeting in the film business was a lunch meeting with Jasmine Guy, and I sat with her at a coffee shop, and she was talking about how she wanted to do the Dorothy Dandridge story, and I asked her to let me write something for her. I'm sitting there thinking to myself, "I'm sitting here with fucking Jasmine Guy," and I go in the middle of campus and [snaps his fingers] tell some cats that I'd just had a meeting with Jasmine Guy and these niggers didn't believe me. Later, I ended up meeting with Russell Simmons. Now, there are different versions of this story, but this is the right version. I had a meeting with Russell, who was looking at doing a production deal with Columbia Pictures because he was thinking about getting in the film business. Stan Lathan [the producer/director] had read Boyz 'N the Hood and loved it and he told me that I had to pitch it to Russell. So I went to the Mondrian Hotel up on Sunset where Russell was staying, and he's from New York and was standoffish, and had the attitude "prove yourself to me" or whatever. And I told him that the script was about L.A. and he wanted me to pitch it to him, and I said, "I don't need to pitch it to you, man. This is L.A., you're from New York, you wouldn't get this." I was basically just being as standoffish as he was. And so I said, "I tell you what, you know how in Jaws before the shark comes you hear the music 'DONNUM, DONNUM'? Well, before there's a drive-by you hear the booming sounds of this car going by and you know something's going to happen." Then Russell keyed in and said, "I'm doing the L.L. Cool J album, The Boomin' System, I get that, I get that." And he wanted to read the script, and at the time there was an airline called the MGM Grand that flew from L.A. to New York, and Russell took that back to New York and read Boyz 'N the Hood, and flipped the fuck out. He said, "This is the best fucking script I've ever read in my life!" He calls Columbia, "You stupid white motherfuckers. This is the first script I want to produce; this is the best script I've ever read." And the folks at Columbia said, Boyz 'N the Hood? Didn't John Singleton the intern write that script? Where is it? Where is it?" I had to call my agent at CAA, and my agent didn't want to give it to them because he wanted to hold on to it for himself, but we had already given it to all of these different production companies and none of them wanted to do it. They weren't feeling it.

But eventually a woman named Karen, who headed up the internship program, got the script to Stephanie Allaine, who was a creative executive at Columbia and the only Black working at the studio who could speak to the powers that be. And Stephanie thought that the script was phenomenal and tried to get Columbia to make it, but they didn't want to make it. She took the script to G-Peck, which was Guber Peters. Jon Peters was running Sony, and he and Peter Guber had their own production company at the same time they were running the studio, and they said that they wanted to do it for $5 million. If they didn't want to make it, Stacy Snider at Universal Pictures said that she wanted to make it.

So now after G-Peck decided that they would make it, Columbia decided that it would do it and wanted to meet with me. So I get my biggest meeting ever, with Frank Price and Michael Nathanson at Columbia. I came in wearing jeans and a Public Enemy T-shirt and acting like I was a bigwig but was really the smallest person on the street and had just caught the bus there, right? And they said, "So we liked your script and you want to direct it?" I said, "Yeah, I'm gonna direct it." And he asked me what I thought if they'd pay me $150,000 for the script and had someone else direct it. And I said, "Well, then, we'd have to end this meeting, because I'm directing this movie," and they asked me what made me think I could direct it. I said, "Because this is the movie I was born to make. It won't cost a lot of money. Instead of renting helicopters in the scenes where the helicopter flies over South Central, I'll use sound and light. I'll let light go past the window and put in the sound. I know who I want in the movie, and I'm gonna make this movie." I ended the meeting, and Frank Price used to say that I had more chutzpah than any other young person he'd met since Steven Spielberg.

GA: [Laughs] *He was probably right. You were pretty gutsy.*
JS: So my agent called me and told me that Columbia wanted to make Boyz 'N the Hood, they wanted me to direct it, and then I got scared. I also got my first office ever, in the Irving Thalberg Building at Columbia. Irving Thalberg was a movie mogul at a young age, so that was phenomenal for me to get my first office in that building, since I was only twenty-two at the time. And they say that it's great to operate from fear sometimes because you learn so much very quickly. I was very cavalier about being a filmmaker before, but I was really scared as hell because I had to fucking prove myself, so I just started watching movies upon movies and movies to figure out how I wanted to direct the film.

GA: *What movies did you watch?*
JS: I watched Drugstore Cowboy, The Color Purple, some Kurosawa films and a lot of Coppola's

work, because the first call I made was to Fish [Laurence Fishburne]. I sent Fish the script and he said, "Oh, this is beautiful, this is so beautiful. I was crying at the end." He told me that he wanted to do it and asked me if I could just add some more scenes with the father.

GA: [Laughs] His part, eh?
JS: Right, an actor's response.

GA: How did you go about working with actors, since this was your first film?
JS: I would ask Fishburne how Coppola rehearsed his actors, and Fishburne would tell me everything that Coppola did on the four or five films that he worked on with Francis, starting with *Apocalypse Now*. I would do acting exercises with the actors that had everything to do with the characters but had nothing to do with the movie. I dealt with the characters' past, present and future and did some improvisation.

GA: How did you run your set that critical first week?
JS: The first day of production I'm shooting in my old neighborhood, in the Bottoms in Inglewood. In the movie you'll see my old neighborhood. I got to the set at five in the morning, the call time was 6:30 or 7:00 A.M. and there was fog everywhere and it's one of the worst neighborhoods in L.A. and I'm there early in the morning, I'm standing there shivering—not shivering because it's cold, I'm shivering because I'm nervous. Then I saw the trucks come and all the people arrive, and I said, "Okay, let's do it, I need the kids over here, I need you guys to start walking, rehearse. I'd look at the shot and they'd rehearse the shot. The first shot in the movie was the most basic of shots—it was a tracking shot with four little kids, and the main character, Trey, is basically standing on the curb waiting for his friends to get there. His friends walk into the shot and they start walking. It's the first shot I ever shot in a movie ever. I went through the whole day shooting, and people were coming out of their apartments, people I hadn't seen since elementary school. They said, "John? What are you doing here?" And I told them I was directing a movie. And they said, "You're directing a movie?"

So we'd do scenes and stuff and there'd be about two hundred people standing to the side, and I'd yell, "Cut," and everybody in the neighborhood would yell, "Yay! Hooray!" And I'm on a roll, I'm shooting a movie, but I'm learning how to direct a movie while directing a movie. I shot most of the movie in continuity, which you never get a chance to do. But Steve Nicolaides, being the good producer that he was, knew that I had to basically shoot part of the film in continuity [the scenes shot in the order of the script, which is unusual], because I was new at it. So the film becomes a better film as it goes along, because I was becoming a better filmmaker day-to-day. I'd be up at two o'clock in the morning, making shot lists and figuring everything out in advance, the nuances and everything, and just poring over the whole thing. I had an outward appearance of confidence, but inside I was nervous for the first week and a half, but once I started watching the dailies, I was cool.

GA: Boyz 'N the Hood *was also accepted to the Cannes Film Festival in France, right?*
JS: Yeah, we got accepted to the Cannes Film Festival, and Spike had *Jungle Fever* there as well, and it was interesting, because my career was really getting started and Spike was going through some messy stuff with another Black director. It was just that whole nigger backbiting shit. Spike and I went to dinner the first night I was in Cannes and we later had lunch on the beach. We'd only known each other peripherally before, because I was in school and he was doing his thing, but then we sat there and we made a pact to never backbite each other in the media. We had a kind of mutual admiration because we both went to film school, and I'm not an elitist person or anything, I'm from the hood, but when you study your craft? When you study this shit? You really realize the strength of having knowledge about the past, and not only film form and film content and what filmmakers have done well, but you also study what they didn't do well and use it to do your own thing. It makes you a better filmmaker. To this day, Spike and I are so cool. I have a natural admiration for what he's accomplished, and it was really cool for us to sit down and talk candidly back then. At that time he was like a big brother to me, and I would say, "I want to grow up and be like you."

GA: *Let's talk about your hip-hop influence on movies?*
JS: I'm the first-generation hip-hop filmmaker. I was eleven years old when *Rapper's Delight* came out, so I've grown up with hip-hop. If you look at all of my movies, they're hip-hop films, because they have a different sensibility than the films from the filmmakers who came before me, like Melvin Van Peebles, Gordon Parks, Michael Schultz, Spike and Eddie Murphy. These people really made inroads into this business. And I mentioned Eddie Murphy because of his phenomenal success as an actor. All of these people who came before me opened the door for me to be able to do what I do in the way that I do it. Nobody's doing it the way I do it even now, because there's a certain mind-set when you choose to do things on your own terms and to not act like you're happy just to have your foot in the door. I've never been like that. So I'm basically a brat, because the first thing I directed, Boyz 'N the Hood was so phenomenally successful that it all led from there, and I've had varying degrees of success since I started doing my thing. When I sit in a meeting with a bunch of executives who just happen to not be Black, I'm thinking, "I'm gonna

do what the fuck I want to, because I've been doing it this way and I've been successful." Why am I going to take your suggestion? I'll be polite, if it's good and constructive criticism, I'll do it, but I'm gonna do what the fuck I want to do. [Laughs]

GA: After Boyz 'N the Hood there were a lot of other "hood" films, but none of the derivative films seemed to have the emotional fortitude of Boyz. Why?
JS: I like that, emotional fortitude. I'm gonna write that down. From an emotional standpoint, when I wrote Boyz 'N the Hood, I was writing about myself. All of these other people were doing it in reaction to wanting success or because they had an excuse to put out a soundtrack. When Jaws was successful three or four Jaws movies were made, and it's the same thing. Whenever anything is successful in Hollywood, it's appropriated.

GA: How were you able to transfer strong emotions to the page?
JS: I don't know, man. I just remember writing the script for Boyz 'N the Hood crying at the computer and smiling. I was writing about my life, about how I was ornery towards my mother when I was twelve years old and she sent me to live with my father, and how that changed me. My father gave me responsibilities and basically said that I was going to take out the trash, wash dishes and wash my ass. I was going to be a man. And he said, "I'm teaching you these things because all your little friends across the street don't have a daddy to teach them and you're going to see how they end up." So I basically just poured my life out. Right now I'm writing a script called Flow—about a young guy who makes a lot of money very quickly and his reaction to it. There're some personal things that I had to deal with when I had a change of lifestyle, and I can put that in the script. So I'm always trying to write from the heart, and that's what I think people key into.

GA: How did it feel to be nominated for the Oscar the first time you directed a movie and to be the first African American director and the youngest person ever?
JS: It was good, but at the time I couldn't really enjoy it, because I was very nervous about so much adulation so soon and I felt that I had to get another movie made quickly. The great thing about that was when I was nominated for the Oscar I was already in preproduction on Poetic Justice.

GA: Did the early success put pressure on you to perform at that level again?
JS: Until Shaft, I don't think I made a film where I didn't feel like I had to say something—I didn't know Boyz was going to be such a powerful thing—I felt that I had to do something powerful every time.

John Singleton **471**

GA: What inspired you to do Rosewood?

JS: I met the survivors of the town of Rosewood, Florida, and they told me their stories and when someone in their seventies or eighties tells you that they saw their whole family killed, it's just so humbling. I was actually prepping another movie at the time—*Makes Me Wanna Holler*, based on Nathan McCall's book, which I had the rights to. I still want to make that film. I just felt that at the time I had to make *Rosewood*. A lady from Rosewood told me, "Baby, either you're gonna do this movie or Steven Spielberg's gonna do it."

GA: But the film didn't perform well at the box office.

JS: Warner Brothers basically shelved the movie. They were ashamed they made the film, and wouldn't even let me take it to the Baptist convention and show it to all the ministers so they could talk about it in their churches.

GA: Why didn't they get behind it?

JS: Because no one wants to hear about the Black struggle. You hear about the struggles of all different kinds of people, but it's like trying to get Germans to do a movie about the Holocaust in Germany. They don't have any empathy for that, because in the back of their minds some of them are very ashamed of what happened.

GA: So why would they invest money to make the movie but not promote it?

JS: I don't know. It was fucked up. I could have done a lot to promote it, and after a while I figured it's not my $30 or $40 million.

GA: How'd you actually convince them to actually make it, though?

JS: It really wasn't a struggle to get the film made, because Jon Peters, who later produced *Ali*, was a big powerhouse producer, so he got it made.

GA: It seems that Blacks avoid films with difficult subject matter like Rosewood. Why is that?

JS: The fallacy of African Americans in this country, and I say this with all my heart and soul, is that unlike Jews, Chinese or Japanese or anybody, we don't lecture on the things that we've struggled through to make us stronger. We've gone through so much in this country to get to where we are today that every Black person should want to fucking read. Everyone should want to be a fucking genius, because it was illegal for us to learn how to read. We should never celebrate ignorance, because it was once illegal for us to have any type of knowledge at all. It's a case of our accepting that we're still being oppressed. Everybody's fucking oppressed, but rise above it. But Rosewood was a good experience for me, because I didn't make it to make money, but because I thought it was the right thing to do. Plus, what better way to get the monkey off my back about being the "urban" filmmaker than to do something radically different?

GA: *It's a disturbing film, but I highly recommend it. Why Shaft?*
JS: After Rosewood I felt like I needed a hit. In this business you're only one movie away from being out in the street. Shaft was one of my most successful films financially, and it was a big Hollywood movie and my first movie with a movie star—Samuel L. Jackson.

GA: *What are your hopes for Black cinema?*
JS: I'm trying to move Black cinema back into having something to say. Right now they're making these stupid-ass comedies. I don't want to blast anybody, but people know what they do is marginal and they know what they could do if they aspired to something more. You can make us laugh without having a minstrel show.

GA: *What are your favorite films?*
JS: Kurosawa's The Seven Samurai, Jaws, Citizen Kane, E.T.: The Extra-terrestrial, Raiders of the Lost Ark and the first Star Wars and The Empire Strikes Back. And then A Clockwork Orange, Annie Hall, The Godfather. And I love westerns like Red River. They're the most American of movie conventions, and every movie I've done references westerns.

GA: *During the Jazz Age a lot of the Black musicians collaborated on projects, and many hip-hop artists collaborate today. Why don't we see the same in film?*
JS: Because everyone is out for themselves. When it does happen, it's beautiful: Denzel, Wesley, Sam, all of the huge stars who are working right now have done their best work with Black filmmakers. The relationship that Denzel and Spike have is phenomenal. Every movie that they've ever done together has been the best that either of them has done. Spike and Denzel did Mo' Betta Blues, Malcolm X and He Got Game. Look at those three performances from Denzel. But everyone is out for his own, and what I hate about this business is how it serves to keep successful Black people apart and how it serves to keep Black stars from working with hot Black directors.

GA: *And how's that?*
JS: It's just that some Black filmmakers have their agents and their managers telling them that

they shouldn't do this movie or whatever. But Denzel Washington is a smart actor. On *Training Day*, Denzel said that he wanted Antoine Fuqua to direct. Antoine Fuqua hadn't had a hit, but he said he wanted Fuqua, and that helped Denzel and it helped Antione's career. And I predicted that he would get his first Best Actor Academy Award, and he did. It's a beautiful thing, and that is the way it should work, because everybody looks out for each other in this business, and Black people need to do the same thing, and this is what I've been about since day one. I don't get on my soapbox and preach, I just do it, but none of these fucking stars, none of the actors that I've ever helped make a star have ever called me up and said that he's got this project, why don't we work together? We're both going to get paid [Laughs], and we're probably going to get paid more by collaborating. But none of those people have ever called me up. That's why every movie I make, I invent new monsters.

GA: *If we could see more collaboration between Black directors, producers and actors, Black cinema might really soar.*
JS: But look at it, man, the big thing in this business is when successful people collaborate, and that doesn't happen that much, but when it does happen, it's beautiful. Look at what Sam Jackson and I did with *Shaft*. We want to do another movie, and when that happens, it'll be powerful.

GA: *There's something about the psychology of Black men that is understood between each other; the subtext is understood.*
JS: Yeah. Because when they're acting on their own and it's a white director, no matter what the director's great intention, they're on their own. They're directing themselves.

GA: *How does fatherhood affect your creativity?*
JS: I have five kids, and fatherhood's made me a better filmmaker, it's given me more patience, and it's made me more compassionate. I thought that fatherhood was going to make me more conservative, more risk adverse and everything, but it's made me even more radical, because I want to try different things that excite me.

GA: *What advice do you have for aspiring directors?*
JS: Write your own scripts. That's the cheapest way to learn how to make a movie.

Forest Whitaker

Forest Whitaker has one of the most recognizable faces in show business. A native of Longview, Texas, Whitaker got his start in film as an actor and has performed in some of the industry's most memorable films including the *The Crying Game*, *Platoon* and *Bird*, for which he won the award for Best Actor at Cannes in 1988.

Whitaker's first film venture behind the camera was in the 1993 HBO film *Strapped*. In 1995, he made his feature film directing debut with the 1995 hit film *Waiting to Exhale*. Based on the best-selling novel by Terry McMillan, the film, which starred Whitney Houston, Angela Bassett, Loretta Devine and Lela Rochon was the highlight of the holiday season and grossed $65 million domestically. The film's soundtrack produced by Babyface generated a smattering of hits.

Showing a penchant for films associated with women, Whitaker next directed *Hope Floats* (1998) with Sandra Bullock. He recently produced the film *Papi Chulo* directed by Linda Mendoza.

GA: *Tell me about creativity and the role it played in your childhood.*
FW: I was born in Texas, but my parents moved to Los Angeles when I was a young child—the first months of my life. My experience in Texas is that every summer I went back there to stay

with my grandparents on their farm. One of my grandfathers was a Baptist preacher. My other grandfather was a retired railroad man who had a farm and all of my relatives lived there. And luckily for me, all of my grandparents were still alive when I visited. In Los Angeles, my parents moved to South Central Los Angeles when I was a little child, and we lived there up until I was about eleven years old then we moved to Carson, California, where I stayed until I was about seventeen when I went off to college. I never took an acting class until I was in college. My mother was a teacher, my father was an insurance man, so the arts were not a big part of my life growing up as a child. The first structured plays I did were musicals in high school because in high school I was a singer. I did two musicals, Jesus Christ Superstar, and Cabaret. I was always singing. Then when I went to college, I had a scholarship in football, and it turned into a scholarship in music, then a scholarship in acting.

GA: What were some of your earliest memories of movies?

FW: I remember Sidney Poitier in Lilies of the Field because I was a kid then and I remember singing the song ["AMEN"] when I got home. I remember watching television because television probably played a more important part for me when I was a young kid because we didn't go to the movies a lot because we were pretty poor. If we did go to the movies, it was usually a drive-in. I didn't really go into a walk-in as I would call it until, maybe high school, possibly college. Now in regards to music, there was a period when I was in a neighborhood do wop group when I was about 13. While I was in elementary school in South Central was the first time I probably saw a play when I saw the opera The Marriage of Figaro. It was traveling from school to school, but I didn't see much theater as a kid.

GA: At what point did you decide that you wanted to be an actor and have a creative career?

FW: When I went to college I wanted to study music, I was studying classical voice to be an opera singer, and I was asked by my speech teacher for music to audition for a play, which was Under Milkwood, a Dylan Thomas play, and I got the lead in the play, I was the narrator. That summer a s well we went to Europe to sing different Renaissance songs across Europe, and I went to the West End and I saw Jonathan Pryce perform a version of Hamlet. I had always had a strange attraction to certain pieces because in junior high when they first showed Franco Zefferelli's movie Romeo and Juliet and we had to read those plays in class, I had an immediate understanding of the words. So it's really kind of circular for me. In the beginning stages of my life, I was just growing up, being a kid. One of my brothers was a music producer, so I would be in the studio with him quite often. We would record rap and hip hop music. My other brother was becoming a painter at the time and I was painting a lot. It's really the combination of different influences that brought me to filmmaking in the traditional sense. I wrote a script when I was in college that Steve Golin at Propaganda Films tried to buy from me. From that, they asked me to direct music videos, and, because of my acting classes in college, some of the other students asked me to direct or help them with their scenes. When we left and were out in the professional world, they asked me to direct plays, so I started directing plays professionally as well. As I started to direct plays and music videos—I was pursuing my interest in music and also in writing—things just started to come together for me as a filmmaker. In some ways, I went through a quiet apprenticeship by watching some of the best filmmakers, I think, in the world as an actor over the last twenty years.

GA: Who are some of your favorite directors?

FW: They all had different things to offer. Barry Levinson was interesting because being a writer he also had a great openness to people creating at the same time. So I watched him work with Bruno Kirby and different people and watched scenes be written overnight for the process, which was interesting to see. I thought Robert Altman was interesting because he had an understanding of being able to take real-world situations and turn them into drama, to be able to set up a party with real people and put people and actors inside of it and actually create scenes. It's an interesting way of working, and I thought that it was a useful tool depending on what you're doing. Oliver Stone was interesting because he has a very clear passion and directed vision about things. He also put the company through a really grueling training process and I don't think the film Platoon (1986) would have been as authentic if we hadn't gone through that.

I've worked with so many different filmmakers, and they all have a different style. David Fincher I found to be quite fascinating because I think he's good with actors, but he's extremely technically savvy and aware. I've worked with Neil Jordan who I found to have a clear statement on making really personal films, and I understood from that process because I've done different types of films, independent films and studio films. It's a certain thing you learn about—what you will do to make a film and how you make it work under any circumstance. In the end, The Crying Game was a really successful film.

GA: To what would you attribute your ability as an actor to work with so many different directors and so many different types of films—over thirty films, since 1982, correct?

FW: Yes. My concern has always been to just create work and to try to do something that's true. That's the thing that's guided me so far. As a filmmaker, there are a lot of things we have to deal with because of the studio and stuff like that, which are different in some ways than a pure art form but are still a part of the process of making a film. That's been my only goal: to do good work and to tell good stories and to be true to the heart of the soul of whatever it was I was doing. It's the same way I approach directing. I approach it from all different angles, but the biggest part is to find the soul of the piece and to let the expression of the movie come from that and to have the capabilities to be able to translate that kind of feeling or thought into a film, to make something that's alive because I believe a film has a soul.

GA: *Now tell me what you mean by a film having a soul.*

FW: I think that a film follows the basic precepts of the laws of creation from every tradition whether it's Christianity, Islam, the Native traditions, the African traditions. Normally, I start off with a void, a blackness and through a vibration, sound. Since you're sitting in a theater the first thing is darkness and then there's this sound, this energy and from that sound you see a life and from that motion you see something that's created. It has a beginning, a middle and an end.

GA: *How did you reach that level of understanding about the soul of a film and that level of clarity for yourself in that regard?*

FW: I don't really divorce my work from the way I live in my life. They're just expressions of the same and because I spend a large portion of my waking hours dealing with my art, I try to relate as a whole, and let it be an expression of the way I think about the world.

GA: *And so much of what you're saying to me sounds like the process of becoming an artist or being in touch with your artistry and being in touch with yourself.*

FW: Yeah, well I think as an actor I've always tried to find the certain thing that connects with everyone. When you're looking at a character you think, maybe he's a killer, maybe he's a murderer, but you think certainly he's connected to me in some way, so how can I go inside of myself and find that thing? That thing is it. The same with film for me. It has a certain character and I take on the little personality of that and it dictates to me the spirit of the piece: how it should be shot, how it should look, the colors, how those colors affect things. By going deep and trying to find that thing. If I do find it then it's ultimately going to relate to people because it's that thing inside of all of us. It's somewhere in there. It has to be.

GA: That approach tends to make your stories universal whether or not you're playing a character or directing the piece?

FW: Yeah, and in that way that's the only way that I can understand the term commerciality because for me it's not about making money because if you can find the fruits of a piece and you truly go deeply enough to see—find the truth of a character and the archetypal thing about it—then ultimately it's going to relate to people or resonate to people in a way that makes them attracted to it and makes them enjoy it in some way or learn from it or grab something from it and that will make people go to the theater. It's not the process of, "Oh, let me look at papers and find statistics: What do people want these days? What are people wearing these days?" That's not the process. Certainly, you can do that. I don't choose to because that's not why I'm making films. But then I am also making films that I hope will relate to my experience. I do want my grandparents in Texas to at least, if it's on video, watch the movie. If it's on cable I hope someone will tell them that it's on tonight and that they'll watch it and hopefully get something from it. It may not be their sensibility, but if it's honest enough and it's true enough, part of it will relate to them. And they may be able to say, "Well, it's not my thing, but it was pretty good."

GA: Now why does Forest Whitaker make movies? You could obviously just have a successful career as an actor and you can sing so you could do stage, but why have you chosen to direct movies?

FW: Well, I really think that making movies is really profound and beautiful. I'm just trying to find ways to express myself and it just so happens that directing is allowing me to express certain areas of myself in a way that it feels more complete. But the reason I go back and forth from directing to acting, I'm in the process of writing a script right now, is that I'm just trying to tell stories, different stories that relate, that explore the experience, the universal experience that brings us closer together in some kind of a weird way. It's the same thing I always did as an actor. I know that we're all connected in some kind of way. I know that these stories, these myths are part of the connection and in all of our psyches and I like being involved with that. I like telling stories. I'm not sure I'm the best storyteller if we were just sitting across from one another, but I keep trying to find my way of expressing what's inside of me.

GA: In terms of making a transition to making your film directing debut with Strapped, how did you do that? I know you had directed theater and music videos, but how did you move to film?

FW: I had acted for HBO and then a guy named Brian Siberell heard that I was directing and writing and he asked me if I would be interested in directing something. At the time I didn't feel prepared to do that.

GA: Why not?

FW: Ummm, it didn't feel right. For about three or four years he would call me periodically and ask me if I was ready and then one day he called and I said, "Well, I do have a script." And I sent it over and he said, "This isn't going to work for us, but I have this other script that I'd like you to read. Would you read it for me?" I said, "Yes, sure." I read it and at the time the story was from the point of view of the police officer and I said to them, "I'll do this movie if I can make it be from the point of view of the kids." They said okay and I began directing on my first film.

GA: What was it like working with actors given your strong acting background?

FW: It was a great experience for me. It felt completely and totally natural to direct a film from the very start. I never felt out of my place. I felt like I had fallen into what I was supposed to do. And acting is something that I had been doing for so long, it was something that I understood really well, because the thing about Strapped was that about 95 percent of the actors in that movie had never acted before. All of the kids, Bokeem [Woodbine], Fredro [Starr], no one had acted.

GA: What's your process for working with people who've never acted before?

FW: We just went through the rehearsal process. Honestly, it depends on the person. I tend to direct specifically to who the person is, to the way I perceive how that person needs to be communicated to. I don't really have a set way of like, "He's never acted, so I think we should do these exercises." No. I always look at the person then see what it is they need and that may be just to sit back in a room with someone who's going to be their lover and listen to music. Or it may be improvising a scene or it may be all of the above. It can be any number of things.

GA: You went from Strapped to Waiting to Exhale, which achieved such phenomenal success. Tell me how you got involved in that.

FW: I don't know how it originally came to me, but I went to meet with the studio and Terry McMillan was there, and at the time I really didn't have a good handle on that book. It was still just a book when I became involved; there was no script. And I told them that I saw it, and that it seemed pretty straightforward to me. Then I went away to New Orleans, I think, and on the plane I had this image of the script. I had listened to the book on tape and I read the book and I had this image of the movie in my head. So what I did was, I took Terry's words and I went to the recording studio and with music I started to weave the movie together, or weave her words and I was creating the style by which I was going to shoot the movie. I felt I had found the spirit of the piece.

GA: *What music did you use during that process?*
FW: It was music that I worked on with my brother and I put that together with Terry's voice. Then I brought the ghetto blaster in to talk to the studio again, and I explained to them the movie based on this new image of how I saw this style and the way the characters interwove in and out of each other. That's how I began it, then I started to work on the script with Terry and Ron Bass. I worked really intimately with them throughout the whole process, sometimes locking ourselves away in a hotel room to work on the piece.

GA: *Was it intimidating working on an adaptation of a book that was so successful and planted in the minds of the readership of mainly Black women?*
FW: Not really, no. Originally, I wasn't sure if I should direct the piece because I did not have the clear inspiration of it. I didn't see the soul, the piece, and it could have very easily turned into a soap opera.

GA: *I like how you use the word soul, and I'd like to focus on that. What did you see as the soul of Waiting to Exhale?*
FW: It was a piece about a person who was trying to break old patterns, who was trying to love herself, care about herself and solve all the problems in between. That piece was based on goddesses for me, so each one of those women was a very particular goddess. As a result of that, every color in their house was based on that particular goddess, every item, the colors in their clothes. The way I shot the camera with them was based on that particular goddess, as well as some of the issues between Angela Bassett and her husband's character [played by Michael Beach]—he was the god of war and she was the god of the sea, the upper part of the sea, the mothering, nurturing part of the sea. There's a story about how the son of this goddess rapes his mother. What he's really talking about is creation, which is talking about the first forms of life. He rapes her and she takes all of his instruments of war and throws them to the different parts of the world. So if you notice, when she gets up in the morning the first time we see her is through an aquarium, fish and things. She proceeds to wage war as he's [her husband is] excised out of her life. She burns the car. And all of the things on the patio generally, a great portion of them that she sells in the yard sale are all war instruments.

GA: Huh. *Interesting. I didn't catch that.*

FW: Inside of Loretta's house when the girls are all there, she's kind of that energy that lives at the bottom of the ocean. The curtains all look like seaweed, there are sea shells all over the table. We're at the soul of the piece, and the piece starts to find itself. The Lela Rochon character was sort of the goddess of love, the sweet waters and the oranges on the trees were the things that are connected with that energy. So the tree's not an orange tree, I just put oranges on it.

GA: OK. Wow.

FW: Then he [Mykelti Williamson] starts throwing them [oranges] back and forth, we replay that *Romeo and Juliet* scene on the balcony. I actually used the original music from the Zeferrelli film.

GA: *I loved that scene because I thought it was true.*

FW: [Laughs]

GA: *Even though he was being rude, it was funny.*

FW: The thing is too, all of those women in that film I felt I personally knew. So I was finding the spirit of each one of those individual characters, then finding the spiritual center of the piece and then the overall theme of healing that happens with each one of the women in different ways of empowerment. It found its way.

GA: *What was the process of assigning the specific goddess qualities and characteristics to the women?*

FW: I looked at the characters and the behaviors and decided those were the stories, the myths and it works. I was shooting the scene when we were in the house. I had talked to my production designer David Gropman about this and how I needed more things the color of black and green in the house, which in my mind are colors of war. They're always associated with the god of war in archetypal images and thoughts. And when I came in, I was so frustrated at the time because it wasn't what I asked for, it wasn't what I needed. He was racing around trying to find these things and I remember, I was sitting out in the grass just trying to figure out how I was going to do it then. My DP [director of photography] came and sat down, and we'd never had this conversation before and he said, "Not quite right." I said, "No." He said, "I don't know. It seems like it needs a little more black, a little more green."

I looked at certain archetypes for those women. They're bigger than life characters for me.

But for me, one of the things that I want to do as a storyteller is to tell stories about the everyday man, the everyday person and not only so that it will lurk inside of them, but also create the contemporary myths, the contemporary archetypes from the mailman, the insurance man—people who do the smallest deed—but which makes them at times heroes. In *Exhale*, I was definitely reaching for that even though it's a fun movie. People think it's like a pop movie.

GA: It was quite a bit of fun and I remember seeing it twice at the theater because one thing is that we go to the movies to first of all be entertained and it was very, very entertaining. How were you able to find truth and honesty in the piece while at the same time make it entertaining?

FW: Because I think that if I do that, the characters are true, they're honest people, I don't really know. I definitely know that there are things that are concerns of mine and interests of mine that probably make things even more accessible. And *Strapped* and *Waiting to Exhale* really invoke an interest in music. Music always bridges an emotional gap for people. But a different philosophy on music. I started work on the music for *Waiting to Exhale* before we had a script.

GA: Did you really?

FW: Yeah, I started working with Babyface. I called him and told him I was doing the movie, and I actually had songs that were completely written for the film before I shot it.

GA: Which songs?

FW: Toni Braxton's track Voices. First, I'll make a choice and I'll say that I'd like a song, like if I want My Funny Valentine. I may play the music just for the crew, just for the dolly grip so he can know the movement of the piece. I'll say, "Look, I need it to move in this way." It's the feeling I need. Just the feeling I need. So if the camera's going to do a move into a window, I want it to feel a certain way. And sometimes they'll get a chance to get the tempo of what it is I'm looking for from that. I did it in *Strapped* too. I do it all the time. It's just a part of it. It's just a whole because I see the pieces continually deepening, deepening and deepening and each level adds something else and brings it further and further and further. *Waiting to Exhale* because people can relate to it, became a commercial piece.

GA: And the women are beautiful.

FW: They're goddesses.

GA: After Waiting to Exhale's success many thought the flood gates would be opened for similar Black cast movies, but it didn't happen at the rate or level some might have hoped.

FW: Well, certainly you saw a number of films being made after it that hadn't been made before. I don't want to take the credit for that, but it definitely happened. They did the Soul Foods, the Eve's Bayous, the Best Mans. They weren't making those films before that. But I don't take the egocentric point of view that it was because of my film entirely. The fortunate thing is that the industry followed Waiting to Exhale with a number of similar movies, but there seems to be sometimes a plateau of about $35 to $40 million that a lot of the films reach [at the box office] for whatever reason and that still hasn't changed the financial equation for the studio to put more money sometimes in those films. Sometimes they have, but Exhale was different for them because it made so much money. It's a low price [$14 million] and it made $67 million bucks [domestic box office], and it had a pretty decent life overseas and the record sales were humongous.

So, I think they've done it a few times and they continue to do it, but I think they were thinking that if we do this for this price [$8 to 12 million, sometimes $15 million] then we'll get a $35 to $40 million movie and it's unfortunate. I don't know which ones have, certainly Scary Movie that Keenen did, but that's a different genre.

GA: I'd like to talk about Hope Floats (1998), because you've not limited yourself to "Black" films. How did you get involved with that project?

FW: I read a breakdown of different projects that were going on in town and I read the premise of this little Texas movie about this woman who was trying to rebuild her life after a divorce, and it appealed to me. I told the studio that I thought it was really interesting and they gave me the job.

GA: And you did a good job.

FW: Thanks. That was a nice piece to work on too. I liked working on it. It's just your little piece of Americana.

GA: You're a man and it seems as though you have an understanding of women's issues, or you've done films that one could categorize as female films. Why do you think you've been able to delve into such subject matter?

FW: I'd like to think that I look at what's going on in the world, not just the world on a big scale, but at the people around me. And as an artist, as an actor for twenty something years,

I've put myself in the mind set of different people as a profession. I'm not a murderer, but I've played many murderers. I can definitely put myself in that space, to try to think about it, to consider it. None of that seemed far fetched to me. The burning of the car doesn't seem far-fetched to me. Nothing. So it's easy for me to try to put myself on that side: I've heard that discussion. I've heard those feelings from different people either inside of my life or peripherally in my life.

GA: *People do burn cars.*
FW: Yeah, scratch them, break them, knock windows out, not just women. I just try to put myself in the space and try to be as true to the people as I can, and luckily for me it seems to resonate with the female audience. They really think part of it to be true. I'm glad the opposite's not the case. What I'm trying to do is look for the truth.

GA: *And you've probably answered this question implicitly, but what are your thoughts on Black directors not limiting themselves to films that are about the Black experience or just Black cast films and opening up the canvas for themselves?*
FW: I think they should tell the stories that they want to tell, whatever that means—the things that appeal to them. I don't think that it's appropriate as a Black filmmaker to say, "I want to direct a white film because it shows my this or that." That's not the reason I directed Hope Floats. Not at all. But I do like the story. I like Sandy Bullock, yeah. I don't think that's the way to go about it. I think to go about it honestly and to look at stories that appealed to them for whatever culture and whatever it means to them, I think they should do that. I think they should pursue whatever is right for them, what stories appeal to them. And depending on the broadness or the thoughts of the person, that will bring them to other cultures, or maybe it will make them even more specific inside their own culture. It depends on their point of view.

GA: *Writers and directors both Black and white will argue that there is lots of pigeonholing in Hollywood—if you've only done comedy, you're labeled as a comedy person, etc. But you defied that right away. You did two Black cast films and then Hope Floats. Did you have to make a strong argument?*
FW: The executive Elisabeth Gabler and producer Linda Obst were surprised that I was interested in the material. But when I sat down and told them the things I thought that needed to be done to make the piece more honest, they felt that my point of view was the best point of view. That's all it really was, there really wasn't any kind of dance or anything. As far as pigeonholing is concerned, pigeonholing happens with all directors. It happens to white directors all the time.

Even Steven Spielberg for a long time was pigeonholed. When he did *Schindler's List* that was a big change in the face of his career. Garry Marshall—people wouldn't go to Garry Marshall to direct *Seven*. Maybe he could do it. And with actors, with artists, with painters. It's like, "Why is he doing that? I think he needs to return to . . ."

GA: [Laughs] It's true. It's human nature in many ways.

FW: Unfortunately, that's a Sebekian kind of point of view, wanting to categorize. They just want to do it.

GA: It's not just Hollywood in many ways.

FW: No, no. It's in every walk of life. We say, "Why is he wearing that purple tie? You can't go in a meeting like that. You're not hip. You're always the guy who is the Rock of Gibraltor, you can't be acting erratic." But I say that being mindful that there have been certain difficulties in getting certain budgets and certain things to happen and hopefully that's going to change as far as Black projects are concerned. It will change only by success with some of the smaller films in some ways, as it does with teen movies.

They follow trends. Hollywood is a business. It's about what's going to make a lot of money. "Well, they tell me the new thing to do is more of a cosmopolitan thing." Like *The Fast and the Furious* with Vin Diesel, they're trying to find movies that they find to be multi-cultural. I want to say, "Do you mean like *The Real World*? It didn't matter before. Woody Allen never had anybody Black walking down the streets of Manhattan. Now it's okay to do that now that *Fast and the Furious* did well? Well, I'm just glad it did well. So maybe you'll do some movies and make a bunch of things because maybe that will help the culture move forward.

GA: Hopefully so. Are movies magical to you?

FW: Yeah, man. It's a Shamanic process. It's a process of creating a reality, creating a space. Maybe you can say that it's imaginary, but certainly it exists on that plane. And the lights, the camera and pulling all of that together, there's an alchemy to it. There's an alchemy to that. Then when you take people and put them in that space and they're elevated to another space, it becomes a spiritual event because that elevation of moving up the energy flow, when you elevate a spirit to put them in another space and develop them in another time where time stands at a different ratio, where you're following time from something else, then how could it not be magical?

You can do anything in film now. You can create some of the images of the mind and then you can have people get in a car and ride with you through them. That's Willy Wonka style, man. "Come with me, and we'll be in a world of pure imagination. Remember that song [laughs] from Willy Wonka & the Chocolate Factory?

GA: I love that song.

FW: It's amazing. It's hard for me to even describe. In some ways it [a movie] can initiate something because sometimes a person can go into that space, like when I saw *American Me* (1992), I went in there and I sat in that theater, I was in New York, and I walked out and I had to wander the streets because I couldn't settle myself. He'd [the director Edward James Olmos] affected my psyche to such a degree. Then other times I've walked in a movie theater and they've lifted me with laughter to a degree and my whole opinion or my existence has changed. There's some magic in that. There's some magic in the lights, there's a magic in the space you go sit in, there's a magic in the creation of it, there's a magic in finding new characters on the set and building things to make them look real that really aren't and to use computers and formalize or create a world, a realm that isn't even physically possible—only in the mind.

GA: That said, it's such a powerful medium as you've explained, are films just entertainment?

FW: Movies can be a myriad of things because movies can transform. I can do films that can change laws, do a film that can change the perspective of a tribe or culture. By that I mean, in our country we can make people see something and understand something that they never did before. Many filmmakers do it where they take you to a place where you have to examine your own morals, your own thoughts or you examine the belief systems of another group or you examine how you are living your relationship or your life. That's why films are so important because they do transform or they do put you in that space where these things can occur. So that's why you have to be careful as to what it is the director does and what it is the director says.

GA: Speaking of being careful about what you choose and what you say, do you think Black filmmakers have a responsibility to do certain films or not do certain films that portray Blacks in any particular way, given the power of the medium?

FW: I think that I am disappointed in any filmmaker who perpetuates negative stereotypes be they Black, white, Mexican or whatever. Certainly, you would think that if it's of your own culture that you would have the sensitivity to know that what you might be doing could be detrimental, unless you're making a statement about those stereotypes. If you're making a *Bamboozled* (2000), or if you're making *Undercover Brother* (2002), then at least you have a consciousness about what you're doing. Whether everyone agrees with what you're doing, you do have a consciousness about it and it's evident. So for me, I would hope that Black filmmakers would have the sensitivity to what it is they're projecting [in a film] and how it can affect people.

Debra Martin Chase

When I met Debra Martin Chase, I immediately knew why her name is associated with some of the most powerful names in show business. Nominated for both an Academy Award and an Emmy, Chase has headed the production companies of actor/director Denzel Washington and singer/actress/producer Whitney Houston. She currently runs her own Disney-based company, Martin Chase Productions, while also serving as Houston's producing partner in BrownHouse Productions.

A native of Pasadena, California, Chase recently produced the hit film *The Princess Diaries* (2001) for Walt Disney. Directed by Garry Marshall and starring Julie Andrews, *The Princess Diaries* has grossed over $109 million domestically.

With Houston, Chase served as executive producer on *Rodgers and Hammerstein's Cinderella* (1997), starring Brandy, Houston and Whoopi Goldberg. The film, which aired on ABC's *Wonderful World of Disney*, gave the network its best Sunday-night ratings in over a decade and generated seven Emmy nominations, including Outstanding Variety, Musical or Comedy Special, and won an Emmy for art production.

As head of Washington's Mundy Lane Entertainment from 1992 to 1995, she worked on the critically acclaimed and stylish film noir *Devil in a Blue Dress* (1995), which starred Washington and was directed by Carl Franklin and based on the novel by Walter Mosley. Chase and Washington also executive-produced *Hank Aaron: Chasing the Dream* (1995), a two-hour documentary on the baseball legend, which aired on the TBS Superstation in April 1995. The film was nominated for an Academy Award and an Emmy and won a Peabody Award, the Crystal Heart Award from the Heartland Film Festival, and was voted Best Documentary by the National Association of Minorities in Cable.

Chase's credits also include *Courage Under Fire* (1996) and *The Preacher's Wife* (1996), a remake of the 1947 classic *The Bishop's Wife*.

A Phi Beta Kappa, magna cum laude graduate from Mount Holyoke College, Chase received her J.D. from Harvard Law School and began her career as an attorney working at several major law firms and Fortune 500 Corporations.

▬ ▬ ▬

GA: *You started out as a lawyer. Tell me about that.*

DC: I didn't like practicing law.

GA: *No?*

DC: No, but I did it for five, six years, big firms and big corporations. And I finally just got to that point in my life where I was said, "Okay, you know, you need to do something about this." Because I realized I couldn't do it for the rest of my life, and I've always loved movies. My father is still the biggest movie buff I know. I grew up in one of those households where movies were on all the time and we talked about movies and I was the kid who went to the movie theater on the weekends and would sit there until my parents came to get me. I didn't know anybody in the business. Even though I spent my formative years in Pasadena, I could have been a million miles away from Hollywood, because it was just so foreign to me. When I hit that point in my life, then I said, "Okay, what do you really want to do?" And the thing I wanted to do more than anything else was make movies, so I tried my hand at it.

GA: *And so you left law to go work at Columbia Pictures, right?*

DC: Yeah. First of all I was in New York, and I spent about a year, year and a half learning about the business. Because literally, I didn't know who did what, I didn't know the mechanics of how things worked. So I read books, went to seminars, met with anybody who'd meet with me just to get information. Then at least I had a sense that it was the studio executive and the producer who actually came up with the ideas for movies, and that's what I thought I wanted to do. Then I did come out to L.A. as a lawyer for Columbia, because that was my most marketable skill at the time, and then I went from there.

GA: Then you were able to segue into producing. How did you get into Columbia? A lot of people, bankers, lawyers, want to work in movies, but it's still pretty hard to penetrate those walls.

DC: It's that combination of luck and perseverance, you know? When I started looking for a job, the sister of a very good friend of mine was in human resources at Columbia Pictures in New York, and she arranged for me to meet with the general counsel. As I was waiting for that interview, I saw some papers on her desk. And Peter Guber had started a program to bring people from different disciplines into the entertainment business, and she said, "You wouldn't really be interested." I said, "Yes, I would." Because the job would give me the chance to try different areas. I came out to L.A. and worked in Columbia's legal department for a year under the auspices of that program. Then one day I was at a luncheon and the studio's new chairman, Frank Price, sat next to me and we really hit it off. Frank had brought his projects over from Price Entertainment, and one project was a book set at Harvard. We talked about it at the end of the lunch, and he said, "If you ever have a chance, take a look at the book, and I'd be interested to hear your thoughts on it." That was a Thursday. So I went home that weekend, barricaded myself in my apartment and read the book twice. I made my notes and I called him Monday morning, and I said, "I just happened to have the chance to read the book over the weekend." He had me come up to his office in the afternoon, and we chatted about it. He liked what I had to say, and we just kept in touch. A few months later, he brought me up as his executive assistant, and that was really my big break. He's my mentor. I'm still very close to him.

GA: How long did you work for him?
DC: A year.

GA: What was that job like?
DC: He wanted me to learn, so I went with him to all of his meetings. I was a troubleshooter. I made sure no issues fell through the cracks, read for him, but most importantly, I got to ask any question I wanted to, because he wanted me to learn. And at the end of each day we would sit in his office and I'd say, "Well, I don't understand. Why didn't you buy that story?" And he would explain to me. Or I'd ask, "Why are you publicizing and marketing the movie in this manner?" And he would explain it to me, so it was an invaluable experience.

GA: That sounds great.
DC: I don't know any African Americans who have had such an opportunity. Then, after a year, there was a whole political upheaval at Sony, and Peter Guber and Jon Peters brought Mark Can-

ton in for the top job, so at that point Frank officially put me on the creative staff at Columbia Pictures and then left the company.

GA: That sounds like a pretty exciting job. What were some of the films you got to see through production at Columbia?

DC: Boyz 'N the Hood (1991), A League of Their Own (1992), Dracula (1992) with Francis Ford Coppola, Hero (1992) and Groundhog Day (1993).

GA: Did you get a chance to sit in on meetings with people like Coppola?

DC: Yes. The job was really quite an extraordinary opportunity.

GA: What was your first creative job like day-to-day?

DC: Well, I had been sitting in on the creative meetings all along and acting, in a sense, as Frank's creative executive. So you're reading scripts and books and voicing your opinion to the group. But I was on the creative staff at Columbia for only about six months, because there was another fluke. It was a Monday, I was walking across the lot and I saw Denzel—he had a deal at Tri-Star at the time and I'd never met him before. And I never go up to stars, because, you know, it's always weird, but I was going to lunch and this little voice in my head said, "You should go introduce yourself." So I went up to him and told him that I was at Columbia and if there was ever a chance that we could work together that would be great. He said, "Oh, great. Well, why don't we get together tomorrow and talk, maybe there are some projects." I said, "Great." Unbeknownst to me, he was on his way to lunch with Doug McHenry and George Jackson because over the weekend he'd parted with his business manager of fourteen years who had run his production company. He wanted suggestions on someone who could take over the company. I've known Doug since I was seventeen. They said, "Oh, we have the perfect person." Denzel says, "I just met her twenty minutes ago." It's so bizarre. So sure enough, the next day Denzel showed up at my office and we sat and talked and it turned out that one of his best friends from college had been a good friend of mine when I worked at Avon Products in New York. It was just a good fit. The next week, I left Columbia and went to go work with him.

GA: Talk about synchronicity, huh?

DC: I know, yeah.

GA: What was your first project with Denzel?

DC: Our first company project was Devil in a Blue Dress. We got Tri-Star to buy the book for us.

GA: *Wonderful film.*

DC: Yes, really, really, great material—the book by Walter Mosley and then Carl Franklin, who's just awesome.

GA: *And the music was phenomenal.*

DC: Music, the whole thing. Thank you. We then did *Courage Under Fire* with Meg Ryan. We found the project—it was a spec script. Denzel and I also produced a little documentary on Hank Aaron for PBS in 1995 with Mike Tollin and Brian Robbins. The documentary was nominated for an Emmy and an Oscar, and it won a Peabody Award. It was just a little labor of love.

GA: *It's a good film.*

DC: It was really special. Then we did *The Preacher's Wife*. People would always talk about Denzel becoming a Black Cary Grant, and I had been looking for a romantic comedy. I went back to the Cary Grant library and found *The Bishop's Wife*, and said, "This would be a great remake for Denzel." So we hooked up with Sam Goldwyn, who owned the rights [to *Bishop's Wife*] and developed the project. It took four years, and Whitney actually had attached herself about a year into the process. So I got to know her and the people in her camp. I'd basically taken the journey with Denzel from very well respected actor to huge movie star. But at the time, Denzel's interest in actively producing movies was starting to wane because he was doing back-to-back films. I understood. And Whitney had wanted to start a production company for a long time, so it was kind of a nice segue over to BrownHouse.

GA: *Tell me what it's like to run a megastar's company day-to-day.*

DC: Well, it's twofold. There are two main areas—one is just the development, and in producing you're looking for good material, you're working with your writers and the studio. You're just trying to find stuff and move it forward. Obviously, when you're working for a star, you are also, in most cases, first and foremost looking for projects for them. But you're obviously also looking for things that they're not going to star in but that they will produce with you. Then there's also the reality of being in a star's life and being an access point to a star.

I guess Denzel in particular, because he tends to be pretty accessible—he's got four kids, he lives in the community. So he'd always run into people. He'd go out and run into somebody and so they would have a script, an idea or whatever and he would tell them to call Debra. Then you've got people coming at you all the time, including agents who are trying to steal the star away and who are trying to bribe you to help them.

GA: [Laughs]

DC: I knew when he'd have a big night out, because I'd get these phone calls the next day: "Oh, you know, Denzel told me to call you. I've got this story and it's . . ." And you have to be diplomatic, because obviously the fan base is really important.

GA: Yes, absolutely.

DC: You don't want to piss people off, but also you . . .

GA: You have a company to run.

DC: I have a company to run!

GA: [Laughs]

DC: Like I said, I think it's because he's more accessible. Denzel would get these people who would just come by the office and sit, hang out, and say, "Oh, I'll just wait for him."

GA: [Laughs] You're making this up, right?

DC: No! I swear. The letters. We would get one asking for money, and again, because we're listed we'd just get stuff. I'll never forget. One incident stands out more than anything else. Some guy hand-wrote the first act of a screenplay and sent it with a note saying, "If ya'll like this, I'll finish the script."

GA: [Laughs]

DC: And you want to say, "Dude, [Laughs] c'mon."

GA: [Laughs] You could make a movie about this stuff.

DC: Okay? Dude.

GA: You're funny.

DC: Anyhow, it's part public relations, but at the end of the day it's a production company and you're running it. I've been fortunate, obviously, in working with two stars who are enormously talented, very well regarded and respected. So it was good, and both were very generous with me in terms of sharing their access and allowing me to be a full partner.

GA: In terms of The Preacher's Wife, describe the process of getting the script to the development process through production. How does Debra Martin Chase do that?

DC: Like I said, we start at the point where I see something and say, "Hey, this would make a great remake for Denzel."

GA: So you pitched the idea to him?

DC: He took a look at it and said, "Yeah, this seems like it would be good." He liked the whole church aspect. Sam Goldwyn, Jr., owned the rights; his father—the legendary producer—left the rights to four movies outright to him, one being The Bishop's Wife. I happen to be good friends with Tom Rothman, who at the time was running Sam Goldwyn's company and now runs Twentieth Century Fox. I called Tommy and I said, "Think about this." And he said, "Well, great, let me have a conversation with Sam." They called me back two hours later and said, "Sam loves this idea. Come on in, let's try to make this work." Denzel had done Much Ado About Nothing for them a couple of years before, so there was a very good rapport. So we went in and discussed our general ideas about the remake and kind of got on the same page. It was about finding a writer. Then it's about who has the voice you want, who's a great writer and who do you think is appropriate for this particular piece of material. So we worked with a couple writers, our first being Jeremy Levin.

GA: And what had he done?

DC: Jeremy is a really smart guy, a former psychiatrist. Subsequently, he wrote and directed Don Juan DeMarco, and there are a couple of other big movies he's done. Well, he did the initial draft of the script for us. About that time Sam decided to go ahead and make a deal with a studio, because he realized that the budget for this movie was greater than what his movies at the Goldwyn Company had been. He had some discussions in general with Disney about doing some business together. They had done a remake of Stella Dallas [together with Bette Midler], so there was some history and a pretty good relationship with Joe Roth. That deal closed and we decided to try and put a director on to continue to develop the script under a director's supervision. And probably at about that time, Whitney heard about the project from her agent, Nicole David at William Morris, loved the idea of the church setting and the opportunity to do a gospel soundtrack, so she became attached to the project. So we put together a list of about ten directors we were most interested in and started contacting them and sending out the script. In the middle of all this, Denzel was, I think, at Armani getting fitted for his Oscar tuxedo and Penny Marshall was in the next dressing room. Penny was on the list but had turned the script down. They started talking, and Denzel said, "I've got a script that I really want to do, and I'd love for you to do it." He called me, I sent the script over to Penny's agent, and she said yes.

GA: *She changed her mind like that?*
DC: Yes.

GA: *That's how it works sometimes.*
DC: Exactly, but they had chemistry—Denzel spoke to her directly as opposed to having it come through her agent. Here's an artist speaking to another artist—I have a vision for this and I'd like you to be involved. It makes a big difference.

GA: *And this is the way it happens a lot in this town?*
DC: Yes, that's the reality. Then, over the next year, Penny hired a couple of writers to work on the script with her, and it was just like a train that's moving forward.

GA: *When do you decide to hire another writer for the rewrite? Describe that process.*
DC: It depends. You just have a sense. You get to a certain point and you analyze what else the script needs and whether or not you think the writer you're working with can do that. It's like anything else. All writers, all artists have their strengths and their weaknesses. Some people are really good with character but they're not funny. Some people have great dialogue but they're not good with action. Some people are funny but they can't write the more serious parts of a character. So when you get to a point where the characters are really great, the dialogue is really good but it needs to be funnier, we need some one-liners, a couple of set pieces, you go to somebody who has that strength and bring them in on the project. As you know, at times the people who come in for rewrites don't get credited.

GA: *Yes, I understand. Now, what do you think makes a good producer?*
DC: [Laughs]

GA: *Still figuring it out, huh? [Laughs] Life is a journey, that's fine.*

DC: When people ask me what a producer does, the real answer is that you do whatever it takes within your own moral parameters to get the job done. So you've got to have perseverance, because it's all problem-solving. You're constantly pushing, constantly trying to convince people to share your vision and join that bandwagon. That kind of determination and perseverance is really important. As a practical matter, you have to have a sense of what material works as a movie, some feel for the marketplace and your audience. That for me personally is really important. I like to see movies in real theaters, with real people, and gauge their reaction. I like to travel and see what people are doing. L.A. and New York are really not reflective of the rest of the country, much less the rest of the world, and we make movies for all people. So that's important, just talking to people and seeing what's going on in their lives. But at the end of the day, it's finding material that is universal.

GA: *Can you give some examples of what you consider universal material?*
DC: Well, *Princess Diaries*. Every girl, and the girl in every woman, wishes that she would wake up one day and find out that she's a princess.

GA: [Laughs] *Right.*
DC: *Cinderella*. Within that story, within that fairy tale, we try to tell a story of a young woman understanding that she has the power within herself to do whatever she wants to do. That if she believes in herself, all things are possible—and that's a big theme in a lot of my work. I think that it's important for all of us to remember—and to be reminded of—that it's really important for kids, while their view of themselves and their view of the world is being formed—to give them that inspiration.

GA: *Yes, both Cinderella and The Princess Diaries were excellent in the way everything came together. And I mean, I'm not a twelve-year-old girl, I'm not your target audience for Princess Diaries.*
DC: [Laughs]

GA: [Laughs] *But I was telling a friend that it was really well done. I can appreciate the work.*
DC: Thank you.

GA: *It's entertaining and well-structured in a clear three-act structure format. To what would you attribute your ability to bring those elements together and still give us something that we perhaps have never seen? Everyone kind of knows fairy tales, but this one was a little different.*
DC: Mmm, hmm. You know, hard work and luck, really. When I sold *Princess Diaries* to Disney, on the wish list for my executives, Karen Glass and Doug Short, and myself were Garry Marshall to direct and Julie Andrews to star as the grandmother. That was the wish list the whole time we

were developing it. Whitney and I had the same agent as Julie, so we had gotten the book to her very early on and made her aware of it. But then, as soon as we got the first draft, Nina Jacobson, the head of the studio, called Garry and asked him to come over, and she gave him the script and said, "Disney would love for you to do this." The next day he called her and said yes. So we got really lucky. And good people want to work for good people, so then it all starts to come together.

GA: *How did you find the material for Princess Diaries?*
DC: The book by Meg Cabot came to me from one of the agents at William Morris in manuscript form. I had just sold something else for him and we had a good relationship. He called me and said, "I just got this book, it just sounds like you." He gave me the two lines, and I said, "This is so me." [Laughs]

GA: [Laughs]
DC: Okay, this is so me. Just let me run with this for a little bit. What's interesting as I've evolved as a solo producer—what I've come to understand is that it's helpful to be defined or associated with a genre so that people know what they're buying, so to speak. If you think about it, the most successful producers are associated with a genre. If I say to you the name Jerry Bruckheimer, you think action movie; if I say Scott Ridley you think more literary properties. I say Lawrence Bender, you think *Pulp Fiction* (1994) because of the Quentin Tarantino stuff. I love the girl stuff, I love that. These are the movies that I love, that I want to go see and that I enjoy making. Not to say that's all I want to make. Obviously, *Courage Under Fire* (1996) is a very different movie, but the girl films work for me and they will probably always be a substantial part of my business—not all of my business, but a substantial part.

GA: *When you were a kid did you like the Lesley Ann Warren version of* Cinderella *and watch it every year on CBS?* [Laughs]
DC: Absolutely. Every year, every year I was right there at the TV and I love the old movies. Again, my father being a movie buff, I loved all the Audrey Hepburn and Grace Kelly movies.

GA: *Glamour, you like glamour?*
DC: Love those, okay? [Laughs] Still love those! I lament the fact there's not more of that in the cinema today.

GA: Those were some great films. So in terms of those qualities that make a good producer, in choosing material, how do you know if it's good?

DC: Well, I tell you, I've actually evolved over the years. I used to make this speech when I'd talk to people, because this business is a marriage of art and business and it's in many ways an unholy union. But it's very much a combination of the two, and in today's Hollywood it's more about business than ever before, so the first question I ask myself today is "Is this a story that warrants being told? Is there something universal about this specific story? Is it a journey that is interesting?" But the second question, which is equally as important, is "Who is the audience, what's the market for this and can I sell this movie both to a financier and in the marketplace?" When I go in here at Disney I say, "Okay, I love this book, I love this script. I want you guys to take a look at it." We have the discussion about whether or not they're going to buy it, and one of the questions asked is "What's the trailer? What in this movie goes in the trailer so we can sell it?" Because that's what this business is right now. If you notice every year come Oscar time, this year being no exception, the majority of the movies that are most acclaimed are those from the smaller studios and the more independent movies, because they can afford to make a movie that maybe is not going to do as well at the box office. They can make it for less, and maybe it doesn't do as well financially, but it'll get the critical acclaim. They're set up for that. The studios really aren't—the studios need to make money, because it's a very expensive operation and now they are all divisions of multinational corporations who are all about shareholders and the bottom line.

GA: They need home runs.

DC: Mmm-hmm.

GA: Was Princess Diaries ever supposed to have a Black cast?

DC: No, never. It's a great book and it's a story about European royalty. Why would I mess with it?

GA: I understand. Tell me this—is Hollywood a tough place for Black women?

DC: Yes.

GA: And why is that?

DC: It's evidenced by the fact that there are so few of us. It's a tough business for everybody and there's a very rich pie, and those who have a slice do not want to give it up or do not want to decrease their slice for anyone, so they're going to use whatever's possible to keep people out.

Also, I realized that very few Black movies are made each year. That's one of the reasons *Princess Diaries* was very important to me as a producer—to expand the breadth of my work. Obviously, it's very important for me to tell African American stories and to tell them in a way that I'm proud of. But as a businesswoman, if every studio is making maybe one Black movie a year, it's important for me to expand my work. Plus, most of the Black movies made are director-driven, so you don't necessarily need an outside producer, because most have a producer they work with. So the odds are not great that one of the few Black films made is going to be yours in a given year. To an extent, I think historically we have limited ourselves. We have limited ourselves to that very, very small piece of the Black business that goes on in this town. And, you know, it's hard to have success with such a small piece of the game. And it's like anything else—It's about building a power base, and a power base is built on success. So if you're getting one movie every four years, it's hard, and it makes it harder to get other stuff done. For me personally, I decided that I needed to be a producer first and foremost, and within that to do girl movies, to do African American films and, like other people, to have a breadth of the types of movies that I do.

GA: And that has allowed you to survive in a very tough industry.
DC: Hopefully.

GA: In terms of Princess Diaries, what has that done for you as a producer?
DC: It's helped tremendously.

GA: It's great, and how many movies can you actually feel comfortable letting children watch these days? That's one of them.
DC: Yeah, yeah.

GA: It's clean. You've been able to navigate the Hollywood system very well. In my assessment, you seem to have very strong relationships—Frank Price, Denzel Washington, Doug McHenry. How important are relationships in Hollywood?
DC: Essential. People say this, but it's really true. It's a relationship business, the assets in this town are people. Most businesses at the end of the day are based on relationships, but in the film business even more so. I've been very fortunate having at this point grown up, so to speak, with a lot of the studio heads of today, like Tom Rothman and Stacy Snider. I've known Stacy Snider for years. When she was at Tri-Star I was running Denzel's company, and so it helps a lot, because at the end of the day people want to work with people they like and whom they trust. There are a lot

of people in this town who are not kosher. I have a good reputation and I've worked hard to get that. The people I've worked with respect me, and I've earned that. I know for me, given the choice between working with an unknown entity and somebody I like and I trust, I'm going to go with the latter every time.

GA: *To what would you attribute that ability to really navigate and make sincere relationships?*
DC: I've worked hard, I'm pretty much a straight shooter and pretty sincere. If I'm wrong, I'll say I'm wrong. You know, there's no secret other than that.

GA: *A thing I understand that is key for a producer is the trust that she must have with the director and the actors.*
DC: Yes, absolutely. Again, that's all based on the relationship, and it's hard, because the thing about movies is that all of a sudden you're throwing people together you don't know and you're living together for six months during the process, and either it's going to work or it's not. Garry was incredibly inclusive and just couldn't have been lovelier to me on *Princess Diaries*. It could have very easily gone the other way. He took a moment to check me out and get to know me, because we didn't know each other. I had worked with Penny before and that helped, but once he figured out that I was okay, he could not have been lovelier or more collaborative, and it was great. I sincerely hope to work with him again real soon.

GA: *Producers, as you said before, are problem solvers. Give me an example of a crisis you had to solve in production.*
DC: Because business has become so dominant I really use my legal skills every day, usually in some rights deal or writer's deal or something where it gets to that point where it's taking forever and there are a couple issues left and nobody is budging. I'll roll up my sleeves and get everybody moving—let's cut through this, I'm getting this done today—and just trying to get those issues resolved. The job is about pulling people together and getting them on a train and making sure the train keeps running. So whether it's an actor who's having a bad day or a fight with somebody or doesn't like what they have to say in the script, you sit there and you talk them through it. Or if a script comes in and it's not good and you have to tell your writer they're being taken off the project because this is just not working.

GA: *So good interpersonal skills are key for a person in your position?*
DC: Yes.

GA: Being able to manage all the personalities but at the same time trying to keep the door open because you may want to work with them on the next project.

DC: That's right, that's right.

GA: That's tough. So why are movies magical?

DC: I think because you're able to be transported out of your life, out of your reality, for two to three hours and enter a completely different world. Again, as a kid who was in the movie theater every weekend, I traveled around the world in the movies—Paris and London—and it increased my appetite for life.

GA: That's really fascinating. Who are some of your favorite movie producers?

DC: Producers?

GA: Do you have any favorite producers?

DC: Samuel Goldwyn and David O. Selznick.

GA: Favorite directors?

DC: For directors, it's Carl Franklin, Steven Soderbergh. There are directors whose body of work I respect very much, like Scorsese. But at the end of the day, it's about the individual movie. Michael Mann's *The Insider* was a brilliantly crafted movie. It could have just as easily been a two-hour television movie, but just the level of artistry in every area elevated it to this little gem, and that's Michael Mann. *Moulin Rouge* is not a perfect movie, but it's spectacular. Visually you're in awe of what Baz Luhrmann and his team have accomplished—it's the costumes, it's the music and it's the choreography. It all comes together, and it's amazing.

GA: Definitely. What does it mean to now have your own shingle at Disney? How did that come about?

DC: I've been doing this for a long time. And as wonderful as Whitney and Denzel had been to me, it was time for me to do it on my own, just as a person, because obviously for both of them, they have other careers and the producing was secondary, as it should be in both cases. Whereas for me, this is my livelihood and it was just time. I'm just enormously grateful that my guys here—Dick Cook, Nina Jacobson—have given me the opportunity to do it on my own.

GA: Was it scary at first?

DC: No. What I do on a daily basis has not changed dramatically.

GA: And what's a typical day for you?

DC: Meetings and phone calls. Like I said, I'm always looking for new material. I'm usually in the process of looking for a writer for something. Then I have all the ongoing projects, and at this point I have my own, the Martin Chase projects and the Brownhouse projects, I'm kind of wearing two hats. So there's always something.

GA: You and Whitney are still partnering on things that could still be possibly for her?

DC: Or just that we have a number of projects that are great and we're still working on them together.

GA: Can you talk about any of them?

DC: Sure, the sequel to the *Princess Diaries* is a BrownHouse project, and that's obviously a high priority. We're also doing a musical version of *Sleeping Beauty* for *The Wonderful World of Disney* at ABC, and we've got a remake of *Diva* the French movie with Will Smith's company at Universal. We are also making a movie *Cheetah Girls*, for the Disney Channel about five girls in New York City who dream of being superstars. It's adorable and will air in summer 2003.

GA: *Diva's* fantastic.

DC: Yeah, and that's for Whitney to star in. You know we've got some good stuff.

GA: Do you have a dream project that you would like to do?

DC: Well, I've been trying to get a remake of *Sparkle* going for a few years now. Best-selling author E. Lynn Harris wrote a great script for me, and we had the late Aaliyah attached to star. Warner Brothers really wanted to make the movie. It's been difficult for all of us to regroup since the tragedy.

GA: How do you stay sane in this city where people always seem to be on the edge of losing it?

DC: The business will drive you crazy, and you get to the point where either you realize you have to take control of your life and your emotions and your priorities, or it will control you and it will destroy you. So I have really good friends, I have a great family, my house is my sanctuary. I travel a lot and I try to stay very much involved in the world at large. In a sense, this is a second life for me. I have a whole other life with people who are not in this business, who don't really care and who are just happy if I'm happy. They couldn't care less. And that's really important in terms of being grounded.

GA: I'm sure. Finally, what advice do you have for aspiring producers or anyone who wants to break into this business?

DC: The best preparation for this business is experience, so I always encourage people to get in the mix. If you want to do this, take a job where you can learn to understand the rhythm of the business, how things work, who's who, what's what, and then if you're good and you're smart and you work hard, you will move quickly. Because, frankly, a lot of people are drawn to this business for the wrong reasons. People come to Hollywood because they want to party, they want to hang out with the stars, they want to be made to feel more than they think they are by their associations, by the external stuff. And they're not about the art, they're not about the craft, they're not about making a contribution. Because at the end of the day, making movies is an incredible opportunity to influence world culture. When I was in Mexico recently I mentioned to someone that I produced The Princess Diaries, and she said, "Oh, my God." She'd seen it. It's an experience that when done right is shared around the world. That's also one of the reasons why I got into the business, because I realized very early on what an impact movies had made upon me growing up in terms of my vision of the world and my perceptions about people. And I certainly realized that as African Americans our images have been very skewed, so with the opportunity comes a real responsibility to perpetuate strong images and values to help shape the views of generations to come.

GA: There's an illusion of glamour.

DC: Totally, and it's not glamorous.

GA: Glamour is about one percent of the business.

DC: This is one of my funny stories. When anyone asks me, throughout most of my life, what thing I wanted to do most, I immediately said, "I want to go to the Oscars."

GA: [Laughs]

DC: To me that would have been like the thing. I'd never gone to a telecast, so finally, when Denzel was up for Malcolm for best actor, Sam Goldwyn called me and said, "Why don't you take my tickets, take my limo." I was in seventh heaven. I thought, "Not only am I going to the Oscars, I've got good seats, I've got the limo, I've got the whole thing."

GA: This is why you moved out here, right?

DC: Right. So I pulled up, walked down the red carpet, Sophia Loren was in front of me, and I'm getting my picture taken everywhere. Up in front of us were Richard Gere and Cindy Crawford, when they were married—it was the whole bit. So I walk in the room, I sit down and I look around, and I say, "These are the same schmucks I meet every day."

GA: [Laughs]

DC: "They just have on sequins and a tux." In the front two rows were Nicholson, Cruise, Pfeiffer and all that kind of stuff, and then as you went back it was all industry. All industry. It was so not glamorous, it was so boring and I was so disillusioned. I went to the dinner afterwards, and that was boring. I talked to Tom Rothman the next day about it because I was depressed. It was really disheartening, and he said, "Debra, Hollywood is a business of smoke and mirrors and illusions, and the Oscars is the biggest illusion of them all." And he was absolutely right. That's why if the only reason you're here is for the glamour, the glitz, it will leave you feeling empty, because there is none—that's fake. People and family and friends and such are what's real. The rest of this is not real.

The Scholar

Manthia Diawara

When speaking with Manthia Diawara the Professor of Comparative Literature, Director, Program in Africana Studies at New York University, you get the immediate sense that you are in the company of a master thinker on the subject of Black studies.

A native of the Western African country of Mali, Diawara is an author, scholar, critic and filmmaker whose works examine the contributions and expressions of people of African descent throughout the world.

Diawara has authored ten books and numerous articles and essays on the culture and politics of the Black diaspora. His book *Black American Cinema: Aesthetics and Spectatorship* (Routlege, 1993), which he edited, is considered the first major collection of essays on Black American cinema. Contributors include Henry Louis Gates, bell hooks, Amiri Baraka, Michelle Wallace, Clyde Taylor, and Houston Baker, Jr. His other books include *Blackface* (Arena Press, 1999), *In Search of Africa* (Harvard University Press, 1998), *African Cinema: Politics and Culture* (Indiana University Press, 1992), *In Search of Africa* (Harvard University Press, 1998) and the forthcoming *Black Aethetics: Collected Essays* (New York University Press).

A film scholar who also gets behind the camera as documentary filmmaker, Diawara films include *Diaspora Conversation* (2000), *In Search of Africa* (1997), *Rouch in Reverse* (1995), *Sembene Ousmane: The Creation of African Cinema* (1994), which he codirected with Ngugi Wa Thiongo, and *Cinema de notre Temps: Souleymane Cisse* (1992), which was directed by Ritti Panh and which he produced.

Diawara earned his Ph.D in comparative literature from Indiana University in 1985 and his master of arts degree from American University 1978. He also received his B.A. in literature from American University in 1976. In 1998 he was awarded the NAACP Top of the Mountain Award .

▬ ▬ ▬ ▬

GA: *Tell me about growing up and the role movies played in your life.*

MD: I grew up in West Africa but also in the early '70s I was in Liberia, which is a kind of backwater of the United States. First of all, when I was really young I grew up watching films by Charlie Chaplin and Buster Keaton like everybody else. People think that Africans need to be educated in film. They really don't know that we were educated in film language like everybody else watching Chaplin and the others. When I went to Liberia that's where I first saw African American films like *Shaft* (1971) and *Cotton Comes to Harlem* (1970). That was my first introduction to Black people occupying the large screen, whether it was stereotypical or whatever. But just seeing a Black man, Black woman in close-ups, long shot. That told me right away that I had to go to America.

GA: *When did you come to the States?*

MD: I first went to France and studied literature and film there and then I came to Washington, D.C., in 1974. D.C. was called Chocolate City then, it was a very political city with Black politicians coming through all the time and Howard University is there. So D.C. was a very exciting place for me.

GA: *At the time did you see yourself pursuing narrative filmmaking?*

MD: At that time, literature for Black Americans was more important than film. Therefore, I wanted to become a writer, I wanted to tell stories. I wanted to emulate people no less than the Toni Morrisons, the James Baldwins, the Richard Wrights because they were telling the best stories. I thought I would teach film at that time, but I did not know that I would actually make films.

GA: *In your writings on film, particularly in your essay on D.W. Griffith's Birth of a Nation (1915) in your book Black American Cinema, you've made great assessments of the overall impact of cinema on Black people in this country. Could you talk about that?*

MD: When you look at the history of Blacks in the United States, it's a history of changing the history books in many ways. It's a history of civil rights struggles, ending slavery, Reconstruction, *Plessey vs. Ferguson, Brown vs. the Board of Education.* So the African American struggle, in a way, changed the law books more than any law or any philosopher. But Hollywood was determined to reverse history and portray Black people as though the times had not changed. *Birth of a Nation,*

1914, 1915, was still constructing American history as if Black people were not human beings. It was not only denying Black people historical evolution, but it was also blaming them for the decline of American democracy in many ways. And when I studied the film in film classes I was being told that technically it was the best. It's a film that experimented for the first time in continuity editing. For example, while one event is taking place in one location, another action is simultaneously occurring someplace else. The camera can show you all of that. Editing really was developed in Birth of a Nation and people wanted you to see that. However, they didn't want you to see that the editing was developed at the expense of Black people. Black people were the savages and white people were civilized. We were also told that when you watch a film, when the lights go down, you relax, you watch the film and you regress. Your motor skills are diminished. So you just enjoy the images on the screen.

Now the images that they're asking us to enjoy in Birth of a Nation are images of Black men raping innocent white women. So it was a case of asking myself, "Do I just relax in the dark and enjoy the movie or do I resist?" No, I'm not this rapist. This is not me. And the way this man's face is painted, he's not a Black man. The movie is trying to portray me in a way that I don't recognize myself." So the whole politics of recognition comes in, and that's what I call "the resistant spectator" in my essay. Normally viewers are not supposed to resist. The viewers are supposed to enjoy the story as it unfolds. They're supposed to suspend the notion of disbelief. They're supposed to say, "This is a story, just enjoy it." But I was finding myself resisting, breaking all of the rules, all of the aesthetic contracts. I thought to myself, "No, this is not me. This man has been painted as Black and he's playing a game that is maligning my culture, my history, my everything, so I don't want to suspend my notion of disbelief. I want to disbelieve this thing." That's what I was trying to do in that essay.

I really believe that the reason we all come to film is that it all hinges on this fundamental notion of recognition, the politics of recognition. You see an image of you as it is put out there by somebody else. You then don't know how to accept that image because you don't feel that it's you. It's not you because of your history, your aesthetics, your creativity because you imagine yourself in an ideal manner, but these images are showing you as somebody else, so again you don't want to recognize that. Sometimes the film industry puts you in a situation where you are actually the enemy of democracy, the barbarian, the lawbreaker, the criminal. After seeing Birth of a Nation, I realized that I had to make my own images.

GA: *Do you think those images in Birth of a Nation still have an impact on cinema today, especially from a Hollywood perspective?*

MD: I honestly believe that Black people have made progress in Hollywood, so far as they use Hollywood to their advantage. And every once in a while there are stories that we'd like to see even though those stories are not often successful. *To Sleep with Anger* by Charles Burnett, is an example and I could name several films like that. Even if Hollywood were taken over by Black people—I think Hollywood would perpetuate stereotypes. I don't think any presence of Blacks could completely put an end to that. There would be some changes, we would see some beautiful stories, but because it's an area where people entertain themselves, people like to make money—it's money first before anything else—Hollywood will always play with stereotypes. And in this country, stereotypes of Blacks and Jews and Italians or women make a lot money. So things have changed, but let's not have illusions. As long as we don't have an alternative to Hollywood, we will have these stereotypes.

GA: *Do you think Black filmmakers could take advantage of opportunities in the independent arena to bring about an aesthetic alternative to Hollywood?*

MD: Spike tried to the extent of his power and knowledge to create an alternative to Hollywood. The difficulties he encountered are so monumental in a sense because when you make a film in Black America or African America, whatever you want to call it, [Laughs] the resistance first comes from Black people and that makes it very difficult to make an independent cinema because Black people have expectations. Because they have been a minority that has been maligned, denigrated, degraded, they have expectations for films that sometimes may go against film language itself. So many of the people who actually criticized Spike Lee—"Oh, he's a bourgeois nationalist. His films don't tell stories. He wants to be a revolutionary but he wants to cash in at the same time."—those are all the things that a filmmaker like Spike Lee should have been doing actually if he wanted to succeed, but we criticized him for all those things. From *Ebony* magazine to *Emerge* to the academics—we all criticized him. Now that I make films, I just think that it's very difficult for somebody to be a Woody Allen, to be a Spike Lee or Coppola and not do those things.

GA: *You just hit on something I was going to ask you. You've been on both sides of the table as a critic and as a filmmaker. Have you seen a transition for yourself in terms of your perspective on the process of filmmaking?*

MD: Yes, I see some transitions. It helps me to understand the filmmakers, because filmmaking is like building a house. You have to have your bricks and you have to lay them one after the other, step-by-step, and that has constraints. You have to tell a story, you have to have a beginning, middle and end, as simple as it seems, but when you are confronted with it, it is so difficult. Whereas when you are a critic, you look at the film, and you talk about what the film tells you in the context of your history. So you analyze it, and the analysis can be also very tedious. You have to know film language, you have to be able to watch the film ten, twenty, thirty times to say some things.

For example, when I was writing about *Birth of a Nation* and *Daughters of the Dust* (1991), I watched them until I couldn't take it anymore. So filmmaking and criticism are very different, and when I make adjustments as a filmmaker I'm not telling myself, "I wish the critics could see this." I think critics should be left in their blindness so they can come up with the critical insight they come up with. Whereas, filmmakers should fight hard to challenge the critics, to listen to them sometimes and to completely ignore them sometimes and just make their films. So I think we live in two completely different worlds, and that's probably a good thing. Because when I'm making a film and my critical eye comes sometimes, I just ignore it because it's not going to help. Then sometimes I think about something that a critic said. For example, that the camera is like a pen and that you have to write with the camera. Then I try to use the criticism. So they inform each other, but they can ignore each other completely.

GA: *Some Black filmmakers argue that sometimes the Black media criticizes Black filmmakers while not fully understanding the constraints and business dynamics present in the film industry. Do you find that to be the case?*

MD: I think that is the case, but I don't agree with the analysis. I think that if you look at the relationship between *Ebony* magazine and blaxploitation, *Ebony* magazine attacked blaxploitation and the Civil Rights Movement attacked blaxploitation to the point that they had to adjust their language to the criticism or get out of the business. Of course there are other issues that are more complex: Hollywood needed money; they couldn't find money with other types of films. But as far as Black people are concerned, they see an image, and I think the critic has every right to criticize that image. I think it's good that the critic criticizes that image and that the filmmaker reads the criticism and decides to choose what is interesting in the criticism and ignores the rest and keeps making films. A Black film critic like an Armond White can rarely kill a film, but I think that we need both the Black film critic and the Black filmmaker, and I really don't think that Black films die because of Black film critics. Because, you know, in many ways *The New York Times* has the kind of power that the Black press does not have when it comes to films, especially films coming out of Hollywood. The Black press can help a film, but it can rarely kill a film from Hollywood.

In terms of criticism, there's a scene in *School Daze* where Spike Lee has a character say, "Wake up!" I saw that film, and I asked myself, "Wake up to what?" And it's good for the critic to bring that out, and it's good for Spike Lee to know that he needs to bring his filmic language to a higher level if he wants people to go see his films. I know the situation is more complex, but I really think that sometimes filmmakers make films that underestimate the sophistication of Black people. White people first underestimate us. They used to say in Africa that when you make a film, if you have a lot of flashbacks, if you have a lot of complex editing techniques, you will confuse the African spectator because they are not used to cinema. Now I'm giving you this simple racist example to go from that to a situation in America where Black filmmakers sometimes think that you have to make films in certain ways to make them understandable to Black people when those same Black people are watching Hollywood films every day. They're watching all kinds of techniques on television every day. They're very sophisticated. So you don't need to belabor anything to them. You don't need to bring down your film language, because cinema is the most democratic medium. Everybody knows it.

I may be a film critic, but some regular viewers knows as much about film as I do. I may be a filmmaker, but I may not know how to watch film as well as some regular person who never went to university because this is a very popular medium. And I think that Black filmmakers, African filmmakers, should take that into account: Viewers are more sophisticated than we think. Our average films are very didactic. Our average films think that you have to go back in history to set the record straight, so you can't jump because if you jump, people are not going to see what really happened. And the viewers know what really happened. [Laughs] So there are all these issues that I think would help our filmmakers to move ahead and not condescend to the audience.

GA: *Based on your analysis, why do you think Black filmmakers tend to burden themselves with the task of condescending to the audience?*

MD: I think it's complex. There are several reasons. First, we don't have opportunities to make films as often as other people do. When we get the money to make that one film, we want to put everything in it. Another reason is that a creative person sees himself as God, as if he's creating a whole world. And in order to create a Black world that is complete, you feel obligated to tell that complex history and story. Also, we have our storytelling techniques sometimes that force us to go around the lot instead of simplifying it.

Film is very simple. I told you before, it's like building a house. That means two things. It means you have to be simple. You've got to put one brick, then the other brick, then the other brick. Another reason is that you have to have a clear story. It can be complex through its simplicity, but not simple through its complexity. When you look at a film of mine, you will probably see all of the things I'm criticizing now. In some cases, we also make the big mistake of thinking that all Black people have the same experiences.

GA: *What do you mean when you say that Black filmmakers make the mistake of thinking all Black people have the same experiences?*

MD: Let's go film by film. Take for example, *Sankofa* (1993), by Haile Gerima, which is a very important film because of the way it was supported by the Black community. Whether it was from the grassroots marketing of the film or the film itself, we have to admit from that point that that movie is an important film. But that film felt obligated to use the same narrative as *Birth of a Nation*, where it literally had to re-create the whole color caste system among Blacks. The scene where the young light-skinned man doesn't want to recognize his mother, so we all have to see this guy as the Judas who betrayed all the Black people—it's very simplistic. It really doesn't go too far. Or the scene in Ghana where the woman is almost being raped by the camera in order to show the violence of slavery.

Cinematically speaking, one can understand, but again, probably a small minority of Black people need to see that. Many of us are way too sophisticated to need to see that scene and it doesn't mean that we let white people off the hook for slavery. If you look at the characters played by Spike Lee himself in his films, they're kind of hip hop, arrested-development characters that the Black middle class may not necessarily identify with. They may recognize them, but they may not see themselves in these young people who never grow up and who are the darlings of this community who may even seem retarded to some people. You see these characters mainly in Spike Lee's films—*She's Gotta Have It* (1986), *Crooklyn* (1994), *Do the Right Thing* (1989). But nobody really knows the truth about a film. It's not that because I'm a film critic that I know more than other people. Film is a popular medium. My son knows the new film language coming from hip hop, MTV, better than I do.

GA: *Do you think there's a Black aesthetic in film?*

MD: I think so because when you look at Charles Burnett's *Killer of Sheep* (1977) and *To Sleep with Anger* (1990), Billy Woodberry's *Bless Their Little Hearts* (1984) and Julie Dash's *Daughter of the Dust* (1991), and then when you look at Spike Lee's films—I just want to stay with these for a moment—you'll see that the overriding theme, all the way to MTV, is the Black vernacular and the Black habitus. Certain things that we have mythologized as Blacks, whether it's true or false, the way they talk, the way the music is played, the way the Black body occupies space, the way it poses, the way we handle ourselves, our clothing, the way we look at each other, the body language—all this is what I call the Black habitus.

Many of these films try to anchor the film language in the mining of this Black vernacular and of course literature did it, jazz musicians did it—people like Lester Young and the composers, the way they dressed—they tried to create Black modernity by tying it to things in the Black culture like Du Bois did with the Fisk Jubilee Singers, taking that as a basis of an aesthetic philosophical statement. Daughters of the Dust takes Black stories as the basis for Black people moving up north. Now as filmmakers, we use the camera to portray these things, to surrender themselves completely to this Black way of seeing the world, they create an aesthetic that we can momentarily call the Black aesthetic, but it doesn't mean it's only a Black thing and no other group of people can do it. But its overriding theme is Black culture. Even after all the bad things one can say about the blaxploitation movement, the films of that era had a Black aesthetic either through the music or the expression of Black masculinity. Whether one rejects it, says it's bad or good, Black aesthetics are present in blaxploitation films. I do believe that there is such thing as a Black aesthetic just as there is a Jewish aesthetic with references to Yiddish culture, a particular Jewish humor, which people like Woody Allen exploit. I think we go wrong when we try to essentialize that, when we try to say, "Only Black people do this," or when we try to tell Black filmmakers, "Don't do this because it's not Black." That's really where I think we make the mistake.

But the aesthetic itself is not offensive. It enriches the world and makes the world more colorful, and I think Blacks, particularly Black America, has contributed to that more than anybody. Because in Africa in many ways, we have been divested of what you call the African vernacular by Islam, Christianity and colonialism. Whereas Black Americans, or so-called "African Americans," because it's really not African, [retains] things that are African as a type of resistance to racism. Therefore, whatever they do in modernity, they try to "Africanize" it. Whereas we as Africans from the continent of Africa don't have any of these rhythms and vernaculars that African Americans talk about and attribute to Africa. Instead, we're either just good Muslims or good Christians and then when we put on traditional African rituals, we only do it for tourists. But Black America in that sense is sending Africans back to Africa and I'm really fascinated by that, so when I say that the Afrocentrics take themselves so seriously, they make me laugh because they are Africanizing us [the Africans]. They're more African than we are and I love that. [Laughs]

GA: [Laughs] That's a very good analysis and I've never heard it quite expressed that way. Could you give me some examples of what you mean by that?
MD: Don't get me started. I'd love to do that. Let's look at James Brown's Live at the Apollo. I was a

young boy in Africa when that came out. He performs by first evoking all kinds of rituals. He's going to bring a lot of soul in to the building, he's going to tear the building down, he teaches people how to do a dance, and when he dances he doesn't say many words but then he says, "Please, please." Then somebody comes and puts a red cape on him, and then he screams because he's trying to be one with his drums, the audience, everything. And this is supposed to be his way of going to the Black church. The Black church is supposed to invoke Africa. So in the sixties when James Brown came to Africa he provoked in us the reactions we did not know at all. Because when James Brown said, "You got it! Let's go!" And you began to dance with James Brown, you were bringing out pre, pre, pre, pre African cultures that existed before slavery, before colonialism, before anything else. James Brown does that to you. But it's not just James Brown, Bob Marley can do that to you, Fela can do that to you. However, if you look at Fela, Fela first imitated James Brown and then James Brown imitated Fela. And you see that today in the Afrocentrists. They go to Africa and they say, "You guys were kings and princes," and it has enabled us to create new things. It's not necessarily bad, but it's humorous to me, I love it, because in that case I was brainwashed by the music, the James Brown and the Black American literature.

So if some people today want to be brainwashed in a positive way by Afrocentrism, so be it. That's really why there is a Black aesthetic, but it's created not in Africa; it's created by the Black Atlantic and the Black American, the Brazilian more and more, and the Haitians' reaction to racism, to colonialism, and sometimes their resistance. Sometimes also the fact that they have been thrown in a place with a machine to work, work, work. They develop habitus, they develop ways of being, ways of talking to their machine. That becomes their alternative to modernity that we are now receiving in Africa. So yes, it's a long answer to your question. I believe in Black aesthetics. I don't believe that Black aesthetics is fixed, I think it keeps evolving with individuals who come into it. And Hollywood keeps stealing from it, which is good. In the music world, white musicians keep stealing from it, and I think that's good too. We have to steal it back.

GA: *We've hit on modernism a bit, but more specifically, what do you think has been the impact of modernism on Black cinema?*
MD: I think that Oscar Micheaux probably would be our first modernist filmmaker in many ways—this is one of the disadvantages of becoming a filmmaker as opposed to spending all of my time in criticism—because when I watch Micheaux's films, the way sometimes they defy the logic of space, they also defy narrative logic sometimes by confusing characters, and many people dismiss him as not knowing how to make films. But this was a man who was taking a film and assembling it one way to show it to the Black community and another way to show to the white

community and traveling around the country like that. So his film language not only participated in narrative development, but he was the one filmmaker from Chicago to New York to the South, approaching different topics like lynching. He was one of the first to make a film on that, and he became a formidable critic of America, always giving responses to America. America is the model of all of the industrialized countries and Black culture becomes modernist right away and Oscar Micheaux in that sense was one of the key critics of American society, American cinema, American culture in general by posing, positing his own cinema.

If you look at Black film in the context of modernism, the L.A. Rebellion [group of UCLA Black filmmakers from the 1970s known for creating socially conscious cinema] that whole group—Charles Burnett, Haile Gerima, Larry Clark—they were modernist in two ways. First they were mostly Marxists and they tied their film language to Third Cinema [third world] in Argentina and Chile and also Cuban cinema. They began to consider the camera as a guerilla weapon: Wherever there is oppression the camera must shed its light on that. So in that sense they were very modernist. They were really brilliant. And they were a group of people like in all modernist movements. They are a group with a manifesto, and my colleague at NYU, Clyde Taylor, calls them the L.A. Rebellion. I'm talking about a moment before *Desperately Seeking Susan* (1985), before the riots in London and the whole Black British movement, before *Do the Right Thing* (1989) and Tarantino. They were talking about the city and the policing of crises and the militarization of the police. They were really unique in that.

Many film languages including Hollywood would come to imitate that language with topics like the police versus the people. The L.A. Rebellion was the first to have done that. So in terms of film language, they made a major contribution, which remained in the background basically as sociological, as documentary and which was not celebrated as film language in Hollywood. But they were the first Black filmmakers in communication with Cinema Nouveau, the African filmmakers like Ousmane Sembene, the French filmmakers like Godard, the whole New Wave and the neo realism. The L.A. Rebellion filmmakers literally said, "Hollywood is bad. Let's go third cinema." And they stuck together. They contributed to film language a lot in that sense and then, as I was saying, people like Spike Lee through films like *She's Gotta Have It* (1986), *Do the Right Thing* (1989) and *Crooklyn* (1994), all the way through *Malcolm X* (1992), and then Julie Dash's *Daughters of the Dust* (1991), *Cameleon Street* (1989), by Wendell Harris, these films in their use of the Black vernacular, of a Black habitus, they again, I think, developed a film language that is now homogenized on MTV, on television, everywhere. They made a serious contribution to modernism.

GA: Why do you think the L.A. Rebellion isn't frequently referenced more by the young Black filmmakers who followed them?

MD: There are several reasons actually. One is that I think that Haile in many ways himself was dictatorial. That may be one reason. His style was, "Do like I do and think like I think, or you are a reactionary." He was more orthodox than Larry Clark or Charles Burnett. In many ways I think people recognize Charles a lot. He gets a lot of references—sometimes for the right reasons and sometimes not. He also had what you need in art—he had prestige because he won the MacArthur and that gave him legitimacy. But in terms of concrete imitation of the film language, the UCLA group was didactic, very, very didactic. And most Black filmmakers want to go to Hollywood, and to go to Hollywood you just can't make any money with didactic film language. Because of that, people do not reference them that much. A lot of that has to do with Spike Lee also. When Spike Lee came out, I remember him at UCLA around 1985 or before there was a big conference and he came. He was a young man from NYU and he said in reference to the L.A. Rebellion films, "I would not make my films like this. I want a film that's going to be shown on the big screen. I don't want to have to pick up my film and go from movie theater to movie theater and beg them to show my film." And he said that about the UCLA films. He said, "I want to make films that people will come out and see." Spike was a young filmmaker. They looked at him and dismissed him. So the L.A. Rebellion films are sociological, thesis films and films that set out to demonstrate a case. That's why I call them didactic. The young filmmakers are not going to reference them. Before they made Eyes on the Prize, these were the films that you had to see to see the Black community on film. However, they're not films where you go and turn off the lights and have five hundred people watch them.

So I think Haile and everyone should be happy that this canon can be studied but I don't think young filmmakers have to necessarily reference them or sample them in their films. And I don't want to exaggerate the influence, because if you didn't study with Haile, Clyde Taylor, Ayoka Chinzera at City College of New York, Teshome Gabriel at UCLA or myself you probably have not seen these films. If you went to USC where Singleton went, you have not seen these films. Spike went to NYU, so he would have had to have gone out of his way to have seen these films, so we should not exaggerate the influence of these films because if I can give you an African analogy, more people outside of Africa have seen African films than Africans have seen African films, so Black people see films that everybody else sees. So I don't want to undermine the influence or the importance of the UCLA filmmakers. At the same time I don't want to exaggerate its impact on the filmmakers. I think its influence is mainly on the film critics.

GA: *Why did you decide that you wanted to get behind the camera?*

MD: I decided to become a filmmaker because there were small things here and there that no one was making films on but which I thought I should make films about. For example, I wanted to make a film on Sembene Ousmane, [*Sembene Ousmane: The Creation of African Cinema* (1994)], because I felt that he deserved to be better known. My subjects came like that. That's the main reason. And I also consider myself more of a documentary filmmaker; I would not go to Hollywood to make a Hollywood film. I would help someone make a big narrative film, but I make films that contribute to what I'm doing at the university. I also think that it's very challenging to make films on Black people, and I really find it very exciting to push Black aesthetics and see how far it goes and to see how one can celebrate Black people with the camera. By and large, my films are very small. I have a very good job [as a professor]. I'm well paid, so my ambition is not that of a filmmaker. I'm a film teacher, that's really what I am; I don't want to be too arrogant about it.

But I think I teach better because I also make films and by talking about the making of these films, and by talking about Black culture, Black vernacular, Black aesthetics, diaspora than trying to just say, "I'm the filmmaker. You've got to see my film!" There are people who can already do that. I think that Haile Gerima is a great filmmaker in spite of any disagreement I may have with his films; I think he is an accomplished filmmaker. Melvin Van Peebles's *Sweet Sweetback's Badaaasss Song* is a seminal film whatever disagreement I may have with Melvin. Spike Lee is a great filmmaker. In fact, I think he's better than most in the sense that he understands cinema better than most, and he understands America better than most. So you have great filmmakers like Charles Burnett and Carl Franklin whose *One False Move* (1992) is brilliant.

GA: *What are your thoughts on Black independent cinema today? Sweetback and She's Gotta Have It were seminal. Will we see more movies like that?*

MD: It's hard. Many things have happened since then. First you had *Eyes on the Prize*, which just stole the show. They made the most incredible documentary that just redefined PBS, so if I wanted to do a film about a woman who played a big part in the Civil Rights Movement but who was overlooked, *Eyes on the Prize* has already done it. So that's one way of complicating things. Another thing is that PBS, which has become central in making cinema has also monopolized film language. I can't watch PBS because all of the films look alike and *Eyes on the Prize* actually defined PBS's film language with archival footage, good sound, good images, with a scholarly committee to advise the production and when you combine all of those elements you are actually censoring independent cinema. So *Eyes on the Prize*, the most incredible series has been imitated: Nobody wants to break from the mold. All of the films since *Eyes* are the same on PBS. Another area where harm has been done to film language are places like New York City's Angelika movie theater where you have films like Mike Leigh's *Naked* (1993) or *The Crying Game* (1992) or even Spike Lee to a certain extent who might make a film with a Miramax or make a film and sell it to Miramax or to a Hollywood studio for distribution. So you make a film for $1 million and market it for $10 million. That has killed independent cinema because if the film is not making money, you're not going to get money to make it. This isn't just for Blacks, it's with Blacks and whites. And we all want to go to Sundance, and Sundance films are ultimately shown in these kinds of theaters. More and more I think you have to go to museums to see a kind of independent film language, experimentation of films installations. It's very difficult now to have a new movie like *She's Gotta Have It* because the technology has developed in such a way that everybody's aiming to make a film for $1 million that's going to make $10, $20, $40 million. So the prospect for Black independent cinema I think is that we'll continue to see PBS doing the biographies, and I think those are bad. Then you more or less have interesting films drawing on sexuality, verging on the edge of pornography or different kinds of sexual practices to make people curious. Those will be the independent films distributed by Miramax or whomever. At the universities, we are trying to do simple films for no more than $50,000 and to do what we want to do because we are not going to depend on distribution. Distribution is really the issue. You see all of us crying about distribution, but once you learn distribution you have to adjust your story to the distributor. We're in a bind. So the independent cinema, we have may have seen the end of it.

GA: What are your hopes for Black cinema going forward?

MD: On the one hand, every Black in America is almost moving toward just being American only. We may be nostalgic about this, but more and more one of the cardinal elements of the Civil Rights Movement was to make Black people Americans, to make them citizens, to give them all kinds of rights. At that moment, except for the nationalists, they were not saying, "Take us with our specificities." They were saying more or less, "Take us as human beings," from Martin Luther King, Jr. on. They were the door to opportunities, in our particular case, the door of Hollywood, and letting Black filmmakers come and make films that they want to make as individuals. That is very perverse because once Hollywood gets hold of you, it's going to do it's best to have you not express any Black culture. At the same time, it is the desire for every filmmaker to be out there, big in Hollywood making Hollywood kinds of films. I'm really conflicted about this because I think it's important for a Black person to become an individual too, but sometimes I say that it's perverse and bad because in the game of Win/Win, Black people are losing most of the time. You win some, you lose some, but Black people lose more than they win. They go to Hollywood and they lose their personality, they lose everything. So I'm very ambivalent about this, but I'm able to look at it in the light of everything else in America like politics.

Today the Bush administration has two very important Black people at the top echelon, but what does that mean to us? I think that same thing is happening in Hollywood. Many people would love for that to happen in jazz, but I don't think it's going to happen. In cinema we're more vulnerable in that sense. Cinema is like politics. They put you there but you have no power. And is that what we want? But if we don't want that, we have to be very careful, do we want to have a ghetto of Black filmmakers doing Black films? These are important questions to me. Can we blame people who want to go to Hollywood and make Hollywood films? We can question them about how perverse it is, but can we blame them if that's our very American dream? Now someone very smart will tell me that it does not have to be either or and I would completely agree with that. And I think that's where your struggle is with your book and my struggle also is as a teacher. It doesn't have to be either or. That's our main challenge. How do we fight in such a way that we fight for freedom and democracy as Black people? Then sometimes we valorize and we celebrate our culture as Black people. I think that's really the challenge, and I don't know how we're going to get out of it. There are certain Blacks who blame Black Americans for accepting America. But I said, "That's what the Civil Rights Movement was all about."

Now, philosophically, if you push that to its extremes—you don't have to—but if you do, then we want to go to Hollywood just as human beings, not as Black or white people. We want to work at the White House, NYU, the same way. You don't want anybody to call you Black and so on, if you push it that way. A friend of mine raised the question that the main problem with Du Bois was that he wanted to become American. I said, "How could you not want to be American at that time? There were no alternatives. You could go to Africa or you could stay a slave." We have a challenge in the film industry. Our challenge is how do we keep rearticulating our positions in this country and in this world? And I think it's very important for us to stay away from fixed positions and saying, "This is what Black is and no more." That would be very dangerous. I think we should just keep articulating and on and on, and that's what will enable Black people to survive and to create magic in cinema.

Gordon Parks DIRECTOR [Solomon
Northrup's Odyssey (1984 TV movie), Leadbelly (1976), The
Super Cops (1974), Shaft's Big Score! (1972), Shaft (1971),
The Learning Tree (1969), The World of Piri Thomas
(1968), Flavio (1964 documentary short)] WRITER
[The Learning Tree (1969)—(also novel), Flavio (1964
documentary short)] PRODUCER [The Learning Tree
(1969)—Producer]

Melvin Van Peebles DIRECTOR
[Bellyful (2000), Gang in Blue (1996), Tales of Erotica
(1996)—(segment "Vrooom Vroom Vrooom" (1995)),
Vrooom Vroom Vrooom (1995 short), The Outer Limits
(1995 TV series), Identity Crisis (1989), Don't Play Us
Cheap (1973), Sweet Sweetback's Badaaasss Song (1971),
Watermelon Man (1970), The Story of a Three-Day Pass
(1968), Cinq cent balles (1963 short), Sunlight (1957
short), Three Pickup Men for Herrick (1957 short)]
PRODUCER [Bellyful (2000)—Delegate Producer,
Classified X (1998 TV documentary)—Executive
Producer, Gang in Blue (1996)—Producer, Vrooom
Vroom Vrooom (1995 short)—Producer, Panther (1995)—
Producer, Identity Crisis (1989)—Producer, The
Sophisticated Gents (1981 TV movie)—Associate
Producer, Sweet Sweetback's Baadasssss Song (1971)—
Producer, Sunlight (1957 short)—Producer] WRITER
[Bellyful (2000), Classified X (1998 TV documentary),
Vrooom Vroom Vrooom (1995 short), Panther (1995)—
(novel Panther), (screenplay), The Day They Came to
Arrest the Book (1987 TV movie), The Sophisticated Gents
(1981 TV movie), Greased Lightning (1977), Just an Old
Sweet Song (1976 TV movie), Don't Play Us Cheap (1973),
Sweet Sweetback's Baadasssss Song (1971), Slogan (1969),
The Story of a Three-Day Pass (1968), Cinq cent ballet
(1963 short), Sunlight (1957 short), Three Pickup Men for
Herrick (1957 short)]

William Greaves DIRECTOR [Ralph
Bunche: An American Odyssey (2001 documentary), Ida B.
Wells: A Passion for Justice (1989 documentary), That's
Black Entertainment (1990 documentary), The Deep North
(1990 TV movie), Black Power in America: Myth or
Reality? (1987), Golden Goa (1985), Beyond the Forest (1985),
Frederick Douglass: An American Life, Booker T. Washington:
Life and Legacy (1983), Space for Women (1981), Where
Dreams Come True (1979), In Search of Pancho Villa (1978),
Nationwide: Gary (1977), Just Doin' It (1976), From These
Roots (1974 documentary), Ali, the Fighter (1971 docu-
mentary), Power vs. the People (1973), Voice of La Raza
(1972), Black Journal, In the Company of Men (1969),
Symbiopsychotaxiplasm: Take One (1968 documentary),
Still a Brother: Inside the Negro Middle Class (1968), The
First World Festival of Arts (1966), Wealth of a Nation
(1964), Four Religions (1960 documentary), Emergency
Ward (1959 documentary short), Smoke and Weather (1958
short), Putting It Straight (1957 short)] PRODUCER
[Ralph Bunche: An American Odyssey (2001 documentary)—Producer, The Deep North (1990 TV movie)—
Producer, Bustin' Loose (1981)—Executive Producer,
From These Roots (1974 documentary)—Producer, Ali, the
Fighter (1971 documentary)—Producer, Black Journal
(1968 TV series)—Executive Producer, Still a Brother
(1968 documentary)—Executive Producer, Symbio-
psychotaxiplasm: Take One (1968 documentary)—
Producer] WRITER [Ralph Bunche: An American Odyssey
(2001 documentary), Ida B. Wells A Passion for Justice
(1989 documentary), The Deep North (1990 TV movie),
Black Power in America: Myth or Reality? (1987), Golden
Goa (1985), Beyond the Forest (1985), Frederick Douglass: An
American Life, Co-Writer, Space for Women (1981), Where
Dreams Come True (1979), Nationwide: Gary (1977), Just
Doin' It (1976) Co-Writer, From These Roots (1974 docu-
mentary), Ali, the Fighter (1971 documentary), Power vs.
the People (1973), Voice of La Raza (1972), In the Company of

523

Men (1969), Symbiopsychotaxiplasm: Take One (1968 documentary), The First World Festival of Arts (1966), Wealth of a Nation (1964), Four Religions (1960 documentary), Emergency Ward (1959 documentary short), Smoke and Weather (1958 short), Putting It Straight (1957 short)]

Ossie Davis DIRECTOR [Countdown at Kusini (1976), Gordon's War (1973), Black Girl (1972), Cotton Comes to Harlem (1970), Kongi's Harvest (1970), Cool Red] WRITER [For Us the Living: The Medgar Evers Story (1983 TV movie), Purlie (1981 TV movie)—(play Purlie Victorious), Countdown at Kusini (1976), Cotton Comes to Harlem (1970), Gone Are the Days! (1963)—(also play Purlie Victorious)] PRODUCER [Hands Upon the Heart (1991)—Producer]

Michael Schultz DIRECTOR [L.A. Law: The Movie (2002 TV movie), Boston Public (2000 TV series), City of Angels (2000 TV series)—(episode "Cry Me a Liver"), The Adventures of Young Indiana Jones: Tales of Innocence (1999 video), Ally (1999 TV series), Family Law (1999 TV series), My Last Love (1999 TV movie), Killers in the House (1998 TV movie), Charmed (1998 TV series)—(episode 2.18 "Chick Flick"), Felicity (1998 TV series), Ally McBeal (1997 TV series), The Practice (1997 TV series), Promised Land (1996 TV series), Young Indiana Jones: Travels with Father (1996 TV movie), Shock Treatment (1995 TV movie), JAG (1995 TV series), Young Indiana Jones and the Hollywood Follies (1994 TV movie), Chicago Hope (1994 TV series), Diagnosis Murder (1993 TV series), The Adventures of Brisco County Jr. (1993 TV series), Day-O (1992 TV movie), Livin' Large! (1991), Jury Duty: The Comedy (1990 TV movie), Tarzan in Manhattan (1989 TV movie), Rock 'n' Roll Mom (1988 TV movie), Disorderlie (1987), The Spirit (1987 TV movie), Timestalkers (1987 TV movie), Krush Groove (1985), The Last Dragon (1985), The Jerk, Too (1984 TV movie), For Us the Living: The Medgar Evers Story (1983 TV movie), Benny's Place (1982 TV movie), Carbon Copy (1981), Bustin' Loose (1981)—(uncredited), Scavenger Hunt (1979), Sgt. Pepper's Lonely Hearts Club Band (1978), Which Way Is Up? (1977), Greased Lightning (1977), Car Wash (1976), Cooley High (1975), Starsky and Hutch (1975 TV series), Phat Beach (1996)—Executive

Producer, Disorderlies (1987)—Co-producer, Krush Groove (1985)—Producer]

Fred Williamson DIRECTOR [Down 'n Dirty (2000), Silent Hunter (1995), South Beach (1992), 3 Days to a Kill (1991 TV movie), Critical Action (1991), Steele's Law (1991), Soda Cracker (1989), Foxtrap (1986), The Messenger (1986/I), The Big Score (1983), The Last Fight (1983), One Down, Two to Go (1982), Mr. Mean (1977), Mean Johnny Barrows (1976), No Way Back (1976), Adiós amigo (1975), Death Journey (1975)] PRODUCER [Down 'n Dirty (2000)—Producer, Night Vision (1997/I)—Producer, Beck 2—spår i mörker (1997)—Producer, Original Gangstas (1996)—Producer, South Beach (1992)—Producer, 3 Days to a Kill (1991 TV movie)—Producer, Steele's Law (1991)—Producer, Taxi Killer (1988)—Producer, Foxtrap (1986)—Producer, The Messenger (1986/I)—Producer, One Down, Two to Go (1982)—Producer, Mr. Mean (1977)—Producer, Mean Johnny Barrows (1976)—Producer, No Way Back (1976)—Producer, Adiós amigo (1975)—Producer, Death Journey (1975)—Producer, Boss Nigger (1975)—Producer] WRITER [3 Days to a Kill (1991 TV movie), Steele's Law (1991), The Messenger (1986/I)—(story), The Last Fight (1983), Joshua (1976), Adiós amigo (1975)]

Spike Lee DIRECTOR [25th Hour (2002), Ten Minutes Older: The Trumpet (2002)—(segment "We Wuz Robbed"), Jim Brown, All American (2002 documentary), A Huey P. Newton Story (2001 TV movie), Bamboozled (2000), The Original Kings of Comedy (2000 documentary), Pavarotti & Friends 99 for Guatemala and Kosovo (1999 TV documentary), Summer of Sam (1999), Freak (1998/I TV movie), He Got Game (1998), 4 Little Girls (1997 documentary), Get on the Bus (1996), Girl 6 (1996), Lumière et compagnie (1995 documentary), Clockers (1995), Crooklyn (1994), Malcolm X (1992), Jungle Fever (1991), Mo' Better Blues (1990), Do the Right Thing (1989), School Daze (1988), She's Gotta Have It (1986), Joe's Bed-Stuy Barbershop: We Cut Heads (1983), Sarah (1981), The Answer (1980), Last Hustle in Brooklyn (1977)] PRODUCER [Rent (2004)—Producer, Good Fences (2003 TV movie)—Executive Producer, 25th Hour (2002)—Producer, Ten Minutes Older: The Trumpet (2002)—Producer (segment "We Wuz Robbed"), Jim Brown, All American (2002

documentary)—Producer, Home Invaders (2001)—
Executive Producer, 3 A.M. (2001)—Co-executive
Producer, Producer, Bamboozled (2000)—Producer, The
Original Kings of Comedy (2000 documentary)—
Producer, Love & Basketball (2000)—Producer, The Best
Man (1999/I)—Producer, Summer of Sam (1999)—
Producer, He Got Game (1998)—Producer, 4 Little Girls
(1997 documentary)—Producer, Get on the Bus (1996)—
Executive Producer, Girl 6 (1996)—Producer, Clockers
(1995)—Producer, Tales from the Hood (1995)—Executive
Producer, New Jersey Drive (1995)—Executive Producer,
Drop Squad (1994)—Executive Producer, Crooklyn
(1994)—Producer, Malcolm X (1992)—Producer, Jungle
Fever (1991)—Producer, Mo' Better Blues (1990)—
Producer, Do the Right Thing (1989)—Producer, School
Daze (1988)—Producer, She's Gotta Have It (1986)—
Producer (as Shelton J. Lee), Joe's Bed-Stuy Barbershop:
We Cut Heads (1983)—Producer] **WRITER** [Bamboozled
(2000)—(written by), Summer of Sam (1999), He Got
Game (1998), Clockers (1995)—(screenplay), Crooklyn
(1994), Malcolm X (1992)—(screenplay), Jungle Fever
(1991), Mo' Better Blues (1990), Do the Right Thing
(1989), School Daze (1988), She's Gotta Have It (1986),
Joe's Bed-Stuy Barbershop: We Cut Heads (1983)]

Ernest Dickerson DIRECTOR [Good
Fences (2003 TV movie)—(as Ernest Dickerson),
Big Shot: Confessions of a Campus Bookie (2002 TV
movie), Monday Night Mayhem (2002 TV movie), Our
America (2002)—(as Ernest Dickerson), Bones (2001)—
(as Ernest Dickerson), Night Visions (2001 TV series)—
(episode "My So Called Life and Death"), (episode
"Still Life"), Strange Justice (1999 TV movie), Futuresport
(1998 TV movie), Ambushed (1998)—(as Ernest
Dickerson), Blind Faith (1998), Bulletproof (1996)—
(as Ernest Dickerson), Demon Knight (1995)—(as
Ernest Dickerson), Surviving the Game (1994), Juice
(1992)] **WRITER** [Juice (1992)—(also story)]

Robert Townsend DIRECTOR [10,000
Black Men Named George (2002 TV movie), Carmen: A
Hip Hopera (2001 TV movie), Holiday Heart (2000 TV
movie), Livin' for Love: The Natalie Cole Story (2000
TV movie), Soul Food (2000 TV series), Little Richard
(2000 TV movie), Up, Up, and Away! (2000 TV
movie), The 20th Century: From Behind Closed Doors
(1999 TV documentary), Fraternity Boys (1999), Jackie's

Back: Portrait of a Diva (1999 TV movie), Love Songs
(1999 TV movie)—(segment "Love Song for Jean and
Ellis, A"), B.A.P.S (1997), The Parent 'Hood (1995 TV
series), The Meteor Man (1993), The Five Heartbeats
(1991), Eddie Murphy Raw (1987), Hollywood Shuffle
(1987)] **WRITER** [The Meteor Man (1993)—(written
by), The Five Heartbeats (1991)—(written by), Eddie
Murphy Raw (1987)—(sketch), Hollywood Shuffle (1987)—
(written by)] **PRODUCER** [The Meteor Man (1993)—
Producer, Hollywood Shuffle (1987)—Producer]

Keenen Ivory Wayans DIRECTOR
[The Incredible Shrinking Man (2003), Scary Movie 3:
Episode I—Lord of the Brooms (2003), Scary Movie 2
(2001), Scary Movie (2000), A Low Down Dirty Shame
(1994), In Living Color (1990 TV series), I'm Gonna Git
You Sucka (1988)] **WRITER** [Most Wanted (1997)—
(written by), A Low Down Dirty Shame (1994)—(written
by), The Five Heartbeats (1991)—(written by), In Living
Color (1990 TV series), I'm Gonna Git You Sucka (1988)—
(written by), Eddie Murphy Raw (1987)—(sketch),
Hollywood Shuffle (1987)—(written by)] **PRODUCER**
[Scary Movie (2000)—Producer (uncredited), Most
Wanted (1997)—Executive Producer, The Keenen Ivory
Wayans Show (1997 TV series)—Executive
Producer, Don't Be a Menace to South Central While
Drinking Your Juice in the Hood (1996)—Producer, Eddie
Murphy Raw (1987)—Producer]

Warrington Hudlin DIRECTOR
[Cosmic Slop (1994 TV movie), Bucket Dance Video (1984),
Color (1983), Capoeira of Brazil (1980), Streetcorner Stories
(1977), Black at Yale (1974 documentary)] **PRODUCER**
[Anti-Vigilante (2002)—Executive Producer, Big
Head People (2002)—Executive Producer, Haters
(2002)—Executive Producer, The Breach (2002)—
Executive Producer, Once Upon A Ride (2002)—
Executive Producer, Corporate Dawgz (2002 short)—
Associate Producer, Ride (1998)—Producer, Cosmic Slop
(1994 TV movie)—Producer, Last Days of Russell (1994
TV pilot)—Producer, Bebe's Kids (1992)—Executive
Producer, Boomerang (1992)—Producer, House Party
(1990)—Producer, Black Film Focus (1984–85 weekly talk
show)—Producer, Bucket Dance Video (1984), Color
(1983), Capoeira of Brazil (1980), Streetcorner Stories
(1977), Black at Yale (1974 documentary)]

Doug McHenry DIRECTOR [Keep the Faith, Baby (2002 TV movie), Kingdom Come (2001/I), Jason's Lyric (1994), House Party 2 (1991)] PRODUCER [Two Can Play That Game (2001)—Producer, The Brothers (2001/I)—Executive Producer, Mr. Murder (1998 TV movie)—Executive Producer, Body Count (1998)—Producer, Malcolm & Eddie (1996 TV series)—Co-executive Producer, A Thin Line Between Love and Hate (1996)—Producer, Scenes for the Soul (1995)—Executive Producer, The Walking Dead (1995)—Producer, Jason's Lyric (1994)—Producer, House Party 3 (1994)—Executive Producer, House Party 2 (1991)—Producer, New Jack City (1991)—Producer, Disorderlies (1987)—Producer, Krush Groove (1985)—Producer]

Euzhan Palcy DIRECTOR [The Killing Yard (2001 TV movie), Ruby Bridges (1998 TV movie), Aimé Césaire: A Voice for History (1994 documentary), Siméon (1992), How Are the Kids? (1990 short)—(segment "Hassane"), A Dry White Season (1989), Rue cases nègres (1983), The Devil's Workshop (1982), The Messenger (1975 TV movie)] WRITER [Aimé Césaire: A Voice for History (1994 documentary), Siméon (1992)—(also story), A Dry White Season (1989)—(screenplay), Dionysos (1986), Rue cases nègres (1983), The Devil's Workshop (1982)—(screenplay), (story), The Messenger (1975 TV movie)—(screenplay), (story)] PRODUCER [Ruby Bridges (1998 TV movie)—Co-producer, Aimé Césaire: A Voice for History (1994 documentary)—Producer, Siméon (1992)—Producer, The Devil's Workshop (1982)—Producer, The Messenger (1975 TV movie)—Producer]

Charles Burnett DIRECTOR [For Reel? (2003 TV movie), The Blues (2002 TV miniseries), Finding Buck McHenry (2000 TV movie), Olivia's Story (2000 short), The Annihilation of Fish (1999), Selma, Lord, Selma (1999 TV movie), Dr. Endesha Ida Mae Holland (1998 documentary short), The Wedding (1998 TV movie), Nightjohn (1996 TV movie), When It Rains (1995 short), The Johnny Johnson Trial (1994), America Becoming (1991), To Sleep with Anger (1990), My Brother's Wedding (1983), Killer of Sheep (1977), The Horse (1973 short), Several Friends (1969)] WRITER [For Reel? (2003 TV movie), The Johnny Johnson Trial (1994), America Becoming (1991), To Sleep with Anger (1990), Bless Their Little Hearts (1984), My Brother's Wedding (1983), Killer of Sheep (1977)] PRODUCER [My Brother's Wedding (1983)—Producer, Killer of Sheep (1977)—Producer]

Julie Dash DIRECTOR [The Rosa Parks Story (2002 TV movie), Love Song (2000 TV movie), Incognito (1999 TV movie), Funny Valentines (1999 TV movie), Women: Stories of Passion (1997 TV series), Subway Stories: Tales from the Underground (1997 TV movie)—(segment "Sax Cantor Riff"), Praise House (1991), Daughters of the Dust (1991), Illusions (1982 short), Diary of an African Nun (1977), Four Women (1975 short), Working Models of Success (1973)] WRITER [Subway Stories: Tales from the Underground (1997 TV movie)—(segment "Sax Cantor Riff"), Daughters of the Dust (1991), Illusions (1982 short)] PRODUCER [Daughters of the Dust (1991)—Producer, Illusions (1982 short)—Producer]

Haile Gerima DIRECTOR [Adwa (1999 documentary), Sankofa (1993), After Winter: Sterling Brown (1985 documentary), Ashes and Embers (1982), Wilmington 10—U.S.A. 10,000 (1979 documentary), Bush Mama (1979), Mirt Sost Shi Amit (1975), Child of Resistance (1972), Hour Glass (1971 short)] PRODUCER [The Cutting Horse (2001)—Executive Producer, Through the Door of No Return (1997 documentary)—Producer, Sankofa (1993)—Producer, Ashes and Embers (1982)—Producer, Bush Mama (1979)—Producer] WRITER [Sankofa (1993), Ashes and Embers (1982), Bush Mama (1979), Mirt Sost Shi Amit (1975)]

Lee Daniels PRODUCER [Monster's Ball (2001)—Producer]

Kasi Lemmons DIRECTOR [The Caveman's Valentine (2001), Dr. Hugo (1998), Eve's Bayou (1997)] WRITER [Dr. Hugo (1998), Eve's Bayou (1997)—(written by)]

St. Clair Bourne DIRECTOR [Dr. Ben (2001 documentary), American Masters: Paul Robeson: Here I Stand (1999 TV documentary), John Henrik Clarke: A Great and Mighty Walk (1996 documentary), Making

"Do the Right Thing" (1989 TV documentary), A Nation of Common Sense (1975), Let the Church Say Amen! (1973 documentary), Nothing But Common Sense (1972), A Piece of the Block (1972), Pusher Man (1972), Ourselves (1971), Something to Build On (1971)] PRODUCER [Half Past Autumn: The Life and Works of Gordon Parks (2000 TV documentary)—Producer, Innocent Until Proven Guilty (1999 TV documentary)—Executive Producer, Rebound: The Legend of Earl 'The Goat' Manigault (1996 TV movie)—Co-producer, Making "Do the Right Thing" (1989 TV documentary)—Producer, The Long Night (1976)—Co-producer, A Nation of Common Sense (1975)—Producer, Let the Church Say Amen! (1973 documentary)—Producer, Nothing But Common Sense (1972)—Producer, A Piece of the Block (1972)—Producer, Something to Build On (1971)—Producer, Statues Hardly Ever Smile (1971)—Producer] WRITER [A Nation of Common Sense (1975), Nothing But Common Sense (1972), Something to Build On (1971)]

Stanley Nelson DIRECTOR [Marcus Garvey: Look for Me in the Whirlwind (2001 documentary), The Black Press: Soldiers Without Swords (1998 documentary)] WRITER [The Black Press: Soldiers Without Swords (1998 documentary)] PRODUCER [Marcus Garvey: Look for Me in the Whirlwind (2001 documentary)—Producer, The Black Press: Soldiers Without Swords (1998 documentary)—Producer, Shattering the Silences: The Case for Minority Faculty (1997)—Producer]

Camille Billops DIRECTOR [A String of Pearls (2002 documentary), Take Your Bags (1998 short), KKK Boutique (1995), Finding Christa (1991 documentary), Older Women and Love (1987 documentary short), Suzanne, Suzanne (1982)] PRODUCER [A String of Pearls (2002 documentary)—Executive Producer, Finding Christa (1991 documentary)—Producer] WRITER [Finding Christa (1991 documentary)]

Kathe Sandler DIRECTOR [The Friends (short), A Question of Color (1992 documentary), Remembering Thelma (short documentary] PRODUCER [The Friends, A Question of Color (1992 documentary), Remembering Thelma (short documentary)]

Orlando Bagwell DIRECTOR [Africans in America: America's Journey Through Slavery (1998 TV mini-series), Frederick Douglass: When the Lion Wrote History (1994 TV documentary), Malcolm X: Make It Plain (1994 TV documentary), Dancing (1993 TV mini-series documentary)—(episode "New Worlds, New Forms")] PRODUCER [Africans in America: America's Journey Through Slavery (1998 TV mini-series)—Executive Producer, Eyes on the Prize (1987 TV mini-series documentary)—Producer] WRITER [Malcolm X: Make It Plain (1994 TV documentary)]

Bill Duke DIRECTOR [Deacons of Defense (2003 TV movie), Angel: One More Road to Cross (2001 video), The Golden Spiders: A Nero Wolfe Mystery (2000 TV movie), City of Angels (2000 TV series)—(episode "Bride and Prejudice"), Hoodlum (1997), America's Dream (1996 TV movie), Sister Act 2: Back in the Habit (1993), The Cemetery Club (1993), Deep Cover (1992), A Rage in Harlem (1991), The Outsiders (1990 TV series), A Raisin in the Sun (1989 TV movie), Tour of Duty (1987 TV series), Flag (1986), Johnnie Mae Gibson: FBI (1986 TV movie), Matlock (1986 TV series), Starman (1986 TV series), Crime Story (1986 TV series), The Twilight Zone (1985 TV series)—(episode "Junction, The (1987)"), Spenser: For Hire (1985 TV series), Hell Town (1985 TV series), The Killing Floor (1984 TV movie), Miami Vice (1984 TV series), Emerald Point N.A.S. (1983 TV series), Cagney & Lacey (1982 TV series)—(episode "Bounty Hunter, The"), (episode "Chop Shop"), Fame (1982 TV series), Falcon Crest (1981 TV series), Hill Street Blues (1981 TV series), Knots Landing (1979 TV series)] PRODUCER [Hoodlum (1997)—Executive Producer, Sweet Potato Ride (1996 short)—Executive Producer] WRITER [Good Times (1974 TV series)]

Carl Franklin DIRECTOR [Out of Time (2003), High Crimes (2002), Partners (1999 TV series), One True Thing (1998), Devil in a Blue Dress (1995), Laurel Avenue (1993 TV movie), One False Move (1992), Full Fathom Five (1990), Eye of the Eagle 2: Inside the Enemy (1989), Nowhere to Run (1989), Punk (1986 short)] WRITER [Devil in a Blue Dress (1995)—(screenplay), Last Stand at Lang Mei (1990), Eye of the Eagle 2: Inside the Enemy (1989), Punk (1986 short)]

Reginald Hudlin DIRECTOR [Serving Sara (2002), The Ladies Man (2000/I), City of Angels (2000 TV series)—(episode "When Worlds Colitis"), The Great White Hype (1996), Cosmic Slop (1994 TV movie), Boomerang (1992), House Party (1990), House Party (1983 short)] WRITER [House Party 3 (1994)—(characters), Bebe's Kids (1992), House Party 2 (1991)—(characters), House Party (1990)—(written by), House Party (1983 short)] PRODUCER [Ride (1998)—Producer, Bebe's Kids (1992)—Executive Producer]

John Singleton DIRECTOR [The Fast and the Furious 2 (2003), Baby Boy (2001), Shaft (2000), Rosewood (1997), Higher Learning (1995), HIStory (1994 video)—(video "Remember the Time"), Poetic Justice (1993), Boyz N the Hood (1991)] WRITER [Baby Boy (2001)—(written by), Shaft (2000)—(screenplay), (story), Higher Learning (1995)—(written by), Poetic Justice (1993)—(written by), Boyz N the Hood (1991)—(written by)] PRODUCER [Baby Boy (2001)—Producer, Shaft (2000)—Producer, Woo (1998)—Executive Producer, Higher Learning (1995)—Producer, Poetic Justice (1993)—Producer]

Forest Whitaker DIRECTOR [Black Jaq (1998 TV movie), Hope Floats (1998), Waiting to Exhale (1995), Strapped (1993 TV movie)] PRODUCER [Papi Chulo (2003)—Producer, The Making of 'Green Dragon' (2002 video)—Executive Producer, Door to Door (2002/I TV movie)—Co-executive Producer, Feast of All Saints (2001 TV mini-series)—Executive Producer, Green Dragon (2001)—Executive Producer, Black Jaq (1998 TV movie)—Executive Producer, A Rage in Harlem (1991)—Co-producer]

Debra Martin Chase PRODUCER [The Princess Diaries (2001)—Producer, Cinderella (1997 TV movie)—Executive Producer, The Preacher's Wife (1996)—Co-producer, Courage Under Fire (1996)—Executive Producer, Hank Aaron: Chasing the Dream (1995 documentary)—Executive Producer]

George Tillman, Jr. DIRECTOR [Men of Honor (2000), Soul Food (1997), Scenes for the Soul (1995)] PRODUCER [Barbershop 2 (2003)—Producer, Barbershop (2002)—Producer, Soul Food (2000 TV series)—Executive Producer] WRITER [Soul Food (1997)—(written by), Scenes for the Soul (1995)]

Malcolm D. Lee DIRECTOR [Undercover Brother (2002), The Best Man (1999), Morningside Prep] WRITER [My Babies' Mamas, The Best Man (1999)]

Gina Prince-Bythewood DIRECTOR [Disappearing Acts (2000 TV movie), Love & Basketball (2000), Bowl of Pork (1997)—(as Gina Prince), Damn Whitey (1997)—(as Gina Prince), Progress (1997)—(as Gina Prince), What About Your Friends (1995 TV movie)—(as Gina Prince), Stitches (1991)—(as Gina Prince)] WRITER [Love & Basketball (2000)—(written by), Felicity (1998 TV series)—(writer), Courthouse (1995 TV series)—(two episodes) (as Gina Prince), What About Your Friends (1995 TV movie)—(as Gina Prince), Sweet Justice (1994 TV series)—(writer) (as Gina Prince), South Central (1994 TV series)—(writer) (as Gina Prince), Stitches (1991)—(as Gina Prince), A Different World (1987 TV series)—(four episodes) (as Gina Prince)] PRODUCER [Biker Boyz (2003)—Producer, Felicity (1998 TV series)—Consulting Producer, Courthouse (1995 TV series)—Co-producer (as Gina Prince)]

Manthia Diawara DIRECTOR [In Search of Africa (1997 documentary short), Rouch in Reverse (1995 documentary), Sembène: The Making of African Cinema (1994)] PRODUCER [Cinema de notre Temps: Souleymane Cisse (1992, directed by Ritti Panh)]